MW00999183

Civil Tax Procedure

Graduate Tax Series

Series Editor

Paul L. Caron
Charles Hartstock Professor of Law
Director, Faculty Projects
University of Cincinnati College of Law

Board of Editors

Ellen P. Aprill
Associate Dean for Academic Programs
John E. Anderson Chair in Tax Law
Past Director, Graduate Tax Program
Loyola Law School

Elliott Manning
Professor of Law
Faculty Chair, Graduate Program in Taxation
University of Miami School of Law

Philip F. Postlewaite
Professor of Law
Director, Tax Program
Northwestern University School of Law

David M. Richardson
Professor of Law
Past Director, Graduate Tax Program
University of Florida College of Law

Civil Tax Procedure

THIRD EDITION

Steve Johnson
DUNBAR FAMILY PROFESSOR OF LAW
FLORDIA STATE UNIVERSITY COLLEGE OF LAW

Jerome Borison
ASSOCIATE PROFESSOR OF LAW
UNIVERSITY OF DENVER STURM COLLEGE OF LAW
OF COUNSEL, ANDERSON & JAHDE, P.C.

Samuel C. Ullman
BILZIN SUMBERG BAENA PRICE & AXELROD LLP
ADJUNCT PROFESSOR OF LAW
UNIVERSITY OF FLORIDA LEVIN COLLEGE OF LAW

CAROLINA ACADEMIC PRESS
Durham, North Carolina

Copyright © 2016
Carolina Academic Press, LLC
All Rights Reserved

ISBN 978-1-63280-965-0
LCCN 2016950497

Carolina Academic Press, LLC
700 Kent Street
Durham, North Carolina 27701
Telephone (919) 489-7486
Fax (919) 493-5668
www.cap-press.com

Printed in the United States of America

Contents

Preface xix
Acknowledgments xxi

Chapter 1 · Structure of Tax Administration and Sources of Tax Law 3
I. Introduction 3
II. Roles of the Three Branches 3
A. Congress 4
B. Executive Branch 6
1. Treasury Department 7
2. IRS 8
3. Department of Justice 12
C. Judicial Branch 13
1. Types of Tax Cases 13
2. Trial Courts 15
3. Appeals 19
III. Administrative Sources and Authorities in Tax 20
A. Regulations 20
B. Revenue Rulings 21
C. Revenue Procedures 22
D. Notices and Announcements 23
E. Other Published IRS Positions 23
F. Private Letter Rulings 24
G. Determination Letters 26
H. Technical Advice Memoranda 26
I. Government Manuals 26
J. Other Government Sources 27
IV. Administrative Law Issues 28
A. Notice and Comment 28
B. "Arbitrary and Capricious" Review 30
C. Deference Generally 30
1. Standards 30
2. Results 31
D. Specific Deference Considerations 32
1. "Bootstrapping" 32
2. Inconsistency in Policy 33

3. Regulations Overruling Case Law 33
4. Vintage 34
E. Phantom Regulations 34
F. Regulatory Flexibility Act 35
G. Retroactivity 35
H. Inconsistency in Enforcement 37
Problems 40

Chapter 2 · Reporting Obligations 43
I. Introduction 43
II. The Electronic Filing Initiative 45
III. Record Keeping 48
IV. Who Is Required To File? 49
A. Income Tax Returns 49
1. Filing Thresholds 49
2. Joint Returns of Income Tax 50
B. Estate and Gift Tax Returns 51
1. Filing Thresholds — Estate Tax Returns 51
2. Filing Threshold — Gift Tax Returns 52
C. Information Returns 53
1. Information Concerning Persons Subject to Special Provisions — Sections 6031–6039J 53
2. Information Concerning Transactions with Other Persons — Sections 6041–6050W 54
3. Expanded Information Reporting 55
V. Signing and Verifying Returns 56
VI. Time and Place for Filing 59
VII. Time and Place for Paying Tax 63
VIII. Extension of Time to File or Pay 64
IX. Disclosure of Reportable Transactions 66
X. Tax Return Preparers 68
XI. Making of Elections 70
XII. Confidentiality of Return Information 71
XIII. Enhanced Return Reporting 72
A. Uncertain Tax Positions ("UTP") 72
B. Foreign Reporting 73
Problem 75

Chapter 3 · Spousal Relief 77
I. Introduction 77
II. Universal Requirements for Relief 79
A. Joint Income Tax Return Filed 79
B. Amount Due Involves Income Tax 80
C. Timely Election 80

D. Not Barred by Res Judicata or a Final Administrative Determination 82
III. Additional Requirements Imposed to Obtain Relief under Section 6015(b) 82
A. There Must Be an Understatement of Income Tax Attributable to the Other Spouse 83
B. The Spouse Seeking Relief Did Not Have Actual or Constructive Knowledge of the Understatement on the Return 84
1. Omitted Income Cases 85
2. Deduction Cases 85
C. It Would Be Inequitable to Hold the Innocent Spouse Liable for the Tax 86
IV. Additional Requirements Imposed to Obtain Relief under Section 6015(c) 87
A. IRS Has Burden to Prove the Electing Spouse's Actual Knowledge 87
B. Spouse Divorced, Separated, or Widowed at Time of Election 90
C. Amount of Deficiency Allocated to Other Spouse 90
D. Anti-Avoidance Rules 91
V. Additional Requirements Imposed to Obtain Relief under Section 6015(f) 92
VI. Appealing an Adverse Determination Administratively And Judicially 94
VII. Other Matters 95
A. Rights of the Nonrequesting Spouse 95
B. Can the IRS Attach a New Spouse's Income or Property to Pay the Purported Innocent Spouse's Prior Tax Debts? 97
C. Disclosure Issues 97
D. Effect of Divorce Decree Allocation of Responsibility for Understatements 98
E. Collection Activity and Statute of Limitations Are Suspended 98
F. Section 6015, Section 66, and Community Property 98
VIII. Conclusion 99
Problems 99

Chapter 4 · Examination of Returns 103
I. Introduction 103
II. Tax Gap 104
III. Selection of Returns for Examination 105
IV. Types of Examinations 108
A. Principal Audit Types 108
1. Correspondence Examinations 108
2. Office Audits 108
3. Field Examinations 108
B. Other Audit Types 109
C. Special Procedures in Aid of Examination 110
V. Audit Strategies and Choices 111
A. Generally 111
B. Extending the Statute of Limitations 113
VI. IRS Information Gathering 114
A. Information from the Taxpayer 114

B. Information From Directly Knowledgeable Third Parties 117
C. General Information 119
D. International Information Gathering 120
E. Taxpayer Protections and Defenses 122
F. Whistleblower Awards 123
VII. Information Gathering by the Taxpayer 124
A. Transaction Planning 124
B. Audit and Administrative Appeal 125
C. Means for Compelling Disclosure 125
1. FOIA 125
2. Other Devices 126
VIII. Appeals Office Consideration 128
A. Paths to the Appeals Office 128
1. Traditional Path 128
2. Early Involvement 129
3. Docketed Cases 129
4. Unavailability of Appeals Consideration 130
B. Appeals Procedures 130
C. Whether to Seek Appeals Consideration 133
1. Possible Benefits 133
2. Possible Drawbacks 133
IX. Conclusion of Examination or Administrative Appeal 135
A. No-Change Cases 135
B. Agreed or Partly Agreed Cases 135
C. Unagreed Cases 137
Problem 138

Chapter 5 · Assessment Procedures and Matters Relating to the Statutes of Limitations on Assessment 141
I. Introduction 141
II. How an Assessment Is Made 142
III. Types of Exceptions to the General Statute of Limitations Rule 143
A. Summary or Automatic Assessments 143
B. Deficiency Assessments 144
C. Jeopardy or Termination Assessments 145
IV. What Is an "Adequate Return" to Start the Statute of Limitations? 146
A. Signed under Penalties of Perjury 146
B. Proper Form 147
C. Proper Filing 148
D. Sufficient Information to Calculate the Tax 148
V. Statute of Limitations on Assessment — General Rule 149
A. Late Filed Returns 149
B. Early Returns 150
C. Due Date on Weekend or Holiday 150

D. The Mailbox (or Postmark) Rule of Section 7502 150
E. Returns Filed Pursuant to an Extension to File 151
F. Amended Returns 151
G. Penalties and Interest 152
VI. Exceptions to the General Statute of Limitations Rule 152
A. The Taxpayer Agreement/Waiver Exception 152
B. The 25% Nonfraudulent Omission of Income Exception 153
1. Avoiding the Extended Statute of Limitations by Adequate Disclosure 153
2. Avoiding the Extended Statute of Limitations by Referencing the Definition of Gross Income 155
C. The Fraud Exception 157
D. Suspended Statute of Limitations Due to the Issuance of a Notice of Deficiency 158
E. Other Frequent Exceptions/Suspensions 159
1. The Taxpayer Assistance Order (TAO) 159
2. Bankruptcy 159
3. Third-Party Summons and Designated Summons 159
4. Transferee Liability 160
5. Partnership Items 160
6. Listed Transactions 160
7. Others 161
VII. Pleading the Statute of Limitations and Burden of Proof 162
A. Spotting a Potential Statute of Limitations Issue 162
B. Pleading the Statute of Limitations 162
C. Burden of Proof 163
D. Res Judicata and Collateral Estoppel 164
E. Joint Return Filers 165
Problems 165

Chapter 6A · Examination of Partnerships (TEFRA) 169
I. Introduction 169
II. Basic Concepts 171
A. The Unified Proceeding 171
1. Classification 172
2. Inefficiencies 173
B. The Duty of Consistency 175
C. The Tax Matters Partner 175
D. Excluded Partnerships 177
III. Administrative Proceedings 178
A. The Notice of Beginning 178
B. Period for Mailing the NBAP 179
C. The Examination 180
1. Participation 180
2. Summary Reports 180

3. Settlement — Partnership Items 181
4. Settlement — Affected Items 181
5. Requests for Consistent Treatment 182
IV. Judicial Review of an FPAA 183
V. Statute of Limitations on Making Assessments 185
VI. Efficacy and the Future 188
Problems 189

Chapter 6B · Examination of Partnerships (BBA) 193
I. Introduction 193
II. Need to Know Both Regimes 194
A. BBA Before 2018 194
B. TEFRA After 2018 194
III. What the BBA Mandates 195
A. Partnership-Level Adjustments 195
B. Partnership Representative 196
C. Procedures of Adjustment 197
D. Administrative Adjustment Requests 198
E. Consistent Reporting 199
F. Miscellaneous Rules 199
IV. Some Challenges and Pitfalls 200
A. Open Issues 200
B. Planning Considerations 201
C. Malpractice Considerations 201
Problem 202

Chapter 7 · Termination and Jeopardy Assessments 203
I. Introduction 203
II. Termination and Jeopardy Assessment and Levy 204
A. Conditions Justifying Expedited Assessment 205
B. Consequences of Expedited Assessment 206
1. Termination Assessment 206
2. Jeopardy Assessment 209
III. Section 7429 Review 210
A. In General 210
B. Administrative Phase 212
C. Trial Phase 212
D. Post-Trial Phase 214
IV. Other Taxpayer Protections and Options 214
A. Abatement 215
B. Bond 215
C. Stay of Sale 216
D. Collection Due Process Rights 217
V. Related Assessment Mechanisms 218

A. Departing Aliens 218
B. Tax-Exempt Organizations 219
C. Corporate NOL Carrybacks 220
D. Passive Foreign Investment Companies 220
E. Receiverships and Bankruptcies 220
F. Possessors of Large Amounts of Cash 221
VI. Practical Difficulty 222
Problem 222

Chapter 8 · Tax Court Litigation of Deficiency Determination 225
I. Introduction 225
II. The "Notice of Deficiency" and Tax Court Jurisdiction 227
A. Meaning of Deficiency 228
B. Types of Tax Subject to Deficiency Determinations 229
C. Content and Form of the Notice of Deficiency 229
D. Mailing the Notice of Deficiency to the Taxpayer's Last Known Address 230
E. Timely Filing the Tax Court Petition 233
F. Issuance of Additional Deficiency Notices 234
G. Tax Court's Exclusive Jurisdiction 235
H. Standard of Review for Deficiency Proceedings 235
III. Overview of a Tax Court Case 236
A. Pleadings 237
B. Discovery 238
C. Settlement 239
D. Stipulations 239
E. Notice of Calendared Case and Pretrial Orders 240
F. Calendar Call, Trial, and Briefs 240
G. Decision 241
H. Finality of Tax Court Decision 243
I. Appeal 243
J. Assessment of Deficiency after Decision 244
IV. Small Tax Cases ("S" Cases) 245
V. Burden of Proof in Tax Court 246
VI. Choice of Forum 248
A. Breadth of Jurisdiction 249
B. Payment Considerations 249
C. Precedent 250
D. Judge vs. Jury and Legal Argument vs. Equitable Considerations 251
E. Concerns about New Issues 251
F. Accruing of Interest 253
G. Costs of Litigation 253
H. Other Factors 254
1. Publicity 254
2. State Law 254

3. Speed of Disposition 254
4. Nationwide Jurisdiction 254
5. Tax Court's Exclusive Jurisdiction 254
6. APA Issues 254
VII. Attorney's Fees and Costs 255
Problems 257

Chapter 9 · Overpayment — Claims for Refund 261
I. Introduction 261
II. Is There an Overpayment? 264
A. What Constitutes Payment? 265
B. The Tax Properly Due 266
III. Can the Taxpayer Establish the Right to a Refund? 268
A. The Requirement of a "Claim" 268
1. Amending the Claim for Refund 269
B. Who Qualifies as a "Taxpayer"? 270
C. The Timely Filing Requirement 271
1. The Statute of Limitations on Filing the Claim 271
2. Extension of the Statute of Limitations on Filing a Claim for Refund 273
3. Special Rules Relating to Income Taxes 274
D. The Section 6511(b)(2) Limitation 276
IV. Can a Valid Refund Be Diverted to Another Use? 278
V. The Refund Jurisdiction of the Tax Court 280
VI. The Refund Jurisdiction of the Federal District Courts and the Court of Federal Claims 281
VII. Administrative Adjustment Requests 283
VIII. Tentative Carryback and Refund Adjustments 284
IX. Penalty 285
Problems 286

Chapter 10 · Judicial and Statutory Rules That Override the Statutes of Limitation 289
I. Introduction 289
II. Judicial Doctrines 291
A. Equitable Recoupment 291
B. Setoff 293
C. Taxpayer Duty of Consistency 294
D. Governmental Duty of Consistency? 295
E. Judicial Estoppel 296
III. Mitigation 296
A. Error Year Barred by Law or Rule of Law 298
B. Determinations 298
C. Circumstances of Adjustment 301
1. The Equitable Basis for Mitigation 301

2. The Original Circumstances of Adjustment 301
3. The Choice of Year Circumstances of Adjustment 303
D. Conditions Necessary for Adjustment 304
1. Section 1311(b)(1): The Original Circumstances of Adjustment 304
2. Section 1311(b)(2): The "Choice of Year" Circumstances of Adjustment 305
E. Related Parties 307
F. Amount and Method of Adjustment 307
G. Evaluation of the Mitigation Provisions 308
Problems 309

Chapter 11 · Penalties 317
Part A: Penalties for Failure to File or Pay Timely 317
I. General 317
II. Prepaying Tax Liability 318
A. Calculating the Penalty 320
B. Defenses to the Estimated Tax Penalty 320
III. Failure to File Returns Timely 322
A. Due Dates, Extensions, and Substitutes for Return 322
B. Failure to File Penalty (FTF) 323
C. Fraudulent Failure to File 324
IV. Failure to Pay Tax Timely (FTP) 325
A. Failure to Pay the Tax Shown as Due on the Return 326
B. Failure to Pay Tax Deficiency 327
C. Combined Late Filing and Late Payment Penalties 327
V. The Reasonable Cause Defense 328
A. Situations That Might, Depending on the Circumstances, Qualify as Reasonable Cause 329
1. Reliance on a Tax Advisor or Other Third Person 329
2. Death, Serious Illness, or Unavoidable Absence 330
3. Erroneous Advice from the IRS 330
4. Fire, Casualty, Natural Disaster, or Other Disturbance 330
5. Service in a Combat Zone 331
6. First Time Abatement 331
7. Automatic Reasonable Cause for Late Payment if Payment within 90% of Tax Liability 331
B. Situations That Generally Do Not Qualify as Reasonable Cause 332
1. Mistake or Forgetfulness 332
2. Time and Business Pressures 332
3. Records Unavailable 332
4. Ignorance of the Law 333
5. Constitutional Objections and Religious Beliefs 333
6. Lack of Funds 333
VI. How and When to Dispute "Late" Penalties 334

A. Some Filing and Payment Penalties May Be Automatically Assessed and Others Are Entitled to Deficiency Procedures 334
1. General 334
2. What to Include in the Presentation 335
3. Burden of Proof and Burden of Production in Court Proceedings 336
VII. Conclusion 337
Problem — Part A 337
Part B: Accuracy-Related and Fraud Penalties 338
I. Introduction 338
A. Procedures Regarding Assessment 338
B. IRS's Burden of Production Relative to the Penalty 339
II. Calculating the Penalty 339
A. Stacking of Penalties 340
B. What Is an Underpayment? 341
C. Impact of Filing a "Qualified Amended Return" 342
III. The Negligence Penalty 343
A. Negligence 343
B. Disregard of Rules and Regulations 344
C. Impact of Disclosure on the Section 6662 Negligence or Disregard of the Rules and Regulations Penalty 345
IV. The Substantial Understatement Penalty 346
V. Substantial Valuation Misstatements 348
A. Substantial Income Tax Overvaluations 348
B. Substantial Estate and Gift Tax Undervaluations 350
VI. The Fraud Penalty 350
A. Statute of Limitations and Fraud 352
B. Res Judicata and Collateral Estoppel 353
VII. The Reasonable Cause Exception 354
A. Reliance on Advice of Tax Professionals 355
B. Special Rules Apply to Charitable Deductions 357
VIII. Tax Shelter Penalties 357
A. Penalty as to Reportable Transactions 357
1. Disclosed Transactions 357
2. Undisclosed Transactions 358
3. Determination of the Understatement Amount 358
4. Coordination with Other Penalties 358
5. Reasonable Cause Defense 358
a. Disqualified Tax Advisor 359
b. Disqualified Opinion 360
B. Strict Liability Penalty 360
IX. Conclusion 360
Problem 361

Chapter 12 · Interest 363
I. Introduction 363
II. Interest on Underpayments 364
A. The Basic Rules 364
B. Modifications to the Basic Rules 366
1. Carrybacks to a Year with an Underpayment 366
2. Suspension of Interest on Underpayments 366
a. Suspension in Case of Delayed Issuance of Notice of Tax Due 366
b. Suspension in Case of Failure to Contact the Taxpayer in a Timely Manner 367
c. Suspension in the Case of a Presidentially Declared Disaster or Terroristic or Military Action 369
d. Sec. 6603. Deposits Made to Suspend Running of Interest on Potential Underpayments 369
3. Abatement of Interest Attributable to Unreasonable Errors and Delays by or Advice from the IRS 370
4. Interest on Penalties, Additional Amounts, and Additions to Tax 372
III. Interest on Overpayments 373
A. The Basic Rules 373
B. Modifications to the Basic Rules 374
1. Rules Affecting the Period Over Which Interest Is Paid 374
2. Netting of Interest for Overlapping Tax Periods 374
3. Carrybacks Creating an Overpayment 375
IV. Tax Court Jurisdiction over Interest Determinations 376
Problem 377

Chapter 13 · Collection of Tax 379
I. Introduction 379
II. Collection Structure 380
III. Assessment 381
IV. Liens 382
A. Creation and Extent 382
B. Notice of Lien 385
C. Priorities 386
V. Enforced Collection 388
A. Administrative Levy 388
B. Administrative Sale 390
C. Judicial Sale 392
VI. Ancillary Procedures 393
VII. Administrative and Hybrid Protections for Taxpayers and Third Parties 395
A. Relief from Tax Liens 395
B. Relief From Levies 396
C. Taxpayer Assistance Orders 396
D. Installment Agreements 396

E. Offer-in-Compromise 397
F. Collection Due Process 400
G. Collection Appeals Program 402
H. Collection During Recession 402
VIII. Judicial Protections for Taxpayers and Third Parties 403
A. Judicial Remedies in the Code 403
B. Judicial Remedies under Other Statutes 404
C. The Anti-Injunction Act 406
D. Non-Starters 406
IX. Statute of Limitations 407
Problems 408

Chapter 14 · The Section 6672 "Trust Fund Recovery Penalty" 411
I. Introduction 411
II. The Employer's Compliance Duties: Withholding Taxes, Making Payments, and Filing Returns 413
III. Liability for Trust Fund Taxes Pursuant to Section 6672 415
A. The "Responsible Person" Element 415
1. Defense Strategies With Respect to the Responsible Person Element 416
a. Establish That Individual Did Not Have Status, Duty, or Authority 416
b. The "I Was Just Following Orders" Defense 417
c. Not a Responsible Person at the Time Taxes Withheld 418
B. The "Willfulness" Element 418
1. Defense Strategies with Respect to the Willfulness Element 419
a. Establish That the Responsible Person Did Not Act "Willfully" 419
b. Establish Reasonable Cause 420
c. Establish There Were No Funds Available at the Time the Person Became a Responsible Person 421
IV. Procedures for Determining Liability for the Penalty 422
A. Protesting the Proposed Penalty to the Appeals Division 423
B. Judicially Appealing an Adverse Determination 425
V. Procedures for Collecting the Penalty 426
VI. Monitoring the Statute of Limitations 428
VII. General Strategies in Section 6672 Cases 429
A. Try to Shift Blame to Others 429
B. Act to Gain More Time 429
C. Evaluate Bringing a Suit for Contribution against Other Potentially Liable Persons 430
D. Designate Payments to Trust Fund Portion of Assessments 430
E. Try to Settle the Case among the Targets 431
Problem 432

Chapter 15 · Transferee and Fiduciary Liability 435
I. Introduction 435

II. Core Idea of Nexus 435
III. Section 6901 and Related Sections 436
IV. Substantive Bases of Liability 439
A. Fiduciary Liability 439
B. Transferee Liability at Law 440
1. Contract 440
2. Federal Non-Fraudulent-Conveyance Statute 441
3. State Non-Fraudulent-Conveyance Statute 441
C. Transferee Liability in Equity 442
1. Actual Fraud 443
2. Constructive Fraud 444
V. Procedural Aspects 445
A. Incorporated Procedures 445
B. Statute of Limitations 446
C. Burden of Proof 447
D. Discovery 448
E. Privity 449
F. Right to Contribution 449
VI. Extent of Liability 450
VII. Alternatives to Transferee and Fiduciary Liability 451
Problems 453

Table of Cases 457

Table of Statutes 483

Table of Secondary Authorities 501

Index 521

Preface

Like all other areas of law, tax law has both substantive and procedural components. This book addresses the procedures by which taxpayers' liabilities are determined and collected. These procedures include the filing of returns, the administrative and judicial mechanisms for resolving disputes about how much tax is owed, the administrative and judicial mechanisms by which unpaid taxes are collected after the extent of the liability has been determined, and penalties for noncompliance with tax rules. The focus of this book is on civil tax procedure. Although criminal tax rules are occasionally mentioned, this book does not examine them in detail.

A great many of the rules of civil tax procedure were created or significantly revised by the Internal Revenue Service Restructuring and Reform Act of 1998, Pub. L. No. 105-206, 112 Stat. 685. Throughout the book, this legislation is referred to as the 1998 Reform Act. Unless otherwise indicated, references to sections in this book are to the Internal Revenue Code of 1986 as amended through June 30, 2016.

In this course, students should focus on the assigned reading materials, principally sections of the Internal Revenue Code and the Regulations promulgated under it. For additional information and as aids in practice, there are numerous books and articles exploring in greater depth the topics addressed in this book. Some of the best are the current editions of: Jerome Borison (ed.), *Effectively Representing Clients Before the "New" IRS* (3 volumes); Michael Saltzman and Leslie Book, *IRS Practice and Procedure*; and William D. Elliott, *Federal Tax Collections, Liens, and Levies.*

Acknowledgments

The authors of this third edition are grateful to Professors Paul Caron, Ellen April, Elliott Manning, Philip Postlewaite, and David Richardson, the editors of the Graduate Tax Series. A double dose of thanks is due to our friend and colleague Professor Richardson, who was part of our authors group for the first two editions of this book. Numerous of his contributions remain in this third edition, and his example and good will continue to inspire the current authors.

We also are grateful to those who have adopted this book and use it in their courses. Many of our adopters have shared thoughts that have improved this edition. We are grateful to the numerous attorneys and scholars with whom we have worked, and from whom we have learned, over the decades. And we are grateful to our students—past, present, and future—for the stimulation of working with them and for the pride we feel watching their careers blossom in service to their clients and the legal system.

Jerome Borison wishes to thank his super family—Meg, Spencer and Georgia—for giving him only a modestly tough time about the hours and hours spent in the basement office working at the computer on this book. Fortunately, he did not have to miss any soccer, baseball, softball, tennis, skiing, basketball, piano or choir activities or performances to do it.

Steve Johnson is grateful for the support of the Dunbar family and of the Florida State University College of Law.

Samuel Ullman would like to acknowledge, with much appreciation, his wonderful family, including his awesome wife Barbara and his terrific daughter and son, Lizzy and Mike.

Portions of this book are derived from Jerome Borison, *Effectively Representing Your Client Before the "New" IRS* (3d Ed.). The authors wish to thank the American Bar Association Section of Taxation, which has kindly granted permission for its use.

Civil Tax Procedure

Chapter 1

Structure of Tax Administration and Sources of Tax Law

IRC: §§6405(a); 7441 to 7443A; 7463; 7803; 7805

Regs.: §§601.601(a), (d)

Rulings: Rev. Proc. 2016-1 (or the corresponding revenue procedure in each subsequent year, such as Rev. Proc. 2016-1, etc.) (skim only)

I. Introduction

This chapter begins with an overview of the roles played by the three branches of the federal government in formulating and applying tax law. It then describes the principal types of administrative sources and authorities in tax. Finally, the chapter addresses prominent issues that arise as to the various kinds of tax authorities.

II. Roles of the Three Branches

Article I, section 8, clause 1 of the Constitution gives Congress the power to "lay and collect Taxes." Article I, section 9, clause 4 prescribes that so-called direct taxes must be apportioned among the states in proportion to population, but this requirement has little significance currently. In a widely criticized case, the Supreme Court invalidated an earlier version of the federal income tax because it was not apportioned.[1] That restriction was swept away when the Sixteenth Amendment was ratified in 1913.

As discussed in Chapter 4, the Fourth Amendment proscription against illegal searches and seizures and the self-incrimination clause of the Fifth Amendment sometimes are invoked (usually unsuccessfully) against IRS information-gathering efforts. Apart from those provisions, constitutional challenges to tax measures are asserted only rarely and succeed even less often.[2]

1. Pollock v. Farmers' Loan & Trust Co., 158 U.S. 601 (1895).

2. *See, e.g.*, United States v. United States Shoe Corp., 523 U.S. 360 (1998) (harbor maintenance tax held in violation of Export Clause); United States v. Carlton, 512 U.S. 26 (1994) (retroactive application of estate tax change held not to violate Due Process Clause).

A. Congress

The role of Congress is to write the tax statutes. The highest authority in tax is the statute, whether the Internal Revenue Code or an uncodified session law. For a tax lawyer, identifying the relevant statute(s) and carefully reading the statutory language are the starting point in every case.

The ideas ultimately embodied in tax statutes may originate with the Administration, with individual members of Congress, or with industry groups or key constituents. The ideas will be put into legislative language by congressional staffers, the Treasury Department, or private interest groups. Bills (proposed legislation) will be introduced in the House, the Senate, or both.[3]

The bills are then referred to the tax-writing committees: the Ways and Means Committee in the House and the Finance Committee in the Senate. Many bills die in committee. Important bills may receive hearings by the committee, involving testimony by experts and others and submission of written statements. However, the hearing process is far less robust than it was a generation ago. The committee may revise the language of bills in "mark up" sessions. Ultimately, the committee votes on the bill.

Bills that pass the committee go to the full House or Senate. Typically, the House and Senate versions will differ. Differences between tax bills passed by the two chambers are reconciled by conference committees convened for that purpose. The reconciled measure is then returned to the House and the Senate. After being passed by them, the measure goes to the President for his signature or veto.[4]

The Joint Committee on Taxation is also important. It is a standing committee with members drawn from both the majority and minority of the House Ways and Means and the Senate Finance Committees. It has a sizeable staff of economists and attorneys. The Joint Committee provides expertise on a continuing basis, contributing significantly to the tax legislation process. Sections 8021 through 8023 describe the duties and powers of the Joint Committee. In addition, under section 6405(a), the Joint Committee reviews proposed refunds over $2,000,000.[5]

---

3. Under Article I, section 7, clause 1 of the Constitution, tax measures are supposed to originate in the House of Representatives, but this requirement typically is finessed. *See, e.g.*, Moore v. U.S. House of Representatives, 733 F.2d 946 (D.C. Cir. 1984) (rejecting challenge to 1982 tax legislation that effectively originated in the Senate), *cert. denied*, 469 U.S. 1106 (1985), *abrogated as to standing issue*, Chenoweth v. Clinton, 181 F.3d 112 (D.C. Cir. 1999).

4. For fuller discussion of the tax legislative process, see Conference Proceedings, *The Tax Legislative Process—A Critical Need*, 10 Amer. J. Tax Pol'y 99 (1992); excerpts from the 1978 FBA Conference on Writing Tax Law, 35 Fed. B.J. 76 (1978).

5. *See* IRS Proc. Reg. § 601.108. In fiscal year 2013, the Joint Committee received about 1300 large refund cases, totaling over $30 billion. It raises concerns in about 5% of the cases. The Joint Committee lacks authority to override the IRS's judgement. (Indeed, having such authority could raise separation-of-powers problems.) Nonetheless, the IRS pays great attention to the Committee's concerns. Eric Kroh, *JCT Will Review a Refund if It's Big Enough,* Tax Notes, Apr. 14, 2014, p. 160; *see also* Thomas J. Callahan, Gregory J. Gawlik & Jon R. Stefanik II, *Joint Committee Refund Review: Twelve Questions to Consider*, J. Tax Prac. & Proc., Oct.–Nov. 2008, p. 19.

In recent decades, Congress has passed major tax acts every few years and several lesser measures each year. Initially, tax acts are enacted as session laws, such as the Tax Reform Act of 1969 or the Tax Equity and Fiscal Responsibility Act of 1982. The great majority of important items are then codified in the Internal Revenue Code. The IRC is Title 26 of the United States Code. Thus, for instance, 26 U.S.C. section 163 and IRC section 163 are two ways of referring to the same statute. Generalist lawyers and judges tend to use the first styling while tax specialists use the second.

Before 1939, federal tax statutes existed in session law form only. The first codification was the Internal Revenue Code of 1939, which was succeeded by the Internal Revenue Code of 1954. The 1954 version enacted many new sections and changed the section numbers of provisions retained from the 1939 Code. The current version is the Internal Revenue Code of 1986, which largely preserved the numbering of sections retained from the 1954 Code.

The Internal Revenue Code is divided into subtitles, such as Subtitle A (the income tax), Subtitle B (the estate, gift, and generation-skipping transfer taxes), and Subtitle F (procedural and administrative sections applying to the Code generally). The subtitles are subdivided into, successively, chapters, subchapters, parts, subparts, sections, subsections, paragraphs, and subparagraphs.

Codes tend to operate on internal structural logic. Thus, courts sometimes look to where a provision is situated in the Code as a clue to the meaning of the provision. However, section 7806(b) provides that no "inference, implication or presumption" shall flow from "the location or grouping of any particular provision" within the Code.

The codified version of a tax statute typically omits some features contained in the session law. For example, the effective date of the statute usually is omitted although commercially available compilations provide effective-date information via notation. Also normally omitted are transitional rules, which exempt (permanently or temporarily) particular taxpayers or activities from the reach of a new provision. Such rules, secured by legislators for important constituents, often are the unavoidable price for getting enough votes to pass a measure, but they may be problematic in terms of fairness, transparency, and democracy.[6]

On occasion, Congress will enact a substantive tax measure in a session law but choose not to codify it in the IRC. This has been done, for instance, with respect to filing relief or tax holidays for American embassy workers held captive in Tehran, 9–11 victims, and soldiers and sailors serving in a variety of combat theaters.[7] Also, on

6. *See, e.g.*, Apache Bend Apts., Ltd. v. United States, 964 F.2d 1556 (5th Cir. 1992), *rev'd*, 987 F.2d 1174 (5th Cir. 1993) (en banc).

7. Perhaps the most important tax provision not codified in the IRS is section 530 of the Revenue Act of 1978, which provides safe harbors for making "employee versus independent contractor" classifications. Pub. L. No. 95-600, § 530, 92 Stat. 2763, 2885 (as subsequently amended).

occasion, Congress codifies tax measures, or more general measures that affect the tax system, under titles of the United States Code other than Title 26.[8]

The tax legislative process generates committee reports and other documents. The types of legislative documents relied on in tax controversies include (i) reports generated by the Ways and Means, Finance, and conference committees, (ii) General Explanations (the so-called Blue Books) prepared by the staff of the Joint Committee after passage of major tax acts,[9] (iii) occasional committee prints prepared for general informational purposes, (iv) pre-enactment versions of the bill, (v) testimony and statements during committee hearings, (vi) colloquies, debates, and statements on the floor of each chamber reported in the Congressional Record, and (vii) presidential, Treasury, and other Executive Branch documents.

Finally, the role of the Government Accountability Office ("GAO") should be acknowledged. The GAO is an investigative arm of Congress. Upon request by a member of Congress, the GAO prepares reports about the efficiency and effectiveness of federal programs and activities, often including those involved in tax administration. Over the years, the GAO has released many reports on IRS operations, some laudatory but many critical. Such reports are important political facts and can influence tax debates and legislation.[10]

B. Executive Branch

The President proposes many tax changes that ultimately become law, and the White House is usually involved in the negotiations over major tax proposals. Two Executive departments are of primary significance in tax matters: the Treasury Department (including the Internal Revenue Service) and the Justice Department.

---

8. Examples are 38 U.S.C. § 5301(a), which provides an income tax exclusion for certain training expense reimbursements provided by the Veterans Administration, and 18 U.S.C. § 1001, which makes it a crime to make false statements or submit false documents to federal officials, including IRS personnel.

9. Use of the Blue Books has been controversial. Under the influence of Justice Scalia and others, the role of legislative history in statutory construction has been under attack for some years. Technically, the Blue Books are not even legislative history in the way that House Ways and Means and Senate Finance Committee reports are. The Blue Book is produced by the Joint Committee staff after enactment of the new law; it is not signed by any member of Congress; and it is not approved by either chamber of Congress. Concern also exists that lobbyists may succeed in having self-serving material inserted into the Blue Book. On the other hand, because of the professionalism and expertise of the Joint Committee staff and the significant role of the committee in matters of tax policy, the Blue Book commands considerable respect. The Supreme Court has held that Blue Books are impermissible guides to statutory interpretation. United States v. Woods, 134 S. Ct. 557, 568 (2013). Nonetheless, even after *Woods*, both taxpayers and the Government continue to cite Blue Books. Moreover, Blue Books are "authority" for purposes of penalty analysis. Reg. § 1.6662-4(d)(3)(iii).

10. In general, requests for GAO investigations of the IRS must be reviewed by the Joint Committee. IRC § 8021(e).

1. Treasury Department

Scores of Code sections (for example, sections 446(b) and 482) refer to "the Secretary." Under section 7701(a)(11), those references are to the Secretary of the Treasury. Treasury is primarily responsible for tax policy.

Treasury is the parent department of the IRS, but other parts of Treasury also are players in tax policy and administration. Within Treasury, tax legislation historically has been the province of so-called "main Treasury," rather than the IRS. The landmark 1998 Reform Act included a "sense of the Congress" measure that the IRS "should provide Congress with an independent view of tax administration" and that front-line IRS technical experts should advise the tax-writing committees as to the administrability of proposed tax law changes.[11] Thus far, the IRS has largely ignored this prompting.

The principal technical tax adviser in Treasury is the Assistant Secretary for Tax Policy. The Assistant Secretary is in charge of both the Office of Tax Legislative Counsel and the Office of Tax Analysis. The Tax Legislative Counsel's office has a staff of lawyers who consider technical questions as to tax legislation, rules, and regulations. This office, working closely with the IRS, also helps to develop and finalize regulations, and often comments on proposed revenue rulings and other important administrative positions. The Office of Tax Analysis is staffed by economists who evaluate economic effects and estimate the revenue consequences of tax features and proposals. Estimating revenue effects of tax proposals is called "scoring." Scoring is central to tax legislation, and the quality and limitations of scoring techniques are frequently controversial.

The Treasury Department also administers the few taxes—such as taxes on alcohol, tobacco, and firearms—responsibility for which has not been delegated to the IRS. Treasury has an Office of General Counsel, which sometimes is involved in tax matters. The 1998 Reform Act created the Office of Treasury Inspector General for Tax Administration ("TIGTA"), whose duties partly overlap those of the Office of Inspector General of the Department of the Treasury.[12] TIGTA studies the IRS and sometimes issues reports on its findings.

Each year, the Treasury and the IRS release a Priority Guidance Plan, which typically is revised during the year. The Plan highlights recently completed regulation and ruling projects, describes ongoing projects, and identifies new projects to be undertaken. Tax practitioners are well advised to review the Plan and its revisions in order to both remain current and monitor changing Government priorities.

The Office of Management and Budget (OMB) periodically publishes lists of proposed and final regulations, including tax regulations. In addition, since 2011, the Office of Information and Regulatory Affairs (OIRA) has required all agencies to periodically review whether any of their significant regulations should be modified or

11. 1998 Reform Act § 4021 (not codified in IRC).

12. *See generally id.* at § 1103; IRC § 7803(d).

repealed to ease compliance burdens. Treasury does so twice a year in Retrospective Review Plan Status Reports. Other useful government reports include (1) the IRS Data Book published annually, (2) periodic reports issued by the IRS's Statistics of Income (SOI) Division, and (3) performance reviews issued occasionally by the Treasury Inspector General for Tax Administration.

2. IRS

Most of the Treasury Secretary's authority over day-to-day administration of the tax laws has been delegated to the IRS.[13] The Commissioner of Internal Revenue is appointed by the President, subject to confirmation by the Senate, for a five-year term with the possibility of reappointment (but is removable at will by the President).[14] The IRS National Office formulates policies and programs while field offices throughout the country (and usually in major foreign business centers) work cases. An organizational chart of the National Office of the IRS, current as of March 2015, is on the last page of this chapter before the problems.

In Fiscal Year 2014, the IRS had gross collections of nearly $3.1 trillion. About 53% was from income taxes on individuals, 11% from income taxes on corporations, 1% from income taxes on estates and trusts, 32% from employment taxes, 2% from excise taxes, and slightly under 1% from estate, gift, and generation-skipping transfer taxes. In the same year, the IRS received approximately 240 million tax returns and other forms (not including various information returns). About 186 million of these were income tax returns.[15]

The IRS's budget for the same year was about $11.3 billion. Of that, approximately $2.2 billion went to taxpayer assistance, $5 billion to enforcement, $3.8 billion to operations support, and $300 million to business systems modernization.[16] Both the IRS's budget (measured in constant dollars) and its work force were lower in 2014 than in 2005.[17]

There is a tendency on the part of some IRS agents to resolve close cases in favor of revenue-maximizing outcomes. However, this approach is not in keeping with either the official policy[18] or the best traditions[19] of the IRS.

---

13. IRC §7803(a).

14. IRC §7803(a)(1).

15. *IRS Data Book, 2014,* at 3 & 4.

16. Testimony of J. Russell George (Treasury Inspector General for Tax Administration), hearings before Senate Comm. on Appropriations, Subcomm. on Financial Services & General Government (Apr. 30, 2014).

17. *IRS Data Book, 2014,* at 65 & 66.

18. The IRS rewords its Mission Statement every few years to reflect shifting priorities. The current Mission Statement (set out in every issue of the Internal Revenue Bulletin) reads: "Provide America's taxpayers top quality service by helping them understand and meet their tax responsibilities and by applying the tax law with integrity and fairness to all." Mission statements, however, are merely aspirational, not judicially enforceable. *See* Adams v. Commissioner, T.C. Memo. 1978-152, *aff'd without opinion,* 609 F.2d 505 (4th Cir. 1979).

19. In the early 1960s, the IRS emphasized: "An exaction by the United States Government ... not based upon law ... is a taking without due process of law, in violation of the Fifth Amendment ...

The IRS undergoes frequent reorganization. The 1998 Reform Act directed a major reorganization, which began in 1999. Before that reorganization, the field offices were geographically arranged. Four regions each contained a number of districts, thirty-three districts in all. Each district had Examination, Collection, and Criminal Investigation divisions. Ten Service Centers had return processing and related responsibilities.

Congress concluded in 1998 that the IRS would function better if its geographical structure were replaced by operating units serving particular groups with similar needs.[20] In addition, it was expected that the reorganization would promote accountability and improve the consistency with which similar taxpayers in different parts of the country would be treated. Subsequently, the IRS recognized that some advantages of geographical organization had been lost. It frequently reorganizes to rebalance geography and function.

Under the reorganization, the IRS consists of a National Headquarters and eleven business units, comprised of:

- Four operating divisions: Wage and Investment, Small Business and Self Employed, Large Business and International, and Tax Exempt and Government Entities,
- Two support divisions: Agency-Wide Shared Services and Modernization, Information Technology and Security Services, and
- Five functional business units: Chief Counsel, Appeals, Criminal Investigation, Communications and Liaison, and the Taxpayer Advocate Service.

The service centers were renamed campuses. They retain responsibility for Submission Processing, Accounts Management, and Compliance, although not all campuses serve all three capacities.

Most IRS personnel serve in one of the four operating divisions. The field personnel of the divisions are organized among area and territory offices. The four divisions are described below.

Wage and Investment Division. W&I deals with the largest number of taxpayers: individuals who have only wage and/or investment income. Monitoring the compliance of those taxpayers is greatly facilitated by extensive third-party information reporting of wages, interest, dividends, and the like via W-2 and 1099 forms.[21] *See*

[An IRS agent] "shall hew to the law and the recognized standards of legal construction ... with strict impartiality as between the taxpayer and the Government, and without favoritism or discrimination between taxpayers." Policy Statement 4–7, IRM 1.2 13.1, 5 (Dec. 23, 1960); *see also* Rev. Proc. 64-22, 1964-1 C.B. 689; 1996-1 C.B. ii; 1976-1 C.B. ii. The vehemence of this language perhaps was influenced by scandals of the 1950s in which several IRS officials, including a Commissioner (the IRS's top official), were convicted of taking bribes from taxpayers. For a brief history of the IRS, see Charles P. Rettig, *At-a-Glance: The Internal Revenue Service, Its Mission and Function*, J. Tax Prac. & Proc., Aug.–Sep. 2006, p. 47.

20. 1998 Reform Act § 1001 (not codified in IRC).

21. Accordingly, proposals to expand required information reporting are routinely included in suggested reforms to increase compliance. *See, e.g.*, Joint Comm. on Taxation, *Description of Certain Revenue Provisions Contained in the President's Fiscal Year 2016 Budget Proposal* 245–53 (Sept. 2015).

Chapter 4. W&I is headquartered in Atlanta. Its functions include CARE (Communications, Assistance, and Research), which provides taxpayer education, assistance, and filing support; CAS (Customer Account Services) which processes returns and payments; and Compliance.

Small Business and Self-Employed Division. SB/SE handles both individuals who are self-employed in whole or in part and corporations and partnerships whose assets do not exceed $10,000,000. SB/SE is headquartered in New Carrollton, Maryland. It contains CARE, CAS, and Compliance functions. Responsibility for wealth transfer taxes, employment taxes, and most collection activities also are centralized in SB/SE.

Large Business and International Division. LB&I is headquartered in Washington, D.C. It deals with business entities with assets exceeding $10,000,000. Reflecting the notion that similar companies will have common tax issues, LB&I is organized into industry segments, such as Communications, Technology, and Media; Financial Services; Heavy Manufacturing and Transportation; Natural Resources and Construction; and Retailers, Food, Pharmaceuticals, and Healthcare. International tax issues are centralized in LB&I.[22]

Tax Exempt and Governmental Entities Division. TE/GE is also headquartered in Washington, D.C. It includes a CAS component. Its other components are customer segments dealing with Employee Plans (deferred compensation plans), Exempt Organizations (charities, private foundations, and political organizations), and Governmental Entities (including Indian Tribes and issuers of tax-exempt bonds).

The IRS frequently revises its technological systems. The IRS uses a number of not-always-compatible information systems. This has inhibited IRS enforcement, undercut taxpayer service, and created friction with Congress. The IRS frequently announces new or revised technological modernization initiatives.

Among the functional units, the Office of Chief Counsel is the principal legal arm of the IRS. Chief Counsel's National Office works on matters of policy embodied in regulations, revenue rulings, revenue procedures, private letter rulings, and other types of guidance. The National Office also assists field personnel handling cases and sometimes handles high-profile cases directly. Chief Counsel's field offices handle cases in litigation and pre-litigation status.[23] Counsel offices are organized in parallel fashion to the four operating divisions. Communication and Liaison has jurisdiction over confidentiality and disclosure issues.

Like the so-called "Commissioner's side" of the IRS, IRS Counsel frequently reorganizes. In 2006, the Chief Counsel's Office announced a major restructuring based

---

22. In late 2015, LB&I began significant organizational changes to deploy resources more efficiently. The changes include creation of four geographically based compliance practice areas and five subject matter practice areas. Aspects will include better training and decreased discretion of large case revenue agents in selecting the issues in their audits. *See* William R. Davis, *LB&I Commissioner Announces Sweeping Changes*, 2015 TNT 181-1 (Sept. 18, 2015).

23. As a result of settlement, trial, or otherwise, in Fiscal Year 2014, the Chief Counsel's Office closed about 30,600 Tax Court cases involving over $6.2 billion in disputed taxes and penalties and 329 refund cases involving $743 million. *IRS Data Book 2014*, at 63.

on a "matrix management approach" combining geographical and functional components. The revised structure includes (i) a national Field Leadership Team, (ii) six Area Teams, and (iii) forty-nine Managing Counsel at field offices throughout the country. This reorganization partly discards and partly confirms principles that guided reorganization after RRA 1998. One of the goals of the new structure is to give taxpayers and their representatives contacts in the field offices to resolve problems.

The Criminal Investigation Division ("CID") does what its name suggests. Serious violations of tax responsibilities can lead to the imposition of criminal sanctions. The federal government initiates relatively few criminal tax cases each year: rarely more than 3000, often fewer. These cases are developed by the Special Agents of the CID.[24]

Appeals' mission is to resolve tax disputes short of trial. It has long played this role in the pre-assessment context (see Chapter 4), and its role in resolving collection disputes has increased substantially in recent years (see Chapter 13).[25] After reorganization, Appeals has a strategic planning function plus three operating units: the Large and Mid-Size Operating Unit, the General Business Unit, and the Tax Exempt and Governmental Entities Unit.

The Taxpayer Advocate Service is the current iteration of the IRS's problem-solving function. It exists to cut through red tape and resolve taxpayer difficulties that exist despite (or perhaps because of) normal IRS procedures. The 1998 Reform Act reconstituted this function in response to concerns about the office's independence and effectiveness. The function is headed by the National Taxpayer Advocate. The national office directs field offices which sometimes correspond to IRS operating division field offices. Taxpayer Advocate offices can resolve difficulties informally or via the issuance of a taxpayer assistance order (TAO). The National Taxpayer Advocate also reports to Congress on systemic problems taxpayers confront and possible solutions to them.[26] Section 7803(c) describes the duties and powers of the Taxpayer Advocate's Office, and section 7811 describes TAOs. A taxpayer requests a TAO by filing a Form 911.[27]

The tax practitioner also should be aware of the Office of Professional Responsibility ("OPR"), which reports to the IRS Deputy Commissioner for Service and Enforcement. Treasury Circular 230[28] governs professional responsibility obligations of attorneys and others who practice before the IRS. Alleged violations of Circular

---

24. For fuller description of substantive and procedural aspects of the criminal tax function, see John A. Townsend, et al., Tax Crimes (2d ed. 2015).

25. *See generally* History of Appeals: Appeals at 60 Years (IRS Document No. 7225) (1987). In Fiscal Year 2014, the Appeals Office closed over 115,000 cases, including about 41,000 Collection Due Process cases; 37,000 examination cases; 9100 penalty appeals; 9000 offers in compromise; and 4100 spousal relief cases. *IRS Data Book, 2014*, at 51.

26. The annual reports of the National Taxpayer Advocate are essential reading for those interested in the problems of our tax system and possible solutions to them.

27. *See* IRC § 7811. In Fiscal Year 2014, the Taxpayer Advocate Service closed about 223,000 cases. Taxpayers received full or partial relief in 174,000 cases, including the issuance of 280 TAOs. *IRS Data Book, 2014*, at 50. Memorandum TAS-13-0614-005 providing guidance on the types of cases to be accepted by the Taxpayer Advocate Service is included in the IRS's Internal Revenue Manual.

28. 31 C.F.R. pt. 10.

230 are considered by OPR, with hearing and appeal rights available. Practitioners determined to have violated Circular 230 face a variety of possible sanctions, including censure, suspension or disbarment from practice before the IRS, and monetary penalties.

The 1998 Reform Act created the IRS Oversight Board to oversee the IRS's organization, support, and execution of its missions. Members of the Board include government officials and six individuals from the private sector. Section 7802 describes how the Board is constituted, what its specific responsibilities are, and what it is supposed not to do. The Oversight Board has not had a major effect on tax administration.

Tax scams have grown alarmingly. They include identity theft and scam artists telephoning taxpayers, posing as IRS agents and demanding immediate payment of bogus tax debts. The IRS has detailed procedures for such cases, as described on the IRS's website and its social media (such as YouTube and Tumblr).

3. Department of Justice

Justice's role is principally in tax litigation. The general pattern goes back to the Administration of Franklin Roosevelt. The IRS Chief Counsel's Office represents the IRS in the Tax Court, while Justice represents the IRS in other courts. In your study of tax law, you will encounter some cases styled as, for example, "Jones v. Commissioner" and others as "Jones v. United States." The former styling connotes that the trial court was the Tax Court (or a predecessor court) and that the government was represented by IRS Counsel. The latter styling connotes that the trial court was either a federal District Court or the Court of Federal Claims (or a predecessor court) and that the government was represented by the Department of Justice.[29]

The Tax Division of Justice is led by an Assistant Attorney General. It has four geographically based civil trial sections. They handle refund suits and all other civil tax litigation in the District Courts and state courts. Litigation in the state courts is rare. The federal government can remove cases from state court to federal District Court,[30] and it nearly always exercises that power. A fifth trial section within the Tax Division handles cases in the Court of Federal Claims.

Civil tax cases may be tried by other government lawyers as well. A large part of Justice (though they sometimes think of themselves as semi-autonomous) is the United States Attorneys Offices in all the federal judicial districts. A tax case in Bankruptcy Court will be handled by an attorney from the geographically appropriate civil trial section of the Tax Division or an attorney from the local United States Attorneys Office.

---

29. Older cases often are styled as "*Lucas v. Earl*," "*Welch v. Helvering*," or "*Corliss v. Bowers*." This goes back to a time when suits were brought against the Commissioner named as an individual or against local collectors named as individuals. Local collectors no longer exist. (Robert Lucas and Guy Helvering were Commissioners of Internal Revenue. Frank Bowers was a Collector of Internal Revenue for the Second District of New York.)

30. 28 U.S.C. §§1442, 1444, 1446.

The Tax Division also has a Criminal Enforcement Section ("CES"). It reviews potential criminal tax cases referred by the Criminal Investigation Division of the IRS. The CES may accept those cases for prosecution, decline them, or return them for further development. In criminal cases that actually reach trial, the government is represented by either the CES or the United States Attorneys Office. The CES also maintains liaison with the various organized crime and drug enforcement task forces.

There are three other tax-relevant components of the Justice Department. First, the Tax Division's Appellate Section represents the government in federal Circuit Court, regardless of the trial court in which the case originated. Second, the Solicitor General's Office makes the ultimate decision about whether to prosecute or defend tax appeals. It also argues tax cases before the Supreme Court and occasionally before circuit courts. Third, the Office of Review coordinates the Tax Division's settlement policies. It also researches proposed legislation on which the Tax Division has been asked to comment.

There are numerous coordination functions and procedures among the IRS, IRS Counsel, and the various components of the Justice Department. They usually work reasonably well because of mutual respect among the participants and because of a shared understanding of the importance of tax enforcement. Nonetheless, occasional strains are inevitable. Sometimes, Justice has a different view of the law than the IRS has. This can produce embarrassing disagreements.[31]

C. Judicial Branch

Constitutionally, "judicial branch" refers to the Article III courts: the federal District and Circuit Courts and the Supreme Court. In the tax world, the term is used more broadly to include all federal courts that hear tax cases, Article I as well as Article III courts.[32] The following briefly describes the types of tax cases, the courts that hear them, and the available avenues of appeal.

1. Types of Tax Cases

There are seven types of tax cases. This chapter describes them briefly; other chapters develop the most important of them in greater detail.[33]

Deficiency actions. In general, federal income, estate, gift, and generation-skipping transfer taxes (above amounts reported on taxpayers' returns) cannot be assessed until the IRS has issued a formal determination of additional tax owing. That addi-

---

31. *See, e.g.*, Campbell v. Commissioner, 59 T.C. Memo. (CCH) 236 (1990), *aff'd in part & rev'd in part*, 943 F.2d 815 (8th Cir. 1991) (IRS prevailed at trial on one theory; on appeal, Justice repudiated that theory but sought unsuccessfully to preserve the victory by offering a different theory).

32. Under Article I, section 8, clause 9 of the Constitution, Congress has the power to create additional courts whose judges do not have Article III life tenure. The Tax Court, the Court of Federal Claims, and the Bankruptcy Court are Article I courts. Article I courts have only that jurisdiction conferred upon them by Congress.

33. *See also* Steve R. Johnson, *Reforming Federal Tax Litigation: An Agenda*, 41 Fla. St. U. L. Rev. 205 (2013).

tional tax is called a deficiency. The formal determination is called a statutory notice of deficiency. The notice also is called a Ninety-Day Letter since the taxpayer has ninety days from the date the notice was mailed to file a petition with the Tax Court challenging the determinations in the notice. In the action following the filing of a Tax Court petition, the taxpayer is the petitioner and the Commissioner is the respondent. *See* Chapter 8.

Refund actions. If the taxpayer failed to file a Tax Court petition or if the tax in question was assessable without the need to issue a notice of deficiency, the IRS will assess the tax plus interest and, if applicable, civil penalties. See Chapter 11 for discussion of civil penalties. A taxpayer who wishes to challenge an assessed liability must pay it, then file a refund claim with the IRS, and then (after the IRS denies or ignores the claim) file a refund suit in either the Court of Federal Claims or District Court. A taxpayer who concludes that she reported and paid too much tax also must file a refund claim and, if necessary, bring a refund suit. *See* Chapter 9.

TEFRA and BBA actions. As a result of the Tax Equity and Fiscal Responsibility Act of 1982 ("TEFRA"), income tax liabilities arising from partnership operations may be determined and litigated under special rules. The rules are a hybrid of entity-level and partner-level audit, collection, and litigation. TEFRA litigation may involve an analog of either Tax Court deficiency actions or refund actions. For tax years beginning after 2017, the TEFRA rules are replaced by different entity-based audit and litigation rules set out in the Bipartisan Budget Act of 2015 ("BBA"). *See* Chapter 6.

Collection actions. The three preceding types of cases involve how much tax the taxpayer owes, therefore how much the IRS may properly assess. Collection suits involve post-assessment matters. They may be brought by the IRS in aid of collection, by taxpayers in opposition to collection, or by third parties (such as other creditors of the taxpayer or co-owners of property) to prevent harm to their interests. Liability issues are sometimes argued in collection contexts, for instance, in post-assessment spousal relief cases, *see* Chapter 3, and in Collection Due Process cases and suits to reduce tax liabilities to judgment, *see* Chapter 13. Most collection cases must be brought in District Court although the Tax Court's jurisdiction has been broadened to include some collection matters.

Miscellaneous civil actions. A variety of special types of civil tax suits may be brought, usually in District Court. Here are some of the more prominent types: (1) the government may seek a writ, order, or injunction to further tax enforcement;[34] (2) the government may request a District Court to enforce a summons issued by the IRS,[35] *see* Chapter 4; (3) the government may ask a District Court to enjoin income tax return preparers who have engaged in misconduct, to enjoin promoters of abusive tax shelters or other schemes, or to enjoin flagrant political expenditures by section

34. IRC § 7402(a).
35. IRC § 7402(b).

501(c)(3) organizations;[36] (4) taxpayers may seek expedited judicial review of IRS jeopardy or termination assessments, *see* Chapter 7;[37] (5) taxpayers and (sometimes) aggrieved third parties may seek monetary damages as a result of wrongful IRS conduct,[38] *see* Chapter 13; and (6) affected persons may bring Tax Court actions for declaratory judgment as to, for example, their status as tax-exempt organizations, status of employees versus independent contractors, or status as qualified retirement plans.[39]

Bankruptcy cases. The IRS is a creditor in a large percentage of bankruptcy cases. Thus, numerous tax issues are tried in Bankruptcy Court. They include liability, collection, and procedural bankruptcy issues. If the IRS believes there are unpaid taxes, it will submit a proof of claim to the Bankruptcy Court, and the merits of the claim may then be litigated. The taxpayer/debtor also can initiate the process of liability determination. The Bankruptcy Court has broad powers to determine tax liabilities.[40] The taxpayer/debtor can trigger such determination by filing a motion with the Bankruptcy Court. Even if the liability is uncontested, there may be litigation in the Bankruptcy Court as to whether and how those liabilities can be collected either within or outside the bankruptcy process.

Criminal tax cases. Egregious tax behavior may be punished criminally.[41] Criminal tax cases are tried in federal District Court. As is usual in criminal cases of all types, the government bears the burden of proof at a "beyond reasonable doubt" standard. The typical rules of criminal procedure apply.

2. Trial Courts

Depending on circumstances, federal civil tax cases may be tried in any of four courts: District Court, Tax Court, Court of Federal Claims, or Bankruptcy Court. In cases involving the extent of liability (as opposed to collection after determination of liability), the taxpayer typically initiates the case, and the taxpayer chooses the court in which the case will be brought. First-year law students learn that forum shopping usually is discouraged. In tax, however, it is accepted.

Which court should the taxpayer select? Taxpayers typically choose the Tax Court, when it is available, because it is a prepayment forum, *i.e.*, the taxpayer can challenge the merits of the IRS's determinations without first paying the amount of tax the IRS believes is owed. When liquidity is not controlling, dozens of considerations can bear on the taxpayer's choice-of-forum decision.[42]

---

36. IRC §§ 7407, 7408, 7409, respectively.

37. IRC § 7429(b).

38. *E.g.*, I.R.C. §§ 7431–7435.

39. IRC §§ 7428, 7436, 7476, respectively. See IRC sections 7477–7479 for additional declaratory judgment possibilities.

40. 11 U.S.C. § 505(a).

41. *E.g.*, IRC §§ 7201–7217; *see* John A. Townsend, et al., Tax Crimes (2nd ed. 2015).

42. The principal considerations are discussed in Chapter 8. *See generally* Nina J. Crimm, *Tax Controversies: Choice of Froum,* 9 B.U.J. Tax Law 1 (1991); David B. Porter, *Where Can You Litigate Your Federal Tax Case?*, Tax Notes, Jan. 27, 2003, p. 558.

District Court. All law students are familiar with District Court. It is the only tax trial forum in which juries may be used,[43] but jury-trial tax cases are not the norm even in District Court. Civil tax cases constitute only a small slice of the typical District Court's docket, and District Court judges are rarely tax experts. On the other hand, some practitioners believe that the generalist nature of District Courts provides a breadth of perspective useful in some situations. For example, although federal tax law is mostly self-contained, state law principles sometimes are important in Federal tax controversies. District Court and Bankruptcy Court judges tend to be much more conversant with state law than are Tax Court and Court of Federal Claims judges.

Tax Court. The Tax Court is the most important trial court as to liability determination. When the modern income tax began in 1913, the first controversy resolution forum was an office within the agency itself (then called the Internal Revenue Bureau). Complaints of pro-government bias and lack of institutional independence led to the creation in the 1920s of the Board of Tax Appeals (B.T.A.) as an Executive Branch agency independent of the Bureau. The modern Tax Court was shaped by legislation in the 1940s and in 1969.[44]

The 1969 legislation established the Tax Court under Congress's power in Article I, section 8 of the Constitution "[t]o constitute Tribunals inferior to the supreme Court." Several decisions have addressed how the Tax Court fits in our constitutional order, but their reasoning cannot be readily harmonized. Taking the cases at face value, the Tax Court seems to be a "Court of Law" which exercises a portion of the judicial power of the United States but is not in the Article III Judicial Branch. Instead, it might be in the Article II Executive Branch although it is independent of Executive control and although the point of the 1969 legislation was to convert the tribunal from an administrative agency to a court. Alternatively, it might be in the Article I Legislative Branch although it is independent of Congress.[45] If you understand what that means, the authors of this text bow down and worship you as a life form higher than human.

As an Article I court, the Tax Court has only the jurisdiction conferred upon it by statute. Legislation over the last several decades has often expanded that jurisdiction, but the court's original purpose—deciding deficiency cases—remains its most important purpose. Sections 7441 to 7487 describe the organization and jurisdiction of the Tax Court.

---

43. *See, e.g.*, Funk v. Commissioner, 687 F.2d 264 (8th Cir. 1982) (neither Seventh Amendment nor statute requires jury trials in Tax Court deficiency actions).

44. The leading history of the Tax Court and its predecessors is Harold Dubroff & Brant J. Hellwig, The United States Tax Court: An Historical Analysis (2nd ed. 2014). *See also* Harold Dubroff & Charles M. Greene, *Recent Developments in the Business and Procedures of the United States Tax Court*, 52 Alb. L. Rev. 33 (1987).

45. This formulation is a distillation of *Freytag v. Commissioner*, 501 U.S. 868 (1991); *Kuretski v. Commissioner*, 755 F.3d 929 (D.C. Cir. 2014), *cert. denied,* 135 S. Ct. 2309 (2015); and *South Carolina State Ports Auth. v. Fed. Maritime Comm'n*, 243 F.3d 165, 171 (4th Cir. 2001), *cert. denied,* 535 U.S. 743 (2002).

December 2015 legislation added the following sentence to Section 7441: "The Tax Court is not an agency of, and shall be independent of, the executive branch of the Government." This cryptic pronouncement may muddy the waters as much as it clarifies them.

When fully staffed, the Tax Court has 19 regular judges (each judge being called a "division" of the court), each appointed (by the President subject to Senate confirmation) for a 15-year term. It has as well a number of special trial judges who act somewhat like magistrate judges in the district courts.[46] In addition, a number of former regular judges continue to hear and decide cases on senior status.

The Tax Court is located in Washington, D.C., where it holds some trials. In addition, Tax Court judges "ride circuit," hearing groups of cases (trial dockets) in approximately 75 cities around the country. Typically, a draft opinion is prepared by the judge who presided over the trial, and the draft opinion is then circulated to the other divisions of the court. Cases of sufficient importance, or as to which the judges are in disagreement, may receive full-court (*en banc*) review. This sometimes results in a complex of plurality, concurring, and dissenting opinions.

The Tax Court issues several types of opinions. In descending order of precedential or influential weight, they are: (1) reviewed opinions (all or most divisions of the court participating), (2) regular opinions (only one division participating but involving an issue not settled by previous decisions), (3) memorandum opinions (only one division and generally involving only the application of settled law), and (4) summary opinions (resolving small-dollar cases and having no precedential value). Reviewed and regular opinions (both identified as "T.C.") are published in an official reporter: the United States Tax Court Reports. Memorandum opinions (identified as "T.C.M.") are collected in unofficial reporters. The Tax Court's official position is that memorandum opinions are not precedential. However, the rest of the world (and even the Tax Court itself often) treats them as precedential. All Tax Court opinions (including summary opinions) are posted on the Tax Court's website at www.ustaxcourt.gov.

Unlike the other available fora, the Tax Court hears only tax cases. Moreover, Tax Court judges usually had substantial experience in tax practice (private, governmental, or both) before donning black robes. Thus, the conventional wisdom (doubted in some quarters) is that the Tax Court is the court to select for taxpayers who have strong cases on the technical merits.

Old cases sometimes suggested that, because of the Tax Court's expertise and its nationwide jurisdiction, Tax Court decisions should be accorded greater weight than decisions of other courts.[47] Congress rejected that approach in 1948 when it directed federal appellate courts to review Tax Court decisions "in the same manner and to the same extent as decisions of the district courts in civil actions tried without a

---

46. Section 7443A allows the chief judge of the Tax Court to assign trials of cases to special trial judges. Rejecting constitutional challenges, the Supreme Court upheld the assignment of complex cases to special trial judges. Freytag v. Commissioner, 501 U.S. 868 (1993). Part of the Court's rationale was that, to become effective, proposed opinions in such cases must be adopted on behalf of the court by a division of the court, thus causing the decision to be rendered by a judge, not by a special trial judge. *See also* Ballard v. Commissioner, 544 U.S. 40 (2005) (invalidating the Tax Court's practice of not including special trial judge reports in record on appeal).

47. *E.g.,* Dobson v. Commissioner, 320 U.S. 489, 502 (1943).

jury."[48] Notwithstanding the statute, one occasionally detects in post-1948 cases a whiff of the older view.[49]

Although it is less prevalent than formerly, some still hold the view that the Tax Court tends to favor the IRS.[50] The view probably arose for three reasons: (1) many Tax Court judges served with the IRS, Treasury, or Justice Department before taking the bench, (2) the IRS appears before the Tax Court in every case, provoking fears of "capture," and (3) the IRS does in fact win (in part or whole) most Tax Court cases. This view is mistaken. Many Tax Court judges have private practice or part private/part governmental backgrounds, and the most convincing explanation of victory rates is that taxpayers appear *pro se* far more often in Tax Court than in the other tax trial tribunals. The best empirical work dispels the myth of Tax Court favoritism towards the IRS.[51]

Court of Federal Claims. The current Court of Federal Claims is the culmination of evolution. For many years, the Court of Claims existed as a forum of national jurisdiction to hear claims against the United States government. It possessed both trial and appellate jurisdiction. In the Federal Courts Improvement Act of 1982, Congress bifurcated the Court of Claims, vesting its trial jurisdiction in a new Claims Court and its appellate jurisdiction (along with appellate jurisdiction over customs and patent cases) in a new Court of Appeals for the Federal Circuit. The Claims Court was an Article I court, while the Federal Circuit is an Article III court. Subsequently, the Claims Court was renamed the Court of Federal Claims.

For tax law purposes, the most important aspect of the court is that it and the District Courts possess concurrent original jurisdiction over suits to recover overpayment of federal taxes.[52] Because they hear and have heard claims against the government, the Court of Federal Claims and its ancestors historically have thought of themselves as "the conscience of the federal government." This has given rise to the view in some quarters that this is the court to choose for taxpayers whose cases are weak on the law but strong in equities. It would be dangerous to place too much weight on this perception.

Bankruptcy Court. Bankruptcy cases are commenced by the filing of a petition in Bankruptcy Court. Typically, the debtor files the petition "voluntarily." The most important types of bankruptcy cases are Chapter 7 (liquidations), Chapter 11 (reorga-

---

48. IRC § 7482(a)(1); *see* Leandra Lederman, *(Un)Appealing Deference to the Tax Court,* 63 Duke L.J. 1835 (2014).

49. *E.g.,* Waterman v. United States, 113 AFTR2d 1169, at n. 10 (S.D. Ohio 2014). *But see* Steve R. Johnson, *The Phoenix and the Perils of the Second Best: Why Heightened Appellate Deference to Tax Court Decisions is Undesirable,* 77 Or. L. Rev. 235 (1998) (criticizing this view).

50. Similar fears are part of the reason why recurring proposals to create a single appellate court to hear all federal tax appeals have failed. *See id.* at 243–47.

51. *See* James Edward Maule, *Instant Replay, Weak Teams, and Disputed Calls: An Empirical Study of Alleged Tax Court Judge Bias,* 66 Tenn. L. Rev. 351 (1991).

52. *See* 28 U.S.C. §§ 1346(a)(1), 1491.

nizations), and Chapter 13 (adjustments of debts for individuals with regular income). As noted, federal tax issues often arise in the course of such cases.

In some instances, there are procedural advantages to handling tax issues in Bankruptcy Court.[53] Some practitioners believe that Bankruptcy Court is a more pro-debtor forum, that its concerns center on rehabilitating the debtor and preserving assets for private unsecured creditors. It would be a mistake, though, to assume that bankruptcy judges are uniformly of pro-debtor stripe.

3. Appeals

Not all Tax Court decisions can be appealed. The taxpayer, with the concurrence of the Tax Court, may choose to have the case heard under streamlined procedures that provide no right of appeal for the losing party. This option (called the S or small case procedure) is available in cases in which the amount at issue does not exceed $50,000 for any year.[54] *See* Chapter 8.

Tax Court decisions not subject to the S procedures are appealable to a federal Circuit Court. Venue lies in the court for the circuit in which the taxpayer resides or, in the case of a corporation, in which the taxpayer has its principal place of business.[55]

District Court decisions are appealable to the circuit of which the district is a part. Court of Federal Claims decisions are appealable to the Court of Appeals for the Federal Circuit. Bankruptcy Court decisions are appealable to the district court or to the circuit's Bankruptcy Appellate Panel.[56]

The losing party in the Circuit Court may seek Supreme Court review via writ of certiorari. About 10,000 certiorari petitions of all kinds are filed with the Supreme Court each year, and only 70 to 100 of these petitions are granted. In a typical year, the Supreme Court hears and decides four or fewer federal tax cases. The two principal reasons for grant of certiorari are (1) administrative importance (principally the amount of revenue at stake nationally as to the issue) and (2) existence of a split between the circuit courts as to the issue.

---

53. A decided advantage of Bankruptcy Court is that, unique among the available tribunals, this court can hear all claims against the debtor/taxpayer from all creditors arising at all times (unless barred by time or other factors). Those who owe money to the IRS typically owe money to others as well. The ability of the Bankruptcy Court to consider all creditors' claims globally can matter much to the debtor/taxpayer unable to satisfy all of her debts.

54. IRC § 7463(a), (b). The Tax Court denies S designation only rarely, usually when an important legal issue is present. Theoretically, the IRS can request S designation if the taxpayer does not. This almost never happens.

55. The government and the taxpayer can select a different circuit by written agreement although this rarely is done. IRC § 7482(b)(1), (2).

56. Section 1233 of the Bankruptcy Abuse Prevention and Consumer Protection Act of 2005, Pub. L. No. 109-8, 119 Stat. 23, amended 28 U.S.C. § 158 to create a certification process to facilitate appeals of some Bankruptcy Court decisions to Circuit Courts. The provision is aimed mainly at cases presenting important, unresolved questions of law.

III. Administrative Sources and Authorities in Tax

Tax statutes are interpreted by cases and by administrative positions. Administrative interpretations of the tax statutes come in numerous forms. The most important are discussed below.

A. Regulations

Regulations are the most authoritative administrative pronouncements in tax. They are drafted by IRS and Treasury lawyers. After many stages of review and amendment a regulation becomes final upon approval by the Secretary of the Treasury.[57]

The tax lawyer should be aware of the steps in the regulation issuance process and should monitor the progress of any regulation project important clients. Word-of-mouth sometimes provides the first warning. More formally, the government signals its work-plan priorities twice a year in the Semiannual Agenda of Regulations (or Priority Guidance Plan).

In some instances, the IRS publishes an Advance Notice of Proposed Rule-making. It describes the positions the government intends to propose and invites public comment on them. When the government actually proposes a regulation, it announces it in a Notice of Proposed Rulemaking, which invites public comments. Written comments always are permitted, and oral hearings sometimes are scheduled.

After considering comments, the government may withdraw the proposed regulation, re-propose a modified version, or adopt the regulation with or without modification. When a strong need exists for immediate guidance, the government may issue the measure simultaneously as a proposed regulation and as a temporary regulation going into immediate effect. New temporary regulations expire not more than three years after the date of their issuance.[58] Section 7805 sets out rules governing promulgation of regulations.

Proposed, temporary, and final regulations are published in the Federal Register and in the IRS's Internal Revenue Bulletin. They are accompanied by Treasury Decisions ("TDs"). The preambles of Notices of Proposed Rulemaking and TDs are not printed in the compilations of final regulations. However, they often contain useful explanations, and they show which comments the IRS took seriously. The thorough tax attorney always examines the preamble(s) in every case in which the meaning of a regulation is at issue.

---

57. In addition to the Treasury regulations, there are a number of internal procedural regulations of the IRS. They describe how IRS functions are performed and the respective roles of taxpayers and IRS personnel in various administrative processes. See Proc. Reg. §§ 601.101 to 801.6. The procedural regulations are issued by the IRS without the necessity of Treasury approval.

58. IRC § 7805(e)(2).

Final regulations are compiled in Title 26 of the Code of Federal Regulations. Thus, as with tax statutes, there are two ways to refer to the same regulation: 26 C.F.R. § 1.162-21 and Treas. Reg. § 1.162-21 identify the same regulation. Tax practitioners typically use the latter styling.

As indicated by the above example, there typically are three components of each regulation citation. The prefix to the left of the period identifies the type of tax or equivalent. As prominent instances, "1" refers to income tax; "20" to estate tax; "25" to gift tax; "31" to some employment taxes; and "301" to procedure and administration.[59] The number immediately to the right of the period identifies the Code section under which the regulation was promulgated. Finally, the number to the right of the hyphen indicates the order in which that regulation is placed among the regulations under that Code section. Thus, section 1.162-21 is the twenty-first regulation under section 162 of the income tax. Temporary regulations are identified with a "T" after the last digit.

Regulations have been written under nearly every Code section. However, many of the older regulations have not been updated to reflect subsequent amendment of the statute. Before relying on a regulation, the practitioner must ascertain whether it is current in material respects.

B. Revenue Rulings

A revenue ruling applies the law, or what the IRS believes the law to be, to a factual situation. The factual situation may reflect an actual scenario encountered by IRS personnel (usually during audits) or an amalgamation of such scenarios. The idea is to provide guidance to taxpayers and IRS agents as to significant matters that are not clearly resolved by statute, regulations, and settled case law.

Revenue rulings are numbered sequentially by year of issuance. For instance, Rev. Rul. 83-179 was the 179th revenue ruling issued in 1983, and Rev. Rul. 2002-4 was the fourth revenue ruling issued in 2002. (The IRS switched to the full year prefix in 2000.) Revenue rulings are published in the IRS's weekly publication, the Internal Revenue Bulletin (the "I.R.B."). Formerly, the I.R.B.s were collected twice yearly in the Cumulative Bulletin (the "C.B."). The IRS stopped publishing the C.B. in 2009 and discontinued paper copies of the I.R.B. in 2013. The electronic version of the I.R.B. is available on, and is searchable through, the IRS's website.

IRS Counsel drafts revenue rulings. Draft rulings are subject to multiple levels of review within IRS, IRS Counsel, and sometimes Treasury. The number of revenue rulings issued has decreased substantially in recent decades. The tax system would benefit from a greater volume of published guidance, but budgetary limitations make significant increase unlikely in the foreseeable future.

---

59. "301" refers to procedural regulations finalized by Treasury, as opposed to the "601" IRS procedural regulations described earlier.

C. Revenue Procedures

Revenue Procedures are also published in the I.R.B. and numbered sequentially. They set forth procedures and practices, such as when and how taxpayers should effect elections permitted by the Code, how they can change accounting methods, etc. In theory, revenue procedures involve only administrative or mechanical matters. Sometimes, though, substantive policy statements slip into revenue procedures.

Certain revenue procedures are reissued each year bearing the same number (except for year) and restating rules in the same area, sometimes with modification from the prior year's rules. For example, Rev. Proc. 20xx-1 each year describes how taxpayers are to go about seeking letter rulings, determination letters, information letters, and similar guidance. Rev. Proc. 20xx-2 each year describes procedures for furnishing technical advice memoranda. Rev. Proc. 20xx-3 identifies areas as to which the IRS will not issue rulings. Rev. Procs. 20xx-4 through 20xx-7 relate to similar but specialized types of guidance. Rev. Proc. 20xx-8 sets out user fee schedules for obtaining various types of guidance.

How punctiliously must the taxpayer satisfy each procedural step specified by a statute, regulation, revenue procedure, notice, or announcement? Will the failure to meet the least jot and tittle doom the taxpayer's attempt to invoke the procedure? One should strive for perfect compliance, of course. If there is some shortfall, however, the taxpayer may explore three options. First, relief provisions particular to specific topics appear some places in the Code.[60]

Second, the judicial "substantial compliance" doctrine may—but usually doesn't—provide relief. This "is a narrow equitable doctrine [used] to avoid taxpayer hardship if the taxpayer establishes that he or she intended to comply with a provision, did everything reasonably possible to comply with the provision, but did not comply ... because of a failure to meet the provision's specific requirements."[61]

Third, in some situations, the so called "section 9100" regulations empower the IRS to grant administrative relief if, among other things, the taxpayer properly requests such relief and shows that she acted reasonably and in good faith, albeit not fully effectively. The principal provisions address extensions of time to make elections, automatic extensions, and other extensions.[62] Actually securing relief under these provisions is the unusual result, not the norm. Moreover, in general, relief under any device is confined to shortfalls as to administrative requirements; compliance with statutory requirements typically must be scrupulous.[63]

---

60. *E.g.*, IRC § 1362(f) (relief for inadvertent invalid Subchapter S elections or terminations).

61. Poppe v. Commissioner, T.C. Memo. 2015-205, at n. 7 (citing cases) (denying relief on the facts of the case); *see* Steve R. Johnson, *Substantial Compliance*, State Tax Notes, July 20, 2009, p. 169.

62. Reg. §§ 301.9100-1, -2, & -3. respectively. Related provisions address more particular situations. *See generally* Vines v. Commissioner, 126 T.C. 279, 290–91 (2006).

63. *E.g.*, Dirks v. Commissioner, T.C. Memo. 2004-138.

D. Notices and Announcements

IRS notices and announcements provide guidance, often in advance of regulations and rulings (which take longer to issue). They are published in the I.R.B. In recent years, notices have largely ousted revenue rulings. In the early 1980s, the IRS issued between 200 and 400 revenue rulings but only 10 to 20 notices each year. Recently, the IRS has been issuing under 50 revenue rulings but around 100 notices each year. Notices are less formal and so are much easier to finalize. The IRS views notices as being on the same precedential or persuasive plane as revenue rulings.[64] Courts, however, seem to treat notices less deferentially.[65]

E. Other Published IRS Positions

The IRS publishes several other types of positions in the I.R.B. They include disbarment notices (of practitioners no longer eligible to practice before the IRS), orders delegating to named offices or officials the power to take certain actions, and acquiescence and nonacquiescence notices. The latter are issued by the IRS as to cases decided adversely to the IRS. An acquiescence signifies that the IRS concedes the correctness of the decision, thus will not continue to litigate the issue. The IRS may acquiesce only in part, or it may "acquiesce in result only," conceding the correctness of the outcome but not of the reasoning on which the court based the outcome. A nonacquiescence means that the IRS disagrees with the result of the case and will continue to set up the issue in other cases.[66]

As the forms of IRS guidance continue to evolve, it might be well to periodically check "Electronic Reading Room" on the IRS website. This link contains information on the types of IRS guidance documents, how they are promulgated, and other topics.

From the IRS website one also can review and download numerous IRS forms and plain-language explanatory publications. These publications do much more good than harm. Nonetheless, statements in them may be incomplete and occasionally are imprecise. Taxpayers may not invoke erroneous statements in IRS publications to defeat deficiencies asserted by the IRS.[67] But reasonable reliance on the publications may deflect accuracy-related penalties.[68]

Responding to a public perception that citizens have no rights when dealing with the IRS, the IRS has issued a Taxpayer Bill of Rights ("TBOR"). According to an IRS press release on June 10, 2014, this document "takes the multiple existing rights em-

---

64. Rev. Rul. 90-91, 1990-2 C.B. 262.

65. *E.g.,* BMC Softwear, Inc. v. Commissioner, 780 F.3d 669, 675–76 (5th Cir. 2015); Costantino v. TRW, Inc., 13 F.3d 969, 980–81 (6th Cir. 1994) (both refusing to defer to IRS notices).

66. Formerly, the IRS's reasoning for appealing or not appealing adverse decisions sometimes was explained in an action on decision ("AOD").

67. *E.g.,* Casa de La Jolla Park, Inc. v. Commissioner, 94 T.C. 386, 396 (1990).

68. *See* Treas. Reg. § 1.6662-4(d)(3)(iii).

bedded in the tax code and groups them into 10 broad categories, making them more visible and easier for taxpayers to find on IRS.gov."

The rights are the rights to: (1) be informed, (2) quality service, (3) pay no more than the correct amount of tax, (4) challenge the IRS and be heard, (5) appeal IRS decisions in independent forums, (6) finality, (7) privacy, (8) confidentiality, (9) retain representation, and (10) a fair and just tax system.[69]

Although the press release calls these rights "cornerstone," "fundamental," and "important," they are matters of administrative policy only and are not judicially enforceable. That remains the case despite December 2015 legislation that amended Section 7803(a)(3) to direct the Commissioner to "ensure that [IRS employees] are familiar with and act in accord with [these] taxpayer rights."

F. Private Letter Rulings

Clients have different levels of risk aversion. Usually, the tax attorney's oral statement setting out his level of confidence in the position to be taken suffices. For extra comfort, the client may request that the lawyer prepare an opinion letter as to tax consequences. When the greatest certainty is needed, the attorney may seek a private letter ruling from the IRS. A favorable private letter ruling is akin to an insurance policy.

The process starts when the taxpayer files a ruling request with the IRS National Office. The request sets out the facts of a proposed transaction, the taxpayer's conclusions as to the effects of the transaction, and the reasoning and authorities in support of those conclusions. As noted above, the "how" of requesting a letter ruling is given by the first revenue procedure of the year in question. An Appendix to that revenue procedure contains a sample format for requesting a letter ruling.

The IRS will consider the ruling request, sometimes conferring with the taxpayer's representative in person or by telephone. If the IRS appears to disagree with the taxpayer's conclusion, the standard strategy is to withdraw the request before a negative letter is issued. The existence of a negative letter makes it very difficult for an IRS Revenue Agent or Appeals Officer to accept the taxpayer's treatment of the issue.

If the National Office agrees with the taxpayer, it will issue a favorable letter ruling. Although letter rulings are not published by the IRS, they are publicly released (in redacted form to preserve the taxpayer's anonymity) and can be researched through private electronic and print media.

Favorable rulings bind the IRS as to the taxpayer who requested the rulings[70] unless there was a material misrepresentation or omission of facts in the ruling request or a significant change of controlling law. Revocation of a letter ruling typically

69. IRS Pub. 1, "Your Rights as a Taxpayer" (2014).

70. The Code does not command this result. The conclusive effect of letter rulings is pursuant to administrative decision. Rev. Proc. 2016-1, 2016-1 I.R.B. 1, § 11.

is on a prospective basis. The IRS will retroactively revoke a ruling only "in rare or unusual circumstances."[71]

For many years, letter rulings were identified by seven digits, signifying year and week of issuance and order of issuance within that week. Thus, PLR 9325003 was the third letter ruling issued during the 25th week of 1993. Now, styling uses the full year, such as PLR 200425003. The IRS usually finalizes a letter ruling within four months of the filing of the request, and the taxpayer may request expedited consideration.

Because of resource limitations, the IRS ruling program has been under pressure for decades, and the number of letter rulings issued annually has been dropping. One reason is that the IRS no longer issues "comfort rulings," i.e., rulings requested as to matters on which the law already is clear. The annual revenue procedure identifying subjects as to which the IRS will not rule, is one attempt to cull such unproductive exercises. In addition, the IRS charges user fees for letter rulings, on a sliding scale ranging from several hundred dollars to around $30,000.

As noted, a PLR typically binds the IRS only as to the taxpayer who requested it. Other taxpayers, even ones situated similarly to the requesting taxpayer, would seem statutorily foreclosed from relying on the PLR since section 6110(k)(3) provides that PLRs "may not be used or cited as precedent."

Does that mean that a taxpayer whose research discloses a favorable PLR issued to another taxpayer, will remain silent as to that PLR? Of course not. First, the taxpayer will, and should, consider the PLR in deciding what return position to take. More often than not, what the IRS thinks in 2000 it will continue to think in 2010, assuming comparable transactions and no significant intervening change in the law. In this regard, the PLR is being used predictively, not as precedent.

Second, the taxpayer will use the PLR during audit and administrative appeals. The revenue agent or appeals officer will assert section 6110(k)(3). Nonetheless, the PLR probably will have some traction, especially if the taxpayer's attorney can credibly argue "based on the PLR, the National Office would find for us if a TAM were sought. We can save ourselves the trouble and delay of going for a TAM if you just give up the adjustment now."

Third, the taxpayer also will try to use the PLR if the case is litigated. Citation of the PLR in the brief will be accompanied by a footnote explaining why the PLR is not really being cited as precedent. This is disingenuous, of course, but courts too sometimes cite PLRs, section 6110(k)(3) notwithstanding.[72]

As the forms of IRS guidance continue to evolve, it might be well to periodically check "Electronic Reading Room" on the IRS website. This link contains information on the types of IRS guidance documents, how they are promulgated, and other topics.

---

71. *Id.* at § 11.06.

72. *E.g.*, Wolpaw v. Commissioner, 47 F.3d 787, 792–93 (6th Cir. 1995); Transco Exploration Co. v. Commissioner, 949 F.2d 837, 840 (5th Cir. 1992).

From the IRS website one also can review and download numerous IRS forms and plain-language explanatory publications. These publications do much more good than harm. Nonetheless, statements in them may be incomplete and occasionally are imprecise. Taxpayers may not invoke erroneous statements in IRS publications to defeat deficiencies asserted by the IRS.[73] But reasonable reliance on the publications may deflect accuracy-related penalties.[74]

G. Determination Letters

Determination letters are similar to private letter rulings except they may be issued (1) by field offices, (2) on matters covered by settled law, and (3) as to completed transactions, not contemplated transactions. Most determination letters relate to whether an entity qualifies as a retirement plan or as a tax-exempt organization.

H. Technical Advice Memoranda

Technical Advice Memoranda (TAMs) are similar in organization and numbering to PLRs. However, they arise in a different manner. During an audit or administrative appeal, the IRS and the taxpayer may agree on the facts but disagree on the law. The Revenue Agent or Appeals Officer may then contact the National Office, requesting its view of the law. Although the IRS field employee is nominally the requesting party, the taxpayer often initiates the process by asking the field employee to submit the request. As noted previously, steps in the TAM process are set forth in the second revenue procedure issued by the IRS each year.[75]

TAMs often receive more careful consideration than PLRs, so many practitioners accord TAMs a slightly higher persuasive status. Before urging that a TAM be sought, the tax practitioner should have considerable confidence in the correctness of the taxpayer's legal position. Issuance of an adverse TAM often eliminates flexibility the field personnel might otherwise have been inclined to show, leaving the taxpayer with only two options: concede the issue or litigate it.

The IRS Chief Counsel's Office also provides guidance to IRS functions through a variety of less formal devices. These devices include both generic legal advice and case-specific advice.[76]

I. Government Manuals

The Internal Revenue Manual (IRM) exists to guide IRS personnel in the performance of their duties. Its text combines command and advice. As one might expect

---

73. *E.g.*, Casa de La Jolla Park, Inc. v. Commissioner, 94 T.C. 386, 396 (1990).

74. *See* Treas. Reg. § 1.6662-4(d)(3)(iii).

75. *See also* Proc. Reg. § 601.201 (procedures as to TAMs and other types of IRS determinations).

76. *See, e.g.*, Chief Counsel Notice CC-2007-003 (Jan. 19, 2007) (describing procedures by which other functions in the IRS can obtain advice from the National Office technical functions).

given the multitude of IRS responsibilities, the IRM is massive. It is divided into parts, covering administration, collection, examination, appeals, criminal investigation, etc. The parts are subdivided variously.

Although the IRM is not "law" in the traditional sense,[77] consulting it can be quite useful to the tax practitioner, especially on matters of procedure. IRS personnel are supposed to follow the IRM. When they do not, pointing out the failure can sometimes give the practitioner a powerful argument while the case remains in administrative posture.

The organization of the IRM creates an obstacle to mining the gold in it. Each successive number is a subdivision of the number immediately preceding it. Numbers over 9 are indicated by parentheses. Thus, a number like 86(12)3 means the third division of the twelfth division of the sixth division of part 8 of the IRM. Without the parentheses, the citation would indicate the third division of the second division of the first division of the sixth division of part 8. More recently, IRM citations usually are rendered with periods separating subdivisions, for example, 86(12)3 may be given as 8.6.12.3. This newer version is an improvement and is the format used in this book.

Commercial services provide print versions of the IRM (often with helpful "How to Use the Manual" explanations). Both the IRS website (www.irs.gov) and commercial sites have versions of the IRM. However, the one on the IRS's site is less complete.

Although less important than the IRM, there are many other government manuals, reports, and digests of potential interest to tax lawyers. They include the IRS Chief Counsel Directives Manual, various Chief Counsel bulletins (dealing with criminal tax enforcement, tax litigation, disclosure litigation, and collection, bankruptcy, and summonses), litigation guideline memoranda, compliance officer memoranda, and various Department of Justice manuals. Many, though not all, government manuals and parts of manuals have been publicly released, either as a result of administrative decision or because of successful litigation under the Freedom of Information Act.

J. Other Government Sources

The discussion thus far accounts for the most important types of administrative sources and authorities in tax, but it is far from exhaustive. At times in your practice, you will encounter references to, among many other sources: service center advice, IRS legal memoranda, IRS information letters, field service advice, industry specialization papers, field directives, etc.[78]

---

77. In general, agency policy manuals do not have the force of law and do not bind the agency. Schweiker v. Hansen, 450 U.S. 785, 789 (1981) (per curiam). Specifically, the IRM "is an internal IRS document issued to instruct personnel in performing their duties, and thus does not create any enforceable rights for taxpayers." Dudley's Commercial & Indus. Coating, Inc. v. United States, 292 F. Supp. 2d 976, 987 (M.D. Tenn. 2003) (citing cases).

78. *See generally* Gail Levin Richmond, Federal Tax Research pt. 3 (9th ed. 2014), U.S. Dep't of Treasury; Understanding IRS Guidance—A Brief Primer (2005); *Inventory of IRS Guidance Documents—A Draft*, Tax Notes, July 17, 2000, at 305; Mitchell Rogovin & Donald L. Korb, *The Four R's*

The line-up changes over time. Sometimes, modalities are replaced, as when revenue rulings replaced ITs (income tax unit rulings). Other times, like old soldiers, they simply fade away, like GCMs (General Counsel Memoranda), which once were important but ceased being issued in the 1990s. Many such changes will occur during your career as a tax attorney.

IV. Administrative Law Issues

A key dynamic in current U.S. tax administration is the overdue acknowledgement that general rules of administrative law apply to tax as well. The Administrative Procedure Act ("APA") clearly applies to Treasury and the IRS,[79] and for generations occasional tax cases applied (or misapplied) one or another of the APA rules.[80] Nonetheless, the tax bench and bar (both private and public) found the APA's applicability to tax to be an inconvenient truth and did their best to ignore it.

The Supreme Court's 2011 *Mayo* decision[81] was the final nail in the coffin of such tax insularity. A major current of tax administration now is and for decades will remain determining precisely what the APA requires in the context of tax. Numerous specific issues will have to be worked out.[82] Some of the most important are sketched below.

A. Notice and Comment

Under the APA, in order to promulgate binding rules (so called legislative or substantive regulations), an agency must publish general notice of its proposed rulemaking and give interested persons opportunity to comment.[83] These requirements do not apply to "interpretative rules, general statements of policy, or rules of agency organ-

Revisited: Regulations, Rulings, Reliance, and Retroactivity in the 21st Century: A View from Within, 46 Duq. L. Rev. 323 (2008).

79. 5 USC § 551(1).

80. *E.g.*, Am. Standard Inc. v. Commissioner, 602 F.2d 256 (Ct. Cl. 1979); Wendland v. Commissioner, 79 T.C. 355 (1982), *aff'd*, 739 F.2d 580 (11th Cir. 1984) *&* 728 F.2d 1249 (9th Cir. 1984), *cert. denied*, 469 U.S. 1034 (1984). In *Wendland*, the IRS conceded that, in general, the APA notice and comment requirements apply to tax regulations. 79 T.C. at 380.

81. Mayo Found. for Med. Educ. & Research v. United States, 562 U.S. 44, 55 (2011).

82. Some are discussed in Steve R. Johnson, *Preserving Fairness in Tax Administration in the* Mayo *Era*, 32 Va. Tax Rev. 269, 300-23 (2012). Litigation under the APA often involves issues—such as constitutional and prudential standing, ripeness, mootness, exhaustion of remedies, and others—that are seen less frequently in traditional tax litigation. *See* 5 U.S.C. §§ 702–706; *e.g.*, Florida Bankers Ass'n v. U.S. Dep't of Treasury, 799 F.3d 1065 (D.C. Cir. 2015); AICPA v. IRS, 114 AFTR2d 6451 (D.D.C. 2014) (both rejecting challenges to tax regulations because the plaintiffs lacked standing to challenge the regulations). The Anti-Injunction Act, IRC § 7421 (discussed in Chapter 13), also plays a major role in APA tax cases.

83. 5 USC § 553.

ization, procedure, or practice."[84] Nor do they apply when "the agency for good cause finds (and incorporates the finding and a brief statement of reasons therefor in the rules issued) that notice and public procedure thereon are impracticable, unnecessary, or contrary to the public interest."[85]

Treasury usually publishes notice of proposed tax rules in the *Federal Register*, invites comments, and considers comments received. However, Treasury sometimes omits these steps on the ground that its regulations are merely interpretive, thus are excepted from the APA requirements.

This reasoning is wrong. Treasury intends its tax regulations to have binding effect, and that makes them legislative, not interpretive.[86] Accordingly, many existing tax regulations may be procedurally invalid.[87] Some Treasury and IRS actions have been struck down on this basis.[88]

The up-to-date lawyer will avoid an error that appeared in many old cases and that some (including the IRS) continue to commit even now. Specific-authority tax regulations are promulgated pursuant to delegations contained in particular substantive Code sections. For example, sections 217(j) and 469(l) authorize Treasury to write regulations addressing deductibility of, respectively, moving expenses and passive-activity losses. Over a thousand such delegations exist in the Code, and their wordings—thus the extent of the delegations—vary considerably. Nonetheless, most tax regulations fall outside such specific delegations. They are general-authority regulations because they spring from the delegation in section 7805(a) of authority to "prescribe all needful rules and regulations for the enforcement of [the Code]."

The old, erroneous view equated specific-authority regulations with substantive, legislative regulations and general-authority regulations with merely interpretive regulations. This approach never had support in the APA or administrative law case law. Appropriately, the Tax Court has repudiated its decisions taking the old view,[89] but it may take some (including the IRS) a while to get the memo.

Treasury may not just "go through the motions" required by the APA. It must take comments seriously. This includes keeping an "open mind" on the issues,[90] responding

---

84. 5 USC § 553(b)(3)(A).

85. 5 USC § 553(b)(3)(B).

86. *See, e.g.*, Chrysler Corp. v. Brown, 441 U.S. 281, 295 (1979); Am. Mining Cong. v. Mine Safety & Health Admin., 995 F.2d 1106, 1109 (D.C. Cir. 1993).

87. *See, e.g.*, Kristin E. Hickman, *A Problem of Remedy: Responding to Treasury's (Lack of) Compliance with Administrative Procedure Act Rulemaking Requirements,* 76 Geo. Wash. L. Rev. 1153 (2008); Kristin E. Hickman, *Coloring Outside the Lines: Examining Treasury's (Lack of) Compliance with Administrative Procedure Act Rulemaking Requirements*, 82 Notre Dame L. Rev. 1727 (2007).

88. *E.g.*, Cohen v. United States, 853 F. Supp. 2d 138, 143 (D.D.C. 2012), *aff'd*, 751 F.3d 629 (D.C. Cir. 2014) (refund procedure created by IRS invalidated for failure to satisfy notice and comment requirements).

89. Altera Corp. v. Commissioner, 145 T.C. No. 3, at n. 10 (2015).

90. *Cf.* Izaak Walton League v. Marsh, 655 F.2d 346, 364 (D.C. Cir. 1981) (non-tax case).

to substantial comments,[91] and finalizing regulations that, if not identical to the originally proposed rules, are at least a logical outgrowth of them.[92]

B. "Arbitrary and Capricious" Review

Under the APA, a court may set aside "agency action, findings, and conclusions" on any of several grounds, including that they are "arbitrary, capricious, an abuse of discretion, or otherwise not in accordance with law."[93] Under the often quoted *State Farm* case, an agency action is arbitrary and capricious "if the agency has relied on factors which Congress has not intended it to consider, entirely failed to consider an important aspect of the problem, offered an explanation for its decision that runs counter to the evidence before the agency, or is so implausible that it could not be ascribed to a difference in view or the product of agency expertise."[94]

APA review is supposed to be "exceedingly deferential."[95] Nevertheless, tax regulations sometimes have been invalidated as being arbitrary and capricious.[96] Loss on such grounds, although inconvenient, typically is not fatal. The government can try again, reproposing the regulation after curing the procedural defect.

C. Deference Generally

The degree of deference[97] courts should accord to Treasury and IRS positions is the most frequently litigated administrative law issue in tax, and recent decisions have rendered obsolete much prior case law and commentary. Although no short discussion can do justice to all the nuances, below we address (1) the major standards in play and (2) results under those standards.

1. Standards

Oceans of ink spilled in previous cases and commentary have been rendered irrelevant by *Mayo* and other recent developments. In general, under current law and depending on the situation, one of three standards will apply to test the validity of an IRS interpretation of a tax statute or regulation: the standards emanating from the *Chevron, Skidmore,* and *Seminole Rock* cases.

---

91. *Altera, supra* (invalidating regulations under section 482 in part on this basis).

92. *Cf.* Shell Oil v. EPA, 950 F.2d 741 (D.C. Cir. 1991) (non-tax case).

93. 5 U.S.C. § 706(2)(A).

94. Motor Vehicles Mfrs. Ass'n v. State Farm Mut. Auto. Ins. Co., 463 U.S. 29, 43 (1983).

95. Fund for Animals, Inc. v. Rice, 85 F.3d 535, 541 (11th Cir. 1996).

96. *E.g.,* Dominion Resources, Inc. v. United States, 681 F.3d 1313 (Fed. Cir. 2012) (failure to articulate cogent explanation); *Altera, supra* (regulation lacked a basis in fact, was contrary to the evidence available to Treasury, and Treasury failed to rationally connect the choice it made to the facts it found); *see also* Steve R. Johnson, *Reasoned Explanation and IRS Adjudication,* 63 Duke L.J. 1771 (2014).

97. Unfortunately, "deference" does not have a single meaning, and the courts have often been unclear as to which meaning they intend. See, e.g., Atchison, Topeka & Santa Fe Ry. Co. v. Pena, 44 F.3d 437, 445 (7th Cir. 1994) (describing three meanings of "deference": delegation, respect, and persuasion).

- *Chevron*[98] applies when the IRS position is an interpretation of a Code section and the interpretation is set out in a regulation promulgated through the notice-and-comment process.[99]
- *Skidmore*[100] applies when the IRS position is an interpretation of a Code section and the interpretation is set out in any form other than a notice-and-comment regulation.[101]
- Absent a recognized exception, *Seminole Rock*[102] applies when the IRS position is an interpretation of a Treasury regulation, not a Code section.[103]

2. Results

Chevron has been heavily criticized, and the Supreme Court's application of it is occasional, inconsistent, and diminishing.[104] The doctrine may be dying in substance, but it continues to be intoned at least nominally. Thus, the lawyer must continue to treat it seriously.

When *Chevron* applies, its famous "two step" directs that a court should defer to the agency's view if that view is an at least reasonable construction of an ambiguous statute.[105] But the spirit in which a rule is applied matters more than the verbal formulation of the rule. *Chevron* was once seen as a pro-agency standard, and many still speak of it as such. However, in recent years, the doctrine has been applied more rigorously and less deferentially at both of its steps. For example, although the IRS prevailed in *Mayo* in 2011, *Chevron* did not save a tax regulation from invalidation in *Home Concrete* in 2012 and all nine justices dispensed with *Chevron* in analyzing, and ultimately upholding, a tax regulation in *King v. Burwell* in 2015.[106] Similarly, despite *Chevron*, lower courts found invalid two Circular 230 regulations in prominent 2014 cases.[107]

---

98. Chevron, U.S.A., Inc. v. Natural Res. Def. Council, Inc., 467 U.S. 837 (1984).

99. *Mayo, supra,* 562 U.S. at 55–58; *see also* Validus Reins., Ltd. v. United States, 786 F.3d 1039, 1049 (D.C. Cir. 2015) (in an excise tax case, rejecting the IRS's claim to *Chevron* deference in part because the IRS rulings failed to take into consideration an important aspect of the problem: a canon of construction).

100. Skidmore v. Swift & Co., 323 U.S. 134 (1944). *Skidmore* was rescued from oblivion by United States v. Mead Corp., 533 U.S. 218, 235–38 (2001).

101. *E.g.,* Taproot Admin. Servs., Inc. v. Commissioner, 133 T.C. 202, 208–09 & n. 15 (2009), *aff'd,* 679 F.3d 1109, 1115–16 (9th Cir. 2012) (both parties and both courts agreed that *Skidmore* is the appropriate standard as to revenue rulings). *See generally* Kristin E. Hickman, *IRB Guidance : The No Man's Land of Tax Code Interpretation,* 2009 Mich. St. L. Rev. 239.

102. Bowles v. Seminole Rock & Sand Co., 325 U.S. 410 (1945). The same principle is often identified by reference to the more recent case Auer v. Robbins, 519 U.S. 452 (1997).

103. *E.g.,* Carpenter Family Invs., LLC v. Commissioner, 136 T.C. 373, 379 n. 4 (2011). For the exceptions to *Seminole Rock's* applicability, see Steve R. Johnson, *Preserving Fairness in Tax Administration in the* Mayo *Era,* 32 Va. Tax Rev. 269, 311–13 (2012).

104. *See, e.g.,* Christine Kexel Chabot, *Selling* Chevron, 67 Admin. L. Rev. 481 (2015); Steve R. Johnson, *The Rise and Fall of* Chevron *in Tax: From the Early Days to* King *and Beyond,* 2015 Pepperdine L. Rev. 14.

105. *Chevron, supra,* 467 U.S. at 843–45 & 865–66.

106. 135 S. Ct. 2480 (2015).

107. Loving v. IRS, 742 F.3d 1013 (D.C. Cir. 2014); Ridgely v. Lew, 55 F. Supp. 3d 89 (D.D.C. 2014).

Each case, of course, stands on its own facts, and the pendulum may swing back towards agency indulgence at some time in the future. Nonetheless, lawyers should not assume that the IRS will prevail whenever *Chevron* provides the governing standard.

As applied to *Skidmore*, "deference" is a misnomer. Under that case, courts decide whether to adopt an agency's construction based on "the thoroughness evident in its consideration, the validity of its reasoning, its consistency with earlier and later pronouncements, and all those factors which give it the power to persuade, if lacking power to control."[108] This is an open-ended "all facts and circumstances" approach. Unsurprisingly, therefore, *Skidmore* "has produced a spectrum of judicial responses, from great respect at one end, to near indifference at the other."[109]

In general, under *Seminole Rock/Auer*, an agency's interpretation of its own regulation is "controlling" unless it is "plainly erroneous or inconsistent with the regulation."[110] Although appearing often in non-tax cases, this doctrine is less common in tax cases. The IRS, less steeped in administrative law than the Department of Justice is, may sometimes forget to assert it. Alternatively, the Tax Court is hostile to the doctrine,[111] so the IRS may deliberately choose to omit it in Tax Court cases.

Empirical studies suggest that the extraordinary attention paid to nuances of deference doctrine may be disproportionate to practical consequences. One study suggested that outcomes are largely uniform across the doctrines—the agency wins about 70% of the time regardless of which deference doctrine is applied.[112]

D. Specific Deference Considerations

Over the decades, numerous particular facts have been debated as possibly enhancing or eroding the customary levels of deference. Uniformity exists as to none of these. Described below are the majority views as to the issues.

1. "Bootstrapping"

Assume the IRS is engaged in litigation, during the course of which the government issues a regulation, ruling, or notice "enacting" its litigating position. That strikes many as unfair, as the government changing the rules after the game has started. Can the IRS get away with that?

---

108. *Skidmore, supra,* 323 U.S. at 140.

109. *Mead, supra,* 533 U.S. at 228. This characterization holds in tax as well. Among the many cases rejecting deference, see Voss v. Commissioner, 796 F.3d 1051 (9th Cir. 2015) (Field Service Advisory, Chief Counsel Advisory, IRM, and Litigation Guideline Memorandum); Validus Reins., Ltd. v. United States, 786 F.3d 1039 (D.C. Cir. 2015) (revenue ruling); Fed. Nat'l Mortgage Ass'n v. United States, 379 F.3d 1303, 1307–09 (Fed. Cir. 2014), *cert. denied,* 552 U.S. 1139 (2008) (revenue procedure).

110. *Auer, supra,* 519 U.S. at 461.

111. *See* Steve R. Johnson, Auer/Seminole Rock *Deference in the Tax Court,* 11 Pitt. Tax Rev. 1 (2013).

112. Richard J. Pierce, Jr., *What Do the Studies of Judicial Review of Agency Actions Mean?*, 63 Admin. L. Rev. 77, 85 (2011). *Auer* produced a higher agency-win rate (at least in the Supreme Court), but this difference may have narrowed in subsequent years.

The blackletter rule is that a regulation does not forfeit deference simply because it "was prompted by litigation."[113] The objection may have more force when the position is taken in a pronouncement below the level of a regulation.[114] Moreover, a litigating position that appears only in a brief usually receives little deference.[115]

2. Inconsistency in Policy

As seen above, the fact that the agency has taken inconsistent positions cuts against it under *Skidmore*. The same is true under *Seminole Rock*. However, agency inconsistency usually is held to be irrelevant for *Chevron* purposes.[116]

The foregoing discusses inconsistency at the level of broad policy, that is, in issued regulations and published rulings. IRS inconsistency in enforcement in specific cases also has generated controversy. This dimension is discussed in Part IV.H of this chapter.

3. Regulations Overruling Case Law

Can an agency overrule a court? That is, after a court has interpreted a statute may the agency issue a force-of-law regulation to command a different result? In the *Brand X* case, the Supreme Court answered the question with a qualified "yes." "A court's prior construction of a statute trumps [a contrary] agency construction otherwise entitled to *Chevron* deference only if the prior court decision holds that its construction follows from the unambiguous terms of the statute and thus leaves no room for agency discretion."[117]

Although *Brand X* was decided over a decade ago, its parameters remain unsettled. The Supreme Court had the opportunity to clarify the situation in 2012 in *Home Concrete*, a tax case, but its 4–1–4 decision failed to do so. The Court invalidated a regulation which sought to undo a previous Supreme Court decision. The plurality reasoned that, like *Chevron*, *Brand X* is premised on an implicit delegation to the agency to fill statutory gaps but that the prior decision fixed the meaning of the statute, leaving no gap for Treasury to fill via regulation.[118]

This approach is not distressing if, as in *Home Concrete* and later cases,[119] it is confined to prior Supreme Court decisions. This would entail only limited contraction of *Brand X*, meaning that agency regulations can trump prior court decisions except

113. Smiley v. Citibank (South Dakota) N.A., 517 U.S. 735, 741 (1996).

114. *See generally* Leandra Lederman, *The Fight Over "Fighting Regs" and Judicial Deference in Tax Litigation*, 92 B.U.L. Rev. 643 (2012).

115. *Cf.* Alaska Dep't of Envtl. Conservation v. EPA, 540 U.S. 461, 487–88 (2004) (non-tax case). *But see* NPR Inv., LLC v. United States, 740 F.3d 988, 1014 (5th Cir. 2014) (rejecting taxpayer's contention that an IRS notice was merely a litigating position and thus was not authority).

116. *E.g.*, United States v. Eurodif S.A., 555 U.S. 305, 316 (2009).

117. Nat'l Cable & Telecomms. Ass'n v. Brand X Internet Servs., 545 U.S. 967, 982 (2005).

118. United States v. Home Concrete Supply, LLC, 132 S. Ct. 1836 (2012); *see* Steve R. Johnson, *Reflections on* Home Concrete, 13 Fla. St. U. Bus. Rev. 75 (2014).

119. *E.g.*, *Validus*, *supra*, 786 F.3d at 1049.

those of the Supreme Court. The broadening of this approach to prior lower court decisions as well, however, would unravel *Brand X*.

4. Vintage

Mayo held that "neither antiquity nor contemporaneity with [enactment of the underlying] statute is a condition of [a regulation's] validity."[120] But this assertion should be refined.

The conditions of antiquity and contemporaneity appear to have more significance positively than negatively. That is, the fact that the regulation or other IRS position has long endured and/or that it was issued at or near the time Congress enacted the underlying statute increases the chance that the courts will embrace the regulation, while their absence does not diminish that chance. As a result, the IRS typically benefits more than the taxpayer from these considerations.[121] Great longevity of a regulation or other position facilitates statutory interpretation arguments that Congress endorsed the position by inaction (not overturning it legislatively) or by reenacting the statute without change.[122] It also increases the plausibility of claims that taxpayers and others reasonably relied on continuation of the old approach. Some judges care about reasonable reliance.[123] And longevity probably creates—psychologically if not legally—a presumption of validity.[124]

E. Phantom Regulations

Assume that a Code section provides as follows: "Under regulations to be prescribed by the Secretary, taxpayers may deduct Type X expenses." Assume further that Treasury has not yet issued the contemplated regulations. May taxpayers deduct Type X expenses even without regulations? Judges and commentators are not of one mind on this question. Some say that permitting the deductions would be to make real what is not real, *i.e.*, to conjure with phantoms. One scholar maintains that tax cases (which tend to treat the statute as operative despite Treasury's failure to issue regulations) are at odds with the general administrative law jurisprudence which take a stricter view.[125]

---

120. 562 U.S. at 55.

121. *Compare* Higgins v. Commissioner, 312 U.S. 212, 216 (1941) (rejecting a negative argument by the taxpayer), *with* United States v. Cleveland Indians Baseball Co., 532 U.S. 200, 219–20 (2001) (embracing a positive argument by the government).

122. These are widely recognized to be weak canons, but they continue sometimes to be used nonetheless. *E.g.*, Bob Jones Univ. v. Commissioner, U.S. 461 U.S. 574, 600 (1983) (remarking that "[o]rdinarily and quite appropriately, courts are slow to attribute significance to the failure of Congress to act on particular legislation" but finding special circumstances to be present in the case).

123. Five justices in *Home Concrete* accepted taxpayer reliance as an important interpretational consideration. 132 S. Ct. at 1847 & 1849 (Scalia, J., concurring in part & in result) & *id.* at 1853 (Kennedy, J., dissenting).

124. *E.g.*, Hall v. United States, 132 S. Ct. 1882, 1890 (2012) (bankruptcy tax case).

125. Amandeep S. Grewal, *Mixing Management Fee Waivers with* Mayo, 15 Fla. Tax Rev. 1 (2014).

F. Regulatory Flexibility Act

The APA is the most important, but not the only, body of administrative law rules that knocks for entry at the portal of tax administration. Another is the Regulatory Flexibility Act ("RegFlex" or "RFA"), which was enacted to obviate unnecessary compliance burdens of small businesses. With stated exceptions, the RFA requires agencies to analyze the impact of new rules on small businesses or to certify the absence of significant impact.[126] Compliance with RegFlex requirements is subject to judicial review.[127] Relatedly, Code Section 7805(f) requires that Treasury submit proposed tax regulations to the Small Business Administration for its comments.

Treasury commonly sets out RegFlex material in Treasury Decisions, the preambles that accompany proposed and final tax regulations. There are suspicions, however, that Treasury does not always give RegFlex analysis all the care it deserves, and commentators occasionally suggest that some tax regulations may be subject to attack on this ground.[128]

So far, the RegFlex adequacy of tax regulations has only rarely been litigated.[129] In non-tax contexts, agencies usually prevail in RFA litigation, which may further damper enthusiasm for mounting similar challenges against tax regulations. It remains to be seen whether the RFA or other administrative law statutes other than the APA will become important in tax.

G. Retroactivity

There are deep—and often unresolved—questions as to the extent to which tax statutes, regulations, and rulings may be applied retroactively. These questions include: (1) what measuring date or event should be used in deciding whether a measure is retroactive?[130] (2) what is the policy of the law generally as to retroactivity? (3) does that general policy apply with equal force to tax law? (4) which doctrines of law—constitutional, statutory, and interpretative—may be deployed to challenge a retroactive tax measure? (5) do these doctrines apply with equal force to tax statutes, tax

---

126. 5 U.S.C. §§603–605.

127. 5 U.S.C. §611.

128. *See, e.g.,* Michael Asimow, *Public Participation in the Adoption of Temporary Tax Regulations,* 44 Tax Law. 343 (1991); Schuyler M. Moore, *New Regulations Violate Regulatory Flexibility Act and Executive Order 12291,* 36 Tax Notes 805 (Aug. 3, 1987).

129. In one case, the district court rejected a RegFlex challenge to tax reporting regulations, but the decision was vacated on lack-of-standing-to-sue grounds, so is without precedential status. Florida Bankers Ass'n v. U.S. Dep't of Treasury, 19 F. Supp. 3d 111, 125–26 (D.D.C. 2014), *vacated,* 799 F.3d 1065 (D.C. Cir. 2015).

130. *See, e.g.,* W. David Slawson, *Constitutional and Legislative Considerations in Retroactive Lawmaking,* 48 Cal. L. Rev. 216 (1960) (describing different meanings of "retroactive"). The parties disagreed as to whether the regulations challenged in *Home Concrete* were retroactively. The majority was able to avoid the issue. The four dissenters believed the regulation did "not have an impermissible retroactive effect." 132 S. Ct. at 1853; *see also* Manhattan Gen. Equipment Co. v. Commissioner, 297 U.S. 129, 135 (1936).

regulations, and tax rulings? and (6) what factors will determine the outcomes of challenges under those doctrines?

Detailed discussion of all these matters is beyond the scope of this book.[131] But the difficulty of the questions when a statute is challenged is reflected in the following contrast. The Supreme Court has declared that "the presumption against retroactive legislation is deeply rooted in our jurisprudence, and embodies a legal doctrine centuries older than our Republic."[132] Yet not since the 1920s has the Court invalidated a tax statute on retroactivity grounds, and the Court, while not expressly overruling the old cases, has remarked that they "were decided during an era characterized by exacting review of economic legislation under an approach that has long since been discarded."[133]

What about retroactive tax regulations? Congress has stated its belief that "it is generally inappropriate for Treasury to issue retroactive regulations."[134] Yet the reach of legal mechanisms to enforce this policy preference is unclear. Some have suggested APA remedies, that unreasonable retroactive regulations may be "arbitrary and capricious" for APA purposes and may traduce the very definition of a "rule" for APA purposes.[135] But these suggestions have not received general acceptance. Similarly, various provisions of the Constitution can in extreme cases be used against retroactive provisions, but they are instruments too blunt to provide a general remedy.[136]

Accordingly, the remedy against retroactive tax regulations is to be found, if at all, in the Code, particularly section 7805(b). Before 1996, that section provided that tax rulings and regulations were presumed to be retroactive but that Treasury could choose to apply them and prospectively. As revised in 1996, section 7805(b)(1) provides generally that tax regulations (including temporary regulations) may not apply to tax years ended before the date on which the public is notified of the intended rulemaking.

This general prohibition is weakened in two ways, however. First, it applies only to regulations under Code sections enacted after the 1996 amendment. Regulations (even new ones) issued under pre-1996 Code sections are still under the pre-1996 rules.

Second, there are exceptions to the general rule, and they may end up swallowing it. For instance, one exception allows Treasury to "provide that any regulation may take effect or apply retroactively to prevent abuse."[137] Prevention of abuse, obviously,

---

131. For more detailed discussion, see Erika K. Lunder, Robert Meltz & Kenneth R. Thomas, *Constitutionality of Retroactive Tax Legislation* (Cong. Res. Serv. Report R42791) (Oct. 25, 2012); James M. Puckett, *Embracing the Queen of Hearts: Deference to Retroactive Tax Rules*, 40 Fla. St. U.L. Rev. 349 (2013).

132. Landgraf v. USI Film Prods., 511 U.S. 244, 265 (1994).

133. United States v. Carlton, 512 U.S. 26, 34 (1994); *see also id.* ("tax legislation is not a promise, and a taxpayer has no vested right in the Internal Revenue Code").

134. H.R. Rep. No. 104-506, at 44 (1996).

135. *E.g.*, Bowen v. Georgetown Univ. Hosp., 488 U.S. 204, 220 (1988) (Scalia, J., concurring); *see* 5 USC §§ 551(4) (defining a "rule" as having "future effect") & 706(2)(A).

136. *See generally* Jeffrey Omar Usman, *Constitutional Constraints on Retroactive Civil Legislation: The Hollow Promises of the Federal Constitution and Unrealized Potential of State Constitutions*, 14 Nev. L.J. 63 (2013).

137. IRC § 7805(b)(3).

is susceptible to multiple interpretations. If construed to apply to everything the IRS suspects may be abusive, this exception could be of oceanic breadth.[138]

However, under section 7805(b)(8), a different rule applies to rulings, defined to include "any administrative determination other than [a] regulation." This retains the pre-1996 presumption of retroactivity. Nonetheless, taxpayers may challenge IRS decisions applying positions retroactively. Courts typically review such challenges on an abuse of discretion standard, and a considerable body of case law exists.[139]

Prospective rules have occasioned far less controversy than retroactive rules. However, when a new rule is more favorable than the prior rule, taxpayers sometimes complain—typically without success—about only prospective application of the new rule.[140]

H. Inconsistency in Enforcement

IRS consistency is highly desirable for many reasons: regularity in government, fairness, protecting reasonable expectations, and facilitating business planning. Encouraging such reliance, the IRS states that revenue rulings and procedures may generally be used as precedents.[141]

The government usually achieves positional consistency. Indeed, elaborate review processes exist to further it. Nonetheless, given the volume and complexity of matters handled by the IRS, there have been many cases over the decades in which the government has taken a litigating or other position at odds with a regulation, revenue ruling, manual, or other published authority.

Earlier, we saw that consistency or lack thereof is one of the *Skidmore* factors. But can the taxpayer get even more mileage out of IRS inconsistency? Can inconsistency alone defeat the IRS adjustment on an estoppel, governmental duty of consistency, or other theory?[142]

---

138. As part of its campaign against abusive tax shelters, Treasury amended a regulation under section 752 and sought to apply it retroactively. The courts split. *Compare* Cemco investors, LLC v. United States, 515 F.3d 749, 752 (7th Cir. 2008) *&* Maguire Partners v. United States, 104 AFTR2d 7839 (C.D. Cal. 2009), *aff'd*, 444 Fed. Appx. 190 (9th Cir. 2011) (upholding retroactive application) *to* Sala v. United States, 552 F. Supp. 2d 1167, 1185 (D. Colo. 2008), *rev'd on other grounds*, 613 F.3d 1249 (10th Cir. 2010) *&* Stobie Creek Inv. LLC v. United States, 82 Fed. Cl. 636 (2008), *aff'd on other grounds*, 608 F.3d 1366 (Fed. Cir. 2010) (rejecting retroactive application).

139. *E.g.*, Automobile Club of Michigan v. Commissioner, 353 U.S. 180 (1957); Lesavoy Foundation v. Commissioner, 238 F.2d 589 (3d Cir. 1956). For discussion of factors bearing on permissible retroactivity of tax regulations, see *Snap-Drape, Inc. v. Commissioner*, 98 F.2d 194, 202 (5th Cir. 1996); and *Klamath Strategic Investment Fund, LLC v. United States*, 440 F. Supp. 2d 608, 623–25 (E.D. Tex. 2006).

140. *E.g.*, Kandi v. United States, 2006 U.S. Dist. LEXIS 2687 (W.D. Wash. Jan. 11, 2006) (holding that the IRS did not abuse its discretion in applying pro-taxpayer proposed regulations only prospectively).

141. *E.g.*, IRS Proc. Reg. § 601.601(d)(2)(v)(e).

142. *See generally* Steve R. Johnson, *An IRS Duty of Consistency: The Failure of Common Law Making and a Proposed Statutory Solution*, 77 Tenn. L. Rev. 563 (2010) (analyzing the cases and noting prior commentary).

There have been a few taxpayer victories, but most of the cases have been to the contrary.[143] Various rationales appear in the cases, including a general reluctance to apply estoppel against the government, the traditional rule that a mistake of law will not give rise to estoppel, a view of IRS manuals and the like as being directory rather than mandatory, and a concern with the disincentive effects of a vigorous rule of preclusion. The courts reason that, if inconsistency with previously published positions could lead to later litigation losses, the government would be tempted to cease publishing positions. Better to have published guidance with occasional inconsistency than not to have published guidance.

One taxpayer victory on the consistency issue is *Rauenhorst v. Commissioner*.[144] In response to that case, the IRS Chief Counsel's office directed its attorneys not to take litigating positions inconsistent with regulations, revenue rulings, revenue procedures, IRS notices, and IRS announcements, and to coordinate litigating positions in tension with other types of guidance issued by the IRS.[145] However, that direction faded quietly into oblivion.

The division in the case law presents an opportunity for artful lawyering. As noted earlier in this chapter, the taxpayer chooses the forum in which a tax case will be tried. The forum most receptive to "the IRS has been inconsistent" arguments has been the Court of Federal Claims.[146] If IRS inconsistency is a major part of the taxpayer's case, the taxpayer's attorney should consider bringing the case as a refund action in the Court of Federal Claims.

---

143. *E.g.*, Sklar v. Commissioner, 549 F.3d 1252, 1264–67 (9th Cir. 2008); Florida Power & Light Co. v. United States, 375 F.3d 119 (D.C. Cir. 2004); Riley v. United States, 118 F.3d 1220 (8th Cir. 1997); Schering-Plough Corp. v. United States, 2007-2 USTC ¶ 50,831 (D.N.J. 2007); In re Dewberry, 158 B.R. 979 (Bankr. W.D. Mich. 1993).

144. 119 T.C. 157 (2002).

145. Chief Counsel Notice CC-2003-014 (May 8, 2003), reproduced at 2003 Tax Notes Today 93-7 (May 14, 2003).

146. *E.g.*, Computer Science Corp. v. United States, 50 Fed. Cl. 388 (2001), *appeal dismissed,* 79 Fed. Appx. 430 (Fed. Cir. 2003).

Chart 1-1 Organizational Chart of the National Office of the IRS

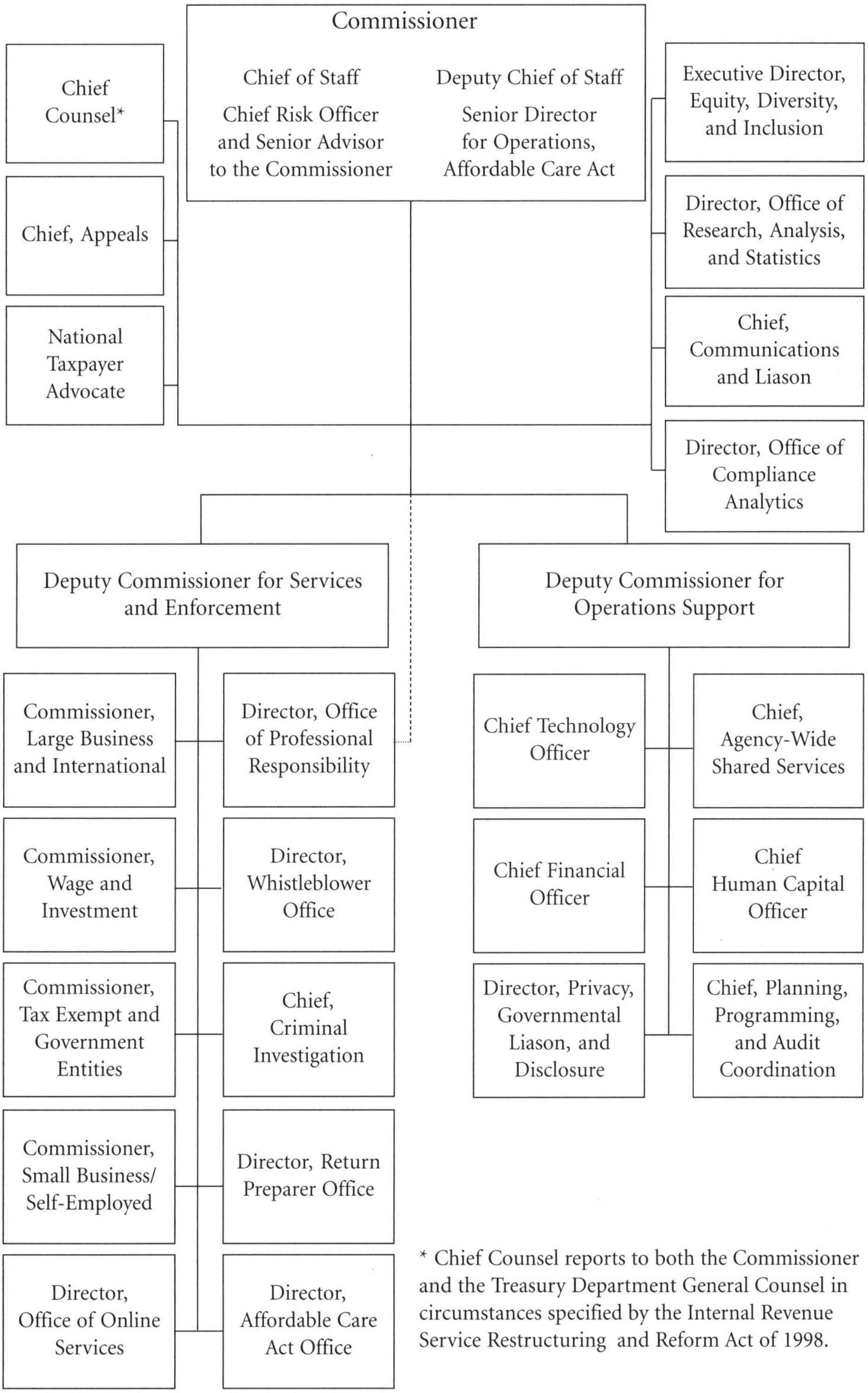

* Chief Counsel reports to both the Commissioner and the Treasury Department General Counsel in circumstances specified by the Internal Revenue Service Restructuring and Reform Act of 1998.

Source: Internal Revenue Service Data Book, 2015.

Problems

1. The National Taxpayer Advocate is required by law (IRC § 7803(c)(2)(B)(ii)) to provide an annual Report to Congress each year. The 2014 Report identified the failure of the IRS to provide service to taxpayers at local IRS offices as among the most serious problems facing tax administration in the United States. The Report concluded that, as a result, taxpayers are experiencing increasing difficulties in meeting their federal tax obligations. The primary obligation, of course, is the filing of a complete and correct tax return each year. But many people file tax returns even though their levels of incomes are below that required for filing. The 2011 Report pointed out, for example, that 15.1% of the population falls below the poverty line. Many of those persons are eligible for the earned income tax credit and other benefits but must file a return in order to obtain them.

Unfortunately, the overwhelming complexity of the tax law, at every level, presents a serious obstacle to filing for many. Albert Einstein once commented that "the hardest thing in the world to understand is the income tax." The 2010 Report noted that the tax law contains 3.8 million words and have averaged more than one change a day for the preceding 10 years. In addition, approximately 20% of the population speaks a language other than English in the home. The IRS prints some forms and publications in Spanish, Chinese, Korean, Russian, and Vietnamese as well as an English. Nonetheless, language and other realities make it nearly impossible for many to file returns without assistance. The IRS is no longer providing that assistance on a regular basis, so it must come from volunteers or from tax return preparation industry.

The preparation of tax returns paid by preparers is largely unregulated. The 2013 Report pointed out that in 2011 the IRS received 142 million individual returns, of which 79 million were prepared by paid preparers. But over 42 million of those returns were prepared by unregulated preparers (54%). The role played by unregulated preparers in the administration of the tax system cannot be overstated. And sadly, their competence has been subject to substantial question for many years. Reports of serious mistakes, many intentional, made by unregulated preparers are frequent. Most involve return inaccuracy and lack of ethical standards. The 2013 Report concluded that the case for oversight of the industry is clear.

In 2011, the IRS issued regulations requiring registration, testing, and continuing education for previously unregulated return preparers. The regulations included penalties for failure to comply. Certified Public Accountants and lawyers, who were already subject to regulation, were not subject to most of those requirements. For authority to issue these regulations, the IRS relied on a statute enacted by Congress and signed into law by President Chester A. Arthur in 1884 authorizing the Treasury Department (of which the IRS is now part) to "regulate the practice of representatives of persons before the Department of the Treasury." 31 U.S.C. § 300(a)(1). That statute was originally enacted as part of the War Department's appropriation for "horses and other property lost during the Civil War in military service."

The unregulated sector of the return preparation industry objected vigorously to the new regulations. Their validity was tested soon in *Loving v. IRS*, 742 F.3d 1013 (D.C. Cir. 2014). After reviewing the text, history, and context of the statute, the court applied the test used by the Supreme Court in *Chevron U.S.A. v. Natural Resources De-*

fense Council, 467 U.S. 837 (1984), for determining whether the administrative agency (including the IRS) has authority to promulgate regulations on a specific subject and, if so, for determining the validity of the regulations. The *Loving* court held that the new regulations failed the first *Chevron* test. The authority to regulate the "... practice of representatives of persons before the Department of the Treasury," as used in the 1884 statute, was "clear and unambiguous...," yet return preparation simply did not rise to the level of "practice" before the IRS. The IRS's authority to regulate return preparers was therefore foreclosed by the plain meaning of the statute. The court, employing the traditional *Chevron* two-step test, invalidated the new regulations.

Soon thereafter, the Supreme Court was asked to use the *Chevron* two-step test to invalidate a regulation, much the way the Court of Appeals had in *Loving*. The Supreme Court, in *King v. Burwell*, 135 S. Ct. 2480 (2015), examined regulations dealing with Affordable Care Act that had been promulgated by the IRS. The Court did not focus on the specific wording of the applicable provision of the statute, as it had in *Chevron* and the Court of Appeals had in *Loving*. Instead, the Court employed a much broader approach for considering whether the IRS has the authority to promulgate the regulations at issue. The Court looked at the statute as a whole and the intentions of Congress in enacting the statute. The court said, *id.* at 2488–89:

> When analyzing an agency's interpretation of a statute, we often apply the two-step framework announced in *Chevron*, 467 U. S. 837. Under that framework, we ask whether the statute is ambiguous and, if so, whether the agency's interpretation is reasonable. *Id.*, at 842–843. This approach "is premised on the theory that a statute's ambiguity constitutes an implicit delegation from Congress to the agency to fill in the statutory gaps." *FDA v. Brown & Williamson Tobacco Corp.*, 529 U. S. 120, 159 (2000). "In extraordinary cases, however, there may be reason to hesitate before concluding that Congress has intended such an implicit delegation." *Ibid.*
>
> This is one of those cases. The tax credits are among the Act's key reforms, involving billions of dollars in spending each year and affecting the price of health insurance for millions of people. Whether those credits are available on Federal Exchanges is thus a question of deep "economic and political significance" that is central to this statutory scheme; had Congress wished to assign that question to an agency, it surely would have done so expressly. *Utility Air Regulatory Group v. EPA*, 573 U. S. ___, ___ (2014) (quoting *Brown & Williamson*, 529 U. S., at 160). It is especially unlikely that Congress would have delegated this decision to the IRS, which has no expertise in crafting health insurance policy of this sort. See *Gonzales v. Oregon*, 546 U. S. 243, 266–267 (2006). This is not a case for the IRS.
>
> It is instead our task to determine the correct reading of Section 36B. If the statutory language is plain, we must enforce it according to its terms. *Hardt v. Reliance Standard Life Ins. Co.*, 560 U. S. 242, 251 (2010). But oftentimes the "meaning—or ambiguity—of certain words or phrases may only become evident when placed in context." *Brown & Williamson*, 529 U. S., at 132. So when deciding whether the language is plain, we must read the words "in their context and with a view to their place in the overall statutory scheme." *Id.*, at 133 (internal quotation marks omitted). Our duty, after all,

is "to construe statutes, not isolated provisions." *Graham County Soil and Water Conservation Dist. v. United States ex rel. Wilson*, 559 U. S. 280, 290 (2010) (internal quotation marks omitted).

a. What did *King v. Burwell* add to the body of law addressing the validity of regulations?

b. Some commentators have said that *King v. Burwell* simply applies step 1 of *Chevron* (the ambiguity test) to the statue as a whole rather than the specific wording in question, but that step 2 remains the same (i.e., if step 1 is met by a finding of ambiguity then step 2 asks whether the approach taken by the administrator and the regulations is reasonable). When is it proper to use the *King v. Burwell* approach in step 1 rather than the *Chevron/Loving* approach?

c. *King v. Burwell* was decided after *Loving*. Would *Loving* have been decided differently if the court of appeals had applied the rationale of *King v. Burwell*? Don't forget that in 1884, the year in which the Act upon which the regulations were based, was enacted there were no "return preparers." Would that matter when reviewing the "overall statutory scheme"?

2. Shortly after the Supreme Court's decision in *King v. Burwell*, the Tax Court examined a different aspect of the authority of the IRS to promulgate tax regulations. In *Altera Corp. v. Commissioner*, 145 T.C. No. 3 (July 27, 2015), the Tax Court struck down a regulation in part because the IRS, after issuing the regulation in proposed form, had ignored numerous comments from the public, thereby violating the "reasoned decisionmaking" requirement of the Administrative Procedure Act, 5 U.S.C. § 706(2)(A), and *Motor Vehicle Mfrs. Ass'n v. the State Farm Mut. Auto Ins. Co.*, 463 U.S. 29 (1983). Although that standard had often been applied by courts to non-tax regulations, *Altera* is among the few cases thus far to apply that standard to tax regulations. *See also Dominion Resources, Inc. v. United States*, 681 F.3d 1313, 1319 (Fed. Cir. 2012). Should tax lawyers be expected to subject every adverse regulation to a "*State Farm* reasoned decisionmaking" test pursuant to *Altera*?

3. On August 7, 2005, United States Court of Appeals for the Ninth Circuit issued its opinion in *Voss v. Commissioner*, 796 F.3d 1051 (9th Cir. 2015). In that case, the IRS argued that Chief Counsel Advice 200911007 (March 13, 2009) should be afforded deference. Citing other judicial authority, the court applied the *Skidmore* test. That is, the court said that the CCA would be entitled to the "measure of deference proportional to the 'thoroughness evident in its consideration, the validity of its reasoning, its consistency with earlier and later pronouncements, and all those factors which give it power to persuade.'" The court said that agency interpretations, such as these, which lack force of law do not warrant *Chevron*-style deference. The court, critical of the CCA, gave it "limited weight." A dissenting opinion, however, said that "in the absence of IRS regulations interpreting [the section], we should defer to the IRS's interpretation" of the statute.

What if the IRS, instead of promulgating regulations addressing return preparers, had issued a sub-regulatory pronouncement, not subject to the APA, but with requirements and penalties similar to those found in the return preparers regulations that were struck down in *Loving*? How would you analyze the enforceability of those pronouncements?

Chapter 2

Reporting Obligations

IRC: §§6001 (first sentence); 6011(a), (e)(1), (f); 6012(a), (b) (skim); 6013(a), (b)(1); 6018(a) (skim); 6019 (skim); 6020(b); 6031(a) (skim); 6032–6053 (skim titles only); 6061(a); 6071(a) (skim); 6072(a), (b), (e); 6075(a), (b); 6081; 6103(a) (skim); 6111, 6112 (skim); 6151(a); 6155; 6159(a) (skim); 6161(a); 6702; 7206(1), (2) (skim); 7502(a); 7503; 66 (skim)

Regs: §§1.451-1(a) (last two sentences); 1.6161-1; 301.7502-1 (a), (d); 301.9100-1(a); 301.9100-3(a)

Rulings: Rev. Proc. 2013-34; IR 2002-135 (12/11/02)

Forms: Skim SS-4; 56; 1127; 8275; 8275-R; 8453; 8879; 9465

I. Introduction

Subtitle F of the Code, entitled "Procedure and Administration," begins with section 6001. That section directs that "[e]very person liable for any tax..., or for the collection thereof, shall keep such records, render such statements, make such returns, and comply with such rules and regulations as the Secretary may from time to time prescribe." The record keeping and return filing obligations stemming from this and other provisions are the heart of the administration of our federal tax system. Taxpayers are required to maintain records and report to the government both underlying information about, and the computation of, their tax liabilities.[1]

Persons who have information relating to the tax liabilities of others also have record keeping and reporting obligations. They are required to file "information returns," the contents of which assist both taxpayers in preparing their returns and the

1. This chapter focuses on the record keeping and reporting requirements stemming from Title 26 of the United States Code. There are, however, other federal statutes that contain record keeping and reporting requirements that are germane to the federal tax system. A notable example is the Currency and Foreign Transactions Reporting Act, 84 Stat. 1118, 31 U.S.C. §§5311–5332 (2004). This Act requires reports and record keeping "where they have a high degree of usefulness in criminal, tax, or regulatory investigations or proceedings, or in the conduct of intelligence or counterintelligence activities, including analysis, to protect against international terrorism." 31 U.S.C. §5311 (2004). Under the Act, certain persons are required to report and keep records of specified transactions involving U.S. or foreign currency or other, broadly defined, "monetary instruments." Compliance with the Act is enforced through civil and criminal forfeiture provisions (31 U.S.C. §5317 (2004)) and through civil and criminal penalties (§§5321 & 5322).

government in auditing those returns.[2] There are several types of information returns. The most often encountered are those that report information concerning: (i) persons subject to special provisions in the Code (sections 6031–6039J), (ii) transactions with other persons (sections 6041–6050W), (iii) wages paid to employees (sections 6051–6053), and (iv) health care coverage (sections 6055–6056).

In connection with both tax returns and information returns, the Code and Regulations provide guidance as to: (i) who is required to file, (ii) how returns are to be signed and verified, (iii) when and where the returns are to be filed, (iv) when and where tax payments are to be made, and (v) whether, and under what circumstances, extensions of time to file or pay are available.

Compliance with the record keeping and reporting obligations is encouraged through a series of penalties that range from relatively minor civil penalties to significant fines and possible imprisonment if the conduct consists of a willful attempt to evade or defeat any tax. The civil penalties for failure to comply with the record keeping, reporting, and taxpaying obligations mentioned in this chapter are discussed in detail in Chapter 11. Tax crimes are left for another course.

To assist taxpayers in fulfilling their obligations, the Service has produced hundreds of forms and thousands of pages of related instructions.[3] The individual income tax return, Form 1040, is only two pages long (exclusive of supporting schedules), but there are about fifty documents and schedules listed on the IRS's website relating to some version of Form 1040. The instructions to Form 1040 are a mind-numbing, if not mind-boggling, two hundred or so pages long.[4] Furthermore, the Service has identified 195 other forms that might be used by individual taxpayers.[5] Discussion of all the recordkeeping, reporting and disclosure obligations is well beyond the scope

2. Responding to concerns about identity theft, Treasury has finalized regulations that cover a multitude of sections allowing information return filers to truncate the payee's tax identification number on payee statements and some other documents. The truncated taxpayer identification number (TTIN) takes the place of a payee's Social Security number, individual taxpayer identification number (ITIN), or adoption taxpayer identification number (ATIN). T.D. 9675, 79 Fed. Reg. 41127-02 (July 15, 2014).

3. In calendar year 2015, the IRS received nearly 243 million returns, including approximately 148 million individual income tax returns, 2 million corporate income tax returns, 3 million estate and trust income tax returns, 36 thousand estate tax returns, 238 thousand gift tax returns, 30 million employment tax returns, 1 million excise tax returns, 3.9 million partnership returns, and 4.7 million S corporation returns. IRS Data Book, 2016, Table 2, available at https://www.irs.gov/uac/returns-filed-taxes-collected-and-refunds-issued.

"In 2009, the IRS had 833 tax forms and 299 sets of instructions posted on its website." David E. Vance, *Unconstitutional Vagueness and the Tax Code*, Tax Notes, May 19, 2014, at 827, 828. The recordkeeping, return preparation, and return filing obligations impose psychic and financial costs on taxpayers and third parties. But the psychic costs are unquantifiable, and estimates of the financial costs vary widely. *E.g.*, Jason Fichtner & Jacob Feldman, *The Hidden Cost of Tax Compliance*, Mercatus Center, George Mason Univ., at 3 (May 20, 2013), *available at* http://mercatus.org/publication/hidden-costs-tax-compliance.

4. The complexity of the forms and their instructions may be mind-boggling, but it is not illegal. *See* Lewis v. Commissioner, 523 F.3d 1272 (10th Cir. 2008) (rejecting the taxpayer's argument that Form 1040 violates the federal Paperwork Reduction Act).

5. In some circumstances, taxpayers may use substitutes for the forms prescribed by the IRS. Because of the possibility of abuse, this option is tightly controlled. *See* Rev. Proc. 2015-55, 2015-49 I.R.B. 788.

of this book. Consequently, this chapter focuses on some of the principal record keeping, reporting, and disclosure obligations, and even as to those that are covered, the discussion is best described as an overview.

More detailed information about a given form, including who is required to file the form, when and where it should be filed, and, in many cases, a line-by-line explanation of information to be provided on the form, is contained in the instructions to the form. Fortunately, most forms, schedules, and attachments required to be filed by taxpayers are readily available on the IRS's website.[6]

II. The Electronic Filing Initiative

As a preliminary matter, it is appropriate to note a current, major policy initiative of the government: facilitating and encouraging electronic filing of returns. Although electronic filing of certain tax and information returns had been available, and in some cases required, for a number of years, Congress provided the impetus for the shift to "e-filing," in the 1998 Reform Act. Congress announced its policy that:

(1) paperless filing should be the preferred and most convenient means of filing federal tax and information returns;

(2) it should be the goal of the Service to have at least 80% of all returns filed electronically by the year 2007; and

(3) the IRS should cooperate with and encourage the private sector to increase electronic filing of returns.[7]

To assist the IRS in establishing a strategic plan to implement the congressional policy, the Act directed the Secretary to "convene an electronic commerce advisory group." To this end, the Electronic Tax Administration Advisory Committee ("ETAAC") was formed. Among other things, ETAAC was charged with providing an annual report to Congress of progress made in achieving the stated congressional electronic filing goals.[8]

In response to Congress' paperless-filing policy, the IRS established an "e-file Program" under which taxpayers can file their Forms 1040, 1040A, or 1040EZ, either

---

6. To find forms and instructions on the IRS website, as configured as of the date this book went to press, go to http://apps.irs.gov/app/picklist/list/formsInstructions.html. On that page, you may find a form or instruction by its product number, title or revision date.

7. 1998 Reform Act, § 2001(a) (not codified in IRC).

8. *Id.* § 2001(d). The 80% e-file goal has been met for individual tax returns for each year starting with the 2012 taxable year. However, excluding the Form 1040 series, the e-file rate is a paltry 46%, with no expectation for improvement in the immediate future. *See* IRS Oversight Board, Electronic Filing 2014 Annual Report to Congress (2014). Budgetary woes have prevented the IRS from implementing new electronic tax administration initiatives. William Hoffman, *E-Filing Grows, but IRS Budget Hampers Progress*, Tax Notes, Feb. 10, 2014, at 618.

With adequate funding, the IRS hopes to raise the electronic filing rate to 90% for individuals and 50% for businesses. According to the IRS's 2014–2017 strategic plan, the IRS plans to "foster a culture of data-driven decision making" to better use information technology for the IRS's internal systems and in expanding electronic interactions with taxpayers. *New Strategic Plan Emphasizes Better IT, "Big Data" to Improve Taxpayer Services*, 33 Bloomberg BNA Tax Management Weekly Rep. 887 (June 27, 2014).

through an Electronic Return Originator (ERO) or by using their personal computer, online access, and commercial preparation software.[9] To compliment electronic filing, the IRS established two electronic payment options—credit card or electronic funds withdrawal. Also, most states and the District of Columbia participate in a Federal/State e-file program.

The availability of e-filing has been dramatically expanded. E-filing is now available to C and S corporations (Forms 1120 and 1120S); employment taxes (Forms 940 and 941); estates and trusts (Form 1041); exempt organizations (Forms 990/990EZ, 990PF, 8868, and 1120-POL); information returns (including Forms 1098 and 1099); and partnership returns (Form 1065). Generally, businesses that are required to file more than 250 returns "of any type" during the calendar year with or within which the business' taxable year ends are required to file returns electronically.[10]

The IRS has issued a number of publications and notices that define the role of "Authorized IRS e-file Providers" (including EROs) in the e-file program.[11] Also, the IRS's website provides a database containing the names of all "Authorized IRS e-file Providers" who are available to taxpayers in preparing and e-filing income tax returns. Finally, the instructions to Form 1040 not only extol the virtues of e-filing, they also state a strong preference for e-filing by the Commissioner.[12]

Hoping to make e-filing more ubiquitous, Congress passed legislation in 2009[13] that requires return preparers who file more than ten individual income tax returns per year[14]—in other words, nearly all return preparers—to e-file such returns.

---

9. Rev. Proc. 2007-40, 2007-1 C.B. 1488.

10. Reg. § 301.6011-2 et seq.

11. *See* Publication 1345, Handbook for Authorized IRS *e-file* Providers of Individual Income Tax Returns; Publication 1345A, Filing Season Supplement for Authorized IRS *e-file* Providers of Individual Income Tax Returns; Publication 1346, Electronic Return Filing of Individual Income Tax Returns; Publication 3112, The IRS *e-file* Application and Participation; Publication 4163, Modernized e-File (Mef) Information for Authorized IRS *e-file* Providers of Forms 1120/1120 S; IRS e-file for Large Taxpayers Filing Their Own Corporate Income Tax Return, dated Feb. 2006; Postings to the Electronic Filing System Bulletin Board (EFS Bulletin Board). All publications are available at http://apps.irs.gov/app/picklist/list/formsPublications.html.

12. Section 6011(e) grants the IRS the authority, with certain limitations, to prescribe Regulations setting forth "which returns must be filed on magnetic media or in other machine-readable form." That section also prohibits the IRS from requiring individuals, estates, or trusts to file other than on paper forms. *See* Reg. § 301.6011-2 et seq.

Rev. Proc. 2011-25 provides guidance to specified tax return preparers regarding the format and content of requests for waiver of the magnetic media (electronic) filing requirement due to undue hardship and guidance to tax return preparers, specified tax return preparers, and taxpayers regarding how to document a taxpayer's choice to file an individual income tax return in paper format when the return is prepared by a tax return preparer or specified tax return preparer but filed by the taxpayer. The burden of compliance with electronic filing requirement contained in IRC § 6011 (e)(3) and Reg. § 301.6011-7 is on the tax return preparer and specified tax return preparer.

13. Worker, Homeownership, and Business Assistance Act of 2009, Pub. L. 111-92 (2009).

14. Section 6011(e)(3)(B) specifies the term "specified tax return preparer" as "any tax return preparer unless such preparer reasonably expects to file 10 or fewer individual income tax returns during such calendar year." Reg. § 301.6011-7(a)(3).

As it relates to most of the rules regarding filing tax returns and paying taxes, e-filing is treated no differently than paper filing. However, a number of special rules were deemed necessary to implement, or encourage implementation of, the policy. For instance, the due date for filing information returns concerning transactions with other persons (sections 6041–6050W) and regarding wages paid to employees (sections 6051–6053) was extended from February 28 to March 31, if they are filed electronically.[15] Also, the "timely-mailing-is-timely-filing" regulations were amended to clarify that a document filed electronically "is deemed to be filed on the date of the electronic postmark ... given by the authorized electronic return transmitter."[16]

One critical aspect of implementing the e-filing program has been developing a mechanism for signing and verifying e-filed returns.[17] In the 1998 Reform Act, Congress added section 6061(b) which directs the IRS to "develop procedures for the acceptance of signatures in digital or other electronic form."

The IRS responded by requiring that taxpayers file with the ERO a paper copy of Form 8453 (U.S. Individual Income Tax Transmittal for an IRS *e-file* Return). By filing this form with the ERO, the taxpayer verifies the accuracy of the prepared income tax return. The ERO must mail the form to the IRS within three business days after receiving the IRS's acknowledgement that the return has been accepted. In the alternative, the taxpayer may sign the return using his self-selected personal identification number (PIN).[18]

In addition to requiring greater use of the Internet for filing returns, the IRS is making more services accessible to taxpayers and tax professionals. E-services is a suite of web-based products that allow tax professionals and payers to conduct business with the IRS electronically. Registration is required. When first launched in the summer of 2004, the e-Services incentive products were reserved for those who e-filed 100 or more individual returns.[19] Now, in order to register, a practitioner needs to file only 5 or more accepted individual and business tax returns electronically during one calendar year. There are many useful tools that a practitioner may access after registration including: Disclosure Authorization, Electronic Account Resolution, and Transcript Delivery Service, eService Registration, Preparer Tax Identification Number, IRS e-file Application and Taxpayer Identification Number Matching.

---

15. IRC §6071(b); Reg. §31.6071(a)-1(a)(3).

16. Reg. §301.7502-1(d)(1).

17. The IRS rejects electronically filed returns that do not conform to IRS-developed requirements. For instance, the rejection rate in 2007 was 7% and in 2013 was 12%. Vance, *supra* in note 3, at 829.

18. The IRS has entered into agreements with tax preparation software companies to provide the free service to taxpayers who meet certain guidelines. Free File products are now available at http://www.IRS.gov/freefile. Nearly 40 million taxpayers have used Free File since it began in 2003. In theory, it is available to those who earn under $62,000 a year, thus about 70% of taxpayers. However, the program has been criticized for confusing implementation and excessive reliance on private sector vendors. *See* Eric Kroh, *IRS Signs 1-Year Extension of Free File Alliance Partnership*, Tax Notes, May 26, 2014, at 915. It has now been extended through 2020.

19. IR-2005-33 (Mar. 21, 2005); *see* http://www.irs.gov/Tax-Professionals/e-services-Online-Tools-for-Tax-Professionals.

III. Record Keeping

In addition to directing persons liable for any tax to file all applicable returns prescribed by the IRS, section 6001 requires those same persons to "keep such records" as the Service prescribes. The Service has issued Regulations that describe, in brief but encompassing language, the record keeping responsibilities with respect to the various tax and information returns.[20]

These Regulations require taxpayers to keep such records as may be required to substantiate the items shown on the return. In the case of income tax returns, the records must be sufficient to permit the Service to determine the amount of any income tax liability and they must "be retained so long as the contents thereof may become material in the administration of any internal revenue law."[21] For most individuals with straightforward returns, records should be retained for at least three years after the return is filed.[22] During that period, the IRS can initiate procedures that can result in the assessment of additional tax for the year.[23] However, there are numerous exceptions that extend the statute of limitations on assessment beyond the basic three-year period, and consequently the record-retention time.[24]

The general record keeping rules are supplemented by specific requirements in situations in which taxpayer record keeping and reporting has proven problematic. For instance, section 274(d) contains record keeping rules for taxpayers who claim deductions under sections 162 or 212 for traveling expenses, entertainment, amusement or recreational expenses, gifts, or with respect to section 280F(d)(4) "listed property."[25] To substantiate the deductions, the Regulations under section 162 suggest that taxpayers maintain a daily diary sufficient to establish both the amount and nature of expenditures such as "travel, transportation, entertainment, and similar business expenses."[26]

Another example of specific record keeping requirements, for which the consequences of noncompliance can be costly, is contained in Regulation section 1.170A-13, "Recordkeeping and return requirements for deductions for charitable

---

20. *E.g.*, Reg. § 1.6001-1(a), (e), relating to income taxes; Reg. § 20.6001-1(a), relating to estate taxes; and Reg. § 25.6001-1(a), relating to gift taxes.

21. Reg. § 1.6001-1(e).

22. For this purpose, an income tax return filed before the due date prescribed by law (April 15 for calendar year taxpayers) is deemed to be filed on the due date. IRC § 6501(b)(1). Taxpayers should retain records for more than three years if the records relate to ongoing or continuing transactions or tax attributes. The most prominent example is information as to the bases of assets that have not yet been disposed of by the taxpayer. Other examples include records relating to installment sales and accounting under the percentage of completion method.

23. IRC § 6501(a).

24. *See* Chapter 5.

25. In connection with these expenses, Regulation sections 1.274-5 and 1.274-5T contain extensive substantiation requirements and specifically preclude deductions for estimated expenditures, superseding *Cohan v. Commissioner*, 39 F.2d 540 (2d Cir. 1930).

26. Reg. §§ 1.162-17(d)(2); 1.274-5T. The IRS has updated rules for determining the amount of employee expenses for lodging, meals, and incidental expenses which will be deemed to be substantiated under an employer-provided reimbursement or other expense allowance arrangement. Notice 2015-63, 2015-40 I.R.B. 461.

contributions." Of particular concern are the substantiation requirements for charitable contributions of property, other than money, having a value in excess of $5,000. In such cases, the taxpayer is required to: (i) obtain a "qualified appraisal" made within a specified period of time, by a "qualified appraiser"; (ii) attach an appraisal summary to the tax return; and (iii) maintain extensive records relating to the gift.[27] Compliance with these substantiation requirements is a necessary predicate to taking a deduction for a charitable contribution.[28]

IV. Who Is Required To File?[29]

A. Income Tax Returns

1. Filing Thresholds

Section 6012(a) lists eight categories of persons[30] required to file income tax returns. The major categories are: (i) individuals having gross income in excess of the exemption amount, (ii) every corporation subject to the income tax, (iii) every estate that has $600 or more of gross income for the year, and (iv) every trust that has taxable income for the year or that has gross income of $600 or more for the year regardless of the amount of its taxable income.

However, in classic Code fashion, apparent clarity, particularly as it relates to filing by individuals in section 6012(a)(1), fades in a smog of definitions, cross references, exceptions, and exceptions to exceptions. Section 6012(a)(1) is one of a number of provisions in federal tax procedure that provides an opportunity to test one's skills at close reading of complicated statutory language. Fortunately, most taxpayers do not have to wade through section 6012(a)(1) because the dollar amounts of the filing thresholds are relatively low and the instructions to the Form 1040 do a good job of translating the section.

---

27. Reg. §§ 1.170A-13(c), 1.170A-13(b)(2)(ii).

28. IRC § 170(a)(1) (stating that a charitable deduction will be allowed "only if verified under regulations prescribed by the Secretary"). Section 170(f)(8) requires contemporaneous written acknowledgment of charitable contributions of $250 or more. For a comedy of errors culminating in disallowance of over $25,000 of contributions made by check to a church, see *Durden v. Commissioner*, T.C. Memo. 2012-140.

29. As seen below, statutes and regulations define which taxpayers are required to file returns of the various kinds. Some taxpayers who are required to file, fail to do so. This creates an enforcement problem, necessitating IRS examinations as described in Chapter 4 and penalties for late filing and payment as described in Chapter 11A.

Conversely, many taxpayers who are not legally required to file returns, nonetheless unnecessarily do file. This creates an efficiency problem: wasted time, effort, and resources by both taxpayers and the IRS. One study found that in the four years 2005 to 2008, approximately eight million unnecessary returns were filed, wasting $390 million and 75 million hours. Vance, *supra* note 3, at 828 (citing reports by the Treasury Inspector General for Tax Administration Office of Audit). That being said, some taxpayers who are not legally required to file a return do so as it is the only way to obtain refunds to which they are entitled and because doing so starts the running of the three-year statute of limitations on assessment.

30. Section 7701(a)(1) defines "person" for purposes of the Internal Revenue Code to include "an individual, a trust, estate, partnership, association, company or corporation."

Nevertheless, section 6012(a)(1) is of interest. By working through the section, one reaches the counterintuitive conclusion that in many cases it is not possible, solely by reference to the Code and Regulations, to determine whether there is an obligation to file an income tax return. This is because critical elements of determining the threshold for filing or, in some situations, calculating the income tax liability itself, depend on dollar amounts that are administratively adjusted for inflation on an annual basis.[31]

2. Joint Returns of Income Tax

Section 6013 permits a husband and wife to file "a single return jointly of income taxes...." Joint returns traditionally are favored because the tax liability of a married couple is usually less when reported on a joint return than when reported on separate returns.[32]

However, section 6013(d)(3) provides a persuasive reason, at least in some cases, why joint income tax returns should *not* be filed. That section makes each spouse jointly and severally liable for the tax liability, including interest and penalties. This has led to particularly harsh consequences when one spouse fails to report income or deductions correctly or fails to pay his or her share of the correct tax liability, and the other "innocent" spouse is pursued by the IRS to pay the deficiency. Early case law led to the enactment of provisions protecting innocent spouses, which provisions are currently found in section 6015. Joint return filing and spousal relief under section 6015 are discussed in Chapter 3.

Eligibility for joint return filing is limited to individuals who have the same taxable year and are spouses.[33] Marital status is determined as of the close of the year.[34] This is true no matter how many days during the year one was married. Thus, if two people married on December 31st, they are treated as married for tax purposes; if they were married all year but divorced on December 31st, they would not be married for return filing purposes. However, if one spouse dies during the taxable year, marital

31. The standard deduction is defined in section 63(c) to be the sum of the basic standard deduction and the additional standard deduction. Both of these components of the standard deduction are subject to adjustment for inflation. IRC § 63(c)(4). The exemption amount, defined in section 151 (d)(1) is also subject to the adjustment for inflation. IRC § 151(d)(4). For 2016 tax returns, the inflation adjusted amounts are reflected in Rev. Proc. 2015-53, 2015-44 I.R.B. 615.

32. The greater the difference in incomes between the spouses, the more advantageous it is to file a joint income tax return; if both incomes are more or less the same, there may not be any dollar advantage to filing jointly. If one spouse has certain deductions that exceed allowable limits if his or her return were filed separately, filing jointly may permit a greater deduction. For example, if one spouse exceeds the 50% contribution limit of section 170(b) based on his/her individual income, the excess might be deductible if both incomes are combined.

33. The Supreme Court invalidated a key portion of the Defense of Marriage Act (DOMA). United States v. Windsor, 133 S. Ct. 2675 (2013); *see also* Obergefell v. Hodges, 135 S. Ct. 2584 (2015). In Rev. Rul. 2013-17, 2013-2 C.B. 201, the IRS interpreted *Windsor*, ruling that "marriage" includes legally married same-sex couples for all federal tax purposes. The IRS recognizes as married those who legally married in any state, regardless of whether their state of domicile recognizes same-sex marriages. However, "marriage" does not include domestic partnerships, civil unions, and similar arrangements.

34. IRC § 6013(d)(1); *see also* IRC § 7703.

status is determined as of the date of death and the taxable year for the joint return ends on the last day of the surviving spouse's taxable year.[35]

As a general rule, joint returns cannot be made if either spouse was a nonresident alien during the taxable year.[36] There is an exception in section 6013(g), however, which treats a nonresident alien married to a citizen or resident of the United States as a resident—thereby permitting them to file a joint return if both spouses so elect. Also, a person who was a nonresident alien at the beginning of the year, but who became a resident alien before the end of the year and is married to a citizen or resident of the United States at the end of the year may, with his or her spouse, elect to be treated as a resident for the taxable year.[37]

B. Estate and Gift Tax Returns

1. Filing Thresholds—Estate Tax Returns

Subject to dollar thresholds discussed below, estate tax returns are required to be filed on Form 706 with respect to every decedent who at the time of death:

(a) was a U.S. citizen;[38] or

(b) was not a U.S. citizen but who

(i) was domiciled in the United States;[39]

(ii) was not domiciled in the United States but some part of whose gross estate was situated in the United States;[40] or

(iii) had been a citizen and, within the 10-year period ending on the date of death, had expatriated to avoid U.S. income taxes.[41]

The liability is imposed, and a return is required, only if the date of death value of the gross estate, increased by certain lifetime gifts, exceeds the "basic exclusion amount."[42] The basic exclusion amount is $5,000,000 for estates of decedents dying after December 31, 2009 (adjusted for inflation for decedents dying in a calendar year after 2011).[43]

In the case of a decedent who, at the time of death, was not a citizen of the United States and was not domiciled in the United States, the estate tax is reported on Form 706-NA. The tax is imposed only with respect to the portion of the estate "situated in the United States" at that time.[44] There are extensive provisions in the Internal Rev-

35. IRC § 6013(c).
36. IRC § 6013(a)(1).
37. IRC § 6013(h).
38. IRC § 2001(a).
39. *Id.*
40. IRC §§ 2101(a), 2106.
41. IRC § 2107.
42. IRC § 6018(a)(1); Reg. § 20.6018-1(a).
43. IRC § 2010(c). For example, the inflation adjusted exclusion amounts for decedents dying in 2015 and 2016 are $5,430,000 and $5,450,000, respectively. Rev. Proc. 2014-61, 2014-47 I.R.B. 860; Rev. Proc. 2015-53, 2015-44 I.R.B. 615.
44. IRC §§ 2103, 2106.

enue Code, related Regulations and international tax treaties[45] that define what property is treated as situated within and outside the United States and the computation of the taxable estate for such decedents.[46] Estates of such decedents are entitled to a $13,000 credit against the estate tax, an amount under the current tax rate schedule equivalent to an exclusion of $60,000 from the taxable estate.[47] A return is required and tax is imposed only if the date of death value of the gross estate situated in the United States exceeds the $60,000 amount covered by the credit.[48]

Gifts made by the decedent during the decedent's lifetime may affect the filing threshold. If the decedent made taxable gifts subsequent to 1976, other than gifts which are includible in the gross estate of the decedent, these must be accounted for when determining if an estate tax return has to be filed.[49] For example, if the decedent made taxable gifts of $2,000,000 during her life, an estate tax return would be due if the taxable estate exceeds $3,000,000, assuming the basic exclusion amount is $5,000,000 (*i.e.*, not adjusted for inflation). The reason is that the $2,000,000 in taxable gifts is added to the amount in the taxable estate and, if combined they exceed the basic exclusion amount, a return is due.

2. Filing Threshold—Gift Tax Returns

Section 6019 imposes a broad reporting requirement on any individual who makes any transfer by gift. Subject to a few exclusions, a Form 709 must be filed anytime a gift is made, even if no tax is due because, for example, the unified credit exceeds the computed tax. In determining whether a donor must file, section 6019 specifically excludes certain gifts: (i) the first $10,000 (adjusted for inflation in $1,000 increments with the amount being $14,000 for gifts made in 2016) of each gift of a present interest made to any person by the donor during the calendar year,[50] (ii) the amount paid, on behalf of another person, to an educational organization for tuition or to a medical care provider for medical care,[51] (iii) subject to certain limitations, the value of interests

---

45. *See, e.g.*, United States Treasury Model Estate and Gift Tax Treaty (Nov. 20, 1980). Treaty text available at Fed. Est. & Gift Tax Rep. (CCH) 75,061, at 86,058 (July 27, 2009); 1 Tax Treaties (CCH) ¶209.

46. IRC §§2101–2108.

47. IRC §§2001(c), 2102(b).

48. IRC §6018(a)(2); Reg. §20.6018-1(b). Regulation section 20.6018-1(b) states that the date of death value above which a return must be filed is $30,000. This Regulation has not been amended to reflect the current $60,000 threshold. For purposes of determining whether the filing thresholds have been exceeded for either estates of U.S. citizens or residents, or estates of persons who are not U.S. citizens and not domiciled in the United States, there is added to the decedent's gross estate (i) the adjusted taxable gifts, determined under section 2001(b), made by the decedent after December 31, 1976, and (ii) the "amount allowed as a specific exemption under section 2521 (as in effect before its repeal by the Tax Reform Act of 1976) with respect to gifts made by the decedent after September 8, 1976."

49. IRC §6018(a)(3).

50. IRC §2503(b)(1), (2); Rev. Proc. 2015-53, 2015-44 I.R.B. 615 (the annual exclusion for each donee is $14,000 for 2016). If both spouses consent, a gift made by one spouse to any person other than his spouse shall be considered as made one-half by him and one-half by his spouse, thus doubling the amount that a couple can gift away before being obligated to file gift tax returns. IRC §2513.

51. IRC §2503(e).

in property transferred to a spouse,[52] and (iv) subject to certain limitations, charitable gifts.[53] Thus, for example, if the donor's only gifts were $100,000 to her spouse, $7,500 to each of six children, and $45,000 directly to University of Denver to pay for her granddaughter's tuition, the donor would not have to file a Form 709. However, if she gave $17,500 to each child, she would be obligated to file a return regardless whether gift tax is due or not.

C. Information Returns

There are five types of information returns specified in the Internal Revenue Code. Two of them—"Registration of and Information Concerning Pensions, Etc. Plans" (sections 6057–6059) and "Information Concerning Income Tax Return Preparers" (section 6060)—are narrowly targeted. They are not discussed here. The reporting obligations for the other three types of information returns are of more general interest and are discussed briefly below.

1. Information Concerning Persons Subject to Special Provisions—Sections 6031–6039J

There are a number of provisions in the Code that either grant favorable treatment to, or impose additional burdens on, entities or individuals. The Code requires that certain persons (generally businesses), directly or indirectly subject to these special provisions, provide information to the government through the filing of an information return. Prominent among the reporting requirements within this type of information return are annual returns filed by three entities: (i) partnerships—section 6031,[54] (ii) exempt organizations—section 6033, and (iii) S corporations—section 6037. Several information reporting requirements of this type are imposed on individuals.[55] Notably, nine of the reporting obligations in this category deal in some manner with non-U.S. persons.

There are significant civil penalties for failure to comply with the information reporting obligations. With respect to information return filing obligations involving

52. IRC § 2523(a). There are significant limitations, generally precluding a deduction from taxable gifts where the donee's interest in the transferred property is terminable and the donor either retains or has transferred or may transfer to another person an interest in the property that may be enjoyed by that person upon the termination or failure of the donee spouse's interest. IRC § 2503(b). The first $148,000 of gifts to a spouse who is not a citizen of the United States is not included in the total amount of taxable gifts. Rev. Proc. 2015-53, *supra*.

53. IRC § 6019(3).

54. However, a partnership which derives its income from tax exempt obligations may not have to file a return. *See* Treas. Reg. § 1.761-2(a)(1), (2); Rev. Proc. 2003-84, 2003-48 I.R.B. 1159.

55. For example, section 6039E requires that individuals applying for a U.S. passport or seeking permanent residency status under the immigration laws file certain information about their status with the application. Section 6039G requires certain individuals who lose their U.S. citizenship to provide information about their status to one of several listed officials of the government who were involved in the loss of citizenship. In both of these cases, the official receiving the information is required to provide a copy to the IRS.

persons subject to special provisions, some penalties are found directly in the section that imposes the filing requirement.[56] Most others are found in section 6652, which establishes specific penalties for failure to comply with a number of the information return filing obligations.[57]

2. Information Concerning Transactions with Other Persons— Sections 6041–6050W

The "transactions with other persons" that result in information-reporting obligations under sections 6041–6050W are primarily payments by a business (upon whom the reporting obligation is imposed) to another party. These transactions include, among others, payment of dividends[58] and interest, share of proceeds or in-kind share of a commercial fishing venture,[59] and royalties.[60] There are also reporting obligations imposed on some "third parties" involved in transactions who neither make nor receive the payment in question. For instance, in the case of each real estate transaction, the "real estate reporting person"[61] is required to file a statement with the IRS containing information about the transferor of the property, a description of the property, the date of closing, and the "gross proceeds" received or to be received (without reduction by the seller's basis).[62]

Section 6050I, though of broad application, is of particular interest to attorneys who may receive significant cash deposits or payments on account of services rendered. Section 6050I imposes reporting obligations on persons who, in the course of their trade or business, receive more than $10,000 in cash in one or more related transactions. For purposes of this section, cash includes U.S. and foreign currencies and certain cashiers' checks, bank drafts, traveler's checks or money orders. The report, filed on a Form 8300, must contain the name, address and taxpayer identification number of the person from whom the cash was received.[63]

Attorneys fought an extended, largely unsuccessful, fight to withhold the names of their clients from whom they received more than the reporting obligation's $10,000 threshold amount. The position advanced was that divulging the name of a client

56. Section 6038(c) imposes a penalty on any U.S. person who controls a foreign business entity and who fails to provide, on an annual basis, certain information about the entity.

57. In 2007, Congress added another civil failure-to-file penalty. Section 6699 applies to S corporations which fail to timely file required returns or file returns that omit required information. The amount of the penalty depends on the length of the delinquency and the number of shareholders the S corporation has. At the same time, Congress revised section 6698, a comparable penalty for failure to file partnership returns.

58. IRC § 6042.

59. IRC § 6050A.

60. IRC § 6050N.

61. Real estate reporting persons include, in the following order as set forth in the statute, the attorney or title company responsible for closing the transaction, the mortgage lender, the seller's broker, the buyer's broker, or anyone else designated by the IRS in Regulations. IRC § 6045(e)(2).

62. IRC § 6045(e); Reg. § 1.6045-4(g); *see also* IRC § 6045(f) (requiring persons, who in the ordinary course of their business make payments to attorneys for services, to report such payments).

63. Reg. § 1.6050I-1(e)(2).

who paid in cash might trigger an investigation of the client, making any such disclosure a violation of the attorney's duty of confidentiality.

Structuring transactions to avoid the reporting requirements is unlawful. For example, one may not make two $6,000 payments or deposits rather than a single $12,000 payment or deposit. Section 6050I(f) imposes civil and criminal penalties for failing to file reports, filing false reports, or structuring or assisting in structuring any transaction, if the purpose therefore was to evade the reporting obligation.

A key feature of most types of reporting obligations that involve "information concerning transactions with other parties" is that they require the person filing the return to provide the same information to the person who is the subject of the report. Generally, this information is required to be provided by January 31 of each year.

Of particular importance are the penalties imposed under sections 6721–6724 for failure to file information returns on time and failure to include all of the required information. The basic penalty is $250 for each such failure during any calendar year, not to exceed $3,000,000.[64] If the failure is corrected within 30 days, the amount of the penalty is reduced to $50 per failure and the annual cap is reduced to $500,000. The annual cap is further reduced for persons with gross receipts of not more than $5,000,000.[65] No penalty is imposed if such persons can show that the failures were due to reasonable cause and not to willful neglect.[66] For purposes of these penalties, "information returns" is broadly defined, but limited to the returns listed in section 6724(d).

3. Expanded Information Reporting

In 1970, the IRS received about 360 million information return documents. It now receives over 2 billion such documents each year, about 10 to 15 for each taxpayer.[67]

More information reporting leads to more tax compliance.[68] Consider this progression: items subject to third-party information reporting and withholding (like wages) are misreported only about 1% of the time; items (like interest and dividends) subject to third-party information reporting, but not withholding, are misreported about 4% of the time; items (like capital gains and losses) subject to partial third-party information reporting are misreported about 8.6% of the time; but items subject

---

64. IRC § 6721(a).

65. IRC § 6721(d).

66. IRC § 6724(a).

67. During Fiscal Year 2014, the IRS received nearly 2.3 billion third-party information returns, nearly 86% of which were filed electronically. IRS Data Book, 2014, table 14.

68. "Overall, compliance is highest where there is third-party information reporting and/or withholding. For example, most wages and salaries are reported by employers to the IRS on Forms W-2 and are subject to withholding. As a result, a net of only 1 percent of wage and salary income was misreported. But amounts subject to little or no information reporting had a 56 percent net misreporting rate in 2006." IR-2012-4 (Jan. 6, 2012).

For a proposal to extend this approach, to require pass-through entities to track and report basis, see James Alm & Jay A. Soled, *Improving Tax Basis Reporting for Passthrough Entities*, Tax Notes, May 19, 2014, at 809.

to neither withholding nor third-party information reporting are misreported over 50% of the time.[69]

Accordingly, expanded information reporting is an important strategy in efforts to improve tax compliance.[70] For example, (1) 2008 legislation added section 6050W requiring banks and others to report gross credit and debit card payments received by merchants during the year,[71] and (2) 2008 legislation required brokers and mutual funds to report basis and other information to investors and the IRS for stock bought in 2011 or later.[72]

V. Signing and Verifying Returns

Section 6061(a) directs that any returns, statements, or documents "made under any provision of the internal revenue laws or regulations shall be signed in accordance with forms or regulations prescribed by the Secretary." Other Code sections and their related Regulations provide additional guidance about signing documents submitted to the IRS. For instance, section 6064 provides that an individual's name signed on the return is "prima facie evidence for all purposes" that the person actually signed the return. A taxpayer desiring to disclaim a return that is apparently signed by the taxpayer would have to overcome this presumption.[73]

The Code also requires that unless the IRS provides otherwise, every "return, declaration, statement, or other document" required to be filed must be signed under penalties of perjury.[74] Saltzman and Book point out that "the phrase 'under penalties of perjury' in the return jurat is an historical relic from the time when taxpayers were

---

69. "By comparison, misreporting rates for wage and interest income, which are subject to withholding or information reporting by financial institutions, are low (about 1 and 4 percent, respectively)." *Tax Gap: A Strategy for Reducing the Gap Should Include Options for Addressing Sole Proprietor Noncompliance*, GAO-07-1014 (July 2007); *see also* Charles P. Rettig, *Nonfilers Beware: Who's That Knocking at Your Door?*, J. Tax Prac. & Proc., Oct.–Nov. 2006, p. 19, 19–20 (reporting IRS data for 2001).

70. *See, e.g.*, Leandra Lederman, *Reducing Information Gaps to Reduce the Tax Gap: When Is Information Reporting Warranted?*, 78 Fordham L. Rev. 1733 (2010); Mark A. Luscombe, *The Tax Gap and the Growth of Third-Party Reporting*, Taxes, Aug. 2010, at 3.

71. Housing Assistance Tax Act of 2008, Pub. L. 110-289 (enacting IRC § 6050W); *see* Treas. Reg. § 1.6050W-1. In 2011, the IRS created Form 1099-K to implement these rules.

72. Energy Improvement and Extension Act of 2008, Pub. L. 110-343; *see* Prop. Reg. REG-101896-09, T.D. 9504, 2010-2 C.B. 670; IRS Notice 2010-67, 2010-2 C.B. 529.

Section 6045A requires every broker that transfers to a broker a security which is a covered security to furnish a written statement to the transferee broker within 15 days after the date of transfer for purposes of meeting reporting requirements.

73. One way to overcome the presumption would be to show that the return was signed under duress. For instance, duress is a defense to joint and several liability under section 6013(d)(3). *See* Reg. § 1.6015-3(c)(2)(v); *see also* Chapter 3, Section II.A. An interesting discussion and successful use of this defense can be found in *In Re Ellen Ann Hinckley*, 256 B.R. 814 (Bankr. M.D. Fla. 2000). Looking at all the facts, the court found that Mrs. Hinckley "could not resist her husband's demands" and that she "would not have willingly signed [the returns in question], but for Mr. Hinckley's constraint on her will." *Id.* at 828 (parenthesis added).

74. IRC § 6065.

required to make their returns under oath, and were prosecuted under the perjury statute in the general Criminal Code if they made a false statement on the return."[75] Prosecution for false statements is now under the felony statute—section 7206(1). Alternatively, the government might choose to prosecute under the general false-statement section: 18 U.S.C. section 1001. A section 1001 conviction can lead to a stiffer sentence than a section 7206(1) conviction.

There is additional guidance in the Code about electronic signatures[76] and signatures on returns of corporations[77] and partnerships,[78] and in the Regulations about returns made by agents[79] and by minors.[80] The courts have also weighed in on several issues, one of which involving joint income tax returns is addressed below. However, in relation to other issues of the administration of the internal revenue laws, the signing requirement has not given rise to much controversy.

The signature requirement, however, has been an issue in connection with joint returns. As indicated earlier, persons who sign joint returns are jointly and severally liable for the tax due for the year.[81] It would seem that a non-signing spouse should not be burdened with joint and several liability if one spouse prepared and filed a joint return either without the non-signing spouse's signature or by signing the return for the non-signing spouse. The non-signing spouse may not even have seen the return. But, regardless of whether or not the non-signing spouse has seen the return,

---

75. Michael I. Saltzman & Leslie Book, IRS Practice and Procedure ¶ 4.03(1)(c) (updated through May 2016).

76. IRC § 6061(b).

77. IRC § 6062.

78. IRC § 6063. This section provides that the partnership's return may be signed "by any one of the partners." However, the instructions to Form 1065 say that a general partner must sign the return. There can be nice questions as to who is the appropriate party to sign returns of entities. *See, e.g.*, Sheldon I. Banoff & Richard M. Lipton, *Who Can Sign an LLC's 1065 Tax Return? It's Still Not Clear,* J. Tax'n, Apr. 2011, at 254; Sheldon I. Banoff & Allan G. Donn, *Who Can Sign a Partnership's or LLC's Tax Returns? Simple Questions; Complex Answers,* J. Tax'n, Sept. 2010, at 144. The IRS has provided guidance on who has authority to execute returns, waivers, and statute extensions with respect to decedents. Chief Counsel Advisory CCA 201334040 (Aug. 23, 2013).

79. Reg. § 1.6012-1(a)(5) authorizes the signing of an income tax return by an agent in certain circumstances and requires that a power of attorney authorizing signing of the return be filed with the return. In *Elliott v. Commissioner*, 113 T.C. 125 (1999), the taxpayer's attorney signed and filed an income tax return for the taxpayer, but at the time did not have (and therefore could not submit with the return) a properly signed power of attorney. By the time a power of attorney was filed, the statute of limitations on assessing additional tax had expired. The Tax Court upheld the Service's argument that an asserted deficiency was timely and said: "Failure to satisfy the requirements for filing a return is fatal to the validity and the timeliness of the return." *Id.* at 128 (citation omitted). *See also* Levi v. Commissioner, T.C. Memo 2015-118. However, in case a spouse cannot sign a joint return by reason of disease or injury, the other spouse, with the oral consent of the incapacitated spouse, can sign the incapacitated spouse's name. Reg. § 1.6012-1(a)(5). An explanation of the circumstances must be attached to the return. Regulation section 1.6012-1(b)(3) contains similar rules with respect to non-resident aliens' returns signed by an agent. However, under certain circumstances the agency appointment itself may be sufficient proof of the agent's authorization to sign the return.

80. Reg. § 1.6012-1(a)(4) (directing that returns of a minor be made by the minor or by the minor's "guardian or other person charged with the care of the minor's person or property").

81. IRC § 6013(d)(3).

the non-signing spouse nevertheless may be found to be jointly and severally liable. One such situation is when a non-signing spouse, who is physically unable to sign the return, orally consents to the other spouse signing the return for him or her.[82] More interesting is the series of cases in which a non-signing spouse's intent to file a joint return was held sufficient to validate the joint return for purposes of imposing joint and several liability. In *In re Hanesworth*,[83] Mrs. Hanesworth filed a Chapter 7 bankruptcy petition when she found out that the IRS was going to seize her home for nonpayment of tax liability for 1978, a year for which a joint return, signed only by her husband, was filed. The Court held in favor of the government, noting that:

> [The wife's] failure of one spouse to sign the return does not negate the intent of filing a joint return by the nonsigning spouse...[F]ailure to object to her liability until she realized her home was actually in jeopardy, the established pattern of joint filings both before and after the year in question, and [her] history of acquiescence in her husband's handling of the family's financial affairs, coupled with the facial declarations on the return, lead to the conclusion that [she] tacitly consented to the filing of a joint tax return for 1978.[84]

Such tacit consent was sufficient to impose joint and several liability on Mrs. Hanesworth even though she did not sign the return.

Note, however, that a joint return signed by a tax preparer is invalid if neither spouse signs the return, even if the spouses intended that the return actually filed be a joint return.[85] In *Olpin*, a joint return was filed for the 1995 tax year. The only signature on the return was that of the Olpin's tax preparer. The facts of the case indicate that the spouses' failures to sign the return were inadvertent. Not having noticed the fact that the taxpayers had not signed the return, the IRS treated the return as filed, processed the return, and accepted payment of the liability shown on the return. In 1996 the parties divorced. Mrs. Olpin then declared bankruptcy in 1997. The IRS asserted a claim against the estate. During her bankruptcy deposition the IRS informed Mrs. Olpin that neither she nor her husband signed the 1995 joint return. The IRS suggested that Mrs. Olpin file a married filing separate return for the 1995 tax year, which she did, because at least part of the deficiency was attributable to unreported income of Mr. Olpin. The IRS then asserted a deficiency against Mr. Olpin based on calculating his liability on the basis of married, filing separately. Mr. Olpin argued that the joint return for 1995 was valid and as such, his 1995 tax liability should not have increased. The spouses both testified that at the time the return was filed both intended to file a joint return. The court held that the IRS did not have the power to waive the signature requirement and thus a joint return was not filed in 1995.[86]

---

82. Reg. § 1.6012-1(a)(5).

83. 1991 U.S. App. LEXIS 13886 (10th Cir. June 26, 1991) (reported as Table Case at 936 F.2d 583).

84. *Id.* at *11–12 (citation omitted).

85. *See* Olpin v. Commissioner, 270 F.3d 1297 (10th Cir. 2001), *aff'g* T.C. Memo. 1999-426.

86. *Cf.* T.A.M. 200429009 (IRS permitted a corporation to ratify a claim for refund where the original claim for refund had a defective signature and the corporation filed a properly signed claim for refund after the expiration of the SOL).

If a taxpayer fails to file a required return, section 6020 allows the IRS to prepare a substitute for return. There are two kinds of "substitute returns," Section 6020(a) allows the IRS to prepare a return from information provided by the taxpayer, with the taxpayer then signing the return. Section 6020(b) allows the IRS to prepare a return (sometimes called a "substitute for return" or SFR) from information the IRS obtains from other sources.[87] Because the return is not signed by the taxpayer, however, it is not a return for purposes of the statute of limitations.

VI. Time and Place for Filing

Due Dates: The basic rule for timely filing of income tax returns is that they must be filed by the fifteenth day of the fourth month following the end of the taxable year.[88] The "fifteenth day of the fourth month" rule applies to income tax returns filed by: individuals, estates, trusts, political organizations, homeowners associations, and estates of individuals under Chapter 7 or Chapter 11 bankruptcy. The "fifteenth day of the fourth month rule," in effect, also applies to the final return of a decedent for the short period ending on the date of death.

Domestic "C" corporations having an office or place of business in the United States are required to file their returns on or before the fifteenth day of the fourth month following the close of their taxable years, that is, April 15 for calendar year corporations.[89] C corporations are entitled to an automatic six-month extension to file.[90]

Foreign corporations that do not have an office or fixed place of business in the United States but which are required to file income tax returns, have until the fifteenth day of the sixth month following the close of the taxable year to file their returns.[91]

S Corporations annually report their items of income, gain, loss, deduction, and credit on Form 1120S. Schedule K-1 of Form 1120S is a summary of the corporation's items of income, gain, loss, deduction, and credit. Schedule K-1 is also used to report to the IRS and to each shareholder the shareholder's share of those items. Form 1120S, including a copy of each K-1, must be filed on or before the "fifteenth day of the third month" following the end of the taxable year (March 15, for calendar-year S

87. The Treasury has revised Reg. §301.6020-1 to facilitate preparation of section 6020(b) substitutes for returns. T.D. 9380, Substitute for Return, 2008-1 C.B. 718. In Chief Counsel Notice CC-2008-22-026 (May 30, 2008), the IRS concluded that section 6020(b) allows revenue officers to prepare employment tax returns in employment tax cases involving worker classification issues.

88. IRC §6072(a).

89. *See* IRC §6072(b); Reg. §1.6072-2(a). The Surface Transportation and Veterans Health Care Choice Improvement Act of 2015, §2006 Pub. L. 114-41 (July 31, 2015), subject to a few exceptions and to various effective dates, changed the due date of C corporate returns to the fifteenth day of the fourth month after the end of the taxable year. Prior thereto they were due the fifteenth day of the third month. Organizations exempt from tax in section 401(a) follow the "fifteenth day of the fifth month" rule. Reg. §1.6072-2(c).

90. The Surface Transportation and Veterans Health Care Choice Improvement Act of 2015, §2006, Pub. L. 114-41 (July 31, 2015), subject to a few exceptions and to various effective dates, changed the number of months an automatic extension is available from three months to six months.

91. Reg. §1.6072-2(b).

corporations). Form 1120S and its related documents can be filed electronically with certain exceptions listed in the instructions.[92]

Partnerships are not required to file income tax returns because the partners, not the partnerships, pay tax on the partnership's income. However, section 6031 states that every domestic partnership that has income, deductions or credits is required to file a Form 1065 information return reflecting, among other things, its income, gains, losses, deductions, and credits and the names, addresses, and identification numbers of its partners.[93] Like S corporations, partnerships must file a schedule K-1 with the return and to each partner. The basic "fifteenth day of the third month" rule applies to the filing of such returns.[94] Generally, partnerships with more than 100 partners are required to file their returns electronically whereas other partnerships may elect to file electronically.[95]

Foreign partnerships that have gross income that is, or is deemed to be, effectively connected with the conduct of a trade or business within the United States, or that have U.S. source income that is not effectively connected, are also required to file annual information returns.[96] However, certain foreign partnerships otherwise required to file, including those with de minimis U.S. source income and U.S. partners with de minimis interests in the partnership, are either relieved of the filing requirement or have reduced filing obligations.[97]

Partnerships must also provide each partner with a Schedule K-1 that includes the partner's name, address, and identification number, the identification number of the

---

92. The exceptions to electronic filing generally involve something unusual that the IRS wants called to its attention. Electronic filing is not permitted for amended returns, bankruptcy returns, final returns, returns with a name change, returns with pre-computed penalty and interest, returns with reasonable cause for failing to file timely, returns with reasonable cause for failing to pay timely, returns with request for overpayment to be applied to another account, short-year returns, and 52–53 week tax year returns.

93. IRC § 6031. For this purpose, partnerships include general and limited partnerships, limited liability partnerships (LLPs), limited liability companies that elect partnership status under the "check-the-box" rules, and any other business entity that is not a corporation and that elects partnership status under the check-the-box regulations.

Section 6698 imposes a potentially expensive penalty on any partnership required to file an information return under section 6031 that either fails to file in a timely manner, *i.e.*, before the due date of the return, including extensions, or files the return but fails to include the required information. The penalty is $195 a month multiplied by the number of persons who were partners in the partnership during any part of the taxable year, for each person who was a partner in the partnership during the year. The section 6698 penalty is in addition to any criminal penalty imposed under section 7203 for willful failure to file a return, supply information, or pay tax. IRC § 6698(a). Section 6698(a) contains a "reasonable cause" exception to the penalty. Based on legislative history relating to the penalty, the IRS has not applied this exception to any domestic partnership that has ten or fewer partners, within the meaning of section 6231(a)(1)(B), provided that all the partners have filed timely income tax returns including their respective shares of the partnership's income, gain, loss, deductions, and credits. *See* Rev. Proc. 84-35, 1984-1 C.B. 509.

94. The Surface Transportation and Veterans Health Care Choice Improvement Act of 2015, Pub. L. 114-41 (July 31, 2015), subject to a few exceptions and to various effective dates, changed the due date of partnership returns to the fifteenth day of the third month after the end of the taxable year.

95. Reg. § 301.6011-3(a).

96. Reg. § 1.6031(a)-1(b)(1).

97. Reg. § 1.6031(a)-1(b)(2), (3).

partnership, and the partner's distributive share of the partnership's separately stated items of income, gain, loss, deduction, and credit, as well as the partner's distributive share of the partnership's non-separately stated items of income, gain, loss, deduction, and credit. The Schedule K-1's must be provided to the partners on or before the due date (the fifteenth day of the third month), including extensions, for filing the partnership's return.[98]

Where to File: According to the instructions to the Form 1040, if not filed electronically, the place where the form must be filed depends on the state (or foreign country) in which the taxpayer is located, whether the taxpayer is submitting payment or not, and whether a private delivery service is used or not.

Form 706 (Form 706-NA for estates of citizens who were neither U.S. citizens nor U.S. residents) is used to report estate and generation-skipping transfer taxes. The form is to be filed by the executor of the estate "within nine months of the date of the decedent's death."[99] According to the Regulations, the due date is "the day of the ninth calendar month after the decedent's death numerically corresponding to the day of the calendar month on which death occurred."[100] If there are two or more executors, each must sign the return. Estate tax returns for citizens of the United States, residents of the United States, resident aliens, and nonresident aliens are to be filed at the Internal Revenue Service Center located at Cincinnati, Ohio.

Gift tax returns (Form 709) must "be filed on or before the fifteenth day of April following the close of the calendar year."[101] An extension of time to file an income tax return also serves as an extension of time to file the gift tax return.[102] According to the instructions to the Form 709, if not filed electronically, the place where the form must be filed (either the Covington, Kentucky or Cincinnati, Ohio Service Center) depends on whether the return is filed by mail or by private delivery service.

There are two rules that often modify the due dates for both filing (and paying) taxes. Section 7502(a) provides that a return or payment addressed to the proper office, mailed by U.S. mail, and postmarked on or before its due date, but which is received after such date, is deemed to have been filed or paid as of the date of the postmark. Long lines at post offices on April 15 each year attest to individual taxpayers' awareness of this "timely mailing is timely filing or paying" rule.

In 1996, Congress expanded the "timely mailing is timely filing" rule to include delivery by private delivery services.[103] To qualify as a designated delivery service, the service must be available to the public, provide regular service comparable to that

---

98. This is intended to solve a long-running problem whereby the returns of individual partners was the same as the partnership but the partners did not have the results of the partnership in time to file their returns.

99. IRC § 6075(a).

100. Reg. § 20.6075-1. However, "if there is no numerically corresponding day in the ninth month, the last day of the ninth month is the due date." *Id.*

101. IRC § 6075(b)(1).

102. IRC § 6075(b)(2).

103. IRC § 7502(f).

available through the U.S. mail, and it must record electronically or mark on the envelope in which the item is delivered the date it received the envelope.[104] This recorded or marked date serves as the postmark for section 7502 purposes. The IRS periodically issues a notice listing the qualified designated service providers.[105] The IRS generally takes the position that section 7502 does not apply to the filing of amended returns.[106]

One question that has come up, in connection with the timely mailing is timely filing rule, is how a taxpayer can establish the time of filing if the return is lost. Courts have not agreed on whether proof other than a registered or certified receipt received at the time of mailing can be used to prove the time of filing.[107] Treas. Reg. section 301.7502-1 establishes the general rule that section 7502 requires actual delivery. The only exceptions are proof of proper use of registered or certified mail or of a duly designated private delivery service.[108] "No other evidence of a postmark or of mailing will be prima facie evidence of delivery or raise a presumption that the document was delivered."[109]

The other rule that often modifies the filing and paying due dates is section 7503—the "Saturday, Sunday, or legal holiday" rule. This rule says that when the last day prescribed for performing any act falls on a Saturday, Sunday or legal holiday, performance of the act on the next day which is not a Saturday, Sunday, or legal holiday shall be considered timely. So, if April 15 falls on a Saturday, application of both section 7502 and section 7503 means that an individual income tax return mailed by U.S. mail, properly addressed, and postmarked on the following Monday, will be considered timely.[110]

According to the instructions to the Forms 1120 (C corporations), 1120-S (S corporations) and 1065 (partnerships), if not filed electronically, the place where the form must be filed (either the Ogden or Cincinnati Service Center) depends on the state (or foreign country) in which the principal office of the business is located, its total assets and whether a private delivery service is used.

---

104. IRC § 7502(f)(2). The IRS publishes a list of private delivery services designated for section 7502 purposes. Notice 2015-38, 2015-21 IRB 984 (May 7, 2015). The list should be reviewed carefully. Not all services offered by all delivery services are designated.

105. *See* Notice 2004-83, 2004-52 I.R.B. 1030. Also, the instruction to Form 4868 provides a list of current valid private delivery services. Notice that private delivery services cannot deliver items to P.O. boxes. Taxpayers must use the U.S. Postal Service to mail any item to an IRS P.O. box address.

106. CCA 201052003 (Aug. 2010) (interpreting Treas. Reg. § 301.7502-1(b)(1)).

107. *Compare* Estate of Wood v. Commissioner, 909 F.2d 1155 (8th Cir. 1990) (taxpayers can present evidence other than registered or certified mail to prove that a return was filed on a certain date), *with* Surowka v. United States, 909 F.2d 148 (6th Cir. 1990) (registered or certified receipt only way to prove filing).

108. REG-138176-02, 69 Fed. Reg. 56377.

109. Reg. § 301.7502-1(e)(2); *see* Stocker v. United States, 705 F.3d 225 (6th Cir. 2013) (following this rule and holding against the taxpayer, who had failed to have the Post Office date-stamp his copy of the certified mail receipt).

110. Operation of these rules was illustrated in 2011. The normal last date for filing individual income tax returns would have been Friday, April 15, 2011. That day, however, was Emancipation Day, a legal holiday in the District of Columbia. Saturday, April 16 and Sunday, April 17 were weekend days. So returns properly mailed on Monday, April 18, were timely.

VII. Time and Place for Paying Tax

Taxes are generally due on the last date for filing the return.[111] Thus, in the case of a calendar year individual whose income tax return is due "on or before" April 15 of the year following the close of the calendar year, payment is due on that April 15. The due date for *payment* is determined without regard to whether the taxpayer has obtained an extension of time for *filing* the return.[112] Also, the date a return is considered filed or a payment is considered made is generally the date the return or payment is received by the government in the proper office.[113] The "timely mailing is timely filing" and "Saturday, Sunday or legal holiday" rules of sections 7502 and 7503, discussed above, apply here also. Payment options include cash, e-pay, credit card, and installment arrangements.[114] Generally, payment is sent to the same location as, and with, the tax return.

With respect to income taxes, there are two significant prepayment requirements. Employers are required to withhold from wages paid to employees a tax "determined in accordance with tables or computational procedures prescribed by the Secretary."[115] This tax is treated as a "refundable credit" that is applied against the taxpayer's income tax liability.[116] If the amount withheld is greater than the employee's income tax liability, the excess is considered an "overpayment,"[117] which, subject to certain offsets,[118] is required to be refunded to the taxpayer, if timely claimed on the taxpayer's income tax return. The employer is required to pay over the amounts withheld to the federal government. This has resulted in a relatively high degree of compliance with the tax laws by wage earners while, at the same time, creating a significant com-

---

111. IRC §6151(c).

112. In the interest of uniformity in applying the statutes of limitations on the government with respect to assessing additional tax, or on taxpayers with respect to obtaining refunds, early returns filed and early payments made are generally "considered" as filed or made on the last day prescribed by law for filing or paying. *See* IRC §§6501(b)(1), 6513(a), (b). See also Chapter 5, dealing with statutes of limitations in deficiency cases, and Chapter 9, dealing with claims for refund.

113. When a taxpayer discovers that her original return was erroneous, she is not currently legally obligated to file an amended return. *E.g.*, Broadhead v. Comm'r, 14 T.C.M. 1284 (1955). For a proposal to create such an obligation, see T. Keith Fogg & Calvin H. Johnson, *Amended Returns—Imposing a Duty to Correct Material Mistakes*, Tax Notes, Sept. 8, 2008, at 979.

114. *See* IR-2010-45 (Apr. 8, 2010). However, payment options do not include bogus promissory notes. A taxpayer who attempted this approach in the context of Collection Due Process proceedings (discussed in chapter 13) was penalized under section 6673 for asserting frivolous positions for the purpose of delay. Goff v. Commissioner, 135 T.C. 231 (2010).

The IRS has a "DirectPay" online system, which allows taxpayers to pay tax or make estimated payments directly from their checking or savings accounts without fees or pre-registration requirements. Taxpayers with valid Social Security numbers can access the system from the IRS website. Over 150,000 taxpayers have used the system to pay over $340 million in taxes. IR-2014-67.

115. IRC §3402(a)(1).

116. IRC §31(a).

117. IRC §6401(b); *see* Chapter 9.

118. IRC §6402.

pliance problem with respect to employers that, for one reason or another, withhold the required taxes but fail to pay them over.[119]

The other significant prepayment requirement with respect to income taxes is that individuals, corporations, trusts, estates, and tax exempt organizations (with respect to their unrelated business taxable income) must estimate their tax liability for the year and make four installment payments. This prepayment obligation is discussed in Chapter 11.

VIII. Extension of Time to File or Pay

As just discussed, the Code contains rules for the time by which returns are to be filed and taxes are to be paid. Nevertheless, section 6081(a) authorizes the IRS to "grant a reasonable extension of time for filing any [required] return, declaration, statement or other document. . . ." and sections 6161 et seq. provide a variety of rules that allow payment to be extended in narrow situations.

Obtaining an extension of time to file an income tax return is relatively simple. For income tax returns of individuals, Regulation section 1.6081-4 permits an automatic six-month extension of time to file without having to provide any justification for the delay.[120] Form 4868 requesting the automatic six-month extension must be filed (either electronically or on paper) on or before the due date of the return.[121] Form 4868 requires the taxpayer to "properly estimate" the tax liability for the year. If the tax liability on the application for extension does not constitute a bona fide and reasonable estimate based on facts available at the time, the extension may be held invalid, subjecting the taxpayer to a late-filing penalty.[122] If the estimate is bona fide and reasonable, the extension is valid even if the actual liability turns out to differ considerably from the estimated liability. There is a safe harbor: if the total amount paid (through withholding, estimated tax payments, and the amount paid with the extension application) is within 10% of true liability, the IRS will presume that the reasonable cause defense properly applies and will not assert the section 6651(a)(2) failure to pay penalty if the balance is paid with the return.[123] Beyond that safe harbor,

---

119. See Chapter 14 dealing with the section 6672 "trust fund penalty" imposed on responsible persons who fail to "collect, truthfully account for, and pay over" tax such as the withholding tax.

120. Reg. § 1.6081-2(a)(1) reduces the automatic extension period from six to five months with respect to partnership returns.

121. The General Instructions to Form 4868 indicate that it is to be used to obtain a six-month extension to file Forms 1040, 1040A, 1040EZ, 1040NR, 1040NR-EZ, 1040-PR, or 1040-SS. Form 4868 can be filed electronically or on paper. *See* Form 4868. If an individual taxpayer (a U.S. citizen or resident) is out of the country on the regular due date, two extra months to file the return and pay any amount due will be granted without an extension request. In other words, June 16, 2014 is the due date for filing and for payment for this calendar-year taxpayer. If this taxpayer still needs some time to file a return, he or she can obtain an additional four months to file a return by filing Form 4868 and checking the box on line 8.

122. *See, e.g.*, Crocker v. Commissioner, 92 T.C. 899 (1989).

123. Reg. § 301.6651-1(c)(3)(i); *see also* Chapter 11.

there is little certainty. Neither the case law nor rulings define clearly the contours of "proper estimate."

C corporations may also get a six-month extension, unless it is on a calender year, in which case the extension is only five months, or a June 30 year in which case it is seven months.[124] It may be necessary for the taxpayer to get an extension of time to file that is longer than six months. Except in the case of "undue hardship," no extension longer than six months normally will be granted unless the taxpayer has first obtained the automatic six-month extension.[125] Taxpayers will be exposed to both late filing and late payment penalties under sections 6651(a)(1) and (2), unless taxpayers are prevented from filing or paying on time in certain circumstances such as major natural disasters. The IRS will grant relief (e.g., extended filing deadlines, extended payment deadlines, and penalty abatement) either by special statutes or by administrative fiat and make announcement through its website.[126]

It is also possible to obtain a six-month extension of time to file an estate tax return by filing a Form 4768. After an estate tax return is filed, one can provide supplemental information by filing another Form 706 with "Supplemental Information" written across the top of page 1. After obtaining an extension, the return must be filed before the end of the extended period and the return "cannot be amended after the expiration of the extension period." However, supplemental information may still be provided to the IRS.[127]

An extension of time to file, even if valid, is not an extension of time to pay.[128] Thus, even if penalties are avoided, interest runs on the underpayment from the original due date of the return until the date of full payment.

Several provisions in the Code may alter the due date for payment of certain taxes. Perhaps most important is section 6161 which authorizes the IRS to extend the time for paying any tax shown or required to be shown on any return "for a reasonable period not to exceed 6 months ... from the date fixed for payment thereof."[129] The IRS is also authorized to extend the time for payment of any deficiency in income tax for up to 18 months and for an additional period, not to exceed twelve months, if payment on the original due date "will result in undue hardship to the taxpayer."[130]

There are several provisions that permit delay of payment of estate taxes either with the permission of the IRS or at the option of the executor. The IRS may extend the time for payment of estate tax for a period not to exceed four years if the estate

---

124. IRC § 6081(b)

125. Reg. § 1.6081-1(b)(1).

126. *See* Tax Relief in Disaster Situations on www.irs.gov/uac/Tax-Relief-in-Disaster-Situations.

127. Reg. § 20.6081-1(d); *see, e.g.*, Estate of Proske v. United States, 2010 WL 2178968 (D.N.J. 2010) (holding that the IRS abused its discretion in denying an estate's request under Reg. § 20.6081-1 for an extension of time to file estate tax return).

128. Reg. § 1.6081-1(a).

129. IRC § 6161(a). The General Instructions to Form 4868 at page 2 state that an extension of time for filing an income tax return also serves to extend the due date of a gift or generation-skipping transfer tax return (Form 709 or 709-A).

130. IRC § 6161(b)(1).

can demonstrate "reasonable cause" for the delay.[131] The executor may elect to defer payment of estate tax on the value of any reversionary or remainder interest held by the estate until six months after the termination of the precedent interest.[132] A further extension of up to three years may be granted for reasonable cause.[133] Finally, the executor may elect to pay the estate tax imposed on an interest in a closely held business in as many as ten equal installments.[134] The first such installment may be made any time within five years from the due date for payment of the tax.[135]

Finally, if the IRS determines that it will facilitate collection, the IRS is authorized to enter into written agreements for the payment of any tax in installments.[136] The provision is most often utilized in collection proceedings and it is discussed in detail in Chapter 13.

IX. Disclosure of Reportable Transactions

In the American Jobs Creation Act of 2004, Congress sought to strengthen the reporting and disclosure responsibilities of persons who provide, for compensation in excess of a threshold amount,[137] "any material aid, assistance, or advice with respect to organizing, managing, promoting, selling, implementing, insuring, or carrying out any reportable transaction...."[138] Such persons, called "material advisors," are required to file a return identifying and describing the tax benefits of the plan. Material advisors are also required to maintain a list of persons whom they advised regarding the reportable transaction.[139]

Taxpayers who participate in any reportable transaction also have disclosure responsibilities which are spelled out in Regulation § 1.6011-4. The Regulations reflect changes in the underlying statutes and add "transactions of interest" as a new reportable trans-

---

131. *See, e.g.*, Baccei v. United States, 632 F.3d 1140 (9th Cir. 2011) (upholding imposition of failure-to-pay penalty when an estate submitted a defective Form 4768 not satisfying the requirements of Reg. § 20.6161-1(b); also rejecting the taxpayer's substantial compliance, equitable estoppel, and reasonable reliance arguments).

132. IRC § 6163(a).

133. IRC § 6163(b).

134. IRC § 6166(a); *see, e.g.*, PLR 200842012 (July 18, 2008) (addressing the section 6166 requirements that the business be closely held and that it be involved in an active trade or business). In *Estate of Roski v. Commissioner*, 128 T.C. 113 (2007), the Tax Court held that the IRS has discretionary power under section 6166 to require that deferred payments be secured by bond or lien, but that the IRS may not require such security uniformly, in every case. *See* Britt Haxton, Note, *The Section 6166 Balancing Game: An Examination of the Policy Behind* Estate of Roski v. Commissioner, 62 Tax Law. 525 (2009).

135. *Id.*

136. IRC § 6159.

137. Pub. L. 108-357, 118 Stat. 1418 (Oct. 22, 2004). The threshold amounts are $50,000 with respect to reportable transactions for natural persons and $250,000 in all other cases. IRC § 6111(b)(1)(B).

138. IRC § 6111(b)(1)(A).

139. IRC § 6112. Material advisor is defined in IRC § 6111(b)(1).

action. Section 6707A imposes a penalty for failure to include in a return "any" information required to be included under section 6011 with respect to reportable transaction.

The Small Business Jobs Act of 2010[140] moderated the former penalty amounts under section 6707A. The current penalty generally is 75% of the reduction in tax on the taxpayer's return that would have resulted from the transactions in question had they not been reportable transactions. The 2010 legislation also establishes maximum and minimum penalty amounts. The maximum as to listed transactions is $100,000 for individuals and $200,000 for other taxpayers ($10,000 and $50,000, respectively, as to non-listed transactions). The minimum is $5,000 for individuals and $10,000 for others.[141]

Also, there is an accuracy related penalty, under section 6662A, equal to 20% of the amount of the understatement attributable to a reportable transaction. This penalty applies to listed transactions and other reportable transactions "if a significant purpose of such transaction is the avoidance or evasion of Federal income tax."[142] The penalty is increased to 30%, and the otherwise available reasonable cause defense will not apply, if the relevant facts are not disclosed as required under section 6011.[143]

The transaction is reported on Form 8886, which requires that the taxpayer identify the type of reportable transaction, indicate whether it was acquired through a corporation or a pass-through entity, and provide the name and address of any person paid a fee for promoting, soliciting, or recommending participation in the transaction or providing tax advice with respect to the transaction. In addition, the Form requires a description of the facts relating to the transaction, the kind of tax benefits expected and the estimated amount of the tax benefits.

Under § 1.6011-4 of the Regulations, reportable transactions include the following.

1. Listed transaction. These are transactions identified by the Service to be tax avoidance transactions, including transactions that are "substantially similar" to any such identified tax avoidance transactions.
2. Confidential transactions. These are transactions "offered to a taxpayer under conditions of confidentiality and for which the taxpayer has paid an advisor a minimum fee."
3. Transaction with contractual protection. These are transactions in which the fee paid is refundable (in whole or in part) if the intended tax consequences are not realized or if the fee paid is contingent on the taxpayer receiving the promised tax benefits.[144]

---

140. Pub. L. No. 111-240, 124 Stat. 2504 (Sept. 27, 2010).

141. Guidance as to the changes is set out in LB&I-20-0211-001, 2011 TNT 80-11.

142. IRC § 6662A(b)(2).

143. IRC §§ 6662A(c), 6664(d)(3)(A).

144. For examples of transactions involving refundable or contingent fees that are specifically excepted from the reporting requirements, see Rev. Proc. 2007-20, 2007-7 IRB 517 (Feb. 12, 2007).

4. Loss transactions. These are transactions in which the taxpayer claims a section 165 loss in excess of a threshold amount. The threshold amount depends on several factors including whether the taxpayer is a corporation (generally $10 million in a single year or $20 million in any combination of years) or an individual (generally $2 million in a single year or $4 million in any combination of years).
5. Transactions with a significant book-tax difference. These are transactions where the amount, which was motivated by tax purposes, of an item or items of income, gain, expense, or loss from the transaction differs by more than $10 million on a gross basis from the amount of the item or items for book purposes determined by the U.S. generally accepted accounting principles (U.S. GAAP) for worldwide income. An exception to application of U.S. GAAP is when a taxpayer, in the ordinary course of its business, keeps books for reporting financial results to shareholders, creditors, or regulators on a basis other than U.S. GAAP consistently from year to year, and does not maintain U.S. GAAP books for any purpose, then the taxpayer may determine the amount for book purposes based on the taxpayer's books.
6. Transactions involving a brief asset holding period. These are transactions involving a claimed tax credit in excess of $250,000 in which the assets giving rise to the credit are "held by the taxpayer for 45 days or less."

The reportable transaction rules continue to evolve. The regulations remove certain categories of reportable transactions but also add a new category: transactions of interest.[145] Treasury and the IRS have frequently refined rules under section 6011 and related sections, by both regulations[146] and lower-level administrative pronouncements.[147]

X. Tax Return Preparers

Many tax advisers—such as lawyers, certified public accountants, and enrolled agents practicing before the IRS—have long been subject to regulation by the IRS under rules set out in Treasury Circular 230.[148] However, the ever-increasing complexity of the tax laws has given birth to an army of commercial tax return preparers numbering in the hundreds of thousands. Such preparers have not been subject to

145. Reg. § 1.6011-4(c)(3)(i)(E).

146. *E.g.*, T.D. 9425, Section 6707A and the Failure To Include on Any Return or Statement Any Information Required To Be Disclosed Under Section 6011 with Respect to a Reportable Transaction, 2008-2 C.B. 1100 (temporary and proposed regulations on section 6707A penalties for failure to disclose reportable transactions under section 6011); REG-129916-07, Patented Transactions, 2007-2 C.B. 891 (proposed regulations making patented tax transactions a category of reportable transactions under sections 6011, 6111, and 6112).

147. *E.g.*, IRS Notice 2008-111, 2008-2 C.B. 1299 (guidance as to "intermediary transactions" as a category of listed transaction); Rev. Proc. 2008-20, 2008-1 C.B. 980 (providing guidance to material advisers required to keep lists of reportable transactions under section 6112); Rev. Proc. 2007-20, 2007-1 C.B. 517 (updated guidance as to exceptions under Reg. § 1.6011-4(b)(4) for reportable transactions with contractual protection).

148. 31 C.F.R. subtitle A, pt. 10.

either federal or (except for California, Maryland, New York, and Oregon) state regulation.

Many—both inside and outside government—believe that incompetence and sometimes dishonesty among unregulated return preparers is at unacceptably high levels. Accordingly, in 2010, Treasury promulgated regulations requiring preparers to obtain preparer tax identification numbers (PTINs) and to pay user fees for obtaining and renewing them.[149] In addition, Treasury promulgated regulations that would have been effective in 2011, mandating competency testing, continuing education, and ethical duties for return preparers.[150]

Key portions of the 2011 regulations were invalidated in 2013 and 2014 in the much discussed *Loving* case.[151] Starting from the premise that agencies—including Treasury and the IRS—cannot wield power beyond what Congress grants them, the *Loving* opinions found that the applicable statute, 31 U.S.C. § 330, confers on Treasury the power to regulate only "representatives" who are "engaged in practice" before the IRS. They read these statutory terms narrowly, holding that return preparers do not represent clients before the IRS and do not practice before it. The 2011 regulations were invalid, *Loving* held, because they went beyond the statutory delegation.

The subsequent *Ridgely* decision took the same tack and substantially invalidated a Circular 230 rule prohibiting contingent fee arrangements for preparing, giving advice as to, and filing specified tax returns and refund claims.[152] If subsequent cases continue in this vein, many other provisions of Circular 230—including those purporting to regulate tax opinions—may be at risk of being invalidated.[153]

Several bills have been introduced in Congress to amend the underlying statute, but their enactment is doubtful. In addition, in 2014, the IRS unveiled its Annual Filing Season Program, which uses various incentives to induce unregulated preparers to do "voluntarily" what the invalidated 2011 regulations would have mandated.[154]

Return preparers may be penalized under section 6694(a) with respect to unrealistic positions on their clients' returns, under section 6694(b) for willful or reckless conduct, or under section 6695 for a variety of associated derelictions.[155] "Tax return preparer" is defined in section 7701(a)(36). With stated exceptions, the term includes "any person

---

149. Reg. § 1.6109-2.

150. Former 31 C.F.R. §§ 10.4(c), 10.5(b), 10.6(d)(6) & (e)(3).

151. Loving v. IRS, 742 F.3d 1013 (D.C. Cir. 2014), *aff'g* 917 F. Supp. 2d 67 (D.D.C. 2013). For discussion of *Loving*, see Steve R. Johnson, *Loving and Legitimacy: IRS Regulation of Tax Return Preparation*, 59 Vill. L. Rev. 515 (2014).

152. Ridgely v. Lew, 55 F. Supp. 3d 89 (D.D.C. 2014).

153. *See* Steve R. Johnson, *How Far Does Circular 230 Exceed Treasury's Statutory Authority?*, 146 Tax Notes 221 (2015).

154. *See* Rev. Proc. 2014-42, 2014-29 I.R.B. 192; FS-2014-8; IR-2014-75. The American Institute of Certified Public Accountants (AICPA) has instituted legal proceedings to block the program. AICPA v. IRS, 804 F.3d 1193 (D.C. Cir. 2015), *rev'g* 2014 WL 5585334 (D.D.C. 2014).

155. There are seven types of punishable conduct under section 6695. They include failure to furnish a copy of the return to the taxpayer, failure to sign returns as preparers, and failure to file correct information returns. IRC § 6695(a), (b), (e); *see* Notice 2008-12, 2008-1 C.B. 280 (specifying which returns require a preparer signature).

who prepares for compensation ... any return of tax ... or any claim for refund of tax.... [T]he preparation of a substantial portion of a return or claim for refund shall be treated as if it were the preparation of such return or claim for refund."[156]

Section 6694 and the regulations under it have been frequently revised in recent years, sometimes in ways cancelling out prior changes. In May 2007, Congress amended section 6694, in part to require that, in order to endorse tax return positions, preparers had to have reasonable belief that the positions were more likely than not correct.[157] This provoked a firestorm of criticism, especially because "more likely than not" was a higher standard than most of the relief standards applicable to penalties on taxpayers.[158]

Responding to the criticism, Congress went "back to the future" in October 2008. It lowered the required confidence standard for return preparers to the "substantial authority" threshold required for taxpayers under section 6662, except that it kept the "more likely than not" standard for reporting positions with respect to tax shelter transactions.[159]

In egregious cases, tax return preparers may also be subject to criminal sanctions. Conspiring with or otherwise willfully assisting taxpayers to evade tax liability is potentially punishable under criminal provisions in both the Internal Revenue Code and other titles of the United States Code.[160] In addition, wrongful disclosure or other use of taxpayer information by tax preparers is criminally punishable under section 7216.

XI. Making of Elections

The Code contains hundreds of elections available to taxpayers. Elections are to be made as prescribed in the applicable statute, regulation, or revenue procedure. Often, elections are required to be made on the return for the tax period in question.

Often, failure to make the election when required is fatal. However, in some cases, relief options exist as to failures to make timely elections.[161] Such relief is popularly called "section 9100 relief." To secure it, taxpayers must satisfy requirements set out

156. IRC §7701(a)(36)(A); Reg. §301.7701-15. The exceptions are in section 7701(a)(36)(B). *See also* IRS Notice 2008-12, 2008-1 C.B. 280 (specifying when a preparer is required to sign a return).

157. U.S. Troops Readiness, Veterans Care, Katrina Recovery, and Iraq Accountability Appropriations Act of 2007, Pub. L. No. 110-28, §8246, 121 Stat. 200 (2007).

158. *See* Chapter 8.

159. Emergency Economic Stabilization Act of 2008, Pub. L. No. 110-343, §506(a), 122 Stat. 3765 (2008).

160. *E.g.*, IRC §§7201, 7206 & 7212(a); 18 U.S.C. §§371 & 1001. For detailed discussion, see John A. Townsend, et al., Tax Crimes (2nd ed. 2015).

161. In some instances, the IRS is empowered to extend time for making elections or to grant relief with respect to elections filed late. *E.g.*, Rev. Proc. 2014-18, 2014-7 I.R.B. 513 (extension of time to make estate tax marital deduction portability election); Rev. Proc. 2013-30, 2013-36 I.R.B. 173 (procedures for granting relief as to late elections with respect to S corporations).

in the applicable regulations.[162] Section 9100 relief is only available for election deadlines established by regulations; it is not available if the deadline is statutory.

XII. Confidentiality of Return Information

Our tax system depends on taxpayers filing complete, accurate, and timely returns. Thus it is important to minimize barriers to such filing. This fact helps explain the strong (though not unlimited) confidentiality that attaches to tax return information. Congress has concluded that voluntary compliance with the tax laws would diminish if taxpayers faced the risk that their privacy would be violated, that their financial disclosures about themselves could become matters of public knowledge.[163]

Section 6103 is the principal section reflecting this conclusion. Section 6103(a) provides that tax "[r]eturns and return information shall be confidential," and it generally prohibits federal employees and designated other persons from disclosing "any return or return information obtained by [them] in any manner in connection with [government service or otherwise under the section]."[164] Section 6103(b) defines tax returns and tax return information broadly.[165]

Section 6103 is complemented by other sections, including section 6110 (allowing redaction of IRS written determinations and background files otherwise open to public inspection), sections 7213, 7213A, and 7216 (criminal provisions as to unauthorized inspection or disclosure of confidential tax information by IRS employees, return preparers, and others), and sections 7431 and 7435 (civil damages for unauthorized inspection, disclosure, or enticement as to tax return information).

Section 6103 is a very long section, however, and its definitional rules and its exceptions allow disclosures of some tax information for purposes deemed to be of sufficient social significance. The IRS is required to report to Congress annually on requests for disclosures, disclosures actually made, and the purposes of such disclosures.[166] Such reports show that the IRS legally discloses billions of items of tax return information each year.[167]

---

162. Reg. §§301.9100-1 to -3; *see* Timothy J. Watt & Thomas L. Evans, *Requesting 9100 Relief*, Tax Adviser, Oct. 2008, at 65; Jasper L. Cummings, Jr., *Relief for Late Regulatory Elections*, Tax Notes, May 13, 2013, at 743.

163. *See generally* Stephen W. Mazza, *Taxpayers Privacy and Tax Compliance*, 51 U. Kan. L. Rev. 1065 (2003).

164. Proposals sometimes are made to relax section 6103 to allow greater disclosure of corporate tax return information. *E.g.*, Joshua D. Blank, *Reconsidering Corporate Tax Privacy*, 11 N.Y.U.J.L. & Bus. 31 (2014); Lee A. Sheppard, *Should Corporate Tax Returns Be Disclosed?*, Tax Notes, Mar. 31, 2014, at 1381.

Greater transparency (that is, less confidentiality) also has been urged with respect to returns of tax-exempt organizations. George K. Yin, *Saving the IRS*, 2014 TNT 87-5 (May 6, 2014).

165. *See* Baskin v. United States, 135 F.3d 338, 340–42 (5th Cir. 1998) (tracing the history of disclosure prohibitions); 1 Joint Comm. on Tax'n, *Study of General Disclosure Provisions* (Jan. 28, 2000).

166. IRC §6103(p)(3).

167. In 2010, for instance, the IRS disclosed 7.1 billion such items to federal and state agencies, including 4.2 billion to the states, 1.5 billion to congressional committees, 1.3 billion to the Census

Outside of section 6103, there is another relevant context. Sometimes discovery of tax returns is sought in "private party versus private party" law suits. The federal courts have crafted a common law privilege that offers some protection—varying from jurisdiction to jurisdiction—against such discovery.[168]

XIII. Enhanced Return Reporting

Chapter 4 describes options available to the IRS for discovering information during audit. That is a "back end" remedy, however. In recent years, Congress, Treasury, and the IRS have increasingly relied on the "front end" approach of requiring taxpayers to report on their returns more information about types of transactions with particularly high potential for noncompliance. Some of the main examples of this approach are described below.

A. Uncertain Tax Positions ("UTP")

This is an area in which financial accounting has driven tax procedure. In 2006, the Financial Accounting Standards Board issued what is commonly called FIN 48, requiring more detailed analysis of income tax contingencies on "certified" financial statements.[169] In 2010, Treasury and the IRS developed the UTP initiative to capitalize on FIN 48 analysis.

Treasury and the IRS rolled out the UTP program through a series of steps, including initial announcements,[170] promulgation of regulatory authority,[171] finalization of Schedule UTP to be attached to the income tax returns of large corporations, and subsequent guidance.[172] The purpose of the program is to require taxpayers to report their uncertain tax positions to the IRS under certain circumstances.

The UTP reporting requirements have been phased in. Schedule UTP is to be included in the returns of corporations which have one or more uncertain tax positions (as defined by the instructions to the schedule) on the return and which meet the applicable total asset threshold. The thresholds are $100 million for 2010, $50 million in 2012, and $10 million for 2014 and later years.

The full consequences of the UTP regime will take years to become clear. Some have suggested that UTP may (1) cause whistleblower claims (*see* Chapter 4) to di-

---

Bureau, 39 million for Medicare premium subsidy adjustments, and 13.6 million to child support enforcement agencies.

168. *See* Nancy T. Bowen, *Strategies for Defending Against Discovery Requests for Tax Returns,* Tax Notes, Jan. 12, 2009, at 217.

169. FASB Interpretation No. 48, Accounting for Uncertainty in Income Taxes, interpreting FASB Statement No. 109; *see* Steven S. Schneider, *FIN 48 for Tax Lawyers—Accounting for Uncertainty in Income Taxes,* 2007 Tax Mgmt. Memo. 139.

170. IRS Announcement 2010-9, 2010-1 C.B. 408, clarified by 2010-13, I.R.B. 515; IRS Announcement 2010-75, 2010-2 C.B. 428; IRS Announcement 2010-76, 2010-2 C.B. 432.

171. T.D. 9510, 2011-6 I.R.B. 453, accompanying Reg. § 1.6012-2.

172. In March 2011, the IRS posted on its website frequently asked questions as to Schedule UTP.

minish, (2) decrease the significance of the controversy over IRS summonses for companies' tax accrual workpapers (see Chapter 4), and (3) along with other rules described below, become the basis for internationally harmonized tax reporting.[173]

The enhanced United States reporting regimes may come to interact with regimes developed by other countries. The Organization for Economic Cooperation and Development (the OECD, a multilateral treaty organization headquartered in Paris) has developed standards for transparency and information exchange for tax purposes, and these standards have been gaining greater international adherence.[174]

B. Foreign Reporting[175]

The Foreign Account Tax Compliance Act ("FATCA") was enacted as part of 2010

---

173. For discussion of some possible consequences, see Jerald David August, *Mandatory Disclosure of Uncertain Tax Positions on Income Tax Returns Filed by Corporate Taxpayers: The IRS's New Weapon,* Practical Tax Law., Winter 2011, at 7; J. Richard "Dick" Harvey, *Schedule UTP Guidance—Initial Observations,* Tax Notes, Oct. 4, 2010, at 115; Melissa A. Dizdarevic, Comment, *The FATCA Provisions of the HIRE Act: Boldly Going Where No Withholding Has Gone Before,* 79 Fordham L. Rev. 2967 (2011).

174. *See* Ed Morgan, *International Tax Law as a Ponzi Scheme,* 34 Suffolk Transnational L. Rev. (2011).

175. Unilateral, bilateral, and multilateral cross-border tax enforcement is one of the most rapidly growing areas of tax procedure. Here are some of the important recent trends and developments:

• Tax treaties: The United States has an expanding web of tax treaty connections with other countries. Many treaties have provisions dealing with mutual assistance in tax enforcement, but the contents of these provisions and the degree to which they are used vary. For an overview, see IRS Publication 901, *U.S. Tax Treaties* (as periodically revised).

• Cooperative action: The IRS and its counterparts in other countries are experimenting with more collaborative activities, including information exchange, joint dispute resolution, and joint audits of taxpayers. *See, e.g.,* PricewaterhouseCoopers, *Emergence of New Examination Approach—Joint Audits,* 2011 TNT 129-40 (July 6, 2011).

In 2012, Treasury finalized regulations requiring U.S. banks to report to the IRS information on accounts of non-U.S. account holders, which information the IRS will share with foreign revenue authorities concerned with their citizens evading their taxes through use of U.S. accounts. T.D. 9584, 77 Fed. Reg. 23,391-01 (2012). Banks challenged the validity of those regulations on a number of administrative law grounds. The district court upheld the regulations. Florida Bankers Ass'n v. Department of Treasury, 19 F. Supp. 3d 111 (D.D.C. 2014), *vacated and remanded,* 799 F.3d 1065 (D.C. Cir. 2015) (plaintiff lacked standing).

• FATCA: Thousands of pages of final and temporary regulations under the Foreign Account Tax Compliance Act, IRC §§ 1471–1474, were issued in 2014, and the IRS released numerous forms and guidance documents as to FATCA compliance. These matters are covered in depth on the IRS website. *See also* Joshua D. Blank & Ruth Mason, *Exporting FATCA*, Tax Notes, Mar. 17, 2014, at 1245.

• FBAR: In 1970, Congress enacted the Currency and Foreign Transactions Report Act, also known as the Bank Secrecy Act. Regulations promulgated under the Act require U.S. persons to report their interests in foreign accounts on Foreign Bank and Financial Account ("FBAR") forms. 31 C.F.R. § 1010.350. *See generally* Robert S. Chase II, Carol P. Tello & Dwaune L. Dupree, *The FBAR Reset: Final Regulations Provide Mixed Guidance,* Tax Notes, Apr. 25, 2011, at 395. In addition, IRS Form 1040 requires taxpayers to acknowledge their having such interests.

Civil and criminal penalties exist for violation of these reporting obligations. *See also* United States v. Williams, 489 Fed. Appx. 655 (4th Cir. 2012) (reversing the district court's holding that the taxpayer's FBAR violations were not willful)

legislation.[176] It increases disclosures required of United States taxpayers who have foreign investments and of foreign financial institutions, trusts, and corporation which invest in the United States. In part, this sweeping legislation establishes a withholding system to encourage foreign entities to disclose the identities of and information about United States persons with whom they do business. This complex regime is being phased in. The IRS has released preliminary guidance on the FATCA provisions.[177]

In addition, persons subject to the jurisdiction of the United States must file Foreign Bank and Financial Accounts Reports ("FBARs") if they have interests in financial accounts abroad exceeding $10,000. This has led to more audit activity. FBAR-related examinations rose by 96% (from 334 to 656) between fiscal years 2004 and 2009. FBAR penalty assessments rose by 388% and FBAR penalty collections by 444%.[178]

Also, section 6038D, enacted in 2010, requires some taxpayers to attach to their returns information as to specified foreign financial assets if the aggregate value of such assets exceeds $50,000.

Under the "required records" doctrine, the Fifth Amendment cannot be invoked to justify nondisclosure of records required by law to be kept. This applies to records required by the Bank Secrecy Act. *E.g.*, In re Grand Jury Investigation M.H., 648 F.3d 1067 (9th Cir. 2011) (upholding imposition of contempt sanctions).

• OVDP: To encourage U.S. holders of undisclosed foreign accounts to "come in from the cold," the IRS has had one or another version of its Offshore Voluntary Disclosure Program since 2009. The current version was revised in 2014. IR-2014-73 (June 18, 2014). The details of the program and forms necessary to participate in it are available at the IRS website.

• Traditional information gathering: The IRS continues to use the full panoply of it information-gathering tools to obtain information as to tax avoidance or evasion through offshore arrangements. *See, e.g.*, Andrew Velarde & Jaime Arora, *District Court Authorizes John Doe Summonses to 5 U.S. Banks*, Tax Notes, Nov. 18, 2013, at 685

• Criminal enforcement: The Department of Justice is aggressively prosecuting U.S. taxpayers engaged in tax evasion through offshore devices as well as the bankers, lawyers, and others who assist them. *See, e.g.*, Scott A. Schumacher, *Magnifying Deterrence by Prosecuting Professionals*, 89 Ind. L.J. 511 (2014); IR-2011-94 (Sept. 15, 2011).

• Other countries: The United States is not alone in policing cross-border tax avoidance and evasion more aggressively. Many other countries—as well as international bodies such as the Organization for Economic Cooperation and Development, G-8, and the United Nations—are working along somewhat similar lines. An effort that has attracted considerable attention is the OECD's Base Erosion and Profit Sharing project. *See, e.g.*, Yariv Brauner, *What the BEPS?*, 16 Fla. Tax Rev. 55 (2014).

• Dispute resolution: Disputes as to the meaning of treaty provisions have long been handled through often cumbersome Competent Authority procedures. Slowly but increasingly, tax treaties contain arbitration clauses. *E.g.*, Maya Ganguly, *Tribunals and Taxation: An Investigation of Arbitration in Recent U.S. Tax Conventions*, 29 Wis. Int'l L.J. 735 (2012).

176. Hiring Incentives to Restore Employment (HIRE) Act of 2010, Pub. L. 111-147.

177. IRS Notice 2011-34, 2011-19 I.R.B. 765; Notice 2010-60, 2010-2 C.B. 329; *see, e.g.*, Mark Leeds, *Passive—Aggressive: IRS Releases Initial Guidance on FATCA Rules*, Tax Management Weekly Report, Nov. 22, 2010, at 1544.

178. Treasury Inspector General for Tax Administration, *New Legislation Could Affect Filers of the Report of Foreign Bank and Financial Accounts, but Potential Issues Are Being Addressed* (2010-30-125). The Treasury's Financial Crimes Enforcement Network (FinCEN) has proposed rules to clarify the reporting obligations of U.S. persons with foreign bank accounts. *See* Charles P. Rettig, *New IRS Guidelines Limit FBAR Penalties*, J. Tax Prac. & Proc., June–July 2015, at 17.

Problem

Tom and Mary were married during the calendar years 20x4 through 20x0. Tom worked as a travelling salesman and Mary worked as a consultant.

Tom and Mary's joint federal income tax returns were prepared by Sally, an accountant whose office was in their neighborhood.

For the year 20x4, Tom and Mary directed Sally to prepare their joint return in paper form, not in electronic form. Tom went to Sally's office to sign the return on April 14, 20x5. Mary didn't go with him because she was out of town on business, so Tom signed Mary's name to the return for her. It was mailed and postmarked that day, and received by the IRS on April 18, 20x5.

For the year 20x5, Tom and Mary again directed Sally to prepare their joint return in paper form, not in electronic form. Again Mary was out of town on business when the return was due. Tom signed the return, but failed to sign Mary's name at all. So the return was filed with Tom's signature alone. Tom mailed the return to the IRS on March 1, 20x6, and it was received on March 5, 20x6.

Tom and Mary both took sabbatical leaves from their jobs for most of 20x6. They traveled the world nearly the whole year. In preparation for the sabbatical leave, however, in early 20x6 Tom had cashed-in an annuity contract so that he and Mary would have spending money for their travels. The proceeds were $120,000. Tom told Sally that none of the proceeds from the contract was taxable. Tom and Mary had only $5,000 of gross income in 20x6, all of which was Tom's. Mary had no income for the year. Tom and Mary timely filed a joint return for the year 20x6 in March 20x7.

Tom and Mary were the sole shareholders of Tomary, Inc., a C corporation, through which they did some consulting work. Because Tom and Mary didn't work in 20x6, Tomary had no gross income that year.

Sally also prepared Tom and Mary's 20x7 joint return, in paper form. Sally mailed the return to them on April 1, 20x8, with instructions to sign and mail it to the IRS. Tom and Mary knew that the due date for returns was April 15th. That date fell on Saturday in 20x8. After Tom and Mary signed the return on April 10, 20x8, Tom put it in his car intending to mail it, but forgot. It was still on the front seat of his car on April 17th, when he and Mary went out to dinner. Mary gasped when she saw the return. Tom admitted that he had simply forgotten to mail it. So on the way home they went to a post office that was open late. They gave the envelope to the clerk in the post office for mailing at 9:30 P.M. It was postmarked immediately, and received by the IRS on April 20, 20x8.

Tom's brother, Bill, who was a U.S. citizen, lived in Greece. Bill had $35,000 of earned income in 20x7, all of which was excluded from income under IRC section 911.

Mary didn't want to repeat the 20x7 experience again for 20x8, so this time she took their signed joint return (for 20x8) to her office on Monday, April 15, 20x9, and sent it to the IRS by FedEx. The FedEx driver picked it up at Mary's office at 6:30 P.M. It was delivered to the IRS on April 16, 20x9.

Tom and Mary had participated in a tax shelter transaction during 20x8. Tom and Mary told Sally about the transaction in February 20x9, so that she could ask whatever questions were necessary. Sally correctly determined that it was a "reportable transaction," but did not make any disclosure of the transaction on the return.

Sally attended a tax lecture in July 20x8, at which she learned that the $120,000 that Tom had received in early 20x6 as proceeds from the annuity contract should have been treated in full as gross income. She promptly advised Tom and Mary.

Sally also prepared Tom and Mary's 20x9 joint return. Tom and Mary were late getting the information to Sally in order for her to prepare the return. They again wanted to file a paper return. So Sally filed an Extension of Time to File (Form 4868) on their behalf, which automatically granted them a 6-month extension of time to file, until October 15, 20x0. Sally mailed the return to them on September 30, 20x0, and after Tom and Mary signed it, Tom mailed it on October 5, 20x0. It was postmarked later that day, and received by the IRS on October 11, 20x0.

1. Is the 20x4 return a valid joint return?
2. Will the 20x4 return be treated as having been filed timely?
3. Is the 20x5 return a valid joint return?
4. Will the 20x5 return be treated as having been filed timely?
5. Were Tom and Mary required to file a return for 20x6?
6. Should Tom and Mary file an amended return for 20x6?
7. Was Tomary required to file a return for 20x6?
8. Was Tom and Mary's 20x7 return filed timely?
9. On what date is the 20x7 return treated as having been filed?
10. Was Bill required to file a return for 20x7?
11. On what date is the 20x8 return treated as having been filed?
12. What is the result to Tom and Mary of their failure to disclose the tax shelter transaction on their 20x8 return? What is the result to Sally?
13. Will the 20x9 return be treated as having been filed timely?
14. On what date is the 20x4 return treated as having been filed?

Chapter 3

Spousal Relief

IRC:	§§ 6013(d)(3); 6015
Regs.:	§§ 1.6013-4(d); 1.6015-1(a)(1), (a)(2), (a)(3), (b), (h), -2, -3a, (b), (c)(1), (c)(2), -4, -5(a), (b)(1)-(3), -6, -7
Cases:	Kellam v. Commissioner, T.C. Memo. 2013-186; Est. of Krock v. Commissioner, T.C. Memo. 1983-551; King v. Commissioner, 115 T.C. 118 (2000)
Rulings:	Rev. Proc. 2003-19; Rev. Proc. 2013-34; Notice 2011-70
Forms:	8379; 8857

I. Introduction

Carol Jones has come to you complaining about her predicament. She recently received a notice from the IRS saying she owes taxes relating to a 20x4 joint income tax return Form 1040 she filed with her ex-husband, John. Carol is presently divorced, financially strapped, and has custody of the children. The divorce was ugly and traumatizing for all. She and her ex-husband do not talk to each other anymore. She is considering marrying Harold Roberts, a very nice man she met recently.

Carol tells you she does not know much about the details of what was on the 20x4 return, as John took care of all the family's finances and had the return prepared by his accountant. She wants to know if you can help her avoid some or all of the tax and keep the tax debt from becoming a financial concern of Harold's, in case they marry. The answer to both questions is, "possibly."

The normal rule when a married couple files a joint return is that each spouse is jointly and severally liable for all tax, penalties,[1] and interest due, regardless of to whom the tax liability is attributable.[2] If the joint return was properly filed, an aggrieved spouse may be able to rely on the "innocent spouse" or "proportional liability" provisions of section 6015 to avoid or reduce the liability.[3]

1. However, section 6663(c) provides a basis for relief from joint and several liability with respect to the fraud penalty, as only the perpetrator of the fraud can be held liable.

2. IRC § 6013(d)(3).

3. The relief provisions were significantly expanded and simplified by Congress in the 1998 Reform Act. This chapter focuses on the relief rules of general applicability under section 6015. A special rule dealing with liability for income items from community property exists under section 66(c). *See, e.g.,* Robert B. Nadler, *A Practitioner's Guide to Innocent Spouse Relief: Proven Strategies for Winning Section*

Three opportunities for relief are described in section 6015,[4] each of which has the effect of allowing a joint filer who makes a timely election to be held responsible for only the portion of the amount due that is attributable to him or her. Two forms of relief—sections 6015(b) and (c)—apply to understatements (deficiencies). The third relief provision—section 6015(f)—applies primarily to underpayments, i.e., the balance due on the joint return filed by the couple. Relief under section 6015(c) is basically automatic whereas relief under sections 6015(b) and (f) is subject to the discretion of the Service.[5] All are reviewable by the Tax Court.[6]

The IRS receives thousands of requests for spousal relief each year. If successful, one is relieved of liability for tax (including interest, penalties, and other amounts) to the extent the liability is attributable to all or a portion of the understatement or underpayment with respect to which the requesting spouse was innocent.[7] Subject to various limitations, refunds are possible in section 6015(b) and (f) cases, but not those filed under section 6015(c) unless paid subsequent to the grant of relief.[8]

Note that throughout this chapter, the spouse seeking relief may be referred to alternatively as the requesting spouse, the electing spouse, or the spouse seeking relief and the other as the nonrequesting spouse.

6015 Tax Cases (2011); G. Michelle Ferreira & Claudia A. Hill, *Innocent Spouse: Untying the Tax Knot*, J. Tax Proc. & Prac., Dec. 2008–Jan. 2009, p. 29 (setting out a helpful summary of the three kinds of section 6015 relief and section 66(c) relief); Scott Schumacher, *Innocent Spouse, Administrative Process; Time for Reform*, Tax Notes, Jan. 3, 2011, p. 113 (arguing that the way the IRS reviews section 6015 cases and section 6015's substantive rules fails to adequately protect innocent spouses). It is important to note that even if relief is granted to a requesting spouse, she may still be liable under the transferee liability rules, making the time and trouble of gaining innocent spouse relief wasteful. This scenario is likely where, for example, one of the spouses died and left significant property to the other without paying the entire tax debt. Reg. § 1.6015-1(j).

4. For detailed discussion of section 6015, see Robert B. Nadler, A Practitioner's Guide to Innocent Spouse Relief: Proven Strategies for Winning Section 6015 Tax Cases (2nd ed. 2014). *See also* Stephanie Hunter McMahon, *An Empirical Study of Innocent Spouse Relief: Do Courts Implement Congress's Legislative Intent?*, 12 Fla. Tax Rev. 629 (2012); Scott Schumacher, *Innocent Spouse, Administrative Process: Time for Reform*, Tax Notes, Jan. 3, 2011, at 113.

5. IRC § 6015(f).

6. *See* note 63, *infra*.

7. CCA 200606001 (Oct. 27, 2005).

8. The IRS takes the position that administrative relief under section 6015 does not constitute an abatement of tax under section 6404; such relief merely reduces the taxpayer's account to zero administratively to prevent the IRS from engaging in collection activity. This is not merely semantical; it has real consequences. For example, in one case, a wife was granted administrative relief under section 6015 for joint income tax liabilities. Later, her husband submitted an offer in compromise as to his liabilities. In the course of investigating his offer, the IRS discovered that the wife had made false statements in her petition for section 6015 relief. By that time, the statute of limitation had closed on the tax year in question. However, the IRS took the position that it could reinstate her previously assessed liabilities and collect them within the normal limitations period as to collection. CCA 200802030 (Oct. 12, 2007).

II. Universal Requirements for Relief

A. Joint Income Tax Return Filed

In order to be held jointly and severally liable under section 6013(d)(3) and, conversely, to be permitted to seek relief therefrom, a joint income tax return must have been filed. An income tax return may be filed jointly by two people who were legally married on the last day of the taxable year in issue.[9] In addition, both persons must intend to file a joint return.[10] Courts hold that intent, rather than the presence or absence of a spouse's signature, is determinative.[11] If a taxpayer can establish that either of these conditions is not satisfied, such as the couple never had a marriage ceremony and did not qualify as married under common law rules, or that one spouse fraudulently signed the return for the other spouse or one of the spouses signed the return because the other spouse forced him or her to do so, the return in question does not qualify as a joint return.[12] The latter situation often arises when duress was involved. In order to prove that a taxpayer signed a joint return under duress, the taxpayer must show (1) that the taxpayer was unable to resist the demands of the taxpayer's spouse to sign the joint return and (2) that the taxpayer would not have signed the joint return absent the constraint that the taxpayer's spouse applied to the taxpayer's will.[13] The determination of whether the taxpayer signed a joint return under duress

9. Following *United States v. Windsor*, 133 S. Ct. 2675 (2013), the IRS has ruled that for all federal tax purposes, it will recognize a marriage of same-sex individuals that was validly entered into in a state whose laws authorize the marriage of two individuals of the same sex even if the married couple is domiciled in a state that does not recognize the validity of same-sex marriages. Rev. Rul. 2013-17. The Revenue Ruling also determined that the terms "spouse," "husband and wife," "husband," and "wife" as used in the Internal Revenue Code include an individual married to a person of the same sex if the individuals are lawfully married under state law, and that the term "marriage" in the Code includes such a marriage between individuals of the same sex. *See also* Obergefell v. Hodges, 135 S. Ct. 2584 (2015).

10. IRC §§6013(a), 7701(a)(38); Reg. §1.6013-4. Joint filling status cannot be revoked once the due date for filing the return, including extensions, has passed. IRM 25.15.1.2. But spouses who file separate returns can, subject to certain limitations, elect to file joint returns at a later time. IRC §6013(b). Rev. Rul. 2005-59, 2005-37 I.R.B. 505 (returns prepared by the IRS pursuant to its authority under section 6020(b) are not joint income tax returns since they are not signed by both spouses; completion of Form 870, 1902 or 4549 are not joint income tax returns, even if signed by both spouses, because they are not signed under penalty of perjury). *See also* Ibrahim v. Commissioner, 788 F.3d 834 (8th Cir. 2015) (a return by a married taxpayer claiming head of household status is a "separate return" for these purposes, thus allowing for a switch to a joint return).

11. Est. of Krock v. Commissioner, T.C. Memo. 1983-551. *See generally* IRM 25.15.1.2.

12. Reg. §1.6015-1(b); *see* Steve R. Johnson, *The Duress or Deception Defense to Joint and Several Spousal Liability*, Tax Prac. & Proc. 15 (Dec. 2004–Jan. 2005); *see also* In re Hinckley, 256 B.R. 814 (Bankr. M.D. Fla. 2000) (to prove duress, the requesting spouse must prove that she could not resist the non-requesting spouse's demand to sign the return, and that the requesting spouse would not have otherwise signed the return); Stephanie H. McMahon, *What Innocent Spouse Relief Says About Wives and the Rest of Us*, 37 Harv. J. of Law & Gender 141 (2014) (argues for limiting relief to cases in which spouse was unable to exercise her free will when signing joint return).

13. Stanley v. Commissioner, 81 T.C. 634 (1983).

or tacitly consented to a joint filing is dependent on the facts and is measured by a wholly subjective standard. The couple's past filing history and, assuming she had enough income to need to file, whether the claimant filed a separate return in the current year are factors courts consider. If the requesting spouse is successful, joint and several liability never attaches and the taxpayer can escape liability without having to prove each of the elements necessary for relief under section 6015.[14] For a more detailed discussion of the requirements for filing a joint return, see Chapter 2.

B. Amount Due Involves Income Tax

The relief provisions of section 6015 are available only with respect to balances due for income taxes and related penalties, additions to tax, and interest.[15] Section 6015 does not provide relief for other taxes that must be reported on a joint federal income tax return, such as domestic service employment taxes under section 3510.[16]

C. Timely Election

Assuming that a joint return was intended and no fraudulent transfers of assets occurred between the husband and wife,[17] either or both of them may, by filing Form 8857,[18] make an election requesting relief under section 6015.[19] If only one spouse

14. Rev. Proc. 2013-34, 2013-43 I.R.B. 397, § 2.03; Raymond v. Commissioner, 119 T.C. 191 (2002). For a wife who is terrified of her ex-husband and who would prefer to forgo her legitimate defenses rather than have to confront him, an added advantage of establishing that a joint return was not intended is the fact that the nonrequesting spouse is not entitled to notice or other rights under section 6015. In this situation, the Service recharacterizes the joint return as two married filing separate returns and assesses the liability associated with them to the proper spouse.

15. Reg. § 1.6015-2(b). Income tax, for these purposes, includes self-employment tax.

16. Reg. § 1.6015-1(a)(3).

17. A spouse may not seek relief if the IRS is able to establish that the spouses fraudulently transferred assets between them to qualify for relief. Reg. § 1.6015-1(d).

18. In *Palomares v. Commissioner*, T.C. Memo. 2014-243, the Tax Court held that the filing of a Form 8379 (Injured Spouse) was not an adequate substitute for the Form 8857. It said:

> Petitioner's Form 8379 did not convey sufficient information to notify Respondent that she was seeking relief from joint and several liability for the 1996 tax year and a refund of amounts that had been applied against the liability for that year. On its face, petitioner's Form 8379 requests only an allocation of items reported on a joint return for 2007. Respondent determined that petitioner did not qualify for an injured spouse allocation because she did not file a joint return for 2007. Upon receipt of petitioner's Form 8379, respondent was unaware of the details of petitioner's personal life, her separation from her husband, or her belief that she should not be held liable for the 1996 tax liability. Though respondent's September 24 letter notes that petitioner may have intended to file a Form 8857 and a copy of that form was included with the letter, this courtesy cannot be construed as reflecting Respondent's awareness that petitioner was seeking a refund based on a request for relief from joint and several liability for the 1996 year.

19. One of the most significant advantages to filing a Form 8857 is that, by statute, the IRS suspends collection from the date the election is filed until the matter is finally resolved plus 60 days. Any improper assessment may be enjoined. IRC §§ 6015(e)(1), 6330(e) (with respect to Collection Due Process hearings); Reg. § 1.6015-7(c).

Since the IRS may not pursue collection once a taxpayer requests relief under section 6015(b) or

makes the election and relief is granted, the electing spouse is responsible only for the portion of the understatement attributable to his or her adjustments; the other spouse remains jointly and severally liable for the entire understatement. If both spouses make the election and each is granted relief, then each owes only the share of the understatement attributable to him or her. One makes the election by completing and mailing Form 8857 to the IRS Service Center in Covington, Kentucky, or, if the case is presently active, by handing it to the IRS employee assigned to the case. Relief can be sought under any or all of the three provisions in section 6015 by completing the form.[20]

A section 6015 election requesting relief may be made at any time after receipt of a notification of an audit or a letter or notice from the IRS indicating that there may be an outstanding liability with regard to that year.[21] It can be made while the return is being examined by a revenue agent or on appeal with an appeals officer or counsel attorney (called a "deficiency" election), after the taxpayer receives a collection notice from the Service but before a "collection due process" hearing is requested (called a "stand alone" election),[22] or during a "collection due process" hearing (called a "CDP" election).[23]

For section 6015(b) and (c) claims, the election must be made no later than two years after the date on which the IRS began "collection activity" with respect to the electing spouse.[24] Regulation section 1.6015-5(b)(2) explains the term "collection activity." The most frequent collection activities that start the two-year clock[25] are the issuance of a collection due process notice directed to the electing spouse, the application of a refund otherwise due the electing spouse against the joint return liability,[26] and the issuance of a notice of levy against property in which the spouse making the election has an ownership interest.

(c), the statute of limitations (SOL) on collection is suspended for the entire period the matter is being considered and then for an additional 60 days. IRC § 6015(e)(2). Neither the SOL on assessment nor the SOL on filing refund claims is affected by a request for relief under section 6015.

20. Reg. § 1.6015-1(a)(2).

21. Reg. § 1.6015-5(b)(5).

22. If the election is filed as part of an offer in compromise, both the Forms 656 and 8857 are submitted. The basis for the offer is that there is doubt as to liability. As such, the matter is transferred to examination personnel for consideration.

23. Reg. § 1.6015-5(b)(3). This is normally accomplished by filing a Form 12153 and an attached Form 8857, with the local Appeals Office. A unique aspect of making the claim in conjunction with a CDP hearing is that the spousal defenses may be raised whether or not other underlying tax liability issues may be raised. IRC §§ 6330(c)(2), 6330(d). *See also* IRM 25.15.3.4.4.

24. Reg. § 1.6015-5(b)(3). An election for innocent spouse relief under sections 6015(b) and (c) made after two years from the time a notice of intent to levy is mailed to the requesting spouse is considered untimely. Actual receipt of a notice of intent to levy is not required to begin the two-year limitation period. Mannella v. Commissioner, 132 T.C. 196 (2009), *rev'd on other grounds*, 631 F.3d 115 (3d Cir. 2011).

25. Collection activity does *not* include the following actions: issuance of a notice of deficiency, issuance of a demand for payment of tax, issuance of a notice of intent to levy under section 6331 (d), or the filing of a Notice of Federal Tax Lien.

26. IRC § 6402; McGee v. Commissioner, 123 T.C. 314 (2004) (the two-year period does not begin until notice of the right to petition for relief under section 6015 is sent to the spouse).

Section 6015(f) requests do not need to be brought within two years. Despite some judicial decisions upholding the validity of the now abrogated regulation setting out the two-year rule,[27] Treasury decided to extend the period for filing a section 6015(f) request in the interests of tax administration and fairness. The new rule is that a request for section 6015(f) relief must be filed with the IRS within the section 6502 period for collection of tax (typically ten years from the date of assessment) or the section 6511 period for seeking refund or credit of tax (typically the later of three years from the date the return was filed or two years from the date tax was paid).[28]

D. Not Barred by Res Judicata or a Final Administrative Determination

Relief from joint and several liability is not available if a court has rendered a final decision on the requesting spouse's tax liability and if relief under section 6015 was at issue in the prior proceeding, or if the requesting spouse meaningfully participated in the proceeding and did not ask for relief under section 6015.[29] Also, any final decisions rendered by a court of competent jurisdiction regarding issues relevant to section 6015 are conclusive and the requesting spouse may be collaterally estopped from relitigating those issues.[30]

A similar rule applies to final administrative determinations, such as a closing agreement or an offer in compromise.[31]

III. Additional Requirements Imposed to Obtain Relief under Section 6015(b)

Section 6015(b) can be used by any joint filer, whether still married and living together or not. However, it is utilized almost exclusively by persons who are not divorced or separated (or by persons who seek a refund). The reason section 6015(b) tends to be used by spouses still married is that the other section that may provide

---

27. While courts were divided on the issue, some appellate courts held that Reg. § 1.6015-5(b)(1) was a valid interpretation of § 6015(f) and that the two-year limitation period applied to § 6015(f) claims. *See* Mannella v. Commissioner, 631 F.3d 115 (3d Cir. 2011); Lantz v. Commissioner, 607 F.3d 479 (7th Cir. 2010).

28. Reg. §§ 1.66-4(j)(2)(ii) & 1.6015-5; Notice 2011-70, 2011-2 C.B. 135.

29. Reg. § 1.6015-1(e).

30. *Id.* A requesting spouse who received notification from the IRS of her ability to seek innocent spouse relief and did not allege innocent spouse relief, signed court documents, participated in settlement negotiations, and voluntarily agreed to income tax deficiencies and penalties was considered to have meaningfully participated in two prior Tax Court proceedings and was denied innocent spouse relief involving the same taxable years. Moore v. Commissioner, T.C. Memo. 2007-156.

31. Reg. § 1.6015-1(c); *see also* Dutton v. Commissioner, 122 T.C. 133 (2004).

relief from understatements, section 6015(c), applies to divorced or separated spouses and the burden of proof is minimal.[32] A spouse seeking relief under subsection (b), by contrast, has a significant burden, *i.e.*, to prove each of the following elements:

1. A joint income tax return was filed (or deemed to have been filed);
2. A timely election was made;
3. There is an understatement in income tax attributable to erroneous items of the other spouse;
4. In signing the return, the spouse did not know there was an understatement on the return and did not have reason to know of its existence; and
5. Taking into account all the facts and circumstances, it would be inequitable to hold the requesting spouse liable for the tax.

The discussion above covered elements (1) and (2). Elements (3), (4) and (5) are discussed below.

A. There Must Be an Understatement of Income Tax Attributable to the Other Spouse

The innocent spouse rule of section 6015(b) is available only with respect to an understatement of income tax.[33] An understatement[34] is nearly identical to a deficiency. Essentially, it represents the additional amount of tax and related penalties owed as the result of a taxpayer's erroneous treatment of items on a tax return that are discovered during an examination by the IRS. An understatement should be contrasted with an underpayment. An underpayment is the balance of the tax reflected as due on the filed return. Relief from liability for an underpayment is possible only under the discretionary provisions of section 6015(f).

In order to obtain relief under section 6015(b)(1)(B), the understatement, or the portion for which relief is sought, must be attributable to the other spouse. To whom an item is attributable normally turns on who would have been required to report the item if separate returns had been filed.[35] If the answer points to one spouse, the other spouse may be eligible for relief. If the answer does not point to either spouse, the understatement is normally attributed to the spouse whose decision-making caused the couple to be involved in the transaction that gave rise to the reporting position. For example, if one spouse invested in a venture and was the sole signatory

32. Section 6015(b) is similar to the relief available under section 6013(e) existing prior to the 1998 Reform Act, but with a potpourri of dollar limitations removed. To the extent the two are alike, old case law is instructive.

33. Reg. § 1.6015-2(b).

34. IRC § 6662(d)(2)(A).

35. Bokum v. Commissioner, 94 T.C. 126 (1990), *aff'd* 992 F.2D 1132 (11th Cir. 1993); Silverman v. Commissioner, T.C. Memo. 1996-69, rec'd 116 F.3d 172 (6th Cir. 1997).

on documents relating to the venture, any erroneous items of the venture would normally be attributed to this spouse.[36] When no clear attribution is possible, allocation rules similar to those discussed in Regulation section 1.6015-3(d) are likely to be utilized. *See* section IV.C below.

B. The Spouse Seeking Relief Did Not Have Actual or Constructive Knowledge of the Understatement on the Return

In order for the requesting spouse to obtain relief under section 6015(b), that spouse must be able to establish that he or she had neither actual knowledge nor reason to know of the understatement on the return. Most cases are decided under the "reason to know" standard. Courts struggle with granting relief under this provision since doing so runs counter to two universally held truisms: (1) everyone is responsible for reviewing their tax returns before signing them and (2) ignorance of the law is no excuse. Consistent with this, before they are willing to grant relief, courts expect the requesting spouse to have inquired about items on, or missing from, the return when a "reasonably prudent person in the taxpayer's position" would have felt obligated to do so.[37] One cannot merely "bury one's head in the sand like an ostrich"[38] when there are indications of error. In other words, say the courts, section 6015 protects the innocent, not the intentionally ignorant.[39]

In determining whether the spouse seeking relief should have inquired further, courts and the Regulations consider six broad factors:

---

36. This is so even if the decision-making spouse believed the items were allowable because of professional advice he received to that effect. Silverman v. Commissioner, T.C. Memo. 1996-69, *rev'd on other grounds*, 116 F.3d 172 (6th Cir. 1997).

37. Price v. Commissioner, 887 F.2d 959, 965 (9th Cir. 1989). The lack of knowledge requirement under section 6015(b) is satisfied where the requesting spouse was not involved with the preparation of the joint returns, signed the documents without reading them because she felt that she did not know enough to understand them, and satisfied her duty of inquiry by questioning her husband and receiving strong and repeated assurances from him that they had to file joint tax returns. Juell v. Commissioner, T.C. Memo. 2007-219.

The requesting spouse's knowledge of the losses from her investment in a limited partnership with her husband gave her reason to know of the understatement. The requesting spouse knew of the investment, was a limited partner in the partnership, received annual reports from partnership listing her losses, was well-educated, had willingly signed tax returns without reviewing them, and balanced the couple's checkbooks. Golden v. Commissioner, T.C. Memo, 2007-299, *aff'd*, 548 F.3d 487 (6th Cir. 2008), *cert. denied*, 556 U.S. 1130 (2009).

Even though the requesting spouse had knowledge of the embezzlement income and knew that taxes would not be paid at the time the *amended* joint return was filed, the court granted relief because the requesting spouse did not have knowledge of the embezzlement income at the time the *original* joint return was filed and did not receive any significant benefit. Billings v. Commissioner, T.C. Memo. 2007-234.

38. Cohen v. Commissioner, T.C. Memo. 1987-537.

39. Hayes v. Commissioner, T.C. Memo. 1989-327.

1. The nature and amount of the item relative to other items;
2. The couple's financial situation and whether the income reported appears low compared to the standard of living of the couple;
3. The requesting spouse's education and business experience;
4. The extent of the requesting spouse's participation in the questioned activity;
5. Whether a reasonable person would have inquired about the item; and
6. Whether the reporting position of the erroneous item on the return represented a departure from reporting positions on previous years' returns.[40]

1. Omitted Income Cases

Relief for understatements due to "omitted income" has been in the Code to varying degrees since 1972. Courts look to whether the spouse requesting relief knew or had reason to know of *either* the omitted income itself or the underlying transaction giving rise to the omitted income. If she did possess that knowledge, relief is denied.[41] For example, in *Cheshire v. Commissioner*,[42] the court ruled that the actual knowledge standard in omitted income cases was actual and clear awareness. Consequently, Ms. Cheshire, who knew her spouse received retirement distributions that gave rise to the deficiency asserted, was not eligible for relief. The court was not moved by the fact that Ms. Cheshire was unaware that the couple's joint return misstated the tax treatment.

This analysis is often criticized for failing to take into account how reasonably the requesting spouse acted under the circumstances to determine if the position was correct, such as whether he or she made inquiry of the other spouse or a return preparer. It also fails to take into account whether the requesting spouse had any knowledge of the *specific* facts of the transaction resulting in the omission.

2. Deduction Cases

With respect to "deduction" cases, some courts, particularly the Tax Court in *Bokum v. Commissioner*,[43] appear to take a tougher position before they are willing to grant relief than is true with omitted income cases. These courts seem to believe that since deductions are plainly visible on the return, the spouse seeking relief has a greater duty of inquiry. Thus, if the spouse knew, or through inquiry should have learned, of the transaction giving rise to an erroneous deduction, relief is denied.

---

40. Reg. § 1.6015-2(c); Friedman v. Commissioner, 53 F.3d 523 (2d Cir. 1995); IRM 25.15.3.6.3(3).

41. *See, e.g.*, McCoy v. Commissioner, 57 T.C. 732 (1972) (even though she did not know that the liabilities exceeded assets and that the transaction resulted in income under section 357(c), wife was not afforded relief because she knew that husband transferred assets and liabilities of a business to a corporation).

42. 115 T.C. 183 (2000), *aff'd*, 282 F.3d 326 (5th Cir. 2002).

43. 94 T.C. 126 (1990), *aff'd*, 992 F.2d 1132 (11th Cir. 1993).

Other courts,[44] seeking to fulfill what they believe was a liberalizing intent by Congress in enacting section 6015 in the 1998 Reform Act, look to the actual words of the statute and focus on whether the requesting spouse had reason to know of the *understatement* rather than whether he or she had reason to know of the *transaction*. As the Fifth Circuit said in *Cheshire v. Commissioner*:

> Accordingly, in erroneous deduction cases, this court questions whether the spouse "knew or had reason to know that the *deduction* in question would give rise to a substantial understatement of tax on the joint return." However, if the spouse knows enough about the underlying transaction that her innocent spouse defense rests entirely upon a mistake of law, she has "reason to know" of the tax understatement as a matter of law.... If "reason to know" cannot be determined as a matter of law, the proper factual inquiry is "whether a reasonably prudent taxpayer in the spouse's position at the time she signed the return could be expected to know that the stated liability was erroneous or that further investigation was warranted."[45]

If the spouse seeking relief had a duty to inquire about the correctness of a deduction taken on the return and did not do so, relief is denied. But if the requesting spouse can show he or she made inquiries, relief can be obtained if the spouse acted reasonably to be assured that the transaction was reflected on the return correctly. This duty can be satisfied by inquiry of the other spouse or of the couple's return preparer.[46] Relief is denied only if a reasonably prudent person would not have agreed to the return position or if, through inquiring, the requesting spouse became familiar enough with sufficient details of the transaction to put him or her on an equal footing with the other spouse.

C. It Would Be Inequitable to Hold the Innocent Spouse Liable for the Tax

The determinative issue in innocent spouse cases is frequently whether, based upon all the facts and circumstances during the marriage and afterwards, it would be unfair to hold the electing spouse liable for the tax. Though this inquiry is broad, including both financial and non-financial considerations, a critical factor is whether the spouse seeking relief received a significant economic benefit that is, in some manner, traceable to the understatement. The most damaging evidence to an innocent spouse's claim of inequity is that the couple lived a very lavish lifestyle in

44. *See* Commissioner v. Neal, 557 F.3d 1262 (11th Cir. 2009); Reser v. Commissioner, 112 F.3d 1258, 1266 (5th Cir. 1997); Hayman v. Commissioner, 992 F.2d 1256 (2d Cir. 1993); Price v. Commissioner, 887 F.2d 959 (9th Cir. 1989); Erdahl v. Commissioner, 930 F.2d 585 (8th Cir. 1991) (citing Stevens v. Commissioner, 872 F.2d 1499 (11th Cir. 1989)).

45. 282 F.3d 326, 334 (5th Cir. 2002) (citations omitted).

46. It is not clear how extensively a relief-seeking spouse must inquire of the other spouse or, if the return was prepared by a professional, of that individual. It appears that the mere inquiry is enough to satisfy this obligation.

the year under review. For this purpose, normal support is not considered a significant economic benefit.[47]

Also problematic for requesting spouses is the situation where the couple divorced and the requesting spouse received substantial financial benefit from the other spouse in the property settlement and the property received is traceable to the understatement. However, if the electing spouse can show that his or her current investments, including property, are traceable to years other than the years in issue or to personal funds, relief is possible.[48]

Since the inquiry into whether it is inequitable to hold the spouse liable is not limited to economic benefit, other facts are also germane. They include physical or psychological abuse, extramarital relations, purchase of assets in a manner that did not benefit the innocent spouse, desertion, failure to pay alimony or child support, separation, and divorce.[49]

IV. Additional Requirements Imposed to Obtain Relief under Section 6015(c)

One of the most dramatic changes to the innocent spouse rules enacted in the 1998 Reform Act was the addition of the right to elect proportionate liability. The section 6015(c) provision is, in a sense, a "no fault" opportunity for relief. Unless the IRS can meet its burden to prove the existence of a condition defeating relief, relief is granted to the extent the spouse seeking relief proves the portion of the understatement that is not attributable to him or her. Unlike section 6015(b), the electing spouse is not required to establish his or her innocence, the other spouse's guilt, or the unfairness of being held liable for the entire tax.

A. IRS Has Burden to Prove the Electing Spouse's Actual Knowledge

A requesting spouse will be denied relief if the IRS establishes that, at the time the return was signed, the requesting spouse had actual knowledge of an erroneous

---

47. Reg. § 1.6015-2(d). The requesting spouse did not receive a significant benefit from the unpaid taxes beyond that of minimal living expenses because the taxpayers did not live extravagantly or take trips, did not have any investments, life insurance or savings, or anything else of value. Beatty v. Commissioner, T.C. Memo. 2007-167.

48. Silverman v. Commissioner, 116 F.3d 172 (6th Cir. 1997).

49. Reg. § 1.6015-2(d); Rev. Proc. 2003-61, 2003-32 I.R.B. 296, modified, Rev. Proc. 2013-43 I.R.B. 397. *See* Steve R. Johnson, *The Duress or Deception Defense to Joint and Several Spousal Liability*, Tax Prac. & Proc. 15 (Dec. 2004–Jan. 2005). Even though the requesting spouse was involved in the business generating the tax liability, relief under section 6015(c) was appropriate because of the abuse present in her relationship with the non-requesting spouse. The non-requesting spouse physically and verbally abused the requesting spouse and her son. The abuse included threats against her and her son's lives, physical assaults, and manipulative and controlling behavior. Wilson v. Commissioner, T.C. Memo. 2007-127.

item giving rise to the deficiency.[50] Regulation section 1.6015-3(c)(2) makes it clear that actual knowledge is a different standard than "reason to know" and that only actual knowledge disqualifies a spouse from proportional relief under section 6015(c).

Three cases, *Charlton*,[51] *Cheshire*,[52] and *Martin*,[53] have helped shape the jurisprudence with respect to omitted income in section 6015(c) cases. *Charlton* and *Cheshire* are both discussed in the following excerpt from *Martin v. Commissioner*:

> In *Charlton v. Commissioner*, ... the taxpayer seeking relief was aware that the source of income was his wife's business, but he did not compare records provided him by his wife with other business records to determine whether his wife had accounted for all of the income. Although Mr. Charlton had actual knowledge of income from a particular source and knew generally of his spouse's source of income, he had no knowledge that all income from that source had not been accounted for as reported. We thus held in *Charlton* that "respondent has not shown that Charlton had actual knowledge of the item causing the deficiency, and that Charlton qualifies for relief under section 6015(c)."
>
> In *Cheshire v. Commissioner*, also an omitted income case, petitioner had actual knowledge of the fact of the omitted income, as well as the amount of income, but submitted that she was entitled to relief because she was unaware of the applicable tax laws. Specifically, petitioner "was aware of the amount, the source, and the date of receipt of the retirement distribution and interest" but did not know the tax consequences of the income. In that case we held that "knowledge" for purposes of section 6015(c) relief disqualification does not require actual knowledge on the part of the electing spouse as to whether the entry on the return is or is not correct. Instead, the electing spouse must have "actual knowledge of the disputed item of income * * * as well as the amount thereof, that gave rise to the deficiency." Thus, in *Cheshire v. Commissioner*, we concluded that ignorance of the applicable tax law is no excuse and that respondent had met his burden of proving knowledge of the omitted income.
>
> [In the instant case, *Martin*], without petitioner's involvement or knowledge, Mr. Martin and certain professionals devised this complex and somewhat devious transaction consisting of a series of steps and involving several

50. If the wife signed the return without having inquired due to a history of abuse by the husband, she is treated as not having actual knowledge. Reg. § 1.6015-3(c)(2)(v). The IRS must plead actual knowledge as an affirmative defense in the answer to a section 6015(c) petition. Chief Counsel Notice 2005-011 (May 20, 2005).

51. 114 T.C. 333 (2000).

52. 115 T.C. 183 (2000), *aff'd*, 282 F.3d 326 (5th Cir. 2002).

53. T.C. Memo. 2000-346.

> entities. The transaction was primarily intended to deceive State insurance regulators into believing that the asset position or picture of Mr. Martin's insurance company was improved. The transaction was further complicated because it was structured for tax purposes to appear that the transfer of property to the corporation(s) was a nontaxable event under section 351. Ultimately, the desired results were not achieved, Mr. Martin was incarcerated due to his fraudulent deceptions, and petitioner was left penniless and bankrupt.
>
> Petitioner knew that Mr. Martin intended to contribute shares in Primera to another corporation, but she had no actual knowledge of the myriad and complex steps or entities involved in the transaction. Petitioner's uncontroverted testimony revealed that she was, at most, superficially aware of only a small portion of the details in these complex transactions. Because petitioner had only a superficial awareness of the transaction, petitioner did not have actual knowledge of the amount of the financial gain that was misreported, nor of the underlying facts that gave rise to the gain. Based on the facts pertaining to the transactions available to petitioner, she would not have known that the stock transfer was not a section 351 transaction or that the corporate sale of land could have resulted in financial gain or income to her husband. Like the taxpayer in *Charlton v. Commissioner*, petitioner possessed only a part of the information, and the information that she did possess was insufficient to supply her with actual knowledge regarding the amount of the financial gain from the transaction, if any.[54]

Another case, *King v. Commissioner*,[55] addressed the actual knowledge issue in the context of a tax deficiency associated with losses claimed by the taxpayer's husband but disallowed under section 183 because they were not incurred in an activity engaged in with the intent to make a profit.

> The question in this case, therefore, is not whether petitioner knew the tax consequences of a not-for-profit activity but whether she knew or believed that her former spouse was not engaged in the activity for the primary purpose of making a profit. Thus, in determining whether petitioner had actual knowledge of an improperly deducted item on the return, more is required than petitioner's knowledge that the deduction appears on the return or that her former spouse operated an activity at a loss.... The Court is satisfied that petitioner's knowledge of the activity in question was that it was an activity that she knew was not profitable but that she hoped and expected would become profitable at some point. Respondent presented insufficient evidence to show that petitioner knew that her former spouse did not have a primary objective of making a profit with his cattle-raising activity. Petitioner, therefore, is en-

---

54. *Id.* at 16–20.
55. 116 T.C. 198 (2001).

titled to relief from the tax liability arising out of this activity under section 6015(c). Since the activity was an activity attributable solely to her former spouse, the relief to petitioner extends to the full amount of the deficiency.[56]

B. Spouse Divorced, Separated, or Widowed at Time of Election

Section 6015(c) relief is only available to unmarried and separated spouses. Marital status is determined at the time of the election. Whether one is divorced or legally separated is decided in the same manner as it is determined in connection with the right to file jointly, i.e., state law controls except in the case of sham divorces that have tax avoidance as their principal purpose.[57] Note that even if the spouses are neither legally separated nor divorced, either may make the election after the couple lived apart for an entire 12-month period.

C. Amount of Deficiency Allocated to Other Spouse

Depending on how complicated the adjustments are, the most challenging aspect of section 6015(c) for the electing spouse may be the requirement of proving the portion of the deficiency allocable to him or her.[58] The regulations are particularly instructive here and should be read carefully by the student. The portion of the total deficiency allocated to the electing spouse can be expressed as follows:

$$\frac{\text{Net Amount of Items Taken into Account in Computing the Deficiency that Are } \textit{Allocable to the Electing Spouse}}{\text{Net Amount } \textit{of All Items} \text{ Taken into Account in Computing the Deficiency}} \times \text{Total Deficiency}$$

Examples of Allocation of Deficiency:

Basic Facts: H and W filed a joint return for 20x4. The IRS examines the return and, as the result of $150,000 in net adjustments to their joint taxable income, determines liabilities of $50,000. H and W later divorce. W timely files a proportionate liability election under section 6015(c); H does not. To the extent W can meet her burden of proof, she will be liable only for the portion of the liability properly allocated to her. H remains liable for the entire $50,000 unless he makes an election also.

Example (1): There is only one source for all the adjustments—H did not report all the income from his business and took some unwarranted business deductions. The $50,000 of liabilities is made up of $40,000 additional income

56. *Id.* at 205–06. See *Rowe v. Commissioner*, T.C. Memo. 2001-325, for an extensive discussion of the Tax Court's approach to analyzing "actual knowledge."

57. Boyter v. Commissioner, 668 F.2d 1382 (4th Cir. 1981); Reg. § 1.6015-3(b)(1), (2). A widow(er) is treated as not married and may make the election. Reg. § 1.6015-3(a).

58. IRC § 6015(c)(2); Reg. § 1.6015-3(d); *see* Est. of Capehart v. Commissioner, 125 T.C. 211 (2005).

tax, $8,000 in accuracy-related penalties, and $2,000 in self-employment taxes. The self-employment taxes, being exclusively attributable to H, are taxed to him regardless of what is true as to the remaining $48,000 in income tax and penalty. However, since none of the items of adjustment relates to W, the percentage of the deficiency allocable to her is 0%. The entire remaining $48,000 deficiency is H's liability. W owes no additional tax.

Example (2): There are two sources for the adjustments: H had unreported income of $100,000 from the sale of stock owned by him in his name. W had a $50,000 casualty loss disallowed with respect to property she owned.[59] Assuming both spouses make the election, 2/3 of the liability is H's and 1/3 is W's. The result would be the same even if some of the casualty loss is disallowed due to the 10% of Adjusted Gross Income floor in section 165(h).

Example (3): Same as (2) except that W only had $35,000 in income. In such case, only $35,000 of deductions attributable to W will be allocated to her; the remainder will be allocated to H.

D. Anti-Avoidance Rules

To prevent the inappropriate use of the election under section 6015(c), two special rules are included in the Code. To quote from the Senate Report:

> [I]f the IRS demonstrates that assets were transferred between the spouses in a fraudulent scheme joined in by both spouses, neither spouse is eligible to make the election under the provision (and consequently joint and several liability applies to both spouses).
>
> [Also], the limitation on the liability of an electing spouse is increased by the value of any disqualified assets received from the other spouse. Disqualified assets include any property or right to property that was transferred to an electing spouse if the principal purpose of the transfer is the avoidance of tax (including the avoidance of payment of tax). A rebuttable presumption exists that a transfer is made for tax avoidance purposes if the transfer was made less than one year before the earlier of the payment due date or the date of the notice of proposed deficiency. The rebuttable presumption does not apply to transfers pursuant to a decree of divorce or separate maintenance. The presumption may be rebutted by a showing that the principal purpose of the transfer was not the avoidance of tax or the payment of tax.[60]

Example (4): Same facts as example (2) above, except that the IRS establishes that H transferred $10,000 of property to W to avoid tax. If the transfer was

---

59. The unreported income and casualty loss would be attributed equally to H and W unless there is clear and convincing evidence that the item is attributable to the ownership of the property by one or the other. The example assumes that such evidence is present. Reg. § 1.6015-3(d)(6) will require an extra step to account for the different tax rates associated with the items that gave rise to the understatement.

60. S. Rpt. No. 105-174, 105th Cong., 2d Sess. 59 (1998), 1998-3 C.B. 595.

not part of a fraudulent scheme, whatever W's share of the deficiency is per the calculation in example (2) above, it will be increased by $10,000. By contrast, if the transfer were part of a fraudulent scheme, neither H nor W could make the proportionate election. Alternatively, if the IRS could prove that W had actual knowledge of H's unreported income, W would not be permitted to elect proportionate liability as to the deficiency flowing from that adjustment, unless she can prove she was forced by the other spouse to sign the return against her will.

V. Additional Requirements Imposed to Obtain Relief under Section 6015(f)

The section 6015(f) election is revolutionary. It expands the availability of relief to underpayments in situations where, taking into consideration all the facts and circumstances, the Service believes it would be inequitable to hold the requesting spouse responsible for more than his or her portion of the unpaid tax. The Conference Committee Report relative to section 6015(f) states:

> The conferees intend that the Secretary will consider using the grant of authority to provide equitable relief in appropriate situations to avoid the inequitable treatment of spouses in such situations. For example, the conferees intend that equitable relief be available to a spouse that does not know, and had no reason to know, that funds intended for the payment of tax were instead taken by the other spouse for such other spouse's benefit.
>
> The conferees do not intend to limit the use of the Secretary's authority to provide equitable relief to situations where tax is shown on a return but not paid. The conferees intend that such authority be used where, taking into account all the facts and circumstances, it is inequitable to hold an individual liable for all or part of any unpaid tax or deficiency arising from a joint return. The conferees intend that relief be available where there is both an understatement and an underpayment of tax.[61]

In 2013, the IRS issued Rev. Proc. 2013-34 to provide guidance on how section 6015(f) would be analyzed.[62] Under paragraph 4.01 of the revenue procedure, the IRS will consider granting equitable relief under section 6015(f) only if the individual can establish that certain threshold requirements are met. The threshold requirements include such things as a joint return having been filed, that relief is not available under 6015(b) or (c), that the claim for relief was made timely, *i.e.*, generally on or before the Collection Statute Expiration Date (CSED) of ten years after assessment,

61. H.R. Conf. Rep. No 599, 105th Cong., 2d Sess. 254-55 (1998), 1998-3 C.B. 1008-09.

62. 2013-2 C.B. 397. This ruling supersedes Rev. Proc. 2003-61, 2003-2 C.B. 296, which itself superseded Rev. Proc. 2000-15, 2000-1 C.B. 447. *Cf.* Erhmann v. Commissioner, T.C. Summary Op. 2014-96 (utilizing Rev. Proc. 2013-23); Torrisi v. Commissioner, T.C. Memo. 2011-235 (utilizing Rev. Proc. 2003-61).

that no impermissible transfers of assets or fraudulent conduct took place, and that the item for which relief is sought is attributable, in full or in part, to the nonrequesting spouse.[63] If the requesting spouse cannot satisfy the last requirement, paragraph 4.01(7) says the Service will still consider granting relief if the reason is due, among other reasons, to the misappropriation of funds or fraud by the nonrequesting spouse, or because the requesting spouse was the subject of abuse that made her unable to challenge the tax treatment of items on the return or the payment of the tax.

If the requesting spouse meets the paragraph 4.01 threshold requirements, the IRS will ordinarily grant streamlined determinations of equitable relief under section 6015(f) if the requesting spouse also satisfies *all* the conditions in paragraph 4.02 of the revenue procedure. The paragraph 4.02 conditions include that the joint filers are no longer married, that the requesting spouse would suffer economic hardship if relief is not granted, and that the requesting spouse had no knowledge or reason to know that the nonrequesting spouse would not pay the income tax liability (or because of abuse, could not challenge her husband about such matters). It is worth highlighting that since section 6015(f) relief is employed primarily with respect to underpayments, the knowledge or reason to know element focuses on the *payment* of the tax, not the proper *reporting* of income or expenses.

If the requesting spouse satisfies the threshold requirements but does not meet the paragraph 4.02 conditions for streamlined determinations, the IRS examiner is instructed to consider all the facts and circumstances of the case in determining whether full or partial equitable relief should be granted. Section 4.03 contains a list of nonexclusive factors to be considered, but stresses that typically no one factor or even a majority of factors will be determinative of the availability of relief.[64] The presence of abuse, however, is a factor that may impact the other factors. The factors considered in determining whether it would be equitable to grant relief include:

1. Whether the requesting spouse is still married to the nonrequesting spouse, with marriage being a neutral factor and no longer being married due to divorce, legal separation or death a factor that weighs in favor of relief;
2. Whether the requesting spouse would suffer economic hardship and could not pay reasonable basic living expenses if relief is not granted;
3. Whether the requesting spouse did not know and had no reason to know—
    a. in the case of an underpayment, that the nonrequesting spouse would not or could not pay the income tax liability at the time the return was filed or within a reasonable time thereafter, or

---

63. Tax Court held relief was not available where the requesting spouse was not able to meet the threshold requirement that the relief sought was attributable to an item of the non-requesting spouse. Hammernik v. Commissioner, T.C. Memo. 2014-170.

64. The requesting spouse was denied relief even when three factors weighed in favor of relief, one weighed against relief, and the remaining factors were neutral as the court was heavily persuaded that the requesting spouse knew or reasonably should have known that her ex-husband would not pay the tax due on the return. Ehrmann v. Commissioner, T.C. Summary Op. 2014-96.

b. in the case of a deficiency, of the item giving rise to the deficiency;

4. Who, as between the requesting spouse or the nonrequesting spouse, has a legal obligation to pay the outstanding income tax liability pursuant to a divorce decree or other legally binding agreement;

5. Whether the requesting spouse received significant benefit (beyond normal support) from the unpaid income tax liability or item giving rise to the deficiency;

6. Whether the requesting spouse is in compliance with income tax laws; and

7. Whether the requesting spouse was in poor physical or mental health at the time the return was filed, including whether the requesting spouse was abused.[65]

VI. Appealing an Adverse Determination Administratively And Judicially

As with all adverse determinations by local or service center personnel, the taxpayer may seek review of a decision denying relief by filing a protest in the Appeals Office of the IRS.[66] If the Appeals Office upholds the denial, either an unfavorable final determination letter or a notice of deficiency is mailed to the taxpayer. Once this letter is received, the requesting spouse can seek judicial review. If he or she wishes to litigate the matter without first paying the asserted deficiency or underpayment,[67] a petition must be filed with the Tax Court[68] within 90 days of the date the IRS mailed

65. Abuse factor weighed in the requesting spouse's favor since her husband was abusing drugs, stealing money from his clients, hot-tempered, and she feared that he would retaliate if she filed a claim for innocent spouse relief. Nihiser v. Commissioner, T.C. Memo. 2008-135.

66. IRS Appeals Memo. 25-0615-0005 (new "quick look" policy to rapidly resolve easy 6015 matters).

67. Section 6015(e) was amended on December 20, 2006, to grant jurisdiction to the Tax Court to hear appeals of equitable relief determinations made under section 6015(f). The Tax Relief and Health Care Act of 2006, Pub. L. No. 109-432, Tit. IV, §408, 120 Stat. 2922, 3052 (2006). The amendment effectively reversed a line of cases that held the Tax Court lacked jurisdiction in such cases. Bartman v. Commissioner, 446 F.3d 785 (8th Cir. 2006); Billings v. Commissioner, 127 T.C. 7 (2006).

68. Ewing v. Commissioner, 122 T.C. 32 (2004); Chief Counsel Notice 2004-026. The cited *Ewing* case (*Ewing II*) was proceeded by Ewing v. Commissioner (*Ewing I*), 118 T.C. 494 (2002), *rev'd*, 439 F.3d 1009 (9th Cir. 2006). *Ewing I* was part of a line of cases questioning whether the Tax Court has jurisdiction to hear "stand alone" section 6015(f) cases. As a result of 2006 legislation, it is now clear that the Tax Court has such jurisdiction. Tax Relief and Health Care Act of 2006, Pub. L. 109-432, div. C, §408, 120 Stat. 3061; *see also* Alioto v. Commissioner, T.C. Memo. 2008-185.

Presently, it is unclear whether one can pay the tax, penalties, and interest, file a claim for refund, and, if the claim is disallowed, litigate in the U.S. District Court or Court of Federal Claims. *See* U.S. v. Popowski, 110 A.F.T.R.2d (RIA) 6997 (D.S.C. 2012) (innocent spouse relief raised as a defense in a suit to reduce joint tax liabilities to judgment); U.S. v. Elman, 110 A.F.T.R.2d (RIA) 6993 (N.D. Ill. 2012) (innocent spouse relief raised as a defense in a suit to enforce federal tax liens on her home).

If these courts will hear innocent spouse claims, some believe they are better suited to hear equitable matters and more predisposed to side with the requesting spouse than the Tax Court. However, it may be difficult for many divorced spouses to get into these courts as the tax asserted by the IRS, including interest and penalties, must be paid in full prior to trial. See Chapter 9 for a discussion of refund actions.

the unfavorable final determination letter or Notice of Deficiency,[69] or if the IRS failed to act on the election, after six months has passed from the date the taxpayer filed the election or request.[70]

The Tax Court has taken a very liberal approach to the cases that have come before it on spousal relief. Rather than merely reviewing the record on an "abuse of discretion" standard and deferring to the agency's determination, the court reviews all the facts of the case on a de novo basis.[71] This approach is often to the benefit of the spouse who was denied relief.

VII. Other Matters

A. Rights of the Nonrequesting Spouse

Unless an election is filed by each spouse in his or her own name, the nonfiling spouse is considered a "nonrequesting spouse." Nonrequesting spouses are entitled to many, but not all, of the rights available to the requesting spouse.

Upon receipt of an election by a requesting spouse, the Service must send notice of the election to the nonrequesting spouse at his or her last known address.[72] The notice must provide the nonrequesting spouse with an opportunity to submit information for consideration in determining liability. Intervention and participation are optional. The nonrequesting spouse may submit whatever information he or she deems relevant to the issue of the appropriateness of relief for the requesting spouse.[73]

---

69. The 90-day limit for filing a petition with the Tax Court is a jurisdictional limit and cannot be equitably tolled, even though there was a district court order stating that the requesting spouse had 30 days to file a petition with the Tax Court. Pollock v. Commissioner, 132 T.C. 21 (2009).

However, the 90-day period did not begin to run when the IRS sent the notice of final determination to an incorrect address. The Post Office had already returned three of the IRS's prior mailings to the taxpayer at that address as undeliverable. The IRS thus had a duty to exercise reasonable diligence to search for a correct address, a duty the IRS failed to satisfy. Terrell v. Commissioner, 625 F.3d 254 (5th Cir. 2010).

70. *See* Reg. § 1.6015-7(b). An automatic stay imposed by a former spouse's bankruptcy proceeding does not preclude the Tax Court from making a determination of whether an individual is entitled to innocent spouse relief when her former spouse filed a notice of intervention and then filed for bankruptcy. Kovitch v. Commissioner, 128 T.C. 108 (2007).

71. The court may consider evidence introduced at trial that was not included in the administrative record in making a determination under section 6015(f). Porter v. Commissioner, 132 T.C. 203 (2009) (holding that the Tax Court will apply a *de novo* standard and may consider evidence not in the administrative record). The IRS concedes that the standard of review for section 6015(f) cases is *de novo* and that the reviewing court is not confined to the administrative record. AOD 2012-07; Chief Counsel Not. CC-2013-011; *see also* Wilson v. Commissioner, 705 F.3d 980 (9th Cir. 2013), *aff'g* T.C. Memo. 2010-134.

72. Reg. § 1.6015-6(a)(1); Chief Counsel Notice 2003-015. Notice is required regardless whether the claim is filed as part of a deficiency proceeding, a CDP hearing, or a "stand-alone" section 6015 request.

73. Reg. § 1.6015-6(b) has a detailed list of the kinds of information that could be submitted.

The Service can share information received from one spouse with the other spouse, but upon request will omit information disclosing a spouse's location.[74]

The nonrequesting spouse may participate during the administrative phase of the case in much the same way as the requesting spouse. By filing a protest with the Appeals Office within 30 days of the notification letter's mailing date, the nonrequesting spouse is even permitted to appeal a preliminary determination granting the requesting spouse partial or full relief.[75]

After hearing the matter, the Appeals Office will render a final determination. At the conclusion of the administrative consideration of the case, both spouses are notified of the Service's determination. Despite the many rights accorded the nonrequesting spouse to have a hearing and to participate in it, the nonrequesting spouse may neither block an administrative settlement offered to the requesting spouse nor file a petition with the Tax Court in his own right to review the determination;[76] only if the requesting spouse files a petition with the Tax Court may the nonrequesting spouse intervene and get judicial review.

If the requesting spouse files a petition in the Tax Court and if the nonrequesting spouse is not already a party to the case, the Commissioner must serve the nonrequesting party with notice of the case.[77] The notice advises the nonrequesting spouse of the opportunity to file a notice of intervention for the sole purpose of challenging the other spouse's entitlement to relief from joint liability pursuant to section 6015.[78] As an intervenor, the nonrequesting spouse has the rights of a quasi-party, including the right to be heard and the right to be a signatory to any proposed settlement.[79]

---

74. Reg. § 1.6015-6(a)(1). A taxpayer who has been the victim of domestic violence and fears that filing a claim for innocent spouse relief will result in retaliation should check the box on the Form 8857 alerting the IRS to this fact. Once so alerted, the IRS will make every effort to protect the privacy of the requesting spouse and will, among other precautions, centralize all correspondence in one location so that the nonrequesting spouse cannot guess the whereabouts of the domestic abuse victim. *See* Steve R. Johnson, *The Duress or Deception Defense to Joint and Several Spousal Liability*, Tax Prac. & Proc. 15 (Dec. 2004–Jan. 2005).

75. Rev. Proc. 2003-19, 2003-1 C.B. 371.

76. Maier v. Commissioner, 119 T.C. 267 (2002), *aff'd* 360 F.3d 361 (2d Cir 2004); Rev. Proc. 2003-19, 2003-1 C.B. 371. *Cf.* King v. Commissioner, 115 T.C. 118 (2000); Corson v. Commissioner, 114 T.C. 354 (2000).

77. Tax Ct. R. 325. Chief Counsel Notice 2005-011 (May 20, 2005).

78. Any intervention shall be made in accordance with the provisions of Tax Ct. R. 325(b).

79. King v. Commissioner, 115 T.C. 118 (2000); Corson v. Commissioner, 114 T.C. 354 (2000); Chief Counsel Notice 2003-015. This includes the right to introduce evidence in support of the electing spouse's claim for relief under section 6015. Van Arsdalen v. Commissioner, 123 T.C. 135 (2004). The intervening spouse has no greater rights than those of other parties and may be dismissed if he or she fails to prosecute the case. Tipton v. Commissioner, 127 T.C. 214 (2006).

A non-requesting spouse's right to intervene and the corresponding right to notification of an innocent spouse relief request survive even after the non-requesting spouse dies. IRS is obliged to take appropriate steps to notify any heirs, executors, or administrators if a requesting spouse files a request for relief. Fain v. Commissioner, 129 T.C. 89, 92 (2007).

As a non-party, the nonrequesting spouse also may not appeal to the circuit courts of appeal a Tax Court decision granting relief to the requesting spouse. Baranowicz v. Commissioner, 432 F.3d 972 (9th Cir. 2005).

B. Can the IRS Attach a New Spouse's Income or Property to Pay the Purported Innocent Spouse's Prior Tax Debts?

If a person owes taxes from years before marriage, those tax liabilities are her separate debts. They may have arisen from separate returns filed or from joint returns filed with a previous spouse. The concern of many people who are considering (re)marriage is whether the person she is marrying will be obligated to pay pre-existing taxes.[80] This was a concern of Carol Jones who we met at the beginning of the chapter.

As a general statement, the new spouse's assets cannot be seized to pay the premarital (separate) debts of the remarrying spouse. Subsequently acquired property purchased with the earnings of the new spouse and titled solely in that person's name are not subject to government seizure to pay the separate debts of the other spouse.[81] This assumes, however, the individuals have not commingled their property. If the property of the new couple is commingled, the IRS will seize the property to satisfy any debts owed to it.

Likewise, the separate earnings of the new spouse are not available to the government to pay the other spouse's debts. Practically speaking, to safeguard refunds attributable to the new spouse from being offset by the Service to pay the other spouse's liability, it is better to file separate returns after the marriage until the debts are paid in full, even though the practice may result in a higher tax bill.

Alternatively, the couple could carefully monitor their withholding and estimated tax payments to insure that they do not overpay their taxes, thus avoiding a refund subject to seizure by the IRS.

If a husband and wife file jointly, they should allocate income and deductions between them,[82] using a Form 8379 for this purpose. This helps avoid the "injured spouse" situation where one spouse's refund is intercepted to pay the other spouse's liability. If the form is filed, the IRS is only allowed to withhold the refund attributable to the liable spouse. To be safest, the form should be filed with the tax return. However, one can file the injured spouse form after the return was filed and the improper offset occurred.

C. Disclosure Issues

Section 6103(e)(8) requires the Service, on request, to disclose certain information to one spouse about the other spouse's payments on a joint income tax liability and about the Service's actions to secure those payments. The spouse is entitled to know

---

For discussion of circumstances under which the participation of the nonrequesting spouse is limited, see Frances D. Sheehy, *The Right to Intervene in Innocent Spouse Cases Disappears when the Affirmative Defense of Innocent Spouse is Withdrawn*, Fla. B.J., Feb. 2013, at 30.

80. The IRS may intercept refunds to apply against the following debts: federal tax, child support, state income tax or federal non-tax debt (e.g., student loan). *See* Chapter 9.

81. *See* Pate v. United States, 949 F.2d 1059 (10th Cir. 1991).

82. Rev. Rul. 80-7, 1980-1 C.B. 296; *see also* SCA 199924056 (Apr. 20, 1990) (IRS must pay a spouse his or her separate interest in a joint refund even if the Service erroneously issued the refund check to the other spouse).

the status of collection on the joint tax liability, but is not entitled to personal information related to the other spouse.[83]

D. Effect of Divorce Decree Allocation of Responsibility for Understatements

Even when a divorce decree indicates that one spouse has taken responsibility for taxes owed, the IRS, not being a party to the divorce decree, may continue to pursue either spouse until the liability is paid.[84] The IRS reasons that the paying spouse can then get contribution from the other spouse.[85]

E. Collection Activity and Statute of Limitations Are Suspended

If an election is filed under sections 6015, a freeze is placed on the taxpayer's account and collection is suspended by statute from the date the election is filed until the matter is finally resolved, plus 60 days.[86] Any improper assessment may be enjoined.[87] Levies served before the claim for relief was filed will normally be released as well.

Since the IRS may not pursue collection once a taxpayer requests relief under section 6015, the statute of limitations (SOL) on collection is suspended for the entire period the matter is being considered plus an additional 60 days.[88]

F. Section 6015, Section 66, and Community Property

Special issues arise when spousal relief is sought in a community property state. Rather than section 6015, relief is controlled by section 66. Sections 66 and 6015 do

---

83. Pursuant to IRM 25.15.1.9.2, the revenue officer *may* disclose the following information, upon request:

- Whether the Service has attempted to collect the deficiency from the other spouse;
- The amount, if any, collected from the other spouse;
- The current collection status (e.g., delinquent status, installment agreement, suspended); and
- The reason for suspension, if applicable (e.g., unable to locate, hardship).

The revenue officer may not disclose the following information:

- The other spouse's location or telephone number;
- Any information about the other spouse's employment, income, or assets; or
- The income level at which a suspended account will be reactivated.

84. IRM 25.18.3.8.

85. Though the allocation of responsibility in the divorce decree is not controlling, the IRS considers it as a factor in whether to grant equitable relief under section 6015(f). *See* Rev. Proc. 2013-34, ¶4.03(2)(d). Even in cases not controlled by section 6015(f), agents consider an allocation to reflect on the equities of the situation.

86. IRC §6015(e)(1); Reg. §1.6015-7(c)(2)(i); IRM 25.15.2.4.2. However, a Notice of Federal Tax Lien may be filed during this period. Beery v. Commissioner, 122 T.C. 184 (2004).

87. IRC §6015(e)(1)(B); Reg. §1.6015-7(c).

88. IRC §6015(e)(2). Neither the SOL on assessment nor the SOL on filing refund claims is affected by a request for relief under section 6015.

not preempt state community property laws for refund purposes. Thus, a taxpayer qualified for section 6015 relief is not eligible for refund of taxes, interest, or penalties paid out of community funds to cover the other spouse's tax liability.[89] In addition, certain tax benefits must be allocated between the spouses in community property states in spousal relief situations. Such allocation is effected by filing Form 8379 "Injured Spouse Allocation."[90]

VIII. Conclusion

Finding oneself liable for the tax transgressions of one's ex-spouse can be a significant emotional and financial burden to a taxpayer. Fortunately, Congress has sought to alleviate the harsh consequences by enacting section 6015. While far from perfect, the provisions attempt to balance the duty of the taxpayer to review a tax return before signing and filing it with the realities of many situations where it would be unfair to hold the innocent spouse liable.

Problems

1. Sue and Mike had been married for 15 years and had three children. Sue, Mike and the children were all in good health. Sue had majored in biology in college, and had taken a few business courses. She was thinking of going to medical school, but instead worked as a medical technician after college to help put Mike through medical school. She did not work outside the home after their first child was born, and had no business experience.

Mike was a surgeon in sole practice and managed the finances of his practice himself. He didn't discuss the finances with Sue. All of Mike's earnings from his practice were deposited in a separate bank account in his name. Sue knew about the account, but had no knowledge of the deposits, withdrawals or balances. Mike paid all the bills for his practice and the major household bills, like the mortgage, utilities, country club, children's schooling and travel. He gave Sue money for household expenses such as food, the children's clothing and miscellaneous items.

Mike also gave Sue money to be used for her clothing and jewelry, separate from the household money. He wanted her to be well-dressed.

Mike made a good living from his medical practice, and the family had a good lifestyle. They belonged to an exclusive country club. Sue frequently took the children there for swimming and tennis lessons. The children also attended "day camp" there during the summers. Sue and Mike frequently played golf and had dinner at the club.

---

89. Ordlock v. Commissioner, 533 F.3d 1136 (9th Cir. 2008); *see* Note, *Interpreting a Visigothic Spanish Civil Law Tradition to Trump the Internal Revenue Code: Section 6015's Uneven Application in Community Property States*, 63 Tax Law. 553 (2010).

90. *See* CCA 201108036 (Feb. 25, 2011).

Sue and Mike travelled together extensively. Their travels included medical meetings held in resort facilities all over the country. Sue didn't attend any of the meetings, but enjoyed the sightseeing and the travel.

Sue and Mike drove expensive late model cars, and the children attended private schools. The family lived in a large lakefront home in an upscale neighborhood. Mike kept a boat on the lake, and sometimes took the family boating.

Mike was a heavy drinker. Sue suspected that he had become an alcoholic, but wasn't sure. He sometimes became violent when he drank. He had threatened her on multiple occasions, and had struck her a few times. She was not seriously injured, and had not sought medical attention or told anyone about the incidents but as the years passed, she became more and more frightened being in his presence.

Mike also had a gambling problem. Sue knew that he gambled, but did not know the extent or seriousness of his problem until later.

Sue had become concerned some years ago about her total dependence on Mike, particularly in light of his drinking and gambling problems. As a result, Sue opened a separate bank account in her own name. Mike didn't know about the account. She made periodic deposits from the money Mike had given her for household expenses, as well as some gifts from her parents who had become concerned about her. Other than the bank account, she had no assets in her own name. The account earned some interest in 20x4 and prior years, but because she had kept the account secret from Mike, the interest was never reported on their joint returns. She felt guilty about not reporting the interest, and changed the account to a non-interest bearing account in late 20x4.

They separated in 20x6 and were divorced in 20x7. The Marital Settlement Agreement between them provided that Mike would be responsible for all federal income tax liabilities for the years they were married. It also provided for a sale of their marital home and other assets, but there was very little cash left after payment of debts. Sue was granted custody of the children. She paid all the expenses for herself and the children from alimony and child support payments she received from Mike. She rarely had any money left over.

Sue and Mike filed joint returns while they were married. The returns were prepared by an accountant, although Sue had no participation in their preparation. After asking the accountant if everything was correct, Sue signed the returns, but otherwise knew little about their content. After their separation in 20x6, Sue stated that she did not want to sign the joint return because she did not trust him any longer. Mike hit her severely and threatened not to pay any alimony unless she signed the return. She signed it.

Mike filed the 20x5 and 20x6 returns. They were joint returns signed by both Sue and Mike. Unknown to Sue, however, Mike did not pay the taxes required to be paid with the returns for either year. Sue says that she thought he had paid the taxes.

Mike had not paid the tax in full for some of the prior years either. In fact, the IRS had begun collection activities for 20x1 and 20x2. Sue knew about those collection activities at the times she signed the 20x5 and 20x6 returns. Sue had also seen some mail that indicated they were behind on other bills and that some of the amounts had been turned over to collection agencies.

The IRS recently conducted examinations of the 20x5 and 20x6 returns, as well as the 20x4 return. Assume that the statute of limitations is not an issue. The IRS did not propose changes for 20x5 or 20x6, but did for 20x4. The 20x4 proposal included disallowance of the deductions taken on the 20x4 return for many personal items, such as the country club charges, the boat and the cars. It also included in income the interest from Sue's separate bank account. The proposal is currently under review by the IRS Appeals Office.

Sue recently received correspondence from the IRS demanding payment of the unpaid taxes as set forth on the joint returns for 20x5 and 20x6. She has asked you to represent her in the matter, and asked for your advice with respect to the proposed changes for 20x4. She has told you that she does not have enough money to pay the taxes, interest, and penalties owed for 20x5 and 20x6 and proposed for 20x4.

a. Is there authority for seeking relief for Sue for 20x5 and 20x6? What about 20x4?

b. What will be your legal arguments for 20x4? For 20x5 and 20x6?

c. What procedure must be followed to seek relief at the administrative level? Is judicial review available in the event administrative relief is not granted?

2. Charles and Mary had been married for ten years. Both of them worked outside the home. They shared in management of their financial affairs and the earnings from their jobs were co-mingled in joint bank accounts. There was no evidence of abuse by either spouse. They filed a joint federal income tax return for the year 20x1. They were not getting along and were divorced in late 20x2, after the 20x1 joint return had been filed.

The IRS conducted an audit of the 20x1 return. The revenue agent's report (RAR) proposed a deficiency in tax of $60,000. The deficiency was based entirely on the denial of losses that arose from an investment made by Charles while they were married that the revenue agent concluded was a tax shelter entered exclusively for tax purposes. There was ample evidence that Mary knew that Charles had made the investment and had used funds from their joint bank accounts to do so. Charles and Mary retained separate counsel to represent them before the IRS Appeals Office in a review of the deficiency proposed by the RAR. In addition to disputing the disallowance of the loss on the merits, the protest filed by Mary's attorney sought relief from joint and several liability for the deficiency under section 6015.

a. Does Charles have the right to participate in the proceedings before the Appeals Office and, if so, to what extent? What paperwork is required?

b. Assume for the purpose of this question only that despite evidence presented by Charles, the Appeals Officer had granted Mary innocent spouse relief and memorialized its decision on Form 870-IS. Charles vehemently disagrees with the determination. Can he petition the Tax Court for a redetermination?

Assume that the Appeals Office issued a Statutory Notice of Deficiency determining a deficiency in the amount of $60,000, consistent with the RAR, and denied innocent spouse relief to Mary. Mary filed a Petition in the U.S. Tax Court under section 6015(e)(1)(A) arguing exclusively that she was entitled to innocent spouse relief.

c. Does Charles have the right to participate in the proceedings before the Tax Court and, if so, to what extent? What paperwork is required?

Shortly thereafter, Mary entered into a Stipulation (agreement) with counsel for the IRS agreeing that she was not liable for any deficiencies and that she was eligible for relief under Section 6015(c). Counsel for the IRS has filed a Motion asking the Court to decide that Mary was eligible for relief under section 6015(c) consistent with the stipulation.

d. Was it proper for the IRS and Mary to enter into the Stipulation?

Chapter 4

Examination of Returns

IRC: §§ 6001; 7522; 7525; 7602(a)–(d)(1); 7604(a); 7605; 7609

Regs.: § 301.7121-1

Proc. Regs.: §§ 601.105; 601.106

Cases and Rulings: United States v. Fern, 696 F.2d 1269 (11th Cir. 1983)

I. Introduction

Ours has often been called a "self assessment" or "voluntary" system of taxation. Tax protesters (those who proclaim, based on spurious constitutional or statutory theories, that they have no obligation to file returns and/or pay taxes) seize on such language. However, the courts have made the following clear:

> The word voluntary is not the equivalent of optional. To the extent that income taxes are said to be voluntary, they are only voluntary in that one files the returns and pays the taxes without the IRS first telling each individual the amount due and then forcing payment of that amount. The payment of income taxes is not optional.[1]

The first step in the process occurs when the taxpayer files a return and pays the tax reported due on that return. For most taxpayers—those whose returns are not audited—the process ends there. However, when a return is examined, a wide array of procedures is engaged. After discussing the tax gap, this chapter discusses those procedures, including selection of returns for examination, types of examinations, audit strategies and decisions, IRS information gathering, taxpayer discovery of information from the IRS, Appeals Office consideration, and conclusion of the audit or of Appeals consideration.[2]

1. United States v. Middleton, 246 F.3d 825, 840 (6th Cir. 2001) (upholding this jury instruction and resulting tax evasion conviction). The IRS website (www.irs.gov) contains detailed refutations of the most common tax protestor arguments.

2. Examination and audit typically are used as synonyms in tax practice. That practice is followed here.

II. Tax Gap

The IRS conducts examinations both to correct inaccuracies that already have occurred and to deter future inaccuracies. The "tax gap" represents the difference between what taxpayers should have paid and what they actually did pay on a timely basis. The IRS estimates that the tax gap has grown over the years, and stands at approximately $450 billion.[3]

The IRS-estimated gap represents a noncompliance rate of about 18%—lower than that of most countries but hardly cause for rejoicing. It is estimated that 85% of the tax gap comes from underreporting on filed returns; 7% relates to nonfiling; and 9% involves the nonpayment of reported taxes. Over half is associated with individual income tax; nearly 20% relates to employment taxes; and the remainder involves corporate income tax, estate and gift taxes, and excise taxes.[4]

Current areas for audit and enforcement emphasis include underreporting by high-income individuals, nonfilers, corporations, tax shelters, offshore accounts and other international transactions, and abusive trusts. However, the IRS budget is inadequate to cover all areas of need.[5] Thus, as the IRS shifts resources to one area to curb tax underpayment there, tax underpayment tends to rise in the area(s) from which the resources had been taken.[6]

A sufficient level of audit coverage is important to the health of the tax system, both to detect honest error and to deter overly aggressive reporting. The income tax audit rate, as officially measured, has been dropping for decades, and compliance has dropped with it. In the mid-1960s, the announced audit rate was in the 4.5 to 5% range and the announced compliance rate was over 90%. Now, the audit rate is consistently below 1% and the compliance rate has fallen to about 82%.

The official audit rate understates coverage because it does not take into account "compliance activity the IRS doesn't call an audit but sure feels like an audit to the taxpayer," activity such as the automated substitute for return, automated underreporter, and math error programs. Taking such activity into account causes the individual audit rate to rise to about 7.4%.[7]

---

3. *See* IRS, Tax Gap Estimates for Tax Years 2008–2010 (Apr. 2016).

4. *Id.*; *see also* Charles P. Rettig, *Nonfliers Beware: Who's That Knocking at Your Door?*, J. Tax Prac. & Proc., Oct.–Nov. 2006, at 15. For slightly different figures, see Mark A. Luscombe, *Tax Protestors: Is the IRS Turning the Corner?*, Taxes, May 2007, at 3. All the above figures are suggestive, not conclusive. They are educated guesses, not facts. The figures are imprecise, and they fluctuate over time.

5. The IRS has been caught in a financial squeeze. Its budget dropped by nearly 20% on an inflation-adjusted basis between 2010 and 2015, but its workload has increased substantially in part because "recent decades have seen a dramatic escalation in tax programs and provisions serving purposes other than revenue raising." Kristin E. Hickman, *Administering the Tax System We Have*, 63 Duke L.J. 1717, 1728 (2014).

6. *See* Steve R. Johnson, *The Future of American Tax Administration: Conceptual Possibilities and Political Realities*, 7 Colum J. Tax L. 5 (2016); Steve Johnson, *The 1998 Act and the Resources Link Between Tax Compliance and Tax Simplification*, 51 U. Kan. L. Rev. 1013 (2003).

7. Nina E. Olson, *More Than a "Mere" Preparer: Loving and Return Preparation*, Tax Notes, May 13, 2013, p. 767, at 773.

On the other hand, it overstates coverage because it fails to distinguish qualitatively among the types of audits. By far the largest group of officially counted "audits" consists of examinations conducted by mail by Service Center personnel.[8] Those audits are decidedly inferior both in comprehensiveness and in level of rigor compared to examinations performed personally by revenue agents.

III. Selection of Returns for Examination

Although the current audit rate is low by historical standards, clients should not put too much stock in the general percentage. A number of factors raise the likelihood of one's return being examined. Each year, the IRS determines approximately how many returns will be examined, and the total is allocated among the IRS divisions. The IRS does not announce the criteria it uses to select returns for examination, and those criteria change over time. The following are some of the numerous events and conditions that can prompt an audit.

(1) *Discriminate Function ("DIF")*. This is a major source of examinations. The DIF program is a multi-factor computer process. It scores returns by assessing patterns of deviation from expected ranges. Returns are divided into classes reflecting income and other characteristics. The items on each return are then analyzed through formulae designed to detect variations from amounts and relationships normal to the return's class. The scores from these formulae are added to yield a DIF score.[9] The higher the score, the greater the return error potential, thus the greater the chance that the return will be examined. Returns with high DIF scores are reviewed by IRS personnel who decide whether the return is to be audited and, if so, which type of audit will be used.

As one would expect, the DIF formulae are secret. By virtue of section 6103(b)(2), neither taxpayers nor other interested persons can force their disclosure under the Freedom of Information Act. From time to time, the IRS does publish data as to the typical ranges of deductions for interest, medical and dental expenses, charitable contributions, etc. However, a taxpayer should not assume that her return is audit-proof even if all her deductions are within such ranges.

(2) *Information matching*. As described in Chapter 2, third-party payors sometimes are required to file information statements with the IRS, with copies to the taxpayer. For example, wage and salary payors must file W-2 forms indicating how much they paid each employee and how much income tax was withheld; banks, savings and loan associations, and others must file 1099-INT forms indicating interest paid to depositors, as well as any tax withheld under the back-up withholding

8. In calendar year 2014, the IRS received approximately 192 million returns of all types. It audited 1.4 million of them (for a 0.7% audit coverage rate). One million of the 1.4 million involved correspondence audits. The remaining 400,000 were field audits. IRS Data Book, 2015, at 23.

9. For many years, the DIF score was based only on deduction and credit items. The IRS is developing income components for DIF purposes.

rules; corporations must file 1099-DIV forms indicating dividends paid to shareholders.[10]

The IRS's computers match or check such reported information with the recipient's tax returns. If there is a discrepancy between the information report and the recipient's return, the IRS (typically the Service Center to which the recipient's return was sent) will send the taxpayer a letter requesting explanation of the discrepancy. A reasonable explanation often will end the matter. If the size, number, or pattern of return errors creates suspicion as to the accuracy of the return generally, the return may be pulled for more searching examination.

Comprehensive information reporting and matching greatly improve the accuracy of tax reporting. According to the IRS, amounts subject to withholding—such as wages and salaries—have a net misreporting rate of about 1.2%. Amounts subject to third-party reporting but not withholding—such as interest and dividends—have a net misreporting rate of 4.5%. Amounts subject to partial third-party reporting—such as capital gains—have a net misreporting rate of 8.6%. Misreporting skyrockets—up to a 53.9% rate—for items subject to neither information reporting nor withholding.[11]

Accordingly, there are frequent proposals to expand information reporting. They include proposals to increase reporting as to government payments for goods and services, as to debt and credit card reimbursements paid to certain merchants, and as to brokerage and mutual fund accounts.[12]

(3) *Economic level of the taxpayer.* In general, the audit rate rises as the taxpayer's economic level rises. The larger the estate, the more likely is an audit of its estate tax return. The higher the net worth of a corporation or the higher the income of an individual, the more likely is an audit of its, his, or her income tax return.

(4) *Return items.* From experience, the IRS knows that there are certain return items as to which taxpayer error is common. Returns claiming such items may be subject to a higher risk of audit. For example, income tax returns claiming office-in-the-home deductions or deductions for home computers face a heightened audit risk. Another example is the Earned Income Tax Credit, which has nearly a 25% error rate (some honest mistake, some fraud). This has led to the counter-intuitive result that returns of the working poor are audited more frequently than returns of many affluent taxpayers.[13]

---

10. Related mechanisms exist. For instance, a taxpayer who claims an income tax deduction for alimony paid to a former spouse must supply the recipient's tax identification number (Social Security number) on his Form 1040.

11. *See* Rettig, *supra*, at 15–16.

12. *See, e.g.*, Joint Comm. on Tax'n, Description of Certain Revenue Provisions Contained in the President's Fiscal Year 2016 Budget Proposal 245–52 (Sept. 2015).

13. In fiscal year 2015, the audit rate was 0.3% for all individual income tax returns (i) with income under $200,000, (ii) which did not report business, farm, or rental activities, and (iii) which did not claim the EITC. However, the audit rate was 1.7% (that is, nearly six times higher) for individuals with under $25,000 of income who did claim the EITC. IRS Data Book, 2015, at 23.

Returns that reflect attempts at manipulation or tax protester devices face a higher audit risk. Examples include (i) returns on which the jurat (the "under penalties of perjury" language above the signature line) has been struck out, (ii) returns which have been tailored via home computer to resemble a Form 1040 or other return but which alter the IRS form in some critical respect, and (iii) returns on which line entries are not numbers but a symbol or abbreviation meaning "refuse to answer: Fifth Amendment privilege against self-incrimination" or something comparably worthless.[14]

(5) *Infection.* Sometimes, a return would not have been examined based on that return taken alone, but is swept into audit because of its relation to other returns that are or were under examination. For example, if audit of a taxpayer's returns for prior years revealed significant deficiencies, the odds increase of his later returns being picked up for examination. Also, audit of an estate tax return raises the likelihood of examination of that estate's income tax returns. Similarly, if a return filed by a closely held corporation is under audit, the returns of the corporation's shareholder(s) may also be drawn into the audit.

(6) *Taxpayer initiation.* Certain actions by a taxpayer may prompt the IRS to examine a return or to accelerate an examination. Examples include the taxpayer's filing an amended return, a refund claim, or a bankruptcy petition.

(7) *Informant.* Third parties sometimes tell the IRS about alleged tax wrongdoing by another taxpayer. Congress has encouraged this by authorizing the payment of tax bounties or rewards under Code section 7623 to informants whose information results in successful adjustments. The most likely informants are disgruntled employees or ex-employees and former spouses or significant others.

(8) *Notoriety.* For instance, if the local newspaper carries a story on the indictment of your client for embezzling from his church's building fund, don't be surprised if the IRS pulls his returns to check whether he reported the embezzlement income.[15] Or, if your firm is defending a prominent drug trafficker at criminal trial, don't be amazed if there is an IRS agent in the gallery, taking notes on the testimony in order to advance a civil tax audit.

In some instances, instead of launching an audit, the IRS uses "soft notice" techniques. That is, when the IRS has reason to doubt the accuracy of a return, the IRS sends the taxpayer a letter directing attention to the problematic item and urging amendment if the original return is in fact erroneous.[16]

---

14. It is settled that, in general, the privilege against self-incrimination does not exonerate failure to file complete and accurate tax returns. *See, e.g.*, United States v. Sullivan, 274 U.S. 259, 264 (1927).

15. Illegally obtained income is taxable. James v. United States, 366 U.S. 213 (1961).

16. *See* Michael Joe & Crystal Tandon, *IRS Issuing New "Soft Notice" to Underreporting Taxpayers*, Tax Notes, Oct. 13, 2008, p. 138.

IV. Types of Examinations

There are three principal types of examinations: correspondence, office, and field. They are described below, after which several specialized types of examinations are discussed. The various audit types differ in their comprehensiveness, rigor, and methods.

A. Principal Audit Types

1. Correspondence Examinations

Correspondence examinations are the most common type of audit. They are conducted by tax examiners at the service centers or in local area offices. The IRS sends the taxpayer a letter inquiring into an apparent return anomaly. The taxpayer is asked to respond by mail, explaining the situation and providing documentation. Typically, the initial interchange is limited to one or a few items that piqued the IRS's interest, but the examination may broaden if other questionable items are identified.

Correspondence exams generally are limited to simple income tax issues that are covered by established examination programs. If the exam turns up issues beyond those covered in the programs, the case may be transferred to a field office for more intensive investigation. Transfer also may occur if the taxpayer requests a personal interview or if the taxpayer is deemed unable to communicate effectively in writing.

2. Office Audits

Office audits are conducted at IRS field offices by personnel known as tax auditors. Office exams often involve more complex issues than those present in correspondence exams. They usually entail some face-to-face contact with the taxpayer or the taxpayer's representative. The exam may involve either individual or business taxpayers.

The scope of the office audit usually is limited to one or a few issues, and the goal is to close the exam after the first interview. Again, though, the possibility exists that the exam may be expanded if the initial interview discloses significant information pointing towards other possible adjustments.

3. Field Examinations

Complex individual and business returns are examined by revenue agents, whose training and experience exceed those of office auditors. Although such exams may take place at IRS offices, they usually are conducted at the taxpayer's place of business or, if different, where the taxpayer's books, records, or other source documents are located. Unlike office audits, field exams often involve multiple meetings over weeks or months, sometimes over a year for complex corporate returns.

B. Other Audit Types

There are variations on the audit types described above. Some have been with us for decades; others are temporary. Here are examples:

Employment tax audits. Employment taxes, such as FICA (Federal Insurance Contribution Act) and FUTA (Federal Unemployment Tax Act) taxes, are imposed by the federal government. The central question in employment tax audits often is whether the worker should be classified as an employee or as an independent contractor.[17] This question is analyzed under a multi-factoral test derived from non-tax common law,[18] leading to frequent confusion and controversy.

An important feature of employment tax audits is plural potential targets. Employers and employees share liability for FICA taxes. The employer is supposed to collect and pay over to the IRS both the employer's and employee's shares. If the employer is a company and it fails to pay, one or more of its so called "responsible persons" may become secondarily liable for part of the taxes. See Chapter 14.

Estate tax audits. Audits of estate tax returns are conducted by estate tax examiners, who typically are attorneys and often have considerable experience. The largest class of issues in such audits involves valuation of assets. The IRS employs a staff of appraisers called Valuation Engineers. They sometimes are assisted by specialized functions, such as the IRS's Art Advisory Panel which consists of well-regarded private sector art experts. In large cases, the IRS may hire non-IRS personnel as valuation consultants or experts.

Coordinated Examination Program ("CEP") and Limited Issue Focused Examinations ("LIFE"). The returns of large corporations are quite likely to be audited.[19] Very large corporations experience essentially perpetual audit.

Large corporate exams are through the CEP. The exams are performed by revenue agents in the highest pay grades. They have the benefit of industry-specific position papers and audit programs developed through and coordinated by the Industry Specialization Program ("ISP") and the Market Segment Specialization Program ("MSSP"). CEP features early involvement by IRS Chief Counsel attorneys to provide legal analysis. The idea is to weed out bad issues early in the process and to see that potentially good issues receive the development they need during audit. CEP also can entail accelerated Appeals Office consideration.

LIFE is one of several approaches the IRS has tried to improve communications with the taxpayers and to streamline exams. Using materiality benchmarks, the audit

---

17. *See, e.g.*, Frank Agostino & Tara Krieger, *Federal Employment Misclassification*, J. Tax Prac. & Proc., June–July 2015, p. 31; Josh O. Ungerman & Matt L. Roberts, *Buckle Your Seatbelts: Employment Taxes Are Back in Vogue and It Will Be a Bumpy Ride*, J, Tax Prac. & Proc., June–July 2015, p. 21.

18. *See, e.g.*, 303 West 42nd St. Enterprises, Inc. v. IRS, 181 F.3d 272 (2d Cir. 1999); Rev. Rul. 87-41, 1987-1 C.B. 296.

19. The income returns of corporations with assets exceeding $20 billion were audited at an 84.2% rate in fiscal year 2014, IRS Data Book, 2014, at 23, but at only a 64% rate in fiscal year 2015, IRS Data Book, 2015, at 23.

focuses on the most significant issues. The revenue agent(s) and the taxpayer enter into agreements as to the process to be followed and time frames within which each will respond to the other's requests.

Early resolution mechanisms. Both taxpayers and the IRS benefit from early resolution of issues. In recent decades, the IRS, with varying success, has tried the following devices, among others: (1) Pre-filing Agreements (PFAs, allowing taxpayers, before their returns are filed, to ask that the IRS consider and resolve specific, typically factual issues),[20] (2) Compliance Assurance Program (CAP, pre-filing resolution of substantial, recurring issues),[21] (3) Advance Pricing Agreements (APAs, pre-filing resolution of section 482 transfer pricing issues),[22] (4) Quality Examination Process (QEP, interactive process for planning and resolving audits of large taxpayers),[23] and (5) Industry Issue Resolution Program (IIRP, addressing complex tax issues common to significant numbers of business taxpayers).[24]

Some initiatives last; some don't; and most are reorganized from time to time. For instance, IIRP was later folded into a larger initiative: the Industry Issue Focus (IIF) program.[25] In addition, the IRS combined the APA function with the Competent Authority function (for resolving tax treaty interpretation questions) to form the Advance Pricing and Mutual Assistance Program.[26]

In some situations, the taxpayer can cause the IRS to accelerate examination. For example, taxpayers who are debtors in bankruptcy cases can request prompt determination of their tax liabilities.[27] Also, executors can request prompt determination of decedents' gift tax and income tax liabilities. The executor is excused from personal liability for any such taxes beyond amounts the IRS determines within nine months of the request.[28] As a practical matter, the constricted time frame often compels the IRS to streamline the audit.

C. Special Procedures in Aid of Examination

Several special procedures exist to support the audit function in unusual situations. For example, subject to a number of requirements, the IRS is authorized to conduct

---

20. Rev. Proc. 2009-14, 2009-3 I.R.B. 324.

21. IR-2011-32 (Mar. 31, 2011).

22. Rev. Proc. 2015-41, 2015-35 I.R.B. 263 (revised procedures for requesting an APA).

23. IRM 4.46; IRS Pub. 4837 Achieving Quality Examinations Through Effective Planning, Execution, and Resolution (3-2010).

24. Rev. Proc. 2003-36, 2003-1 C.B. 859; IR-2004-100 (July 29, 2004).

25. *See, e.g.*, David L. Click, *LMSB's Industry Issue Focus Initiative: What Does It Achieve?*, Tax Notes, May 28, 2007, p. 863.

26. Notices 2013-78 & 2013-79, 2013-50 I.R.B. 633 & 653; *see also* Rev. Proc. 2015-40, 2015-35 I.R.B. 236 (guidance as to seeking Competent Authority relief).

27. 11 U.S.C. § 505(a).

28. IRC § 6905(a). *See also* § 6501(d) (permitting requests for prompt assessment of certain taxes by fiduciaries and corporations).

undercover operations.[29] In addition, section 7623 has long authorized the IRS to pay amounts deemed necessary for enforcing the revenue laws. The Tax Relief and Health Care Act of 2006 added whistleblower provisions to be administered by a new Whistleblower Office in the IRS. A whistle-blower may receive an award of between 15% to 30% of amounts collected as a result of information he or she provides.[30]

Audit reconsideration is sometimes a useful device, especially when important new evidence has been unearthed or when counsel entered a case late. A taxpayer may request audit reconsideration if she (1) did not appear for the audit, (2) moved or did not receive correspondence from the IRS, (3) has additional information not presented during the audit, or (4) disagrees with the assessment resulting from the audit.[31] Whether to grant an audit reconsideration request is discretionary with the IRS.

V. Audit Strategies and Choices

A. Generally

"Hope for the best; prepare for the worst." The prudent taxpayer, though hoping there will be no audit, begins preparing for it even before filing the return for the tax period. She does so by taking reasonable return positions and by gathering and retaining documentation supporting them. The following briefly discusses the general features of the audit process and tactical choices that often arise during it.

The audit starts when the IRS sends the taxpayer an initial contact letter. The letter identifies the IRS office, the tax return(s) or tax period(s) in question, and the IRS contact person and telephone number. The letter typically states the issue(s) the IRS wants the taxpayer to explain or substantiate and sets a date and time for an appointment, or date for response in writing. From these items, it will be apparent which type of audit the IRS intends to conduct.

The taxpayer and the taxpayer's representative should begin preparing the response as soon as possible. They should do so by reviewing records, assessing the merits of the taxpayer's return positions, ascertaining whether exposure exists as to other return positions for this year and other years should the examination broaden, and planning the audit defense strategy.

In most cases, a cooperative approach is best. This includes complying in timely manner with reasonable requests by the examining agent. Agents dislike delays and unfulfilled promises. If a problem develops, inform the agent early rather than late. However, the touchstone is always the best interests of the taxpayer, consistent with the attorney's own ethical obligations. Balancing the considerations can require considerable skill.

29. IRC §7608(c).

30. IRC §7623(b); *see* Paul D. Scott, *Tax Whistle-Blowers To Receive Increased Rewards*, Tax Notes, Jan. 29, 2007, at 441.

31. IRS Pub. 3598, The Audit Reconsideration Process (Rev. 7-2012).

In responding to questions asked by the IRS agent, the usual strategy is to provide the requested information but not to volunteer additional information. Counsel usually meets with the agent without the taxpayer being present. Unwise disclosures (as well as the other extreme, stonewalling) might cause the IRS to broaden the examination. The attorney should always be alert to any changes in the pace or tenor of the contacts with the agent. An especially worrisome sign is if the agent abruptly and without explanation ceases all contacts. That might mean that the case has been referred for criminal investigation. Clients should be instructed always to ask for the title of any IRS person who contacts them. Contact from Special Agents (the agents working for the IRS's Criminal Investigation function) signifies that the matter has changed from civil to criminal.

Sometimes, it is helpful to retain an economic, valuation, or other expert to assist the taxpayer and the attorney during the examination. To preserve the possible applicability of the attorney-client privilege, the expert should be retained by the attorney, not by the client, and communications with the expert should not be outside the circle of confidentiality.[32]

In most instances, examining agents behave courteously and professionally. Taxpayer complaints about agents are taken seriously by the IRS. Moreover, IRS agents often are under demanding case management schedules. It is in the agents' self-interest to maintain good relations with taxpayers in order to move cases expeditiously. Nonetheless, instances arise in which the taxpayer thinks the agent is behaving unreasonably or, perhaps more frequently, has an erroneous view of the applicable law.[33] What can be done in such circumstances?

The taxpayer has a right to elevate the matter to the agent's group manager. Some fear that "going over the agent's head" will antagonize the agent, leading to even more adjustments being set up. That fear is misplaced. Supervisory conferences are a routine, accepted part of the system, and agents realize they have more to lose than to gain by engaging in reprisals.[34]

The taxpayer typically has the opportunity for administrative appeal through the IRS Appeals Office, as described in Section VIII below. If the point of contention is a legal issue, the taxpayer may consider asking the agent to obtain a TAM from the National Office, as described in Chapter 1.

The taxpayer may also consider resort to the local Taxpayer Advocate or the National Taxpayer Advocate. As noted in Chapter 1, the Taxpayer Advocate function will not intervene in a dispute about the law, but it can be useful if a procedural problem arises.

---

32. *See, e.g.*, United States v. Kovel, 296 F.2d 918 (2d Cir. 1961).

33. Many experienced taxpayer representatives think this is happening more frequently, as a result of shrinking budgets curtailing the training IRS agents receive.

34. Under the 1998 Reform Act, IRS agents can lose their jobs if they violate IRS rules and regulations for the purpose of retaliating against or harassing a taxpayer or taxpayer's representative. *See* Act § 1203(b)(6) (not codified).

B. Extending the Statute of Limitations

A frequent and difficult decision involves the statute of limitations ("SOL") on assessment. The SOL is discussed in detail in Chapter 5, but some discussion of it is appropriate here because of the important choices it entails.

Under section 6501(a), the normal SOL period—the period within which the IRS must assess tax—is three years from the later of when the return was filed or was due. This period is extended or suspended under a number of conditions, including, under section 6501(c)(4), the execution by the taxpayer and the IRS of an agreement extending the SOL.

If an examination or Appeals Office consideration is underway but completion is not imminent and only a few months remain in the SOL period, agents are supposed to request that the taxpayer voluntarily agree to extend the SOL. The taxpayer must then decide whether to execute an extension.[35]

It seems counterintuitive to voluntarily enter into an agreement giving the IRS more time to examine the return. However, tax practitioners frequently recommend agreeing to the extension. This is because of burden of proof matters and the cost of resolving matters in court versus doing so administratively.

If the taxpayer does not consent to the extension, the agent is supposed to issue a Notice of Deficiency based on the information developed to that point. The result may well be an inflated amount of deficiency. Once adjustments are included in a notice of deficiency, the taxpayer usually must overcome the presumption of correctness that attaches to the IRS's determination.[36] This may be difficult, and it can be expensive if trial occurs. It is sometimes better to sign an extension and give the agent more time to examine the return, anticipating that the agent will narrow the issues rather than expand them. This is particularly true when the taxpayer is confident the return under examination is, by and large, correct.

If the taxpayer agrees to extend the SOL, the next choice is whether to use Form 872 or Form 872-A. Form 872 is referred to as a "closed-ended" or "fixed period" extension. It extends the SOL to a future date certain. If additional extensions are necessary, another form or forms must be executed by the taxpayer and the IRS. Form 872-A, on the other hand, is an "open-ended" extension. It extends the SOL until 90 days after either the IRS or the taxpayer takes certain actions. If no such action is taken, the SOL extends indefinitely. Either the taxpayer or the IRS can unilaterally terminate the extension at any time.

If the taxpayer is willing to extend the SOL only for some issues, the taxpayer and the IRS can execute a "restricted consent."[37] However, the IRS may be reluctant to

---

35. The IRS is required to give the taxpayer written notice of the right to refuse to execute the consent and the right to limit a consent to specified issues or a specified period of time. IRC §6501(c)(4)(B).

36. *E.g.*, Welch v. Helvering, 290 U.S. 111 (1933).

37. The restricted consent must contain the statement: "The amount of any deficiency assessment is to be limited to that resulting from any adjustment to (description of the area(s) of consideration) including any consequential changes to other items based on such adjustment."

agree to a restricted consent since doing so could preclude the Service from making valid adjustments the agent might later discover.

VI. IRS Information Gathering

Audits are about facts. The taxpayer presumably knows the facts that underlie his tax return positions. The IRS needs to learn enough of the facts to confirm or to correct those return positions.

The IRS can develop facts through three main sources: the taxpayer himself, third parties knowledgeable about the particular transactions, and relevant sources of general information. These sources are discussed below. Also discussed below are the special tools for gathering information abroad and the defenses and protections available to taxpayers and others against IRS information gathering.

A. Information from the Taxpayer

Whether the examination is by letter or in person, the audit will begin with the IRS identifying the issues to be explored and requesting the taxpayer to produce the documents or other information relevant to those issues. If the taxpayer refuses or procrastinates, the IRS agent may give the taxpayer a Form 4564 Information Document Request ("IDR"). IDRs should not be used to force a taxpayer to create documents not already in existence.[38]

IRS policy and training emphasize best practices in information gathering. Large case agents are instructed that IDRs must be issue focused, that is, the agent must identify and state the issue that caused the IDR to be issued. Moreover, the agent must discuss the IDR with the taxpayer before issuing it, and the parties must determine a reasonable timeframe for response. The goal is to make the IDR process more efficient, reducing the need to enforce the IDR through a summons. However, the IRS has indicated its intention to issue summonses more often, and seek their judicial enforcement more often, if the taxpayer ignores a best-practices IDR.[39]

If the production still is not forthcoming, the agent may simply process the case based on the information at hand. The taxpayer typically bears the burden of proof in civil tax litigation, particularly when the taxpayer fails to honor IRS requests for information.[40] If the taxpayer fails to provide the requested information in support of claimed deductions, the agent may reduce or wholly disallow those deductions.

---

38. Nor may IRS summonses force a taxpayer to do so. *E.g.*, United States v. Davey, 543 F.2d 996, 1000 (2d Cir. 1976); IRM 25.5.4.2.1 (1).

39. LB&I-04-0613-004 (June 18, 2013) (affecting IRM 4.46.4).

40. IRC § 7491(a)(2); *see* Steve R. Johnson, *The Dangers of Symbolic Legislation: Perceptions and Realities of the New Burden-of-Proof Rules*, 84 Iowa L. Rev. 413 (1999).

However, when the stakes are high or when the adjustment involves underreporting of income rather than exaggeration of deductions,[41] the IRS may issue a summons to the taxpayer for the information sought. Sections 6201(a) and 7601(a) provide general authority to the IRS to make inquiries to ascertain tax liability. More specifically, under section 7602(a), the IRS is authorized to issue summonses to compel the taxpayer to produce "books, papers, records, or other data," to give testimony under oath, or both. The prospect of a summons lies behind all informal information requests by field agents. However, summonses are not issued in correspondence or office audits.

The summons must be served either by hand-delivering an attested copy to the taxpayer or by leaving an attested copy at the taxpayer's residence. When documents or data are sought, they must be described in the summons "with reasonable certainty."[42]

The attorney should impress upon his client the importance of taking seriously any contact with the IRS, particularly a summons. Potentially damaging documents need to be produced if the IRS request, reasonably construed, calls for them. If the taxpayer lies to an IRS agent, that can be a felony under Code section 7207 or 18 U.S.C. section 1001. If the taxpayer destroys documents, that can be a crime under 18 U.S.C. sections 1503 and 1505. If the taxpayer's representative does the lying or destroying, the representative is also punishable under the above statutes.[43] If the taxpayer's representative helps the taxpayer in lying or destroying, the representative is punishable criminally under Code Section 7206(2), 18 U.S.C. sections 2 (aiding and abetting) or 18 U.S.C. section 371 (conspiracy). In addition to criminal considerations, taxpayers' representatives are under an ethical obligation not to mislead IRS personnel.[44] An attorney breaching that duty can be fined or censured, or can be suspended or disbarred from practicing before the IRS. That attorney may face discipline under state law as well.

The IRS summons is broad, but it is not self-enforcing. In the event of noncompliance with the summons, the IRS may ask the Department of Justice to file suit in District Court for enforcement of the summons.[45]

---

41. Although the ultimate burden of persuasion is on the taxpayer in unreported income cases, some courts have imposed a burden on the IRS to make an initial showing. *See, e.g.*, Bradford v. Commissioner, 796 F.2d 303, 305 (9th Cir. 1986).

42. IRC § 7603(a).

43. *See, e.g.*, United States v. Fern, 696 F.2d 1269 (11th Cir. 1983) (affirming conviction of accountant under 18 U.S.C. § 1001 for making false statement to IRS tax auditor).

44. *See, e.g.*, 31 C.F.R. § 10.22 (diligence as to accuracy); *see also id.* at §§ 10.20 (information to be furnished to IRS), 10.50-10.52 (sanctions for violations).

45. It might appear that the government could seek immediate contempt sanctions under section 7604(b) or could criminally prosecute under section 7210. However, some courts take the view that a summoned party may not be criminally prosecuted under section 7210 or be subject to contempt sanctions under section 7604(b) for failure to comply with an IRS summons until a federal court has issued an order enforcing the summons and the summoned party has failed to comply after reasonable opportunity to do so. Reisman v. Caplin, 375 U.S. 440 (1964); Schulz v. IRS, 413 F.3d 297 (2d Cir. 2005).

In fact, the IRS's most common response is to forgo enforcement—the resource expenditure often would be too great compared to the utility of the information sought. In addition, unlike a designated summons,[46] issuance of a regular summons to the taxpayer does not toll the statute of limitations on assessment. Thus, even "successful" summons enforcement litigation could result in the IRS receiving the desired information only after expiration of the limitations period. In addition, the very fact that the IRS issued a summons with which the taxpayer did not comply, will help the IRS persuade the Tax Court that it needs and deserves discovery should the case later be litigated.

The key case as to summons enforcement is the Supreme Court's *Powell* decision.[47] Under *Powell*, the government's affirmative case entails four elements: (i) the examination is being conducted for a legitimate purpose; (ii) the information sought may be relevant to that purpose; (iii) the IRS does not already possess the information; and (iv) the administrative steps required by the Code have been followed.[48]

If the revenue agent's affidavit accompanying the complaint establishes these elements to the satisfaction of the judge, the court will issue an order requiring the taxpayer to appear and show cause why the taxpayer should not be compelled to comply. The burden of going forward now shifts to the taxpayer to negate at least one of the four elements or to establish an affirmative defense. Defenses may include procedural matters (such as objections to the time and place for production called for in the summons) or substantive matters (such as objections that the taxpayer does not possess the documents sought and cannot readily obtain them, that the summons is overly broad and burdensome, that the summons was issued in bad faith,[49] or that the information sought is protected by a privilege).[50] In potentially criminal cases, the taxpayer may be able to invoke the Fifth Amendment privilege against self-incrimination.

Contesting a summons is difficult, both doctrinally and pragmatically. Doctrinally, affirmative defenses are construed narrowly, and the four *Powell* elements are construed liberally in the government's favor. For example, the courts have upheld IRS summonses for copies of the taxpayer's returns for prior years, rejecting the contention that, since the original returns had been filed with IRS service centers, the information was already

46. *See* IRC § 6503(j) (discussed in Chapter 5).

47. United States v. Powell, 379 U.S. 48 (1964).

48. See *United States v. Norwood*, 420 F.3d 888 (8th Cir. 2005), for a good discussion of the elements of and defenses to summons enforcement.

49. A taxpayer resisting a summons on the ground of bad faith on the part of the IRS is entitled to an evidentiary hearing only when she alleges specific facts plausibly raising an inference of improper motive. United States v. Clarke, 134 S. Ct. 2361 (2014). The fact that the IRS violated its own procedural rules in issuing the summons does not prevent enforcement unless the taxpayer can show bad faith by the IRS or harm or prejudice to the taxpayer. Adamowicz v. United States, 531 F.3d 151 (2d Cir. 2008).

50. In a case involving discovery under court rules, not an IRS summons, the Tax Court allowed the taxpayer to use the technique of predictive coding to separate discoverable from privileged documents, subject to subsequent right of the IRS to object if it finds the production to be incomplete. Dynamo Holdings Limited Partnership v. Commissioner, 143 T.C. 183 (2014).

in the IRS's possession. Nor does the fact that the IRS had previously seen, but not copied, the information mean that the information is already in the IRS's possession.[51]

Pragmatically, judges may reason that merely allowing the IRS to have information doesn't harm the taxpayer and that the trial judge will have the opportunity to prevent or cure any prejudice during trial of the merits. Moreover, the judge realizes that, if both sides have access to the facts, the case is more likely to be settled without the need for trial. The government wins the overwhelming majority of summons enforcement cases.[52]

One controversial area is issuing a summons to obtain tax accrual workpapers. Such workpapers are prepared by a corporation's financial auditors. They identify and evaluate questionable positions that may have been taken on the corporation's tax returns. They are prepared to ascertain the adequacy of the corporation's reserves for contingent tax liabilities for financial statement purposes. Given their nature, tax accrual workpapers are a virtual roadmap for an IRS audit of the corporation.

In general, the IRS summons can reach tax accrual workpapers.[53] In recent cases, taxpayers have argued attorney-client and work product privileges, with mixed results.[54] However, this issue has diminished in significance. The IRS has created attachments for the Form 1120 filed by corporations. Schedule M-3 and especially Schedule UTP (Uncertain Tax Positions) typically give the IRS the clues it desires, thus obviating the IRS's need to obtain the corporation's tax accrual workpapers.[55]

B. Information From Directly Knowledgeable Third Parties

The IRS often must seek information from third parties who have knowledge of the events and transactions relevant to the taxpayer's return. For instance, (i) the taxpayer may not have, or may claim not to have, some information that is material; (ii) the information supplied by the taxpayer may need to be corroborated; or (iii) information earlier supplied by the third party (such as W-2 or 1099 forms) may have been rebutted by the taxpayer, necessitating checking the information further with the third party.

Under section 6201(d), in a court proceeding involving an income adjustment based on an information return, the IRS often cannot rely solely on the information return. The IRS bears "the burden of producing reasonable and probative information" supporting the adjustment "in addition to such information return." This provision

51. United States v. Texas Heart Inst., 755 F.2d 469 (5th Cir. 1985).

52. *E.g.*, National Taxpayer Advocate 2006 Annual Report to Congress, Executive Summary 111-1 (Jan. 2007) (in 2005–2006, the government won 93 summons enforcement cases, taxpayers won three, and there were five split decisions).

53. United States v. Arthur Young & Co., 465 U.S. 805 (1984).

54. *Compare* Wells Fargo & Co. v. United States, 112 AFTR2d 5380 (D. Minn. 2013) (IRS victory), *with* United States v. Deloitte & Touche USA LLP, 610 F.3d 129 (D.C. Cir. 2010) (taxpayer victory).

55. *See* Charles Boynton *et al.*, *A First Look at Schedule M-3 Reporting and Schedule UTP*, Tax Notes, July 21, 2014, p. 253. Schedule UTP is discussed in Chapter 2. The IRS has broad authority to specify the information taxpayers must report on their returns. IRC §§ 6001 & 6011(a).

operates whenever the taxpayer "asserts a reasonable dispute" as to the adjustment and has "fully cooperated" with the IRS during the audit. This provision reflects the fact that W-2s and 1099s sometimes contain innocent errors. They also may intentionally overstate the payment(s) to the taxpayer, as when an employer wants to inflate section 162 deductions for wages paid and issues wrong W-2s that appear to support the overstatement.

Section 7434(a), which allows the person as to whom the false information return was filed (the employee in a W-2 case) to bring a civil action for damages against "any person [who] willfully files a fraudulent information return." Under section 7434(d), a copy of the complaint in such an action is to be filed with the IRS, so that the IRS can pursue its own remedies against the information reporter. Those remedies may be civil (as under section 6674) or criminal (as under section 7204).

Third parties usually comply with informal IRS information requests. The 1998 Reform Act added section 7602(c), under which the IRS generally may not contact third parties "without providing reasonable notice in advance to the taxpayer that contacts with persons other than the taxpayer may be made." The IRS routinely does that via a standardized notification. In addition, the IRS must periodically give the taxpayer a record of third parties contacted and also must provide that record upon the taxpayer's request.

It can be useful to the taxpayer to know with whom the IRS has talked. Nonetheless, section 7602(c) usually is of limited significance. It is a notification section only. It does not prevent the IRS from contacting anyone nor does it prevent the third party from providing information in response to the contact. Moreover, section 7602(c)(3) contains exceptions—consent, jeopardy to collection, prospect of reprisal, and criminal investigation—that permit the IRS to contact third parties without giving notice to the taxpayer.

In some cases, the IRS will have to issue a summons to the third party. The third party's refusal to comply with the informal request is an obvious instance. Other times, the third party may be willing to comply but fears being sued by the taxpayer. The third party may then ask the IRS agent to issue a so called "friendly summons," which provides suit protection under section 7609(i)(3).

In general, the enforceability of a third-party summons turns on many of the same factors as govern the enforceability of a summons to the taxpayer, including the *Powell* factors described above.[56] Special rules apply to third-party summonses. Previously, special rules applied only if the summoned person was a "third party recordkeeper" as defined by the statute. The 1998 Reform Act broadened section 7609 to apply to summonses to all third parties, save those identified in the exceptions in section 7609(c)(2), (f), and (g).

---

56. *See, e.g.*, United States v. Monumental Life Insurance Co., 440 F.3d 729 (6th Cir. 2006) (reversing the district court and denying enforcement of a third-party summons because the IRS already had many of the documents in its possession and because some of the documents were too far removed from the investigation to be relevant). The lengthy summons issued to the third party is reproduced at the end of *Monumental*. Students may find it instructive to read or skim the summons.

When the IRS issues a summons to a third party calling for testimony or production of documents or computer software source codes, section 7609(a) directs that the IRS notify the taxpayer of the third-party summons, provide a copy of the summons, and inform the taxpayer of the right of intervention. Notice must be given within three days of service of the summons and not less than twenty-three days before the date for compliance stated in the summons. Some deviation from these timing rules may be excused if the taxpayer is not actually prejudiced.[57]

Under section 7609(b), the taxpayer has twenty days to initiate a District Court proceeding to quash the summons. The summoned party may intervene in the taxpayer's suit. If the summoned party brings brought suit, the taxpayer has the right to intervene.

Under section 7609(d), the IRS may not examine the summoned documents (if received) until expiration of the twenty-day suit period or until conclusion of the proceeding (absent consent or court order). Under section 7609(e), the pendency of a proceeding to quash suspends the running of both the civil and criminal statutes of limitations.

The IRS sometimes suspects that a tax liability exists but does not know the identity of the taxpayer. A summons to a third party in this situation is known as a "John Doe" summons. Under section 7609(f), a John Doe summons cannot be issued unless the IRS obtains permission via an ex parte application to a federal District Court. The IRS's application must establish that (1) the summons relates to a tax investigation of a person or group of persons; (2) a reasonable basis exists for believing that the person or group may have failed to comply with the Code; and (3) the information the IRS seeks is not readily available from other sources.[58] A prominent recent example of the IRS's use of this tool is its issuance of John Doe summonses to financial institutions as part of an investigation of unidentified taxpayers who may have used offshore credit cards or bank accounts to evade U.S. income tax.

C. General Information

Sometimes taxpayer-specific information is unavailable or incomplete. In those situations, the IRS may seek general information.

For example, in unreported income cases, the IRS often must endeavor to approximate the taxpayer's income through indirect methods. Under the expenditures method, the IRS estimates what the taxpayer spent during the tax period at issue. The premise is that such expenditures, to the extent they exceed non-taxable sources of income, must have been defrayed by taxable income. Since it is rarely possible to

---

57. *See, e.g.*, Sylvestre v. United States, 978 F.2d 25 (1st Cir. 1992). Courts sometimes have held violation of the 23-day requirement to be fatal to the summons. However, based on "harmless error" analysis, most decisions are to the contrary. *See* Jewell v. United States, 749 F.3d 1295 (10th Cir. 2014).

58. *E.g.*, In re Tax Liabilities of: John Does, 96 AFTR 2d 6656 (N.D.N.Y. 2005) (summons to ascertain the identities of holders of putatively tax-exempt bonds issued by the City of New Orleans).

ascertain how much the taxpayer actually spent on food, entertainment, etc., the IRS often relies for this part of the expenditures calculation on average living standard/living costs statistics compiled and published by the Bureau of Labor Statistics. Under section 7491(b), the IRS bears the burden of proof "with respect to any item of income which was reconstructed by the [IRS] solely through the use of statistical information on unrelated taxpayers." Typically, the IRS does not depend on BLS statistics "solely," but uses them as only one element of the reconstruction.

Another indirect method—one used for approximating business receipts—is the "percentage mark-up" method. The IRS determines the taxpayer's likely mark-up for the tax year(s) in question through a combination of factors. They include the taxpayer's own markup in other years (if that can be ascertained), mark-ups used by similar companies in the area, and industry-wide average mark-ups. By combining the estimated mark-up with the taxpayer's volume of sales, the taxpayer's receipts can be approximated.

D. International Information Gathering

United States persons doing business abroad may have to pay U.S. tax with respect to their earnings abroad,[59] and foreign persons doing business here may be subject to U.S. tax on their U.S.-source earnings.[60] Full discussion of information gathering in the transnational context is beyond the scope of this book. The main points are sketched below.

The task of gathering information as to international transactions can be quite challenging. A multinational enterprise may keep records in a number of locations; complex corporate ownership and affiliation arrangements may blur lines of control; and some foreign jurisdictions have laws forbidding or limiting the disclosure of business records.

The IRS has three major sets of tools for gathering documentary and testimonial information from abroad as well as a number of lesser tools. One major set involves FATCA and other reporting requirements described in Chapter 2.

A second important device is the administrative summons. If a company or a financial institution has a branch in the United States, the IRS may serve a summons on it calling for information the company or financial institution has anywhere, that is, information held by the foreign branches as well as information held by the U.S. branch. Such summonses are subject to the rules discussed above governing summonses generally, with some modifications to reflect jurisdiction and international comity.[61]

---

59. The United States generally imposes income tax on the worldwide income of its citizens and resident aliens, and the constitutionality of this practice has been upheld. *E.g.*, Cook v. Tait, 265 U.S. 47 (1924).

60. *See, e.g.*, IRC §§ 871, 881.

61. *See, e.g.*, United States v. Bank of Nova Scotia, 691 F.2d 1384 (11th Cir. 1982), *cert. denied*, 462 U.S. 1119 (1983), *further proceedings*, 722 F.2d 657 (11th Cir. 1983), *appeal after remand*, 740 F.2d 817 (11th Cir. 1984), *cert. denied*, 469 U.S. 1106 (1985).

A major battleground has been use of John Doe summonses served on multinational banks and other financial institutions to discover bank, credit card, and other accounts held abroad by Americans, income with respect to which was not being reported on the Americans' tax returns. This evolved into a multi-prong effort including as well Overseas Voluntary Disclosure Initiatives, whistleblower reports, criminal prosecutions, Deferred (Non) Prosecution Agreements imposing heavy fines and revised procedures on foreign banks assisting Americans to evade U.S. taxes, and agreements with other countries.[62] Many of the battles—administrative, judicial, and diplomatic—have been fought with Swiss banks, and the IRS and DOJ are now targeting banks headquartered in other jurisdictions as well.

Third, the IRS may use "exchange of information" provisions under treaties and executive agreements. The United States has comprehensive bilateral tax treaties with about 70 other countries. Those treaties typically contain provisions for mutual administrative assistance, which can include help in gathering some kinds of information. In addition, the United States has tax information exchange agreements and mutual legal assistance treaties with a number of countries with whom we do not have comprehensive tax treaties. A multilateral agreement, the Hague Evidence Convention, also has proved useful to IRS information-gathering efforts in some instances.

Cross-border tax evasion is a problem shared by all economically substantial countries. This realization has prompted growing international revenue-enforcement cooperation that would have been unthinkable a generation ago.[63] Information exchange is a two-way street. If the IRS expects to receive information from foreign revenue authorities, it must be able to offer information to them in return. A regulation directing U.S. banks to furnish information to the IRS to be given to foreign revenue agencies survived judicial challenge.[64]

One of the lesser devices is the centuries-old device of letters rogatory, under which one government may ask a foreign government for help. The foreign government need not accede to the request, but often will for reasons of comity. Although this device is slow and uncertain, the IRS sometimes has prevailed upon foreign governments to take testimony under oath or to provide documents needed by the IRS.

Another lesser device is Code Section 982. It precludes a taxpayer from introducing at trial foreign evidence that the taxpayer did not produce to the IRS when requested. This has occasionally been useful to the IRS. However, the IRS's greater need usually is to obtain information, not to preclude its admission.

---

62. *See, e.g.*, Kathryn Keneally & Charles P. Rettig, *The End of an Era: The IRS Closes in on Offshore Bank Accounts*, J. Tax Prac. & Proc., Apr.–May 2009, p. 11.

63. For instance, the IRS is working with the United Kingdom's Her Majesty's Revenue and Customs and the Australian Tax Office to develop data on complex offshore structures used by wealthy individuals and companies to conceal assets. IRS Press Release, May 9, 2013 (07:19 EDT). In addition, the IRS has begun to do joint audits of some taxpayers with other countries' tax agencies.

64. Florida Bankers Ass'n v. U.S. Dep't of Treasury, 19 F. Supp. 3d 111 (D.D.C. 2014) (rejecting plaintiffs' procedural and substantive challenges), *vacated & remanded*, 799 F.3d 1065 (D.C. Cir. 2015) (holding that the Anti-Injunction Act barred suit), *cert. denied*, 84 U.S.L.W. 3429 (June 6, 2016).

Courts also may fashion remedies. For example, under some circumstances a court may direct a taxpayer subject to its jurisdiction to repatriate records or assets held abroad.[65] However, information is most useful to the IRS when it is available early, during audit, well in advance of litigation.

E. Taxpayer Protections and Defenses

Some protections available to taxpayers as the IRS gathers information have already been noted. Others include the following:

(1) Section 7605 contains rules dealing with time and place of examinations. Under section 7605(a), the time and place fixed by the IRS must be "reasonable under the circumstances." Under section 7605(b), taxpayers shall not "be subjected to unnecessary examination or investigation, and [generally] only one inspection of a taxpayer's books of account shall be made for each taxable year."

However, the "only one inspection" rule is of limited significance. First, by its terms, it does not prohibit a second examination, only second inspection of the taxpayer's "books of account," which is a narrow concept.[66] Second, even this limited stricture is fairly easily circumvented. For example, the IRS may be able plausibly to argue that its first inspection had not ended (merely gone on hiatus), thus that there was no second inspection, just a resumption of the first. Third, section 7605(b) states no remedy for violation, and courts have been reluctant to fashion a meaningful remedy.[67] Fourth, section 7605(b) provides that a second inspection may occur if the taxpayer so requests or the IRS "after investigation, notifies the taxpayer in writing that an additional inspection is necessary."[68]

(2) Section 7521 contains a number of rules as to IRS interviews of the taxpayer. Under section 7521(a), the taxpayer, upon advance request, may make an audio recording of any interview. The IRS also may record any interview as long as it gives the taxpayer prior notice and, if requested by the taxpayer, provides the taxpayer a copy (at the taxpayer's expense).

Under section 7521(b), the IRS is required, at or before the first meeting, to explain the audit process and the taxpayer's rights in it. If, during an interview (other than pursuant to a summons), the taxpayer expresses a desire to consult with a federally authorized advisor,[69] the interview must be suspended. Moreover, unless the taxpayer is directed to testify pursuant to a summons, the taxpayer need not personally meet with an IRS agent but may send an authorized representative instead.

---

65. *E.g.*, United States v. Ghidoni, 732 F.2d 814 (11th Cir. 1984), *cert. denied*, 469 U.S. 932 (1984).

66. *See, e.g.*, Benjamin v. Commissioner, 66 T.C. 1084, 1097–99 (1976), *aff'd*, 592 F.2d 1259 (5th Cir. 1979).

67. *See, e.g.*, Council of British Societies in Southern California v. United States, 42 A.F.T.R.2d 6014 (C.D. Cal. 1978) (denying § 7605(b) relief).

68. *See* Rev. Proc. 2005-32, 2005-2 C.B. 1206 (setting forth procedures for reopening examinations under section 7605).

69. Such an advisor is anyone authorized to practice before the IRS pursuant to the rules of Treasury Circular 230. IRC § 7525(a)(3)(A).

Under section 7602(d), the IRS may not issue a summons nor may it begin an action to enforce a summons after (i) the case been referred to the Department of Justice for criminal prosecution or (ii) a disclosure request has been made by Justice to the IRS.[70]

(4) Under section 7611, special restrictions apply to tax examinations and investigations involving churches.

(5) In proper cases, evidentiary privileges may be asserted against IRS information gathering, including summonses. Privileges may arise from the Constitution (such as the Fifth Amendment privilege against self-incrimination),[71] a statute (such as section 7525), or the common law (such as the attorney-client privilege and the work product doctrine).[72] Privileges were sharply controverted in the tax shelter wars.[73] Congress enacted section 7525 in 1998 to extend to taxpayer communications with non-attorney tax advisors the same protection as attaches under the attorney-client privilege to taxpayer communications to attorneys. However, the section 7525 privilege attaches only in noncriminal matters, and it does not attach to written communications regarding tax shelters.[74]

(6) The Internal Revenue Manual and IRS policies also provide taxpayer protections. Here are three examples. First, the IRS has a policy against repetitive audits of the same taxpayer, especially as to the same issues. The attorney should review the details of this policy whenever the client has been audited in the recent past. Second, although collectability usually is not considered at the audit stage, the Manual instructs agents to consider indicators of the taxpayer's financial weakness in deciding the scope and depth of the audit. Third, large corporations are audited every year. Over time, animosities (or excessive cordiality) may build up. To minimize this possibility, IRS policy limits the number of consecutive years that IRS examiners and specialists can be involved in audits of the same taxpayer.[75]

F. Whistleblower Awards

In 2006, Congress revised section 7623 to increase awards to third parties providing useful information on tax underreporting by substantial taxpayers (that is, taxpayers whose gross income exceeds $200,000 when the extra liabilities exceed $2 million). The award ranges between 15% and 30% of the additional amount collected by the IRS.[76]

---

70. *See* IRC §6103(h)(3)(B).

71. *See, e.g.*, Braswell v. United States, 487 U.S. 99 (1988).

72. *E.g.*, United States v. Rexworthy, 457 F.3d 590 (6th Cir. 2006).

73. *See generally* Martin J. McMahon, Jr. & Ira B. Shepherd, *Privilege and the Work Product Doctrine in Tax Cases*, 58 Tax Law. 405 (2005).

74. *See generally* Valero Energy Corp. v. United States, 569 F.3d 626 (7th Cir. 2009) (rejecting section 7525 defense); Countryside Limited Partnership v. Commissioner, 132 T.C. 347 (2009) (upholding section 7525 defense).

75. *See, e.g.*, *IRS Establishes Five-Year Duration on Continuous Audits of Taxpayers*, Tax Management Weekly Report, Dec. 4, 2006, at 1811.

76. IRC §7623(b).

The IRS reports to Congress each year on the program and posts the report on the IRS's website. In fiscal year 2014, the IRS received over 14,400 whistleblower claims; it made 101 awards, totaling $52 million. In fiscal year 2013, the comparable figures were about 10,500 claims, 122 awards, totaling $53 million.

Nonetheless, the path often is challenging for the whistleblower. (1) The IRS may choose not to act on the information. (2) The IRS may contend that it had information from independent sources, rendering the whistleblower's information superfluous. (3) A disappointed whistleblower may obtain judicial review but only if she files a Tax Court petition within 30 days after the IRS makes it determination.[77] (4) Typically, it takes five to seven years from the time the whistleblower submission is made for the IRS to analyze, investigate, and collect additional taxes. (5) Federal law provides little protection against retaliation whistleblowers may face.[78]

In short, the whistleblower program has not yet lived up to the hopes that accompanied it in 2006. Revisions will be needed to maximize its impact.[79]

VII. Information Gathering by the Taxpayer

At times, taxpayers must obtain information from the IRS. In litigation, the taxpayer has the same discovery options as the government plus the benefit of a few special devices authorized by the Code.[80] Our attention now, however, is on other taxpayer attempts to get information from the IRS.

A. Transaction Planning

Especially where the tax stakes are considerable and the law unclear, the taxpayer will need to carefully research the IRS's positions and practices. For the most part, this is comparatively easy now. The IRS discloses a great deal of information through the *Internal Revenue Bulletin*, rulings, memoranda, advisories, and the like which are released to and published by private companies. Freedom of Information litigation over several decades triggered disclosure of private letter rulings (redacted under section 6110(c) to excise the requesting taxpayer's identity and some other information),

77. IRC § 7623(b)(4); *see, e.g.*, Friedland v. Commissioner, T.C. Memo. 2011-90 (dismissing petition filed outside the 30-day window). Precisely what constitutes a "determination" for this purpose is less than fully settled. *See, e.g.*, Comparini v. Commissioner, 143 T.C. 274 (2014) (full-court reviewed).

78. For a proposal to strengthen such protection, see Joint Comm. on Taxation, *Description of Certain Revenue Proposals Contained in the President's Fiscal Year 2014 Budget Proposal* 175 (Dec. 2013).

79. For some proposals, see Joint Comm. on Taxation, *Description of Certain Revenue Proposals Contained in the President's Fiscal Year 2016 Budget Proposal* 276 (Sept. 2015); *see also* Treasury Inspector General for Tax Administration, *Deficiencies Exist in the Control and Timely Resolution of Whistleblower Claims* (2009).

80. *See, e.g.*, IRC § 6902(b) (special discovery rule for transferees in Tax Court cases). See Chapter 8 for discovery in Tax Court.

large portions of the Internal Revenue Manual, denials and revocations of tax exemptions, and many varieties of internal IRS memoranda.[81]

Nonetheless, taxpayers planning transactions sometimes need more detailed or current information than that which has been published. A private letter ruling request, as described in Chapter 1, sometimes is a good option. Sometimes, a telephone call to IRS Counsel's National Office will be productive. How does the practitioner know whom to call? IRS rulings identify the names and telephone numbers of personnel principally responsible for drafting them, and those who drafted topically relevant rulings are good starting contacts. Also, the IRS sometimes publishes lists of persons responsible for areas and their contact information. If the practitioner does not have the name of a particular IRS attorney, the inquiry can be directed to the relevant National Office unit. With patience and perseverance, the right person likely will be reached.[82]

B. Audit and Administrative Appeal

Taxpayer information gathering has a predictive purpose when done at the planning stage. The goal is to assess the likelihood of the IRS challenging the taxpayer's treatment of an item on a return. By the time the return is audited, the goal has shifted. The taxpayer has taken a return position, and, if the IRS challenges it, the objective now is to vindicate that position or at least to settle the dispute on acceptable terms.

Information gathering may be critical to achieving this objective. In some instances, the aim is to uncover facts not previously available to the taxpayer. In other instances, the quest is to locate prior IRS rulings, announcements, position papers, and the like which directly or inferentially support the taxpayer's return treatment. Discovery of such items might persuade the IRS to drop the matter or, at least, to refrain from asserting a penalty.

C. Means for Compelling Disclosure

1. FOIA

Congress enacted FOIA in 1966 as a way of opening the actions of federal agencies to the light of public scrutiny. Codified as 5 U.S.C. section 552, FOIA applies to

81. *See, e.g.*, Hawkes v. IRS, 467 F.2d 787 (6th Cir. 1972), *appeal after remand*, 507 F.2d 481 (6th Cir. 1974); Taxation with Representation Fund v. IRS, 485 F. Supp. 263 (D.D.C. 1980), *aff'd in part and remanded in part*, 646 F.2d 666 (D.C. Cir. 1981).

82. Calling the Chief Counsel's Office should be distinguished from the option, available to all taxpayers, of calling the IRS's toll-free number to ask substantive tax questions. The IRS's toll-free responders are not equipped to answer sophisticated questions. Indeed, they are of diminishing utility as to routine questions. The IRS, allegedly because of budget cuts, pulled resources away from taxpayer service. As a result, many callers cannot get through to responders at all or can do so only after inordinate delays, and the answers they receive are too often wrong. *See, e.g.*, IRS Data Book, 2015, at 47 (call and walk-in assistance events dropped from nearly 100 million in 2012 to around 60 million in 2015).

federal agencies generally, including the IRS.[83] Section 552(a) describes agency material that is subject to disclosure, and section 552(b) lists categories that are exempt from disclosure. Additional exclusions exist under section 552(c). Since subsection (a) is a broad principle of disclosure, the "action" in FOIA cases is at the level of the exemptions. The IRS must disclose information fairly within the taxpayer's FOIA request unless one of the exemptions applies. FOIA exemptions are narrowly construed in favor of disclosure.[84] The main exemptions in the tax context are section 552(b)(3), (5), and (7).

Exemption 3 permits non-disclosure of information which is specifically shielded by some other, non-FOIA statute. The major Code section declaring tax returns and tax return information to be confidential, section 6103, is such a statute for FOIA purposes.[85] Under section 6103(b)(2), tax return information includes all information collected to determine the taxpayer's liability.

Exemption 5 permits non-disclosure of internal agency memoranda which the agency could not be compelled to reveal via discovery in litigation. In essence, this reduces to whether a recognized evidentiary privilege applies. The IRS, no less than private parties, may assert the attorney-client privilege and the work product doctrine. In addition, IRS materials sometimes are covered by the governmental deliberative privilege—a limited privilege which protects predecisional, deliberative communications.[86]

Exemption 7 shields investigatory records compiled for civil or criminal law enforcement purposes. As examples, witness statements, memoranda revealing investigative techniques, and the identities of informants have been held protected.[87]

In addition to the statutory exceptions, the courts have limited FOIA requests when necessary to protect judicial process. Thus, "a FOIA request cannot be used as simply a way to get around the discovery rules, and limitations, of a civil action."[88]

2. Other Devices

Section 534(b) authorizes the IRS to notify a corporate taxpayer in writing that it contemplates making an accumulated earnings tax adjustment before issuing the statutory notice of deficiency. Such notification is routine since, under section 534(a), the IRS bears the burden of proof on the issue if it fails to give such notification.

---

83. *See generally* P. Stephen Gidiere III, The FOIA Information Manual (2d ed. 2013).

84. *See, e.g.*, Vaughn v. Rosen, 523 F.2d 1136 (D.C. Cir. 1975). A sampling of cases suggested that the IRS improperly withheld information sought under FOIA about 12% of the time. Treasury Inspector General for Tax Administration, *Fiscal Year 2015 Statutory Review of Compliance with the Freedom of Information Act* 4 (Sept. 18, 2015).

85. *See, e.g.*, Chamberlain v. Kurtz, 589 F.2d 827 (5th Cir.), *cert. denied*, 444 U.S. 842 (1979).

86. *See, e.g.*, Marriott Int'l Resorts, L.P. v. United States, 437 F.3d 1302 (Fed. Cir. 2006); Tax Analysts v. IRS, 416 F. Supp. 2d 119 (D.D.C. 2006).

87. *See, e.g.*, Barney v. IRS, 618 F.2d 1268 (8th Cir. 1980); Kanter v. IRS, 478 F. Supp. 552 (N.D. Ill. 1979).

88. United States v. Chrein, 368 F. Supp. 2d 278, 284 (S.D.N.Y. 2005).

Under section 7517, when the IRS makes a determination of the value of an asset for gift, estate, or generation-skipping transfer tax purposes, the IRS must furnish the taxpayer a written statement as to the determination. The statement must explain the basis of the valuation, set forth computations, and include any expert appraisal by or for the IRS. The statement is to be furnished within 45 days after the taxpayer requests it.

The Privacy Act was enacted in 1974 and is codified at 5 U.S.C. section 552a. The principal thrust of the Privacy Act is to stop unauthorized disclosure from federal agency files of personal information on individuals (not entities). The Privacy Act also allows individuals the right, upon request, to view the information on them in agency files. Access is not available to third-party records or internal agency documents in those files. Individual taxpayers might consider making Privacy Act requests for access to IRS files on them. If the information therein is inaccurate, the taxpayer can demand its correction.

As a practical matter, however, the Privacy Act adds little to the options available to taxpayers under FOIA. First, under 5 U.S.C. section 552a(b), access is unavailable as to "any information compiled in reasonable anticipation of a civil action proceeding." Second, under section 552a(k)(2), agencies are permitted to issue rules excluding access to categories of information, including investigatory materials compiled for law enforcement ends. The IRS has used this authority to exempt most information gathered on audit or during Appeals consideration. Third, section 7852(e) precludes use of the Privacy Act to attempt to revise the IRS's determination of "any tax, penalty, interest, fine, forfeiture, or other imposition or offense." Fourth, as the more specific section, section 6103 tends to control over the Privacy Act as to tax confidentiality.[89]

Some Appeals Officers are posted at the service centers. Most are dispersed among local offices. The great majority of taxpayers reside within a few hours of an Appeals Office. Because of specialized expertise, local workloads, or staffing problems, taxpayers may discover, to their surprise, that their cases have been assigned to less proximate offices. This is unusual but may be occurring with increasing frequency. In such cases, meetings sometimes are telephonic rather than in person.

The Appeals Office is a crucial part of our tax administration apparatus. The system could not function if the cases settled by Appeals instead proceeded to trial. At the start of the 2016 fiscal year, approximately 53,000 cases were pending in Appeals, comprised of 20,700 deficiency-type cases; 19,900 CDP cases (see Chapter 9); 3500 penalty abatement cases; 4200 offer-in-compromise cases; 1300 spousal relief cases; 1300 general industry cases; 400 coordinated industry cases; and 1700 cases involving matters such as interest abatement, CAP, professional responsibility, and miscellaneous penalties. In fiscal year 2015, Appeals received nearly 114,000 cases and closed nearly 118,000 cases.[90]

---

89. *See, e.g.*, Gardner v. United States, 213 F.3d 735 (D.C. Cir. 2000).

90. IRS Data Book, 2015, at 52.

VIII. Appeals Office Consideration

A. Paths to the Appeals Office

Our focus here is on Appeals' role in reviewing deficiency determinations.[91] A deficiency matter can reach Appeals through any of three routes: the traditional "undocketed" path, the early involvement path, and the docketed path.

1. Traditional Path

If the issues cannot be resolved at the audit stage, the examining agent will write up the proposed adjustments in a Revenue Agent's Report ("RAR"). That document is also called a Thirty-Day Letter because the taxpayer has thirty days from the issuance date to request Appeals consideration.

The thirty-day period can be extended. The IRS typically grants an additional thirty days, upon taxpayer request, unless a special circumstance is present. One special circumstance is imminent expiration of the statute of limitations on assessment. If the limitations period will expire within six months, the IRS will ask the taxpayer to execute a consent extending the limitations period. The IRS is disinclined to extend the thirty-day period beyond an additional thirty days unless the taxpayer advances a strong justification.

The taxpayer invokes Appeals' jurisdiction by filing a Protest. A Protest filed on the taxpayer's behalf by a representative should be accompanied by an executed Form 2848 Power of Attorney. The Protest sets out the taxpayer's view of the facts and the law. The IRS may reject an insufficiently explanatory Protest although this is rare. When the amount at issue in each tax period does not exceed $25,000, the taxpayer, in lieu of a Protest, can file a simple statement saying that Appeals consideration is desired.

A Protest is simply a letter sent to the IRS Area Director for the relevant operating division. No particular form is required. The contents the IRS expects in a Protest are described in Procedural Regulation section 601.106(f)(5) and in IRS Publications 5 "Your Appeal Rights and How To Prepare a Protest If You Don't Agree" and 556 "Examination of Returns, Appeal Rights, and Claims for Refund."

There are two schools of thought as to the Protest. Some attorneys believe that the taxpayer should submit the skimpiest Protest possible. The theory is that the taxpayer thereby preserves maximum space for maneuvering during the ensuing discussions. The other theory (which is more widely held) is that the Protest should be detailed and complete. The notion is that the taxpayer and her representative have greater credibility with the Appeals Office if they aren't perceived as trying to "hide the ball" or spring arguments "in ambush." In addition, there have been cases in which the Appeals Officer has conceded particular issues from the start of the discussion, having been persuaded as to them by a full and careful Protest.

---

91. See Chapter 8 for discussion of deficiency determinations and Chapter 13 for discussion of collection.

2. Early Involvement

The traditional path to Appeals consideration has been modified to permit earlier Appeals intervention. In the 1990s, the IRS created the Early Referral Program under which, in certain cases, Appeals could consider some issues while the revenue agent was still considering other issues. This has been broadened to make the Program available to all taxpayers.[92]

The IRS also created the Fast Track Settlement program, with the aim of concluding administrative appeal within 120 days.[93] Originally available to only LB&I taxpayers, the program has been expanded to include small businesses as well. The IRS also has established rapid-settlement mechanisms as part of its efforts to deal with corporate tax shelters.[94]

3. Docketed Cases

Under the traditional path, Appeals consideration occurs after audit but before litigation. However, a case may reach Appeals after Tax Court pleadings have been completed.

(1) The taxpayer may have done nothing after receiving the Thirty-Day Letter because of strategy or inadvertence. When no Protest is filed within the thirty days, the IRS issues a statutory Notice of Deficiency (Ninety-Day Letter). When a Tax Court petition contesting the statutory notice is filed, the normal practice of IRS Counsel is to refer the case to Appeals after the pleadings are complete unless there are reasons to believe that Appeals consideration would be unavailing. If Appeals cannot resolve the case, it is then returned to Counsel for trial preparation.

(2) The taxpayer may have requested Appeals consideration after audit but was properly denied it under established policies—for example, if too little time remained on the limitations period and the taxpayer refused to extend that period. In that event, IRS Counsel will refer the case to Appeals after close of the Tax Court pleadings. The statute of limitations is no longer a concern because, under section 6503(a), issuance of the statutory notice suspends the running of the limitations period.

(3) The taxpayer may have requested Appeals consideration but was improperly denied it before issuance of the statutory notice. This is not common, but it does happen. This is a particularly appropriate circumstance for post-pleadings Appeals consideration. It is settled that the improper initial denial of administrative appeal does not invalidate the statutory notice.[95]

(4) The taxpayer may have gone through Appeals after audit without being able to resolve the case there. Normally, in such instances, IRS Counsel begins trial prepa-

92. IRC § 7123(a); Rev. Proc. 99-28, 1999-2 C.B. 109.

93. Rev. Proc. 2003-40, 2003-25 I.R.B. 1044.

94. Announcement 2006-61, 2006-2 C.B. 390. 87 *See, e.g.*, Rev. Proc. 2002-67, 2002-2 C.B. 733.

95. *E.g.*, Luhring v. Glotzbach, 304 F.2d 560 (4th Cir. 1962). *See generally* Rev. Proc. 2016-22, 2016-15 I.R.B. 577 (Appeals procedures in docketed cases).

ration. However, if the taxpayer, Appeals, and Counsel agree that settlement potential still exists, the case nonetheless can return to Appeals.

Appeals usually settles about half of the docketed cases it receives. The docketed status imposes some urgency. The timing ultimately is in the hands of the Tax Court, not the parties. If the court calendars the case for trial, the parties must choose between further settlement efforts and trial preparation. The Tax Court often is receptive to continuance if the parties jointly represent that settlement would be probable with more time, but judges differ in their receptivity and one who assumes that a continuance will be granted proceeds at his peril.

4. Unavailability of Appeals Consideration

There are situations in which normal administrative appeal is foreclosed. Typically, these situations are ones in which appeal would be fruitless or could disrupt matters requiring special coordination. These include: (i) cases in which criminal prosecution has been recommended or is pending, (ii) tax protester cases, and (iii) cases which have been designated as litigation vehicles, where obtaining a precedent to govern a class of cases is more important than disposing of any given case in that class.

B. Appeals Procedures

When the taxpayer submits the Protest, it will receive initial review to determine whether the Protest is adequate for processing. The review also decides whether, in light of the points raised by the Protest, the RAR should be modified, the case should be returned to the agent for further factual development, or the opinion of Counsel should be sought on legal questions.

Once a case has been accepted by Appeals, that office will contact the taxpayer or taxpayer's representative, scheduling a conference. The general view among experienced tax attorneys is that the representative usually should attend the conference without the taxpayer. At the conference, the taxpayer's representative and the Appeals Officer exchange their views of the facts and the law. Since the purpose of the conference is settlement, under Federal Rule of Evidence 408, their remarks during the conference should not be admissible as evidence if the case must be tried.

Appeals conferences are conducted informally. Testimony is not taken under oath, and transcripts are not made. Under section 7521, the taxpayer may record the meetings, in which case the Appeals Office will do so as well. The rules of evidence do not apply. Theoretically, potential evidence problems would be part of each side's hazards of litigation calculus. However, as a practical matter, such problems rarely loom large in Appeals discussions.

Especially in non-docketed cases in which the taxpayer is prepared to extend the statute of limitations, Appeals consideration may stretch over months. A case becomes "over age" under Appeals guidelines after a year. If new facts or law develop, the taxpayer should supplement the protest with additional memoranda or letters.

The 1998 Act prohibited Appeals Officers from engaging in *ex parte* communications with other IRS personnel.[96] In general, this provision has produced more friction and wasted motion than genuine taxpayer protection, but it may be of use in some situations.

Responding to criticisms of its impartiality and independence, Appeals has announced its Appeals Judicial Approach and Culture ("AJAC"), under which Appeals Officers (1) are to be less involved in developing information (instead deciding on whatever information is presented to them), (2) are discouraged from raising new issues, and (3) in some situations, should require more time before expiration of the statute of limitations on assessment as a condition of accepting a case.[97]

Unless Appeals is persuaded to concede the case, it will expect the taxpayer to make a settlement offer. If that offer is unacceptable, Appeals may make a counter-offer. The offer must reflect the merits, and "nuisance value" typically is disregarded. Many Appeals Officers follow an "80/20" approach. That is, if Appeals believes the IRS has an over 80% chance of prevailing on a given issue, it will expect the taxpayer to concede that issue in full. If Appeals believes the IRS has an under 20% chance of prevailing, it will concede the issue in full.

If Appeals' evaluation puts the issue in the range between 20% and 80%, it is empowered to settle the case on a basis reflecting the perceived "hazards of litigation." Examination agents theoretically do not have this power; they are supposed to "write up" each adjustment with merit that they find, even if hazards exist as to it. However, examination agents do engage in hazards-based settlement, in fact though not in name. They do so by trading issues. For example, when there are two potential audit adjustments with significant hazards for both sides, the agent may set up one, which the taxpayer will concede in return for the agent not setting up the other issue. Nonetheless, hazards-based settlement is more common at Appeals than at audit. Formerly, a common settlement strategy was to trade penalty issues for deficiency adjustments. In theory at least, Appeals has ended this practice. It will still settle penalty issues, but only on the merits and not by way of tradeoff.[98]

Settlement practice has been affected by the 1998 Reform Act. Under section 7430, the IRS may have to pay the taxpayer's reasonable professional fees and costs incurred during the administrative and judicial phases of a controversy. The 1998 legislation added section 7430(g) dealing with "qualified settlement offers" ("QSO"s). If the taxpayer makes a QSO which the IRS rejects, the taxpayer will be considered the prevailing party if the judgment ultimately entered in the case is for an amount equal to or less than the amount of the taxpayer's offer. The taxpayer will then be entitled to recover

96. IRS Restructuring & Reform Act of 1998, § 1001(a)(4), 112 Stat. 689; *see* Rev. Proc. 2012-18, 2012-10 I.R.B. 455 (updated rules re *ex parte* communications).

97. *See* SBSE-04-0714-0024 (July 9, 2014); AP-08-0714-0004 (July 2, 2014); AP-08-0713-03 (July 18, 2013).

98. Chief Counsel Notice CC-2004-036 (Sept. 22, 2004), *reproduced at* 2004 Tax Notes Today 1869.

fees and costs incurred after the QSO was made.[99] If litigation appears a possible outcome, the taxpayer should seriously consider whether to make a QSO.

Cases taken to Appeals usually are resolved there. Depending on the kind of case and the particular office, Appeals usually resolves 80% to 90% of the cases it takes, whether by full concession by the IRS, full concession by the taxpayer, or compromise.

If settlement appears to be unlikely through normal means, the taxpayer may consider ancillary procedures. If the taxpayer believes the Appeals Officer misunderstands the law, she may request the Officer to seek advice from the National Office via a TAM (described in Chapter 1) or less formally from the local IRS Counsel's Office.

Another approach would be to invoke alternative dispute resolution mechanisms created as adjuncts to Appeals consideration. The 1998 Reform Act created both arbitration and mediation routes. Section 7123(b)(2) directed the IRS to establish a pilot program under which the taxpayer and Appeals may jointly request binding arbitration. After several years of testing, and despite limited success during testing, the IRS formally established the Appeals Arbitration Program in 2006. In light of continued anemic results, however, Appeals eliminated its arbitration program in late 2015.[100]

Outside of the Appeals context, arbitration is making only limited inroads into tax controversy resolution. Tax Court Rule 124 permits voluntary binding arbitration in docketed cases, but it is rarely used. Also, arbitration provisions have been included in several tax treaties to which the United States is a party.

Mediation continues to be available. It can come early or late in the Appeals process. The Fast Track mediation program allows SB/SE, LB&I, and the taxpayers under their jurisdiction to mediate disputed issues, using an Appeals Officer as the mediator. Most disputes are resolved within sixty days, considerably faster than the regular Appeals process.

Section 7123(b)(1) directed the IRS to establish procedures under which the taxpayer or Appeals may request non-binding mediation of any issue unresolved at the conclusion of Appeals consideration. The IRS has established a mediation process in which the mediator may be an outside party or, more often, a specially trained Appeals Officer. Mediation is available as to most types of issues, factual or legal, regardless of amount. However, it is not available as to collection cases, docketed cases, cases designated as litigation vehicles, cases in which the taxpayer asserts frivolous issues or acts in bad faith, or cases in which mediation would be inconsistent with sound tax administration.[101]

---

99. *See generally* Reg. § 301.7430-7.

100. Rev. Proc. 2015-44, 2015-38 IRB 354. During the 14 years of its availability, only two cases were resolved through the Appeals arbitration program. *Id.* § 3.

101. Rev. Proc. 2014-63, 2014-53 I.R.B. 1014.

C. Whether to Seek Appeals Consideration

Taxpayers are not required to avail themselves of the Appeals Office. Most taxpayers choose to do so, and that often is the right choice. Nonetheless, the decision must be made on the circumstances of each case.

1. Possible Benefits

(1) The most important consideration is the prospect of resolving the case efficiently and on a satisfactory basis. As noted above, Appeals has a high resolution rate. Moreover, resolution at Appeals is usually faster and significantly less expensive than litigation.

(2) Appeals resolution may be more comprehensive. The Tax Court typically has jurisdiction only for those tax years as to which the IRS has asserted deficiencies and which are included in the petition. Appeals can take a more holistic approach. Via closing and collateral agreements, Appeals can settle items in related tax years or periods, such as those in which the same kind of issue arises and those which involve the multi-year effects of a single transaction. Similarly, Appeals can resolve matters involving parties transactionally related to the taxpayer, such as spouses, sellers and their buyers, transferors and their transferees, and fiduciaries and beneficiaries.

(3) Appeals involves less publicity than does litigation. Judicial proceedings typically are open to the public and may be covered by the media. Appeals proceedings are private and confidential, except insofar as settlement documents in docketed cases are incorporated into Tax Court decision documents.

(4) Appeals consideration often is necessary to the taxpayer's exhaustion of administrative remedies. As described more fully in Chapter 8, if the taxpayer ultimately prevails in litigation, she sometimes is able to receive from the IRS reimbursement of attorneys fees and costs under section 7430. However, under section 7430(b)(1), such reimbursement is possible only if the taxpayer exhausted administrative remedies available within the IRS, which includes the Appeals Office.

On the other end of the spectrum, if the taxpayer loses in the Tax Court, the court is authorized by section 6673 to impose an additional penalty on the taxpayer (or on the taxpayer's attorney) if the taxpayer's position was frivolous or the taxpayer instituted or maintained the action primarily for delay. Section 6673(a)(1)(c) lists the taxpayer's unreasonable failure "to pursue available administrative remedies" as an additional basis for imposition of the penalty. The Tax Court does not use failure to go through Appeals as an independently sufficient basis on which to impose section 6673 penalties, but it does consider such failure as part of an overall "facts and circumstances" section 6673 inquiry.

2. Possible Drawbacks

Despite the above benefits, there are times when Appeals consideration may be undesirable.

(1) Examining agents sometimes miss possible adjustments that may be larger or stronger than the ones they did set up. In such a circumstance, experienced coun-

sel in years gone by sometimes chose to forgo Appeals consideration before issuance of the statutory Notice of Deficiency and perhaps to forgo it entirely. The concern was that the Appeals Officer might raise the issue(s) the examining agent missed. Appeals Officers were discouraged from raising new issues unless they were substantial.[102] But, of course, it is precisely those adjustments about which taxpayer would be concerned.[103]

Taxpayers finding themselves in such a situation have several options, depending on the taxpayer's level of risk aversion and the magnitude and strength of both the adjustments that already have been raised and the as yet undiscovered adjustment(s). First, the taxpayer could just concede the adjustments that have been raised. As a matter of administrative realities, that would make it highly unlikely that the potential issue ever would surface.

Second, the taxpayer could default both the Thirty-Day Letter and the Ninety-Day Letter. The IRS would then assess the tax, and the taxpayer would pay it. Then, after the section 6501 limitations period for assessments had expired but before the section 6511 limitations period for seeking a refund expired, the taxpayer would file a refund claim with the IRS, then a refund suit if necessary. See Chapter 9. The taxpayer would contend in the claim and the suit that the adjustments reflected in the assessment were substantively unfounded. This could prompt the IRS to examine the whole return. In general, though, the IRS could use the new issue (even if found) only as an offset to the claimed refund and, because of the statute of limitations, could not use it as a basis for an additional assessment. Great care must be taken, however, to be sure that no exception to the statute of limitations on assessment applies.[104]

Third, if the taxpayer needs or wants to litigate in Tax Court, the strategy would be to default the Thirty-Day Letter, file a Tax Court petition contesting the Ninety-Day Letter, and go through Appeals in docketed status. If the Appeals Officer or the IRS Counsel attorney finds the new issue, it could be raised, but only via the IRS's answer or an amendment to the answer. The IRS would then bear the burden of proof on the new issue under Tax Court Rule 142(a). In contrast, if Appeals discovers the new issue during undocketed consideration, it would be included in the Ninety-Day Letter, with the result that the taxpayer likely would bear the burden of proof as to that issue during ensuing litigation. See Chapter 8.

(2) As noted previously, if the end of the limitations period on assessment is near, the taxpayer usually can get Appeals consideration in undocketed status only by con-

---

102. IRS Policy Statement 8-2; IRM 1.2.17.1.2.

103. Under the AJAC described above, Appeals is not supposed to raise new issues. The jury is still out on how rigorously this injunction will be followed. This drawback cannot yet be dismissed from consideration.

104. *See, e.g.*, Trans Mississippi Corp. v. United States, 494 F.2d 770 (5th Cir. 1974) (taxpayer brought a refund suit for $78,000 but wound up with an additional assessment exceeding $370,000; the new assessment was timely because of the fraud exception of § 6501(c)(1)). See Chapter 5 for discussion of the assessment statute of limitations.

senting to extend that period, which may be undesirable. Under section 7430(b)(1), refusal to grant such an extension is not tantamount to failure to exhaust administrative remedies.

(3) In some instances, Appeals Officers have little flexibility, little ability to settle on any basis short of concession by the taxpayer. For example, the issue may be an Appeals Coordinated Issue ("ACI"). These are issues (often CEP or ISP) as to which the IRS particularly desires nationwide uniformity of treatment. Proposed settlements must be approved by an ACI or ISP coordinator, who rarely permits deviation from the national settlement position. Or, the case may have been designated by IRS Counsel as a litigation vehicle. Or, the examining agent's adjustment may be supported by an extant TAM or revenue ruling.

In instances such as these, there may be little to hope for from Appeals. However, if the case contains other adjustments not subject to such strictures, Appeals consideration may still be worthwhile, to achieve resolution of those other adjustments, even if the controlled issue may have to be litigated.

IX. Conclusion of Examination or Administrative Appeal

A. No-Change Cases

If the examining agent accepts the return as filed, the IRS will issue a "no change" letter to the taxpayer. The letter is not precedential. If a similar issue arises as to another tax year, the no-change letter does not preclude the adjustment (although it may help to deflect a penalty). Nor is the letter binding even as to the tax period for which it was issued. Assuming other rules (like the statute of limitations) are not traduced, the IRS can reopen the period even after issuing a no-change letter. However, the IRS rarely reopens absent fraud, material misrepresentation, clear error in applying IRS positions, or other unusual condition.[105]

B. Agreed or Partly Agreed Cases

If the examining agent concludes that adjustments are appropriate and the taxpayer chooses not to contest their assessment (so called "agreed cases"), the IRS and the taxpayer will execute one of several forms. The most common are Forms 870, 870-AD, 866, and 906. The extent to which the parties are bound as to the tax period(s) in question depends on which form was executed.

The key provision in this regard is section 7121. Section 7121(a) authorizes the IRS to enter into written closing agreements as to a taxpayer's liability for any tax for any tax period. Section 7121(b) provides that such closing agreements are "final and

---

105. Proc. Reg. §601.105(j).

conclusive" and may not be reopened, set aside, or modified "except upon a showing of fraud or malfeasance, or misrepresentation of a material fact."[106]

The courts have held that only Forms 866 and 906 are closing agreements under section 7121.[107] Form 866 "Agreement as to Final Determination of Tax Liability" is used to close the total liability of the taxpayer for one or more tax periods ending prior to the date of the agreement. Form 906 "Closing Agreement as to Final Determination Covering Specific Matters" is partial. It is used to close one or several issues affecting the taxpayer's liability for prior tax periods and/or for subsequent periods. It is useful when there is a recurring issue or a transaction with multi-year effects, obviating the need to refight the same battles each year.

Forms 870, 870-AD, and their ilk are not closing agreements. They have effect only as their terms provide under contract, contract-like, or estoppel principles. Form 870 deals with income tax; Form 890 with estate tax; and similar forms with other types of taxes. They are waiver forms. By executing them, the taxpayer consents to the immediate assessment of the tax without further notification. Under sections 6211 through 6213, this has the effect of eliminating the opportunity for Tax Court review. Under section 6601(c), such execution suspends the running of interest on the liability for the period starting on the thirty-first day after the agreement and ending on the date the IRS makes notice and demand for payment. If there is an overpayment, the form operates as a claim for the refund or credit of it.

However, the 870 and its cognates do not foreclose further adjustment and dispute. Nothing on the forms prevents the IRS from asserting an additional deficiency for the covered period(s) (although this is not common) or prevents the taxpayer from filing a refund claim or suit. Indeed, the language of the forms expressly permits both additional assessments and refund claims.

Form 870 and its cognates are used at the audit level. Similar agreement reached at Appeals is memorialized on Forms 870-AD, 890-AD, and their ilk.[108] Their wording differs from the wording of Form 870 and its near kin. The 870-AD states that, if the IRS accepts the offer, "the case shall not be reopened in the absence of fraud." The IRS takes this language seriously. Some taxpayers, however, have filed refund claims even after executing 870-ADs, usually waiting to do so until after the limitations period on further assessment has expired. The courts are split on whether the 870-AD precludes a refund suit.[109] Even in circuits where the 870-AD is not itself preclusive, the IRS may be able to rely on some other doctrine of law to achieve the same result.[110]

---

106. For closing agreement procedures, see Proc. Reg. § 601.202; Rev. Proc. 68-16, 1968-1 C.B. 770, *modified by* Rev. Proc. 94-67, 1994-2 C.B. 800.

107. *See, e.g.*, Maloney v. Commissioner, 51 T.C. Memo. (CCH) 572 (1986) (Form 870 is not a binding closing agreement).

108. *See generally* IRM 8.8.1.

109. *Compare* Uinta Livestock Corp. v. United States, 355 F.2d 761 (10th Cir. 1966) (suit not precluded) *with* Kretchmar v. United States, 9 Cl. Ct. 191 (1985) (suit barred by doctrine of equitable estoppel).

110. In the Ninth Circuit, for example, "standing alone[, Form 870-AD] should not stop the executing taxpayer from seeking a refund." Whitney v. United States, 826 F.2d 896 (9th Cir. 1987). On

An assessment based on a closing agreement can be invalid if the taxpayer did not waive restrictions on assessment.[111] The IRS has developed procedures for securing such waivers in connection with closing agreements.[112]

The agreements discussed above may be supplemented by collateral agreements. A collateral agreement may address a matter not directly at issue but still appropriate for clarification, such as future year effects. Or, a collateral agreement may be with a related taxpayer, in order to forestall the possibility of the IRS being whipsawed by inconsistent positions. Whether to enter into a collateral agreement and on what terms always are matters of strategy and negotiation.

When Appeals settles a docketed case, the agreement will be memorialized in decision documents to be filed with the Tax Court. Theoretically, IRS Counsel may reject the settlement reached by Appeals and litigate the case or settle it on different terms, but this is exceedingly rare. Counsel and the taxpayer jointly execute the documents, and they are filed with the Tax Court. In the normal course, they are signed (stamped) by a Tax Court judge, and the stipulated terms become the decision of the court. Again it is theoretically possible for the court to refuse to accept the settlement, and again such refusal is exceedingly rare.

After a case is resolved administratively by execution of one of the forms described above, or after the parties' agreement in a docketed case is entered as a stipulated decision of the Tax Court, the mechanics enter their final phase. The deficiency, interest, and penalties, if any, will be assessed. Within a few months, the taxpayer will receive a bill from the relevant service center for the assessed amounts.

C. Unagreed Cases

If the examining agent and the taxpayer are unable to reach agreement fully resolving the case, the IRS will issue the Thirty-Day Letter. In cases subject to the deficiency procedures of sections 6211 through 6213, if the taxpayer fails to seek Appeals review, the IRS will then issue the Ninety-Day Letter, leading to the opportunity for Tax Court review described in Chapter 8.

If an undocketed case goes to Appeals and less-than-full resolution is achieved there, Appeals will prepare and issue the Ninety-Day Letter. If Appeals receives the case in docketed status and is unable to resolve it, the case is returned to IRS Counsel for trial preparation.

In cases not subject to the deficiency procedures, the IRS will directly assess whatever underpayment it believes exists. Thereafter, the taxpayer may pay the tax, file a refund claim, and institute refund litigation, as described in Chapter 9.

---

particular facts, the IRS concluded that neither equitable estoppel nor the duty of consistency, *see* Chapter 10, provided an alternative basis of preclusion. CCA 200738010. On different facts, they might.

111. Manko v. Commissioner, 126 T.C. 195 (2006).

112. Chief Counsel Notice CC-2006-017 (Aug. 17, 2006).

Problem

Will and Joan received a letter from the Internal Revenue Service in late 20x4 informing them that their joint federal income tax returns for the years 20x2 and 20x3 had been selected for an "office audit." Both returns included itemized deductions. The letter asked them to come to the office of the IRS at 10:00 A.M. on January 15, 20x5, to meet with B. Chops, Tax Auditor, and bring documentation in regard to the following items that were included in the returns:

- Charitable contribution deductions for 20x2 and 20x3.
- Casualty loss deduction for 20x2, including insurance recoveries in connection with the loss.
- Deduction for alimony paid by Will to a former spouse in both 20x2 and 20x3.
- Income reported on the 20x3 return for which no Form W-2 or Form 1099 was received by Will or Joan.
- Estimated taxes paid for 20x2 and 20x3.

1. Will and Joan have asked you to represent them in the examination. You have not provided legal services to them in the past. In fact, you've never even met them. You have scheduled a conference with them in your office for next week. Will and Joan would like P. Pusher, the accountant who prepared the returns, and M. Fund, their financial advisor, to attend the conference as well.

(a) What advice will you give them in advance of the conference?

(b) What will be your response to Will and Joan's request to have Pusher and Fund attend the conference with them. Why?

(c) What can you learn from the letter from the IRS?

(d) During the meeting, Will and Joan told you that Will plays in some high stakes poker games a few nights a week and has done quite well. In fact, his net winnings were $35,000 in 20x2 and $55,000 in 20x3, all in cash. Those winnings were not reported on their returns, however, because they thought cash was not taxable. What advice will you give them when you learn of this unreported income?

(e) What document will you need to represent Will and Joan before the IRS?

(f) What is the role of the Tax Auditor with respect to the facts? The law?

2. The meeting with Ms. Chops did not go well. In fact, she told you during the meeting that she will request additional documents. What will you expect to receive from Ms. Chops formalizing her request for the additional documents? What will be the likely result if you fail to comply with her request?

3. Shortly after the meeting, Ms. Chops informed you that she would like the taxpayers to agree to extend the statute of limitations.

(a) What procedure is used to accomplish the extension?

(b) Will you recommend the extension? Why or why not?

(c) What are the different documents the IRS might ask the taxpayers to sign in order to effectuate the extension of the statute of limitations? What are the advantages and disadvantages of each?

(d) By what date must the extension be effectuated for 20x2? For 20x3? What is the result if the extension is not effectuated timely?

4. You proposed a settlement to Ms. Chops pursuant to which the taxpayers would concede certain issues and the IRS would concede others. What procedure will be used to document the settlement in the event Ms. Chops accepts your proposal?

5. Unfortunately, your settlement proposal was not acceptable to Ms. Chops. As a result, she proposed a deficiency in tax, plus penalties and interest. Will and Joan feel there is merit to their case and would like to press further.

(a) What further opportunities are available for settlement with the Internal Revenue Service?

(b) What procedures must the taxpayers follow in order to avail themselves of those opportunities?

6. A conference was held soon thereafter with Appeals Officer S. Ment. Mr. Ment told you that he felt that there were not enough facts for him to evaluate one of the issues. He also discovered a new issue.

(a) What is likely to happen with respect to the underdeveloped issue?

(b) What is likely to happen with respect to the new issue?

7. What role will the strength of your legal arguments play in a proposed settlement at the Appels Office?

8. Notwithstanding your efforts, you were not able to agree on a settlement at the Appeals Office.

(a) What document will be issued by the Appeals Office to Will and Joan?

(b) What is the significance of that action?

Chapter 5

Assessment Procedures and Matters Relating to the Statutes of Limitations on Assessment

IRC:	§§6201; 6203; 6211–6213; 6501(a), (b)(1) & (3), (c), (d), (e); 6503(a); 7421(a); 7454(a); 7481(a), (b); 7485 (skim); 7502; 7503
Cases, etc.:	Colony, Inc. v. Commissioner, 357 U.S. 28 (1958); Barkett v. Commissioner, 143 T.C. 149 (2014); T.C. Rule 142(a), (b)
IRS Forms:	Skim 8275; 8275-R

I. Introduction

Before the IRS can start to collect taxes, penalties, and interest, it must post the amounts due in the Service's computer system. This process is called assessment. The government does not have an unlimited time to make an assessment. Generally, the IRS has three years from the date the taxpayer files a return to assess taxes it believes are due.[1] There are, however, many exceptions and circumstances that suspend or extend the limitation's period. The principal focus of this chapter is to explore the general rule and the exceptions[2] and to consider what happens if the IRS does not make an assessment timely. Along the way, you will learn to challenge a perceived untimely assessment.

The reason it is critical to know whether an assessment was made timely or not is that, unless one of the judicial or statutory rules overrides the statute of limitations

1. If the assessment is timely, the IRS has ten years from the date of assessment to collect the tax administratively. At the end of ten years, the statute of limitations (SOL) on collection expires (referred to as the Collection Statute Expiration Date (CSED)), unless the government takes appropriate judicial action to extend the collection period. Thus, without even considering exceptions that might extend either the Assessment Statute Expiration Date (ASED) or CSED, it is apparent that the IRS can be involved in a client's life for as much as thirteen years. The SOL relative to collection is discussed in Chapter 13. *See* IRM 25.6 *et seq.* for provisions relating to the SOL.

2. As one reads the Internal Revenue Code to identify the exceptions and circumstances causing suspension of the SOL on assessment, it is important to distinguish those sections that affect the ASED from those that affect the ten-year CSED. For example, the Code suspends the collection statute, but not the assessment statute, when offers in compromise (section 6331(k)(3)(B)), installment agreements (section 6331(k)(3)(B)), collection due process hearings (section 6330(e)(1)) and innocent spouse relief (section 6015(e)(2)) are requested.

(SOL)[3] an assessment made beyond the Assessment Statute Expiration Date (ASED) is void and uncollectible. This means that the taxpayer does not owe the tax and associated penalties and interest. In other words, the taxpayer enjoys a complete victory without ever having to litigate the merits of the tax return positions at issue.[4]

Whether an assessment has been made and the date it was done are significant for other reasons also.

- It represents the first step in the 10-year collection process that includes notices, liens and levies.
- It is the start of the 240-day period a taxpayer must wait before filing a petition in bankruptcy in order to be eligible for discharge of assessed income tax liabilities.[5]
- It is the date the tax lien comes into existence.[6]

Before proceeding with a discussion of the SOL on assessment, however, it is important to understand how assessments are made, what the different types of assessments are, and what constitutes an adequate return for purposes of starting the SOL clock.

II. How an Assessment Is Made

An assessment is nothing more than the recording of a tax debt due on the books of a taxing authority. It is similar to what businesses do every day when they enter an account receivable on their books and records for a sale made on credit.

Just as businesses first record sales and corresponding receivables before sending out statements of amounts owed, so too does the IRS assess the tax owed before making attempts to collect it. Without an assessment, any collection action by the Service is unlawful.

In the federal context, section 6203 of the Code and section 301.6203-1 of the Regulations establish the methodology for assessment. Mechanically, an assessment is made when a duly authorized IRS official (an assessment officer) signs a summary record of assessment[7] containing the following four elements: the identity of the tax-

---

3. *See* Chapter 10.

4. If the SOL has expired by the time an assessment is made or collection activity pursued, the taxpayer has an absolute right to the return of money collected subsequent thereto and to have any liens removed. IRC §§ 6325(b), 6401.

5. 11 U.S.C §§ 507(a)(8)(a)(ii), 523(a)(1)(A). *See* Chapter 13.

6. *See* Chapter 13.

7. Originally, the summary record was a Form 23-C; thus, tax professionals often refer to the assessment date as the "23-C date." More recently, the IRS uses a computer-generated RASC Report-006. Assessments are presumed to be correct. *E.g.*, Sullivan v. U.S., 618 F.2d 1001, 1008 (3d Cir. 1980). Nonetheless, courts sometimes invalidate assessments which are premature or otherwise defective. *See* William D. Elliott, *Tax Practice—Assessment Irregularities*, J. Tax Prac. & Proc., Aug.–Sept. 2010, p. 21 (discussing the cases).

payer, the type of tax, the tax period, and the amount assessed.[8] An assessment does not create a tax liability. Instead, its purpose is to enable collection of the tax.[9] Upon request, taxpayers are entitled to a copy of the record of assessment.[10] In practice, it is rare that one needs to see the record of assessment. Rather, a "transcript (or record) of the tax account information" usually provides one with the information needed, such as the dates and amounts of assessments, payments and lien filings.[11]

III. Types of Exceptions to the General Statute of Limitations Rule

There are three main types of assessments: (i) automatic or summary, (ii) deficiency, and (iii) jeopardy or termination. The different types of assessments are based principally on when in the tax process they are made and whether the IRS must comply with certain procedures before making them. However, regardless of the *type* of assessment, the *method* of recording it (as just described) is identical. As we will see, while any of the assessment types can run afoul of the SOL, disputes typically arise from deficiency assessments, as they take place later in the taxing process.

A. Summary or Automatic Assessments

Our tax system is primarily one of self-assessment. This means that taxpayers initially determine the amount of the assessment, either by filing a tax return or making a payment of tax. Since the taxpayer acknowledges the amount of the liability, the Code authorizes the government to automatically assess the liability without first having to comply with additional procedures to safeguard the taxpayer's rights.

Most of the situations that give rise to automatic assessments involve either self-assessment or common errors taxpayers make when self-assessing. These situations include:

(1) Taxes determined by the taxpayer on a filed return;[12]

(2) The amount of tax paid by the taxpayer;[13]

8. Reg. 301.6203-1; IRC §6203; *see* United States v. Galletti, 541 U.S. 114, 122 (2004).

9. For an insightful discussion of the nature and role of assessments, see *Principal Life Ins. Co. v. U.S.*, 95 Fed. Cl. 786, 790–92 (2010).

10. Regulation section 301.6203-1 states that "[i]f the taxpayer requests a copy of the record of assessment, he shall be furnished a copy of the pertinent parts of the assessment which set forth the name of the taxpayer, the date of assessment, the character of the liability assessed, the taxable period, if applicable, and the amounts assessed."

11. IRM 3.5.20.3.6. The request can be made telephonically or by sending the government a letter to that effect or checking the appropriate box on a Form 4506-T.

12. IRC §6201(a)(1).

13. IRC §6213(b)(4).

(3) The tax resulting from a mathematical or clerical error appearing on a taxpayer's return;[14] and

(4) Taxes and penalties the taxpayer consents to have assessed by completing a Waiver of Restrictions on Assessment.[15]

Automatic assessments are also permitted with respect to:

(1) Additional taxes and penalties the IRS asserts are due for which the deficiency procedures do not apply, (these primarily encompass employment and excise taxes and related penalties);[16] and

(2) Interest, even if it relates to a deficiency assessment, as it more closely resembles the cost of borrowing money than a tax liability.[17]

Summary assessments rarely run afoul of the ASED as most are made shortly after a return is filed, payment is received, or a waiver is executed. They must be made within the three-year period, unless one of the exceptions applies.

B. Deficiency Assessments

A deficiency assessment is one made with respect to *additional* income taxes, gift or estate taxes, or certain excise taxes the IRS determines are due. In the case of income taxes, this is the result of an increase in taxable income attributable to additional income or disallowed deductions or credits following an examination of the taxpayer's return.[18]

---

14. IRC §6213(b)(1), (g)(2). The Service must send the taxpayer notice of the error and of the right to request abatement of the assessment. If the taxpayer makes the request, the IRS is obligated to send a Notice of Deficiency so the taxpayer can petition the Tax Court for judicial review. Because math errors are common and taxpayers rarely seek to litigate them, Congress believed it was appropriate to permit assessment of the difference automatically and put the onus on the taxpayer to request a different procedure. *But see* Winter v. Commissioner, 135 T.C. 238 (2010) (holding that the Tax Court has deficiency jurisdiction over inconsistencies between S corporation returns and shareholder returns despite such inconsistencies being treated as math errors). For 2013 and 2014 individual income tax returns the IRS processed during 2015, "IRS sent almost 1.7 million notices to taxpayers for 2.2 million math errors identified on their returns." Math errors associated with calculation of income and other taxes (34%) and misreporting the number and amount of exemptions (24.8%) were the most common errors. IRS Data Book, 2016, Table 15.

15. IRC §6213(d). This is accomplished via one of the 870 forms, such as the Form 870, Form 870-AD, or Form 4549.

16. IRC §6201(e). The definition of a deficiency in section 6211(a) includes only income taxes, estate and gift taxes, and certain excise taxes. Automatic assessment of deficiencies of these taxes is prohibited. Also not permitted is automatic assessment of (i) the portion of late filing and late payment penalties that are calculated as a percentage of a deficiency and (ii) underestimated tax penalties if no return was filed for the taxable year. IRC §§6665(b), 6671(a).

Despite the fact there is no statutory prohibition to automatic assessment of other taxes the IRS determines are due, the IRS usually offers some level of administrative review before making the assessment. *See, e.g.*, Reg. §601.106.

17. IRC §6601(e).

18. *Id.* The deficiency procedures prior to assessment also apply to penalties calculated as a percentage of the deficiency, such as the accuracy-related penalty of section 6662, the fraud penalty of section 6663, and the portion of the late filing/late payment penalty so calculated. Interest, on the other hand, may be added to any assessed amount without formal process.

Because the IRS seeks to hold the taxpayer responsible for more tax than the person agreed to on the filed return and because there are no exigent circumstances that would justify jeopardy procedures, the taxpayer is provided something akin to due process rights, *i.e.*, notice and an opportunity to be heard in a court of law *prior* to assessment. As earlier stated, the government cannot exercise its substantial collection authority until it makes an assessment. Basically, what this means is that the taxpayer is entitled to a Notice of Deficiency and the right to review of the deficiency determination by the Tax Court before the assessment can be made.

How do these rights affect assessment? Unless the taxpayer executes a Form 870 (or a related form) agreeing to the automatic assessment of the deficiency,[19] section 6213(a) prohibits the IRS from assessing the proposed amount until these rights are afforded the taxpayer. Consequently, the government may not assess the asserted deficiency unless it properly mails a Notice of Deficiency to the taxpayer and, until expiration of:[20]

(i) The ninety-day period available to the taxpayer to petition the U.S. Tax Court, and

(ii) If a timely petition is filed by the taxpayer, until the decision of the U.S. Tax Court becomes final.[21]

Since an assessment of the deficiency happens late in the tax process, usually some number of months or even years after the return was filed, it is the type of assessment that most often gives rise to the question of whether the SOL expired before the assessment was made. Like all taxes, deficiencies must be assessed within the normal three-year period, unless one of the extensions or suspensions applies. While any of these exceptions or suspensions could apply to a deficiency, the one most often encountered is the suspension of the SOL upon issuance of a Notice of Deficiency found in section 6503.

C. Jeopardy or Termination Assessments

A jeopardy or termination assessment is an alternative way for the Service to assess and collect taxes. It is a significant collection tool used by the IRS when it believes col-

19. IRC § 6213(d).

20. If the IRS erroneously assesses the tax during the restricted period, the assessment is void and section 6213(a) allows the taxpayer to seek an injunction. This is one of the very few exceptions to IRC § 7421, the so-called Anti-Injunction Act.

21. IRC § 6213(a), (c). *See* IRC § 7481 for when the decision of the Tax Court becomes final. *See also* IRC §§ 7482(a)(3), 7485 (unless an appropriate amount of bond is posted, the IRS may assess the amount determined by the Tax Court even though the taxpayer appeals to a Circuit Court; however, the taxpayer need not have paid the assessment to be entitled to appellate review). To expedite the assessment of a deficiency agreed upon by the parties in a case before the U.S. Tax Court, the taxpayer can execute a Stipulated Settlement, which waives the restriction imposed on the Service to wait until the decision becomes final.

lection of the tax is in jeopardy.[22] For example, jeopardy action is appropriate if the IRS ascertains that a taxpayer is in the process of either transferring property out of the country or otherwise concealing it, which would leave nothing for the Service to attach. Under such exigent circumstances, sections 6851 and 6861 authorize the IRS to assess and collect the tax immediately. These sections provide that a Notice of Deficiency be given to the taxpayer *after* assessment and collection rather than before.[23]

While it is possible for the SOL to expire before a jeopardy assessment is made, it is rare because there are many levels of review within the Service before such assessments are entered. Rather, other issues tend to take center stage. Jeopardy and termination assessments are discussed in detail in Chapter 7.

IV. What Is an "Adequate Return" to Start the Statute of Limitations?

The SOL does not begin to run until the taxpayer files an "adequate return." Whether such a return has been filed is therefore very important. In order for a return to be adequate for this purpose, it must:

- Be signed under penalties of perjury,
- Be on the proper form,
- Be filed correctly, and
- Have sufficient information on it to allow the IRS to calculate tax liability and represent an honest and reasonable attempt by the taxpayer to satisfy the requirements of the tax law.[24]

A. Signed under Penalties of Perjury

In order for a return to be treated as adequate for purposes of starting the limitations period, it must be signed by the taxpayer under penalty of perjury.[25] A return

22. IRM 5.1.4.2.

23. IRM 5.1.4.3.4.

24. Beard v. Commissioner, 72 T.C. 766 (1984), *aff'd* 793 F.2d 139 (6th Cir. 1986); IRC § 6065. According to the IRS, a valid return is "a document that: (1) purports to be a return, (2) is executed under penalties of perjury, (3) reports sufficient data to calculate the tax liability, and (4) most importantly, constitutes an honest and reasonable attempt to satisfy the requirements of the law." CCA 200651015 (Dec. 22, 2006) (*citing* Beard v. Commissioner).

The bankruptcy courts have taken a slightly different approach when considering the dischargeability of income taxes, adding the requirement of timeliness. Bankruptcy Code § 523(a)(1)(B) requires the debtor to have filed a return. In the case of *In re McCoy*, the Fifth Circuit held that save for the narrow exception of IRC § 6020(a), a late filed 1040 can never qualify as a return. In re McCoy, 666 F.3d 924 (5th Cir. 2012). *See also* In re Justice, 817 F.3d 738 (11th Cir. 2016) (a return filed late after the IRS has already assessed the tax fails the last prong of the *Beard* analysis).

25. IRC § 6065.

sent to the IRS unsigned, or with the *jurat* "under penalties of perjury" crossed out or otherwise modified, is not a return for this or any other purpose.[26]

If a taxpayer has not filed a return within a reasonable time after the due date, the Service will send a notice requesting that the delinquent return be filed. If the taxpayer does not do so, the IRS will prepare a return pursuant to its authority under section 6020(b), with the proposed increase in taxes treated as a deficiency.[27]

This kind of return is called a Substitute for Return (SFR). It does not start the running of the SOL because it is missing the taxpayer's signature.[28] Despite the misleading language in section 6020(b)(2) that such a return is "prima facie good and sufficient for all purposes," a SFR is the equivalent of no return for SOL purposes. The SFR-generated deficiency must be assessed in the same manner as any other deficiency, but without the three-year SOL clock running, *i.e.*, because no return was filed by the taxpayer. The taxpayer can respond to the SFR by filing a return of his or her own making,[29] thus starting the SOL.

The section 6020(b) SFR also does not affect filing refund claims;[30] is not treated as an examination under section 7602;[31] does not affect the computation of a deficiency under section 6211(a); does not obviate the IRS's obligation to issue a Notice of Deficiency, does not deprive the taxpayer of the opportunity for Tax Court review;[32] and is not a return for purposes of bankruptcy discharge.[33] However, as described in Chapter 11A, a properly prepared SFR is a return for purposes of the section 6651(a)(2) late payment penalty.

B. Proper Form

To start the SOL, the document mailed must purport to be a return. The return should be on the official form (including authorized computer-generated forms) and not, for example, on a plain piece of paper or on a tampered form.

As a practical matter, filing on the correct form is rarely a problem as courts look to the good faith of the taxpayer to determine if an honest mistake was made. If an

26. IRC §§ 6061, 6064, 6065. Frequently, a taxpayer will have inadvertently failed to sign a return, only to have it sent back by the IRS. If that happens, the SOL does not begin to run until the return is refiled. Late filing penalties generally will be waived if the return is refiled with a signature within 30 days, as there is reasonable cause for the lateness.

27. Any deficiency resulting therefrom is entitled to deficiency procedures, since it represents an amount of tax in excess of that to which the taxpayer self-assessed. Spurlock v. Commissioner, 118 T.C. 155 (2002); CCA 200149032. (Oct. 22, 2001).

28. IRC § 6501(b)(3). The only information used by the Service as the basis for income and expenses when preparing a SFR is what is reported to it on Forms W-2, 1099, and the like.

29. SFRs are notoriously wrong because the IRS does not include any deductions, credits, exclusions or basis of sold property when it prepares the SFR. A taxpayer can usually reduce the amount of taxable income calculated on the SFR by filing his or her own return.

30. Healer v. Commissioner, 115 T.C. 316 (2000).

31. CCA 200518001 (Mar. 29, 2005).

32. Spurlock v. Commissioner, 118 T.C. 155 (2002).

33. 11 U.S.C. § 523(a). *See also* note 24 *supra*.

honest mistake was made, the return actually filed will be accepted for the return that should have been filed.[34] On the other hand, where a taxpayer alters the official form or uses homemade forms, the IRS may treat the form as not being in "substantial compliance" if there is insufficient data to calculate the tax liability, the line titles are altered, or the *jurat* is obliterated.[35]

C. Proper Filing

To be effective for SOL purposes, returns must be filed in an appropriate manner with the Service.[36] This can be by mail or by electronic submission. Depending on the type of return involved, the residence of the taxpayer or business and the method of submission, different rules apply for determining the correct IRS Service Center at which it should be filed. Mailing a return to the local office or handing it to an agent, while normally acceptable, may be treated as improper filing until it reaches the proper office.[37]

D. Sufficient Information to Calculate the Tax

When a taxpayer prepares a return in good faith and includes relevant items of income and expense, the return is adequate for SOL purposes even if there are mistakes on it. The test to determine if the return includes enough information is whether the return affords the IRS the ability to calculate *a* tax liability, not necessarily the *correct* tax liability.[38]

Whereas most taxpayers make an honest and genuine effort to satisfy the law, a group of persons sometimes referred to as "tax protesters" do not. These individuals use a plethora of techniques to avoid filing returns or avoid reporting income correctly. Some of the more common approaches they use are: (1) claiming that the Fifth Amendment provides them with complete protection against including anything at all on the return;[39] (2) placing zeroes or asterisks on each line

34. Knollwood Mem'l Gardens v. Commissioner, 46 T.C. 764 (1966) (taxpayer filed a Form 990 instead of a Form 1120, erroneously but honestly believing it was a tax-exempt organization). See IRC § 6501(g) for statutory exceptions.

35. CCA 200107035 (Jun. 16, 2001) (citing Badaracco v. Commissioner, 464 U.S. 386 (1984); Columbia Gas Sys., Inc. v. United States, 70 F.3d 1244 (Fed. Cir. 1995)).

36. IRC § 6091(b); Winnett v. Commissioner, 96 T.C. 802 (1991). Hand delivery is especially important with certain returns, such as estate and gift tax returns.

37. Dingman v. Commissioner, T.C. Memo. 2011-116 ("For a taxpayer to secure the benefit of a limitations period bar ... one such requirement is that a return be filed at the designated place of filing returns.") (citing Winnett v. Commissioner, 96 T.C. 802 (1991)).

38. Germantown Trust Co. v. Commissioner, 309 U.S. 304 (1940).

39. Some taxpayers fear completing the return, or portions of it, for justifiable reasons. If it can be established that the taxpayer has a legitimate reason to believe that the information supplied on the return might lead to criminal sanctions, courts are willing to grant a limited exception to the completeness requirement. For example, if the taxpayer were a drug dealer, it would be reasonable to be concerned that if income from the sale of illegal drugs is voluntarily reported, the admission could be used in a drug dealing prosecution. Therefore, it would be appropriate to claim the Fifth Amendment as to the source, but not the amount, of any illegal income. Note, however, that where

of the return;[40] or (3) asserting constitutional objections to the existence of the tax laws.[41] Taxpayers' creative reasons for not reporting income and paying taxes are limited only by their imaginations. Courts uniformly brush aside these frivolous justifications for not filing tax returns. Such "returns" normally also result in civil and criminal penalties.[42]

V. Statute of Limitations on Assessment — General Rule

Throughout the legal world, statutes of limitations are arbitrary deadlines meant to provide fairness to the parties by keeping old and stale matters from being litigated.[43] The same is true with respect to taxes.[44] Unless the SOL is extended or suspended, the last day the IRS may make a timely assessment is three years from the *later* of the return's filing date or its due date. In the case of income tax returns for individuals and C corporations, the due date is the 15th day of the fourth month after the end of the year, normally April 15th for individuals.[45]

A. Late Filed Returns

For a return filed after the due date, including any extensions that might have been granted, the assessment period runs three years from the date of filing. Consequently,

---

information on a return might subject a taxpayer to civil penalty only, the obligation to file a return complete in all respects cannot be avoided. *See, e.g.*, United States v. Josephberg, 562 F.3d 478 (2d Cir. 2009).

40. In re McKay, 430 B.R. 246 (Bankr. M.D. Fla. 2010); Coulton v. Commissioner, T.C. Memo. 2005-199.

41. United States v. Mosel, 738 F.2d 157 (6th Cir.1984); United States v. Rickman, 638 F.2d 182(10th Cir. 1980); United States v. Moore, 627 F.2d 830 (7th Cir. 1980). *Cf.* United States v. Long, 618 F.2d 74 (9th Cir. 1980).

42. In addition, under section 6702, tax protester returns are normally considered to be frivolous and not processible. This means that a $5,000 penalty is assessed according to section 6702(a), the SOL on assessment does not begin to run, and no interest accrues in the taxpayer's favor if a refund is justified. IRC § 6611(g). *See* Rev. Rul. 2005-17 to 2005-21, 2005-14 I.R.B. 817–824. The penalty applies to both (i) frivolous purported tax returns and (ii) frivolous CDP requests, installment agreement applications, offer in compromise applications, and taxpayer assistance order applications. IRC § 6702(a).

43. "Statutes of limitation sought to be applied to bar rights of the Government, must receive a strict construction in favor of the Government." E.I. DuPont de Nemours & Co. v. Davis, 264 U.S. 456, 462 (1924); *see also* Badaracco v. Commissioner, 464 U.S. 386, 392 (1984).

44. In the tax context, the SOL not only eliminates litigating old claims but also establishes a reasonable period during which taxpayers must keep records.

45. IRC § 6072(a). Where a husband and wife originally did not file a joint return but elect to do so later, sections 6013(b)(3) and (4) establish the date the joint return is deemed filed for purposes of the SOL on assessment and collection. In no event, shall it be less than one year from the date of the joint filing. Due dates for other returns are found in sections 6072 and 6075.

the SOL for a 20x1 individual income tax return filed on December 12, 20x3, would extend to December 12, 20x6.[46]

B. Early Returns

A return filed before the due date is deemed filed on the due date for SOL purposes.[47] Thus, the ASED for a 20x1 individual income tax return filed on February 25, 20x2, would be April 15, 20x5.

C. Due Date on Weekend or Holiday

If the due date for filing a tax return falls on a weekend or holiday, section 7503 extends it until the next business day. This modification of the due date gives taxpayers one or two extra days to file. For example, individual income tax returns for the 20x1 year would be due April 17, 20x2, if April 15, 20x2 was a Saturday.

Section 7503 does not affect the starting date from which the running of the SOL on assessment is measured, however. The traditional due date and the actual filing date are what control. For example, if a 20x1 return were filed on April 1, 20x2, the return would be deemed filed early and the Service would have only until April 15, 20x5, three years from the "regular" filing date, to assess, even if April 15, 20x2 was a Saturday. With respect to a return received by the Service on April 17, 20x2, the ASED of April 17, 20x5, is likewise unaffected by section 7503.[48]

D. The Mailbox (or Postmark) Rule of Section 7502

A return is normally considered filed when it is received by the IRS.[49] As discussed in Chapter 2, a different rule applies when a return is postmarked on or before the due date, but not received until after it.[50] Section 7502, which is the statutory em-

---

46. When computing time periods for tax purposes, the day on which the event happens is excluded. In re Moore, 359 B.R. 665 (Bankr. E.D. Tenn. 2006) (citing Burnet v. Willingham Loan & Trust Co., 282 U.S. 437, 439 (1931)). The counting begins with the next day. A month is a calendar month and a year is a calendar year. A year means a twelve-month period, regardless whether it contains 365 or 366 days. Rev. Rul. 72-42, 1972-1 C.B. 398.

For example, assume one wishes to determine certain time periods following July 17, 20x1. In all cases, July 18, 20x1, is day #1.

- Thirty days after July 17, 20x1, is August 16, 20x1.
- One month after July 17, 20x1, is August 17, 20x1.
- Ninety days after July 17, 20x1, is October 15, 20x1.
- Three months after July 17, 20x1, is October 17, 20x1.
- One year after July 17, 20x1, is July 17, 20x2.
- Three years after July 17, 20x1, is July 17, 20x4.

47. IRC §6501(b)(1).

48. Brown v. United States, 391 F.2d 653 (Ct. Cl. 1968); Rev. Rul. 81-269, 1981-2 C.B. 243.

49. First Charter Financial Corp. v. United States, 669 F.2d 1342 (9th Cir. 1982).

50. Estate of Mitchell v. Commissioner, 250 F.3d 696 (9th Cir. 2001) (section 7502 applies only when the return is received after the due date).

bodiment of the common law "mailbox rule,"[51] states that the U.S. Postmark date[52] "shall be deemed to be the date of delivery or the date of payment" when a timely mailed return is received by the government after its due date.[53]

The principal focus of the "timely-mailed is timely-filed" rule is to consider returns postmarked on or before the due date, but received after the due date as timely filed, thus avoiding the late filing penalty. But it also establishes the filing date for purposes of the running of the SOL. For example, if a 20x1 return is postmarked April 15, 20x2, and received by the IRS on April 18, 20x2, the postmark date would be deemed the filing date unless the postmark date is before the due date. An assessment on April 18, 20x5, three years from the date of receipt, would be untimely.[54]

E. Returns Filed Pursuant to an Extension to File

If a taxpayer requests an extension of time to file a tax return, all the rules discussed above, except the early return rule, apply with equal force. Thus, the three-year statute for a 20x0 return filed on July 17, 20x1, for which an extension was granted to October 15, 20x1, would expire on July 17, 20x4, not October 15, 20x4.

F. Amended Returns

The date the original return is filed establishes the starting date for the running of the SOL. Amended returns, *filed after the due date*,[55] do not affect the statute of

---

51. For a description of the common law mailbox rule and development of the law in this area, see *Maine Med. Center v. U.S.*, 675 F.3d 110, 114–16 (1st Cir. 2012). In some cases, the common law rule may be broader than section 7502. The circuits have been split as to whether section 7502 is exclusive, *i.e.*, whether the common law rule survived enactment of section 7502 or not. *See, e.g.*, Martinez v. United States, 101 Fed. Cl. 688, 692 (2012) (describing the circuit split). Reg. § 301.7502-1 supports the "section 7502 is exclusive" view. Hopefully, its promulgation will alleviate the judicial disagreement. There is a special "prison mailbox rule" for documents filed by inmates. *E.g.*, Hatch v. Commissioner, 364 Fed. Appx. 401 (10th Cir. 2010). Under this rule, timeliness is measured by the date the document is given to the prison officials for mailing.

52. Section 7502(f) treats delivery to certain "designated delivery services," such as FedEx, the same as delivery to the U.S. Post Office. In addition, with respect to returns e-filed, Reg. § 301.7502-1(d) provides that the timely-mailed/timely-filed rule applies as of the date an "authorized electronic return transmitter" electronically postmarks the return.

53. Taxpayers should be advised to mail their returns by certified or registered mail, return receipt requested, or its designated delivery service equivalent, as doing so provides proof of mailing and is prima facie evidence of delivery.

54. Pansier v. United States, 2011 U.S. Dist. LEXIS 45539. *See also* Hotel Equities Corp. v. Commissioner, 546 F.2d 725 (7th Cir. 1976). Section 7502 also applies if the due date for the tax return was extended to August 15, 20x2, and the return was placed in the mail on August 15th but not received until August 17th. However, section 7502 does not apply (and the regular "date-received is date-filed" rule applies) if, in the preceding example, the return was mailed July 10, 20x2, and received July 13, 20x2.

55. A corrected return filed before the due date is not treated as an amended return for SOL purposes. Instead, such a return is treated as a substitute return and replaces, rather than amends, the original. *E.g.*, Glenn v. Oertel Co., 97 F.2d 495 (6th Cir. 1938).

limitations.[56] In *Badaracco v. Commissioner*,[57] the taxpayer filed timely but fraudulent returns for the tax years 1965–1969. In 1971, he filed non-fraudulent amended returns and paid the additional taxes. Six years later, the Commissioner issued notices of deficiency for these years. The taxpayer argued that the amended returns started the running of the three-year statute and superseded the application of section 6501(c)(1), which allows assessment at any time in the case of a false or fraudulent return. The Supreme Court disagreed. "Nothing is present in the statute that can be construed to suspend its operation in the light of a fraudulent filer's subsequent repentant conduct. Neither is there anything in the wording of section 6501(a) that itself enables a taxpayer to reinstate the section's general 3-year limitations period by filing an amended return."[58]

G. Penalties and Interest

Penalties and interest are generally assessed and collected in the same manner as the underlying tax.[59] For example, if a certain tax can be assessed automatically, a penalty related to that tax can be assessed automatically also. This rule of symmetry between taxes and their associated penalties and interest extends to the SOL. Thus, if the SOL for a tax expires after three years, the SOL for assessing penalties and interest on that tax likewise expires after three years.[60]

VI. Exceptions to the General Statute of Limitations Rule

A. The Taxpayer Agreement/Waiver Exception

One of the most frequent reasons the SOL extends beyond the normal three years is because the taxpayer consents to its extension. This is accomplished by executing a Form 872 or 872-A (or one of its kin).[61] Extensions are available for all taxes, except

56. Though filing an amended return will not affect the ASED, it may still be wise to file it and pay the tax due for several reasons: it may be deemed a voluntary disclosure for criminal purposes (so long as the IRS has not yet begun its investigation); it may keep the IRS criminal investigative division away from the taxpayer; and, it may be treated as a "qualified amended return" resulting in the elimination of certain accuracy related penalties. *See* Reg. § 1.6664-2(c).

57. 464 U.S. 386 (1984). *See also* Potter v. Commissioner, T.C. Memo. 2014-18 ("Once a fraudulent return has been submitted, however, subsequent conduct, such as filing amended returns, does not purge the original fraudulent conduct.") (citing *Badaracco*, 464 U.S. at 393–94).

58. Badaracco, 464 U.S. at 393.

59. IRC §§ 6665(a), 6671, 6601(e)(1), 6601(g).

60. There is no SOL for assessing penalties under sections 6694(b) (a willful attempt in any manner to understate the liability for tax by a person who is an income tax return preparer), 6700 (promoting abusive tax shelters), and 6701 (aiding and abetting understatement of tax liability). IRM 20.1.6.21. There are special rules for the sections 6694(a) and 6695 penalties on return preparers in section 6696(d)(1).

61. IRC § 6501(c)(4); IRM 25.6.22.4.1. With respect to partnerships and S corporations, similar agreements are available.

estate taxes.[62] In order for the extension to be valid, both the taxpayer and the IRS must execute the extension agreement within the limitations period.[63] Once validly extended, the assessment SOL can be extended further in the same manner.

The IRS and the taxpayer sometimes disagree about the meaning of language in particular agreements. In the case of agreements that purport to extend the limitations period, courts typically conceptualize such agreements as unilateral waivers, not contracts. However, contract-like principles often are employed in construing the language of such agreements.[64] For example, a consent is invalid if the IRS coerced the taxpayer into signing it. The cases conflict as to what rises (or falls) to the level of coercion or duress for this purpose. One point of judicial dissension is whether the IRS's threatening to take an action it is legally empowered to take constitutes coercion.[65]

Chapter 4 contains a complete discussion of whether to extend the SOL and, if so, which form to sign.

B. The 25% Nonfraudulent Omission of Income Exception

Employing its authority under section 6501(e), the IRS occasionally will assert that a six-year SOL applies. The six-year SOL applies if a taxpayer omits gross income from the return, and the amount of the omission is greater than 25% of the amount of gross income reported on the return.[66] For the six-year statute to apply, it does not matter whether the omission was intentional, negligent, or accidental.[67] The determination is simply mathematical. Of course, if the omission was fraudulent, the unlimited SOL of section 6501(c) would apply instead.

1. Avoiding the Extended Statute of Limitations by Adequate Disclosure

Though determination of a 25% omission is initially mathematical, things in tax law are rarely that simple. The IRS is given the extra three years to make an assessment

---

62. IRC § 6501(c)(4). Because gift tax liability of a deceased individual becomes part of the deceased's estate, the personal representative cannot agree to extend the SOL for either the gift or estate tax. E-mail Advice ECC 200848060 (July 30, 2008), 2008 TNT 232-45.

63. If a taxpayer filed a Chapter 7 bankruptcy petition, the debtor, not the trustee, is the appropriate person to execute a waiver with respect to prepetition tax debts. ILM 200210032.

64. *See generally* John A. Townsend & Lawrence R. Jones, Jr., *Interpreting Consents to Extend the Statute of Limitations*, 98 Tax Notes Today 16–108 (Jan. 26, 1998) (concluding that "contrary to the consensus, the consent is a contract rather than a waiver and is governed by commonly understood and applied contract interpretation tools").

65. Robert W. Wood & Dashiell C. Shapiro, *Tax Payments and Waivers Voided by Duress*, Tax Notes, Feb. 10, 2014, at 671; *see, e.g.*, Shasta Strategic Inv. Fund, LLC v. United States, 2014 WL 3852416 (N.D. Cal. 2004) ("A finding of duress simply cannot reasonably arise from Agent Doerr's position as an agent of the IRS or the fact that the Service might pursue lawful IRS action, even one that might result in serious financial implications for the taxpayer.").

66. For estate and gift taxes, the 25% yardstick relates to items that were omitted from the gross estate or total gifts. IRC § 6501(e)(2). For excise taxes, the 25% omission is with respect to tax that should have been reported. IRC § 6501(e)(3).

67. Heckman v Commissioner, 788 F.3d 845 (8th Cir. 2015) (6 year SOL applies even if taxpayer made honest error and even if IRS had prior knowledge of the omission).

when a substantial amount of income has been omitted because discovering omitted income is more difficult and time-consuming than discovering mistakes in deductions and credits reported on the return.

However, if the taxpayer provided enough information on the return to inform the IRS that there might be an omission, the Service is no longer at a disadvantage. Thus, section 6501(e)(1)(B)(ii) states that an item will not be treated as omitted *for purposes of the 25% test*[68] "if such amount is disclosed in the return, or in a statement attached to the return, in a manner adequate to apprise the Secretary of the nature and amount of such item."

Proving adequate disclosure is the taxpayer's burden. The statute requires disclosure of both the nature and amount of the item omitted; it does not require disclosure of all the relevant facts affecting the item's treatment.[69] Each case is unique. Depending on how complicated and detailed the transaction involved was, different levels of disclosure are expected.[70]

The seminal case on what constitutes adequate disclosure is *Colony, Inc. v. Commissioner*.[71] In *Colony*, the taxpayer had understated the gross profit on the sales of certain lots of land as a result of having overstated its basis due to having included in its cost certain unallowable items of development expense. The Court held that since the return included the amount of income, though incorrect, and disclosed the source of the income, the IRS had sufficient notice (a "clue") to examine the income item and did not need the extra number of years to audit provided by the statute. Though the *Colony* decision preceded enactment of the present disclosure requirement in section 6501(e)(1)(B)(ii), the "clue" standard continues to apply, as the Supreme Court's decision in *United States v. Home Concrete & Supply, LLC*,[72] confirmed. In *Home Concrete*, the facts were quite similar to those in *Colony*. However, subsequent to *Colony*, Treasury promulgated regulation § 301.6501(e)-1(a)(1)(iii) that said "an understated amount of gross income resulting from an overstatement of unrecovered cost or other basis constitutes an omission from gross income." The government posited that its regulation should be granted deference as an agency's interpretation of an ambiguous statute. Citing its opinion in *Colony*, the Supreme Court disagreed that the statute was ambiguous and held the regulation invalid. While the Surface

68. While an adequately disclosed omission is not taken into account for purposes of section 6501 (e), it is, nevertheless, still part of the deficiency if the taxpayer cannot establish that the SOL has expired.

69. The disclosure required under section 6501(e)(1)(B)(ii) is not identical to the disclosure required to avoid certain accuracy-related penalties under section 6662(d)(2)(B)(ii)(I). Schmidt v. Commissioner, T.C. Memo. 1989-188 (holding the disclosure required under section 6501 is less than that required under section 6662, citing staff explanations accompanying the 1982 enactment of the predecessor of section 6662 in Tax Equity and Fiscal Responsibility Act of 1982 (TEFRA)).

70. *See, e.g.*, CC&F W. Operations, Ltd. Partnership v. Commissioner, T.C. Memo. 2000-286, *aff'd*, 273 F.3d 402 (1st Cir. 2001).

71. 357 U.S. 28 (1958).

72. 132 S. Ct. 1836 (2012).

Transportation and Veterans Health Care Choice Improvement Act of 2015 reversed *Home Concrete*, section 6501(e)(1)(B) now treats an overstatement of unrecovered cost or basis as an omission, and the basic thrust of *Colony* with respect to providing a "clue" is still valid.[73]

Where the omitted item of gross income on an individual's return relates to income of a flow-through entity, such as a partnership or S corporation, the question of adequate disclosure requires an examination of both the entity's and owner's returns. First, the entity's return must provide adequate disclosure of the omitted item or provide the necessary clue.[74] Second, the owner's Form 1040 must notify the IRS that he or she is an owner of the entity.[75]

2. Avoiding the Extended Statute of Limitations by Referencing the Definition of Gross Income

Gross income is the measuring stick for both what was included on the return and what was omitted. As used in section 6501(e), gross income generally has the same meaning as in section 61. Thus, gross income is not reduced by any deductions, including losses from a business or losses from property transactions, which are deductions above-the-line per section 62, or for any other expenses.[76]

The definitions of gross income in section 61 and section 6501(e) part company, however, with respect to how income from an activity that qualifies as a "trade or business" is treated.[77] Under section 61, gross income from a business is computed by reducing gross receipts by the cost of sales or services. For purposes of section 6501, however, section 6501(e)(1)(B)(i) says gross income has no such offset. In other words, with respect to businesses, "gross income" refers to gross receipts and sales with no reduction (*i.e.*, prior to diminution) for the cost of goods sold or services.[78]

---

73. Pub. L. 114-41 (July 31, 2015).

74. IRC § 702(c); Benderoff v. United States, 398 F.2d 132 (8th Cir. 1968). How the changes to the partnership audit rules affect this is yet to be determined. Pub. L. No. 114-74, Title XI, § 1101, 129 Stat. 625 (2015). Applicable to returns filed for partnership taxable years beginning after Dec. 31, 2017. *See* Chapter 6, Part B.

75. Reuter v. Commissioner, T.C. Memo. 1985-607. *See also* United States v. Lovlie, 2008 U.S. Dist. LEXIS 85458 (D. Minn. 2008) (rejecting the taxpayer's argument "that the IRS should have looked to Jan Lovlie's corporate tax return for the Lovlies' individual actual income.... The IRS cannot be required to extrapolate from a corporate tax return the income for the individual who owns that corporation."); Heckman v. Commissioner, T.C. Memo. 2014-131, *aff'd* 788 F.3d 845 (8th Cir. 2015) (neither alleged oral notice nor return of corporation owned by taxpayer constituted adequate disclosure).

76. CCA 200609024 (Jan. 18, 2006).

77. Connelly v. Commissioner, T.C. Memo. 1982-644. One should review section 61 to remind oneself what is included in the definition of gross income. Significantly, it only includes income from a business and gains from dealings in property. Expenses of a business or losses from dealings in property are "above-the-line" deductions per section 62, despite the way they are presented on the tax return for the IRS's convenience. In addition, gains from dealings in property mean that the adjusted basis and expenses of sale reduce the gross proceeds.

78. CCA 201023053 (June 11, 2010).

Example: Julius has gross receipts and costs from an activity, as follows:

Gross Receipts Reported on Return	Cost of Sales Reported on Return	Gross Receipts Omitted from Return	Cost of Sales Omitted from Return
$1,500,000	$1,200,000	$350,000	$250,000

If the activity does not rise to the level of a trade or business, the amount of gross income reported on the return is $300,000 ($1,500,000 less $1,200,000); gross income omitted is $100,000 ($350,000 less $250,000), or 33%. If the activity qualifies as a trade or business, the gross income (for this purpose, gross receipts without reduction for cost of sales) reported is $1,500,000 and the omission is $350,000, only 23%.

A few cases have sought to extend this rule of section 6501(e)(1)(B)(i) to sales of property by a business. In other words, the argument goes, when a business sells an asset, gross income stated and omitted should be computed based on the sales price without diminution for the cost of the property, *i.e.*, its basis. As one can see from the example above, this approach would oftentimes produce a better result for the taxpayer. Not surprisingly, the government has argued that this section only applies to sales of *goods*, not to sales of *investment assets,* with the result being that the section 61(a)(3) definition of gross income, *i.e.*, gains derived from dealings in property, is the correct measure. The government has been successful in these cases.[79]

In *Home Concrete*,[80] the government sought to use regulations it issued interpreting section 6501(e)(1)(B)(i) to exclude the cost of an asset, *i.e.*, its basis, from the determination of income that was omitted. As presented above, the Supreme Court followed the reasoning laid out in *Colony* that section 6015(e) required a literal "omission." The Court stated that "Congress intended overstatements of basis to fall outside the statute's scope."[81] In so doing, the Court rejected the validity of a regulation promulgated in 2010 that sought to interpret omission differently. In its view, "*Colony* has already interpreted the statute, and there is no longer any different construction that is consistent with Colony and available for adoption by the agency."[82] It is unclear whether these results will differ due to changes to section 6501(e) made by the Surface Transportation and Veterans Health Care Choice Improvement Act of 2015, which reversed *Home Concrete* and added section 6501(e)(1)(B) and now treats an overstatement of unrecovered cost or basis as an omission.[83] Since the changes to section 6501(e) did not affect subsection (1)(B)(i), it is possible it will have no effect.

79. Barkett v. Commissioner, 143 T.C. 149 (2014); Insulglass Corp. v. Commissioner, 84 T.C. 203 (1985).

80. 132 S. Ct. 1836 (2012). For discussion of the decision, *see* Steve R. Johnson, *After the Cheering, Problems*, 31 ABA Sec. of Tax'n News Q. 1 (Summer 2012); William J. Wilkins, *Implications of* Home Concrete, 31 ABA Sec. of Tax'n News Q. 25 (Summer 2012).

81. 132 S. Ct. at 1844 (citing *Colony*, 357 U.S. at 35–36).

82. 132 S. Ct. at 1843.

83. Pub. L. 114-41 (July 31, 2015).

As was true with respect to the disclosure (the clue) exception, flow-through entities in which the taxpayer has an ownership interest are treated as part of the taxpayer's return. The Code and a variety of cases hold that the taxpayer's pro-rata percentage of the gross receipts from the entity's business is added to both the "included" and "omitted" gross income calculations on the taxpayer's individual tax return.[84]

> *Example:* Assume the facts in the previous example, and that Julius also was a 10% partner in a partnership that reported gross receipts of $100,000,000. Assume further that the partnership did not omit any income on its return. According to the line of cases mentioned above, $10,000,000, 10% of the partnership income, would be added to Julius' reported income, bringing the total to $11,500,000. Therefore, before the six-year statute would apply, Julius would have had to omit more than $2,875,000 (25% of $11,500,000) from gross income on his individual return.

C. The Fraud Exception

If a taxpayer[85] files a tax return that is false or fraudulent with the intent to evade tax, no time limit is imposed on when assessment may occur.[86] The IRS can pursue the taxpayer at any time in the future.[87] The IRS has the burden of affirmatively plead-

---

84. IRC §§ 702(c) (partnerships), 1366(c) (S corporations); Roschuni v. Commissioner, 44 T.C. 80 (1965); Rev. Rul. 55-415, 1955-1 C.B. 412. *See also* Harlan v. Commissioner, 116 T.C. 31 (2001) (the rule applies to all partnerships, no matter what tier they are). *See* note 75 *supra*.

85. The IRS has also held that fraud committed by one's return preparer can affect the ASED. FSA 200126019 (Mar. 30, 2001). The limitations period is indefinitely extended under section 6501(c)(1) if a return is fraudulent, regardless of whether the fraud was committed by the taxpayer or the taxpayer's preparer. Allen v. Commissioner, 128 T.C. 37 (2007); *see* Bryan T. Camp, *Presumptions and Tax Return Preparer Fraud*, Tax Notes, July 14, 2008, p. 167; Bryan T. Camp, *Tax Return Preparer Fraud and the Assessment Statute of Limitations*, Tax Notes, Aug. 20, 2007, p. 687 (criticizing *Allen*). Subsequent cases have split. In one case, the Tax Court held that *Allen* applies when the preparer's motivation was to commit fraud against the IRS but does not apply when the preparer's motivation was to commit fraud against the client (by concealing the preparer's embezzlement). The Second Circuit reversed, however, and endorsed *Allen*. City Wide Transit, Inc. v. Commissioner, T.C. Memo. 2011-279, *rev'd*, 709 F.3d 102 (2d Cir. 2013).

In a later case, the Court of Federal Claims rejected *Allen* and held that only the taxpayer's fraud triggers section 6501(c)(1). BASR Partnership v. United States, 113 Fed. Cl. 181 (2013). The Federal Circuit affirmed the *BASR* decision at 795 F.3d 1338 (Fed. Cir. 2015). For discussion of *Allen*, *City Wide*, and *BASR*, see Bradley D. Kay, *Whether the Statutory Language of Code Sec. 6501(c)(1) Should be Amended*, J. Tax Prac. & Proc., Dec. 2013–Jan 2014 at 33; Bryan C. Skarlatos & Joseph Septimus, *Can an Innocent Taxpayer Be Subject to an Unlimited Statute of Limitations Because of the Return Preparer's Fraud?*, J. Tax Prac. & Proc., Dec. 2013–Jan. 2014, at 13.

86. What constitutes fraud and the defenses thereto for purposes of section 6501(c)(1) are the same as those that apply for criminal and civil fraud penalties under sections 6663 and 7201. A discussion of penalties is available in Chapter 11 of this text.

87. By contrast, if the taxpayer initially failed to file, even if with the intent to defraud, the subsequent filing of a correct return starts the normal three-year period to make an assessment. Rev. Rul. 79-178, 1979-1 C.B. 435 (a case where the taxpayer did not timely file an income tax return in a willful attempt to evade income tax but, after an IRS investigation began, filed a correct, but delinquent, return).

ing and proving the existence of fraud by "clear and convincing" evidence (rather than by a "preponderance of the evidence").[88] However, once the IRS meets its burden regarding the fraud, the normal rules apply as to the amount of the tax liability, *i.e.*, the taxpayer has the burden of overcoming the presumption of correctness that attaches to the deficiency determination of the IRS. The student is directed to Chapter 11, Part B, Section VI for a detailed discussion of what constitutes fraud.

D. Suspended Statute of Limitations Due to the Issuance of a Notice of Deficiency

As a matter of fairness and quasi-due process, the Code provides that before the IRS can assess additional tax, the taxpayer is entitled to a notice of the proposed deficiency, *i.e.*, the statutory Notice of Deficiency.[89] With this "ticket," the taxpayer has ninety days to petition the Tax Court for a hearing on the matter without first having to pay the proposed deficiency amount.

The IRS may not make an assessment at any time before the issuance of the notice of deficiency plus the expiration of the 90-day petition period and, if the taxpayer does timely petition the Tax Court, until the decision of the court becomes final. This being so, fairness dictates that this time should not be counted toward the government's three-year assessment period. Thus, section 6503 provides that the running of the SOL is suspended until either (i) the ninety-day period lapses and no petition is filed, or (ii) if a petition is filed, the decision of the court regarding liability becomes final. In addition, the IRS is given a sixty-day window after the expiration of the later of the preceding two events to take whatever assessment action is needed.

> *Example:* Carol filed her 20x1 Form 1040 timely on April 15, 20x2. On April 15, 20x5, the IRS mailed Carol a Notice of Deficiency as required by section 6212. The IRS may not assess the tax at any time earlier than July 15, 20x5, as Carol has the right to petition the Tax Court for a pre-assessment redetermination until July 14, 20x5.
>
> If Carol does not petition the Court within the allotted ninety days, the IRS then has sixty days, beginning July 15 and ending September 12, 20x5, to assess the deficiency. If, on the other hand, Carol timely petitions the court and the court's decision is entered November 7, 20x6, the IRS is precluded from assessing until February 5, 20x7, the day the decision became final. At that point, the sixty-day window begins to run, giving the IRS from February 6 to April 6, 20x7 to make a timely assessment.

---

88. IRC § 7454(a); Christians v. Commissioner, T.C. Memo. 2003-130. Once the IRS has met its burden to prove fraud for SOL purposes, it has automatically also met its burden for civil fraud purposes. If the fraudulent intent to evade was evidenced by the non-filing of a return rather than the fraudulent filing of a return, the unlimited nature of the SOL can be cut to three years from the first filing of a late correct return. Bennett v. Commissioner, 30 T.C. 114 (1958).

89. The taxpayer is entitled to these procedures under section 6211-6213. However, the taxpayer may waive the right to a notice and/or to filing a petition to the Tax Court by executing an appropriate form, like a Form 870, 4549, or 1902-B.

Example: Assume the same facts as above except that the IRS issued the Notice of Deficiency on March 31, 20x5, when fifteen days remained on the normal three-year SOL. Those fifteen days are added to the sixty-day window for assessment provided in section 6503. Thus, if Carol does not petition the Tax Court, the IRS's window for assessment would begin June 30, 20x5 (the day following the ninety days to petition) and end on September 12, 20x5 (75 days later).[90]

E. Other Frequent Exceptions/Suspensions

1. The Taxpayer Assistance Order (TAO)

In this era of substantive and procedural tax complexity, it is not uncommon for a taxpayer to find his or her wages unexpectedly levied by the IRS. This often creates a hardship for the taxpayer, such as being unable to pay rent or buy food. In such situations, the taxpayer may file a Form 911 (Application for a Taxpayer Assistance Order) asking the Taxpayer Advocate's office to intervene. Doing so suspends all limitations periods from the date the application is received by the Taxpayer Advocate until a decision is reached, plus whatever period is specified in the TAO.[91]

2. Bankruptcy

A debtor/taxpayer who files under Title 11 of the United States Code for bankruptcy relief is entitled to the benefits of the automatic stay provisions. Among other restrictions, prior to October 21, 1994, the IRS could not assess a tax debt until the automatic stay was lifted. Therefore, the SOL on assessment was suspended for the entire period of the stay, plus sixty days.[92] Currently, however, 11 U.S.C. section 362 (b)(9)(D) permits the IRS to assess outstanding taxes unrestricted by the automatic stay; consequently, section 6503(h) has little current significance.[93] *See* Chapter 13.

3. Third-Party Summons and Designated Summons

An extended statute of limitations might result where the IRS issues a John Doe summons or a third party summons for which the taxpayer is entitled to notice under section 7609.[94] If the taxpayer institutes, or intervenes in, a proceeding with respect to the enforcement of the summons, the SOL on assessment is suspended during the period of the proceeding and appeal regarding the summons.[95]

---

90. Aufleger v. Commissioner, 99 T.C. 109, 117–119 (1992).

91. IRC § 7811(d).

92. IRC § 6503(h).

93. *But see* Rev. Rul. 2003-80, 2003-2 C.B. 83 (IRC § 6503(h) has continued vitality in certain situations where the IRS issued a Notice of Deficiency).

94. Reg. § 301.7609-5; IRM 25.5.6.5.

95. IRC § 7609(e). However, to extend the SOL on assessment, the summons must have been issued to determine a deficiency and have a substantive tax purpose. A challenge to a summons issued for collection purposes only does not extend the SOL on assessment.

In addition, section 6503(j) gives the IRS the ability to issue a "designated summons"—no more than one per return—to a corporate taxpayer.[96] If the summons is challenged in court, the running of the SOL on assessment is suspended during the period of the challenge (or another stated period).[97]

4. Transferee Liability

The SOL for the assessment of taxes, interest, and penalties against transferees and fiduciaries, as provided in section 6901, is longer than that regarding the taxpayer. According to section 6901(c), the SOL is one year longer for each transferee than it is for the immediately preceding transferor, up to an additional three years. *See* Chapter 15.

5. Partnership Items

The statutory scheme for the audit and litigation of partnership tax items was revised by the enactment of the Tax Equity and Fiscal Responsibility Act (TEFRA) of 1982.[98] It created a single unified procedure for determining the tax treatment of all partnership items at the partnership level, rather than separately at the partner level.

Section 6229 provides that, except as otherwise provided in that section, such as fraud or a 25% omission of gross income on the partnership return, "the period for assessing any tax imposed by subtitle A with respect to any person which is attributable to any partnership item (or affected item) for a partnership taxable year shall not expire before the date which is 3 years after the later of (1) the date on which the partnership return for such taxable year was filed, or (2) the last day for filing such return for such year (determined without regard to extensions)." Courts are in accord that where section 6229 and 6501 both have application because of the timing involved in assessing a partnership item, section 6229 provides a minimum period of time for the assessment of any tax attributable to partnership items notwithstanding the period provided for in section 6501, which is ordinarily the maximum period for the assessment of any tax.[99] The partnership rules have again been modified. *See* Part B of Chapter 6.

6. Listed Transactions

Section 814 of the American Jobs Creation Act of 2004[100] amended section 6501(c) by adding a new paragraph (10). Section 6501(c)(10) provides that the limitations period on assessment with respect to a listed transaction that the taxpayer fails to disclose, as required under section 6011 (an "undisclosed listed transaction"), shall not expire before one year after the earlier of (1) the date on which the Secretary is furnished the information required under section 6011, or (2) the date that a material

96. *See* IRC § 6503(j)(2) (setting out requirements for designated summonses).

97. Treasury has issued final regulations as to designated and related summonses. T.D. 9455, 2009-2 C.B. 239.

98. Pub.L. No. 97-248, title IV, 96 Stat. 324 (1982).

99. Rhone-Poulene Surfactants & Specialties, L.P. v. Commissioner, 114 T.C. 533, 542 (2000); Grapevine Imports, Ltd. v. United States, 71 Fed. Cl. 324 (2006).

100. Pub. L. No. 108-357, 118 Stat. 1418 (2004).

advisor meets the requirements of section 6112 with respect to a request by the Secretary under section 6112 relating to the undisclosed listed transaction.[101]

A "listed transaction" is a reportable transaction that is the same as, or substantially similar to, a transaction identified by the Secretary as a tax avoidance transaction for section 6011. Generally, if a taxpayer is required to disclose information regarding the transaction, the taxpayer must complete Form 8886, Reportable Transaction Disclosure Statement, for each listed transaction and attach the Form 8886 to the taxpayer's return for each year in which the taxpayer participated in the listed transaction.[102] A copy of the disclosure statement must also be sent to the Office of Tax Shelter Analysis (OTSA) at the same time that any disclosure statement is first filed by the taxpayer.[103] The Form 8886 must provide the information requested and be completed in accordance with the instructions to the form.[104]

Section 6112 requires material advisors to maintain lists of investors and other information with respect to reportable transactions, including listed transactions, and to furnish that information to the Secretary upon request.

Rev. Proc. 2005-26[105] provides additional ways for the taxpayer or material advisor to disclose a listed transaction to start the running of the SOL.

7. Others

There are at least a dozen Code sections in which the SOL on assessment is suspended until, or shall not expire before, a certain period after the taxpayer notifies the IRS of the occurrence of an event. For example, in connection with losses from certain activities, section 183(e) provides:

> If a taxpayer makes an election under paragraph (1) with respect to an activity, the statutory period for the assessment of any deficiency attributable to such activity shall not expire before the expiration of 2 years after the date prescribed by law (determined without extensions) for filing the return of tax under chapter 1 for the last taxable year in the period of 5 taxable years (or 7 taxable years) to which the election relates. Such deficiency may be assessed notwithstanding the provisions of any law or rule of law, which would otherwise prevent such an assessment.

Similarly, the limitations period remains open when the taxpayer neglects to report international transactions involving any of eight foreign information forms unless reasonable cause for the failure exists.[106] Also, gift tax as to a transfer may be assessed

---

101. May v. United States, 2015 U.S. Dist. LEXIS 76962 (D. Ariz. June 15, 2015) (while taxpayer and IRS agreed to extend the SOL generally, there was no special mention of the section 6707A penalty, so the later assessment was untimely), appeal filed, Case No. 15-16599 (9th Cir. 2015).

102. *See* Treas. Reg. § 1.6011-4(e).

103. *See* Treas. Reg. § 1.6011-4(d), (e).

104. *See* Treas. Reg. § 1.6011-4(d).

105. Rev. Proc. 2005-26, 2005-17 I.R.B. 965.

106. IRC § 6501(c)(8) (unlimited assessment period when U.S. transferor of property to foreign transferee fails to supply required information). *Cf.* 18 U.S.C. § 3292 (suspending the limitations period for criminal tax prosecution to permit obtaining evidence abroad).

at any time if the value and valuation methods used as to gifted property are not adequately disclosed on a return.[107]

Similar provisions exist in sections 453(e)(8), 547(f), 860(h), 982(e), 1033, 1042 (f), 2032A(f), 2055(e), 2056(d), 6038A(e), 6501(c)(8) & (10), 6872, 7507(c), and 7611(d).

VII. Pleading the Statute of Limitations and Burden of Proof

A. Spotting a Potential Statute of Limitations Issue

The first clue to a possible violation of the ASED by the IRS is that the government is proposing to make an assessment more than three years beyond the due date of the return in question. For example, if the IRS mailed a Notice of Deficiency on November 18, 20x5, with respect to a 20x1 tax return, a SOL issue appears to be present.

The notices of adjustment or deficiency issued by the Service may provide possible answers to why things appear untimely. For example, if the IRS is proposing a late filing penalty in the notice, this would suggest that the return was filed late and that the three-year assessment period began later than the due date. Likewise, if the Service is asserting the omission of a large amount of income, this signals that the six-year ASED for a substantial omission of gross income under section 6501(e), or even fraud under section 6501(c)(1), may apply.

B. Pleading the Statute of Limitations

The purported expiration of the SOL is an affirmative defense the taxpayer has to raise. Normally this is done informally with the revenue agent during the examination of the return.[108] However, if the issue cannot be resolved informally and the matter proceeds to trial, the taxpayer must raise it in the pleadings. While the issue of the SOL is typically raised when the petition or complaint is first filed,[109] the taxpayer may amend the pleadings at any time during the proceedings with the court's permission.[110] The SOL is usually decided by a motion for summary judgment or by a

---

107. IRC § 6501(c)(9); Reg. § 301.650(c)-1(f); CCA 201024059 (June 18, 2010).

108. Most often an undeniable violation of the ASED by the IRS can be resolved administratively. A phone call to the responsible IRS employee or to the Taxpayer Advocate's Office is usually sufficient. If that does not resolve the matter, one might have to appeal the case to a supervisor and so forth up the chain of command. Other administrative approaches include filing an offer in compromise or a refund claim, or requesting either a refund (if the tax has already been paid) or an abatement (if not).

109. *See, e.g.*, Tax Ct. R. 39.

110. Permission to amend the pleadings is typically granted unless the IRS would be unduly prejudiced, such as could happen if inadequate time would exist for needed factual development. Tax Ct. Rule 41 ("leave [to amend the petition] shall be given freely when justice so requires"); Balunas v. Commissioner, 546 F.2d 415 (3d Cir. 1976) (Third Circuit suggested that on remand, a pro se taxpayer be permitted to amend his petition to raise the bar of the statute).

motion to dismiss. If the taxpayer fails to timely raise the SOL defense, it will be held to have been waived.

Example: The IRS mails the Notice of Deficiency to Lauri at an address other than the section 6212-required "last known address."[111] Lauri does not receive the notice within the ninety days required to petition the Tax Court. The first time Lauri learns of the Notice of Deficiency is during the IRS's collection efforts. By this time, we'll assume, the three-year SOL has expired. Even though the ninety-day period to file a petition has run, Lauri may file a petition raising the expiration of SOL in the pleadings. The IRS typically will file a motion to dismiss claiming the ninety-day filing period expired. Lauri will file a motion to dismiss claiming the SOL expired. Her claim would be that because the Notice of Deficiency was mailed incorrectly, it was void and did not suspend the SOL. In this situation, the case will never go to trial but will, instead, be decided by the court by granting the motion to dismiss of one of the parties.

C. Burden of Proof

The burden of proof with respect to SOL issues is with the party raising the affirmative defense, *i.e.*, the taxpayer.[112] As will be seen, while the burden of going forward switches between the parties, the burden of ultimate persuasion never shifts from the party who pleads the bar of the SOL.

The taxpayer has the burden of going forward. He or she must establish the date of filing and the date the Service assessed the tax or issued the notice of deficiency.[113] If the taxpayer makes a prima facie showing that more than three years have elapsed between the two events, the burden of going forward shifts to the IRS. The government must plead and prove the application of an exception.[114] The Service might, for example, introduce a timely completed Form 872 signed by the taxpayer evidencing a valid extension of the SOL. Normally, the IRS must prove the application of an exception by a preponderance of the evidence. However, if the government seeks to establish fraud as the basis for the exception, its burden is by the clear and convincing evidence standard.[115]

If the Service succeeds in establishing that an exception applies, the burden of going forward with the evidence returns to the taxpayer to show that the alleged exception is invalid or otherwise not applicable. This might be established, for ex-

---

111. The IRS must take significant steps to determine taxpayer's correct mailing address and is generally required to conform its database to information that comes from the U.S. Postal Service National Change of Address database. CCA (Jan 9, 2008), 2008 TNT 240-29. (Dec. 12, 2008).

112. Tax Ct. R. 39, 142(a).

113. Waltner v. Commissioner, T.C. Memo. 2014-133.

114. *Id.*

115. IRC § 7454. If the Service meets its burden to establish fraud for purposes of the SOL, it automatically also meets its burden to establish that the fraud penalty under section 6663 should be imposed.

ample, by proving that the Form 872 extending the statute was signed by the taxpayer under duress.

D. Res Judicata and Collateral Estoppel

Res judicata and collateral estoppel[116] sometimes play a role in meeting one's burden of proof in SOL situations. The IRS may invoke them to obviate the need to prove certain facts a second time. For example, assume the government previously won a criminal fraud conviction under section 7201 against the taxpayer. During a civil tax proceeding involving the deficiency in tax attributable to the fraud, and the related section 6663 penalty, the taxpayer would be collaterally estopped from denying that the tax returns were fraudulent and therefore subject to the unlimited SOL of section 6501(c)(1).[117] The reason is that once having met the higher "beyond a reasonable doubt" standard of proof, the government does not have to present the evidence again in a trial where the standard of proof is lower, *i.e.*, "clear and convincing."

The IRS can also invoke collateral estoppel to avoid having to reprove certain facts already adjudicated in another court. For example, if a state court found an individual guilty of embezzlement in the amount of $400,000, the IRS need not prove either the fact of embezzlement or its amount in a civil tax case. The government would, nevertheless, still have to prove that fraud, rather than negligence, animated the non-reporting.[118]

These doctrines are not always available to the parties. For example, a prior criminal conviction may not have preclusive effect in a subsequent civil case if in the two cases the government advanced different theories as to why the taxpayer's behavior constituted fraud.[119] Moreover, a taxpayer might wish to use them as a shield during a civil proceeding where the IRS unsuccessfully prosecuted the taxpayer criminally for tax evasion. In such a case, the taxpayer would argue that since the government failed to prove

116. The doctrine of res judicata bars relitigating the same cause of action. The doctrine applies to a claim if it was, or could have been, litigated as part of the cause of action in a prior case. The doctrine of collateral estoppel, or issue preclusion, provides that once an issue of fact or law is "actually and necessarily determined by a court of competent jurisdiction, that determination is conclusive in subsequent suits based on a different cause of action involving a party to the prior litigation." For collateral estoppel to apply, resolution of the disputed issue must have been essential to the prior decision. Morse v. Commissioner, T.C. Memo. 2003-332, *aff'd*, 419 F.3d 829 (8th Cir. 2005). *See generally* Grover Hartt, III & Jonathan L. Blacker, *Judicial Application of Issue Preclusion in Tax Litigation: Illusion or Illumination?*, 59 Tax Law 205 (2005).

117. Courts unanimously agree with this proposition, so long as apples are compared to apples, *i.e.*, that the elements of the crime proven in the criminal prosecution are the same elements the government must prove in the civil case to establish an exception to the SOL. For example, the elements for fraud under sections 7201 (criminal) and 6663 (civil) and under section 6501(c) (SOL) are the same and therefore satisfy this requirement. The elements to gain a section 7206(1) conviction (criminal perjury) and those for civil fraud, on the other hand, are not alike. Thus the IRS cannot rely on res judicata or collateral estoppel based on the perjury conviction and must prove fraud in the civil case. Wright v. Commissioner, 84 T.C. 636 (1985).

118. Allen v. McCurry, 449 U.S. 90 (1980); Meier v. Commissioner, 91 T.C. 273, 286 (1988).

119. Barrow v. Commissioner, T.C. Memo. 2008-264.

fraud in the criminal tax proceeding, the IRS is precluded from trying to prove fraud during the civil phase of the tax matter. Courts, however, are unanimous in holding that neither res judicata nor collateral estoppel applies in this situation. In a criminal case, the Service must prove fraud "beyond a reasonable doubt," but in the civil proceeding the government's burden is the lower "clear and convincing" standard. Merely because the government could not convince a jury of the taxpayer's criminal intent to evade tax does not mean it cannot convince the trier of fact of the fraud in the civil matter.

E. Joint Return Filers

Assuming it is decided that one of the exceptions to the SOL on assessment applies, the tax liability for the entire return is open to determination. The liability is not determined on a taxpayer-by-taxpayer basis. Thus, for example, if a couple filed a joint return and one of them committed fraud,[120] the IRS may examine the return positions of both spouses.[121] What this means is that if the IRS ultimately prevails on the SOL issue, both spouses are put to their burden of proof on the underlying tax.

> *Example:* Assume that five years after the joint return was filed, the IRS sought to prove that Claudia fraudulently omitted income. Assume further that the IRS sought to prove that various deductions taken by her husband, Alex, were erroneous. If the IRS cannot establish that Claudia was fraudulent or that one of the other SOL exceptions applies, the SOL for the year under review will have expired and neither Claudia nor Alex would be liable for any of the proposed adjustments. On the other hand, if the IRS is successful in proving Claudia's fraud, the correctness of the entire tax return would be in issue. Therefore, not only would the adjustments attributable to Claudia be scrutinized but those solely attributable to Alex would also be swept into the controversy.

Problems

1. Sally and Tom were married and properly filed a joint return for the year 20x4 on March 30, 20x5. The return reported $200,000 of gross income and a tax liability of $40,000. A total of $37,500 in taxes had been withheld from their salaries during the year.

(a) How much tax can the IRS assess immediately?

(b) On what date is the return considered to have been filed?

(c) Would your answer to (b) be different if April 15, 20x5 were a Saturday or Sunday?

---

120. The fraud penalty, rather than the tax itself, attaches only to the person(s) who were fraudulent. Garavaglia v. Commissioner, T.C. Memo. 2011-228, *aff'd*, 521 Fed. Appx. 476 (6th Cir. 2013).

121. Benjamin v. Commissioner, 66 T.C. 1084 (1976), *aff'd*, 592 F.2d 1259 (5th Cir. 1979). However, if only one spouse signed an extension agreement, the SOL is extended as to that spouse only, not as to the other (non-signing) spouse as well. Jordan v. Commissioner, 134 T.C. 1 (2010), supplemented T.C. Memo, 2011-243 (2011).

(d) What would be the last date on which the IRS could assess additional tax for the year 20x4?

(e) Would your answer to (d) be different if April 15, 20x5 had been a Saturday of Sunday?

(f) What would be the last date the IRS could assess additional tax if—

(i) Sally and Tom filed an amended return on April 10, 20x5?

(ii) Sally and Tom filed an amended return on August 30, 20x5?

(g) Now assume that April 15, 20x5 was a Saturday. Sally and Tom filed their joint return on Monday, April 17, 20x5. What would be the last date the IRS could assess additional taxes for the year 20x4?

2. Now assume that the return was mailed on Tuesday, April 15, 20x5, postmarked that day, and received by the IRS on Friday, April 18, 20x5.

(a) On what date was the return deemed filed?

(b) What would be the last date on which the IRS could assess additional taxes for the year 20x4?

3. Now assume that Sally and Tom did not file a return for 20x4 at all.

(a) How much tax can the IRS assess immediately?

(b) What would be the last date on which the IRS could assess additional tax?

(c) The IRS prepared a Substitute for Return for Sally and Tom. What would be the last date the IRS could assess additional tax?

4. Now assume that Sally had been paid an additional $60,000 for some consulting work that she had done. But Sally and Tom had inadvertently failed to report it on their return.

(a) What is the last date the IRS could assess additional taxes?

(b) Would your answer to (a) be different if Sally and Tom had intentionally failed to report it on their return?

(c) Would your answers to (a) or (b) be different if the amount were $40,000?

(d) Now assume Sally and Tom were overwhelmed with guilt for their intentionally failing to report the income and asked you whether they should file an amended return reporting the income. What would you advise them and why?

(e) Assume that they did file the amended return, reporting the income, on August 15, 20x5. Would that affect your answer to (b)?

5. Now assume that Tom owned some undeveloped land that he had inherited many years ago. His basis in the land was $10,000. During 20x1, when the land was worth $100,000, he exchanged it (in a transaction to which section 1031 applied) for some other undeveloped land. Shortly after the exchange, an interstate highway was built near the land. In 20x3, a new interchange was built only a few hundred yards from the new land, which caused the land to increase in value. So he sold it in 20x4 for $250,000. Sally and Tom's timely filed (without an extension) joint return for

20x4 reported $250,000, the selling price, as the amount realized, but reported the basis as $100,000. What would be the last date that the IRS could assess additional tax for the year 20x4?

6. What would be the last date on which the IRS could assess additional tax for 20x4 if—

(a) Sally and Tom believed that income taxes were unconstitutional? They filed the return and paid the tax due because they didn't want to go to jail, but they refused to sign the return. Instead they wrote "We won't sign because income taxes are illegal" on the signature line.

(b) Sally and Tom signed and filed the return, but because they believe that income taxes are unconstitutional they filled in every line with a zero?

7. Now assume the facts in Problem 1. The IRS began an examination of the return in December 20x7, but needed more time to complete the examination. So it asked Sally and Tom to extend the SOL pursuant to Section 6501(c)(4).

(a) Assume that a Form 872 was executed on April 1, 20x8 extending the SOL until March 31, 20x9. What would be the last date on which the IRS could assess additional taxes?

(b) Would your answer to (a) be different if the Form 872 were executed on April 20, 20x8?

8. Now assume the facts in Problem 1 only. The IRS mailed a Notice of Deficiency to Sally and Tom on April 15, 20x8. What would be the last date on which the IRS could assess tax if—

(a) Sally and Tom did not file a petition in the Tax Court?

(b) The Tax Court issued its opinion on April 1, 20x9 and entered its decision on June 30, 20x9?

(c) Would your answer to (b) be different if the Notice of Deficiency had been mailed on April 10, 20x8?

Chapter 6A

Examination of Partnerships (TEFRA)

IRC: §§ 6031(a), (b); 6221; 6222; 6223(a), (b); 6224; 6226(a)–(c); 6229; 6231(a)–(c), (g); 6233(e), (g), (h)*

Regs.: §§ 301.6222(a)-1(a), (b) & (c); 301.6223(g)-1; 301.6224(c)-1; 301.6224(c)-2; 301.6624(c)-3; 301.6231(a)(3)-1; 301.6231(a)(5)-1; 301.6231(a)(6)-1; 301.6231(a)(7)-1 (skim)*

I. Introduction

A great deal of business activity in the United States and abroad is conducted through partnerships of various kinds. This is especially true because, by virtue of the so called check-the-box regulations,[1] most multi-member limited liability companies (LLCs) are treated as partnerships for federal tax purposes.

Substantively, section 701 declares that partnerships do not pay income tax themselves but rather that the partners are liable in the partners' separate or individual capacities for tax on partnership profits. Procedurally, there have been three principal eras in federal income taxation of partnership profits and losses. First, before 1982, the IRS audited partnership items by examining the returns of the partners. The IRS proposed any adjustments at the partner level; the partner individually invoked Appeals Office and judicial review of the adjustments; and any determined deficiencies were paid by the partner.

However, special regimes existed during portions of this first era. For instance, under section 7704, certain publicly traded partnerships (PTPs) are treated as corporations, thus are subject to entity-level audit, litigation, and collection. Also, under sections 771 through 776 and 6240 through 6255, electing large partnerships (ELPs)[2] were subject to unified audit rules under which the tax treatment of partnership items was determined at the entity level rather than the owner level.

* All IRC and Reg. references in this Chapter 6A are to the "old" sections, i.e., the sections as they stood before enactment of the Bipartisan Budget Act in November 2015.

1. Reg. §§ 301.7701-1 to 301.7701-3.

2. To be eligible to elect, the partnership must have had at least 100 partners in the tax year. IRC § 775(a)(1)(A). Relatively few partnerships made this election. In 2012, for example, only 103 ELP returns were filed.

Second, 1982 legislation created the TEFRA regime under which the audit and litigation of partnership items occurred at the entity level but with extensive opportunities for owner participation. Additional tax ultimately was still paid by the partners individually. Moreover, because of exceptions, TEFRA often did not apply, in which case the pre-TEFRA owner-level audit and litigation continued. The PTP and ELP regimes remained in place in this second era. The TEFRA rules are discussed in this Chapter 6A.

Third, in late 2015, the Bipartisan Budget Act (BBA) replaced the TEFRA and ELP rules with a radically different set of rules. The PTP rules remain. Under the BBA, audit and litigation will occur at the entity level without owner participation and determined deficiencies will be paid by the entity. However, by virtue of exceptions, elections, and effective dates, aspects of both the original partner-level approach and the TEFRA hybrid approach still can operate in this third era. The BBA rules are discussed in Chapter 6B.

The Tax Equity and Fiscal Responsibility Act of 1982 (TEFRA)[3] dramatically changed the manner in which errors in reporting partnership items for federal income tax purposes are corrected. Congress chose to act because of syndicated tax shelter partnerships in the 1960s and 1970s that resulted in both the administrative and the judicial branches of the government being bogged down in controversies about the correct determination of partnerships' taxable income. Before TEFRA, error correction had to take place at the partner, not the partnership, level. Consequently, a single syndicated tax shelter with several hundred partners had the potential to produce several hundred separate proceedings. The traditional "audit, deficiency notice, Tax Court" procedure for resolving the disputes could not efficiently handle the volume of cases.

The TEFRA solution shifted the focus of the inquiry from the individual partners to the partnership itself. Congress wanted to preserve each partner's right to participate in the error correction proceedings. The solution was to withdraw "partnership items" from the traditional "audit, deficiency notice, Tax Court" procedure and create a similar, but separate, procedure for partnership items. TEFRA is centered on a single, unified, partnership-level proceeding that binds all partners who have not individually resolved their tax liability with the IRS.[4]

---

3. Pub. L. No. 97-248, 96 Stat. 324 (1982). For discussion of the origins of TEFRA, see Steve R. Johnson, *Reforming Federal Tax Litigation: An Agenda*, 41 Fla. St. U. L. Rev. 205, 231–33 (2013); Jerome Kurtz, *Auditing Partnerships*, Tax Notes, Feb. 20, 2012, p. 977; *ABA Section of Taxation Proposal as to Audit of Partnerships*, 32 Tax Law. 551 (1979).

4. Section 6233 extends the TEFRA partnership audit provisions, to the extent determined by Regulations, to entities that file partnership returns but are subsequently determined not to be partnerships, or that are subsequently determined not to be entities. In either case, the Regulations, in effect, respect and apply the TEFRA audit results. Reg. § 301.6233-1. As an example, Regulation section 301.6233-1(a) provides that a determination under the TEFRA partnership audit provisions "that an entity that filed a partnership return is an association taxable as a corporation will serve as a basis for a computational adjustment reflecting the disallowance of any loss or credit claimed by a purported partner with respect to that entity." Section 6234 deals with a situation that arises as a result of the separation from the normal deficiency procedures of procedures relating to partnership audits.

Although the impetus for change was the flood of deficiency cases, overpayment cases based on partnership-level errors also generated multiple administrative and judicial proceedings. Thus, TEFRA also created a procedure, similar to the traditional refund procedure, that again involves a single, partnership-level proceeding that binds all partners who have not individually resolved their tax liability with the IRS. The partnership equivalent of the traditional refund procedure—an administrative adjustment request[5]—is discussed in Chapter 9.

Separate from the TEFRA partnership provisions, sections 6240–6255 contain rules that govern audit procedures involving "electing large partnerships" (ELPs). Congress enacted these rules in 1997 to reduce the inefficiency and complexity of applying TEFRA provisions to audits of large partnerships.[6] These provisions apply only to partnerships that have at least 100 partners and elect application of the rules.[7] Adjustments to an electing large partnership's return "are either reported by the partnership in the year the examination results are determined, or the partnership can elect to pay an imputed underpayment."[8] If a large partnership does not make the election, any audit of that partnership will be conducted under the TEFRA provisions.[9]

Below we consider basic concepts,[10] administrative proceedings,[11] judicial review,[12] and the statute of limitations.[13] We conclude with a word about the flaws in the TEFRA regime that led Congress to enact the BBA rules.

II. Basic Concepts

A. The Unified Proceeding

Section 6221 provides that "the tax treatment of any partnership item (and the applicability of any penalty, addition to tax, or additional amount which relates to

5. IRC §§6227 & 6228; *see, e.g.*, Jewell v. United States, 548 F.3d 1168 (8th Cir. 2008) (holding that a partner did not have standing to sue for refund of part of a tax penalty paid by the partnership pursuant to a closing argument); Samueli v. Commissioner, 132 T.C. 336 (2009) (holding that an amended return did not constitute an administrative adjustment request because it omitted required information and was not accompanied by Form 8082 "Notice of Inconsistent Treatment or Administrative Adjustment Request (AAR)").

6. H.R. Rep. No. 105-148, §1222, at 218–28 (1997), 1997-4 C.B. 319, 540–550.

7. IRC §§6255(a), 775(a). Section 775(b)(2) does not allow an election by a partnership if substantially all of its partners perform substantial personal services in connection with the partnership's activities.

8. IRM 8.19.1.3.

9. *Cf.* IRC §6240(b)(1). For additional discussion of ELPs, see Joint Comm. on Taxation, *Description of Certain Revenue Provisions Contained in the President's Fiscal Year 2016 Budget Proposal* 258–62 (Sept. 2015).

10. IRC §§6221, 6222, & 6231. There are many aspects of the TEFRA regime beyond the basic concepts. For the IRS's position on nearly 50 TEFRA issues, see Chief Counsel Notice CC-2009-027 (Aug. 26, 2009, as periodically updated).

11. IRC §§6223–6225 & 6230.

12. IRC §6226.

13. IRC §6229.

an adjustment to a partnership item) shall be determined at the partnership level." Partnership items include any item relating to the determination of the partnership's taxable income that, under regulations, "is more appropriately determined at the partnership level than at the partner level."[14] The Regulations broadly define partnership items as including, among other things, "[i]tems of income, gain, loss, deduction or credit of the partnership."[15]

Unsurprisingly, an item that is not a "partnership item" under the above standard is a "nonpartnership item."[16] And there is yet a third important category. Adjustment of a partnership item may in turn require revision of one or more items not obviously linked to the partnership. These are called "affected items."[17]

This tripartite classification scheme is fundamental to TEFRA, but it is problematic. First, it often is challenging to decide into which of the three boxes particular tax items should be put. Second, even with perfect categorization, inefficiencies result from the interaction of TEFRA and non-TEFRA processes.

1. Classification

Taxpayers, the IRS, and the courts have invested much labor and many resources in deciding how numerous tax items fit into the tripartite scheme. Regulation section 301.6231(a)(3)-1 has an unsurprising partial list of partnership items. Other items continue to be litigated. Sometimes parties and courts disagree on the right categorization. Sometimes too a given item is held to be a partnership item in one context but not a partnership item in another context.[18]

Here are some items that have been held to be *partnership items*: (1) whether a transaction is a sham or tax-motivated,[19] (2) whether the statute of limitations remains open,[20] (3) basis of property distributed by a disregarded partnership,[21] (4) inside basis,[22] (5) extent of partner's basis in property contributed by the partner to the partnership,[23] and (6) partnership's release of a partner's capital account deficit restoration obligation.[24]

---

14. IRC § 6231(a)(3).
15. Reg. § 301.6231(a)(3)-1.
16. IRC § 6231(a)(4).
17. IRC § 6231(a)(5). For example, under section 213(a), medical expenses are deductible only to the extent they exceed 10% of the taxpayer's adjusted gross income for the year. Assume that Eve is a partner in a TEFRA partnership and that, as a result of a TEFRA proceeding, the partnership is held to have had more income than reported. Eve's pass-through share and thus her adjusted gross income would rise, causing deductible medical expenses to decrease. Eve's section 213 deduction is an affected item.
18. *See generally* Chad D. Nardiello, *Is It a Partnership Item?*, Tax Notes, Sept. 30, 2013, p. 1557.
19. *E.g.*, Prati v. United States, 603 F.3d 1301, 1309 (Fed. Cir. 2010), *cert. denied*, 562 U.S. 1139 (2011).
20. *E.g.*, Weiner v. United States, 389 F.3d 152 (5th Cir. 2004), *cert. denied*, 544 U.S. 1050 (2005).
21. Arbitrage Trading, LLC v. United States, 108 Fed. Cl. 588, 606–08 (2013).
22. *E.g.*, 106 Ltd. v. Commissioner, 136 T.C. 67 (2011).
23. *E.g.*, Nussdorf v. Commissioner, 129 T.C. 30 (2007).
24. Bassing v. United States, 563 F.3d 1280 (Fed. Cir. 2009).

Here are some items that have been held to be *nonpartnership items*: (1) identity of a partner in the partnership[25] and (2) tax treatment on a consolidated return of the parent company's payment to a partnership in which the parent is not a partner.[26]

Here are some items that have been held to be *affected items*: (1) extent of gain or loss on disposition of bona fide partnership interest, as long as the amount could be affected and (2) legal expenses paid by a partnership disregarded as a sham tax shelter.[27]

One somewhat *mercurial item* is whether a given person is a partner.[28] This matter depends on the facts and circumstances although it usually is seen as a partnership item if it affects the distributive shares of the other partners.[29]

Considerable controversy has attended classification of the extent of outside basis. A regulation provides that outside basis "is an affected item to the extent it is not a partnership item." Yet a transferee's outside basis is a partnership item when the partnership has made the section 754 election.[30] The Tax Court has held several times that outside basis can be a partnership item under certain circumstances, but appellate courts have not always agreed.[31] The IRS has sometimes argued that outside basis is a partnership item but other times argued that it is an affected item.[32] The Supreme Court has held that outside basis is a partnership item when the partnership is a sham.[33]

The IRS has been "burned" many times, losing untold revenue because the courts construed TEFRA differently from how the IRS had. Does TEFRA apply to the case at hand or not? In situations of doubt, the IRS often issues both a Notice of Deficiency and an FPAA (the cognate in the TEFRA context of a deficiency notice). Whichever the court dismisses, the IRS will have stopped the running of the limitations period on the surviving process.

2. Inefficiencies

Even if one can reliably classify items under the above scheme, the structures created by TEFRA cause procedural inefficiencies. Every first year law student learns that our legal system discourages claims-splitting. Yet that is TEFRA's inevitable result. Consider the following examples.

---

25. *E.g.*, Alpha I, L.P. *ex rel.* Sands v. United States, 86 Fed. Cl. 126 (2009).

26. Rev. Rul. 2006-11, 2006-1 C.B. 635.

27. Greenwald v. Commissioner, 142 T.C. 308 (2014).

28. *E.g.*, Blonien v. Commissioner, 118 T.C. 541, 551 (2002).

29. Reg. § 301.6231(a)(5)-1(b).

30. Reg. § 301.6231(a)(3)-1(a)(3).

31. *E.g.*, Petaluma FX Partners LLC v. Commissioner, *rev'd*, 591 F.3d 649 (D.D.C. 2010). *But see* Greenwald v. Commissioner, 142 T.C. 308, 314 (2014) (stating that outside basis "generally" is an affected item).

32. *E.g.*, Am. Milling, LP v. Commissioner, T.C. Memo. 2015-192, at n. 10 (noting the IRS's shift of position in two related tax shelter cases).

33. United States v. Woods, 134 S. Ct. 557, 564 (2013); *see also* Logan Trust v. Tigers Eye Trading, LLC, 616 Fed. Appx. 426 (D.C. Cir. 2015).

First, although the tax treatment of partnership items is determined through a partnership-level proceeding, the tax treatment of nonpartnership items continues to be determined in a traditional, partner-level proceeding. Thus, a taxpayer may be involved in both a *partnership-level* proceeding (or, if more than one partnership is involved, multiple partnership-level proceedings) and a *partner-level* proceeding with respect to the same year.[34]

Second, to further complicate matters, there are several situations in which partnership items "become" nonpartnership items.[35] As will be seen, partnership items that experience this metamorphosis may or may not trigger application of the traditional deficiency notice procedures.

Third, although penalties arising out of the reporting of a partnership's income are determined in the partnership level proceeding, partner-level defenses[36] can be asserted only in a traditional refund proceeding following assessment and payment of the penalties.[37] Therefore a partnership level proceeding that results in an assertion of a penalty can result in a traditional partner-level refund proceeding by a partner seeking recovery of the penalty.

The contortions all this requires is illustrated by the following slice of history. Several circuit courts had held that, because outside basis is an affected item requiring

---

34. Section 6234 deals with a problem that arose because of the TEFRA requirement that partnership items be dealt with under a procedure different than, and possibly conducted in parallel with, the traditional deficiency procedure. The problem arises in the situation in which a partner's income tax return shows no taxable income and shows a net loss from partnership items. In that case, if an audit produces a deficiency with respect to non-partnership items but which is eliminated by the net loss from partnership items, there would be no deficiency. If a separate TEFRA partnership proceeding were to result in a reduction in the net loss from partnership items sufficient to create an actual deficiency in tax liability from the non-partnership items, then it might happen that the statute of limitations on assessing that deficiency would expire before the TEFRA proceedings were completed. This would prevent the IRS from collecting the deficiency. In such case, the IRS is authorized under section 6234(a) to issue a "notice of adjustment" with respect to the deficiency resulting from the audit of the non-partnership items, and the taxpayer is given the right to seek Tax Court review of the proposed adjustment. When the notice of adjustment procedure is final (whether because no petition was filed with the Tax Court, or there was such a petition and the order of the Tax Court has become final), the results of the notice of adjustment procedure are "taken into account in determining the amount of any computational adjustment that is made in connection with a partnership proceeding." IRC § 6234(g)(1). The results of the notice of adjustment procedure are taken into account notwithstanding the fact that the statute of limitations on making assessments has expired. IRC § 6234(g)(1).

35. IRC § 6230(b)(1). For example, a partner may elect to have her partnership items for a given tax year treated as nonpartnership items. IRC § 6223(e)(3)(B). This is an "all or nothing" election. A partner cannot elect out for only some of her items or interests. *E.g.*, JT USA, LP v. Commissioner, 771 F.3d 654 (9th Cir. 2014), *cert. denied*, 136 S. Ct. 120 (2015); Exxon Mobil Corp. v. Commissioner, 484 F.3d 731, 734 (5th Cir. 2007).

36. Partner-level defenses are "those that are personal to the partner or are dependent upon the partner's separate return and cannot be determined at the partnership level." Reg. § 301.6221-1(d).

37. *E.g.*, New Millennium Trading, L.L.C. v. Commissioner, 131 T.C. 275 (2008); Fears v. Commissioner, 129 T.C. 8 (2007). The defenses that are personal to a partner may be raised either before payment in a collection due process hearing under sections 6320 or 6330 or following payment in a refund action. Reg. § 301.6221-1(d).

partner-level determinations, the section 6662 penalty for overstatement of outside basis cannot be considered in a partnership-level proceeding.[38] The Supreme Court rejected this view stating:

> We hold that TEFRA gives courts in partner-level proceedings jurisdiction to determine the applicability of any penalty that could result from an adjustment to a partnership item, even if imposing the penalty would also require determining affected or non-partnership items such as outside basis. The partnership-level applicability determination, we stress, is provisional: the court may decide only whether adjustments properly made at the partnership level have the potential to trigger the penalty. Each partner remains free to raise, in subsequent, partner-level proceedings, any reasons why the penalty may not be imposed on him specifically.[39]

The TEFRA regime was supposed to increase efficiency, but in practice it has been the antithesis of efficiency.[40]

B. The Duty of Consistency

The TEFRA provisions require that partnership items be reported on each partner's return in the same manner that they are reported on the partnership's return.[41] This consistency requirement is waived if the partner notifies the IRS of any inconsistency in reporting.[42] If a partner reports inconsistently, but does not notify the IRS of the inconsistency, the IRS may impose consistency without the normal procedures (discussed below) that permit partners to contest an asserted deficiency without first paying it.[43] Furthermore, any partner who does not disclose an inconsistency in reporting may be subject to the section 6662(b)(1) accuracy-related penalty for disregard of the rules. The IRS has in place a matching program to ensure that partners report consistently with the partnership return.[44]

C. The Tax Matters Partner

To facilitate the administrative and judicial proceedings, TEFRA created, and gave certain powers and responsibilities to, the "tax matters partner" (TMP). The TMP is the person the partnership designates who either: "(i) [w]as a general partner in the partnership at some time during the taxable year for which the desig-

---

38. *E.g.*, Jade Trading, LLC v. United States, 598 F.3d 1372, 1380 (Fed. Cir. 2010); Petaluma FX Partners, LLC v. Commissioner, 591 F.3d 649, 655–56 (D.C. Cir. 2010).

39. United States v. Woods, 134 S. Ct. 557, 564 (2013).

40. *See, e.g.*, Tigers Eye Trading LLC v. Commissioner, T.C. Memo. 2009-121, at 81–82 (TEFRA proceedings can create the necessity "to educate two different courts (or at least two different judges) in the operation of the same complex set of transactions").

41. IRC § 6222(a).

42. IRC § 6222(b).

43. IRC § 6222(c).

44. *See* IR-2003-27.

nation is made or (ii) [i]s a general partner in the partnership as of the time the designation is made."[45] The Regulations contain an extensive discussion of the designation or selection of the TMP as well as some special rules relating to the designation or selection of the TMP for a limited liability company.[46] Of particular interest are the TMP's significant responsibilities in connection with administrative and judicial proceedings relating to the determination of the partnership's taxable income.

(a) The TMP is required to notify partners, who are not required to be notified directly by the IRS, about significant developments in partnership administrative and judicial proceedings.[47]

(b) In the case of administrative proceedings initiated by the IRS that result in proposed changes in the partnership's taxable income or loss, the TMP can enter into a settlement agreement with the IRS that other partners will be permitted to adopt and that will be binding on partners that have less than a 1% profits interest in a partnership with more than 100 partners.[48]

(c) The TMP has the power to extend the period of time within which the IRS can make assessments with respect to all partners.[49]

(d) The TMP has the right to seek judicial review of the proposed changes and to determine the court in which to seek such review.[50]

(e) The TMP has the right to request an administrative adjustment of partnership items on behalf of the partnership, to seek judicial review of the requested adjustment if it is denied, in whole or in part, and to determine the court in which to seek such review.[51]

---

45. Reg. § 301.6231(a)(7)-1(b).

46. Reg. § 301.6231(a)(7)-2. Regulation section 301.6231(a)(7)-1 provides rules for the designation or selection of a partnership's TMP by the partnership or, in certain circumstances, by the IRS. The Tax Court has held that the Service, when it has the right to select a TMP, is not compelled to act so long as the other partners are provided adequate notice of how to protect their interests through commencing a partnership proceeding. *See* Seneca, Ltd. v. Commissioner, 92 T.C. 363 (1989), *aff'd*, 899 F.2d 1255 (9th Cir. 1990); *see also* Cinema '84 v. Commissioner, 412 F.3d 366 (2d Cir.), *cert. denied sub nom.* Reigler v. United States, 546 U.S. 1004 (2005) (IRS has no duty to appoint TMP).

47. IRC § 6223(g); Reg. § 301.6223(g)-1(a)(1) to (3). However, if the TMP fails to notify a partner (who is not entitled to notice by the IRS) of a proceeding, the partner's due process rights are not violated because "TEFRA's notice provisions are 'reasonably calculated' to apprise all partners of tax adjustments and administrative proceedings involving the partnership." Kaplan v. United States, 133 F.3d 469, 475 (7th Cir. 1998).

48. IRC § 6224(c)(3).

49. IRC § 6229(b). As is true of all types of extensions, issues sometimes arise as to whether the party signing the extension was authorized to do so. *E.g.*, Summit Vineyard Holdings LLC v. Commissioner, T.C. Memo. 2015-140 (upholding the validity of a consent on "apparent authority" grounds); Chief Counsel Advisory CCA 200952051 (Dec. 7, 2009) (concluding that state law controls which persons are permitted to act as TMP on behalf of an LLC taxed as a partnership).

50. IRC § 6226(a).

51. IRC § 6228(a)(1).

(f) If the IRS mails a Notice of Beginning of Administrative Proceeding to the TMP, the TMP is required to provide the IRS the name, address, profits interest, and identification number of any person who was a partner anytime during the year.[52]

The TMP's power to act on behalf of the partnership can terminate in certain circumstances.[53] Upon termination, the TMP cannot act to bind the partners or the IRS.[54] For example, the TMP's authority to extend an assessment period of limitations for a partnership terminates if the IRS notifies the TMP that she is under criminal investigation for violation of the internal revenue laws.[55]

D. Excluded Partnerships

Congress excluded from the reach of the TEFRA provisions partnerships with ten or fewer partners (at any time during the year), whose partners include only: (i) individuals who are not nonresident aliens, (ii) the estates of partners, and (iii) C corporations.[56] However, any such small partnership is permitted to elect to have the TEFRA provisions apply to it. The election is made by attaching a statement, signed by all persons who were partners at any time during the year, to the partnership

52. IRC § 6230(e). Tax Court rules establish additional responsibilities of the TMP. *See* Tax Ct. R. 241(f)(1), 241(g), 248.

53. Reg. § 301.6231(a)(7)-1(l). For example, dissolution ends the ability of an entity to act as TMP. Reg § 301.6231(a)(7)-1(l).

54. Computer Programs Lambda, Ltd. v. Commissioner, 89 T.C. 198 (1987) (forbidding the TMP to continue as TMP in a partnership proceeding after the TMP entered into bankruptcy); *see also* Barbados #7 v. Commissioner, 92 T.C. 804 (1984) (holding that a bankruptcy-terminated TMP could not automatically be redesignated as TMP for the same year under the "largest profits interest" rule of section 6231(a)(7)(B)). *See generally* Chief Counsel Advisory CCA 201109019 (Mar. 3, 2011) (addressing issues as to the effect of bankruptcy on TEFRA procedures).

55. IRC § 6231(c); Reg. §§ 301.623(c)-5(a), 301.6231(a)(7)-1(l)(1)(iv). Also, the Second Circuit has ruled that the TMP's authority to act on behalf of the partnership can terminate even if the Service fails to inform the TMP that his partnership items have become nonpartnership items. The court, in *Transpac Drilling Venture 1982-12 v. Commissioner*, 147 F.3d 221 (2d Cir. 1998), held that a TMP may not bind the partnership by extending the assessment limitations period if the TMP is under criminal investigation and ultimately cooperates with the IRS regarding the criminal prosecutions of the partnership. Merely being under criminal investigation is not by itself disqualifying. The TMP must be notified that she is under criminal investigation. "[T]here is no automatic termination of TMP status by virtue of [a criminal] investigation." Phillips v. Commissioner, 272 F.3d 280, 288 (2d Cir. 2002).

Some cases have held that, when a serious conflict of interests exists, the TMP may not be allowed to act on behalf of the partnership. *Compare* Leatherstocking 1983 Partnership v. Commissioner, 296 Fed. Appx. 171 (2d Cir. 2008), *and* River City Ranches #1 Ltd. v. Commissioner, 401 F.3d 1136 (9th Cir. 2005) (taking this view), *with* United States v. Martinez, 564 F.3d 719 (5th Cir. 2009) (rejecting this view).

56. IRC § 6231(a)(1)(B)(i). A husband and wife are counted as one partner. For discussion of spousal relief in the TEFRA context (Chapter 3), see *Andrews v. Commissioner*, T.C. Memo. 2010-230.

An LLC that is a "disregarded entity" under Regulation section 301.77013(b)(1)(ii) can nonetheless be a partnership. If it holds an interest in a partnership, the partnership will not qualify for the small partnership. Rev. Rul. 2004-88, 2004-2 C.B. 165.

return for the first year for which the election is to be effective.[57] Also excluded from the TEFRA provisions are partnerships that have validly elected out of partnership status under section 761(a)[58] and publicly traded partnerships treated as corporations under section 7704(a). Even if the partnership is disregarded as a tax sham, the TEFRA procedures can still apply as long as the entity filed a partnership return.[59]

III. Administrative Proceedings

A. The Notice of Beginning

An audit of a partnership's return begins when the IRS mails by certified mail (or hand delivers) to the TMP a notice of the beginning of an administrative proceeding ("NBAP").[60] The date the NBAP is issued to the TMP starts a 45-day period within which the revenue agent can determine whether the case will be "No-Changed." If it is determined that the case will be No-Changed, the NBAP issued to the TMP will be withdrawn and no notices will be delivered to the notice partners.[61]

If the case is not No-Changed and is still in process 60 days after the NBAP was issued, the NBAP is mailed to all notice partners.[62] The date of this mailing starts a 120-day period which must elapse before an FPAA (final partnership administrative adjustment) can be sent to the partnership.[63]

Partners whose names and addresses are known to the Service (other than partners who have less than a 1% interest in the profits of a partnership that has more than 100 partners) are considered notice partners.[64] For TEFRA purposes, the word "partner" includes not only actual partners in a partnership, but also "any other person whose income tax liability ... is determined in whole or in part by taking into account directly or indirectly partnership items of the partnership."[65]

One example is persons who hold an indirect interest in a partnership through a "pass-through" partner such as a partnership, estate, trust, S corporation, or nominee. Such persons are known as "indirect partners."[66] The pass-through partner is supposed to keep indirect partners informed of developments relating to the administrative pro-

57. Reg. § 301.6231(a)(1)-1(b)(2). Intent to make the election must be apparent from the face of the return. The IRS is not required to stitch together hints and snippets to infer the intent. *E.g.*, Nehrlich v. Commissioner, T.C. Memo. 2007-88, *aff'd*, 327 Fed. Appx. 712 (9th Cir. 2009).

58. IRM 4.31.2.1.2(1).

59. IRC §§ 6231(g), 6233; Reg. § 301.6223-1(b).

60. IRC § 6223(a)(1); IRM 4.31.3.3.1(1)(G).

61. IRM 4.31.2.2.9.1(2)(B).

62. IRM 4.31.2.2.9.2(1)(B), (C).

63. *Id.* at (1)(F).

64. IRC § 6223(b). Partners with less than a 1% interest in partnership profits in a partnership with more than 100 partners can join with other partners to create a "5-percent group." The 5% group is entitled to designate one of its members to serve as a partner who is entitled to notice. IRC § 6223(b)(2).

65. IRC § 6231(a)(2)(B).

66. IRC § 6231(a)(9), (10).

ceeding.[67] However, "indirect partners" whose names, addresses, and profits interests are provided to the IRS are entitled to receive the NBAP directly from the IRS.[68]

Another example of a person who is not an actual partner, but whose income tax liability is determined by taking into account partnership items, is a spouse who signs a joint return with an actual partner. Since the non-partner spouse is jointly and severally liable for the tax shown on the return, the non-partner spouse is subject to the TEFRA partnership audit provisions and entitled to receive the notices that the partner spouse is entitled to receive.

B. Period for Mailing the NBAP

No specific date is set forth within which the NBAP must be mailed to the notice partners. However, the Code directs the IRS *not* to mail the FPAA to the TMP until at least 120 days after the NBAP is mailed.[69] As in the case of the traditional Notice of Deficiency, the FPAA must be mailed before the statute of limitations on assessment expires, and upon its mailing the running of the statute is suspended.[70]

This might lead one to believe that the NBAP must always be mailed at least 120 days before the statute of limitations expires. Otherwise, the FPAA would be ineffective because it could not be mailed until after the period for assessment expired. However, in a case in which both the NBAP and the FPAA were mailed within the 120 days before expiration of the statute of limitations, the Tax Court ruled that the FPAA was timely and suspended the running of the statute of limitations.[71]

In that situation, a partner's only recourse is that set forth in section 6223(e), which describes what happens if the IRS fails to send any notice to a notice partner in a timely manner. If the administrative or judicial proceedings are still in progress, the partner becomes a party to the proceeding, unless the partner elects either to adopt any settlement agreement previously entered into by any other partner or to have all partnership items of the partner treated as non-partnership items.[72] However, if all administrative and judicial proceedings are finished when the untimely notice is mailed, then the partner's partnership items are treated as nonpartnership items unless the partner elects to adopt any settlement agreement previously entered into by any other partner.[73]

67. IRC § 6223(h); Reg. 301.6223(h)-1(a).

68. IRC § 6223(c)(3). The IRS's duty to furnish the NBAP arises only when the IRS is given such identifying information in readily available form, either on the return itself or on a written statement satisfying Regulation section 301.6223(c)-1T. *E.g.*, Murphy v. Commissioner, 129 T.C. 82, 86 (2007).

69. IRC § 6223(d)(1). This awkwardly worded section purports to fix the date for taking the first action (the mailing of the NBAP) by reference to the date on which the second action (the mailing of the FPAA) is taken. White & Case v. United States, 22 Cl. Ct. 734 (1991).

70. IRC §§ 6225(a), 6229(a), (d).

71. *See* Wind Energy Tech. Assocs. III v. Commissioner, 94 T.C. 787 (1990).

72. IRC § 6223(e)(3).

73. IRC § 6223(e)(2). Section 6223(e) provides the exclusive remedies available when the IRS fails to provide timely notice. *Wind Energy, supra*, 94 T.C. at 792–94; Green Gas Delaware Statutory Trust v. Commissioner, T.C. Memo. 2015-168.

If the FPAA was not mailed prior to the expiration of the statute of limitations on assessment, this fact should be raised in the resulting judicial proceeding under section 6226. If the issue is not raised, partners may not be allowed to raise the defense later in a refund suit.[74]

If the IRS has issued to a partner an FPAA for a partnership tax year, it may not issue a second FPAA to the partner for the same year of the same partnership absent "a showing of fraud, malfeasance, or misrepresentation of a material fact."[75] The statute does not require that the FPAA take any particular form.[76]

C. The Examination

1. Participation

All partners, including less than 1% profits interest partners in partnerships with more than 100 partners and indirect partners whose names, addresses, and profits interests have been provided to the IRS, have the right to participate in all administrative proceedings.[77] However, any partner who wishes to attend meetings with the revenue agent or otherwise participate in the proceedings must make arrangements with the TMP to obtain notice of the date, time, and place of any such meetings or other steps in the audit process.[78]

2. Summary Reports

At the end of the audit, the revenue agent prepares a summary report which provides "a detailed explanation of each proposed adjustment for each examined year, including facts, law, argument and conclusion for each proposed adjustment...."[79] A separate report for "affected items" is also prepared.[80] A copy of the report(s) is given to the TMP, who, in turn, is required to provide a copy to all partners.[81] The revenue agent then schedules a closing conference, at which the TMP and other participating partners can discuss with the revenue agent the issues spelled out in the summary report. At the conference, the partners will be given the opportunity to

---

74. *See* Weiner v. United States, 389 F.3d 152 (5th Cir. 2004), *cert. denied*, 544 U.S. 1050 (2005); Chimblo v. Commissioner, 177 F.3d 119, 125 (2d. Cir. 1999).

75. IRC §6223(f); *see, e.g.*, Wise Guys Holdings, LLC v. Commissioner, 140 T.C. 193, 194–200 (2013). *But see* Am. Milling, LP v. Commissioner, T.C. Memo. 2015-192 (taxpayer's section 6223(f) contention rejected because, although they were substantive similar, the two FPAAs were issued as to different years of different (albeit related) partnerships); NPR Inv. LLC v. United States, 732 F. Supp. 2d 676 (E.D. Tex. 2010) (allowing the IRS to issue a second FPAA when the partnership misrepresented that it was not subject to the TEFRA rules, causing the IRS initially to issue a no-change letter).

76. *E.g.*, Clovis I v. Commissioner, 88 T.C. 980, 982 (1987) (analogizing FPAAs to Notices of Deficiency).

77. IRC §6224(a).

78. Reg. §301.6224(a)-1.

79. IRM 4.31.2.2.9.3(1)(D).

80. *Id.* at (1)(E).

81. Reg. §301.6223(g)-1(b)(1)(ii).

settle the matter, including partnership items, penalties, additions to tax, additional amounts, and, if present, affected items. Form 870-PT is used if there is agreement as to partnership items but not affected items. Form 870-LT is used if there is agreement as to both partnership items and affected items.

If agreement is not reached as to all partners at the conference, the IRS will send the TMP and each unagreed partner a copy of the Revenue Agent's Report ("RAR") and a 60-day letter. Any unagreed partner may file a protest within the 60-day period and ask for an Appeals conference. All unagreed partners are entitled to attend the conference. If any partners remain unagreed at the conclusion of the Appeals conference, the IRS will issue an FPAA, in response to which, first the TMP and then the remaining unagreed partners have the right to seek judicial review.

3. Settlement—Partnership Items

When a partner enters into a settlement agreement with either the IRS or the Justice Department, that partner's partnership items become nonpartnership items on the date of the settlement.[82] But the traditional deficiency procedures (deficiency notice and opportunity for prepayment judicial redetermination by the Tax Court) are not available. Instead, the IRS can immediately assess and collect any increase in the partner's tax liability that results from the agreed treatment of the partnership items. This increase is referred to as a "computational adjustment."[83]

The conversion of partnership items into nonpartnership items by reason of an agreement triggers a special rule regarding the statute of limitations on assessment. In order to give the IRS time to make the assessment, section 6229(f) provides that the statute of limitation on assessment "shall not expire before the date which is one year after the date on which the items become nonpartnership items." This rule also applies to other circumstances, described in section 6231(a), in which partnership items are converted into nonpartnership items.

4. Settlement—Affected Items

A change in the treatment of a partnership item may affect other items on the returns of the partnership or the partners. If the change in tax treatment of such "affected items"[84] does not require a "partner-level determination," the IRS may immediately assess and collect the additional tax due.[85] Immediate assessment is appropriate when the additional tax is determined solely by a mathematical computation using known amounts. An example is a change in a partner's tax liability resulting from a change in the threshold amount of the medical expense deduction that is triggered by a change in a partnership item.[86]

---

82. IRC § 6231(b)(1)(C). Only the items covered by the settlement are converted. Schell v. United States, 84 Fed. Cl. 159 (2008), *aff'd*, 589 F.3d 1378 (Fed. Cir. 2008), *cert. denied*, 562 U.S. 897 (2010).

83. IRC § 6231(a)(6).

84. IRC § 6231(a)(5).

85. IRC § 6230(a)(1).

86. Reg. § 301.6231(a)(6)-1(a)(2).

However, if the tax liability attributable to the affected item could not be determined without fact-finding at the partner level, a partner-level determination, involving a deficiency notice and opportunity for pre-assessment judicial review in the Tax Court, would be required.[87] An example of a change in an affected item that would require a partner-level determination is the determination of "a partner's at-risk amount to the extent it depends upon the source from which the partner obtained the funds that the partner contributed to the partnership."[88]

Whether or not a partner-level determination is required, the deficiency procedures are not required with respect to any penalty generated by a partnership item.[89] All such penalties are determined at the partnership level and are treated as computational adjustments that may be assessed and collected without a deficiency notice. Individual taxpayer defenses to any such penalties can be raised only in a traditional refund procedure.

5. Requests for Consistent Treatment

If a settlement agreement is reached with one or more partners *before* the IRS mails the FPAA to the TMP, the other partners can request settlement terms that are consistent with the settlement agreement.[90] To do so, they must file their request for consistent treatment within 150 days after the day the FPAA is mailed to the TMP.[91] The 150-day period coincides with the period within which the partners may seek judicial review of the FPAA.[92] In effect, for those partners who choose to litigate, the option of requesting terms consistent with a settlement agreement entered into before the FPAA is mailed to the TMP is taken off the table. If the partners do not like the terms of the settlement agreement, they can wait for the FPAA and, when it is issued, challenge it in court.

Although the Code expressly imposes a time limit on requests for consistent treatment with respect to settlement agreements entered into *before* the FPAA is issued, no such statutory limitation applies with respect to requests for consistent treatment with settlement agreements entered into *after* the FPAA is issued. However, apparently in the interest of encouraging settlements, the Regulations provide that a request for

87. IRC § 6230(a)(2)(A)(i). If, while a partnership-level proceeding is still in progress, the IRS sends a notice of deficiency for an affected item that results from a partnership adjustment, the notice is invalid and the Tax Court lacks jurisdiction over the matter. GAF Corp. v. Commissioner, 114 T.C. 519 (2000).

88. Reg. § 301.6231(a)(6)-1(a)(3). *See generally* Napoliello v. Commissioner, 655 F.3d 1060 (9th Cir. 2011) (holding that the IRS properly issued an affected-item Notice of Deficiency because partner-level determination was necessary, thus rejecting the taxpayer's argument that the notice was invalid because the IRS should instead have made a computational adjustment).

89. IRC § 6221; Reg. § 301.6231(a)(6)-1(a)(1), (3).

90. "No statute requires the IRS to treat identically two or more entities just because they have some partners in common." Cemco Investors LLC v. United States, 515 F.3d 749 (7th Cir.), *cert. denied*, 555 U.S. 823 (2008).

91. IRC § 6224(c)(2).

92. IRC § 6226(a), (b)(1).

consistent treatment with respect to a settlement agreement entered into *after* the FPAA is mailed to the TMP must be filed by the *later* of the 150th day after the day the FPAA is mailed to the TMP or the 60th day after the day on which the settlement agreement is executed.[93]

IV. Judicial Review of an FPAA

At the conclusion of the partnership administrative proceeding, if a settlement acceptable to all partners has not been reached, the IRS is required to mail an FPAA to the TMP and, within 60 days thereafter, to mail a copy of the FPAA to all other partners entitled to receive the notice.[94] After the IRS mails an FPAA to the TMP, the TMP has a period of 90 days within which to file a "petition for a readjustment" of the proposed changes with the Tax Court, a District Court, or the Court of Federal Claims.[95] If the TMP does not file a petition within the 90-day period, then any notice partner (including the TMP) and any 5% group is permitted to file such a petition with any one of those courts within the next 60 days.[96] The court with which any petition is filed has jurisdiction to determine: all partnership items for the year, the allocation of the items among the partners, and all penalties.[97]

As is the case in a traditional deficiency procedure, the Tax Court is generally the choice of forum because payment of the asserted liability is not a jurisdictional requirement.[98] If the petition for review of the FPAA is filed with the District Court or the Court of Federal Claims, the petitioning partner must, as a jurisdictional requirement, deposit the amount of tax that would be due, determined as if the adjustments proposed in the FPAA were correct.[99] If the petition in the District Court or the Court of Federal Claims is filed by a 5% group or by a pass-through partner,

---

93. Reg. § 301.6224(c)-3(c)(3). If a partner fails to accept a consistent settlement offer within the specified time period, the Service is under no duty to extend the time period even if the partner failed to meet the deadline because the TMP failed to provide notice to the partner. Drake Oil Tech. Partners v. Commissioner, 211 F.3d 1277 (10th Cir. 2000); Vulcan Oil Tech. Partners v. Commissioner, 110 T.C. 153 (1998), *aff'd sub nom.* Tucek v. Commissioner, 198 F.3d 259 (10th Cir. 1999).

94. *See* Section III.A., *supra*.

95. IRC § 6226(a). If the petition for readjustment is filed in the District Court, it must be filed in "the district in which the partnership's principal place of business is located." IRC § 6226(a)(2).

96. IRC § 6226(b)(1). Copies of the FPAA mailed to notice partners and to the designated member of any 5% group show the date the FPAA was mailed to the TMP.

97. IRC § 6226(f).

98. Trial by jury is not available in TEFRA partnership proceedings. In the Court of Federal Claims, jury trials are generally not permitted. McElrath v. United States, 102 U.S. 426, 440 (1880) (holding that the Seventh Amendment does not require the Court of Claims, a predecessor of the Court of Federal Claims, to conduct jury trials since there is no right at common law to sue the government). In the Court of Federal Claims, jurisdiction over TEFRA cases is under 28 U.S.C. § 1508. In the District Courts, 28 U.S.C. § 2402 precludes a jury trial in cases, like the TEFRA cases, that are brought under 28 U.S.C. § 1346(e). Tax Court trials never involve juries. IRC § 7459(a).

99. IRC § 6226(e). The partner is not required to pay other outstanding tax liabilities to satisfy this jurisdictional requirement. Reg. § 301.6226(e)-1(a)(1).

each member of the group or each indirect partner must make the jurisdictional deposit.[100]

Any amount so deposited is not considered a "payment of tax" except for purposes of interest computations.[101] This treatment permits the IRS to proceed with collection of any deficiency of that partner that is not based on partnership items without taking into consideration, in determining whether there is a deficiency, the amount of the deposit.

If the petition that goes forward is filed in the Tax Court, no assessment of a deficiency attributable to partnership items can be made until the decision of the Tax Court has become final.[102] However, if the petition that goes forward is filed in either a District Court or the Court of Federal Claims, there is no prohibition on assessment during the pendency of the proceeding. Normally, the IRS will commence collection activities against all the partners without waiting for the conclusion of the District Court or Court of Federal Claims case.

Because this approach could easily result in multiple proceedings, the Code establishes an order of priority. First, if the TMP files a petition, the other partners are precluded from doing so because their right to file is conditioned on the TMP not having filed.[103] If the TMP does not file, the first Tax Court petition that is filed goes forward and any other actions are dismissed.[104] If no Tax Court case is filed, the first action filed in either the District Court or the Court of Federal Claims goes forward.[105]

As can be seen, the FPAA serves the same purpose as a Notice of Deficiency serves in a traditional audit. It staves off assessment and collection action for a period of 150 days, during which the partnership and the partners have an opportunity to seek prepayment judicial review in the Tax Court.[106]

Unlike the traditional Notice of Deficiency, the FPAA also serves as a key to a post-payment judicial review. In the traditional approach, if the taxpayer does not respond to the Notice of Deficiency, the tax is assessed and the IRS sends a Notice of Tax Due. The taxpayer has to pay the tax, or collection activities will begin. After paying the tax, the taxpayer has a period of two years within which to file a claim for refund.[107] If the Commissioner denies the claim, the taxpayer has an additional two years to file suit in the District Court or Court of Federal Claims to recover the claimed overpayment.[108]

However, in the partnership context, once the FPAA is mailed to the TMP, if no suit is filed in any court within the 150-day filing period, the IRS assesses the tax due from

---

100. Section 6226(e)(1) permits correction of a shortfall in the jurisdictional deposit provided that the original amount was determined in good faith. *See* Maarten Investerings Partnership v. United States, 2000-1 U.S. Tax Cas. ¶50,241, 85 A.F.T.R.2d P-H 2000-1086 (S.D.N.Y. 2000).

101. IRC §6226(e)(3).

102. IRC §6225(a).

103. IRC §6226(b).

104. IRC §6226(b)(2), (4).

105. IRC §6226(b)(3).

106. IRC §§6225(a), 6226.

107. IRC §6511(a).

108. IRC §6532(a).

each partner and sends each partner a Notice of Tax Due.[109] Again, the partners must pay the tax they owe. But thereafter they have no opportunity to contest the liability because that right can only be exercised pursuant to a timely response to the FPAA.[110]

If any partner files a petition for a readjustment of partnership items, then all partners are treated as parties and are allowed to participate in the proceedings.[111] If the petition that goes forward is filed in a District Court or in the Court of Federal Claims, the partner filing the petition is required to deposit with the IRS an amount equal to the filing partner's tax liability that would result from making the adjustments called for in the FPAA.[112]

V. Statute of Limitations on Making Assessments

It is "settled that nothing in the statutory scheme of TEFRA demands that an FPAA be issued within a certain time period." However, it is equally settled that "although the IRS may issue an FPAA at any time," the IRS ultimately "may only assess partners for tax years that were open when the FPAA was issued."[113]

Section 6229(a) provides that the statute of limitations for assessing tax attributable to any partnership item (or affected item) "shall not expire before" the date which is three years from the later of the due date of the return, determined without regard to extensions (for returns filed on or before that due date), or three years from the filing of the return (for returns filed after that due date).[114] The phrase "shall not expire before" in section 6229(a) indicates that the section does not establish a free-standing statute of limitations with respect to partnership items (and affected items), and that its sole function is to extend the period of limitations defined elsewhere.

---

109. It is possible for either the TMP or a partner to file a "request for an administrative adjustment" (in effect, a claim for refund), but such a request cannot be filed after an FPAA has been mailed to the TMP. IRC § 6227(a)(2).

110. A few limited opportunities exist for partner-level refund actions. *See* IRC § 6228(b) (allowing a partner to bring a refund suit after the IRS determines to treat as nonpartnership items partnership items relating to a timely request for administrative adjustment), 6230(c) (allowing a partner to bring a refund suit based on allegedly erroneous computation by the IRS) & 7422(h). A prerequisite for the "erroneous computation" refund action is that a refund claim be filed within six months after the IRS mails the notice of computational adjustment to the partner. IRC § 6230(c)(1)(A)(ii) & (2)(A); *see* General Mills, Inc. v. United States, 123 Fed. Cl. 576, 583-86 (Ct. Fed. Cl. Oct. 14, 2015).

111. IRC § 6226(c). This includes nonpetitioning partners. IRC § 6226(d). Thus, if the IRS loses in a partnership refund proceeding, all partners—petitioning or not—are entitled to refunds. Chief Counsel Advisory CCA 201030030 (July 30, 2010). However, it sometimes is challenging to determine just who is a partner. *E.g.*, Sugarloaf Fund LLC v. Commissioner, 141 T.C. 214 (2013) (holding that an investor was neither a direct nor an indirect partner, thus was not permitted to intervene).

112. IRC § 6226(e).

113. Russian Recovery Fund Ltd. v. United States, 101 Fed. Cl. 498, 503 (2011).

114. IRC §§ 6229(a), 6501(a). The question of whether an FPAA was issued within the statute of limitations is a partnership item that must be litigated in a partnership level proceeding. Weiner v. United States, 389 F.2d (5th Cir. 2004), *cert. denied*, 544 U.S. 1050 (2005).

The only period that might be so modified by section 6229(a) is the general period of limitations in section 6501(a), discussed in Chapter 5. Section 6501(a) applies to "the amount of any tax imposed by this title" and, subject to a number of exceptions, requires the tax to be assessed "within 3 years after the return was filed." For this purpose, returns filed before the due date (determined without extensions) are treated as filed on the due date.[115]

Initially, there was uncertainty as to whether section 6229 created an independent statute of limitations or merely extended the section 6501 statute of limitations. The "independent" construction could hurt the IRS because the section 6229 period could end before the section 6501 period, in which case the IRS would be unable to assess additional liabilities resulting from TEFRA items. The "merely extends" view could only help the IRS because the period for assessing TEFRA-related liabilities could only be enlarged by section 6229, never contracted below the period allowed by section 6501.

The uncertainty was bred by the "distressingly complex and confusing" nature of section 6229,[116] the result of "poor drafting" creating an "ambiguous" statute with "multiple plausible meanings" and "legislative history [that] is not reliable [but] is equivocal."[117] After years of controversy, the pro-IRS view prevailed. It is now settled that section 6229 can extend the limitations period for assessment of TEFRA items, but not contract it.[118]

Section 6229 contains special rules relating to extension of the limitations period by agreement,[119] fraudulent returns,[120] returns omitting substantial amounts of income,[121] failure to file returns,[122] and returns filed by the IRS.[123] These rules are largely modeled on comparable special rules in section 6501, and they typically provide for the same result. For example, substantial income omission leads to a six-year limitations period, and fraudulent returns create an infinite period for assessment.

In *Ginsburg v. Commissioner*,[124] the taxpayer asked for summary judgment on the question of whether a deficiency notice, which was mailed within the period set forth

115. Reg. § 301.6501(b)-1(a).

116. Rhone-Poulenc Surfactants & Specialties, L.P. v. Commissioner, 114 T.C. 533, 540 (2000), *appeal dismissed*, 249 F.3d 175 (3d Cir. 2001).

117. AD Global Fund, LLC v. United States, 67 Fed. Cl. 657 (2005), *aff'd*, 481 F.3d 1351 (Fed. Cir. 2007).

118. *E.g.*, Andantech L.L.C. v. Commissioner, 331 F.3d 972 (D.C. Cir. 2003); Russian Recovery Fund Ltd. v. United States, 101 Fed. Cl. 498 (2011); Curr-Spec. Partners, L.P. v. Commissioner, T.C. Memo. 2007-289, *aff'd*, 579 F.3d 391 (5th Cir. 2009), *cert. denied*, 560 U.S. 924 (2010).

119. IRC § 6229(b). Included in this special rule is a provision that coordinates agreements under section 6229(b) with similar agreements under section 6501(c)(4). The special rule limits the applicability of any agreement under section 6501(c)(4) to the section 6229 statute of limitations to those section 6501(c)(4) agreements that expressly acknowledge their application to partnership items.

120. IRC § 6229(c)(1).

121. IRC § 6229(c)(2).

122. IRC § 6229(c)(3).

123. IRC § 6229(c)(4).

124. 127 T.C. 75 (2006).

in the ninth consecutive Form 872, was timely as it related to certain affected items. The taxpayers had also executed a series of Forms 872-P (extension of the time for assessing tax attributable to partnership items), but, at the time in question, the last of the extended due dates with respect to partnership items had expired. One might think that if section 6229(a), when applicable, merely extends the underlying section 6501 statute of limitations, then the otherwise valid Form 872 would apply and the deficiency notice would be timely.

But the Tax Court noted the limitation in section 6229(b)(3) that an agreement under 6501(c)(4) (i.e., Form 872) is applicable to partnership items only if the agreement specifically so states. After some preliminary interpretation of the statute to demonstrate that partnership items for this purpose include affected items, the court concluded that, because the last executed Form 872 did not specifically refer to partnership items, the statute of limitations on assessing tax with respect to both partnership items and affected items had expired.

An entity-level extension of the statute of limitations on assessment must be made either by the TMP or by a person authorized in writing by the partnership to sign the extension. If a person other than the TMP is authorized to sign the extension, the partnership is required to file a statement confirming the authorization, specifying the years for which the authorization is effective and containing the signature of "all persons who were general partners at any time during the year or years for which the authorization is effective."[125] A Form 2848 Power of Attorney, if signed by all general partners, will normally be sufficient for this purpose.

The forms used for extending the statute for partnership items are Form 872-P for a specific period of time extension and Form 872-O for an indefinite extension. Open-ended extensions may be terminated by either the IRS or the partnership by delivery of Form 872-N. Understandably, the IRS has a strong preference for entity-level extensions of the statute of limitations. However, partner-level extensions, extending the statute only for partners who sign them, are permitted in certain circumstances.[126]

The running of the period of limitations on assessment in TEFRA partnership proceedings is suspended upon the issuance of an FPAA for the period within which a petition for readjustment of partnership items can be filed (a total of 150 days) and, if no petition for readjustment is filed, for one year thereafter. If a petition is filed, the suspension lasts for one year after the court's decision becomes final.[127] The

125. IRM 8.19.1.6.6.8.1.2(2).

126. IRM 8.19.1.6.6.8.2.1; *see, e.g.*, Candyce Martin 1999 Irrevocable Trust v. United States, 739 F.3d 1204 (9th Cir. 2014) (consent restricted as to certain items of lower-tier partnership); Russian Recovery Fund Ltd. v. United States, 101 Fed. Cl. 498 (2011)(consent restricted as to indirect partner).

127. IRC §6229(d); *see, e.g.*, Gingerich v. United States, 77 Fed. Cl. 231 & 78 Fed. Cl. 164 (2007) (holding assessments to be time barred because they were made more than one year after Tax Court stipulated decision), *judgement amended sub nom.* Liebovich v. United States, 104 AFTR2d 5976 (Fed. Cl. 2009).

period for assessing income tax attributable to any partnership item (or affected item) is also suspended, under certain circumstances, with respect to an unidentified partner until one year after the partner is identified to the IRS.[128]

VI. Efficacy and the Future

This chapter has chronicled uncertainties and inefficiencies that continue to bedevil the audit and litigation of partnership and partner returns. Lawyers and commentators lament that TEFRA is beset by "unanswerable questions."[129] Judges frequently despair that the TEFRA rules are "fiendishly complicated"[130] and a "statutory labyrinth."[131] The complaint of one court some years ago remains a problem today. "It is a rare statute—even in the world of Federal taxation—that continues to spawn jurisdictional disputes nearly thirty years after its enactment. But as many recent cases would attest, TEFRA is among that uncommon breed."[132]

Taxpayers and the IRS routinely make mistakes in applying TEFRA rules.[133] They also routinely engage in strategic maneuvering based on the unpredictability of TEFRA outcomes. For instance, partnerships that would fit within the small partnership exception sometimes elect into TEFRA to afford themselves the possibility of the IRS misapplying the TEFRA rules. The IRS often issues both Notices of Deficiency and FPAAs because it is not sure which regime applies. And the IRS, uncertain of just who the partners are and where they are, frequently sends multiple FPAAs to multiple parties at multiple addresses.[134] Such conduct does not speak well for the system that breeds it.

Even worse, in 2014, it was revealed that the IRS—for several reasons including the complexity of TEFRA—audits only 1% of returns filed by partnerships whose assets exceed \$100 million.[135] This gave rise to a widespread sense that "many investors

128. IRC § 6229(e).

129. Michael J. Desmond, *quoted by* Shamik Trivedi & Jeremiah Coder, *TEFRA Raises Complex Jurisdictional Issues, Judge Says,* Tax Notes, May 21, 2012, p. 985.

130. Tigers Eye Trading LLC v. Commissioner, 138 T.C. 67, 94 n. 29 (2012).

131. Prati v. United States, 81 Fed. Cl. 422, 427 (2008); *see also* Waterman v. United States, 113 AFTR2d 1169, at n. 5 (S.D. Ohio 2014) (noting that disparate timing consequences under TEFRA entailed "a peculiar result, but the plain language of § 6230(d)(1) and § 6229(c)(3) appears to compel it").

132. Prestop Holdings, LLC v. United States, 96 Fed. Cl. 244, 244 (2010).

133. *E.g.,* Bedrosian v. Commissioner, 143 T.C. 83, 84 (2014)(noting TEFRA "missteps by both the agency [the IRS] charged with administering this [TEFRA] system and [the taxpayers'] representatives"). Sometimes the IRS's errors are excused on "harmless error" grounds; sometimes they are not. *E.g.,* Bush v. United States, 599 F.3d 1352, 1363–65 (Fed. Cir. 2010) (applying "harmless error" doctrine to IRS's failure to make demand for payment before collection), *vacated,* 400 Fed. Appx. 556 (Fed. Cir. 2010).

134. *E.g.,* Stone Canyon Partners v. Commissioner, T.C. Memo. 2007-377, *aff'd sub nom.* Bedrosian v. Commissioner, 358 Fed. Appx. 868 (9th Cir. 2009).

135. Government Accountability Office, *Large Partnerships: Growing Population and Complexity Hinder Effective IRS Audits* (GAO-14-746T) (July 22, 2014).

who are required to pay taxes on their shares of partnership income are effectively immune to meaningful IRS review of the reporting positions taken on the underlying partnership returns."[136]

Some proposed piecemeal changes to TEFRA.[137] Others—convinced that TEFRA's problems are inherent and irremediable—urged that the regime be torn out and discarded root and branch.[138] There is precedent for repeal. A TEFRA-like regime once existed for S corporations under former Code sections 6241 to 6245. Most of that regime was repealed in 1997.[139]

The Administration,[140] leading members of Congress,[141] and various private sector individuals and groups[142] all advanced proposals. The culmination of these efforts is described in Chapter 6B.

Problems

1. Gizmo Florida, Inc., a C corporation, owned and operated a successful business that manufactured and sold widgets in the Florida. Seven years ago, an unrelated company that manufactured and sold widgets in Alabama went out of business. Management of Gizmo Florida decided to expand its business into Alabama to fill the void.

Two issues had to be considered. First, an entity separate from Gizmo Florida would be required to own and operate the business in Alabama for state law purposes. And second, substantial capital would be required for manufacturing operations.

After consideration, the management of Gizmo Florida decided to form a new limited liability company, Gizmo Alabama, LLC, to own and operate the new business in Alabama. Gizmo Alabama would be treated as a partnership for federal tax purposes. The plan called for Gizmo Alabama to be owned by Gizmo Florida, three mid-level managers of Gizmo Florida (Tom, Dick and Harry), and some unrelated investors.

---

136. Donald B. Susswein & Ryan P. McCormick, *Fixing the Partnership Audit Process*, 2015 TNT 193-19 (Oct. 6, 2015) (noting the view but questioning it).

137. *E.g.*, N. Jerold Cohen & William E. Sheumaker, *When It's Broke, Fix It! It's Time for TEFRA Reform*, Tax Notes, Aug. 13, 2013, p. 815.

138. *E.g.*, Steve R. Johnson, *The E.L. Wiegand Lecture: Administrability-Based Tax Simplification*, 4 Nev. L.J. 573, 596–600 (2004) (urging repeal of the TEFRA rules except for the two consistency rules described above); Peter A. Prescott, *Jumping the Shark: The Case for Repealing the TEFRA Partnership Audit Rules*, 11 Fla. Tax Rev. 503 (2011).

139. Small Business Job Protection Act of 1996, Pub. L. 104-188, § 1307(c)(1), 110 Stat. 1781; *see* New York Football Giants, Inc. v. Commissioner, 117 T.C. 152 (2001). The portion that remains is a consistency rule similar to section 6222 discussed above. *See* IRC § 6037(c); Winter v. Commissioner, 135 T.C. 238 (2012).

140. *See* Jt. Comm. on Taxation, *Description of Certain Revenue Provisions Contained in the President's Fiscal Year 2016 Budget Proposal* 256–69 (Sept. 2015).

141. *E.g.*, Amy S. Elliott, *Camp Draft Forgoes Unified Passthrough Regime*, Tax Notes, Mar. 3, 2014, p. 886.

142. *See* Susswein & McCormick, *supra* (noting some of the proposals and advancing some).

Soon thereafter, Gizmo Alabama was formed. Its members were as follows:

Gizmo Florida	15%
Tom	5%
Dick	5%
Harry	15%
Five investors (12% each)	60%
	100%

Tom, Dick and Harry were not related to each other, to any of the shareholders, officers or directors of Gizmo Florida or to any of the five investors. Neither Tom, Dick nor Harry was a nonresident alien. Similarly, the five investors were unrelated to each other or to any of the other members. The five investors consisted entirely of individuals, none of whom was a nonresident alien. Gizmo Florida was selected as the managing member of Gizmo Alabama for state law purposes.

All capital, interests in the profits and losses, and allocations were proportional to ownership of the membership interests.

Gizmo Alabama recently received a letter from the IRS informing it of an examination of some of its recently filed tax returns.

(a) Is Gizmo Alabama subject to the TEFRA rules set forth in IRC secs. 6221–6234?

(b) Would your answer to (a) be the same if the IRS, during the examination, erroneously determined that the TEFRA rules applied?

(c) Assume for the rest of this problem 1 that Gizmo Alabama was subject to the TEFRA rules. Gizmo Florida was named as the tax matters partner (TMP) in the first return of Gizmo Alabama. Who would be deemed to be the TMP if Gizmo Florida resigns or is no longer willing to serve and no replacement TMP was appointed?

(d) How would Gizmo Florida's status as TMP be affected if it files a petition in bankruptcy?

(e) Assume for this question 1(e) that Harry properly became the TMP. Shortly thereafter, the IRS began an investigation of Harry for criminal tax fraud unrelated to Gizmo Florida or Gizmo Alabama. Harry was advised of the investigation, but none of the other members of Gizmo Alabama or was aware of it. Shortly thereafter, and during the IRS examination, Harry signed an appropriate document agreeing to extend the statute of limitations for Gizmo Alabama. The other members of Gizmo Alabama learned of the investigation a year later. The examination was still in progress at that time, but the statute of limitations for one of the years under examination had expired, without regard to the agreement signed by Harry. The other members of Gizmo Alabama took the position that the statute of limitations for that year had expired because Harry's criminal tax fraud investigation had the effect of terminating Harry's status as the TMP. Does their position have merit?

(f) Assume for this Problem 1(f) that Gizmo Florida was the TMP. Toward the conclusion of the examination, Gizmo Florida was undergoing some changes in management. It concluded, as a business decision, that it no longer wanted to be TMP of Gizmo Alabama, but did not formally resign or designate another member as TMP.

The IRS had mailed an FPAA to Gizmo Florida as TMP of Gizmo Alabama 75 days earlier. A decision had been made to petition the Tax Court, but the petition had not yet been filed. Gizmo Alabama management asked Harry to take over as TMP and sign the petition. Harry did sign the petition, and it was timely filed on the 90th day. The IRS argued that the petition was invalid because Harry had not properly become the TMP. Does the IRS's position have merit?

2. LLC 1 was a Florida limited liability company treated as a partnership for federal tax purposes. It was organized on January 1, 2013.

The members of LLC 1 were as follows:

LLC 2	17%
Trust A	15%
Z Corporation	4%
Eight individuals (8% each)	64%
	100%

LLC 2 was also a Florida limited liability company treated as a partnership for federal tax purposes. Its members were all individuals who were unrelated and none of whom was a non-resident alien.

Trust A had four equal income beneficiaries, to whom all of Trust A's income was required to be distributed no less often than annually. It also had three remaindermen.

Z Corporation was a Florida corporation and a C corporation for federal tax purposes.

None of the eight individual members of LLC 1 was related to each other, and none was a non-resident alien.

All capital, interests in the profits and losses, and allocations were proportional to the membership interests.

LLC 1 timely filed its Form 1065 (U.S. Return of Partnership Income) for the calendar year 2013, without extension and named Z Corporation as its TMP. Forms K-1 were timely sent to each of its eleven members.

On March 1, 2016, the IRS sent an NBAP for the calendar year 2013 to Z Corporation, as TMP of LLC 1, by certified mail pursuant to IRM 4.31.2.2.5.1(1) and Reg. § 301.6223(a)-2(a).

(a) To which of the persons identified above would the IRS send the NBAP?

(b) What is the obligation, if any, of the trustee of Trust A to its income beneficiaries with respect to the NBAP? To its remaindermen?

(c) Which persons are entitled to participate in the administrative proceeding?

(d) The NBAP starts the running of a period during which certain action must be taken by the IRS.

(i) What is the action?

(ii) By when must the action be taken?

(e) What effect would the failure of Trust A to receive the NBAP have on the income beneficiaries?

(f) During the examination, the Revenue Agent proposed the adjustment of a series of items which together increased the taxable income of LLC 1 by $225,000. The TMP and LLC 2 entered into a settlement agreement with the IRS with respect to those items. Who is bound by the agreement?

(g) What alternatives are available to those members who are not bound?

(h) During the examination of LLC 1, the IRS and one of the members entered into a settlement agreement in which the tax treatment of two partnership items of LLC 1 were resolved as to that member. The settlement agreement also resolved three nonpartnership items of that member. Are the other members of LLC 1 entitled to the same treatment with respect to the partnership items under the "consistent settlement provisions" of IRC § 6224(c)(2)?

(i) Within what period of time must the IRS issue the FPAA?

(j) What effect does the mailing of the FPAA have on the statute of limitations?

(k) Assume for this Problem 2(k) and Problem (l) below that the IRS sends an FPAA to Z Corporation, as TMP of LLC 1, on January 15, 2017.

(i) What is the last date by which judicial review can be sought?

(ii) What alternatives are available for judicial review?

(l) Assume for this Problem 2(l) that Z Corporation does not seek judicial review of the FPAA.

(i) What alternatives are available to the other members of LLC 1?

(ii) By what date must action be taken?

(m) What action should Z Corporation take if the FPAA is sent on August 15, 2018?

(n) Assume for this Problem 2(n) that the TMP files a petition in the Tax Court with respect to five issues. The TMP prevails on three of the issues and the IRS prevails on two of the issues. Who is bound by the Tax Court decision when it becomes final?

Chapter 6B

Examination of Partnerships (BBA)

IRC: §§6221(a), 6221(b)(skim), 6222(skim), 6223, 6225(a), 6223(b)&(c)(skim), 6226(a), 6227(a), 6231(a), 6232(a)-(d)(skim), 6234(a)-(c), 6235(a), 6235(b)-(d)(skim)*

Other: IRS Notice 2016-23, 2016-13 IRB 490 (Mar. 28, 2016)

I. Introduction

Chapter 6A noted that the ELP regime was little used and that the TEFRA regime was beset by severe, indeed intractable problems. As a result, Congress dismantled both regimes in late 2015 in the Bipartisan Budget Act (BBA), replacing them with a new regime for audit and litigation of partnership tax items.[1]

The BBA continues a lamentable trend in recent federal tax legislation: excessive haste with inadequate deliberation, leading to murky and problem-laden statutes. The statutory language effectively was made public for the first time when the bill was referred to the House Rules Committee on October 28, 2015. The bill was passed by the House on the same day. It was passed by the Senate on October 30 and signed by the President on December 2.

This deliberative dearth is somewhat ameliorated by the fact that the BBA regime bears similarities to previous, unsuccessful bills and by the fact that some well-connected interest groups learned of the measure and made suggestions, some of which led to modifications of the bill. Nonetheless, the unusually truncated and opaque legislative process caused at least three problems: (1) inequality of participation because affected but less well connected taxpayers were unable to present their views, (2) defects that could have been avoided, and (3) paucity of interpretive materials. Neither the House Ways and Means Committee nor the Senate Finance Committee held public hearings, had mark-up sessions, or issued an authoritative report on the new regime. The staff of the Joint Committee on Taxation did issue a "Blue Book."[2] However, as noted in Chapter 1, the Supreme Court has unanimously held that Blue Books are not legitimate devices of statutory interpretation (although many continue to cite them).[3]

---

* All IRC references in this Chapter 6B are to the "new" sections, i.e., the sections as revised by the BBA as amended.

1. Pub. L. 114-74, §1101, 129 Stat. 584, 625, *amended by* Protecting Americans from Tax Hikes Act of 2015, Pub. L. 114-113, div. Q, §411, 129 Stat. 3103.

2. General Explanation of Tax Legislation Enacted in 2015, at 45-84 (JCS-1-16) (Mar. 14, 2016).

3. United States v. Woods, 134 S. Ct. 557, 568 (2013). *But see* Reg. §1.6662-4(d)(3)(iii)(Blue Books are authority for penalty defense purposes)

In late March 2016, the IRS announced its intention to issue regulations under the BBA regime and requested comments from the public.[4] As of June 2016, no such regulations had been proposed.

Regulations will eventually be proposed, and it is probable that the statute will be amended in currently unforeseeable ways. Based on what is currently known, it was justifiable for Congress to abolish TEFRA and ELP, but it is far from clear to what extent the new BBA rules are an improvement.

Below, three questions are addressed: (1) Does the tax practitioner have to know both the TEFRA rules and the BBA rules? (2) What do the BBA rules require and how do they differ from the TEFRA rules? And (3) what will be some of the major challenges faced by taxpayers and their representatives under the BBA?

II. Need to Know Both Regimes

As if Subchapter K and Subtitle F weren't complicated enough already, unfortunately, "yes," for the foreseeable future, the competent tax advisor must be able to navigate both TEFRA and the BBA.

The BBA changes are generally effective for partnership tax years beginning after December 31, 2017.[5] Nonetheless, the tax advisor must know about the BBA before 2018 and must know about TEFRA well after 2017.

A. BBA Before 2018

Despite the general effective date, partnerships may make an "early in" election, choosing to have the BBA apply to their 2016 and/or 2017 returns.[6] Moreover, as will be apparent below, the new rules will often require partnerships and LLCs to revise their organic documents to prescribe how BBA choices are to be made and to realign partnership interests or to provide compensatory offsets so that BBA changes do not disturb the economic outcomes intended by the partners. This process will be difficult and time consuming. It should be begun well before 2018 and cannot be effectively managed without detailed understanding of the Brave New BBA World.

B. TEFRA After 2018

For entities not making the "early in" election, TEFRA will continue in place for 2016 and 2017. Moreover, audits and litigation of complex transactions often take years (sometimes over a decade) to complete, as has been the case with many tax shelters organized as TEFRA partnerships. For instance, assume the IRS begins in 2017 an audit of a complicated partnership return for tax year 2015. Ensuing pro-

---

4. IRS Notice 2016-23, 2016-13 IRB 490 (Mar. 28, 2016). The Notice's "bare bones" description of the BBA provisions adds little to the statute or the Blue Book.

5. BBA § 1101(g)(1)(not codified).

6. *Id.* § 1101(g)(4)(not codified).

ceedings may not conclude until 2025 or later, and attorneys handling those proceedings will be using the TEFRA rules.

III. What the BBA Mandates

The BBA rules fall into six categories: (1) partnership-level adjustments, (2) partnership representative, (3) procedures of adjustments, (4) administrative adjustment requests, (5) consistent reporting, and (6) miscellaneous rules.

A. Partnership-Level Adjustments

The Introduction to Chapter 6A described the three eras of IRS adjustment of partnership items. The first era entailed complete diffusion, with the IRS making partnership-related adjustments wholly at the owner level, *i.e.*, each partner had to be audited. The second era (TEFRA) was more centralized, with audits at the entity level but with owner participation and with exceptions. The third era (BBA) is yet more centralized, eliminating owner participation. However, as seen below, special rules cause individual partner characteristics to still matter in some situations.

Under the BBA, "[a]ny [IRS] adjustment to items of income, gain, loss, deduction, or credit of a partnership ... (and any partner's distributive share thereof) shall be determined, [and] any tax attributable thereto shall be assessed and collected ... at the partnership level."[7] However, unlike C corporations which pay tax at a rate unconnected to the tax rates of their shareholders,[8] the amount of tax BBA partnerships will pay as to IRS adjustments bears some correlation to the tax rates of the partners. The tax amount is called the "imputed underpayment,"[9] which is the net amount derived from all adjustments multiplied by the highest rate set out by section 1 (rates for individuals, estates, and trusts) or section 11 (rates for corporations)[10] for the reviewed year. The reviewed year is the partnership tax year at issue.[11]

Although the imputed payment is calculated by reference to the reviewed year, the partnership becomes liable for it in the adjustment year and reports the amount on its return for the adjustment year. The adjustment year is the year the adjustments are finalized after judicial review, if any.[12] Treasury is directed to establish procedures under which the imputed underpayment amount may be modified consistent with

---

7. IRC § 6221(a). Determination, assessment, and collection of interest and penalties also occur at the partnership level. *See* IRC § 6233.

8. *See* IRC § 11.

9. IRC § 6225(a)(1). Section 6225(a)(2) addresses adjustments that do not result in imputed underpayments.

10. IRC § 6225(b)(1)(A).

11. IRC § 6225(d)(1).

12. IRC § 6225(d)(2).

stated principles as to amended returns, tax-exempt partners, passive losses of publicly traded partnerships, and other conditions.[13]

There are two important elective exceptions. First, a partnership may elect to compel those who were partners in the reviewed year to take into account and pay tax on the IRS adjustments, avoiding the adjustment-year partnership liability.[14] This "push-up" election must be made within 45 days after the IRS issues a Notice of Final Partnership Adjustment to the partnership, and it requires that the partnership provide (at such time and in such manner as required by the IRS) to the reviewed-year partners and to the IRS a statement of each partner's share of any adjustment made by the IRS.[15]

Second, certain partnerships are permitted to elect out of the BBA rules entirely. In general, this option is available only if there are 100 or fewer partners, each of which is an individual, a corporation (including foreign entities that would be treated as C corporations were they domestic[16]), or an estate of a deceased partner.[17] The election is to be made annually on a timely filed partnership return[18]; the partnership must disclose the name and taxpayer identification number of each partner[19]; and each partner must be notified of the election.[20] Special rules apply for determining the number of partners when a partner is an S corporation.[21] Treasury is authorized to prescribe further requirements.[22]

For partnerships making this "opt out" election, partnership items will be adjusted at the partner level. This is a curious choice which Congress may be compelled to reconsider. The BBA "100 or fewer" elective exception is broader than TEFRA's "10 or fewer" exception.[23] Many eligible partnerships may choose to make this BBA election. Yet, as described in Chapter 6A, the difficulties of owner-level audit and litigation constituted a main driver of enactment of the TEFRA rules. The BBA exception threatens to recreate the environment that prompted enactment of the TEFRA rules.

B. Partnership Representative

Under TEFRA, the IRS dealt with a partnership principally through its Tax Matters Partner (TMP) although other partners (especially so called notice partners) had rights to be notified of actions and in some cases to participate in them.[24] The BBA

13. IRC § 6225(c).
14. IRC § 6226(b)&(c).
15. IRC § 6226(a).
16. *Cf.* Reg. § 301.7701-2(b)(8) (identifying types of foreign entities treated as corporations under the "check the box" rules).
17. IRC § 6221(b)(1)(A),(B)&(C).
18. IRC § 6221(b)(1)(D)(i).
19. IRC § 6221(b)(1)(D)(ii).
20. IRC § 6221(b)(1)(E).
21. IRC § 6221(b)(2)(A).
22. IRC § 6221(b)(2)(B)&(C).
23. *See* pre-BBA IRC § 6231(a)(1)(B)(i) (discussed in Chapter 6A).

replaces TMPs with "partnership representatives" (PRs) whose selection and powers differ somewhat from those of TMPs.

Each partnership will select its PR in the manner to be prescribed by the Treasury. Unlike a TMP, the PR need not be a partner although the PR must have "a substantial presence in the United States."[25] The PR has "the sole authority to act on behalf of the partnership."[26] "Notice partner" and similar TEFRA classifications are abolished. Should the partnership fail to do so, the IRS "may select any person" as the PR.[27]

C. Procedures of Adjustment

Sections 6231 to 6235 set out various procedural rules. These rules include the following:

- The IRS is to mail to the partnership and the PR (at their last known addresses) the following notices: Notice of Administrative Proceeding (NAP—replacing the TEFRA NBAP), Notice of Proposed Partnership Adjustment (NPPA), and Notice of Final Partnership Adjustment (NFPA—replacing the TEFRA FPAA). An NFPA may not be issued earlier than 270 days after issuance of the NPPA.[28]
- Paralleling section 6212(c)(1) as to Notices of Deficiency, the BBA prohibits issuance of a second NFPA for the same year if the partnership has filed an action in court challenging the first NFPA unless the IRS shows "fraud, malfeasance, or misrepresentation" by the partnership.[29]
- The IRS, with the partnership's consent, may rescind BBA notices.[30]
- An imputed underpayment "shall be assessed and collected in the same manner as if it were a tax imposed for the adjustment year."[31]
- Paralleling the deficiency procedures discussed in Chapter 8, additional taxes usually may not be assessed or collected during the 90-day judicial petition period or, if a petition is filed, before the court's decision becomes final.[32] Exceptions exist as to math errors, clerical errors, and partnership waivers.[33] Notwithstanding the Anti-Injunction Act, premature assessment or collection can be enjoined.[34]

---

24. *See* pre-BBA IRC § 6223(b) (discussed in Chapter 6A).
25. IRC § 6223(a).
26. *Id.* The partnership and all the partners are bound by the PR's actions and by final decisions in proceedings involving the PR. IRC § 6223(b)(1)&(2).
27. IRC § 6223(a).
28. IRC § 6231(a).
29. IRC § 6231(b).
30. IRC § 6231(c).
31. IRC § 6232(a).
32. IRC § 6232(b).
33. IRC § 6232(d).
34. IRC § 6232(c).

- Partly comparably to the deficiency and TEFRA processes, the BBA permits partnerships to challenge NFPAs by filing within 90 days a Tax Court, District Court, or Court of Federal Claims petition.[35] To invoke the jurisdiction of the latter two courts, the partnership must make a deposit (not treated as a payment of tax) generally equal to the imputed underpayment amount.[36]
- The trial court's decision may determine all relevant issues, and the decision is appealable.[37]
- The BBA statute of limitations rules are generally similar to those applicable to deficiency proceedings, described in Chapter 5. The normal limitations period as to adjustments is three years from the later of when the partnership return was filed or was due to be filed. The period can be expanded by agreement of the parties, fraud, and substantial income omissions,[38] and its running is suspended by issuance of an NFPA.[39] As alternatives to the normal three-year period, adjustments may be made within 270 days (or more in the case of extensions) after modification of an imputed underpayment pursuant to section 6225(c) or 270 days after issuance of an NPPA.[40]

As described in Chapter 6A, the TEFRA limitations rules are viewed as extending and never contracting the section 6501 limitations periods. Thus, the IRS could issue an FPAA at any time and could assess and collect against any partners whose individual 6501 periods happened to be open as of the date of such issuance. That cannot happen under the centralized BBA approach.

D. Administrative Adjustment Requests

The TEFRA version of section 6227 allows both TMPs on behalf of the partnership and partners acting on their own behalf to file administrative adjustment requests (AARs). Such requests could involve either increased or decreased tax. However, the principal significance of the device was as the vehicle by which refund claims were made in the TEFRA context.

The BBA version of the section eliminates partner-initiated AARs. It provides generally that a partnership may file one or more AARs.[41] Any resulting adjustment is determined and taken into account for the partnership year in which the AAR is made.[42] In general, the partnership may not file an AAR more than three years after the partnership return for the year was filed, and it is prohibited from filing an AAR

35. IRC § 6234(a).
36. IRC § 6234(b).
37. IRC § 6234(c)&(d). Generally, dismissal of an action is considered a decision that the NFPA is correct. IRC § 6234(e).
38. IRC § 6235(a)(1).
39. IRC § 6235(b),(c)&(d).
40. IRC § 6235(a)(2)&(3).
41. IRC § 6227(a).
42. IRC § 6227(b).

after the IRS issues an NAP for the year.[43] If the AAR involves an increase of tax, the additional amount is to be paid along with the AAR.[44]

Significant issues as to the BBA remain to be resolved as to tiered partnerships. As relevant to this context, the Blue Book asserts: "In the case of tiered partnerships, a partnership's partners that are themselves partnerships may choose to file an [AAR] with respect to their distributive shares of an adjustment. [They] may choose to coordinate the filing of [AARs] as a group to the extent permitted by the [Treasury]."[45]

E. Consistent Reporting

As described in Chapter 6A, TEFRA had consistency rules as to both return reporting positions and settlements. The entity-level centralization of BBA obviates the need for the settlement consistency rules. The BBA retains reporting consistency rules similar to those of TEFRA.

Thus, partners are directed on their returns to treat partnership items as they were treated on the partnership's return.[46] The IRS generally may immediately assess as math errors additional tax attributable to inconsistent reporting,[47] and the inconsistency may give rise to a penalty. [48] Inconsistent reporting is excused if the partner notifies the IRS of the inconsistency or if the partner received incorrect information from the partnership.[49]

F. Miscellaneous Rules

Numerous special rules are sprinkled throughout the BBA sections. They include the following:

- No income tax deduction is allowed for any payment a partnership is required to make under the BBA regime.[50]
- If a partnership ceases to exist before a partnership adjustment is made, the adjustment is taken into account by the former partners.[51]
- Similarly to the TEFRA rules, if an entity files a partnership return but is later determined not to be a partnership, the BBA provisions will nonetheless apply.[52]
- Partnerships whose principal place of business is outside the United States are treated as being located in the District of Columbia.[53] This has significance for

43. IRC § 6227(c).
44. IRC § 6232(a).
45. General Explanation, *supra* n. 2, at 71.
46. IRC § 6222(a).
47. IRC § 6222(b).
48. *See* IRC § 6222(e); General Explanation, *supra* n. 2, at 61.
49. IRC § 6222(c)(1)&(2).
50. IRC § 6241(4).
51. IRC § 6241(7).
52. IRC § 6241(8).
53. IRC § 6241(3).

various purposes, including venue for District Court actions and venue for appeal from Tax Court decisions.[54]

- When a partnership is a debtor in a bankruptcy case, the periods of limitations for adjustment, assessment, or collection are suspended, as is the period of limitation for seeking judicial review of a BBA adjustment.[55]
- An issue determined in a partnership adjustment proceeding may not be reconsidered as part of a Collection Due Process hearing.[56]

IV. Some Challenges and Pitfalls

Below, we consider open issues as to the BBA regime, planning considerations, and malpractice possibilities.

A. Open Issues

The BBA is at best a skeleton. Much meat will have to be put on its bones. The IRS has acknowledged this. As noted previously, in late March 2016, the IRS requested public comments to inform the process of writing regulations under the new regime. The IRS invited comments as to 12 areas, most of them divided into sub issues. The twelve are: (1) the opt-out election, (2) designation of the PR, (3) determination of the imputed payment, (4) modification of the imputed payment, (5) adjustments not resulting in imputed payments, (6) the section 6225 alternative payment election, (7) AARs, (8) effect of adjustments on inside and outside basis, (9) the consistency requirement, (10) the effects of bankruptcy and cessation of partnership existence, (11) procedural rules, and (12) "[a]ny other issues relevant to the implementation of the [BBA], including ... the interaction of these rules with international tax provisions."[57]

As of the time this book went to press, numerous individuals and groups had responded to the challenge, their comments ranging from the narrow and targeted to plenary.[58] Undoubtedly, numerous additional suggestions will be offered in the future.

Years, if not decades, will be required to provide needed regulatory guidance, and some statutory changes are likely. The magnitude of the task is suggested by the excellent comments given to the IRS by the American Bar Association Section of Taxation on

---

54. *See, e.g.*, IRC § 7482(b)(1).

55. IRC § 6241(6)(A)&(B).

56. BBA § 1101(d)(amending IRC § 6330(c)(4)(C)). The Collection Due Process procedures are discussed in Chapter 13.

57. *See* Notice 2016-23, *supra*, part III.01.

58. Some of the thorniest issues will involve applying the BBA to tiered partnerships and partnerships with many partners. *See, e.g.*, Curtis Beaulieu, *New Audit Rules for Partnerships: Heartburn for MLPs*, Tax Notes, Nov. 9, 2015, at 813.

June 6, 2016. The comments identify over a hundred flaws, limitations, and ambiguities in the BBA and in some instances suggest appropriate changes or clarifications.[59]

B. Planning Considerations

Some regulations will be issued before 2018.[60] However, issuing all or even most of the needed guidance would be an herculean effort even under the best of circumstances, and the IRS's current budgetary woes are hardly the best of circumstances.[61] Undoubtedly, tax planners and advisors will confront difficult questions with inadequate guidance for years to come.

The difficulties may be compounded from a different quarter. Chapter 1 described the growing prominence in tax of principles of general administrative law, and it noted instances in which tax regulations and other guidance have been invalidated by the courts because they were formulated in violation of Administrative Procedure Act requirements. If history is a guide, some BBA regulations will be challenged—perhaps successfully—on notice-and-comment, arbitrary-and-capricious, phantom regulation, "goes beyond the statute," or other administrative law grounds.[62] Having a sense of which BBA guidance may be vulnerable would be helpful to practitioners in the years to come.

C. Malpractice Considerations

Some lawyers specialize in bringing or defending legal and accounting malpractice suits. The BBA may prove to be a bonanza for them, as the following four perspectives suggest.

First, lawyers and accountants will sometimes fail to address issues needing attention under the BBA. Countless existing partnership and LLC agreements refer expressly to TEFRA, and countless others have TEFRA-inspired provisions without identifying TEFRA expressly. These provisions should be reviewed before 2018 and frequently will have to be changed. Similarly, agreements governing all new partnerships and LLCs will have to make BBA-related choices, choices that will demand research, careful analysis, clear advice to clients, and often hard bargaining.

Inevitably, some of the needed work will "fall through the cracks," especially because lawyers and accountants serving mutual clients are not famous for effective coordination. Malpractice actions will ensue.

---

59. These comments are organized under ten headings. Some are the same as topics in Notice 2016-23. In addition, the ABA comments address the early-in election, statutes of limitations, and BBA notices.

60. On March 28, 2016, the IRS announced that it and Treasury intended to publish "in the near future" guidance as to the early-in election. Notice 2016-23, *supra*, part I.

61. *See, e.g.*, Steve R. Johnson, *The Future of American Tax Administration: Conceptual Alternatives and Political Realities*, 7 Colum. J. Tax L. 5 (2016).

62. These and other administrative law challenges to regulations are addressed in Chapter 1.

Second, in some cases, needed discussions will occur, needed changes will be made—but they will be made late, forfeiting some benefit or incurring some disadvantage. Damages in this second class of cases will be smaller than in the first class but probably won't be negligible.

Third, in some cases, the "wrong" choices will be made, saddling the partners with sub-optimum outcomes. Given the complexity of the BBA and the dearth of guidance, such wrong choices are inevitable.

Fourth, many of the elections available under the BBA will create conflicts of interest.[63] If anticipated, such matters sometimes could be hashed out in the give-and-take of negotiation among the owners. Absent such decisions embodied in clearly written provisions, PRs, lawyers, and accountants will have to do the best they can. Perhaps they'll make the "right" choices, in the sense that their choices will secure the best overall results. But they may be sued anyway. Where the interests of owners conflict, a choice good for partners A and B may be bad for partner C. C will not always take the high road or take a global view of the matter.

In short, for various reasons, tax advisors should work hard before 2018 to anticipate and resolve controversial matters before problems arise. But they also should acknowledge the possibility that, despite their best efforts, disharmony and litigation may occur in some cases. They should take this into account, for example, in deciding whether to undertake certain representations, what retainers to charge, what warnings to give to clients, what written acknowledgements to demand from their clients, and whether to serve as PR if requested.

Problem

Return to Problem 1 concluding Chapter 6A (Gizmo and related persons). Assume the same facts, making necessary contextual alterations. Thus, for example, references to "TMP" in Problem 1 would convert to references to "PR." Answer the questions in Problem 1 from the standpoint of the BBA rules rather than the TEFRA rules.

63. For example, the push-up election will help current partners at the expense of historic partners.

Chapter 7

Termination and Jeopardy Assessments

IRC: §§6851; 6861; 6863; 6867; 7429

I. Introduction

As described in Chapter 8, taxpayers typically must be afforded the opportunity for Tax Court review before the IRS can assess deficiencies in income, estate, and gift taxes. Yet audit, administrative appeal, and Tax Court review may consume years. During that time, changes in the taxpayer's financial condition might sharply erode the IRS's ability to collect the deficiencies should the IRS prevail in Tax Court. Furthermore, during that time, some taxpayers with substantial, readily accessible financial resources might attempt to escape responsibility for their tax liabilities by hiding themselves or their assets, or by transferring their assets to relatives, friends, or controlled entities.

There are criminal provisions that can be used to attack such schemes. For example, under section 7201, "[a]ny person who willfully attempts in any manner to evade or defeat any tax ... or the payment thereof" may be found guilty of a felony. Moreover, under 18 U.S.C. section 371, anyone who cooperates with the taxpayer in a scheme of evasion may be found guilty of criminal conspiracy. However, few such criminal prosecutions are brought each year, and even successful criminal prosecution does not make the IRS whole for revenues lost. Thus, some civil mechanisms must exist by which the IRS can preserve the viability of collection.

Those mechanisms are termination assessment under section 6851, jeopardy assessment under sections 6861 and 6862, and related procedures. When they are invoked, the IRS may assess and collect allegedly due taxes immediately, without prior judicial review.[1] Such amounts include any deficiency for the tax period plus, if appropriate, interest and penalties. The importance of these techniques is underscored by the fact that our system has had expedited means of assessment for as long as it has permitted pre-payment challenge to IRS determinations.

---

1. Chapter 13 describes the collection tools available to the IRS after tax has been assessed. An important tool is administrative levy, i.e., the IRS taking possession of property of the taxpayer. Following a jeopardy or termination assessment, the IRS may virtually immediately make jeopardy levy on the taxpayer's assts.

But the peril in expedited assessment is apparent. The deficiency procedures were established for important taxpayer-protection reasons, and their abrogation, even occasionally, is no light matter. Thus, section 7429 provides collateral procedures to afford prompt post-assessment administrative and judicial review to taxpayers subject to expedited assessment. Because they are based on particular need, pose heightened dangers, and entail special procedures, the expedited assessment devices of termination and jeopardy assessments have rightly been called "a singular weapon in the Service's armamentarium."[2]

II. Termination and Jeopardy Assessment and Levy

Termination assessments and jeopardy assessments are similar procedures applied to different tax years and sometimes different taxes. These two techniques are applied when the IRS concludes that collection of tax liabilities would be imperiled by allowing the normal processes of assessment and collection to work their course.

A termination assessment under section 6851 is used with respect to income taxes for years that have not yet closed or for which the returns are not yet due. A termination assessment is made during a tax year that has not yet ended, or at any time before the due date (including any extensions) of the taxpayer's return for the preceding year. A termination assessment terminates the year for purposes of computing the tax to be assessed and collected.

A jeopardy assessment is used, typically, for tax periods already closed and for which the return either has been filed or is past due (taking into account properly obtained extensions). Section 6861 authorizes jeopardy assessment of income, estate, gift, and certain excise taxes. Section 6862 authorizes jeopardy assessment of other taxes. Section 6862 assessments are the sole exception to jeopardy assessment being confined to old tax periods. Under section 6862(a), jeopardy assessment may be made "whether or not the time otherwise prescribed by law for making return and paying such tax has expired." The Regulations give this example:

> [A]ssume that a taxpayer incurs on January 18, 1977, liability for tax imposed by section 4061 [the now repealed gas guzzlers' tax], that the last day on which return and payment of such tax is required to be made is May 2, 1977, and that on January 18, 1977, the district director determines that collection of such tax would be jeopardized by delay. In such case, the district director shall immediately assess the tax.[3]

Normally, the IRS uses jeopardy assessments and termination assessments when the taxpayer was engaged in criminal activities, such as illegal drug trafficking, money laundering, illegal gambling, and organized crime. However, the techniques are not

2. Revis v. United States, 558 F. Supp. 1071 (D.R.I. 1983).

3. Reg. § 301.6862-1(a). The IRS reorganization mandated by the 1998 Reform Act, § 1001, eliminated the position of district director. The authority formerly vested in district directors has been re-delegated to other IRS officials.

confined to those areas. Expedited assessments also are made against legal-source, legal-activity taxpayers who nonetheless meet the conditions justifying expedited assessment.

The expedited assessment techniques of termination and jeopardy assessment should be distinguished from other sorts of rapid or expedited assessment. For example, under section 6213(a), the deficiency procedures described in Chapter 8 apply only to income, estate, gift, generation-skipping transfer, and some excise taxes. Thus, the IRS can immediately assess other types of taxes after audit without issuing a Ninety-Day Letter and without Tax Court review. Moreover, in certain circumstances (such as mathematical or clerical errors on the return), section 6213(b) permits the IRS to immediately assess even those taxes that normally are subject to the deficiency procedures. These direct or immediate assessments are outside sections 6851 and 6861, and related sections, and are not topics of this chapter. The focus of this chapter is only on termination assessment, jeopardy assessment, and related mechanisms.

A. Conditions Justifying Expedited Assessment

The trigger common to termination and jeopardy assessments is also the justification for them: emergency, a state of peril which would compromise ultimate collection of tax if normal processes were allowed to run their course. Section 6851(a)(1) allows the IRS to make a termination assessment if it determines that

> a taxpayer designs quickly to depart from the United States or to remove his property therefrom, or to conceal himself or his property therein, or to do any other act (including in the case of a corporation distributing all or a part of its assets in liquidation or otherwise) tending to prejudice or to render wholly or partially ineffectual proceedings to collect the ... tax.

Both sections 6861(a) and 6862(a) refer to assessment or collection being "jeopardized by delay," but they do not set out criteria with the specificity of section 6851(a)(1). The section 6851 regulations provide:

> A termination assessment will be made if collection is determined to be in jeopardy because at least one of the following conditions exists.
>
> (i) The taxpayer is or appears to be designing quickly to depart from the United States or to conceal himself or herself.
>
> (ii) The taxpayer is or appears to be designing quickly to place his, her, or its property beyond the reach of the Government either by removing it from the United States, by concealing it, by dissipating it, or by transferring it to other persons.
>
> (iii) The taxpayer's financial solvency is or appears to be imperiled.[4]

---

4. Reg. § 1.6851-1(a)(1). The same Regulation clarifies that the insolvency ground "does not include cases where the taxpayer becomes insolvent by virtue of the accrual of the proposed assessment of tax, and penalty, if any." This contrasts with the measurement of insolvency for "in equity" transferee liability cases in which the tax liability is taken into account. *See* Chapter 15.

The sections 6861 and 6862 regulations both refer to the section 6851 regulations. They provide that a state of jeopardy exists when at least one of the these three termination assessment conditions exists.[5] The Government need not show that collection was actually in peril, only that "the circumstances *appear* to jeopardize collection."[6]

It is occasionally argued that, by enumerating these three conditions, the regulations exclude other possible bases for jeopardy or termination assessment. The cases are not entirely consistent, but many decisions look beyond the three grounds in the regulations. In particular, many courts have found that the taxpayer's involvement in criminal activity (especially involving large amounts of cash, as in narcotics trafficking) constitutes strong, sometimes virtually dispositive, support for the appropriateness of expedited assessment.[7]

Another matter of interpretation involves the word "quickly," which appears in the first and second of the three grounds enumerated in the regulations. Just how imminent do the taxpayer's acts have to be? A cramped reading of "quickly" could significantly undercut the utility of the summary device. Recognizing that, the courts have interpreted the word functionally and broadly. If the course of action on which the taxpayer appears to have embarked could significantly erode collection potential before normal procedures have run their course, the "quickly" term will be held to have been satisfied.[8]

The IRS does not make expedited assessments lightly. The expedited assessment procedures are important to the viability of the system. Knowing that, the IRS tends to reserve expedited assessment for clear cases involving substantial dollar amounts.[9] The concern is to avoid creating a body of adverse precedents that could undermine expedited assessment in future cases. Although that is the IRS's usual approach, there are exceptions. The unfortunate fact is that, on occasion, a long, frustrating, and acrimonious course of dealing with a particular taxpayer tips the balance in favor of expedited assessments that might better have been omitted. To minimize such occurrences, expedited assessments require multiple stages of review and approval within the IRS, including by IRS Counsel.[10]

B. Consequences of Expedited Assessment

1. Termination Assessment

Termination assessment may be made with respect to a given tax year either during that year or before the return for the year is due. Two examples clarify this rule. First,

5. Reg. §§ 301.6861-1(a), 301.6862-1(a).

6. Wellek v. United States, 324 F. Supp. 2d 905, 911 (N.D. Ill. 2004) (emphasis in original).

7. *See, e.g.*, Albury v. United States, 88-2 U.S. Tax Cas. (CCH) ¶ 9511 (S.D. Fla. 1988).

8. *See, e.g.*, French v. United States, 79-2 U.S. Tax Cas. (CCH) ¶ 9538 (E.D. Okla. 1979).

9. Restraint is particularly enjoined when the assessment would create public inconvenience, such as when it is against a newspaper, bank, public utility, or other communally important entity. In addition, the IRS sometimes forgoes defensible expedited assessments in order to protect the identity of a confidential informant.

10. *See, e.g.*, IRC § 7429(a)(1)(A); Rev. Proc. 78-12, 1978-1 C.B. 590.

in January 20x4, the IRS determines that collection of the taxpayer's income tax for 20x3 is in jeopardy. The IRS can make a termination assessment as of December 31, 20x3, and collect the determined tax for all of 20x3.[11] Second, on May 1, 20x4, the IRS determines that collecting the taxpayer's income tax for the current year is in jeopardy. The IRS can make a termination assessment and collect the determined tax for the short period January 1, 20x4 through May 1, 20x4.[12]

Upon assessment, the tax "shall immediately become due and payable." If a short period was assessed, the year continues until its normal end. The taxpayer is still obligated to file a return for the full year and at the normal time (typically April 15 of the year following the tax year).[13]

The calculation of the tax for the assessed period includes all income the IRS believes pertains to that period. The taxpayer must be allowed all pertinent deductions and credits, including, if a short period is assessed, full personal exemptions.

In conducting an examination which may lead to termination, revenue agents are instructed to make "reasonable" computation of the tax liability, taking into account all known assets, liabilities, income, and expenses of the taxpayer. Additionally, agents are supposed to interview the taxpayer when feasible (preferably before the assessment is made) to give the taxpayer the opportunity to explain the circumstances. When illegal-source income is suspected, agents are supposed to consult non-tax law enforcement officials, when possible, with knowledge of the activities.[14] Estimates of income and expenses are permitted, but they must relate to specific facts and not entail speculative extrapolations.[15]

Chapter 13 describes the normal rules dealing with post-assessment collection of tax. Those rules are telescoped following a termination assessment. The IRS sometimes does not rapidly seek to collect after an expedited assessment. When it chooses to, however, it can proceed with such collection within a matter of days, even hours, after the expedited assessment.

The IRS must make demand for payment, and, within five days after making the termination assessment, notify the taxpayer of the assessment and the IRS's basis for it.[16] Notification may be served in person or by certified mail to the taxpayer's last known address.[17] The IRS typically files notices of tax lien immediately. Whether it also levies on the taxpayer's property depends upon how the IRS evaluates the circumstances of the particular case. The taxpayer must be given an opportunity—

---

11. What if the IRS did not determine the condition of jeopardy until April 16, 2004? Assuming the taxpayer had not obtained a proper extension, the year would be closed and the IRS's remedy would be jeopardy assessment, not termination assessment.

12. Manual provisions governing termination assessments and jeopardy assessments are set out at IRM 5.1.4.

13. IRC § 6851(a)(1); Reg. § 1.6851-1(a)(3).

14. Frequently, federal or state law enforcement officials will inform the IRS about the illegal activity.

15. *E.g.*, Auth v. United States, 79-2 U.S. Tax Cas. (CCH) ¶ 9726 (D. Utah 1979).

16. IRC §§ 6851(a)(1), 7429(a)(1)(B).

17. IRM 5.1.4.6.

however brief—to pay before seizure is effected.[18] Section 6331(a) provides that, after notice-and-demand, the IRS may take enforced collection action, including levies, without waiting the usual ten-day period.[19]

After making a termination assessment, the IRS is required to issue a statutory Notice of Deficiency to the taxpayer. Under section 6851(b), this must be done within 60 days of the later of (i) the due date for the taxpayer's return for the full year (considered with regard to any properly obtained extension) or (ii) the date the return is filed. Section 6851(b) states that the deficiency determined in the notice may be greater than, less than, or the same amount as was assessed. If the assessed amount exceeds the determined deficiency amount, the excess is to be abated. If the excess has already been collected, the IRS will not make a refund until the case is closed. The deficiency is to be calculated on the basis of the full year, not a period shortened as a result of the assessment.

A pitfall exists for unwary taxpayers in this regard. Returns for years for which there was a termination assessment are to be filed with IRS offices identified in the regulations, not with the usual Service Center.[20] If the return is submitted to the wrong office, it is deemed not to have been filed. As a consequence, the sixty-day period for the issuance of the statutory Notice of Deficiency does not begin to run.

If the return is timely filed and the IRS fails to issue the Notice of Deficiency within the 60-day period, the termination assessment is nullified. However, the IRS may make a new termination assessment or a jeopardy assessment, as long as the section 6501 limitations period has not yet expired and a condition of jeopardy continues to exist. Alternatively, the IRS could follow the deficiency procedures. The failure of the IRS to issue the Notice of Deficiency within the sixty-day period does not compel the IRS to return any amounts collected pursuant to the now-invalidated termination assessment—as long as the IRS properly makes a new assessment and properly issues a Notice of Deficiency.[21]

Upon issuance of the Notice of Deficiency, the taxpayer has the usual options, including filing a petition for redetermination with the Tax Court (with the possibility of Appeals Office consideration once the pleadings are complete). If the taxpayer files a timely petition,[22] the Tax Court has jurisdiction even if the Notice of Deficiency is filed after the 60-day period as long as it was timely issued under section 6501.[23] Any amounts collected under the termination assessment are treated as tax payments for the year.[24] However, under section 6211(b)(1), they are not considered payments in computing the deficiency, and therefore do not affect the Tax Court's jurisdiction.

---

18. *See, e.g.*, Mettenbrink v. United States, 71 A.F.T.R. 2d (RIA) ¶93-3642 (D. Neb. 1991).

19. Under section 6330(f), the Collection Due Process protections do not apply in termination or jeopardy situations.

20. IRC §6091(b); Reg. §1.6091-2.

21. *See, e.g.*, Estate of McDonald v. United States, 79-1 U.S. Tax Cas. (CCH) ¶9182 (N.D. Cal. 1979).

22. Typically, the petition must be filed with the Tax Court within 90 days after the IRS issues the Notice of Deficiency. *See* Chapter 8.

23. *See, e.g.*, Ramirez v. Commissioner, 87 T.C. 643 (1986).

24. IRC §6851(a)(3).

If the IRS eventually concludes that jeopardy to collection did not exist, it may abate the termination assessment. In that event, section 6851(e) directs that the applicable limitations period on normal assessment is determined as if no assessment had been made, except that the running of the period is suspended from the date the assessment was made until 10 days after the assessment was abated.

2. Jeopardy Assessment

As noted, jeopardy assessment is the immediate assessment of an "old" tax year. Typically, it is made before a statutory Notice of Deficiency is issued and Tax Court review is requested. However, if the condition of jeopardy arises after a Notice of Deficiency was issued and during a Tax Court proceeding, jeopardy assessment still is permitted. However, no jeopardy assessment may be made after any decision by the Tax Court has become final or the taxpayer has filed a petition seeking review of the Tax Court's decision. Usually, the assessment may be greater than, less than, or the same amount as determined in the Notice of Deficiency. However, if the assessment is made after the Tax Court decision is rendered (but before it becomes final), the assessment "may be made only in respect of the deficiency determined" in the court's decision. Before the decision is rendered, the IRS may abate part or all of the assessment if it believes the assessment was excessive. If the IRS jeopardy assesses during a Tax Court case, it must notify the court of assessed amounts and abated amounts.[25]

Many of the consequences and procedures as to jeopardy assessments resemble those as to termination assessments. The amount assessed becomes immediately due and payable. Computation typically is easier than with respect to termination assessments because completed tax years are involved. Again, notice and demand for payment must be made and, within five days after the assessment, the IRS must notify the taxpayer of it.[26] The IRS may take collection action immediately after making notice and demand, if payment is not made.

Again, the IRS is required to issue a statutory Notice of Deficiency,[27] but the timing differs from that in the termination assessment context. Section 6861(b) directs the IRS to issue the Notice of Deficiency within 60 days of making notice and demand. This is so only for section 6861 jeopardy assessments since the taxes subject to section 6862 jeopardy assessments do not involve the deficiency procedures. The cases are split as to whether the failure to meet the sixty-day requirement renders the jeopardy assessment unenforceable.[28]

Occasionally, the IRS makes multiple jeopardy assessments for the same tax year. This might happen, for instance, if the IRS later concludes that its prior jeopardy

25. IRC § 6861(c)–(g).

26. IRC §§ 6861(a), 6862(a), 7429(a)(1)(B).

27. This requirement is met if the IRS timely sends the notice to the taxpayer's last known address even if the taxpayer does not receive the notice. "The statute does not require receipt of the notice by the taxpayer." Royal Denim for Import & Export, Inc. v. United States, 371 F. Supp. 2d 569, 571 (S.D.N.Y. 2005).

28. *Compare* United States v. Ball, 326 F.2d 898 (4th Cir. 1964) (yes), *with* Cohen v. United States, 297 F.2d 760 (9th Cir. 1962) (no).

assessment was inadequate in amount. However, each additional jeopardy assessment requires additional notice and demand and an additional Notice of Deficiency. Each of the assessments is independent. Thus, for example, a proper second jeopardy assessment will be upheld even if the first jeopardy assessment was defective for some reason.[29]

The IRS has authority to abate improper or excessive jeopardy assessments before finality of Tax Court decision. The normal limitations rules apply, except that the running of the limitations period is suspended from the date the jeopardy assessment was made until 10 days after it was abated.[30]

The normal sequence is jeopardy assessment followed by jeopardy levy. However, in appropriate circumstances, jeopardy levy may be used after assessment has been effected through normal processes.[31]

III. Section 7429 Review

A. In General

Before 1976, the only judicial recourse available to a taxpayer subject to an expedited assessment was either (i) paying the amount assessed and bringing a normal refund suit or (ii) seeking an injunction under the *Williams Packing* exception to the Anti-Injunction Act.[32] Neither was satisfactory: the former entailed great delay and burden on the taxpayer and the latter was available only in very limited circumstances.

In response to serious concerns about the fairness and perhaps constitutionality of the expedited assessment regime,[33] Congress in 1976 enacted a considerably better review mechanism: section 7429.[34] Suit under section 7429 is now one of the statutory exceptions to the Anti-Injunction Act. Section 7429(a)(1)(A) reinforces pre-assessment review by requiring approval by IRS Counsel both for jeopardy assessment and for levy within 30 days after notice and demand for payment. More importantly, section 7429 creates an elaborate scheme of expedited post-assessment review. However, section 7429 does not suspend the ability of the IRS to collect the assessed tax. Moreover, section 7429 review is available only as to termination and jeopardy assessments, not other types of IRS actions.[35] Here are the main aspects of the rather complex section 7429 post-assessment review scheme:

---

29. *See, e.g.*, Berry v. Westover, 70 F. Supp. 537 (S.D. Cal. 1947).

30. IRC § 6861(g).

31. *E.g.*, Prince v. Comm'r, 133 T.C. 270 (2009).

32. *See* Commissioner v. Shapiro, 424 U.S. 614 (1976); Enochs v. Williams Packing Co., 370 U.S. 1 (1962). For discussion of the Anti-Injunction Act (IRC § 7421) and the Williams Packing exception to it, see Chapter 13.

33. *See, e.g.*, Laing v. United States, 423 U.S. 161 (1976).

34. For further discussion of the origins of section 7429, see Steve R. Johnson, *Reforming Federal Tax Litigation: An Agenda*, 41 Fla. St. U. L. Rev. 206, 229–31 (2013).

35. *E.g.*, Israel v. Everson, 2007-1 U.S.T.C. ¶ 50, 319, at 87,778 (S.D. Iowa 2005), *aff'd per curiam without published opinion*, 210 Fed. Appx. 549 (8th Cir. 2007).

- Within five days after the termination or jeopardy assessment or levy is made, the IRS is required to provide the taxpayer with a written statement of the information upon which the IRS relied in making the assessment or levy.
- Within 30 days after the written statement is provided (or within 30 days after the last date on which it was supposed to have been provided), the taxpayer may request that the IRS review the assessment or levy.[36] This review is conducted by the Appeals Office. The Appeals Office is directed to determine whether the making of the assessment or levy is "reasonable under the circumstances" and whether the amount assessed or demanded is "appropriate under the circumstances."
- If the taxpayer is dissatisfied with the result of this administrative review, he or she may obtain judicial review. Within 90 days after the earlier of (i) the date the Appeals Office notified the taxpayer of its determination or (ii) the sixteenth day after the taxpayer made the request for administrative review, the taxpayer may bring a civil action against the United States in federal District Court challenging the summary assessment or levy. The Tax Court has concurrent jurisdiction, but only in cases in which the IRS jeopardy assessed after the taxpayer petitioned the Tax Court for redetermination of determinations in a statutory Notice of Deficiency for the same or some of the same tax year(s).
- Within 20 days after the action is commenced, the court is to decide the case. The twenty-day period may be extended up to 40 additional days if the taxpayer so requests and establishes reasonable grounds therefor. The government cannot request extension. Saturday, Sunday, or a legal holiday in the District of Columbia cannot be the last day of any section 7429 period.
- The government bears the burden of proof as to whether it was reasonable to make the expedited assessment or levy.[37] In other words, the government must establish that a condition of jeopardy exists. As to the reasonableness of the amount of the assessment, the government must provide a written statement containing the information on which the IRS's determination of the amount assessed was based. Thereafter, the burden of proof on the amount issue shifts to the taxpayer. The court's review is de novo,[38] and the court's decision (at least as to substantive issues) is "final and conclusive and shall not be reviewed by any other court."[39]

The following is a more detailed exploration of the phases of the section 7429 review scheme.

---

36. The 30-day period is not amenable to equitable tolling. Abraitis v. United States, 709 F.3d 641 (6th Cir. 2013).

37. "Reasonable under the circumstances means something more than not arbitrary and capricious [but] something less than supported by substantial evidence." Pircher v. United States, 2009-1 U.S.T.C. ¶ 50,138, at 87,151 (W.D. Tex. 2008) (internal quotation marks omitted).

38. *See, e.g.*, Loretto v. United States, 440 F. Supp. 1168 (E.D. Pa. 1977).

39. IRC § 7429(f).

B. Administrative Phase

It is important that the taxpayer properly seek Appeals consideration. Failure to timely request Appeals consideration is viewed as a failure to exhaust administrative remedies, which precludes the taxpayer from obtaining judicial review.[40] Also, if the taxpayer brings suit before expiration of the time prescribed for administrative review, the case will be dismissed as premature.[41]

The Appeals Office, in considering the request for redetermination, may take into account not only information available at the time the assessment was made, but also after-acquired information. This also is true for a court conducting subsequent judicial review.[42]

C. Trial Phase

Venue is determined pursuant to 28 U.S.C. section 1402(a). Thus, in District Court actions, venue for individual taxpayers is in the district where he or she resides; venue for corporate taxpayers is in the district where the corporation has its principal place of business or filed its return; venue is in the District of Columbia district if the previous rules cannot be applied. If the action is filed in the Tax Court but that court concludes that it lacks jurisdiction, the Tax Court may transfer the action to the proper District Court if the interests of justice so require. A transferred case then proceeds as if it had been filed in that District Court on the date it was filed in the Tax Court.

As noted, the IRS is directed to furnish to the taxpayer within five days after the expedited assessment a written statement of the information on which it relied in making the assessment. The purpose is to give the taxpayer the opportunity to identify erroneous or incomplete information on which the IRS may have relied. To fulfill that purpose, the IRS's statement should be detailed and comprehensive and it should state specific facts. Sometimes, IRS statements do not fit this description but instead contain only general conclusory language, perhaps merely repeating the predicate language in the Regulations.

Taxpayers sometimes have argued that an excessively general IRS statement should cause invalidation of the assessments. The courts have usually rejected this argument, often on a "no harm, no foul" theory.[43] The taxpayer typically gets or has the opportunity to get the detailed information omitted from the statement, by informal communication with the IRS, during Appeals consideration, or via discovery. Thus, the courts reason, the taxpayer is not prejudiced by the generality of the statement and invalidation of the assessment is too drastic a remedy.[44]

---

40. *See, e.g.*, Friko Corp. v. United States, 91-1 U.S. Tax Cas. (CCH) ¶ 50,195 (D.D.C. 1991).

41. *See, e.g.*, Daniels v. United States, 88-1 U.S. Tax Cas. (CCH) ¶ 9196 (N.D. Ga. 1987).

42. *See, e.g.*, Reg. § 301.7429-2(b); Haskin v. United States, 444 F. Supp. 299 (C.D. Cal. 1977).

43. The cases are discussed in Steve R. Johnson, *Reasoned Explanation and IRS Adjudication*, 63 Duke L.J. 1771, 1806–08 (2014).

44. *See, e.g.*, Evans v. United States, 672 F. Supp. 1118 (S.D. Ind. 1987). *But see* Walker v. United States, 650 F. Supp. 877 (E.D. Tenn. 1987) (invalidating the assessment).

A somewhat similar question arises when the court has failed to render its decision within 20 days. Courts usually have rejected taxpayer claims that the assessments should be invalidated on account of such delay.[45] A number of rationales have been offered, including: (1) the taxpayer failed in his or her duty to alert the court to the extraordinary time requirement, (2) the taxpayer suffered no prejudice from the delay, and (3) the statute states no consequence for failure to decide the case within 20 days.

Discovery usually is limited in section 7429 cases, but sometimes can be obtained on a showing of need or other special factors.[46] Both as to the making of assessment or levy and as to the amount assessed, the IRS's determination will be upheld if the court finds it to have been reasonable. The standard of proof has been described as something more than "not arbitrary and capricious" but something less than "substantial evidence."[47] Section 7429 review has been likened to preliminary examination for probable cause in a criminal proceeding but under a different standard: reasonableness. The review is de novo.[48] Typically, the courts will admit any information they feel is probative as to the issues, unconstrained by the usual rules of evidence.[49]

Reasonableness as to the making of the assessment always turns on the facts and circumstances of the particular case. Thus, beyond general points, cases have limited precedential value. Numerous factors have been noted by courts as part of their discussion of whether the government carried its burden of proof with respect to the existence of a condition of jeopardy. Non-exhaustively, they include the taxpayer's use of multiple names or multiple addresses, use of large amounts of cash, transfer or concealment of assets, failure to provide information, involvement in illegal activities, history of not filing returns or of filing inaccurate returns, insolvency, and unexplained travel, especially foreign travel.[50]

After the IRS explains its basis for the amount assessed, the taxpayer bears the burden of proof on the reasonableness of amount issue. The taxpayer does not satisfy that burden simply by attacking the IRS's computation.[51] There are several reasons for this. First, the taxpayer is closer to the facts and should be encouraged to bring them out rather than simply criticize the IRS's attempts. Second, the circumstances prompting expedited assessment make approximation more typical than precision. Third, the taxpayer sometimes is to blame for any imprecision because of failing to

---

45. *See, e.g.*, United States v. Doyle, 482 F. Supp. 1227 (E.D. Wis. 1980), *app. dismissed*, 660 F.2d 277 (7th Cir. 1981). *But see* Clarke v. United States, 553 F. Supp. 382 (E.D. Va. 1983).

46. *See* Steve Johnson, *Discovery in Summary Assessment Proceedings*, 93 Tax Notes, Oct. 10, 2001, at 539.

47. *See, e.g.*, Harvey v. United States, 730 F. Supp. 1097 (S.D. Fla. 1990).

48. *E.g.*, Wellek v. United States, 324 F. Supp. 2d 905, 911 (N.D. Ill. 2004).

49. *See, e.g.*, Daniels v. United States, 88-1 U.S. Tax Cas. (CCH) ¶ 9295 (N.D. Ga. 1988).

50. *See, e.g.*, Varjabedian v. United States, 339 F. Supp. 2d 140, 155–57 (D. Mass. 2004) (upholding the making of an income tax jeopardy assessment against a gas station owner when, among other indicia, the taxpayer maintained large cash hoards, structured postal money order transactions, held numerous assets in his sister's name, and left in his business files specific references to avoiding the IRS).

51. *See, e.g.*, Robinson v. Boyle, 46 A.F.T.R.2d (P-H) ¶ 80-5078 (E.D. Va. 1980).

keep or to produce records.[52] Fourth, there will be the opportunity for more detailed consideration of the alleged deficiency in subsequent Tax Court litigation.

The taxpayer sometimes is given the opportunity through discovery to probe the bases of the IRS's computation. Sometimes too, courts have reduced the amount of the assessment, especially when information developed after the assessment clarified liability. However, when a condition of jeopardy exists, it is rare for a reviewing court to entirely invalidate an expedited assessment because of concerns about the amount assessed.

In general, courts have felt themselves constrained as to what they can decide and order in section 7429 cases, limiting themselves to upholding the expedited assessment in full, invalidating it in full, or invalidating it in part and upholding the remainder of it. Rare decisions have gone beyond this, directing the IRS, the taxpayer, or both to undertake broad courses of action or remediation.[53]

D. Post-Trial Phase

Section 7429(f) states: "Any determination made by a court under [section 7429] shall be final and conclusive and shall not be reviewed by any other court." The reason for this rule of non-appealability is that expedited assessment is only a provisional remedy. The idea is to freeze the situation to prevent erosion of collection potential, but not to determine with finality the underlying merits of the case. The merits will be ascertained in a subsequent Tax Court case contesting the statutory Notice of Deficiency or in a subsequent refund action. The section 7429 proceeding is substantively and procedurally unrelated to a subsequent trial on the merits, and the section 7429 determination has no binding or persuasive effect in the subsequent trial.

Despite the seemingly clear language of section 7429(f), some circuits have held that section 7429 decisions are appealable for limited purposes, such as challenges that the district court exceeded its authority, improperly evaluated the plaintiff's standing to sue, or committed procedural errors.[54] Other circuits do not permit appeal even of such matters. No circuit allows appeal of substantive decisions as to reasonableness of assessment or reasonableness of amount.

IV. Other Taxpayer Protections and Options

A taxpayer need not seek section 7429 review. A number of other protections are available that may be used instead of or in addition to section 7429. These include

---

52. *E.g.*, Varjabedian v. United States, 339 F. Supp. 2d 140, 158 (D. Mass. 2004).

53. As an extreme example, see *Fidelity Equipment Leasing Corp. v. United States*, 462 F. Supp. 845 (N.D. Ga. 1978). The court's attempt at micromanagement predictably failed and was abandoned. *See* 47 A.F.T.R.2d (P-H) ¶ 81-1117 (N.D. Ga. 1981) (vacating the court's previous order in part and entering a new order largely upholding the jeopardy assessment and levy).

54. *See, e.g.*, Morgan v. United States, 958 F.2d 950 (9th Cir. 1992); Schuster v. United States, 765 F.2d 1047 (11th Cir. 1985).

(1) administrative abatement, (2) bond in lieu of collection, and (3) judicial review of intended sale of seized property.

A. Abatement

The taxpayer can request the IRS to abate the assessment. The IRS has the power to abate an expedited assessment "in whole or in part, if it is shown to [the IRS's] satisfaction that jeopardy does not exist."[55] An advantage of abatement is that it is not subject to the compressed time frame applicable to Appeals Office consideration under section 7429. The request for abatement may be made at any time before a Tax Court decision is rendered in the case. Section 6404(b) provides that a taxpayer may not file a claim for abatement of income, estate, gift, or generation-skipping transfer tax. Thus, abatement of expedited assessment of such taxes is a matter of administrative discretion. The taxpayer may informally request the IRS to effect abatement. However, if the IRS rejects or ignores the taxpayer's informal request, the taxpayer has no recourse as to abatement.

B. Bond

Under section 6863, the taxpayer may respond to an expedited assessment by filing a bond with the IRS. The purpose is to preempt enforced collection which might prove to be even more disruptive. The bond may be in an amount equal to all or to only part of the assessment, and it should include interest on the portion of the assessment on which collection is to be stayed. The bond may be filed

> (i) at any time before levy is authorized, (ii) after levy is authorized but before it has been effected, or (iii) in the discretion of the IRS, after levy has been made but before expiration of the collection limitations period.[56]

Additional rules apply in the case of taxes actually or potentially subject to the jurisdiction of the Tax Court. If the bond is given before a Tax Court petition is filed, the bond must contain a condition that, if a Tax Court petition is not timely filed, then the amount whose collection is sought to be stayed, together with interest, will be paid on notice and demand [the section 6863 notice and demand] after expiration of the Tax Court petition period. In addition, the bond must be conditioned on payment of so much of the assessment as is not abated by a final Tax Court decision.[57]

The taxpayer may waive the stay of collection pursuant to the bond in whole or in part at any time. Once the bond has been given, it can be reduced if part or all of the assessment is paid or satisfied by levy, if the IRS abates part or all of the assessment, or if the Tax Court holds that part or all of the assessment exceeded correct tax liability.[58]

---

55. Reg. § 301.6861-1(f)(1).

56. IRC § 6863(a); Reg. § 301.6863-1(a). For discussion of the collection statute of limitations, see Chapter 13.

57. IRC § 6863(b).

58. IRC § 6863(a), (b)(2).

Taxpayers rarely avail themselves of the option to file a bond to stay collection on an expedited assessment. Filing such a bond rarely offers substantial advantages over other taxpayer remedies and protections. Moreover, the very conditions that created or appeared to create the condition of jeopardy often render it infeasible to obtain the requisite bond.

C. Stay of Sale

As stated previously, under certain circumstances, the IRS may levy immediately after making an expedited assessment. However, as described below, when non-cash property has been seized, the Code and the regulations limit the IRS's ability to sell that property. The amount the IRS realizes in cash as a result of administrative sale of seized property often is considerably less than the true value of the property. The sale-limitation rules protect the taxpayer from such leakage of value in most cases.

In general, sale of property seized pursuant to an expedited assessment is prohibited as long as the taxpayer continues to invoke review rights under section 7429 and subsequent Tax Court adjudication of the merits. Thus, sale typically cannot be effected until after the last of these events occurs: (i) the period for seeking administrative review of the expedited assessment expires without the taxpayer requesting such review; (ii) the period for filing an action to review the expedited assessment expires without the taxpayer filing such an action; or (iii) the court's decision in the action becomes final.[59]

Moreover, property seized pursuant to an expedited assessment may not be sold until after issuance of the required statutory Notice of Deficiency and either (i) the section 6213(a) period for filing a Tax Court petition challenging that notice expires without the taxpayer filing such a petition or (ii) the decision of the Tax Court in the case resulting from the filing of a petition becomes final. However, these additional limitations on sale with respect to actual or potential Tax Court review do not apply if a termination assessment was made and the taxpayer fails to file a timely return for the terminated year(s), taking properly obtained extensions into account. Moreover, appeal of the decision of the Tax Court does not prevent sale of the seized property unless the taxpayer files a bond as provided under section 7485.[60]

There are exceptions to the above general rules as to stay of sale. The seized property may be sold if the taxpayer consents to the sale, or if the IRS determines that expenses of conserving and maintaining the property will greatly reduce the net proceeds of sale, or if the property consists of perishable goods within the meaning of section 6336. If a Tax Court petition has been filed, the Tax Court has jurisdiction to review the IRS's determination that special circumstances exists. The review is commenced

59. IRC § 6863(c).

60. IRC § 6863(b)(3)(A); Reg. § 301.6863-2(a).

on motion of either the taxpayer or the IRS. The court's order disposing of the motion is appealable in the same manner as other Tax Court decisions.[61]

If a taxpayer submits such a motion, he or she must assert "grounds that are plausible and believable." Thereafter, the IRS must show by a preponderance of the evidence that one of the above exceptions to the stay exists. The Tax Court may consider "affidavits, appraisals, or other appropriate information" in making its decision. The court has authority to issue a temporary stay on sale pending resolution of the motion.[62]

D. Collection Due Process Rights

In 1998, Congress added the Collection Due Process ("CDP") rights provisions—sections 6320 and 6330—to the Code. These provisions are described in Chapter 13. Under these provisions, taxpayers may obtain administrative and judicial review when the IRS determines to levy against property, including jeopardy levies pursuant to jeopardy assessments. The CDP process is unlikely to be a major weapon for taxpayers contesting jeopardy and termination assessments, but the CDP process has been tried in some cases.[63]

A 2009 case illustrates the potentially complex interactions of law possible in this area.[64] In a 2002 Notice of Deficiency, the IRS determined income tax deficiencies for 1997, 1998, and 1999. The taxpayer filed a Tax Court petition. While the Tax Court case was pending, the local police department seized over $260,000 from the taxpayer on suspicion of fraudulent credit card transactions. Later, the Tax Court held for the IRS. The IRS assessed the liabilities in January 2004, and the IRS filed a Notice of Federal Tax Lien in April 2005.

In June 2005, the taxpayer filed a Chapter 7 bankruptcy petition. His schedule of assets did not include the funds seized by the police. The bankruptcy court issued an order in January 2006 discharging the taxpayer from all dischargeable debts.

In early December 2007, the police informed the taxpayer that the seized funds would be returned to him. On December 7, 2007, the IRS (i) served a notice of jeopardy levy on the local district attorney as to the taxpayer's seized and not yet returned funds and (ii) sent the taxpayer a notice of jeopardy levy.

The taxpayer responded by seeking CDP review. The Tax Court held for the IRS. It rejected the taxpayer's arguments that (1) the assessments were erroneous; (2) all of the seized money belonged to other persons; (3) the assessments were discharged in the bankruptcy proceeding; (4) the jeopardy levy was inappropriate; (5) the Appeals Officer was biased against him; and (6) the IRS did not timely issue notice of the jeopardy levy.

61. IRC §6863(b)(3), (c).

62. Williams v. Commissioner, 92 T.C. 920 (1989).

63. *See, e.g.*, Bussell v. Commissioner, 130 T.C. 222 (2008) (rejecting taxpayers' CDP claims and other arguments as to jeopardy levies).

64. Prince v. Commissioner, 138 T.C. 270 (2009).

V. Related Assessment Mechanisms

The termination and jeopardy assessment mechanisms are the principal means of addressing collection emergencies, but they are not the only means. Here are six others. The characteristic common to them is that they are topical—addressed to highly particular circumstances—rather than general in their application.

A. Departing Aliens

In general, "[n]o alien shall depart from the United States unless he first procures from the [IRS] a certificate that he has complied with all the obligations imposed upon him by the income tax laws."[65] To obtain such a certificate, the departing alien must file certain statements with the IRS, appear before the IRS if required, and pay any tax due.[66]

The departing alien must, at his or her point of departure, present either the above certificate or evidence that he or she is excepted from obtaining one. Failure to satisfy these conditions will subject the departing alien to examination by the IRS at the point of departure and to the necessity of completing returns and statements and paying tax pursuant to a termination assessment.[67]

Some aliens are categorically excepted from the requirement to obtain the certificate. They include employees of foreign governments or international organizations; students, exchange visitors, and industrial trainees admitted under designed visa types and having limited income; tourists, business visitors, and aliens in transit under designated visa types; alien military trainees of the Department of Defense; and residents of Canada or Mexico who frequently commute between their home country and the United States for employment and whose wages are subject to tax withholding.[68]

In considering an application for a certificate of compliance, the IRS will determine whether the intended departure would jeopardize collection of income tax for the current year or the preceding year. If the IRS determines that it would, the tax period will be terminated and the alien will be required to file returns and make payment for the shortened period. If the IRS determines that the departure would not jeopardize collection, the alien may be required to file certain information but will not be required to pay income tax before the usual due date.[69]

If the alien is a United States resident, the intended departure will not lead to termination unless the IRS has information indicating that the alien intends to avoid

65. IRC §6851(d)(1).
66. Reg. §1.6851-2(a)(1).
67. IRC §6851(d)(2); Reg. §1.6851-2(a)(1).
68. Reg. §1.6851-2(a)(2).
69. Reg. §1.6851-2(b)(1)(i).

tax payment through the departure. The intended departure of a nonresident alien will lead to termination unless he or she establishes to the satisfaction of the IRS that return to the United States is intended and that departure will not jeopardize collection. The determination is made based on all facts and circumstances. Evidence tending to negate jeopardy includes "information showing that the alien is engaged in trade or business in the United States or that he leaves sufficient property in the United States to secure payment of his income tax for the taxable year and of any income tax for the preceding year which remains unpaid." If the IRS does make a termination assessment, the departing alien may post a section 6863 bond in order to postpone until the usual time the payment of the determined tax.[70]

B. Tax-Exempt Organizations

An organization otherwise described in section 501(c)(3) can face serious consequences if it makes prohibited political expenditures. The organization may lose its section 501 exemption, and it may be required to pay an excise tax under section 4955. Section 6852 creates a termination assessment remedy to support those taxes.

Under section 6852(a), if the IRS finds that a section 501(c)(3) organization has made political expenditures which "constitute a flagrant violation of the prohibition against making political expenditures," the IRS is directed immediately to determine any income tax payable by the organization for the current and immediately previous tax years. The IRS also is directed immediately to determine any excise tax payable under section 4955 by the organization or any manager of the organization for those years. Those taxes "become immediately due and payable." The IRS is to immediately assess the tax (plus any interest and penalties), give notice of it, and make immediate demand for payment.[71] Since this is a termination assessment, the provision does not apply to a preceding year after the due date of the organization's return, determined with regard to properly obtained extensions.[72]

A section 6852 termination assessment is made only if the flagrant violation results in revocation of the organization's tax exemption. The organization is not liable for income taxes for any period before the effective date of the revocation.[73]

The protections available as to termination and jeopardy assessments typically also are available as to section 6852 assessments. Specifically, the IRS has administrative abatement authority; a statutory notice must be issued within 60 days, creating the opportunity for Tax Court review; the taxpayer may post a bond to stay collection; and the section 7429 review procedures apply.[74]

70. Reg. § 1.6851-2(b)(1).

71. IRC § 6852(a)(1). The key statutory terms have the same meanings as they have under section 4955. IRC § 6852(b)(1).

72. IRC § 6852(a)(4).

73. Reg. § 301.6852-1(b).

74. IRC §§ 6852(b)(2), 6863(a), 7429(a), (b); Reg. § 301.6852-1(c).

C. Corporate NOL Carrybacks

Under section 6164(a), if a corporation files with the IRS a statement with respect to an expected net operating ("NOL") loss carryback for that year, the time for the payment of the corporation's income tax for the immediately preceding tax year is extended. However, if the IRS believes that collection of the amount to which the extension relates is in jeopardy, it is directed to immediately terminate the extension, notify the taxpayer, and demand payment.[75]

D. Passive Foreign Investment Companies

Sections 1291 through 1298 establish a regime of income taxation with respect to passive foreign investment companies ("PFIC"s). Section 1294 provides an election by which the taxpayer may extend the time for payment of tax on undistributed PFIC earnings. However, if the IRS believes that collection is in jeopardy, it is directed to immediately terminate the extension, notify the taxpayer, and demand payment. The amount of undistributed earnings with respect to which the extension is terminated is left to the discretion of the IRS.[76]

E. Receiverships and Bankruptcies

On the appointment of a receiver for the taxpayer in any receivership case, whether state or federal, the IRS is permitted to immediately assess any deficiency (plus interest and penalties) in any of the taxes otherwise subject to the deficiency procedures.[77] Similarly, when a bankruptcy petition has been filed, the IRS may immediately assess any deficiency (plus interest and penalties) in tax otherwise subject to the deficiency procedures. The deficiency to be assessed may be owed by the debtor's estate in the bankruptcy proceeding, or it may be owed by the debtor but (in the latter situation) only if the liability has become res judicata in the bankruptcy case.[78]

Typically, the taxpayer's assets are under the control of the court in bankruptcies and receiverships. However, any assets not under such control may be subject to levy after the assessments.[79] The normal protections available with respect to jeopardy assessments, including section 7429 review, do not apply. For example, no subsequent Notice of Deficiency need be issued. However, the IRS will send a letter "to the taxpayer or to the trustee, receiver, debtor in possession, or other like fiduciary, notifying him in detail how the deficiency was computed." The taxpayer may furnish to the IRS information disputing the deficiency unless a Tax Court petition had been filed before the assessment.[80]

75. IRC §§6164(h), 6864.
76. IRC §1294(c)(3); Reg. §1.1294-1T(e)(5).
77. IRC §6871(a).
78. IRC §6871(b).
79. Reg. §301.6871(a)-2(a).
80. Reg. §301.6871(b)-1(c).

F. Possessors of Large Amounts of Cash

Illegal drug trafficking and other criminal activities often lead to situations in which individuals are found in possession of large amounts of cash, yet they deny they own the cash and deny knowledge of who the owner is. The odds are high that the money represents untaxed income and that one of the conditions of jeopardy exists. However, without an owner, who is the taxpayer and against whom can the IRS make a summary assessment?

Congress responded to these difficulties by enacting section 6867. This section applies when an individual in physical possession of over $10,000 does not claim the cash as his or "as belonging to another person whose identity the [IRS] can readily ascertain and who acknowledges ownership of such cash." In this circumstance, it is presumed for termination and jeopardy assessment purposes that the cash represents income of an unknown single individual for the tax year in which the possession occurs and that collection of tax will be jeopardized by delay.[81] The income is treated as taxable income and is taxed at the highest rate specified in section 1(c).[82]

For this purpose, "cash" includes cash equivalents such as foreign currency, bearer obligations, and, pursuant to regulations, any medium of exchange of a type which frequently has been used in illegal activities. Bearer obligations are taken into account at face amount and other cash equivalents at fair market value. The cash equivalents identified by the regulations include coins, precious metals, jewelry, precious stones, postage stamps, traveler's checks, and certain negotiable instruments, incomplete instruments, and securities.[83]

In general, the possessor of the cash is treated as the taxpayer for purposes of assessment, collection, and the section 7429(a)(1) requirements. Thus, the possessor will receive a statutory Notice of Deficiency, but solely in his or her capacity as possessor of the cash, not in his or her individual capacity. The possessor may file a Tax Court petition contesting the Notice of Deficiency. Also, the possessor will receive the written statement described in section 7429(a)(1)(B). However, the possessor is not treated as the taxpayer for other section 7429 purposes, so may not seek administrative or judicial review of the expedited assessment. Nor may the possessor file a refund claim or bring a refund suit.[84]

If the expedited assessment later is abated and replaced by an assessment against the true owner of the cash, that replacement assessment is treated for all lien, levy, and collection purposes as relating back to the date of the expedited assessment.[85] The true owner may request administrative and judicial review under section 7429, but any suit must be preceded by a request for administrative review made by the true owner within 30 days after the IRS furnishes the written statement of expla-

81. IRC § 6867(a); Reg. § 301.6867-1(a).
82. IRC § 6867(b).
83. IRC § 6867(d); Reg. § 301.6867-1(f).
84. IRC § 6867(b)(3); Reg. § 301.6867-1(d).
85. IRC § 6867(c).

nation to the possessor. The true owner, after levy, may bring a section 7426 action to recover the cash within the nine-month period prescribed by section 6532(c). The true owner may, with the permission of the Tax Court, appear in an action brought by the possessor challenging a Notice of Deficiency issued to the possessor, but the true owner may not bring that action him or herself. However, if the assessment against the possessor is abated and the IRS issues a statutory Notice of Deficiency to the true owner, the true owner may file a Tax Court petition contesting that notice.[86]

VI. Practical Difficulty

Taxpayers subject to expedited assessment and levy face practical problems. As the foregoing makes clear, there are many complex rules and options in these situations. A taxpayer in such a situation needs a competent attorney.

However, the assessments and levies may leave the taxpayer strapped for the resources to hire an attorney. The IRS does not have to release jeopardy liens so that the taxpayer can pay a lawyer.[87] Occasionally, the obligation to pay attorneys' fees is used to help establish that a condition of jeopardy exists (for example, as part of the solvency calculation).[88] Moreover, the expedited assessments and levies may be occurring at the same time as other events (like civil or criminal asset forfeiture, or the pressing of claims by other creditors) that exacerbate the difficulty of paying an attorney.

The attorney accepting one of these cases typically will want payment in advance. Sometimes the taxpayer can make the payment, for example if levy has not yet been made or the taxpayer has resources beyond those levied on. Sometimes, the taxpayer can get from a friend or relative the money needed. Sometimes, the attorney thinks that the taxpayer's case is good enough that the attorney is willing to wait for payment until after the victory at Appeals or in court. Sometimes, a lawyer is willing to take such a case on a pro bono basis.

Problem

Tony was a citizen and resident of the United States. He majored in mechanical engineering in college, and hoped to work on the design and construction of large, ocean-going ships. Instead, he took a job after college as an engineer with a company that owned and operated cargo ships engaged in international commerce. For the first few years he worked on different ships and after a few promotions he was appointed chief engineer for the company. He traveled the world extensively, meeting ships when they were in port to visit with crews, deal with local government officials, and supervise work being done on the ships.

86. Reg. § 301.6867-1(e).

87. *See, e.g.*, Shapiro v. Commissioner, 73 T.C. 313 (1979).

88. *See, e.g.*, Mesher v. United States, 736 F. Supp. 233 (D. Or. 1990).

In addition to the substantial salary Tony earned, he also had income from rental properties he inherited. Unknown to his employer, he had undertaken some very well-paying consulting work in the maritime industry. The jobs were all overseas, so he was paid in foreign currency and no reports of his earnings (such as Forms W-2 or 1099) were filed with the Internal Revenue Service. He referred to this work as his "consulting business."

Tony also earned money bringing merchandise, mostly legal, to sell to friends and business acquaintances in foreign countries in the course of his travels. Sometimes he brought merchandise into the United States from foreign countries to sell as well. He referred to this as his "import business." He bought all the merchandise for cash and sold it all for cash. He never declared any of the items to local customs officials as required. Although the customs officials in the United States and a few foreign countries had become suspicious, they had never been able to catch Tony with any goods. He never reported any of the sales for tax purposes.

Both the consulting business and the import business were begun in 20x0 and were conducted regularly thereafter.

Tony had an accountant in the United States who prepared his tax returns. Because Tony was frequently out of the country, he often did not provide the information to his accountant in time to file his returns on a timely basis. So Tony's returns were frequently filed late, even though the accountant filed extensions.

For the year 20x0, Tony had given his accountant the details of the earnings from his consulting business. This created a problem for Tony, however, because it resulted in his having income for which there had been no withholding and he was hard-pressed to pay the resulting tax liability. In fact, for the year 20x0, he had not only filed the return late, but had not paid all the tax due with the return. He had received some correspondence from the IRS in regard to the unpaid tax, and had been paying it slowly. He avoided the problem in later years by simply not reporting the consulting fees for tax purposes. Tony figured that since the fees were paid outside the country, he would not get caught.

Although Tony was based in the United States, and owned a home there, he also owned apartments in London, Shanghai, and Capetown that he used when he traveled. He kept automobiles in each of those locations and took lavish vacations. He also had substantial bank accounts in foreign countries, most of which had not been reported for tax or other purposes.

In January 20x4, the IRS conducted an examination of Tony's 20x0 and 20x1 tax years. The Revenue Agent knew that Tony continued to owe tax from 20x0. She concluded that the unpaid 20x0 tax was caused by his consulting income for which there had not been any withholding or estimated tax payments. She noticed that he had reported no consulting income in 20x1 and later years. Tony's accountant, who was representing him in the examination, did not have any explanation. So, with the approval of her manager, the Revenue Agent expanded the examination to 20x2. That return, which had also been filed late, did not include any consulting income either.

The Revenue Agent asked Tony's accountant to arrange an interview with Tony personally. But Tony cancelled the scheduled interview because he was traveling. In fact, he cancelled two other interviews for the same reason. Even when the Revenue Agent was finally able to interview Tony, he acted in a very uncooperative manner. She reported to her manager that he was "belligerent and verbally abusive" towards her. In fact, her report stated that Tony told her to stop wasting her time with him because he paid more than enough taxes and she wasn't going to get any more money from him.

On April 1, 20x4, on the recommendation of the revenue agent, the IRS assessed additional taxes for 20x0, 20x1, 20x2, and 20x3. The 20x3 return had not been filed yet.

After the assessments were made, the following occurred:

1. The Revenue Agent conducted a brief net worth analysis, and concluded that Tony's assets appeared to far outweigh his purchasing power based on the income reported on his returns.
2. The Revenue Agent learned that Tony was being investigated by customs officials, both in the United States and abroad. She noted that there was no income or deductions on any of his tax returns from any import activities.
3. The Revenue Agent learned that Tony had bank accounts in foreign countries that had not been reported.
4. On April 5, 20x5, the IRS filed a Notice of Federal Tax Lien in the jurisdictions in which Tony's home, rental properties, and U.S. bank accounts were located, and levied on those accounts.

Discuss in detail the issues raised by the foregoing. Among other matters, identify the types of assessments the IRS likely made, the adequacy of the grounds therefor, and the protections and defenses available to Tony. Evaluate the strengths and weaknesses of both cases.

Chapter 8

Tax Court Litigation of Deficiency Determination

IRC:	§§6211(a); 6212; 6213(a), (b)(4), (c), (d); skim 6214(a), (b); 6215(a); 6503(a)(1); 6512(b); skim 6603(a)–(c); 6673(a), (b)(1); 7422(e); 7430; 7454(a)–(e); 7463; 7481(a), (b); 7482(c)(4); 7483; skim 7485; skim 7491
Regs.:	§301.6212-1, -2
Cases and Rulings:	Rev. Proc. 87-24, 1987-1 C.B. 720; Rev. Proc. 2005-18, 2005-1 C.B. 798; Rev. Proc. 2010-16, 2010-1 C.B. 664; Abeles v. Commissioner, 91 T.C. 1019 (1988); John C. Hom & Assocs. v. Commissioner, 140 T.C. 210 (2013); Est. of Ming v. Commissioner, 62 T.C. 519 (1974)
Forms:	Skim 8822; Thirty-Day Letter; Notice of Deficiency; Petition to Tax Court for Regular Cases; Petition to Tax Court for "S" Cases; Decision of the Tax Court

I. Introduction

Taxpayers seek court review of IRS determinations in many situations in the tax controversy arena.[1] This chapter explores the most common of them, *i.e.*, Tax Court

1. According to the 2013 *IRS Data Book*, the unpublished tabulations presented by representatives of the Tax Court, Court of Federal Claims, and the IRS Chief Counsel's Office at the May 2014 meeting of the American Bar Association Section of Taxation Court Procedure and Practice Committee, the following statistics represent the amount and types of claims received by the Tax Court.

Between 1969 and 2013, the Tax Court has closed about 1.3 million docketed cases. About 28,000 new cases are filed in the Tax Court annually, with about the same number being closed. The court's inventory of pending cases was about 27,000 in 2013. Taxpayers proceed pro se in 70% to 80% of the cases. About 40% of the cases are S cases; 35% are non-S under-$50,000 cases; and 15% involve alleged deficiencies of $1 million or more.

Of the approximately 31,000 cases closed by the Tax Court in 2013, about 5,300 were dismissed; 17,000 were settled by the Appeals Office; 8,000 were settled by the Chief Counsel's Office; and 700 were tried and decided. The court holds trials in about 75 cities throughout the country. Of the Notices of Deficiency that led to Tax Court deficiency cases in 2013, about 13,000 were issued by the service centers, 8,000 by field examination functions, and 3,000 by the Appeals Office. Over 1,800 of the 2013 Tax Court filings were Collection Due Process cases. Taxpayers were represented in about one-third of the CDP cases. In 2013, 380 cases decided by the Tax Court were on appeal as were a total of 57 decided refund cases.

review of a determination that the taxpayer has a deficiency in income, estate, or gift tax.[2] Other situations in which taxpayers seek judicial relief are discussed elsewhere in this book as part of the coverage of a particular subject matter. For example:

- *Relief from Joint and Several Liability.* A spouse who seeks relief from joint and several liability under one of the provisions of section 6015 can get Tax Court review if the Service disallows the claim or does not act within six months of the filing of the claim. *See* Chapter 3.
- *Jeopardy and Termination Assessments.* When collection is in peril, the IRS is empowered to circumvent the normal assessment and collection procedures by making a jeopardy or termination assessment and levy. Affected taxpayers can obtain expedited review of such assessments in District Court or, less often, in Tax Court. *See* Chapter 7.
- *Interest Abatements.* The Tax Court has jurisdiction to determine whether the IRS abused its discretion in not abating interest under section 6404. *See* Chapter 12.[3]
- *Collection Due Process.* Regardless of the type of tax involved, one may seek Tax Court review within thirty days of an adverse Appeals Office determination in a collection due process hearing following the issuance of a Notice of Intent to Levy under section 6330 or Notice of the Filing of a Tax Lien under section 6320. *See* Chapter 13.
- *Trust Fund Recovery Penalty.* If the IRS assesses the trust fund recovery penalty pursuant to section 6672 against a purported responsible person for willful failure to pay over withheld taxes, review is possible in District Court or the Court of Federal Claims but not in the Tax Court. *See* Chapter 14.
- *Transferee and Fiduciary Liability.* Under certain circumstances, the IRS may seek to collect a taxpayer's liability from recipients of assets of the taxpayer, from representatives of the taxpayer, or from other third parties. In such circumstances, the IRS issues notices of transferee or fiduciary liability. The Tax Court and other courts are empowered to hear challenges to such notices. *See* Chapter 15.

Congress has also granted the Tax Court jurisdiction to redetermine the employment status of workers who the Service believes have been misclassified[4] and the power to

---

In contrast, the total inventory of refund actions, *i.e.*, those filed with the Court of Federal Claims or a U.S. District Court, has been falling, with the current inventory standing at about 1,000. In 2013, 189 new refund cases were filed in district court and 74 in the Court of Federal Claims. But refund actions tend to be larger. The 27,000 cases in the Tax Court's 2013 inventory involved about $22 billion while the 1,000 refund cases in inventory involved about $9 billion.

2. For the history of the development of Tax Court deficiency actions, see Steve R. Johnson, *Reforming Federal Tax Litigation: An Agenda*, 41 Fla. St. U. L. Rev. 205, 217–19 (2013). For a description of the expansion of the Tax Court's jurisdiction to areas beyond the deficiency cases, see *id.* at 246–52. For a proposal to expand that jurisdiction yet more, and give the Tax Court almost plenary civil tax jurisdiction, see *id.* at 249–52.

3. In *Hinck v. United States*, 550 U.S. 501 (2007), the U.S. Supreme Court held that the Tax Court has exclusive jurisdiction to determine whether the IRS abused its discretion in not abating interest under section 6404(h).

4. IRC § 7436.

render declaratory judgments as to a variety of matters, including qualification of certain retirement plans, valuation of gifts, tax-exempt status of state and local bonds, eligibility for deferred payment of estate tax, and tax-exempt status of organizations.[5]

II. The "Notice of Deficiency" and Tax Court Jurisdiction

We began the discussion of deficiency determinations in Chapter 4, where we looked at the examination process and a taxpayer's right to appeal the determination administratively. If the matter is not resolved with examination personnel or with the Appeals Office, the IRS is obligated to issue a Notice of Deficiency. The Notice of Deficiency, sometimes referred to as the ninety-day letter or statutory (or stat) notice, is the "ticket to the Tax Court," providing the jurisdictional basis for the court's review. Although the Notice of Deficiency is thought of as the "ticket to the Tax Court," it is the Internal Revenue Code, not mere issuance of a Notice of Deficiency, which confers jurisdiction on the Tax Court.[6] Thus, for instance, an invalidly issued Notice of Deficiency does not create jurisdiction.[7]

There are five conditions that must be satisfied for the Tax Court to have jurisdiction to review the Service's determination.

---

5. IRC §§7476(a), 7477(a), 7478(a), 7479(a), 7428(a). A matter of increasing importance in declaratory judgment cases involves the point at which the IRS has made a determination that is sufficient for judicial review. *Cf.* 5 U.S.C. §704 (Administrative Procedure Act provision declaring: "Agency action made reviewable by statute and final agency action for which there is no other adequate remedy in a court are subject to judicial review."). For example, section 7436(a) empowers the Tax Court to review IRS decisions as to classification of workers as employees or independent contractors. The Tax Court has held that, although there must be an IRS determination for the court to review, that determination need not be set out in only one particular type of IRS document bearing a particular title or in a particular format. SECC Corp. v. Commissioner, 142 T.C. 225 (2014).

6. *E.g.*, Thompson v. Commissioner, 137 T.C. 220, 224–26 (2011), *rev'd on other grounds*, 729 F.3d 869 (8th Cir. 2013). This principle was raised in a case involving a specialized exception to the normal deficiency rules. When a U.S. taxpayer claims foreign tax credits on her return and later receives a refund of the foreign taxes, the taxpayer is supposed to report the refund to the IRS, so that correct U.S. tax liability can be recomputed. IRC §905(c)(1). The IRS may collect the additional liability via notice and demand, without the usual deficiency procedures. IRC §§905(c), 6213(h)(2). Instead of proceeding in this expedited fashion, the IRS in one case issued a Notice of Deficiency. The taxpayer filed a Tax Court petition. The IRS, arguing that it issued the deficiency notice in error (because the IRS should have proceeded under its expedited powers), filed a motion to dismiss the Tax Court case. Finding that factual disputes existed as to whether the predicates of the expedited procedure had been met, the court denied the IRS's motion to dismiss. Sotiropoulos v. Commissioner, 142 T.C. 269 (2014).

7. For example, one case involved section 6707(a), the penalty for failure to provide information as to a reportable transaction. The IRS assessed the penalty. It also issued a Notice of Deficiency disallowing benefits claimed as a result of the transaction. The taxpayer filed a Tax Court petition challenging the deficiency notice. The court held that it could not review the section 6707(a) penalty. The penalty was not "determined" in the Notice of Deficiency; the IRS had assessed it separately. The Tax Court lacked jurisdiction to consider the penalty. The taxpayer's only recourse for the penalty was a refund claim and refund suit. Smith v. Commissioner, 133 T.C. 424 (2009).

1. The Commissioner must determine a deficiency in tax, as defined in section 6211.
2. The deficiency must relate to the kind of tax specified in section 6211, *i.e.*, income, estate, or gift tax, or certain excise taxes.
3. The IRS must send the taxpayer a notice of the deficiency that conforms to certain form and content specifications identified in section 6212.[8]
4. The IRS must send notice of the deficiency to the taxpayer at the taxpayer's last known address in accordance with section 6212.[9]
5. The taxpayer must file a petition with the Tax Court for a redetermination of the deficiency within ninety days (150 days if the notice is addressed to a person outside the United States) after the IRS mailed the Notice of Deficiency.[10]

A. Meaning of Deficiency

In the typical case, a deficiency is simply the excess of the taxpayer's correct liability over the amount shown on the return, adjusted for other assessments and rebates. Both the correct liability and the tax shown on the return are determined without regard to withholding and quarterly estimated prepayment credits.[11] In the first instance, a deficiency is the additional tax proposed to be assessed by the IRS in the thirty-day and ninety-day letters. In the end, however, the amount of the deficiency that may be assessed is what the Tax Court decides, or the parties agree, is owed.

> *Example (1):* The Smiths timely filed their tax return reflecting $200,000 in taxable income and $60,000 in tax liability. Since they had prepaid $45,000 through withholding and quarterly estimated tax payments, the Smiths submitted a check for the $15,000 balance when they filed the return. A year later, the IRS examines the Smiths' return, making three adjustments that collectively increase taxable income from $200,000 to $300,000 and tax from $60,000 to $90,000. These amounts are reflected in a ninety-day letter. At this point in the process, the proposed deficiency in tax is $30,000. The Smiths and an Appeals Officer meet and agree to only one adjustment to taxable income in the amount of $40,000, resulting in an increase in tax of $12,000. The tax deficiency subject to assessment is $12,000.
>
> *Example (2):* The facts are the same as example (1), except that the withholding and estimated quarterly payments were $75,000. This resulted in a refund of $15,000 when the Smiths filed their return. The amounts of the proposed assessment ($30,000) and agreed deficiency ($12,000) are the same

8. If the IRS issued the ninety-day letter, it can rescind the notice with the taxpayer's consent. IRC §6212(d); Form 8526. *See also* Rev. Proc. 98-54, 1998-2 C.B. 529. This provides more time for filing a protest with the Appeals Office without first having to file a petition with the Tax Court. In practice, the IRS rarely rescinds ninety-day letters.

9. IRC §6212.

10. IRC §6213(a).

11. Reg. §301.6211-1(a), (b).

as in the previous example. The deficiency is the difference between the correct amount of tax ($60,000 + $12,000 = $72,000) and the amount shown on the return ($60,000). Withholding and quarterly estimated prepayment credits are disregarded in determining the amount of the deficiency.

B. Types of Tax Subject to Deficiency Determinations

Only certain taxes are entitled to the protections afforded by the deficiency procedures. According to section 6211(a), they include "income, estate, and gift taxes imposed by subtitles A and B and excise taxes imposed by chapters 41, 42, 43, and 44," *i.e.*, those excise taxes associated with qualified plans and private foundations.

Also subject to the deficiency procedures are penalties calculated as a percentage of a deficiency in tax, such as accuracy-related penalties.[12] Employment taxes, consumption-oriented excise taxes, and assessable penalties are not eligible for these procedures. Interest, being merely the cost of borrowing money, is also excluded from the deficiency procedures by section 6601(e)(1).

C. Content and Form of the Notice of Deficiency

If a deficiency is determined, section 6212(a) requires the Commissioner to notify the taxpayer of the determination and to provide the taxpayer with information on how to proceed if he or she disagrees with it. While the IRS has established a series of administrative forms and pattern letters for Notices of Deficiency, the statute does not mandate any particular form. Since the purpose of the Notice of Deficiency is "to advise the person who is to pay the deficiency that the Commissioner means to assess him, anything that does this unequivocally is good enough."[13]

Typically, the notice recites that the Commissioner has determined that there is a deficiency in tax and that the letter constitutes notice of the deficiency. The notice also normally contains the following:

1. A statement showing how the IRS computed the deficiency;
2. Notice of the taxpayer's right to have the deficiency reviewed in the Tax Court, before it becomes an assessment (and therefore collectible) by filing a petition within ninety days (150 days if addressed to a taxpayer outside of the United States) from the mailing date of the deficiency notice;
3. Notice of the taxpayer's right to utilize the more simplified small tax case procedure for "S" cases, if the tax dispute is not for more than $50,000 for any year;
4. A form for the taxpayer to sign and return in case the taxpayer wishes the IRS to assess the deficiency quickly to limit the accruing of interest; and

---

12. IRC § 6665(a). *But see* IRC § 6665(b).

13. Olsen v. Helvering, 88 F.2d 650, 651 (2d Cir. 1937); *see also* Estate of Rickman v. Commissioner, T.C. Memo. 1995-545 (holding that absent extraordinary circumstances, courts will not "probe into [the IRS's] motives and procedures leading to the issuance of the Notice of Deficiency.").

5. Notice that the Service will assess and collect the tax if a timely petition is not filed with the Tax Court within the ninety-day (or, if applicable, the 150-day) filing period.

Section 6212(a) provides that a Notice of Deficiency "shall include a notice to the taxpayer of the taxpayer's right to contact a local office of the taxpayer advocate and the location and phone number of the appropriate office." In some cases, the deficiency notice omitted the address and phone number of the local taxpayer advocate's office and instead invited the taxpayer to visit an IRS website titled "Contact a Local Taxpayer Advocate." On a harmless error theory, the court has held the omission is not fatal to the notice, at least as to taxpayers who have computers.[14] The Tax Court also applies a harmless error approach to errors as to its own procedures.[15]

D. Mailing the Notice of Deficiency to the Taxpayer's Last Known Address

The Code states that the IRS must either hand-deliver or mail the notice of deficiency by certified mail to the taxpayer at his or her "last known address."[16] Though the Code uses the term "last known address" in many sections,[17] it fails to define it anywhere. The Code also fails to state what remedies are available for improperly mailed notices. These questions have been left to litigation to resolve.

Courts have generally held,[18] and the Regulations agree,[19] that the taxpayer's last known address is the address on the return most recently filed, not the address shown on the return under examination. Mailing to the address on the most recently filed return entitles the IRS to a presumption of correctness.[20] The taxpayer can rebut the

14. *E.g.*, John C. Hom & Assoc. Inc. v. Commissioner, 140 T.C. 210 (2013).

15. *See* Tax Ct. R. 160.

16. If a husband and wife filed a joint return, the IRS normally sends a single joint notice of deficiency to the two of them at their last known joint address. *See* IRC § 6015(d). However, if either spouse notifies the IRS that they established separate residences, the IRS must, where practicable, send separate notices relating to the joint return to each individual. IRC § 6212(b)(2). *See* Abeles v. Commissioner, 91 T.C. 1019 (1988) (the filing of subsequent year's returns with separate addresses is sufficient notification).

17. The concept of mailing a notice to the "last known address" is central to a variety of proposed actions. Some of the more important sections include:

- Section 6212(b)—Notice of Deficiency;
- Section 6303(a)—notice of demand for tax;
- Section 6320(a)(2)(C)—notice of the right to a Collection Due Process (CDP) hearing following filing of a tax lien;
- Section 6330(a)(2)(C)—notice of right to a CDP hearing before levy;
- Section 6331(d)(2)(C)—notice of intent to levy;
- Section 6335(a) and (b)—notices of seizure and sale;
- Section 6672(b)—notice of assertion of so-called 100% penalty;
- Section 6901(g)—notice of liability in transferee case; and
- Section 7609(a)(2)—notice of third-party summons.

18. Abeles v. Commissioner, 91 T.C. 1019 (1988).

19. Reg. § 301.6212-2(a).

20. *Id.*

presumption with evidence that he or she gave the IRS *clear and concise notification* of a different address.[21] Courts expect the IRS to exercise reasonable care in ascertaining whether the taxpayer gave the requisite notification.[22]

Whether the taxpayer gave proper notice and whether the IRS properly discharged its duty are questions of fact.[23] According to Rev. Proc. 2010-16, a taxpayer who no longer wishes the address of record to be the one shown on the most recently filed return can affect a change of address by providing clear and concise notification to the Service of a change of address. This can be accomplished in a variety of ways, such as by filing a Form 8822,[24] or in less direct ways.[25] However, under this procedure, the notification will not be effective until at least 45 days after its receipt by the IRS.

---

21. Rev. Proc. 2010-16, 2010-1 C.B. 664, explains how to notify the IRS of a change of address. *See* note 24 *infra*.

22. Monge v. Commissioner, 93 T.C. 22 (1989). A good example of a situation where the Tax Court found that the taxpayer had given clear and concise notification of a different address is *Hunter v. Commissioner*, T.C. Memo. 2004-81. In that case, the taxpayer moved from Gallatin to Hendersonville, Tennessee. After the move he hired new accountants to represent him, filed a power of attorney form with the IRS directing it to send copies of all correspondence to a Nashville office, and listed his new address as Hendersonville. In 1999, the IRS sent deficiency notices to Hunter at his old address, but he never received them. The IRS didn't send duplicates to the new address or to the accountants.

The Tax Court rejected the IRS's argument that the power of attorney form isn't sufficient notice of a change of address. The court also noted that the IRS failed to act on what it knew after the notices were returned as unclaimed, and didn't keep trying to find the correct address. The court noted that the stipulated facts showed no effort was made to redeliver the notices even after the IRS began using Hunter's Hendersonville address in correspondence and meeting with the accountants in settlement talks. The court, noting the IRS can protect itself from those problems by sending a notice to each possible address, concluded that Hunter's inclusion of his Hendersonville address on the power of attorney form provided the IRS with clear and concise notification of the change of address. The court held that the Notice of Deficiency was not valid and granted Hunter's motion to dismiss for lack of jurisdiction and denied the IRS's motion to dismiss.

23. Cyclone Drilling Inc. v. Kelley, 769 F.2d 662 (10th Cir. 1985).

24. Rev. Proc. 2010-16, 2010-1 C.B. 664. If the taxpayer does not use Form 8822 but wishes to clearly notify the Service of a change of address, the following information is required (this can either be written or oral notification and includes electronic notification):

- The old address;
- The new address;
- The taxpayer's full name, social security number or employer identification number, and signature; and
- A statement that the notice is a change of address notice.

25. United States v. Zolla, 724 F.2d 808 (9th Cir. 1984) (knowledge of the change of address by persons in one division cannot be imputed to persons in another division of that same office); Howell v. United States, 1992 U.S. App. LEXIS 32709 (notice of a new address given relative to a different type of tax does not constitute clear and concise notice with regards to income tax); Pyo v. Commissioner, 83 T.C. 626 (1984) (where the IRS is notified of a new address or establishment of separate residences for a year other than the one at issue and the IRS has corresponded successfully with the taxpayer at the new address, the taxpayer may reasonably expect future notices to come to the new address as well); Berg v. Commissioner, T.C. Memo. 1993-77 (one IRS agent's knowledge of the current address, however obtained, is imputed to all other agents in the same division of that office). *See also* note 22.

Normally, giving notification of a change of address to another branch of government is not sufficient notice to the IRS. However, Regulation section 301.6212-2(b)(2) says that a change of address provided to the U.S. Postal Service (USPS) on its official form will satisfy the taxpayer's obligation to provide notice to the IRS. In fact, the cited Regulation says that until the taxpayer gives clear and concise notification to the contrary, the taxpayer's address in the USPS National Change of Address database is the last known address for section 6212 purposes.

The purpose of the last known address requirement is to ensure that the taxpayer receives a copy of the notice and has time to petition the Tax Court for review of the deficiency determination. If the IRS mails the notice as directed in the statute, the notice is valid irrespective of whether the taxpayer receives it.[26] This unfortunate event happens frequently when a taxpayer moves and fails to provide the USPS with a forwarding address or when the USPS erroneously fails to deliver the notice to a forwarded address on file. If this occurs, the taxpayer is basically out of luck and will be precluded from getting pre-assessment review in the Tax Court.[27]

The converse is not necessarily true. A deficiency notice is *not* per se invalid merely because the Service mailed it to an incorrect address.[28] Since the purpose of the Notice of Deficiency is to inform the taxpayer of actions the IRS intends to take and give the taxpayer an opportunity for pre-assessment judicial review, a Notice of Deficiency mailed to the wrong address is still effective if the taxpayer receives it with "ample time" to file a Tax Court petition.[29]

If, however, the IRS *fails* to mail the notice as the statute prescribes *and* the taxpayer does not receive it with ample time remaining on the ninety-day period to petition the Tax Court, subsequent actions by the IRS, *e.g.*, assessments and levy or seizure and sale, are *voidable* by the taxpayer. In order to proceed, the government would have to issue a new Notice of Deficiency. Since an improperly mailed notice does not suspend the running of the three-year statute of limitations on assessment,[30] the government may find itself time-barred from issuing a valid notice.

If the taxpayer has moved and the IRS has not updated its computer to reflect the new address, the IRS normally will send the thirty- and ninety-day letters to the old location. The first time the taxpayer might learn tax is owed is many months or years later when the Service discovers the taxpayer's present address and sends col-

---

26. *See* Estate of Rule v. Commissioner, T.C. Memo. 2009-309.

27. IRC § 6213(a).

28. Frieling v. Commissioner, 81 T.C. 42 (1983).

29. Clodfelter v. Commissioner, 527 F.2d 754 (9th Cir. 1975). *Compare* Manos v. Commissioner, T.C. Memo. 1989-442 (38 days left on the ninety-day period was sufficient time to consider what course of action to take, including whether to file a Tax Court petition), *with* Looper v. Commissioner, 73 T.C. 690 (1980) (17 days left was not enough; of importance to the court was the fact that the notice was of transferee liability and not one respecting the taxpayer's own liability about which he would have been aware of a problem).

30. IRC § 6503(a).

lection notices there. If it turns out the IRS mailed the Notice of Deficiency to the wrong place, the proper way for the taxpayer to proceed is to bring this to the attention of someone at the IRS. If the problem cannot be resolved administratively, the taxpayer should file a petition with the Tax Court even though doing so is well outside the ninety-day period from the issuance of the Notice of Deficiency. In this situation, both parties normally file Motions to Dismiss for Lack of Jurisdiction. The IRS's motion will argue that the Tax Court should dismiss the case because the taxpayer filed the petition untimely. The taxpayer's motion will argue that the Tax Court should dismiss the case because the notice was defective and void due to the improper mailing. The court will decide the case by granting one of the motions and denying the other.

If the court grants the taxpayer's motion, the IRS will have to issue a new notice and do so within the statute of limitations, remembering that the statute of limitations was not suspended from the date of the issuance of the improperly mailed notice. If the court rules in favor of the government, the IRS is entitled to assess the deficiency. If the taxpayer wishes to contest the determination, he or she must pay the deficiency and file a refund claim and, if necessary, a refund suit.

E. Timely Filing the Tax Court Petition

Section 6213(a) requires the taxpayer to file a petition with the Tax Court within ninety days of the date the IRS mails the Notice of Deficiency.[31] The date the Tax Court receives a document is normally treated as its filing date. However, section 7502 says that documents received after the prescribed period are treated as timely filed if the envelope contains an official United States postmark, or certain designated delivery service marks, dated *on or before* the end of the prescribed filing period.[32] To be treated as timely filed under section 7502, the envelope or outside wrapper must be properly addressed to the Tax Court in Washington, D.C., with sufficient postage.[33] See Chapters 2 and 5 for discussions of the "timely mailed (or postmarked) is timely filed" rule of section 7502 and the weekend and holiday rule of section 7503.[34]

The 90-day period is extended in certain situations, the most common being: (1) where the last date for filing specified by the IRS on the Notice of Deficiency is later

31. Estate of Cerrito v. Commissioner, 73 T.C. 896, 898 (1980).

32. IRC § 7502.

33. In one case, taxpayers' attorney left the envelope at a UPS store to be picked up by the Post Office within the period allowed by sections 6213 and 7502. The envelope never reached the Tax Court because it was severely damaged by the Post Office. Three months later, it was returned to the attorney, who then sent a new copy of the petition to the Tax Court. The IRS's motion to dismiss was denied. Van Brunt v. Commissioner, T.C. Memo. 2010-220.

34. *See also* Hale E. Sheppard, *It's in the Mail, Right? Recent Decision Emphasizes Limitation on the Mailbox Rule,* Practical Tax Law., Summer 2008, p. 15 (discussing *Gibson v. Commissioner*, 264 Fed. Appx. 760 (10th Cir. 2008)).

than the 90th day, (2) where the taxpayer files for bankruptcy relief after the issuance of the notice,[35] or (3) where the notice was addressed to a person who was outside the country, even if temporarily while on vacation.[36]

In the latter situation, the taxpayer has 150 days to file the petition. If the taxpayer regularly resides outside the United States but happens to be in the country when the Notice of Deficiency is mailed to her, the 150-day period still applies.[37]

What happens when the 150-day petition period interacts with the section 7502 "timely mailed is timely filed" rule? In one case, a taxpayer abroad mailed his petition to the Tax Court on the 145th day after issuance of the Notice of Deficiency. The taxpayer used the registered mail service of the foreign country. The envelope containing the petition entered the U.S. domestic mail service on the 147th day. The Tax Court received it on the 153rd day. The Tax Court held that the petition was timely filed.[38]

The Tax Court petition must also be filed by a proper petitioner. Under Tax Court Rule 60, a proper petitioner is the person against whom the deficiency or liability was determined, or a fiduciary representing such person. In cases involving corporations, where a corporation's legal status has been terminated or suspended at the time it files a Tax Court petition, the corporation lacks capacity to file.[39]

F. Issuance of Additional Deficiency Notices

The Service normally issues only one statutory Notice of Deficiency. However, it can issue another notice, if necessary, under certain circumstances. If the taxpayer did *not* file a petition with the Tax Court in response to the first Notice of Deficiency and if the statute of limitations on assessment has not expired, the IRS may issue a valid second Notice of Deficiency for the same taxpayer, tax, and period covered by the first deficiency notice. If the taxpayer petitions the Tax Court within ninety days of the second notice, the issues raised in both notices are properly before the court. This situation is most likely when the IRS did not mail the first notice to the taxpayer's last known address.

On the other hand, if the taxpayer timely petitioned the Tax Court in response to the first deficiency letter, section 6212(c)(1) precludes the Commissioner from determining an additional deficiency. The only way the government can raise a new

35. IRC § 6213(f)(1) ("the running of the time prescribed by subsection (a) for filing a petition in the Tax Court with respect to any deficiency shall be suspended for the period during which the debtor is prohibited by reason of such case from filing a petition in the Tax Court with respect to such deficiency, and for sixty days thereafter").

36. Levy v. Commissioner, 76 T.C. 228 (1981).

37. Smith v. Commissioner, 140 T.C. 48 (2013) (majority opinion); Hamilton v. Commissioner, 13 T.C. 747 (1949). The judges dissenting in *Smith*, however, thought that physical presence comports with the language of section 6213(a) better than residence does. For them, the 90-day period should apply unless the taxpayer is physically outside the U.S. or the notice is sent to a foreign address. 140 T.C. at 60–72 (Halpern, J., dissenting).

38. Boultbee v. Commissioner, T.C. Memo. 2011-11.

39. *E.g.*, David Dung Le M.D. Inc. v. Commissioner, 114 T.C. 268 (2000), *aff'd*, 22 Fed. Appx. 837 (9th Cir. 2001); *see also* John C. Hom & Assoc. Inc. v. Commissioner, 140 T.C. 210 (2013).

issue would be if the court were satisfied that the taxpayer was not unduly prejudiced and granted the government's motion to amend its pleadings. The IRS normally bears the burden of proof on new issues.[40]

The prohibition against a second Notice of Deficiency only applies if the second notice is for the same tax and taxable year and is with respect to the same taxpayer as the first notice. A second notice issued to the same taxpayer for another taxable year but the same tax, or for another tax but the same taxable period as covered by the first notice, is not a prohibited second deficiency notice under section 6212(c)(1). The limitations also do not prevent the IRS from asserting an additional deficiency in the case of fraud or jeopardy.[41]

G. Tax Court's Exclusive Jurisdiction

The Tax Court has priority to hear tax deficiency cases. Once it acquires proper jurisdiction as a result of the taxpayer filing a timely adequate petition, no other court may consider the case. A taxpayer may not get the case dismissed without prejudice once the Tax Court has acquired jurisdiction.[42] Section 6512(a) bars a refund suit for a taxable year as to which the taxpayer filed a Tax Court deficiency action. In one case, a taxpayer sued in the Court of Federal Claims for refund of interest and late-payment penalties, items which were not, of course, included in the Notice of Deficiency that precipitated a prior Tax Court case. The court dismissed the refund suit because the Tax Court's jurisdiction, once invoked, "extends to the entire subject of the correct tax for the particular year."[43]

In addition, section 7422(e) provides that if the taxpayer already has a refund action before a District Court or the Court of Federal Claims and, prior to the hearing of the suit, the IRS mails a Notice of Deficiency, the refund action is stayed to give the taxpayer time to decide whether to petition the Tax Court. If the taxpayer does so, the District Court or the Court of Federal Claims loses jurisdiction and the Tax Court acquires it. On the other hand, if the taxpayer does not file a petition with the Tax Court for a redetermination of the asserted deficiency for a matter presently before one of the other courts, the United States may counterclaim in the taxpayer's suit and bring the issues in the notice before the court.

H. Standard of Review for Deficiency Proceedings

The traditional view is that the Notice of Deficiency represents the official determination of the IRS and that the courts will not "look behind the notice" to probe

---

40. IRC § 6214(a); Tax Ct. R. 41.

41. IRC § 6212(c); Zackim v. Commissioner, 887 F.2d 455 (3d Cir. 1989), *rev'g* 91 T.C. 1001 (1988) (the court held that, despite the doctrine of res judicata, the fraud exception prevails even if the Tax Court already decided the matters before it arising from the first Notice of Deficiency).

42. Estate of Ming v. Commissioner, 62 T.C. 519 (1974) (denying taxpayer's motion to dismiss his Tax Court case without prejudice to filing a refund action).

43. The Cheesecake Factory, Inc. v. United States, 111 Fed. Cl. 686 (2013).

the thought processes by which that determination was reached. Accordingly, Tax Court deficiency cases are *de novo* proceedings.[44]

Nevertheless, this view is subject to limited exceptions, such as when it is clear from the face of the notice that the IRS made no determination or when it is clear that the IRS's determination was utterly without factual foundation.[45] It now is clear, however, that general administrative law applies to tax. Part of judicial review under the "arbitrary and capricious" standard of the Administrative Procedure Act is whether the agency adequately explained the reasons for its decision.[46]

III. Overview of a Tax Court Case

The Tax Court recently initiated its electronic access system, which provides taxpayers and practitioners with electronic access to their case filings through the Internet.[47] Access to case filings is currently limited to parties and their counsel.

The general public is allowed only remote access to the Tax Court's online docket record, court opinions, and orders. Furthermore, privacy concerns resulting from the large amount of personal information contained within case filings has led the Tax Court to amend Rule 27 to direct taxpayers to redact their taxpayer identification numbers, dates of birth, names of minor children, and financial account numbers from their filings with the court.[48]

eFiling is mandatory for most parties represented by counsel (practitioners).[49] eFiling in a case can be commenced only after a petition has been filed in the Tax Court in that case. Initial filings, such as the petition, may be filed only in paper form.

The Tax Court recently prepared an eight-part video entitled, "An Introduction to the United States Tax Court." It is available for viewing on the court's website. It is an excellent production that will help practitioners, students, and the general public understand the operation of the court and its procedures better.

---

44. *E.g.*, Greenberg's Express Inc. v. Commissioner, 62 T.C. 324 (1974). *But see* Michael Kummer, *The De Novo Doctrine: Irrelevant to Irrelevancy in Civil Tax Litigation*, 14 Fla. Tax Rev. 115 (2013). *See also* Lewis v. Reynolds, 284 U.S. 281, 283, modified, 284 U.S. 599 (1932); O'Dwyer v. Commissioner, 266 F.2d 575 (4th Cir. 1959). As stated by the court in one case, "[w]hy a given IRS employee felt that penalties should be imposed [in the given case] has nothing to do with [the] litigation." Principal Life Ins. Co. v. United States, 116 Fed. Cl. 82, n. 7 (2014); Vons Cos., Inc. v. United States, 51 Fed. Cl. 1, 6 (2001).

45. *E.g.*, United States v. Janis, 428 U.S. 433, 442 (1976); Scar v. Commissioner, 814 F.2d 1363, 1370 (9th Cir. 1987).

46. Does this impose a higher duty of explanation with respect to Notices of Deficiency and other IRS determinations than the courts traditionally have required? This question is explored in Steve R. Johnson, *Reasoned Explanation and IRS Adjudication*, 63 Duke L.J. 1771 (2014).

47. As of early 2014, about 19,000 practitioners and 28,000 others had registered for e-access to the Tax Court's website.

48. Tax Ct. R. 27.

49. *See* Tax Ct. R. 26(b).

A. Pleadings

In a deficiency redetermination matter, the taxpayer initiates a case by filing a petition with the court within ninety days of the mailing of the notice of deficiency. Petitions may only be filed in paper form, regardless of the court's general move toward e-filing. Along with the petition, the taxpayer, now known as the petitioner, designates a place for the trial and remits $60 as the filing fee.[50] Where the amount of tax and penalty at issue does not exceed $50,000,[51] the taxpayer may request, as part of the petition, that the court hear the case under the simplified procedures associated with "S" cases. According to Tax Court Rule 31(a), this petition, or the taxpayer's pleading, must give the other party and the court "fair notice of the matters in controversy and the basis for their respective positions."

Upon receipt of the petition, the Tax Court serves a copy of it on the Commissioner, the respondent. Within sixty days of service, an attorney in IRS Chief Counsel's office files an answer. The answer must respond to each material allegation in the petition.[52] Failure to challenge a material allegation is deemed a concession on that issue. A reply by the petitioner to the government's answer is not required, unless the Court orders otherwise, or the IRS moves that the affirmative allegations in the answer be deemed admitted.[53]

In general, the pleadings and additional information filed with the Tax Court are matters of public record, allowing anyone to inspect tax returns and other potentially sensitive information.[54] The problems this can cause are potentially exacerbated by the fact that the records in Tax Court cases are available on the Internet through the Tax Court's website, search engines, and databases.[55]

It is difficult to balance such privacy concerns against our long held belief in transparency in judicial administration. The system has developed a variety of responses although they are only partial. First, as noted above, Rule 27 allows for redacting personal information like taxpayer identification numbers and dates of birth. Second, as noted in Chapter 3, a taxpayer who has been a victim of domestic violence will receive some privacy protections in a spousal relief case. Third, Tax Court rules allow

---

50. The filing fee can be waived for indigent taxpayers. In non-deficiency cases, such as a CDP case, the pleadings are similar to those that must be filed in deficiency cases though the time limits for doing so may be different.

51. For innocent spouse cases, the small case procedure is available if the amount of the spousal relief sought does not exceed $50,000 for all years combined. Collection due process cases can only be heard as a small case if the total amount of unpaid tax for all years combined does not exceed $50,000. *See* Tax Ct. R., Form 2, Information About Filing a Case in the United States Tax Court (2016).

52. Until recently, if the case was petitioned as an "S" case, no answer was required, unless the IRS raised an issue with respect to which it bore the burden of proof. However, for petitions filed after March 13, 2007, the government must file an answer regardless whether it is an "S" case or not. Tax Ct. R. 173(b).

53. Tax Ct. R. 37.

54. IRC §7461(a).

55. E-Government Act, Pub. L. 107-347, 116 Stat. 2899 (2002) (codified at 44 U.S.C. §3501).

limiting disclosure when harm can be shown.[56] Fourth, in extraordinary cases, the Tax Court may allow a taxpayer to litigate anonymously.[57]

Consistent with modern pleading practice, Tax Court pleadings may be amended, sometimes by right and other times by leave of the court, which "leave shall be granted freely when justice so requires."[58] The main exception is attempted amendment that raises a matter requiring factual development when the amendment is so near the trial date that the other party's ability to prepare its case would be unduly prejudiced.

B. Discovery

After the pleading stage is complete, the parties may begin discovery.[59] Unlike many other courts, the Tax Court requires that the parties exchange information informally to the extent possible before resorting to the more formal methods of discovery, like interrogatories, depositions, requests for production of documents, electronic information,[60] and requests for admissions. After a case by the same name, this is referred to as a Branerton conference.[61] In "S" cases, formal discovery is rare since there is such a short time between when the case is petitioned and when it is tried.

On motion of a party, the court can limit discovery where: (1) the discovery demands are unreasonably cumulative or duplicative, (2) the information sought is obtainable from a more convenient source, (3) the demands are unduly burdensome or expensive, or (4) the party had ample opportunity to obtain the information from other sources. While the information sought via discovery must be relevant to the subject matter of the case at hand, it does not need to be admissible. Instead, as is true in other American courts, all that is necessary is that the requested information be reasonably calculated to lead to the discovery of admissible evidence.

In 2010, Federal Rule of Civil Procedure 26(b)(4) was amended to provide that drafts of expert witness reports and some communications between attorneys and experts are not discoverable. Tax Court Rule 70(c) was amended in 2012 to largely mirror FRCP 26(b)(4).

---

56. *See* Alison Bennett, *IRS Concerned by Tax Court Proposal to Allow Redacted Petitions, Official Says*, Tax Management Weekly Rep., Apr. 23, 2007, at 583.

57. *E.g.*, Anonymous v. Commissioner, 127 T.C. 89 (2006); *see* Note, *The Anonymous Taxpayer: What the Tax Court Failed to Reveal in* Anonymous v. Commissioner, 61 Tax Law. 999 (2008).

58. Tax Ct. R. 41(a).

59. Under Rule 70, electronically stored information is subject to discovery in Tax Court proceedings, and Rule 104 permits the Tax Court to issue sanctions for failing to provide such information. For discussion of Rule 70 and other rules, see Jeremiah Coder, *Tax Court Proposes Numerous Rule Changes*, Tax Notes, Apr. 6, 2009, at 33.

60. Rule 70(b)(3) of the Tax Court provides limitations on discovery of electronically stored information to alleviate unnecessary burden on parties subject to discovery obligations. *See generally* CC-2010-008 (May 4, 2010) (updating guidance on complying with new electronic discovery rules).

61. Branerton v. Commissioner, 61 T.C. 691 (1974); *see also* Alex E. Sadler & Daniel G. Kim, *Scope of Pretrial Discovery: A Key Difference in Litigating Tax Cases in the Tax Court and Refund Tribunals*, J. Tax Prac. & Proc., Apr.–May 2009, at 39 (comparing discovery options in the tax trial fora).

C. Settlement

During or after discovery, the parties normally begin to discuss settlement. The vast majority of cases are settled rather than litigated. If the Appeals Office has not already considered the case, negotiations will occur with an Appeals Officer rather than an attorney for the IRS. If the taxpayer already had a "bite at the Appeals' apple," a second conference generally is not made available, unless the parties believe there is settlement potential. If the taxpayer is unsuccessful in reaching a settlement with Appeals, the Area Counsel attorney will begin to prepare the case for trial. Settlement is still possible once the attorney takes over the case as the facts become better developed and each side can better evaluate the likely success of trying the case.

Settlements reached between the representatives for the taxpayer and the government are subject to the approval and concurrence of the taxpayer and the manager of the government agent. This was made clear in *Keil v. Commissioner*,[62] in which the Tax Court set aside a settlement because the attorney for the taxpayers was not authorized by them to agree to settle on their behalf without their prior concurrence. Taxpayers specifically had told their attorney at the time of his retention that he could not accept any settlement that affected their liability without their consideration and approval of it. Despite this and unbeknownst to the taxpayers, the attorney caused to be filed with the Court a settlement stipulation that showed their liability computed on the basis of the settlements. The Court entered a stipulated decision that reflected the amounts shown therein. A month later, the taxpayers moved the Court to vacate the stipulated decision and to set aside the related stipulations of settlement. The court granted the taxpayers' motion.

The Tax Court has an arbitration program, but unlike many other federal courts, the Tax Court's program is not mandatory. Rule 124 of the Tax Court allows voluntary binding arbitration between taxpayers and the IRS on factual issues, which may be handled before a Tax Court judge or an outside party. The order of the arbitrator is considered final unless a stipulated decision document is filed. Parties rarely agree to Rule 124 arbitration.

D. Stipulations

A defining characteristic of Tax Court practice is emphasis on the stipulation process. Tax Court Rule 91(a)(1) mandates that the parties stipulate to "the fullest extent to which complete or qualified agreement can or fairly should be reached ... all evidence which fairly should not be in dispute." The parties must stipulate to those facts, conclusions, and documents whose truth is not disputed. The parties are required to stipulate to as much as possible to minimize trial time. If a party does not stipulate to certain evidence, the other party can file a motion to compel that party

62. T.C. Memo. 2005-76.

to show cause why the matters covered by the motion should not be deemed admitted.[63] In egregious situations, the Tax Court may dismiss the case.[64]

E. Notice of Calendared Case and Pretrial Orders

At some point after the pleadings have been filed, the parties get a notice from the Tax Court that the case has been calendared for trial for a specific date. Along with this notice, the parties receive a pretrial order from the judge assigned to the case. The pretrial order requires a status report from each party 45 days prior to the assigned trial date indicating whether the case has been settled and, if not, the likelihood that it will be litigated and the anticipated length of the trial.

The pretrial order requires the parties to prepare pretrial memoranda. The memorandum should give each party's version of the facts and law and identify whom the party plans to call as witnesses and to what the witnesses will likely testify. Failure to list a proposed witness may result in that person being precluded from testifying at trial.

If a party intends to call an expert witness, the party must submit to the court and the other party a copy of the expert's report. This serves as the witness's direct testimony. The report must be submitted not less than thirty days before trial. The expert is not normally entitled to testify unless the report is timely submitted.[65]

F. Calendar Call, Trial, and Briefs

The date and time specified on the pretrial notice as the trial date is usually a Monday morning. The time mentioned signals what is referred to as the "calendar call," rather than the trial date. The parties are required to be present at calendar call to inform the judge of the status of the case.

If trial is required, the judge will want to know when the best time is to hear the case during the week or two that the judge is "sitting" in the particular city. Factors the judge will consider in deciding when to schedule a trial are the availability of the parties and witnesses and whether the taxpayer will incur additional costs if the case is not heard until later in the session. Especially in low dollar cases, judges normally give out-of-town petitioners preference to have their trials on the same day as the calendar call so that their inconvenience and costs are minimized. It is sometimes possible to arrange a "date and time certain" for trial before the calendar call. This normally requires both parties arranging a conference call with the judge or the judge's clerk.

All proceedings before the Tax Court are recorded on audiotape by an independent court reporting service that has a contract with the Tax Court.[66] Transcripts of pro-

63. Tax Ct. R. 91(f).

64. Williams v. Commissioner, 1993 U.S. App. LEXIS 34203 (9th Cir. 1993) (unpublished opinion).

65. Tax Ct. R. 143(g).

66. The Tax Court has changed its evidence submission rules under Rule 143 in order to facilitate live video testimony from a different location in open court proceedings.

ceedings can be ordered from the reporting service for a per-page fee. There is a court reporter in the courtroom who can assist taxpayers who want to order a transcript.

The evidence that parties fail to introduce at trial sometimes is as important as the evidence they do introduce. Consistent with other courts, the Tax Court holds that, when a party is in control of relevant evidence and chooses not to introduce it at trial, the court is entitled to presume that the evidence, had it been introduced, would have been adverse to the party.[67] As to evidence offered at trial, the Tax Court has the reputation of being more lax in applying the rules of evidence than the district courts. It may be dangerous to place too much weight on this lore, however.[68] This is especially true now that Congress directed the Tax Court to follow the Federal Rules of Evidence.[69]

Some time after the conclusion of the presentation of the case, the parties are required to file post-trial briefs, unless the trial judge specifies otherwise. In "S cases," the pretrial memorandum is usually sufficient for this purpose. A post-trial brief is a summary of the facts and the law raised in the trial. Tax Court Rule 151 details the requirements of post-trial briefs.

The trial judge may require the parties to file simultaneous briefs or seriatim briefs. If the judge requires simultaneous briefs, both parties must file opening briefs within 75 days after the conclusion of the trial. The parties file reply briefs 45 days thereafter. If the judge requires seriatim briefs, the party designated by the judge files its opening brief within 75 days after the trial, the other party files its reply brief within 45 days thereafter and the first party files its reply brief within 30 days after that. Each brief is expected to be a response to the previous brief. Upon request of a party, the judge may enlarge any of the periods.

G. Decision

After the parties present their cases and file briefs, the judge reviews all the evidence and drafts a report. This may take months or even years in complex cases. The trial judge forwards his or her report to the Chief Judge.[70] The report of the trial judge

---

67. Wichita Terminal Electric Co. v. Commissioner, 6 T.C. 1158, 1165 (1946), *aff'd*, 162 F.2d 513 (10th Cir. 1947).

68. *See generally*, Joni Larson, A Practitioner's Guide to Tax Evidence: A Primer on the Federal Rules of Evidence as Applied by the Tax Court (2013).

69. Protecting Americans from Tax Hikes Act of 2015, Pub. L. No. 114-113, § 425 Stat. - amending IRC section 7453; Tax Ct. R. 143.

70. IRC § 7459. In many cases, Special Trial Judges act as the trial judges. They hear the evidence and prepare a report of recommended findings of fact and conclusions of law. The report is reviewed by the Chief Judge. If the case is either an "S" case, a case in which the amount of the deficiency placed in dispute is under $50,000, or a lien or levy action, the Chief Judge may authorize the Special Trial Judge to issue the report as the opinion of the court. Tax. Ct. R. 182(b).

If the case involves a deficiency greater than $50,000, the Special Trial Judge's report of recommended findings of fact and conclusions of law gets served on the parties. The parties may object to the recommendation in which case the Chief Judge has several options. If the Chief Judge agrees with the objections raised, he may require additional briefing, hearings, or the like. If he does not agree with the objections, he may adopt the recommendations as the opinion of the court.

becomes the opinion of the court unless, within 30 days of the date the report is submitted to the Chief Judge, the Chief Judge refers the case for review by the nineteen presidentially appointed judges.[71]

Eventually, the court issues its report, or opinion. Under section 7460, the Chief Judge classifies opinions in regular cases.[72] Court review is directed if the report proposes to invalidate a Regulation, overrule a published Tax Court case, or reconsider, in a circuit that has not addressed it, an issue on which the Tax Court has been reversed by a court of appeals.[73] Court review is also directed in cases of widespread application where the result may be controversial, where the Chief Judge is made aware of differences in opinion among the judges before the opinion is released, or, occasionally, where a procedural issue suggests the desirability of obtaining a consensus of the judges.

The opinion is different from the decision. The opinion states how the court decides the issues presented to it. It does not inform the parties of the dollar amount resulting therefrom. That is the role of the decision. All decisions of the Tax Court, except those dismissing a case for lack of jurisdiction, must specify the dollar amount of the deficiency, liability or overpayment determined by the court. Unless the court finds entirely in favor of either the taxpayer or the government, the parties must prepare a Tax Court Rule 155 computation. There are two types of Tax Court Rule 155 computations: agreed and unagreed.

If the parties agree on the dollar amount of the deficiency, liability, or overpayment, an original and two copies of the agreed computation, reflecting such dollar amount, are filed with the Tax Court. When the parties are unable to agree on the appropriate computation of the deficiency, liability, or overpayment, either party, or both parties, may file a computation it believes is consistent with the court's findings of fact and opinion. The court will then decide which computation to accept and issue its decision.

Tax Ct. Rul. 183. Rule 183 notes that the Tax Court judge must give due regard to the Special Trial Judge's findings of fact, which "shall be presumed to be correct." These requirements with respect to larger cases were added to the Tax Court's rules in response to *Ballard v. Commissioner*, 544 U.S. 40 (2005), in which the U.S. Supreme Court said that the previous practice of withholding such reports failed to disclose how much the judges modified or diverged from the Special Trial Judge's findings as part of its collaborative process. For discussion of *Ballard*, see Steve R. Johnson, *Reforming Federal Tax Litigation: An Agenda*, 41 Fla. St. U.L. Rev. 205, 237–40 (2013).

71. IRC § 7460(b).

72. "[Some opinions are released as memorandum opinions] instead of a published Tax Court opinion, or division opinion. IRC §§ 7459, 7460. Division opinions officially published by the court are those in which a legal issue of first impression is decided, a legal principle is applied or extended to a recurring factual pattern, a significant exception to a previously announced general rule is created, or there are similarly significant and precedentially valuable cases. On the other hand, cases involving application of familiar legal principles to routine factual situations, nonrecurring or enormously complicated factual situations, obsolete statutes or regulations, straightforward factual determinations, or arguments patently lacking in merit will be classified as memorandum opinions." Mary Ann Cohen, *How to Read Tax Court Opinions*, 1 Hous. Bus. & Tax. L.J. 1 (2001).

73. Golsen v. Commissioner, 54 T.C. 742 (1970), *aff'd*, 445 F.2d 985 (10th Cir. 1971).

The date of entry of the decision is important in terms of fixing the time at which the appeal period begins to run. It is also important because the restrictions on assessing deficiencies imposed on the IRS end on this date.

The losing side has two separate post-trial motions to file with the Tax Court requesting another hearing or reconsideration of the opinion or decision.[74] Parties rarely file these, and the court even more rarely grants those filed.[75] In general, the grounds warranting reconsideration of an opinion—prior to the decision becoming final—include: (1) "an intervening change in the controlling law, (2) new evidence previously unavailable, and (3) the need to correct clear error or prevent manifest injustice."[76]

H. Finality of Tax Court Decision

Unless a notice of appeal is filed within 90 days after the entry of the Tax Court decision, the decision becomes final on the 90th day after such entry.[77] Decisions that are appealed do not become final during the pendency of the appeal and thereafter until the time for filing a petition for certiorari expires. If a petition for certiorari is filed, the decision becomes final when the petition is denied or, if the Supreme Court accepts review of the case, 30 days after the date of issuance of the Supreme Court's decision.

Once a Tax Court decision has become final, there are only a few narrow grounds on which it can be vacated: (1) the court lacked jurisdiction to enter the decision, (2) there has been a fraud upon the court, and, possibly, (3) the decision was based on a stipulation which both parties acknowledge was mistakenly entered into. According to the Tax Court, even the third of these grounds is questionable, and no grounds beyond the three (or two) suffice. For example, the Tax Court states that it cannot vacate a final decision because of newly discovered evidence, intervening change in the law, or excusable neglect.[78] Thus, the grounds for vacating a final decision are much narrower than the grounds on which reconsideration of a not-yet final decision may be sought.

I. Appeal

In a regular case, the losing party can file an appeal with the appropriate Federal Circuit Court of Appeals within 90 days after the decision is entered. Neither party

---

74. Tax Ct. Rs. 161 (Motion for Reconsideration of Findings or Opinion), 162 (Motion To Vacate or Revise Decisions). A second motion for reconsideration that is substantially similar to the first motion does not extend the period to appeal a decision of the Tax Court. Peery v. Commissioner, 610 Fed. Appx. 566 (6th Cir. 2015).

75. For examples of unsuccessful motions to vacate or reconsider, see *Estate of Quick v. Commissioner*, 110 T.C. 440 (1998), and *Superior Trading, LLC v. Commissioner*, T.C. Memo. 2012-110, *aff'd*, 728 F.3d 676 (7th Cir. 2013).

76. Servants of Paraclete v. Does, 204 F.3d 1005, 1012 (10th Cir. 2000).

77. IRC §7481.

78. Snow v. Commissioner, 142 T.C. 413 (2014); *see also* Seven W. Enterprises, Inc. v. Commissioner, 723 F.3d 857 (7th Cir. 2013).

may appeal an "S" case. Filing a notice of appeal with the Clerk of the Tax Court and paying a filing fee is necessary in order to perfect the appeal.

Venue for appellate review of a Tax Court decision, in the case of an individual taxpayer, typically lies in the judicial circuit where the taxpayer resides. In the case of a corporate taxpayer, venue is in the circuit in which the taxpayer has its principal place of business or principal office at the time of filing the petition.[79]

From time to time, proposals are offered to remove appeals of tax cases from the existing circuit court's jurisdiction and to vest jurisdiction in a new National Court of Tax Appeals.[80] Part of the opposition to such proposals is concern that the new court would tend to favor the IRS. Those having this fear sometimes believe that the Tax Court is pro-IRS. There is no good support for this belief.[81] At the other end of the spectrum, the old view (still occasionally voiced today) was that, by virtue of its specialized expertise and experience, decisions of the Tax Court should be accorded extra influential weight by generalist courts. Congress rejected that view, however, by directing circuit courts to review Tax Court decisions "in the same manner and to the same extent as decisions of the district courts in civil actions tried without a jury."[82]

Beginning in 1986, Congress allowed for interlocutory appeals in special circumstances. Under section 7482(a)(2), interlocutory appeals are permissible only when the trial judge certifies that the appeal: (1) involves a controlling question of law; (2) offers a substantial ground for difference of opinion as to the correct application of the law; and (3) will materially advance the ultimate termination of the litigation.[83]

J. Assessment of Deficiency after Decision

The IRS is restricted from making an assessment after it sends a statutory Notice of Deficiency for the period during which the taxpayer may file a petition in the Tax Court and, if the taxpayer does so, until the Tax Court's decision becomes final. The prohibition on assessment remains in effect during the 90-day period after entry of the Tax Court's decision. If the taxpayer does not file an appeal within the ninety-day period, the Tax Court decision becomes final at the expiration of the appeals period and the prohibition on assessment (and collection thereon) is lifted.[84] However,

79. IRC § 7482.

80. *See* Steven R. Johnson, *Reforming Federal Tax Litigation: An Agenda*, 41 Fla. St. U.L. Rev. 205, 252–54 (2013) (arguing against such a change).

81. *See, e.g.*, James E. Maule, *Instant Replay, Weak Teams, and Disputed Calls: An Empirical Study of Alleged Tax Court Judge Bias*, 66 Tenn. L. Rev. 351 (1999).

82. IRC § 7482(a)(1); *see* Leandra Lederman, *(Un)Appealing Deference to the Tax Court*, 63 Duke L.J. 1835 (2014); Steve R. Johnson, *The Phoenix and the Perils of the Second Best: Why Heightened Appellate Deference to Tax Court Decisions is Undesirable*, 77 Or. L. Rev. 235 (1998).

83. *See* Kovens v. Commissioner, 91 T.C. 74 (1988).

84. IRC § 7481.

even if the taxpayer files a timely notice of appeal within the 90-day period, the prohibition on assessment (and collection thereon) terminates with the filing of the notice. From that point on, the IRS will try to collect in the normal way, as described in Chapter 13. To stay assessment and collection of any deficiency determined by the Tax Court, the taxpayer must file an appeal bond.[85]

IV. Small Tax Cases ("S" Cases)

A taxpayer challenging an IRS determination in Tax Court must consider whether to elect that the case be treated as a small tax case, generally referred to as an "S" case. This is important, as the rules of procedure and review are quite different between "S" cases and regular cases.

The main reason for allowing "S" designation is to allow easier access to the court for taxpayers with relatively small amounts in controversy where it is not economically feasible to retain an attorney. The "S" procedures provide an expedited, less expensive way to resolve tax cases than is normally the case. "S" cases are in the tax world what small claims cases are in the non-tax world.

Generally, if a taxpayer is not familiar with courtroom procedures or the rules of evidence, and especially if he or she will be self-represented (pro se), it is wise to elect small tax designation in situations where it is available. One can designate a case as an "S" case where the amount of deficiency, including penalties but excluding interest, placed in dispute does not exceed $50,000 for any one taxable year.[86] The key to eligibility for "S" case status is the amount "placed in dispute." Thus, if the Notice of Deficiency states a deficiency in income tax of $47,000 and an addition to tax of $6,000, and the taxpayer concedes $5,000 of the deficiency in the petition, the case is eligible for "S" case status ($47,000 + $6,000 – $5,000 = $48,000).[87]

The decision of the trial court in an "S" case is final and cannot be appealed. Both the taxpayer and the IRS have only one shot at the case.[88] In addition, the decision has no precedential value. Though the Tax Court operates under the Federal Rules of Evidence, these rules are applied less rigidly in "S" cases. Other courtroom procedures and rules are also relaxed in "S" cases to make it easier for laypersons to represent themselves.[89] Opening arguments and briefs are not required. Knowledge of procedure

85. IRC § 7485; Estate of Kanter v. Commissioner, T.C. Memo. 2006-46 (demonstrating the need to post bond after an adverse Tax Court decision if one wishes to avoid assessment of the tax deficiency while the case is on appeal).

86. IRC § 7463(a)(1). In a collection due process case (CDP) under section 6330, if the aggregate liability for the years at issue before the Tax Court exceeds $50,000, the taxpayer cannot seek an "S" case designation, notwithstanding the fact that the $50,000 requirement is met for any single year at issue. Schwartz v. Commissioner, 128 T.C. 6 (2007).

87. Kallich v. Commissioner, 89 T.C. 676 (1987). *See also* note 51 *supra*.

88. IRC § 7463(b).

89. Tax Ct. R. 174.

and evidence is not necessary. In fact, the judges frequently assist taxpayers to develop the facts by asking questions of the taxpayer and other witnesses. Ordinarily, Special Trial Judges hear and decide "S" cases.

Normally, the taxpayer is the party that seeks "S" designation. However, either party may do so. The parties can make the request at any time up to and including the time the trial begins.[90] If the taxpayer has sought or seeks "S" status and the IRS opposes it, the court will generally allow the designation.

Exceptions to this occur when the case has a set of facts or legal principles common to other cases before the court or involves an issue that has significance to the taxpayer over a series of years, such as the basis of depreciable property.[91]

V. Burden of Proof in Tax Court

The burden of proof on most matters raised in the ninety-day letter is on the petitioner. (Fraud determinations are the most common exception.) This is so because the Notice of Deficiency is presumptively correct.[92] "[The Commissioner's] ruling has the support of a presumption of correctness and the petitioner has the burden of proving it to be wrong."[93] The standard of proof is usually by a preponderance of the evidence.[94] The burden of proof is substantially the same in all three forums.

In certain situations, the burden of proof shifts to the IRS. These situations include: (1) where the IRS raises a matter not presented in the Notice of Deficiency and (2) with respect to all affirmative defenses raised in the government's answer, such as res judicata, collateral estoppel, waiver, duress, transferee liability, fraud, and statute of limitations.[95] In the case of fraud, the government has to prove its case by clear and convincing evidence.[96]

The Code also places the burden of proof on the IRS if the taxpayer "introduces credible evidence with respect to any factual issue relevant to ascertaining the liability of the taxpayer," (sometimes referred to as the "burden of going forward").[97] This rule

---

90. Tax Ct. R. 171.

91. Page v. Commissioner, 86 T.C. 1 (1986); IRM 8.4.1.2.

92. For discussion of the burden of proof in valuation cases, see John A Townsend, *Burden of Proof in Tax Cases: Valuation and Ranges*, Tax Notes, Oct. 1, 2001, at 101, and Leandra Lederman, *Arbitrary Stat Notices in Valuation Cases, or Arbitrary Ninth Circuit?*, Tax Notes, July 9, 2001, at 231.

93. Welch v. Helvering, 290 U.S. 111, 115 (1933).

94. *See* Tax Ct. R. 142.

95. *See* Tax Ct. Rs. 142(a), 39.

96. *See* IRC §§ 6902, 7454; Tax Ct. R. 142.

97. IRC § 7491; Tax Ct. R. 142(a)(2); Griffen v. Commissioner, T.C. Memo. 2004-64 ("credible evidence," for purposes of interpreting and applying section 7491, is "the quality of evidence which, after critical analysis, the court would find sufficient upon which to base a decision on the issue if no contrary evidence were submitted (without regard to the judicial presumption of IRS correctness)"). For this provision to apply, the taxpayer must have complied with all substantiation requirements in the Code. This includes, where applicable, the requirement that an item be substantiated to the satisfaction of the IRS, like travel and entertainment in section 274(d). In addition, the taxpayer must have retained all records required by the Code and, within a reasonable time, cooperated with rea-

is irrelevant, however, with respect to legal issues.[98] The fact that one party presents unopposed testimony on a matter does not guarantee that the court will find that testimony credible. The court is entitled to disregard evidence it finds unreliable.[99] The IRS also has the burden of production in any court proceeding with respect to penalties asserted against individual taxpayers.[100]

As a result of section 7491's various conditions, the burden of proof usually does not shift to the IRS or the shift is of little practical significance.[101] Because the "preponderance of the evidence" standard is met by even a slight shift from equipoise, the burden of proof matters little in cases in which the evidence has been fully developed. Many judges defer ruling on motions as to the burden of proof until after the trial. This dodge is intensely frustrating to trial counsel and underlines the practical insignificance of section 7491.

In unreported income cases, the taxpayer might be able to shift the burden of proof to the IRS by showing that the IRS's determination of unreported income was arbitrary. One court stated that: "[w]here it lacks a rational basis, the presumption [of correctness] evaporates. Otherwise the Commissioner could, merely by arbitrarily issuing a naked assessment, place upon the taxpayer the unfair ... burden of proving a negative, that he or she did not receive the illegal income assessed against him."[102]

---

sonable requests by the IRS for (access to) witnesses, information, documents, meetings, and interviews. Cooperation includes not only providing reasonable assistance to the IRS in obtaining access to and inspection of the such persons and items not within the control of the taxpayer but also exhausting one's administrative remedies, such as Appeal rights (short of being required to consent to extend the statute of limitations).

The burden of proof really has two separate components. There is the burden of going forward with the evidence (sometimes referred to as the burden of production) and the burden of ultimate persuasion. In nearly all non-fraud matters, the latter burden requires that the weight of the evidence be more than fifty percent on your side, *i.e.*, the scales tip (even if ever so slightly) in your favor. Because the taxpayer must first introduce credible evidence in order to shift the burden of ultimate persuasion, the taxpayer continues to bear the burden of going forward with the evidence. Since very few, if any, cases after trial are a perfect draw, most practitioners believe there is more rhetoric than substance in the burden of proof shift. For excellent discussions, see Nathan Clukey, *Benefits of Shifting the Burden of Proof to the IRS Are Limited*, 1999 TNT 20-136 (Feb. 1, 1999); Steve R. Johnson, *The Danger of Symbolic Legislation: Perceptions and Realities of the New Burden-of-Proof Rules*, 84 Iowa L. Rev. 413 (1999); Janene R. Finley & Allan Karnes, *An Empirical Study of the Change in the Burden of Proof in the United States Tax Court*, 6 Pitt. Tax Rev. 61 (2008); Philip N. Jones, *The Burden of Proof 10 Years After the Shift*, Tax Notes, Oct. 20, 2008, p. 287; John A. Lynch, Jr., *Burden of Proof in Tax Litigation Under I.R.C. § 7491—Chicken Little Was Wrong!!*, 5 Pitt. Tax Rev. 1 (2007).

98. Nis Family Trust v. Commissioner, 115 T.C. 523 (2000).

99. *E.g.*, Olive v. Commissioner, 139 T.C. 19, 30 (2012), *aff'd* 792 F.3d 1146 (9th Cir. 2015).

100. IRC § 7491(c).

101. *See, e.g.*, Rigas v. United States, 2011 U.S. Dist. LEXIS 46730 (S.D. Tex. May 2, 2011) (in the same order, granting the taxpayer's motion to shift the burden of proof to the IRS, then granting the government's motion for summary judgment).

102. Llorente v. Commissioner, 649 F.2d 152, 156 (2d Cir. 1981); *see also* Portillo v. Commissioner, 932 F.2d 1128 (5th Cir. 1991), *rev'd on other grounds*, 988 F.2d 27 (5th Cir. 1993); Weimerskirch v. Commissioner, 596 F.2d 358 (9th Cir. 1979), *rev'g* 67 T.C. 672 (1977).

Res judicata and collateral estoppel sometimes play a role in tax cases. These related doctrines are discussed at length in Chapter 5.

VI. Choice of Forum

There are three routes available to taxpayers to get judicial review of a proposed deficiency.[103] The route that is the focus of this chapter is the "deficiency route," by which the Tax Court's jurisdiction is invoked to redetermine the amount proposed by the IRS *before* the deficiency is assessed and payment required. The Tax Court hears the vast majority of all tax cases in which a deficiency was involved.[104]

The second route arises when the taxpayer bypasses Tax Court review, permits the IRS to assess the deficiency, makes payment, and then sues in the District Court or Court of Federal Claims for a refund of all or a portion of the tax paid. Taxpayers seek review in this manner in only a small percentage of deficiency cases. However, litigation of non-deficiency tax controversies is available only by paying the disputed amount and seeking a refund. The "refund route" is discussed in Chapter 9.

The third route is "bankruptcy." For this avenue to apply, the taxpayer/debtor has to have filed a bankruptcy petition and a deficiency determination must have been made by the IRS either before, or as a consequence of, the filing. Bankruptcy courts decide a very small percentage of tax deficiency cases.

Tax cases are unique in the fact that there are many ways to proceed to litigate a proposed tax deficiency. This gives taxpayers the opportunity to "forum shop" for the best trial court. Some of the more important factors that go into determining which court to choose are discussed below.[105]

---

103. While the three routes are different procedurally, the bottom line should be the same if the courts reach the same conclusion. For example, assume the IRS asserts two adjustments to taxable income. The total tax deficiency is $30,000, $20,000 of which is attributable to the first adjustment and $10,000 of which is attributable to the second. Assume further that each court would agree with the taxpayer on issue #1 and with the IRS on issue #2. Thus, the bottom line would be that the taxpayer owes $10,000 tax.

Under the deficiency route, the taxpayer would have to pay $10,000 (plus interest) only after the Tax Court's decision becomes final and the tax is assessed. A somewhat similar result would follow from a bankruptcy situation. By contrast, if the taxpayer chooses to litigate in refund status, he or she would have to first pay the entire $30,000 (plus interest) and then sue for its refund. After the decision in favor of the taxpayer on issue #1, the taxpayer would be entitled to a refund of $20,000 (plus interest) with respect to issue #2.

See David B. Porter, *Where Can You Litigate Your Federal Tax Case?*, 98 Tax Notes 558 (2003).

104. *See supra* note 1.

105. There is extensive literature of choice-of-entity considerations in tax litigation. *E.g.*, Nina J. Crimm, *Tax Controversies: Choice of Forum*, 9 B.U. J. Tax L. 1 (1991); Thomas D. Greenaway, *Choice of Forum in Federal Civil Tax Litigation*, 62 Tax Law 31 (2009); Gerald A. Kafka, *Choice of Forum in Federal Civil Tax Litigation (Part I)*, Practical Tax Law., Winter 2011, at 55 & *(Part II)*, Practical Tax Law., Spring 2011, at 51; David B. Porter, *Where Can you Litigate Your Federal Tax Case?*, Tax Notes, Jan. 27, 2003, at 558.

A. Breadth of Jurisdiction

The Tax Court has limited jurisdiction and can only hear certain types of tax cases.[106] The Tax Court's principal area of jurisdiction is over cases in which the IRS determines a deficiency[107] in income, estate or gift taxes. Other matters over which the Tax Court has jurisdiction were presented above in Section I.

By contrast, District Courts and the Court of Federal Claims can hear almost all kinds of tax cases. These courts may, like the Tax Court, resolve disputes that originally gave rise to a deficiency in income, estate, and gift taxes. More often, however, these courts are called upon to resolve disputes affecting other taxes and penalties, such as employment and excise taxes, and disputes initiated by the taxpayer, such as where the taxpayer requests a refund on an amended return.

While the Bankruptcy Court also has very broad jurisdiction, it can only review the propriety of tax debts when a debtor is engaged in a bankruptcy proceeding under Title 11 of the U.S. Code.[108]

B. Payment Considerations

The most significant *practical* reason the vast majority of taxpayers go to the Tax Court for review of deficiency determinations is that one does not have to have paid the disputed amount for the court to have jurisdiction. Instead, the Tax Court decides the amount of the liability, if any, and only then does the taxpayer have to pay it.

By contrast, in order to take a case to the District Court or the Court of Federal Claims, one must pay the *entire* amount asserted by the government *before* suing for a refund of the disputed amount.[109] Prepayment may not be possible for the taxpayer, mooting all other considerations.

---

106. Holding that such issues are partnership level matters, the Tax Court held that it has jurisdiction to review a Final Partnership Administrative Adjustments (FPAA) asserting that the partnership is a sham and should be disregarded for tax purposes, as well as a partner's outside basis and any penalties resulting from a FPAA. Petaluma FX Partners LLC v. Commissioner, 131 T.C. 84 (2008), *aff'd in part & rev'd in part*, 591 F.3d 649 (D.C. Cir. 2010), *supplemental opinion*, 135 T.C. 581 (2010). *But see* Chapter 6, Part B.

107. Even when a Tax Court case begins as a deficiency matter, the taxpayer could end up with a refund due. This is because of the court's jurisdiction to decide all issues associated with the year before it. IRC § 6512(b) (granting Tax Court jurisdiction to determine overpayments).

108. Bankruptcy Court is only available to those taxpayers involved with bankruptcy proceedings. In a sense, it is not an "optional" choice like the other forums.

The Bankruptcy Court can determine the tax liability or overpayment of a taxpayer. 11 U.S.C § 505. Furthermore, the Bankruptcy Court can discharge tax liabilities. 11 U.S.C § 523. Decisions of the Bankruptcy Court are appealable to the District Court.

If the taxpayer petitioned the Tax Court before filing a petition in bankruptcy, the Tax Court proceeding is automatically stayed, unless there was a binding decree. 11 U.S.C § 362(a)(1). The Bankruptcy Court can allow the tax issue to be decided by the Tax Court or decide it itself. If the matter is complex, such that the specialization of the Tax Court is highly beneficial to the resolution, the Bankruptcy Court may defer jurisdiction over the deficiency to the Tax Court. In addition, the District Court sometimes withdraws a tax issue from the Bankruptcy Court in order to decide the issue itself.

109. Flora v. United States, 362 U.S. 145 (1960).

C. Precedent

The most important *legal* factor to consider when choosing a forum is the precedent the court will follow in deciding a case. For example, it would make no sense for the taxpayer to take a case to the Tax Court if the court has already addressed the issue and held in favor of the government. Instead, one should review the decisions of other courts and choose the most favorable forum.

To make this judgment, one must know which decisions each trial court is obligated to follow. Under our system of common law and stare decisis, each court will follow its own opinions. Thus, the Tax Court will follow prior Tax Court cases (including cases decided by the Tax Court's ancestor: the Board of Tax Appeals), and the Court of Federal Claims will follow decisions of the Court of Federal Claims and its predecessors—the Court of Claims and the Claims Court. Since it is unusual for a District Court to hear enough tax cases to build a body of decisional law on a given issue, precedent within a particular district is not usually important.

Each trial-level court will also follow the decisions of the Circuit Court of Appeals to which the case is appealable and of the Supreme Court. As discussed in Chapter 1, Tax Court cases and District Court cases are appealable to the circuit court responsible for the location in which the taxpayer resides.

Court of Federal Claims' cases are appealable to the Circuit Court of Appeals for the Federal Circuit.

> *Example* (1): The IRS disallowed a deduction for points on mortgage refinancing for a taxpayer who resides in Denver, Colorado. The Tax Court has decided this issue favorably to taxpayers in previous cases. The Court of Federal Claims has not. The Tenth Circuit, to which appeals in Denver are filed, has not addressed the issue in the past. Other circuits that have considered the issue have uniformly held in favor of the IRS. All other factors being equal, the taxpayer should take the case to the Tax Court. The taxpayer is sure to win at the trial level. If the IRS appeals the loss to the Tenth Circuit, the court will decide the case as one of first impression. While the Tenth Circuit may look to the opinions of other circuits for guidance, it is not bound by them.
>
> *Example* (2): Same as example (1) above except that the Tenth Circuit has held for the IRS in the past and the Federal Circuit Court of Appeals has held in favor of the taxpayer. The taxpayer should avoid the Tax Court since it will follow the precedent established in the Tenth Circuit, even though contrary to its own decisional law.[110] Instead, assuming the taxpayer can pay the

110. Golsen v. Commissioner, 54 T.C. 742 (1970), *aff'd*, 445 F.2d 985 (10th Cir. 1971). In one case, the court chose not to follow the precedent of the circuit to which the appeal would lie because that precedent had been based on a concession by a party. Tigers Eye Trading, LLC. v. Commissioner, 138 T.C. 67, 75–77 (2012) (also holding that a court is not bound to accept a concession as to a matter of law).

entire asserted tax, he or she should take the case to the Court of Federal Claims, as it is obligated to follow the decisions of the Federal Circuit Court of Appeals.

D. Judge vs. Jury and Legal Argument vs. Equitable Considerations

Because the District Court is the only forum in which a jury is available, it is the best court in which to bring a case that relies heavily on equitable considerations by the trier of fact that might be lost if examined under the microscope of the law. While taxpayers have fared well in Tax Court on this issue, innocent spouse cases fit this description. This might also be the best forum if the case involves a very complex provision of the tax law that most people cannot understand and with respect to which the taxpayer honestly sought to comply.

By contrast, cases in the Tax Court are heard by judges who have significant backgrounds in tax law. They are tax specialists who understand the nuances of complex tax provisions. If one is trying to advance a logical but novel position, the Tax Court may be the best place to litigate. If one is relying on the trier of fact to apply equity, the Tax Court is not the court to petition.[111]

The Bankruptcy Court is specifically designed for equity and to help debtors emerge from bankruptcy with a "fresh start." For this reason, the ability to litigate a tax controversy in Bankruptcy Court might be one of a number of factors to consider when determining whether to file for bankruptcy.

E. Concerns about New Issues

A final decision on the merits is res judicata as to all issues that were raised or could have been raised for the year. Issues raised thereafter are barred, no matter their validity. On the other hand, issues raised before the court renders its final decision normally are not precluded. If it is the IRS that raises a new issue, dramatically different results can come about depending on the route taken and whether the IRS raises the issue before the statute of limitations on assessment expires.

In Tax Court, the IRS can raise a new issue in its answer. If it failed to do so, the IRS can ask the court's leave to raise a new issue by amending its answer and seeking a greater deficiency.[112] Since the statute of limitations on assessment is stayed until

---

111. The Pension Protection Act of 2006, P.L. 109-280, Title VIII, Subtitle E, §85(a) amended IRC §6214(b) to permit the Tax Court to apply the doctrine of equitable recoupment in the same manner as other courts may in civil tax cases.

112. With respect to the new issue, the IRS automatically has the burden of proof. The presumption of correctness that applies to the original assessment does not apply to new issues. *See* Abatti v. Commissioner, 644 F.2d 1385 (9th Cir. 1981). The burden of proof and presumption of correctness matters are still important even after the 1998 Reform Act's shift of the burden to the IRS in tax litigation. This is because the new rules require certain prelitigation action by the taxpayer before the shift occurs,

the decision of the court becomes final,[113] a successfully argued new issue can result in an increased deficiency. A dramatic example of this occurred in *Raskob v. Commissioner*.[114] The taxpayer petitioned the Tax Court with respect to a deficiency of only $16,000, but the IRS successfully argued a new issue and the taxpayer left the Tax Court with a tax liability of $1,025,000!

By contrast, refund actions do not suspend the running of the statute of limitations on assessment. If the taxpayer brings the refund action while the statute of limitations on a refund action is still open, but after the statute of limitations on assessment has expired,[115] the IRS would be time-barred from assessing amounts the court found in its favor attributable to a new issue. If a refund would otherwise be due the taxpayer for the same year, the best the government can do is offset or reduce the amount of the refund by the amount that cannot be assessed.[116]

> *Example*: In a Notice of Deficiency mailed April 15, 20x5, the IRS claims that Bill Wilson omitted income in the year 20x1 by treating compensation as a loan. The resulting proposed deficiency in tax is $15,000 (issue #1). The IRS wishes to raise a new issue disallowing tax shelter deductions, the impact of which would be an additional $100,000 deficiency (issue #2). Assume that Bill prevails on issue #1 and the IRS prevails on issue #2. The litigation takes place during December 20x6, more than three years after the tax return was filed.
>
> If Bill litigated the deficiency in Tax Court, he would emerge owing $100,000 (having won on issue #1 but having lost on issue #2). The IRS could assess the $100,000 because section 6503(a) suspends the statute of limitations on assessment for the entire period the case is in Tax Court.
>
> If Bill paid the $15,000 deficiency and waited until after September 12, 20x6 (the date the statute of limitations on assessment would have run after considering section 6503) to sue for a refund, the result would be quite different. Although the IRS would be time-barred from assessing and collecting the $100,000 associated with the tax shelter, it could retain the $15,000 to offset against the $100,000.

---

whereas with respect to a new issue, the burden shift to the IRS occurs whether or not the taxpayer has met the prelitigation requirement. *See* IRC § 7491.

113. IRC § 6503.

114. 37 B.T.A. 1283 (1938), *aff'd sub nom* 118 F.2d 544 (3d Cir. 1941). Dupont v. Commissioner, 118 F.2d 544 (3d Cir. 1941).

115. If the refund action is brought when the statute of limitations on assessment is still open, the IRS will try to issue a timely Notice of Deficiency. If the government does so, the result would be the same as that demonstrated in *Raskob*.

116. Lewis v. Reynolds, 284 U.S. 281, 283 (1932) ("An overpayment must appear before refund is authorized. Although the statute of limitations may have barred the assessment and collection of any additional sum, it does not obliterate the right of the United States to retain payments already received when they do not exceed the amount which might have been properly assessed and demanded"), modified, 284 U.S. 599 (1932).

F. Accruing of Interest

Interest normally accrues on an outstanding tax liability from the due date of the return until the taxpayer pays it. In refund litigation, the continued accruing of interest while the court reviews the determination is not a problem since the taxpayer has to make full payment of the balance to invoke the jurisdiction of the refund courts.

By contrast, continuing accrual of interest is a significant problem when one seeks Tax Court review of a proposed deficiency. As a result, taxpayers wishing to litigate in Tax Court look for ways to stop the interest from accruing.

- The taxpayer can make full payment of an expected deficiency prior to the IRS issuing a ninety-day letter. For example, one might pay the amount on the thirty-day letter. However, since doing so eliminates the deficiency, the government no longer has a basis for issuing a Notice of Deficiency. Without a Notice of Deficiency, the taxpayer cannot seek a hearing in the Tax Court.
- The taxpayer can make partial payment of an expected deficiency prior to the IRS issuing a ninety-day letter. This would leave a balance due, thus preserving Tax Court jurisdiction. By doing so, the interest stops running to the extent of the amount paid. If it turns out that the tax was overpaid, the IRS will send a refund for the overpayment, with interest from the date of payment.
- The taxpayer can make full or partial payment of a deficiency after the IRS mails the ninety-day letter. Tax Court jurisdiction is not adversely affected by payment at this time since all that is required is issuance of a ninety-day letter. It is not necessary that the deficiency continue to exist throughout the proceedings. Interest on the deficiency stops accruing to the extent of the payment and, if it is later determined that the taxpayer overpaid, a refund with interest will be sent.
- The taxpayer can designate a remittance as a "deposit in the nature of a cash bond."[117] Since remittance in this manner is *not* treated as a payment, it does not pay down the deficiency, thus preserving Tax Court jurisdiction. Interest stops accruing against the taxpayer to the extent of the deposit.

G. Costs of Litigation

Although the Tax Court is physically located in Washington, D.C., the judges travel nationwide to conduct trials in various cities. The District Court and the Bankruptcy Court are local forums. The Court of Federal Claims is located in Washington, D.C. Its trials typically occur there, even though the court will travel, depending on the circumstances. Because of the costs associated with having counsel and witnesses fly to, and lodge in, Washington, D.C., litigation in the Court of Federal Claims can be significantly more expensive than in other courts.

---

117. IRC § 6603 (discussed in Chapter 12); Rev. Proc. 2005-18, 2005-13 I.R.B. 798.

The Tax Court is less expensive than the other courts for other reasons also. The Tax Court requires informal discovery discussions between the parties prior to expensive formal discovery. The other courts do not. The Tax Court also requires the parties to stipulate to as much as possible rather than requiring the parties to prove every fact in a time-consuming and expensive trial. In addition, the representative of the government in Tax Court is an attorney in a local office of Area Counsel rather than an attorney with the Department of Justice located in Washington, D.C., which helps keep attorney travel costs down.

H. Other Factors

1. Publicity

If publicity is a concern, the District Court should be avoided. While it is common for reporters to cover litigation in the local District Court, it is rare for them to report on litigation in Tax Court, Bankruptcy Court, or the Court of Federal Claims.

2. State Law

The District Court is significantly more familiar with state law issues since it is a local court, rather than a national court. Thus, if the case involves complicated issues regarding state law that favor the client, it may be desirable to litigate in District Court.

3. Speed of Disposition

The District Court is a court with broad jurisdiction and its caseload is considerable. It may take anywhere between several months and several years before the case comes to trial. The Tax Court normally resolves cases more quickly. This consideration may be affected by the fact that district courts sometimes require mediation, which may protract resolution of the dispute.

4. Nationwide Jurisdiction

The Tax Court, Bankruptcy Court, and Court of Federal Claims are "national" courts and their power is nationwide. They can serve process on and subpoena anyone within the country. The District Court, by comparison, is a regional court and can only serve process on and subpoena people within its jurisdiction.

5. Tax Court's Exclusive Jurisdiction

As discussed in Section II.G., once the Tax Court acquires proper jurisdiction over a case by the taxpayer filing a timely petition, no other court may consider the case. Therefore, decisions on the best forum in which to litigate a tax case should be made before a petition is filed with the Tax Court.

6. APA Issues

Chapter 1 demonstrated that an important trend in tax law is the growing significance of general administrative law, particularly issues under the Administrative Procedure Act ("APA").[118] The Court of Federal Claims lacks jurisdiction to review IRS actions on APA grounds.[119] The district courts historically have displayed greater interest in and sophistication as to the APA than has the Tax Court.[120] Accordingly, if the situation permits, a taxpayer wishing to make an APA argument should consider bringing the case in federal district court unless there are compelling reasons to the contrary.

VII. Attorney's Fees and Costs

Under section 7430, a taxpayer who prevails in proceedings with the IRS or in litigation involving a tax matter may be able to recover costs incurred in the proceedings, including attorney's fees. Before 1982, attorney's fees were recoverable by a prevailing taxpayer under the Equal Access to Justice Act ("EAJA")[121]—but only where the taxpayer prevailed in a suit in federal district court. The EAJA did not provide for attorney's fees and costs incurred in Tax Court proceedings.[122]

In 1982, Congress remedied this glitch by enacting section 7430. Several times since 1982, Congress has expanded the scope of section 7430. The most significant changes include: (1) shifting the burden of proof from the taxpayer (to establish that the government's position was unreasonable) to the government (to prove that its position was substantially justified);[123] (2) allowing taxpayers to recover costs incurred during administrative proceedings as well as during litigation;[124] and (3) establishing clearer guidelines and presumptions for when the government's position is not substantially justified or the taxpayer is deemed to be the prevailing party.[125] Today, to recover costs under section 7430, a taxpayer must satisfy the following requirements:

- The costs must be incurred either in an administrative or court proceeding in connection with the determination, collection, or refund of tax, interest, or penalties or in the case deciding the taxpayer's right to attorney's fees and costs, *i.e.*, fees for fees;[126]

---

118. 5 U.S.C. § 551 *et seq.*

119. *E.g.*, Martinez v. United States, 333 F.3d 1295, 1313 (Fed. Cir. 2003); Strategic Housing Finance Corp. v. United States, 86 Fed. Cl. 518, 552 (2009) (calling this principle "well-settled"), *aff'd*, 608 F.3d 1317, 1332 (Fed. Cir. 2010).

120. *See, e.g.*, Diane L. Fahey, *Is the United States Tax Court Exempt from Administrative Law Jurisprudence when Acting as a Reviewing Court?*, 58 Clev. St. L. Rev. 603, 604 (2010) (arguing that the Tax Court should apply the APA more rigorously).

121. 28 U.S.C. § 2412 (1988).

122. Smith v. Brady, 972 F.2d 1095 (9th Cir. 1992).

123. IRC § 7430(c)(4).

124. IRC § 7430(a)(1).

125. IRC § 7430(c)(4)(B), (E). *See generally* Amy Barnes & Robert E. Dallman, *Opportunities for Taxpayers to be Reimbursed for Costs Incurred in Tax Audits and Cases*, J. Tax'n, Apr. 2011, at 215.

126. Huffman v. Commissioner, 978 F.2d 1139, 1149 (9th Cir. 1992); Powell v. Commissioner, 891 F.2d 1167 (5th Cir. 1990).

- The taxpayer must exhaust all administrative remedies with the IRS, including review by the Appeals Office;
- The taxpayer must not unreasonably protract the proceedings;
- The taxpayer must be the prevailing party with respect to the amount in controversy, or the most significant issue or set of issues presented. In order for the taxpayer to be the prevailing party, the government must not be able to establish its position in the proceeding was substantially justified. (Only costs incurred during the time the government's position was unjustified are recoverable under section 7430. Interest does not accrue on section 7430 awards.);[127] and
- The taxpayer must satisfy certain net worth requirements.[128]

A particularly interesting provision—the Qualified Settlement Offer rule—was added in the 1998 Reform Act. If the judgment in the court proceedings is in an amount that is equal to or less than the amount of the taxpayer's last offer (the "qualified offer"), the taxpayer is treated as the prevailing party for costs and fees incurred thereafter.

The taxpayer is not required to use any specific form for requesting administrative costs from the IRS. However, the request must be in writing and contain the information specified in Regulation section 301.7430-2(c)(3). The taxpayer must file the request with the IRS for administrative costs within ninety days of the final decision of the IRS regarding the underlying tax, addition to tax, and penalties.[129] The request should be filed with the IRS office that has jurisdiction over the underlying tax matter.

If a taxpayer's request for a section 7430 award of administrative costs is denied in whole or in part by the IRS, the taxpayer may appeal to the Tax Court.[130] If the IRS sends its notice of denial to the taxpayer by certified or registered mail, the taxpayer has ninety days from the date of the notice to file a Tax Court petition appealing the denial.

The Tax Court, District Court, the Court of Federal Claims, and the Bankruptcy Court may all grant section 7430 awards.[131] If the IRS and the taxpayer settle the case,

---

127. Miller v. Alamo, 992 F.2d 766 (8th Cir. 1993). Because of the requirement, it is very difficult to obtain reimbursement in cases presenting novel issues. *See* Hale E. Sheppard, *Seeking Cost Reimbursement in Cases of First Impression: Zealous Advocacy or Pushing Your Luck?*, Practical Tax Law., Spring 2007, at 15. Similarly, reimbursement usually will not be granted simply because the IRS proceeded in bad faith. Centex Corp. v. United States, 486 F.3d 1369 (Fed. Cir. 2007). *But see* Dixon v. Commissioner, 132 T.C. 55 (2009) (allowing attorneys' fees and interest as sanctions under section 6673 for egregious IRS conduct).

128. Individuals with net worth over $2 million and entities with net worth over $7 million are excluded from eligibility for reimbursement. IRC § 7430(c)(4)(A)(ii); 28 U.S.C. § 2412(d)(2)(B). All assets of the taxpayer are included in this calculation. Smith v. United States, 107 AFTR2d 1228 (D. Conn. 2011).

129. Reg. § 301.7430-2(c)(5); *see* Eric L. Green, *Making the IRS a Qualified Offer It Can't Refuse: Using Qualified Offers to Help Settle Tax Cases and Obtain Reimbursement of Costs*, J. Tax Prac. & Proc., Apr.–May 2010, at 19.

130. IRC § 7430(f)(2).

131. IRC § 7430(c)(6). The wording of this section—"'court proceeding' means any civil action brought in a court of the United States"—includes the Bankruptcy Court. Kovacs v. United States, 739 F.3d 1020 (7th Cir. 2014). However, it is worth noting that the Bankruptcy Court also gives its

including issues relating to recovery of costs, any section 7430 award must be included in the stipulation agreement. Otherwise, the taxpayer must make a separate written motion for a section 7430 award. Any evidence pertaining only to the section 7430 motion should not be presented in the main case.

The Tax Court will include its decision regarding recovery of fees and costs under section 7430 with its decision in the case. If the taxpayer loses and it is determined that the section 7430 request was frivolous, the taxpayer could be subject to sanctions under section 6673(a)(2).[132]

A court order granting or denying all or part of an award for reasonable litigation costs is subject to appeal in the same manner as the court's decision or judgment.[133] In order for the reviewing court to determine whether the denial was appropriate, the trial court must include a statement of reasons, not merely a conclusory statement.[134] The standard of review is "abuse of discretion" and the appellate court will "reverse only if [it has] a definite and firm conviction that the [trial] court committed a clear error of judgment in the conclusion it reached upon weighing the relevant factors."[135]

Problems

Bill and Mary were married and filed joint federal income tax returns. They received a letter from the IRS dated November 10, 20x5, telling them that their returns for the years 20x3 and 20x4 were under examination, and asking them to call the Revenue Agent assigned to the case to schedule a meeting. Bill and Mary engaged a lawyer to represent them in the examination.

Bill and Mary separated in mid-20x5 and were considering a divorce. Mary didn't trust Bill, and filed a separate return for that year. Bill failed to file a return at all.

The 20x3 and 20x4 returns showed as their address the home that they had occupied together. Mary continued to live there after they were separated. Bill moved to an apartment in the same city, and provided his local post office with a "change of address" form. On the advice of the lawyer they had engaged to represent them in the examination, Bill also wrote a letter to the IRS dated December 30, 20x5, informing the Service of his new address together with the other required information.

The Revenue Agent conducting the examination for 20x3 and 20x4 asked for a copy of their 20x5 return. The lawyer gave the Agent a copy of Mary's 20x5 return, and informed the Agent that Bill had not filed. Shortly thereafter, the IRS sent Bill a letter saying that it had prepared a return for him based on payee information it had received (W-2s and 1099s). Except for a personal exemption, the return did not include any deductions.

---

courts the authority to impose sanctions, including an award of attorneys' fees and costs, either under its general powers or as a result of a particular infraction. *See, e.g.*, 11 U.S.C. §§ 105, 362(k); *see also* In re Parker, 515 B.R. 337 (Bankr. M.D. Ala. 2014), *aff'd*, 634 Fed. Appx. 770 (11th Cir. 2015).

132. Bragg v. Commissioner, 102 T.C. 715, 720–21 (1994).

133. IRC § 7430(f)(1).

134. Liti v. Commissioner, 289 F.3d 1103 (9th Cir. 2002).

135. *Id.* at 1105–06.

The report of the Revenue Agent addressed to Bill and Mary proposed deficiencies in tax for 20x3 and 20x4 of $10,000 and $12,000, respectively. The Revenue Agent issued a separate report for 20x5, addressed to Bill, proposing a deficiency in the amount of $20,000.

The lawyer filed protests for all three years, and argued the cases before the Appeals Office. Unfortunately, however, the Appeals Officer to whom the cases had been assigned decided against Bill and Mary on all issues.

The IRS sent a Notice of Deficiency to Bill and Mary for 20x3 and 20x4 dated February 1, 20x7, addressed to the home that was still occupied by Mary. Mary sent Bill a copy.

1. What should the attorney have discussed with Bill and Mary?

2. In what court or courts could Bill and Mary seek judicial review of the Notice of Deficiency for 20x3 and 20x4?

3. Would Bill and Mary have to pay the deficiency in tax proposed by the IRS in the Notice of Deficiency for 20x3 and 20x4 as a prerequisite to seeking judicial review in the Tax Court?

4. What is the last date by which Bill and Mary must file a petition in the U.S. Tax Court for the years 20x3 and 20x4? Can the date be extended?

5. Assume that the attorney advised Bill and Mary that the precedents for the issues in their case were much better in the District Court than in the Tax Court. Can they seek judicial review in the District Court? What is the procedure? What are the advantages? The disadvantages?

6. Assume that Bill and Mary chose to seek judicial review in the Tax Court. Can the case be tried in the Tax Court under its small case ("S") procedures? What are the advantages to Bill and Mary? The disadvantages? What procedure should be followed to carry out the choice? What will the court do if the IRS opposes the request?

The lawyer filed a petition in the Tax Court on behalf of Bill and Mary for the years 20x3 and 20x4 on April 1, 20x7.

7. Assume that Bill and Mary later decided that they should have gone to the District Court. Can they do that?

8. Which party has the burden of proof in the Tax Court? What is the standard of proof?

9. Assume that Bill and Mary decided not to use the small case procedure. What must their attorney do upon receipt of the following:

a. The IRS answer to the petition filed by their lawyer?

b. A letter from the lawyer for the IRS asking for an informal (Branerton) conference?

c. A letter from the lawyer for the IRS asking for a stipulation conference?

d. A notice from the Tax Court that the case has been calendared for trial?

e. A pretrial order from the judge to whom the case has been assigned?

Bill and Mary were unable to settle their case, and it went to trial in the Tax Court in 20x8. Bill and Mary won on two issues and lost on one issue. The opinion, issued on March 1, 20x9, said that the decision would be entered under Rule 155.

10. What caused the Court to specify that the decision would be entered under Rule 155? What should Bill and Mary's attorney do?

11. Assume that the Tax Court issued its decision on June 1, 20x9.

a. How long did Bill and Mary have to decide whether to appeal?

b. When does the decision of the Tax Court become final?

c. When can the IRS make an assessment against Bill and Mary for 20x3 and 20x4?

d. To which Court of Appeals would the decision be appealed?

The IRS also sent a Notice of Deficiency for 20x5 to Bill dated February 1, 20x7. It was addressed to Bill at the home that was occupied by Mary. The postal carrier, who did not know about Bill's change of address form, but knew that Bill no longer lived there, sent it back to the IRS with a notation that it was undeliverable because Bill was no longer at that address. The notice was never delivered to Bill and he knew nothing about it.

12. Is the Notice of Deficiency sent to Bill for 20x5 valid?

13. Assume for this question only that the postal carrier had delivered the Notice of Deficiency as addressed, and Mary had sent it to Bill a few days later. Would your answer to question 12 be different?

14. Assume for this question only that Bill had not provided his local post office with a "change of address" form, and had not written a letter to the IRS informing it of his new address. The postal carrier simply returned the Notice of Deficiency for 20x5 to the IRS as undeliverable. Is the notice valid?

The IRS assessed tax against Bill for 20x5 on July 1, 20x7 and sent letters to Bill attempting to collect the tax. Like the Notice of Deficiency, the letters were sent to the home occupied by Mary but sent back to the IRS as undeliverable. They were never received by Bill. Bill finally learned of the assessment when his bank informed him that the IRS was levying on his bank account to collect the tax due for 20x5.

15. Bill called the attorney when he found out the IRS was levying on his bank account to collect the 20x5 tax. What should the attorney advise Bill to do?

16. Assume for purposes on this question only that the Notice of Deficiency was not valid. What would prevent the IRS from issuing a second Notice of Deficiency, this time to his real last known address?

Chapter 9

Overpayment — Claims for Refund

IRC: Skim §§6164(a)–(f); 6401(a), (b)(1), (c); 6402(a), (b); 6404(a); 6405(a), (b); 6407; 6411(a), (b); 6511(a)–(d)(2)(A), (h); 6512; 6513(a)–(d); 6514; 6532(a)(1)–(4), (b); 6611(a); 6621(a); 7422(a), (e); 7502(a), (d); see also 28 U.S.C. §2401(a)

Regs.: §§301.6401-1(a), (b); 301.6402-1; 301.6402-2(a)(1), (b); 301.6402-3(a); 301.6402-4

Case: Flora v. U.S., 362 U.S. 145 (1960)

Forms: Skim 843; 1040X; 2848

I. Introduction

Taxpayers sometimes find that they have paid more than the amount of tax that is due. The Code contains an extensive set of rules that, if followed, permit taxpayers to claim refunds of the amount overpaid. The most often encountered claims for refund are on income tax returns. This occurs when a return shows an overpayment, i.e., that the tax withheld on wages,[1] the amount of any estimated taxes paid,[2] and overpayments from a prior year applied to the current year, exceed the reported liability. If there is an overpayment, the IRS will normally send a check to the taxpayer in that amount or will deposit it directly into a specified bank account.[3] (Alternatively, the taxpayer can elect to have the overpayment applied to the following year's estimated tax liability.)[4] Absent any concerns that the taxpayer was the subject of identity theft,[5]

1. Technically, the tax withheld on wages under sections 3401–3406 is treated as a refundable credit under section 31. Refundable credits are credited against the taxpayer's income tax liability, and any excess is refunded to the taxpayer. IRC §36. If the taxpayer is also entitled to non-refundable credits, those credits are applied first to the tax liability, thereby preserving for the taxpayer the maximum amount that can be received from the refundable credits. IRC §6401(b).

2. Payments of estimated income tax are considered payment on account of the taxpayer's income tax for the year. IRC §6315.

3. In 2011, the IRS unveiled IRS2GO, a smartphone application that lets taxpayers check the status of their tax refunds and also obtain various other types of tax information. IR-2011-8 (Jan. 24, 2011).

4. IRC §6402(b).

5. The filing of mass numbers of returns claiming bogus refundable credits is a major problem. In 2013, the IRS "protected $17.8 billion from refund fraud, initiated 1400 investigations and obtained over 1,000 indictments and 400 convictions" related to refund fraud and identity theft. Prepared remarks of Commissioner of Internal Revenue John Koskinen before National Press Club (Washington, D.C.), Apr. 2, 2014, at 7. The IRS has responded in many ways, including slowing the speed of paying

the IRS will send the refund to the taxpayer or deposit it within a few weeks of the return being filed.

These kinds of claims for refund are simple in part because they are associated with the taxpayer's annual return filing responsibility and the IRS's normal processing of returns. When the taxpayer discovers an overpayment later or if it is discovered in connection with an audit of a return, getting a refund is more complicated. In those situations, the taxpayer most likely will have to file a claim for refund, most often on an amended return.[6] An alternate approach to asserting an overpayment was created by the Internal Revenue Service Restructuring and Reform Act of 1998.[7] The legislation gave taxpayers the right to a Collection Due Process hearing if the IRS files a notice of lien or a notice of intent to levy on a taxpayer's assets. These hearings are discussed in Chapter 13. For purposes of the topic of this chapter, however, taxpayers are entitled to "raise challenges to the existence or amount of the underlying tax liability" at such hearings,[8] including the existence of an overpayment, so long as the taxpayer either did not receive a notice of deficiency or have an opportunity to contest the liability.[9]

The basic procedural structure for obtaining a refund is simple: (1) there must be an overpayment; (2) a claim for refund must be filed in a timely manner; and (3) the amount of the claim must be tested against certain statutory limitations. However, the law is infused with numerous exceptions and rules that deal with specific circumstances. For instance, although the basic statute of limitations on filing a claim for refund is the later of three years from the time the return was filed or two years from the time the tax was paid,[10] under various circumstances the statute of limitations on

---

claimed refunds in some situations (to allow operation of multiple levels of anti-fraud screening), limiting to three per year the number of refunds electronically deposited into the same bank account, and cracking down on personal accounts held by tax return preparers into which multiple refunds are deposited. Written Testimony of Commissioner John A. Koskinen, 2014 Filing Season and Improper Payments, Before Subcomm. On Oversight of House Ways & Means Comm. (May 7, 2014); Written Testimony of Commissioner John A. Koskinen, IRS Actions to Reduce Improper Payments, Before Subcomm. On Government Operations of House Oversight & Government Reform Comm. (July 9, 2014). Similarly, under the Delinquent Return Refund Hold Program, the IRS may delay paying a refund for up to six months while it investigates whether the taxpayer was delinquent in filing returns in prior years. In 2012, the Delinquent Return Refund Hold Program collected over $240 million, which was applied to amounts due with respect to prior years. Treasury Inspector General for Tax Administration, *Expansion of the Delinquent Return Refund Hold Program Could Improve Filing Compliance and Help Reduce the Tax Gap* (TIGTA No. 2014-30-023) (June 3, 2014).

6. In Fiscal Year 2012, the IRS received over 4 million amended returns. Based on a sampling, the Treasury Inspector General for Tax Administration (TIGTA) thinks the IRS error rate in processing amended returns may be as high as 17%, potentially causing erroneous refunds of over $400 million per year. Treasury Inspector General for Tax Administration, *Amended Tax Return Filing and Processing Needs to be Modernized to Reduce Erroneous Refunds, Processing Costs, and Taxpayer Burden* (TIGTA 2014-40-028) (July 9, 2014).

7. Pub. L. 105-206, 112 Stat. 685 (July 22, 1998).

8. IRC § 6330(c)(2)(B) (as to any proposed levy). Challenges to the existence or amount of the asserted liability may also be raised in a collection due process hearing under section 6320. *See* § 6320(c).

9. IRC § 6330(c)(2)(B).

10. IRC § 6511(a).

claiming a refund[11] is longer than the three-year/two-year periods,[12] or is extended,[13] suspended,[14] or capable of being reopened.[15]

If a refund claim is filed within the applicable statute of limitations and the amount requested is within the statutory limits, the IRS has the discretion to accept and pay the claim, to deny part or all of it, or to simply ignore it. If the IRS accepts the claim and pays the requested refund in its entirety, this is usually the end of the matter; the taxpayer is happy and has no reason to proceed further. On the other hand, if the IRS denies part or all of the claim, or fails to respond to it, the taxpayer can file a refund suit in a United States District Court, the Court of Federal Claims, or in certain limited circumstances, the Bankruptcy Court.[16]

It is worth noting that the Tax Court does not have general jurisdiction to determine the validity of refund claims. Its principal role is as a forum for taxpayers to seek a redetermination of a deficiency proposed by the IRS without the requirement of having to pay the tax first. However since the Tax Court's role in a deficiency proceeding is to determine the correct amount of tax, if it finds that an overpayment has occurred, it has jurisdiction to require the government to make a refund.[17]

Added to the procedural maze created by special rules is the fact that while a taxpayer may otherwise be entitled to a refund of an overpayment, the refund may be diverted to pay other debts that are owed. For instance, the statute authorizing the IRS to refund overpayments also authorizes the IRS to first apply an overpayment against any other tax liability owed to the federal government by the taxpayer, and then directs the IRS to use the balance, to the extent necessary, to satisfy certain other debts of the taxpayer to federal and state agencies, like past due child support and state income taxes.[18] Any such diversion of an otherwise proper refund obviously reduces the amount refunded to the taxpayer.

---

11. A taxpayer seeking a refund may not look outside the procedural structure provided in the Code to some other statute that may have a longer statute of limitations for recovery, even when the claim stems from unconstitutionally collected taxes. United States v. Clintwood Elkhorn Mining Co., 128 S. Ct. 1511 (2008) (taxpayer suing for refund of taxes collected in violation of Export Clause of United States Constitution could not proceed under the Tucker Act when his suit did not meet time limits for refund actions in the Internal Revenue Code).

12. IRC §6511(d).

13. IRC §6511(c).

14. IRC §6511(h).

15. IRC §§1311–1314. *See* Chapter 10.

16. The complexity of this area results in part from the principle of sovereign immunity. The government cannot be sued without its consent, and statutes conferring such consent are read strictly. *E.g.*, United States v. Mitchell, 463 U.S. 206, 212 (1983); United States v. Testan, 424 U.S. 392, 299 (1976). The party challenging the government bears the burden of showing that sovereign immunity has been waived. *E.g.*, Tri-State Hosp. Supply Corp. v. United States, 341 F.3d 571 (D.C. Cir. 2003). A taxpayer who has had his refund claim decided by a bankruptcy court is barred by res judicata from seeking a refund in another court. Isley v. United States, 272 Fed. Appx. 640 (9th Cir. 2008).

17. IRC §6512(b).

18. IRC §6402.

Presently, amended returns have to be filed on paper, not electronically. As a result, amended returns are not subject to the same automated filters and verification processes as are original returns filed electronically. IRS employees reviewing amended returns must manually check math computations and otherwise determine eligibility for claimed refunds. Not only does this increase the likelihood of an amended return being examined but it also increases the chance of the IRS issuing an erroneous refund.[19]

This chapter first discusses three primary questions associated with overpayments and claims for refund: (1) Is there an "overpayment"? (2) Can the taxpayer establish the right to a refund, including whether the claim was filed timely and whether the amount for which a refund is sought was paid within certain time limits? (3) Can the payment of a refund be diverted to another use? After considering these questions, the refund jurisdiction of the courts, tentative carryback and refund adjustments, and penalties for excessive claims are discussed. Although many of the procedures mentioned in this chapter apply to other taxes as well, unless otherwise noted, the discussion pertains to federal income taxes.[20] Claims for refund with respect to partners and partnerships are discussed in Chapter 6.

II. Is There an Overpayment?

Neither the Code nor the Regulations contain a comprehensive definition of an overpayment.[21] The Supreme Court has defined the term "in its usual sense, as meaning any payment in excess of that which is properly due."[22] This definition invites consideration of what constitutes "payment" and how the amount "properly due" is determined.

---

19. Treasury Inspector General for Tax Administration, *Amended Tax Return Filing and Processing Needs to be Modernized to Reduce Erroneous Refunds, Processing Costs, and Taxpayer Burden* (TIGTA No. 2014-40-028) (Apr. 25, 2014). The IRS agrees with TIGTA's recommendation that e-filing should be expanded to include amended returns.

20. In addition to the general requirements, special requirements exist as to refund claims of particular types. *E.g.*, IRC § 6416 (excise taxes); Reg. §§ 31.6413(a)-1 to 31.6413(c)(1) (employment taxes).

21. Section 6401 describes certain things included in the term "overpayment," such as any amount assessed or collected after the applicable statute of limitations, but neither that section nor its related Regulations purports to define the term comprehensively. In *Williams-Russell & Johnson v. United States*, 371 F.3d 1350 (11th Cir. 2004), the Eleventh Circuit Court of Appeals was faced with the question of whether payments actually owed and made in a timely fashion but assessed after the expiration of the statute of limitations should be refunded. The taxpayer argued that any such payments are, by definition, "overpayments" under section 6401(a). The court, citing the principles established in *Lewis v. Reynolds*, 284 U.S. 281 (1932), modified, 284 U.S. 599 (1932), concluded that "a taxpayer's claim for refund must be reduced by the amount of the correct tax liability for the taxable year, regardless of the fact that the Commissioner can no longer assess any deficiency for the taxable year" (*citing Bachner v. Commissioner*, 109 T.C. 125, 130 (1997), *aff'd*, 172 F.3d 859 (3d Cir. 1998)).

22. Jones v. Liberty City Glass Co., 332 U.S. 524, 531 (1947).

A. What Constitutes Payment?

Just as the amount of an overpayment is determined "in its usual sense," so too is the amount paid as tax. Thus, taxes paid with the return or with a request for extension of time to file, taxes reported on the return but paid later, taxes paid in response to a notice of deficiency, and taxes paid in installments are all payments. Likewise, prepayments, such as estimated taxes[23] and taxes withheld on wages, are considered payments.

One area where it is not intuitive whether an amount paid is determined in its usual sense is when a taxpayer deposits money with the IRS to suspend the running of interest on a proposed tax liability. This occurs most often when the IRS has concluded an examination of the taxpayer's return and is proposing a deficiency. Rather than letting the interest accrue in case the IRS proves successful, the taxpayer might like to "stop the bleeding" if possible. The dilemma the taxpayer faces is that if he makes full payment of the proposed deficiency before a Notice of Deficiency is issued, there will not be a deficiency in tax for which a notice can be issued. This would then preclude Tax Court review. For example, if the 30-day letter is proposing a deficiency of $25,000 and if the taxpayer pays the entire amount to stop the accruing of interest, there remains no deficiency in tax and therefore no opportunity to litigate the issues in the Tax Court.

So, the question is how can a taxpayer make a payment for interest purposes but not have it treated as a payment for deficiency purposes.[24] Sounds like a job for Houdini, or Congress. While the topic is more fully covered in Chapter 12, it has significance here because of the procedures associated with the return of the remittance (and associated interest) if the taxpayer requests it or is otherwise entitled to it.

The solution to the problem is in section 6603 and Revenue Procedure 2005-18.[25] The latter provides rules for making and withdrawing deposits under section 6603. In order for a remittance to be treated as a deposit, the taxpayer must designate it as such in a letter to the IRS. A remittance that is not designated as a deposit will be treated as a payment by the taxpayer and assessed by the IRS upon receipt.[26]

So long as the remittance is considered a deposit, *i.e.*, before the Service has treated the deposit as a payment and assessed the tax, the taxpayer may request the return of all or part of it (including interest that will have accrued in the taxpayer's favor)[27]

23. IRC § 6315.

24. In the tax field, the distinction between deposits and payments was a judicial creation. *See* Rosenman v. United States, 323 U.S. 658, 662–63 (1945); *see also* Principal Life Ins. Co. v. United States, 95 Fed. Cl. 786, 796–98 (2010) (providing a good history of this issue).

25. Rev. Proc. 2005-18, 2005-13 I.R.B. 798, which superseded Rev. Proc. 84-58, 1984-2 C.B. 501.

26. IRC § 6213(b)(3).

27. To protect against taxpayers purposefully depositing more than the anticipated liability in order to earn interest, section 7 of Revenue Procedure 2005-18 limits the amount of the deposit on which interest will be paid to the amount "attributable to a disputable tax." Taxpayers are required to identify the amount and nature of the disputable tax (determined by any "reasonable method") at the time the deposit is made or, in the case of re-designation of deposits in the nature of a cash bond, at the time of the re-designation.

by sending a letter to the IRS to that effect. A request for the return of a deposit is not subject to the procedures associated with a claim for credit or refund as an overpayment. Importantly, such a request can be made at any time, meaning it is not subject to the three- and two-year statute of limitations rules discussed in Section III.C below.

Once a deposit under section 6603 is applied to a liability, it is treated as a payment, the date of which is when the IRS assesses the tax. This means that the normal rules, *i.e.*, those discussed throughout this chapter, apply to its refund. Treating the payment as having been made on the date the tax is assessed is beneficial to the taxpayer because the lateness of the date (rather than the date the deposit is received by the IRS) makes it more likely that the payment is within the two-year look-back limitation period discussed below.

When the taxpayer has not followed the procedures in Revenue Procedure 2005-18, the taxpayer may find it difficult to prove that a remittance was meant to be a deposit rather than a payment. "In determining whether a remittance is a deposit or a tax payment, the court applies a 'facts-and-circumstances' test, considering (1) when the tax liability is defined, (2) the taxpayer's intent in remitting the money, and (3) how the IRS treats the remittance upon receipt."[28]

B. The Tax Properly Due

An overpayment is, generally speaking, the excess of the tax paid over the amount of tax properly due. For refund claim purposes, the amount of tax properly due and the amount of an overpayment is, in the first instance, normally determined on the tax return filed by the taxpayer. Except in situations where the IRS suspects identity theft or the like, the amount claimed as an overpayment on the original return is refunded to the taxpayer within several weeks and is rarely, if ever, subjected to examination by the IRS at that time.[29]

The amount reflected on the tax return, while initially treated as the tax due, may not be the tax properly due. Both the taxpayer and the IRS are entitled to make changes, if they feel it is necessary. If the taxpayer subsequently believes that the original return was incorrect in some respect and concludes there was an overpayment, he can file a refund claim (usually an amended return that claims a refund).[30] Likewise, the IRS may audit a tax return or a refund claim and conclude there is no overpayment or, worse, that there is an underpayment. If either of these situations occurs, the

28. Syring v. United States, 112 AFTR2d 4197143 (W.D. Wis. 2013) (remittance treated as a payment, resulting in the denial of a refund of $144,000 because the statute of limitations on claiming a refund had run); *see also* Ewing v. United States, 914 F.2d 499, 503 (4th Cir. 1990) (similar); Principal Life Ins. Co. v. United States, 95 Fed. Cl. 786, 798–807 (2010) (discussing when a deposit converts into a payment).

29. While the IRS rarely examines a tax return prior to issuing a refund, the fact that the government did not do so when it was filed does not preclude the IRS from performing an examination at a later time.

30. Reg. § 301.6402-3(a).

amount of tax properly due will eventually be determined by agreement of the parties or by a decision of a court.

An interesting situation can arise as a result of the interplay of the taxpayer's filing of a refund claim and the authority of the IRS to examine the claim or the tax return. Assume the taxpayer timely filed the refund claim. The basis for the claim is that he failed to take a deduction of $15,000 on his 20x1 tax return, resulting in an overpayment of $5,000. Upon receiving the claim for refund, the IRS decides to examine the tax return. The IRS concludes that the expenditure was allowable and should have been deducted. However, as a result of the examination, the IRS also determines that the taxpayer treated a $200,000 item as a loan that should have been reported as gross income, resulting in an additional tax liability of $50,000. The taxpayer agrees. Consequently, the IRS will make two adjustments, the net of which is an increase in income of $185,000 and an increase in tax due of $45,000.

If the statute of limitations on assessment is still open, the IRS will assess the $45,000 and send the taxpayer a bill for it (plus interest). But what if the taxpayer filed the refund claim on April 1, 20x5 (which would be timely) and by the time the IRS examined the return and determined that the loan should have been gross income, the statute of limitations for assessment of the tax had expired? Is the taxpayer entitled to the $5,000 refund? In 1932, the United States Supreme Court answered that question in *Lewis v. Reynolds*.[31] The taxpayer asserted that because the statute of limitations on assessment had expired, the IRS was precluded from requiring the inclusion of the item of income and recalculating the tax liability as if it was included. The taxpayer further argued that the only thing the IRS could do was to allow or disallow the adjustment requested in the timely filed claim for refund. Since the IRS agreed that the expenditure was an allowable deduction, he should have received a refund of $5,000.

The Supreme Court disagreed with the taxpayer. The Court said, "Although the statute of limitations may have barred the assessment and collection of any additional sum, it does not obliterate the right of the United States to retain payments already received when they do not exceed the amount which might have been properly assessed and demanded."[32] In other words, the tax properly due may be determined irrespective of the right of the government to make an assessment. The IRS may offset the two items and not give a refund but it cannot demand payment of the tax associated with the gross income item. This is sometimes referred to as the "offset doctrine."

Lewis v. Reynolds suggests that before a claim for refund is filed, consideration should be given to whether, and to what extent, there are items that the IRS might raise to reduce or eliminate the claimed refund. This is particularly important if, when the claim is filed, the IRS has time to audit the return and perhaps assess and collect a deficiency. Filing a timely claim for refund near the end of the statute of

---

31. 284 U.S. 281 (1932) modified, 284 U.S. 599 (1932).

32. *Id.* at 283; *see also* R.H. Donnelley Corp. v. United States, 684 F. Supp. 2d 672 (E.D.N.Y), *aff'd*, 641 F.3d 70 (4th Cir. 2011) (applying *Lewis* in the context of credit carrybacks).

limitations on assessment preserves the claim for refund and provides some protection against exposure to deficiency assessments, though not against an offset.

III. Can the Taxpayer Establish the Right to a Refund?

A. The Requirement of a "Claim"

Regulation section 301.6402-2(b)(1) establishes the standard for an effective claim. "The claim must set forth in detail each ground upon which a credit or refund is claimed and facts sufficient to apprise the Commissioner of the exact basis thereof." While the regulation does not mandate that a specific form has to be used, the IRS has created forms for this purpose. Whether a claim is sufficient is a question of fact. The relevant inquiry is whether the claim is sufficient to notify the IRS that the party is asserting a right to a tax refund, and to enable the IRS to begin an examination of the claim.[33] Pursuant to traditional administrative law principles, the taxpayer needs to provide the agency, here the IRS, with enough information from which to reach a conclusion. "The requirement for filing a proper refund claim 'is designed both to prevent surprise and to give adequate notice to the Service of the nature of the claim and the specific facts upon which it is predicated, thereby permitting an administrative investigation and determination.'"[34]

As previously mentioned, most claims for refund are reflected on an originally-filed tax return. A return is treated as a claim for refund if it contains a statement setting forth the amount determined as an overpayment and requests that such amount be refunded to the taxpayer. When that is the case, the return itself sufficiently apprises the IRS of the grounds and the facts upon which the claim is based. As the return and the claim are one and the same document, a claim for refund reflected on a tax return can never be untimely.[35]

For taxpayer-initiated claims for refund other than one reflected on the original tax return, the IRS has provided different forms. For income taxes, this is accomplished on Form 1040X for individuals, Form 1120X for corporations, Form 1065X for partnerships, and a revised Form 1120S for S corporations. Claims for refund of estate tax, gift tax, employment tax, assessable penalties, and certain excise taxes, as well as claims for refund or abatement of interest, are filed on Form 843 (Claim for Refund and Request for Abatement). If the claim is made on an amended return, an explanation in compliance with the regulation is required. Refund claims on these forms are considered formal claims.[36]

There is a significant body of case law dealing with taxpayers who have failed to file formal claims within the statute of limitations, but who, to some extent, have in-

33. Furst v. United States, 678 F.2d 147, 151 (1982).
34. Computervision Corp. v. United States, 445 F.3d 1355, 1363 (Fed. Cir. 2006).
35. Rev. Rul. 76-511, 1976-2 C.B. 428.
36. Reg. § 301.6402-3(a).

formed the IRS that they believe they are entitled to a refund. "Informal claims," such as correspondence between the taxpayer and an IRS agent stating a claim, are recognized[37] provided that: (1) the IRS was put on notice that the taxpayer was actually asking for a refund for the year in question; (2) the taxpayer made clear both the factual and the legal bases for the claim; and (3) there is a written document relating to the claim. "The determination of whether a taxpayer has satisfied the requirements for an informal claim is made on a case-by-case basis and is based on the totality of the facts."[38]

It is worth noting that there are situations where a refund will be granted even though no claim for refund has been filed. For example, if the IRS examines the taxpayer's return and if it is determined that the taxpayer failed to deduct all allowable expenses or he erroneously included in income certain items, the IRS should agree to a refund at the conclusion of the audit, or at the appeals level using a Form 870-type agreement (including Form 4549). Similarly, it is possible that the Tax Court, upon a petition by the taxpayer in response to a notice of deficiency, will determine that there was an overpayment.

1. Amending the Claim for Refund

After filing a claim for refund, the taxpayer may realize it was incorrect and that it needs to be revised. This might happen, for example, if the original refund claim stated only that he failed to take a deduction for travel and entertainment and he

---

37. IRM 34.5.2.1; *see, e.g.*, Mobil Corp. v. United States, 67 Fed. Cl. 708 (2005); Wall Indus. v. United States, 10 Cl. Ct. 82 (1986); American Radiator & Standard Sanitary Corp. v. United States, 318 F.2d 915 (Cl. Ct. 1963). An application for an automatic extension of time to file an amended return on Form 4868 can constitute an informal claim for refund. Kaffenberger v. United States, 314 F.3d 944 (8th Cir. 2003), acquiesced AOD CC-2004-04, 2004 Lexis 4. *See also* Estate of Wilshire v. United States, 2008 U.S. Dist. LEXIS 91920 (S.D. Ohio 2008) (written and oral communications between executor and IRS constituted informal refund claim); Stevens v. United States, 2007 WL 2556592 amended, 2007 WL 2688466 (N.D. Cal. 2007) (numerous phone calls and written communications between taxpayer and IRS stating basis for claim clear example of informal claim doctrine); ILM 200736027, 2007 TNT 175-13 (informal claim considered valid where taxpayer sent a single letter to the IRS stating the basis for his refund); CCA 201116017 (Apr. 22, 2011) (documents filed with Taxpayer Advocate Service and TAOs do not constitute informal refund claims).

38. Donahue v. United States, 33 Fed. Cl. 600, 608 (1995). In *Palomares v. Commissioner*, T.C. Memo. 2014-243, a case denying an innocent spouse refund claim filed incorrectly on a Form 8379 (Injured Spouse) rather than on a Form 8857, the Tax Court, quoting from *Jackson v. Commissioner*, T.C. Memo. 2002-44, "explained that the relevant inquiry is 'whether, under all the facts and circumstances, petitioner gave sufficient notice of the basis for his refund claim to respondent so that respondent could investigate the claim and make a determination on the merits.'" Further quoting from *Jackson*, the court said:

> It has long been recognized that a writing which does not qualify as a formal refund claim nevertheless may toll the period of limitations applicable to refunds if (1) the writing is delivered to the Service before the expiration of the applicable period of limitations, (2) the writing in conjunction with its surrounding circumstances adequately notifies the Service that the taxpayer is claiming a refund and the basis therefor, and (3) either the Service waives the defect by considering the refund claim on its merits or the taxpayer subsequently perfects the informal refund claim by filing a formal refund claim before the Service rejects the informal refund claim.

later determines he also failed to take a charitable contribution deduction. In such situations, the taxpayer's success will depend on whether the statute of limitations has expired by the time he wishes to make the revision. If it has not, then the taxpayer should either amend the original claim or file a new claim for refund.

If the statute of limitations on filing a claim has expired, the IRS will not consider either new claims or new legal theories that vary from the original claim.[39] The "variance doctrine" is based on long-standing requirements that the claim must be timely and must set forth both the facts and law that support the requested refund. If the claim proceeds to trial, the taxpayer-plaintiff will be precluded "from substantially varying... the factual bases of its arguments from those raised in the [timely] refund claims it presented to the IRS."[40] While claims and legal theories that were not before the IRS for its review will not be entertained by courts, "[i]t is immaterial that the size of the refund sought ... substantially exceeds the amount originally sought.... As long as the nature of the claim was timely given, differences in amount—even large differences—are immaterial."[41]

B. Who Qualifies as a "Taxpayer"?

Generally, the person who is liable for the tax is the person entitled to file a claim for refund. Section 6402(a) says that the IRS may credit the amount of the overpayment against any liability of the person who made the overpayment and shall refund any balance to such person.

But can a person who paid the tax for another file a claim for refund? In *United States v. Williams*,[42] the Supreme Court was asked to decide whether Ms. Williams, who was not personally liable for the tax but who paid it under protest on behalf of her ex-spouse, could file a suit in District Court to recover the tax. Ms. Williams paid the tax in order to remove a tax lien against her former husband that attached to property she owned jointly with him. The government took its long-held position that the refund procedures were only available to "taxpayers"—people against whom the tax could be assessed.[43] According to the government, since the tax in question could not be assessed against Ms. Williams, she was not a taxpayer and thus could not avail herself of the refund procedures.

After resolving a sovereign immunity issue raised by the government, the Court held for Ms. Williams, saying that she fell squarely within the wording of section

39. *E.g.*, Dominion Resources, Inc. v. United States, 97 Fed. Cl. 239, 260 (2011), rev'd on other issues, 681 F.3d 1313 (Fed. Cir. 2012); Mobil Corp. v. United States, 52 Fed. Cl. 327 (2002); John Keenan, Rona Hummel & Whitney Lessman, *Supplemental Claims: Acceptable Amendment or New Claim?*, Tax Adviser, Mar. 2011, at 149.

40. Ottawa Silica Co. v. United States, 699 F.2d 1124 (5th Cir. 1983).

41. Parker Hannifin Corp. v. United States, 71 Fed. Cl. 231, 234–35 (2006).

42. 514 U.S. 527 (1995).

43. *Compare* Snodgrass v. United States, 834 F.2d 537 (5th Cir. 1987), *and* Busse v. United States, 542 F.2d 421 (7th Cir. 1976) (holding that only the person against whom the tax was assessed has the right to maintain a refund suit), *with* Martin v. United States, 895 F.2d 992 (4th Cir. 1990) (allowing the wife who voluntarily paid her former husband's liability to maintain a refund suit).

6402(a). This section, said the Court, posits that the test for who can file a claim is the person who made the overpayment, not the person who could be assessed. In reaching this result, however, the Court expressly withheld decision as to whether "a party who volunteers to pay a tax assessed against someone else [rather than pays the tax under protest to release a lien] may seek a refund under § 1346(a)."[44]

C. The Timely Filing Requirement

When a taxpayer files a claim for refund that meets the conditions discussed above, there are two interconnected, time-related tests that must be addressed to determine whether the taxpayer is entitled to a refund and in what amount. The first question, addressed in this section, is whether the claim was filed within the statute of limitations set forth in section 6511(a). The second question, addressed in Subsection D, is whether the amount that can be refunded is limited under section 6511(b)(2).

1. The Statute of Limitations on Filing the Claim

To be effective, a claim for refund must be in writing[45] and it must be filed "within 3 years from the time the return was filed or 2 years from the time the tax was paid, whichever of such periods expires the later...."[46] In other words, a refund claim must be filed by the *later* of three years from the time the return is filed or two years from the time the tax is paid.

Unless a claim is filed in a timely manner, no refund is allowed. Should a refund be made (or credit given) erroneously after the expiration of the statute of limitations on filing a *claim*, it is considered void and is recoverable by the government. Likewise, if a timely claim is filed but part or all of the claim is disallowed, any refund made (or credit given) with respect to the disallowed portion after the period for filing *suit* has expired is erroneous and considered void.[47]

---

44. 514 U.S. at 540; *see also* Robinson v. United States, 95 Fed. Cl. 480 (2011) (alleged threat of imprisonment of son insufficient to support claim that after paid son's liabilities to IRS under duress). It is important to note that refund claims, similar to other claims against the United States, are non-assignable under 31 U.S.C. § 3727.

45. Wrightsman Petroleum Co. v. United States, 35 F. Supp. 86, 96 (Ct. Cl. 1940), *cert. denied*, 313 U.S. 578 (1941) ("an oral claim made to a Revenue Agent is not a sufficient compliance with the statute requiring the *filing* of a claim by the taxpayer. An oral claim cannot be filed. The claim must be in writing. This is a requirement, not of the regulations, but of the statute and, therefore, is something which the Commissioner has no right to waive."); Mills v. United States, 890 F.2d 1133, 1135 (11th Cir. 1989) ("There are no rigid guidelines except that an informal claim must have a written component and 'should adequately apprise the Internal Revenue Service that a refund is sought for certain years.'").

46. IRC § 6511(a); Strategic Housing Finance Corp. v. United States, 608 F.3d 1317 (Fed. Cir. 2010), *cert. denied*, 131 S. Ct. 1513 (2011); RadioShack Corp. v. United States, 566 F.3d 1358 (Fed. Cir. 2009).

47. IRC § 6514(a); CCA 201110011 (Mar. 11, 2011). Section 7405(a) authorizes the United States to bring a civil action to recover any erroneously made refund, and section 6532(b) requires such an action to commence within two years of the erroneous refund or, if "the refund was induced by fraud or misrepresentation of a material fact," then within five years. The Supreme Court has held that the limitations period begins to run on the receipt of "payment." O'Gilvie v. United States, 519 U.S 79

As is true with most documents that need to be filed with the IRS, the date it is received is treated as the date it is filed. Therefore, a refund claim for 20x1 that would need to be filed by April 15, 20x5, i.e., three years from the due date of April 15, 20x2, is timely if received any time before then but untimely if received thereafter. However, under the "timely-mailing (or postmarking)-is-timely-filing" rule of section 7502, a properly addressed claim that is received by the IRS after the due date, but which is postmarked (or recorded or marked by a designated private delivery service) on or before the due date, is deemed to be delivered on the date of the postmark. Thus, in the example above, if the claim was received by the IRS on April 17, 20x5, but was postmarked April 14, 20x5, it would be considered timely filed. Also, under section 7503, if the last day of the period within which a claim can be filed falls on a Saturday, Sunday or legal holiday, a claim filed on the next succeeding day (which is not a Saturday, Sunday or legal holiday) is considered timely filed.[48] Therefore, if in the example, April 15, 20x5, was a Saturday, the due date for the filing of the refund claim would be extended to Monday, April 17, 20x5.

In calculating the three- and two-year dates, a return filed before the due date is treated as filed on the due date.[49] Similarly, tax prepaid during the year, such as through withholding, estimated payments, and prior years' overpayments applied to the current year, is considered paid on the due date of the return (without extensions).[50] As we will see when we discuss the limitation on the amount refundable, the fact that these payments are treated as being paid on April 15 of the year following the tax year is of critical importance. If no return is filed, the claim for refund must be filed within two years from the time the tax was paid. IRC § 6511(a). However, in the case of income taxes, a return that is filed claiming an overpayment serves as both a return and a claim for refund. If such a return is filed late, it is always a timely claim for refund because a claim, made on the return itself, is clearly filed within three years of the time the return was filed.[51]

(1996). For this purpose, receipt of payment of the erroneous refund has been held to be either the date the check cleared, United States v. Greener Thapedi, 398 F.3d 635 (7th Cir. 2005); United States v. Commonwealth Energy, 235 F.3d 11 (1st Cir. 2000), or the date of receipt of the check, Paulson v. United States, 78 F.2d 97 (10th Cir. 1935). In a related matter, the IRS has announced in AOD 2006-02 that it does not acquiesce in *Pacific Gas and Electric Co. v. United States*, 417 F.3d 1375 (Fed. Cir. 2005). That case held that the IRS could not offset a refund of taxes and interest due for 1982 by an erroneous refund of interest for that year because the offset was made after expiration of the section 6532(b) limitations period for the government to file suit for the erroneous refund. For a comprehensive analysis of procedures relating to erroneous refunds, see Bryan T. Camp, *The Mysteries of Erroneous Refunds*, Tax Notes, Jan. 15, 2007, at 231.

48. See Weisbart v. U.S. Dept. of Treasury, 222 F.3d 93 (2d Cir. 2000); Rev. Rul. 2003-41, 2003-1 C.B. 814 (containing examples of the impact of the Saturday, Sunday, legal holiday rule on claims for refund).

49. IRC § 6513(a).

50. IRC § 6513(b).

51. See Weisbart v. U.S. Dept. of Treasury, 222 F.3d 93 (2d Cir. 2000); Rev. Rul. 1976-511, 1976-2 C.B. 428.

Applying the basic statute, if a taxpayer files his return timely and pays all tax shown as due on the return before or at the time of filing the return, a claim for refund of tax that is filed within the next three years will be timely. For example, if the taxpayer files the calendar year 20x1 return on April 15, 20x2, a claim for refund of 20x1 taxes filed on or before April 15, 20x5, is timely pursuant to the three-year rule. Even if additional tax is paid after the return is filed, but within one year of filing, the three-year rule still establishes the last day for which a timely claim can be filed.

The two-year statute of limitations rule is relevant only with respect to tax paid more than one year after the return was filed. In that situation, the two-year rule will be the one that must be satisfied with respect to the later-paid tax, because it will be later than the date computed using the three-year rule. Thus, if the taxpayer files the 20x1 return on April 15, 20x2, and pays additional tax for the year on June 30, 20x4 (usually as the result of a deficiency assessment), then the two-year rule applies as to that additional tax and a claim for its refund must be filed no later than June 30, 20x6, to be timely.

There are numerous nuanced exceptions and special rules, so much so that the IRS acknowledges: "the section 6511 rules are so complicated that the system cannot currently be programmed to figure out every situation."[52] However, as seen below, numerous special rules can apply. That being the case, counsel for a taxpayer should independently and carefully calculate the RSED (refund statute expiration date).

2. Extension of the Statute of Limitations on Filing a Claim for Refund

The statutes of limitations relating to the government's ability to assess additional tax[53] and the taxpayer's ability to claim a refund are, in a sense, related. In the usual case of a taxpayer who files a timely return and pays the tax shown on the return in a timely manner, the government can assess additional tax, and the taxpayer can file a claim for refund, within the same three-year period.[54] Similarly, if the IRS and the taxpayer agree, in a timely manner, to an extension of the statute of limitations on *assessment* by executing a Form 872 or Form 872A, then the statute of limitations on filing a *claim for refund* also is extended. Form 872 extends to a certain date the latest when the IRS must either assess the tax it asserts to be due or send a Notice of Deficiency. Form 872A is more open-ended and extends the statute of limitation on assessment for the IRS until 90 days after either the taxpayer or IRS terminates it. Both forms state that a taxpayer generally has six months after the date the agreement ends to file a claim for refund.[55]

52. CCA 201321022 (May 2, 2013).

53. IRC §6501(a).

54. IRC §6511(a).

55. IRC §6511(c)(1). Extension under section 6511(c) of the period for filing a refund claim depends upon the proper execution of the extension as to the period for assessment. To be valid, a Form 872 must be executed by both the taxpayer and the IRS before the assessment limitations period expires. *E.g.*, King v. Commissioner, T.C. Memo. 2006-112. In one case, the IRS received within the assessment limitations period a Form 872 duly signed by the taxpayer, but the IRS itself did not sign until after that period had expired. Since the 872 was invalid, section 6511(c) did not operate to

While extending the statute of limitations on assessment also extends the statute on filing a claim for refund, there is no provision in the Code that authorizes the Service and the taxpayer to agree to extend the statute of limitations only on filing a claim for refund. As such, when an extension respecting assessment is not entered into, taxpayers must be vigilant in monitoring the basic three-year/two-year period to preserve their positions. This is especially important when the IRS is examining one year that could result in a refund in another year.

For instance, if the IRS is proposing that a deduction taken in year one should have been taken in year two, the taxpayer must make sure that the year two statute of limitations on claims for refund does not expire while the issue of the correct year is being resolved. Similarly, if the IRS was taking the position that an item of income included in year one should have been included in year two, the taxpayer needs to take action to preserve a possible refund in year one.

In such cases, because the IRS and the taxpayer cannot agree to extend the statute of limitations on filing a claim for refund, the taxpayer needs to file a "protective claim for refund" before the statute of limitations expires. The protective claim is the same as a regular claim in all respects except that the words "Protective Claim for Refund" are written on the top of the first page. The IRS understands that a timing issue is in the process of being resolved and it places the protective claim in suspense pending resolution of the underlying issues.[56]

3. Special Rules Relating to Income Taxes

Under certain circumstances, the three-year/two-year period for filing a claim for refund is too short. For instance, because determining the year that a debt or security becomes worthless is often difficult, an extended statute of limitations is needed where a taxpayer's choice of timing, if wrong, could result in the correct year being barred. Thus, in lieu of the basic rule, a "seven years from the due date of the return for which the claim for refund was filed" rule applies with respect to the deductibility of a worthless debt or security.[57]

---

extend the period available to the taxpayer for later filing a refund claim. Chief Counsel Advisory CCA 201402003 (Oct. 31, 2013).

56. Protective claims may also be used when taxpayers are paying taxes in installments. Generally, claims for refund may not be filed until the entire tax liability is paid. Flora v. United States, 362 U.S. 145 (1960). The IRS may permit protective claims to be filed while the installments are being paid and not act on the claims until the tax liability is paid in full. *See* Gen. Couns. Mem. 38786 (Aug. 13, 1981); Burgess J.W. Raby & William L. Raby, *Protecting the Protective Refund Claim*, Tax Notes, Apr. 28, 2003, at 529.

In e-mailed advice, the Service provided a general overview of protective claims that are filed to preserve the taxpayer's right to claim a refund when the right is contingent on future events and may not be determinable until after the limitations period expires, noting that the Service has discretion in deciding how to process such claims. IRS E-Mail Chief Counsel Advice ECC 200848045 (July 17, 2008), 2008 TNT 232-54. Additionally, in CCA 201526007 (June 26, 2015), the Service said that a timely filed protective refund claim can be supplemented and amended up to the point at which final action is taken on the claim.

57. IRC § 6511(d)(1).

Extra time on the statute of limitations on claims for refund is also necessary in order to implement the statutorily authorized carryback of net operating losses[58] and capital losses.[59] In this case, the statute of limitations with respect to the years to which a net operating loss or a capital loss can be carried remains open until the later of (i) three years after the due date (including extensions) of the return for the year which gave rise to the loss or (ii) if there has been an agreement extending the statute of limitations on assessment with respect to the year which gave rise to the loss, six months after the expiration of the period within which assessment may be made pursuant to the agreement.[60]

Another situation warranting a modification of the statute of limitations on claims for refund arises when an individual taxpayer is physically or mentally unable to file timely refund claims.[61] By the time a guardian is appointed to act on behalf of the taxpayer, the statute of limitations on filing a claim may have expired. Section 6511(h) suspends the running of the statute of limitations during the period that the taxpayer is "financially disabled," until a guardian or other person authorized to act on behalf of the taxpayer is appointed.[62] Financially disabled does not refer to limited income

---

58. Section 172 permits carryback of a net operating loss (NOL) to the two years immediately preceding the year in which the loss occurred. Section 6164 permits a corporation that expects a NOL for the current year to defer, for a certain period of time, paying a portion, or perhaps all, of the tax owed for the immediately preceding year.

59. IRC § 1212.

60. IRC §§ 6511(c)(1), 6511(d)(2)(A).

61. *See, e.g.*, United States v. Brockamp, 519 U.S. 347 (1997). In *Webb v. United States*, 850 F. Supp. 489 (E.D. Va. 1994), the government prevailed on its motion to dismiss a refund suit because the underlying claim for refund was filed after the statute of limitations on filing the claim expired. The facts alleged by the taxpayer and treated as true by the court in considering the motion to dismiss were as follows:

> By virtue of Parsons' advanced age, trusting nature, emotional vulnerability, declining health and drug dependence, she became a victim of the fraud and undue influence and control of her doctor, Alvin Q. Jarrett, and her lawyer B. Roland Freasier, Jr. As Parsons' fiduciaries, Jarrett and Freasier took over her personal and business affairs so totally that they were able to transfer to themselves substantially all of her stock holdings in 1980. Thereafter, and during the relevant period of 1980 to July 1987, Jarrett and Freasier limited Parsons' contact with friends, and Jarrett regularly administered pain-killing drugs, sleeping pills and tranquilizers. Parsons was confined to her bed in Virginia and was given inadequate medical care while her household staff was cut back and her contacts with the outside world were limited still further. Parsons was totally dependent on Jarrett to manage all of her physical, emotional, and financial needs, and she was neither aware of, nor able to inform herself about, the fraud and self-dealing of her fiduciaries.

Id. at 490. The total gift tax paid was $10,862,876.88. Of this amount, $7,038,054.34 was paid within two years of filing the claim for refund. The refund suit was brought to recover the balance of gift tax paid. Section 6511(h), enacted in the IRS Restructuring and Reform Act of 1998, P.L. 105-206, § 3202(a), was a response to Webb and several other cases.

62. *See, e.g.*, Bova v. United States, 80 Fed. Cl. 449 (Fed. Cl. 2008) (taxpayer was not entitled to an extension of the statute of limitations based on "financial disability," because the durable power of attorney executed by the taxpayer authorized an attorney to act on the taxpayer's behalf during the entire period of her financial disability and did not restrict attorney from taking necessary actions).

or assets. Instead, in order for the statute of limitations on filing a claim to be suspended under this provision, it must be established that the taxpayer has a medically determinable disability "which can be expected to result in death" or "to last for a continuous period of not less than 12 months."[63]

Finally, even if the statute of limitations on filing a claim for refund has expired, under certain circumstances, the claim for refund may be treated as filed timely under the mitigation provisions.[64] The mitigation provisions are discussed in Chapter 10.

D. The Section 6511(b)(2) Limitation

Even if an otherwise valid claim for refund is filed timely, the taxpayer may not be eligible for a refund of the entire underpayment. This is because the amount that may be refunded is limited to amounts paid within a specified "look-back" period.[65] The Supreme Court calls this provision a "lookback,"[66] explaining that it is not a "statutory time ... limitation[ ]" but rather a "substantive limitation[ ] on the amount of recovery."[67]

Just as the three-year rule for the timeliness of the claim usually applies to situations where a refund is sought relative to changes to the filed return and the two year statute generally applies to taxes paid at a later date, so too does this division usually hold for the limitations of section 6511(b)(2). If a claim for refund is filed within the three-year period of section 6511(a), the look-back period runs from the date the claim is filed, back for a period of three years.[68] In the simplest case, assume a calendar year individual's 20x1 return is filed on or before April 15, 20x2.[69] A refund claim filed no later than April 15, 20x5, would be timely and the three-year look-back period would run to and including April 15, 20x2. Thus, the maximum amount potentially recoverable would include (and be limited to) any and all taxes paid or *deemed paid* during that three-year look-back period.[70] For these purposes, it is critical to understand that tax paid or deemed paid on April 15,

63. Two statements must accompany a claim for relief under section 6511(h). One is a statement by the person signing the claim that no one was authorized to act for the person during the period that the taxpayer was unable to manage his financial affairs. The other is a certified statement by the taxpayer's physician containing certain representations about the taxpayer's physical or mental impairment. Rev. Proc. 99-21, 1999-1 C.B. 960.

64. IRC §§ 1311–14.

65. IRC § 6511(b).

66. Commissioner v. Lundy, 516 U.S. 235, 240 (1996).

67. United States v. Brockamp, 519 U.S. 347, 348, 352 (1997).

68. The IRS considers a refund claim included on a late-filed return to be filed the same day as the return. ILM 200751025, 2007 TNT 247-18.

69. For this purpose, returns filed before the due date are deemed to have been filed on the due date. IRC § 6513(a).

70. If a return is mailed on April 17th (a Monday) of year one and a claim for refund is mailed on April 16th in year four, the IRS accepts that the date of deemed filing, April 15th of year one, will be included in the look-back period. AOD 2000-09, 2000 AOD Lexis 7.

20x2, includes not only tax paid with the return, but also (1) any tax for 20x1 prepaid through withholding, (2) by estimated tax payments, (3) through application of a prior year's overpayment to the current year,[71] and (4) refundable credits, such as the earned income credit and the child tax credit.[72] The significance of treating all these payments as being made on April 15, 20x2, is that this date gets captured by the three-year look-back calculation; without doing so, they would fall outside the look-back period because they were actually paid during the taxable year and not on April 15 of the following year.

When a return is filed after the original due date, the look-back rules get more complicated. If the tax return for which a refund is requested was filed late and the taxpayer did not seek and receive an extension of time to file, a refund claim filed at the end of the third year following the filing of the return would be a timely claim under section 6511(a) but might allow for only a limited amount of tax to be refunded under section 6511(b). Using the example above, assume the tax return was filed late without an extension on July 21, 20x2, and the refund claim was filed on July 5, 20x5. The refund claim would be timely since it was filed within three years of the filing of the tax return. However, when we do a three year look-back, none of the taxes that were paid or deemed paid on April 15, 20x2, like withholding, are recoverable. The only taxes available for refund would be those paid with the return and those paid subsequently.

By contrast, if the reason the tax return was filed after the due date is because the taxpayer got an extension of time to file the return, the statute provides that the three-year look-back period includes the period represented by the extension.[73] This permits recovery not only of taxes actually paid or deemed paid on the original due date, as discussed just above, but also any payments made during the extension period. Returning to the example above, assuming there had been a six-month extension to file until October 15, 20x2, and the return was filed July 21, 20x2, a refund claim filed on July 5, 20x5, would not only be timely but would permit refund of any taxes paid or deemed paid between April 15, 20x2, (the date prepaid taxes are deemed paid) and when the refund claim was filed.

In the case of a refund claim filed more than three years after the return was filed, regardless of whether an extension to file the tax return was timely requested, the amount that can be refunded is limited to the tax paid within two years of the date the claim was filed.[74]

---

71. IRC §6513(b).

72. Israel v. United States, 356 F.3d 221 (2d Cir. 2004).

73. CCA 201526013 (June 2, 2015) (where taxpayer filed for an extension to file, the look-back period is the three years and four months; it doesn't matter if the taxpayer actually filed within the four-month extension period—the taxpayer still gets the benefit of the extension period for purposes of the look-back).

74. IRC §6511(b)(2)(B). In *Baral v. United States*, 528 U.S. 431 (2000), the Supreme Court rejected the taxpayer's contention that estimated taxes and withholding taxes could only be considered "paid" when the income tax return was filed and the tax shown thereon assessed. The taxpayer's income tax return, on which he claimed a refund, was filed several years late. If the estimated taxes and withholding taxes were not "paid" until the income tax shown on his late filed return was assessed, then they were

A return that shows an overpayment filed more than three years after the due date of the tax return will constitute a timely claim for refund since the return and the claim for refund are one and the same document. However, the refund will be limited to taxes paid during the three-year look-back period. For example, if a return for the year 20x1, is filed on November 28, 20x6, the return would constitute a timely claim for refund but only taxes paid within the three prior years could be refunded.[75] Consequently, the taxpayer might be denied any refund since the deemed payment date of April 15, 20x2 is outside the three years.[76]

The discussion so far has focused on the inter-connected three-year statute of limitations on filing a claim and the three-year look-back limitation. If the taxpayer does not file the claim timely pursuant to those rules, the two-year rule might save him. This rule says that the claim must be filed within two years of the (read as "any") tax being paid and that the amount refundable is limited to the taxes paid during the two-year look-back period. Needless to say, this rule is of no value to getting a refund of the taxes paid or deemed paid on April 15 of the year following the tax year in question. So, of what value is the two-year rule? It is used most often in connection with taxes paid following an IRS examination. For example, assume the IRS examines the taxpayer's 20x2 return during 20x5. The IRS denies certain deductions and proposes a tax of $38,000. Taxpayer waives the restrictions on assessment and pays the tax on August 2, 20x7. Later, he decides to litigate the question in the Court of Federal Claims. So long as he files a refund claim by August 2, 20x9, his claim will be timely but his maximum refund is limited to the $38,000 paid within the two-year period.

IV. Can a Valid Refund Be Diverted to Another Use?

Section 6402(a) authorizes the IRS to apply any overpayment (and accrued interest) otherwise payable to a taxpayer, against any current or future liability of the taxpayer

"paid" within the two year look-back period. The Court agreed with the IRS that sections 6513(b)(1) and (2) "settle the matter." Those sections provide that withheld and estimated taxes are "deemed" to have been paid of the due date of the return determined without regard to extensions. That being the case, even though the claim was considered timely, the two year look-back period was not long enough to make the withheld and estimated tax payments available for the claimed refund.

75. Regs. § 301.6511(b)-1(b)(1)(i); Rev. Rul. 76-511, 76-2 C.B. 428.

76. A particularly vexing and disappointing result might happen when the taxpayer has not filed returns for many years and "wishes to come clean and set the record straight." For example, let's assume in late 20x9, the taxpayer files tax returns for 20x1–20x7. Some years show tax due and some show overpayments. Since the statute of limitations to assess does not begin to run until a tax return is filed, the IRS may assess tax for the years there are amounts owing. However, while the refund claims would all be timely, no refunds would be available for older years, i.e., 20x1–20x5, because of the section 6511(b)(2) limitation. The limitation not only would preclude a refund in this situation but it also would prohibit the overpayment from being used as a credit against taxes owed for other years.

for any internal revenue tax.[77] This "refund offset program" has proven to be an efficient and effective way of collecting tax liabilities. For example, if a taxpayer owes taxes for 20x3 and files a 20x5 return reflecting an overpayment, the IRS may intercept the refund and apply it against the 20x3 balance due.[78]

Congress also has tapped into the refund stream three additional ways to achieve collection from taxpayers by offsetting refunds to pay: (1) certain past-due support payments,[79] (2) debts owed to federal agencies,[80] and (3) past-due state income tax obligations.[81] Any balance remaining is then refunded to the taxpayer.

Increasing the number of creditors who have access to any given refund required Congress to establish the order in which the several creditors are accommodated. Thus, any refund that would otherwise be paid to a taxpayer is first applied to the taxpayer's debts, if any, in the following order:

1. Any *existing* liability in respect of an internal revenue tax.
2. Any past-due support of which the Secretary has been duly notified by a state.[82]
3. Any past-due, legally enforceable debt owed to a federal agency of which the IRS has been duly notified by the agency.[83] For this purpose, a debt owed to a federal agency includes "any overpayment of benefits made to an individual under title II of the Social Security Act" and any amounts the taxpayer has collected via fraudulent employment compensation.[84]

---

77. The IRS considers a current liability to arise no later than the date on which a notice of deficiency is issued. Consequently, the Service says it may credit an overpayment or a decrease in tax resulting from a tentative carryback adjustment against unassessed internal revenue tax liabilities that have been determined in a notice of deficiency sent to the taxpayer. Rev. Rul. 2007-51, 2007-3 C.B. 573. The general rules and procedures applicable to the collection, through the Treasury Offset Program (TOP), of delinquent, nontax debts owed to federal agencies are contained in 31 CFR part 285.

78. The IRS also may apply an individual's overpayment against a proposed but not yet assessed deficiency. Perry v. Commissioner, T.C. Memo. 2010-219; Rev. Rul. 2007-51, 2007-2 C.B. 573; *see* Note, *Revenue Ruling 2007-51; Why the IRS is Keeping Your Money*, 59 Syracuse L. Rev. 311 (2008).

79. IRC § 6402(c) (added by the Omnibus Budget Reconciliation Act of 1981, Pub. L. No. 97-35, § 2331(c)(2), 95 Stat. 357).

80. IRC § 6402(d) (added by the Deficit Reduction Act of 1984, Pub. L. No. 98-369, § 2653(b)(1), 98 Stat. 494).

81. IRC § 6402(e) (added by the Personal Responsibility and Work Opportunity Reconciliation Act of 1996, Pub. L. No. 104-193, § 110(I)(7)(B)–(C), 110 Stat. 2105).

82. Section 6305 requires the Secretary to assess and collect the amount of certain delinquent amounts payable under court order or state administrative process for child and spousal support. This approach is different than the section 6402 offset approach. The two approaches "may be used separately or they may be used in conjunction with each other." Reg. § 301.6402-5(a)(1).

83. In *Bosarge v. United States Dept. of Educ.*, 5 F.3d 1414 (11th Cir. 1993), the taxpayer, who had defaulted on a student loan, sought to enjoin application of the refund offset procedure which, if implemented, would have resulted in the refund to which he was otherwise entitled being offset against the unpaid student loan debt. Bosarge claimed that Alabama state law exempted $3,000 of personal property from levy or sale for the collection of debts. The court found that neither Alabama law nor the Federal Debt Collection Procedures Act of 1990 (which incorporates state law exemptions) demonstrated that Congress intended the offset procedure to be subject to state law exemptions.

84. IRC §§ 6402(d)(3)(D), 6402(f) (as amended by "SSI Extension for Elderly and Disabled Refugees Act," P.L. 110-328, § 3(a), (d), 122 Stat. 3570 (2008)).

4. Any past-due, legally enforceable, state income tax obligation of which the Secretary has been duly notified by the state.
5. Any *future* liability in respect of an internal revenue tax.[85]

If a refund is applied as above, while it might appear the taxpayer has a dispute with the IRS for applying the refund to another debt instead of actually refunding (or crediting) the tax to the taxpayer, the fact is that the person's problem is with the agency that reported the past-due debt to the IRS, unless it was for a tax debt per items 1 and 5 above. It is with this agency that the individual must resolve the matter.[86]

A refund due with respect to a joint return presents the question of to whom the refund is to be paid. Courts have determined that refunds should be paid to the spouses in proportion to their respective contributions to the overpayment.[87] A spouse whose interest in a refund relating to a joint return has been or is expected to be offset under section 6402 can file Form 8379, entitled "Injured Spouse Allocation." This form requires a proposed allocation of items on the joint return and related documentation. The form may be filed with the joint return or filed separately if the joint return has already been filed.

V. The Refund Jurisdiction of the Tax Court

In response to a Notice of Deficiency, if a taxpayer files a timely petition in the Tax Court, the court has jurisdiction to determine not only whether there is a deficiency and the amount thereof, but also whether there might have been an overpayment.[88] In essence, because the Tax Court has exclusive jurisdiction to redetermine deficiencies according to section 7422(e), the Tax Court is responsible for determining the correct tax liability for the year regardless of whether its determination results in a deficiency or a refund. An overpayment in a Tax Court case might arise if the taxpayer discovers previously unclaimed deductions, or if the IRS agrees with the taxpayer that one or more items of income were overstated or belonged in another year. An overpayment might also occur if the taxpayer petitions the Tax Court for a redetermination of a deficiency but, in an effort to minimize accrual of interest, pays the asserted tax liability. If the Tax Court determines there is an overpayment, the taxpayer does not have to file a claim for refund; the decision of the court provides the basis for the right to the refund.

---

85. The Service takes the position that it may credit an overpayment or a decrease in tax resulting from a tentative carryback adjustment against unassessed internal revenue tax liabilities when the liabilities are identified in a proof of claim filed in a bankruptcy case. Rev. Rul. 2007-52, 2007-2 C.B. 575; *see also* Nichols v. Birdsell, 491 F.3d 987 (9th Cir. 2007) (refund is an asset of the bankruptcy estate to be applied to the taxpayers' future tax obligations). Similarly, the IRS has authority under section 6402 to apply an overpayment of the nondeferrable part of estate tax to the estate's outstanding estate tax liability deferred under section 6166. Estate of McNeely v. United States, 2014-1 U.S.T.C. ¶ 60,679 (D. Minn. 2014); *see* IRC § 6403.

86. IRC § 6402(g).

87. Michael I. Saltzman & Leslie Book, IRS Practice and Procedure ¶ 11.07[1] (rev. 2016).

88. IRC § 6512.

If the Tax Court finds an overpayment but the IRS files a notice of appeal, the IRS is authorized to refund or credit the uncontested portion of the overpayment. In any event, once the Tax Court's decision becomes final, the IRS must refund or credit the amount of the overpayment, or so much of the overpayment as has not already been refunded or credited. If the IRS fails to refund or credit the overpayment within 120 days after the Tax Court decision becomes final, the taxpayer can file a motion with the court for an order directing the IRS to refund the overpayment.[89]

VI. The Refund Jurisdiction of the Federal District Courts and the Court of Federal Claims

As previously stated, after the taxpayer files a claim for refund, the IRS may examine the claim and either allow or disallow it. If the government allows the claim in full, it will issue a Letter 570 (or a similar letter) notifying the taxpayer of its findings.[90] On the other hand, if the IRS proposes to disallow all of a part of the claim, it will issue Letter 569.[91] As is true for any determination of the Service, the taxpayer may request an administrative review by the Appeals Division by filing a protest.[92]

If unsuccessful administratively, a taxpayer's right to a refund of an overpayment may ultimately have to be determined in a civil action initiated by the taxpayer in a U.S. District Court or the Court of Federal Claims. Section 7422(a) provides that no such action may be filed "until a claim for refund ... has been duly filed with the Secretary." The fact that a refund claim must be filed before a refund suit can be brought is not surprising based on the discussion above. However, if the taxpayer's refund claim is merely an informal one, like correspondence with the IRS, it is important to note that "failure to subsequently perfect the claim by complying with the formal claim requirements will bar the court from exercising jurisdiction over the claim."[93]

Both the federal District Courts and the Court of Federal Claims have jurisdiction to hear claims for refund of overpaid federal taxes.[94] A lawsuit for the recovery of an overpayment cannot be filed until the IRS has had at least six months to consider the claim for refund. If the IRS disallows the claim before the six months have passed, the taxpayer can file suit immediately.[95]

89. IRC § 6512(b)(2).

90. IRM 4.71.8.5.

91. IRM 4.19.16.1.4.1.

92. IRM 8.7.7.1.

93. Pennoni v. United States, 86 Fed. Cl. 351, 363 (2009).

94. In principle, a tax refund suit derives from the common law cause of action for indebitatus assumpsit. Lewis v. Reynolds, 284 U.S. 281 (1932). For a description of the origins and evolution of federal tax refund litigation remedies, see Steve R. Johnson, *Reforming Federal Tax Litigation: An Agenda*, 41 Fla. St. U. L. Rev. 205, 212–15 (2013). For a proposal to divest the Court of Federal Claims of its tax refund jurisdiction (while expanding the Tax Court's tax refund jurisdiction) see *id.* at 249–50 & 254–58.

95. IRC § 6532(a)(1).

If the IRS mails a notice of disallowance in response to a claim for refund, the lawsuit must be filed within two years from the date of mailing of the notice.[96] The IRS may reconsider its disallowance of a taxpayer's claim for refund, but such administrative reconsideration does not extend the two-year period during which the taxpayer must file suit for recovery.[97] Similarly, the issuance of a second denial of the same claim does not refresh the section 6532 limitation period.[98] Taxpayers are permitted to waive the notice of disallowance requirement, in which event the two-year statute of limitations on commencing suit begins on the date the waiver is filed. Also, taxpayers and the IRS are permitted to extend the two-year statute of limitations on filing a suit.[99] Form 907 is used for this purpose.

The federal district courts and the Court of Federal Claims have jurisdiction only if the full amount of the assessed tax is first paid.[100] The full-payment rule also requires payment of asserted penalties but, according to *Flora*, not interest.[101]

The full-payment rule does not apply to all assessments, some of which can be divided into many parts. These "divisible" taxes include those that involve separate transactions, such as withholding taxes or the trust fund penalty tax under section 6672. A taxpayer facing a trust fund penalty,[102] can obtain judicial review by paying the amount involved for one employee for each calendar quarter in question and posting a bond.[103] The IRS will then counterclaim for the amount involved for the rest of the employees.[104]

---

96. IRC § 6532(a)(1). Thus, the conventional wisdom is that, if the IRS never sends the notice, there is an unlimited period of filing the refund suit. *E.g.*, Detroit Trust Co. v. United States, 130 F. Supp. 815 (Ct. Cl. 1955) (holding a refund suit timely when brought nearly thirty years after the refund claim had been filed because the IRS had not denied the claim). However, there is some authority that the suit must be commenced within the six-year general federal limitation statutes; 28 U.S.C. §§ 2401(a), 2501. *E.g.*, Finkelstein v. United States, 943 F. Supp. 425 (D. N.J. 1996); Nancy T. Bowen, *A Trap for the Unwary: Is the Six-Year General Statute of Limitation an Outside Limit for Refund Suits?*, Practical Tax Law., Spring 2009, at 5. The IRS rejects the idea that the six-year limitation statutes limit refund suits. CCA 201044006 (Nov. 5, 2010). *But see* Wagenet v. United States, 104 AFTR2d 7804 (C.D. Cal. 2009); CC-2012-012 (June 1, 2012).

97. ILM 200828028.

98. Leonard v. United States, 85 Fed. Cl. 435 (2009).

99. IRC § 6532(a)(2). However, a Form 872 agreement to extend the time to assess the tax does not extend the time to file a refund suit. Brach v. United States, 107 AFTR2d 1242 (Fed. Cl. 2011).

100. Flora v. United States, 362 U.S. 145 (1960), *aff'd on reh'g*, 357 U.S. 63 (1958). For detailed discussion of *Flora* and a proposal to overturn it, see Steve R. Johnson, *Reforming Federal Tax Litigation: An Agenda*, 41 Fla. St. U. L. Rev. 205, 219–22, 267–71 (2013).

101. *See, e.g., id.* at 175, n.37(d). *But see* DiNatale v. United States, 12 Ct Cl. 72,74 (1987) (holding that "[f]ull payment of the tax liability, penalties, and interest is thus a prerequisite to maintaining a tax refund action in the Claims Court") (citations omitted).

102. This penalty is really a collection device. It is imposed on control persons of an employer who willfully fail to collect or pay over to the IRS the employee's share of FICA and withholding taxes. *See* Chapter 14.

103. IRC § 6672(c).

104. *Id.*

A suit for refund in a U.S. District Court or the Court of Federal Claims is no different than other actions in those courts. A jury is available in the district courts but not the Court of Federal Claims.

One issue that sometimes surfaces in tax cases that is a bit of an outlier is how the courts handle issues or legal theories presented by the taxpayer for the first time at trial rather than during the administrative phase. Such a situation is called a "variance." This is discussed in Section III.A.1 above. It is possible that the government may have intentionally, or more likely, unintentionally waived its variance defense by failing to timely raise the objection and by acting on the new issue or new theory.[105]

VII. Administrative Adjustment Requests

As indicated in Chapter 6, Congress withdrew error correction for partnerships to which TEFRA applies from the established deficiency notice and claim for refund procedures. Congress replaced deficiency notice procedures with final partnership administrative adjustment ("FPAA") procedures, and replaced taxpayer initiated amended returns and claims for refund procedures with administrative adjustment request procedures. Thus, any partner who believes there was an error on the partnership's return may file an administrative adjustment request asking the IRS to correct the error.[106]

Whether made by the Tax Matters Partner ("TMP") on behalf of the partnership, or by any partner on the partner's own behalf, administrative adjustment requests must be filed within three years after the *later* of (i) the due date of the partnership return determined without extensions, or (ii) the date the partnership return for the year was actually filed.[107] Additionally, if the IRS has initiated a partnership proceeding, the request must be filed before the notice of FPAA is mailed to the TMP.

When an administrative adjustment request is filed, the IRS has four main options. The Service can: (1) accept and make the proposed adjustments, (2) conduct a partnership proceeding, (3) ignore the request, or (4) disallow the request in whole or in part.[108]

Procedurally, the simplest response is for the IRS to agree to make the requested adjustments.[109] Thus, the IRS can treat a request by the TMP on behalf of the partnership as a substituted return.[110] In this case, the requested changes are deemed "mathematical or clerical errors." As such, the resulting refunds are paid or the defi-

105. *See* Margaret C. Wilson, *The Variance Doctrine: No Forks in the Road to Refunds*, 55 Tax Law. 605 (Winter 2002).

106. IRC § 6227(a).

107. IRC § 6226(a)(1).

108. IRC § 6227(c)(2)(A).

109. IRC § 6227(c).

110. IRC § 6227(c)(1).

ciencies are assessed under section 6213(b)(1) without further proceedings.[111] If the administrative adjustment request is filed by a partner on the partner's own behalf, the IRS can: (1) treat the request as if it were a claim for refund by that partner with respect to non-partnership items, (2) assess the tax resulting from the requested adjustment, (3) notify the partner that all the partner's partnership items will be treated as nonpartnership items, or (4) conduct a partnership proceeding.[112]

If the IRS responds to a request for administrative adjustment by initiating a partnership proceeding, the issues raised in the request are resolved in the course of that proceeding.[113] Once the IRS mails its notice of the beginning of an administrative proceeding, the TMP may no longer petition a court for judicial review of the disallowed administrative request.[114]

The IRS is not required to respond to a request for administrative adjustment.[115] If the IRS does not respond to a request made by the TMP on behalf of the partnership, or responds but disallows any part of the request, the TMP can seek judicial review by filing a petition in the Tax Court, a District Court, or the Court of Federal Claims.[116] The petition must be filed before the IRS mails a notice of beginning of an administrative proceeding and during the period beginning after the request has been on file for six months and ending "before the date which is 2 years after the date of [the] request."[117] If the IRS either does not respond to an administrative adjustment request, or responds by disallowing any part of the request, and the TMP seeks judicial review, all persons who were partners in the partnership at any time during the partnership's year in question are treated as parties and permitted to participate in the proceedings.[118]

VIII. Tentative Carryback and Refund Adjustments

Section 6411 permits taxpayers to apply for a quick, tentative refund of taxes for a prior taxable year affected by a carryback of a net operating loss, a net capital loss, or an unused general business credit. The quick refund procedure is also available for an overpayment of tax resulting from a claim of right adjustment under section 1341(d). Application for the tentative refund must be made within one year after the year in

---

111. IRC §§6227(c)(1), 6230(b)(1). A partner who does not agree with any such error correction may, by notice to the IRS, not accept the proposed changes. The notice must be filed by the partner within sixty days after the day the IRS mails a notice of correction of the error to the partner. IRC §6230(b)(2).

112. IRC §6227(d)(2).

113. IRC §§6227(c)(2)(A)(ii) (with respect to requests filed by the TMP on behalf of the partnership), 6227(d)(4) (with respect to requests filed by a partner on the partner's behalf).

114. IRC §6228(a)(1)(B).

115. IRC §6227(c)(2)(A)(iii).

116. IRC §6228(a)(1).

117. IRC §6228(a)(2).

118. IRC §6228(a)(4). The above rules as to Administrative Adjustment Requests are summarized in *Rigas v. United States*, 2011-1 U.S.T.C. ¶50,372 (S.D. Tex. 2011).

which the net operating loss, net capital loss, unused business credit, or claim of right adjustment arose, but it may not be filed before the return for that year is filed.

Although the taxpayer could file normal refund claims for the amounts subject to the tentative carryback and refund adjustments, the "quick refund" procedure is preferred by taxpayers. This is because the IRS is required to respond to the tentative carryback and refund adjustment procedure within 90 days of the later of the date the application is filed or the due date of the return for the year in which the loss, unused credit, or claim of right adjustment occurred.[119] The IRS must still meet this 90-day deadline to process the tentative refund even if it selects the taxpayer's Form 1045 for audit.[120] No such accelerated response is required in the case of a normal claim for refund.

The quick refund procedure is tentative in the sense that if the IRS ultimately determines that the amount refunded is excessive it will treat the excess as a mathematical or clerical error. As such, the IRS is permitted to assess and collect the excess, without giving the taxpayer the benefit of either a notice of deficiency or the right, normally available in the case of mathematical or clerical errors, to request abatement. The IRS may also decrease the amount of any tentative carryback adjustment by the amount of any unassessed liabilities the IRS has identified in a proof of claim filed in a bankruptcy proceeding,[121] or against unassessed internal revenue tax liabilities that have been determined in a notice of deficiency sent to the taxpayer.[122]

IX. Penalty

Section 6676, enacted in 2007,[123] imposes a 20% penalty on a taxpayer who makes a claim for an income tax refund or credit for an "excessive amount," i.e., the amount by which the refund or claim exceeds the amount allowable under the Code.[124] The taxpayer can avoid the penalty by showing that there was a reasonable basis for the claim.[125]

There are rules coordinating section 6676 with other sections that could apply, such as the accuracy-related, reportable transactions understatement, and fraud penalties of sections 6662, 6662A, and 6663, respectively (all discussed in Chapter 11).[126] The section 6676 penalty is immediately assessable; the IRS need not issue a notice of deficiency.

---

119. IRC § 6411(b).

120. Field Att'y Adv. 20075001F (Dec. 14, 2007), 2007 TNT 242-21.

121. Reg. § 1.6411-2T; Reg. § 1.6411-3T; Rev. Rul. 2007-52, 2007-2 C.B. 575; Rev. Rul. 2007-53, 2007-2 C.B. 577.

122. Rev. Rul. 2007-51, 2007-2 C.B. 573.

123. Small Business and Work Opportunity Tax Act of 2007, § 8247, Pub. L. 110-28.

124. IRC § 6676(a), (b).

125. The statute does not define "reasonable basis." It remains to be seen whether sections 6662(d)(2)(C) and 6694(a)(2)(C) sense of the term will be imported into section 6676.

126. IRC § 6676(c).

Problems

1. Daisy timely filed her federal income tax return on Form 1040 for the year 20x5. The return reported $150,000 in gross income, all from her job. Her employer had properly withheld a total of $45,000 in tax from her monthly paychecks. Her return reported a tax liability of $40,000 and an overpayment of $5,000.

(a) Assume she filed the 20x5 Form 1040 on April 15, 20x6. Will Daisy have to file a separate claim for refund in order to have the overpayment refunded to her? Is the refund claim timely? How much of a refund would she be entitled to?

(i) How would your answer to part (a) differ if Daisy owed the IRS $8,000 from 20x3? What if she was in default on her federally guaranteed student loans by $8,000? What if she was in default on her Mastercard bill by $8,000? What if the proposed $8,000 tax liability was pending before the Tax Court and therefore not yet assessed?

(b) Answer part (a) assuming she filed the Form 1040 on October 15, 20x6, having received an automatic six-month extension to file her income tax return as the result of having timely filed a Form 4868? Will she be entitled to interest on any refund to which she is entitled?

(c) Assume Daisy got a refund of $5,000 after she timely filed her 20x5 Form 1040. Several years later, her financial planner noted that she failed to claim a $20,000 interest deduction associated with her home mortgage when she filed her 20x5 tax return. Had she taken the deduction, her tax liability would have been reduced by $6,000. What procedure should she follow to obtain a refund? If she filed a claim for refund on the following dates, would it be considered timely and would she be able to get a refund of the full $6,000? Answer each twice, first assuming the facts of part (a) above and then part (b) above.

(i) March 5, 20x9?

(ii) July 5, 20x9?

(iii) November 5, 20x9?

(d) Assume Daisy filed the claim for refund noted in part (c) on March 5, 20x9.

(i) The Internal Revenue Service denied her claim for refund on June 30, 20x9, and Daisy would like to sue for a refund. By what date must she bring suit?

(ii) The Internal Revenue Service neither denied nor admitted her claim for refund. By what date must she bring suit?

(iii) What courts have jurisdiction to hear her case?

(e) Assume Daisy filed her 20x5 Form 1040 on April 15, 20x6. She filed the claim for refund (for $6,000) noted in part (c) on March 5, 20x9. The Revenue Agent who reviewed the claim for refund agreed with Daisy that she was entitled to the interest deduction. However, the agent also discovered that Daisy failed to report income of $40,000 from an independent contracting gig she had for a couple of months in 20x5. The tax on the $40,000 would be $12,000. Daisy waived the restrictions on assessment and delivered the waiver to the Revenue Agent pursuant to section 6213(d) in a timely manner. The Internal Revenue Service assessed $12,000 in tax relating to the unreported income on the following dates. What would be Daisy's tax situation in each case?

(i) April 14, 20x9.

(ii) May 3, 20x9.

(iii) June 29, 20x9.

(f) Take the facts of part (e) above. The $40,000 item of income mentioned was reported by her on her 20x6 return. However, the agent thought it should be reported in 20x5. While Daisy and her accountant strongly disagree and believe the agent misunderstands the facts and law, Daisy would like to protect herself against the possibility of having the same item of income taxed twice—once as reported in 20x6 and also in 20x5 if the agent is correct. What would you recommend to mitigate this possibility?

(g) Take the facts of part (e) above. Daisy disagreed that the $40,000 was income, believing instead that it was a non-taxable loan. She informed the agent of her disagreement and the agent issued a Notice of Deficiency on April 15, 20x9 in which the IRS took the position that the $40,000 was income in 20x5, but allowed Daisy the $20,000 interest deduction. The deficiency in the notice was in the amount of $6,000 ($12,000 less $6,000).

(i) Can Daisy petition the U.S. Tax Court for a redetermination? If she can, by what date must she do so? If Daisy were to succeed in the Tax Court, she would be entitled to a refund of $6,000. Can the Tax Court enter a decision reflecting an overpayment?

(ii) Daisy determined that the precedent in the Court of Federal Claims is more favorable to her position. She signs a waiver of restrictions on assessment (Form 870) and the IRS makes an assessment of $6,000. Having given the IRS the permission to assess, can she still contest the issues raised in the Notice of Deficiency administratively and judicially? If she can, what must she do procedurally and by when?

(h) Take the facts in part (a) above. Assume that Daisy received the $5,000 refund. Her 20x5 income tax return was examined during the year 20x7. The Revenue Agent found that Daisy had failed to report some income, and proposed additional tax of $12,500. Daisy agreed and paid the tax on September 15, 20x7. Daisy was having her estate plan reviewed during the year 20x9. The lawyer who was working on the estate plan reviewed Daisy's tax returns, including the results of the examination for the year 20x5. He told her that the Revenue Agent had made an error, and that the deficiency in tax should have been $5,000. He advised her to file a claim for refund for $7,500. What would be the result if Daisy filed the claim for refund on the following dates:

(i) March 1, 20x9.

(ii) July 1, 20x9.

(iii) October 1, 20x9.

(i) Take the facts in part (h) above except that during the examination, the Revenue Agent asked Daisy to extend the statute of limitations on tax assessments pursuant to section 6501(c)(4) because he did not believe he could finish the examination on time. Daisy agreed, and signed the appropriate papers to extend the statute of limitations until December 31, 20x9. Daisy paid the additional tax of $12,500 on the unreported income on January 15, 20x0. After she was informed by her estate planning lawyer that the additional tax should have been only $5,000, she filed a claim for refund for $7,500. What would be the result if Daisy filed the claim for refund on the following dates:

(i) May 15, 20x0.

(ii) May 15, 20x1.

(iii) February 1, 20x2.

2. Ace Corp. incurred a loss in its business in 20x5. Ace has been advised by its accountant that it can carry the loss back to 20x3 and obtain a refund of tax paid for that year. Ace is a "C" corporation and uses the calendar year.

(a) Assuming that Ace did not request an extension of time to file its 20x5 return that would be due March 15, 20x6, by when must Ace claim a refund for 20x3 if it uses the procedure set forth in section 6411?

(b) Answer part (a) if Ace does not use the procedure set forth in section 6411?

(c) If Ace uses the procedure set forth in section 6411, and files its 20x5 return on March 10, 20x6, when should it expect to receive the refund of taxes it paid for 20x3?

Chapter 10

Judicial and Statutory Rules That Override the Statutes of Limitation

IRC: §§ 1311–1313

Regs.: §§ 1.1311(a)-1; 1.1311(a)-2; examples under 1.1311(b)-1 through 1.1312-4; 1.1313(a)-4; 1.1313(c)-1

I. Introduction

Normally, errors in overpaying or underpaying federal income taxes must be corrected within a specified period of time. In the case of overpayments, taxpayers must file a claim for refund "within three years from the time the return was filed or two years from the time the tax was paid, whichever of such periods expires the later, or if no return was filed by the taxpayer, within two years from the time the tax was paid."[1] This period is extended if the taxpayer and the IRS agree to an extension of time for assessing additional tax.[2] It is also extended in certain special situations, such as overpayments triggered by bad debts or worthless securities,[3] or by net operating or capital loss carrybacks.[4]

In the case of underpayments, the IRS generally must assess additional tax within three years after the return was due or was filed, whichever was later.[5] In some circumstances, the period of limitations on assessment may be longer than three years. For instance, it may be extended by agreement between the taxpayer and the IRS[6] and is extended to six years in the case of a "substantial omission of items."[7] Also, the period of limitations on assessment is suspended upon issuance of a Notice of Deficiency, and, if a petition for redetermination of the deficiency is filed in the Tax Court, it is further extended until sixty days after the court's decision becomes final.[8]

1. IRC § 6511(a). For this purpose, returns filed before their original due date are deemed to have been filed on that due date. IRC § 6513(a); see Chapter 9.
2. IRC § 6511(c).
3. IRC § 6511(d)(1).
4. IRC § 6511(d)(2); see Chapter 9.
5. IRC § 6501(a). For this purpose, returns filed before their original due date are deemed to have been filed on that due date. IRC § 6501(b)(1).
6. IRC § 6501(c)(4).
7. IRC § 6501(e).
8. IRC § 6503(a).

If the taxpayer does not file a return or files a false or fraudulent return, the tax can be assessed "at any time."[9]

There are separate sets of rules applicable to the assessment of tax or the filing of a claim for refund relating to "partnership items." Depending on the set of rules applicable to the particular situation, audit and litigation of items reported on partnership returns may proceed at either the entity or the owner level.[10]

If the taxpayer fails to correct an overpayment or the IRS fails to correct an underpayment within the applicable limitations period, correction of the error is normally not possible. In such cases the IRS raises the statute of limitations as a defense against a late filed claim for refund, or the taxpayer raises the defense against a late issued deficiency notice.

In certain situations, application of the statute of limitations results in particularly harsh consequences to a taxpayer attempting to get a refund or to the IRS attempting to assess a deficiency. These situations usually arise when an item of income or deduction is reported in the wrong taxable year by the taxpayer or in any year by the wrong, related taxpayer. In either case, the facts relating to the treatment of the item in the open year are considered in a timely fashion, and resolution of the matter in the open year reveals an erroneous treatment of the item in a barred year.

For example, assume that John, a calendar year, accrual basis, sole proprietor and manufacturer of hunting arrows, ships an order to a customer on September 15, 20x0. He encloses a bill for $5,000 with the shipment. He receives payment on January 15, 20x1. As an accrual basis taxpayer, John should include the $5,000 in his income for the year 20x0, but he mistakenly includes the payment in his income in 20x1, the year in which he is paid. Realizing his error, on July 15, 20x4, John files a timely claim for refund with respect to 20x1. The IRS accepts John's position and sends him a check for the refund.

At this point, John has not paid tax on the $5,000 income item in either 20x0 or 20x1. However, the statute of limitations on assessment of additional tax for the correct year, 20x0, expired on April 15, 20x4. Since John recovered the tax erroneously paid with his 20x1 return on this item of income, it would be inequitable to permit him to use the statute of limitations defense to avoid paying tax with respect to the item for the correct year, 20x0.

There are both judicial doctrines and statutory provisions that open otherwise barred years to permit correction of errors of this kind where strict application of the statute of limitations would produce inequitable results. In addition, under certain circumstances, the judicially created "duty of consistency" requires that an error in a barred year be corrected in an open year. This chapter deals first with the judicial

9. IRC § 6501(c)(1), (3); see Chapter 5.

10. IRC § 6231(a)(3). In addition, the partnership rules contain their own set of consistency rules limited to that context. See Chapters 6A and 6B.

doctrines and then the statutory provisions that mitigate the sometimes harsh consequences of the applicable statutes of limitations.

II. Judicial Doctrines

The principal focus here is on three case law rules that potentially ameliorate harsh consequences of the statute of limitations: equitable recoupment (available to both taxpayers and the IRS) and setoff and the taxpayer duty of consistency (both available only to the IRS, not to taxpayers). These three doctrines are founded on equitable principles and have their origins in cases decided in the 1930s.[11] The three doctrines are discussed below.

After discussing the taxpayer's duty of consistency, we address the alleged governmental duty of consistency, which does not involve the statute of limitations and which may or may not exist as a judicially enforceable rule. Thereafter, we discuss the doctrine of judicial estoppel. This is a general rule of litigation. Although principally used in other contexts, judicial estoppel can be asserted, on proper facts, in tax cases.

A. Equitable Recoupment

Equitable recoupment was first incorporated into federal tax law by the Supreme Court in *Bull v. United States*.[12] In that case, for estate tax purposes, the value of a partnership interest owned by the decedent was determined by a provision in the partnership agreement. Under the agreement, in exchange for the partnership interest, the estate received its proportionate interest in partnership profits for one year after the decedent's death.

Initially, the IRS required the estate to include the amount so determined in the decedent's gross estate for estate tax purposes. Because estate tax was paid on that amount, the executor did not include that amount in the estate's income tax returns. Several years later, the IRS notified the executor that the estate had an income tax deficiency because the profits received from the partnership were not reported as income on the estate's income tax return.

The Board of Tax Appeals sustained the IRS's position that the profits interest was properly includible in the estate's income. The executor then paid the income tax deficiency and filed a claim for refund. The executor's position was that the decedent's partnership interest was either property of the estate and thus includible in the decedent's estate for estate tax purposes, or income of the estate and thus includible in the estate's income tax return, but the partnership interest could not be both property and income. The Court of Claims held that the payment was properly

11. Stone v. White, 301 U.S. 532 (1937); Bull v. United States, 295 U.S. 247 (1935); Lewis v. Reynolds, 284 U.S. 281 (1932), *modified by* 284 U.S. 599 (1932).

12. 295 U.S. 247, 259–63 (1935).

treated as income but declined to address the resulting estate tax overpayment because, by that time, the statute of limitations for filing a claim for refund of estate taxes had expired.[13]

The Supreme Court agreed with the Court of Claims that the post-death profits share was income to the estate. But because the business of the partnership was providing services, and the partners had not contributed any capital to the partnership and the partnership had no tangible assets, the Court held that the partnership interest did not enhance the gross estate, thus should not have led to estate tax.[14] This left the Court with the question of whether the estate could recover the overpayment in estate tax when the statute of limitations on filing a claim for refund had expired.

The Supreme Court said that if the Commissioner brought suit against the estate for the income tax deficiency, the estate could raise the overpayment of the estate tax related to that same item as a defense. In that case, the estate could "equitably recoup" the overpaid estate tax by, in effect, requiring the IRS to apply the estate tax overpayment against the income tax liability. This defense would be available despite expiration of the statute of limitations on filing a claim for refund of the overpaid estate tax.

The Court acknowledged that in this case the estate was the plaintiff seeking a refund of income taxes and, as plaintiff, technically the estate was not in a position to raise equitable recoupment of the overpaid estate tax as a defense. However, the Court found that equitable recoupment is available even though the taxpayer pays the asserted income tax deficiency, files a claim for refund, and then pursues the matter as a plaintiff in suit to recover the overpayment. Even as a plaintiff in a refund suit, the taxpayer is clearly challenging the IRS's determination and the procedural posture of the case should not affect the availability of equitable relief. Consequently, the estate could recoup the time-barred estate tax overpayment against the income tax liability.

Subsequent cases have limited application of the doctrine of equitable recoupment to situations in which a single item is involved, as was the case in *Bull*.[15] The doctrine has also been applied to permit the IRS to apply an income tax refund due to one taxpayer against an otherwise time-barred income tax deficiency of an economically related taxpayer.[16]

---

13. *Id.* at 254.

14. *Id.*

15. *See also* Karagozian v. Commissioner, T.C. Memo. 2013-164 (rejecting application of equitable recoupment; although FICA taxes "paid in the time-barred years were paid on the same type of transaction [compensation] as in 2008, ... the overpaid FICA taxes from 2002 to 2007 are separate transactions, separate items, and separate taxable events from [the taxpayer's 2008 federal income tax deficiency]"), *aff'd*, 595 Fed. Appx. 87 (2d Cir. 2015), *cert. denied*, 136 S. Ct. 370 (2015).

16. Stone v. White, 301 U.S. 532 (1937). In *Stone*, the decedent created a testamentary trust leaving his wife the net income of the trust. She accepted the interest in the trust rather than electing against the will to take her statutory allowance. The trustees paid tax on the trust's income. Although Mrs. Stone received the income, she did not report it on her income tax return based on several circuit court cases holding that the income was not taxable until the value equaled that of the statutory allowance she would have been entitled to receive. The Supreme Court later held such income fully taxable to the beneficiary. The trustees then filed a claim for refund of the taxes they had erroneously paid on the income in question. At that time, the IRS could not assert a deficiency against the wife

In *Estate of Buder v. Commissioner*,[17] an estate planning attorney died. His estate deducted as QTIP property a trust for his wife's benefit. When his wife later died, her estate included the trust in her gross estate. Later, her estate brought a refund action. The IRS and the estate agreed that the QTIP election had been improper. Thus, the trust should have been taxed in the husband's estate, not in the wife's estate. However, the Government argued, under the doctrine of equitable recoupment, that the refund due the wife's estate should be reduced by the tax improperly avoided by the husband's estate and also by interest thereon. The District Court (1) agreed that equitable recoupment applied but (2) denied recovery of the interest. The Circuit Court affirmed in both respects. As to the interest issue, it held that the District Court had not abused its discretion "given the countervailing equitable considerations."[18]

There once was controversy as to whether the Tax Court, as an Article I court of limited jurisdiction, could apply equitable principles. Congress resolved the matter, at least as it relates to equitable recoupment. Congress added a sentence to section 6214(b), confirming that the Tax Court can apply the doctrine "to the same extent that it is available in civil tax cases before the district courts ... and the ... Court of Federal Claims."[19]

B. Setoff

Setoff is another of the equitable doctrines that, in effect, permits opening an otherwise barred year. It comes up in situations in which a taxpayer files a claim for refund. The IRS may use the occasion to audit the return for the taxable year of the claim to see if there are any other errors. If the IRS discovers omitted income or improper deductions, the Supreme Court has held that even though the statute of limitations on assessing additional tax with respect to the newly discovered items has expired, the IRS can use the new items to reduce the amount of the refund otherwise due to the taxpayer.[20]

A taxpayer is entitled to a refund only when the amount paid exceeds proper tax liability. The taxpayer's obligation to pay the correct amount of tax arises at the time

because the statute of limitations on assessing additional tax had expired. The Supreme Court allowed the IRS to recoup Mrs. Stone's otherwise barred income tax liability by applying against that liability the income tax refund to which the trust was otherwise entitled. *See also* IES Industries Inc. v. United States, 349 F.3d 574 (2003) (government was allowed to equitably recoup underpayment in one year from overpayments made in prior, different years).

17. 372 F. Supp. 2d 1145 (E.D. Mo. 2005), *aff'd*, 436 F.3d 936 (8th Cir. 2006).

18. *See* Wendy C. Gerzog, Bruder*: The Extent of Equitable Recoupment*, Tax Notes, Mar. 20, 2006, at 1361.

19. Pension Protection Act of 2006, Pub. L. 109-280, § 858(a), 120 Stat. 1020. *See, e.g.*, Menard, Inc. v. Commissioner, 130 T.C. 54 (2008) (holding that the Tax Court may apply equitable recoupment to offset Medicare tax overpayments against income tax liabilities even though the Tax Court has no subject matter jurisdiction as to Medicare tax). *But see* CCA 2101033030 (Aug. 20, 2010), 2010 TNT 162-18 (despite section 6214(b), the IRS cannot apply equitable recoupment or other judicial doctrines to recoup gift tax that was not timely assessed and so was not paid, but was used in calculating a deduction on the estate tax return for gift tax paid or payable; this would be an affirmative collection of tax, not defensive use).

20. Lewis v. Reynolds, 284 U.S. 281, 283 (1932). See also Chapter 9, Section II. B.

of required filing, and it persists whether or not the IRS assesses the tax. Thus, the failure of the IRS to assess an unpaid amount does not prevent the IRS from retaining an amount the taxpayer paid as to the liability before expiration of the limitations period for assessment.[21] However, the IRS cannot retain and set off amounts paid or collected after expiration of that period.[22] Nor can the IRS collect an unassessed tax, the assessment of which is barred by the statute of limitations, by setoff against an otherwise valid refund.[23]

C. Taxpayer Duty of Consistency

The duty of consistency is an equitable doctrine that found its first clear expression in *R. H. Stearns Co. v. United States*[24] and *Alamo Nat'l Bank of San Antonio v. Commissioner*.[25] The duty of consistency requires that a taxpayer taking a favorable, though incorrect, position with respect to an item in a barred year, report the item in later years consistently with the manner of reporting in the earlier, barred year.[26] For example, if for estate tax purposes the estate uses a low value for an office building owned by the decedent, the duty of consistency would require the estate to use that value as the basis of the property on a subsequent sale after the statute of limitations on assessing additional estate tax expired.[27] Consistent reporting would be required even though the estate could establish that the value of the office building had been understated for estate tax purposes.[28]

The statutory mitigation provisions, discussed below, also deal with inconsistent reporting. However, unlike the duty of consistency, which addresses the barred year

---

21. Principal Life Ins. Co. v. United States, 95 Fed. Cl. 786 (2010).

22. IRC § 6401(a).

23. IRC § 6402(a); El Paso CGP Co., L.L.C. v. United States, 748 F.3d 225, 230 (5th Cir. 2014) (such collection is barred unless the statutory mitigation provisions, discussed later in this chapter, reopen the closed year).

24. 291 U.S. 54 (1934).

25. 95 F.2d 622 (5th Cir. 1938).

26. For a detailed discussion of the duty of consistency, see Steve R. Johnson, *The Taxpayer's Duty of Consistency*, 46 Tax L. Rev. 537 (1991).

27. The judicial doctrine is no longer needed in this context. 2015 legislation (1) requires that the basis of property acquired from a decedent not exceed the property's basis determined for estate tax purposes, (2) requires estates filing estate tax returns to notify both the IRS and beneficiaries of the values of properties, to facilitate consistent reporting, and (3) makes inconsistent reporting a basis for imposition of the accuracy-related penalty. Surface Transportation and Veterans Health Care Choice Improvement Act of 2015, § 2004, Pub. L. 114-41, 129 Stat. 443 (creating IRC §§ 1014(f), 6035, 6662(b)(8), 6662(k)).

28. A representation by one taxpayer can be binding on another taxpayer when the two taxpayers are in privity. In *Janis v. Commissioner*, T.C. Memo. 2004-117, taxpayers who were coexecutors and beneficiaries of their father's estate and co-trustees and beneficiaries of a testamentary trust were held to be in privity with the estate. In Tech. Adv. Mem. 200407018 (Feb. 13, 2004), the decedent's estate was determined to be in privity with the estate of the decedent's spouse. In *Estate of Posner v. Commissioner*, T.C. Memo. 2004-112, the court assumed *arguendo* that the decedent's estate was in privity with the estate of the decedent's spouse but rejected application of the duty of consistency because other elements were not satisfied.

error by imposing incorrect reporting of the item in an open year, the mitigation approach permits correction of the error in the otherwise barred year. The duty of consistency doctrine also differs from mitigation in that the mitigation provisions are limited to inconsistencies in reporting of an item for income tax purposes, whereas the duty of consistency can apply to deal with inconsistent reporting involving different kinds of tax.

Courts have taken different positions on the duty of consistency. The majority of the courts follow the standard set forth in *McMillan v. United States*,[29] articulating three elements necessary for application of duty. Those elements are: (1) the taxpayer makes a representation or reports an item for tax purposes in one tax year; (2) the IRS acquiesces in or relies on that fact for the year; and (3) the taxpayer wishes to change the representation of the item after the statute of limitations for the year has expired.[30] While most cases adopting the duty of consistency generally apply these three elements, some courts have added additional elements in determining whether to apply the duty of consistency.[31] Moreover, a minority of courts has refused to recognize the duty of consistency, preferring to rely on common law estoppel principles.[32]

D. Governmental Duty of Consistency?

Courts and commentators sometimes refer to a governmental duty of consistency. The taxpayer duty of consistency is fundamentally different from the governmental duty of consistency (if the latter truly exists). As seen above, the taxpayer duty involves the same taxpayer at different points in time, *i.e.*, the same taxpayer taking inconsistent positions at different times in order to erect a statute of limitations barrier to IRS efforts to correct improper tax benefits the taxpayer obtained in a different tax year.

In contrast, a government duty involves two different taxpayers. For instance, assume that Damon and Pythias engage in essentially equivalent transactions and report them the same way on their returns. Assume further that their identical treatment is wrong—they both claimed a tax benefit on their returns as a result of the transaction but that benefit was not properly allowable under the law. The IRS audits Damon's return and unwisely accepts the improper tax benefit claimed on that return. Later, the IRS audits Pythias' return and (correctly under the law) disallows the claimed tax benefit.

According to some commentators and a few cases, the IRS should be under an enforceable duty to treat similarly situated taxpayers similarly.[33] Thus, the courts

---

29. 64-2 U.S.T.C. (CCH) ¶ 9720, 14 A.F.T.R. 2d (P-H) 5704 (S.D. W. Va. 1964).

30. *Id.* (citing *Alamo Nat'l Bank*, 956 F.2d at 623).

31. *See* Shook v. United States, 713 F.2d 662 (11th Cir. 1983); Garner v. Commissioner, 42 T.C. Memo. (CCH) 1181, T.C. Memo (P-H) ¶ 81,542 (1981).

32. *See* Crosley Corp. v. United States, 229 F.2d 376 (6th Cir. 1956); Commissioner v. Union Pac. R. Co., 86 F.2d 637 (2d Cir. 1936); Marco v. Commissioner, 25 T.C. 544 (1955).

33. *E.g.*, Vesco v. Commissioner, 39 T.C.M. 101, 129 (1979); Stephanie Hoffer, *Hobgoblin of Little Minds No More: Justice Requires an IRS Duty of Consistency*, 2006 Utah L. Rev. 317.

would force the IRS to allow to Pythias the tax benefit it allowed Damon—notwithstanding the fact that the law does not allow the benefit. This approach prefers consistency over accuracy. The weight of the authority rejects this extreme view.[34]

E. Judicial Estoppel

Under the doctrine of judicial estoppel, a party may be precluded from taking a position in court that is inconsistent with another position that same party (or a party in privity) previously took in court.[35] The doctrine is designed to protect the dignity and integrity of judicial proceedings. It can be applied against any party, and it sweeps more broadly than just statute of limitations situations.

Judicial estoppel does not appear frequently in tax cases, but, on proper facts, the doctrine can be applied in tax, to the benefit of the taxpayer or the IRS as the case may be. For example, in one federal tax collection case, a woman asserted an interest in property the IRS had seized and sold to pay the tax debts of the woman's ex-husband. The IRS was awarded summary judgment against her claim. In a prior bankruptcy case, she had asserted that she had no interest in the property. Her position in the tax collection case (that she had interest in the property) was inconsistent with her position in the bankruptcy case that she had no such interest. Her position in the bankruptcy case was a good faith error. Nonetheless, she was held to be estopped from arguing in the collection case that she had an interest in the property.[36]

III. Mitigation

In particular areas, Congress sometimes writes statute-of-limitations mitigation rules of narrow application.[37] The mitigation rules of most general application, however, are set out in sections 1311 to 1314. The ancestors of these provisions were enacted in 1938, and they were substantially revised in 1953.

Enactment of the statutory mitigation regime reflects the preference that, when possible, tax rules should be established by Congress through statutes (or by the Treasury though regulations pursuant to delegations of authority from Congress) rather

34. For detailed discussion of the alleged IRS duty of consistency, see Steve R. Johnson, *An IRS Duty of Consistency: The Failure of Common Law Making and a Proposed Statutory Solution,* 77 Tenn. L. Rev. 563 (2010).

35. *See generally* Zedner v. United States, 547 U.S. 489, 503–06 (2006); Steve R. Johnson, *The Doctrine of Judicial Estoppel,* Nev. Law., Dec. 2003, at 8.

36. Galin v. IRS, 563 F. Supp. 2d 332, 338 (D. Conn. 2008).

37. *E.g.,* IRC § 6521 (providing for mitigation when (1) an amount is erroneously treated as self-employment income or wages, (2) correcting the error would require assessing one tax and refunding or crediting a different tax, and (3) some rule of law (other than compromise of liabilities under section 7122) would prevent making one or another of the required corrections). *See, e.g.,* CCA 200918021 (May 1, 2009) (applying section 6521).

than by the courts. Sections 1311 to 1314 cover a number of situations that the judicial doctrines might also cover. Appropriately, the courts hold that, when applicable, the mitigation provisions preempt the judicial doctrines.[38]

Congress enacted the first part of the mitigation provisions in 1938. The original "circumstances of adjustment," i.e., the original set of factual situations to which the mitigation provisions apply, were limited to the following:

(a) section 1312(1)—double inclusion of an item of gross income;

(b) section 1312(2)—double allowance of a deduction or credit;

(c) section 1312(3)(A)—double exclusion of an item of gross income where the item was included in the return or the tax paid with respect to the item;

(d) section 1312(5)—inconsistent correlative deductions and inclusions for trusts or estates and legatees, beneficiaries, or heirs;

(e) section 1312(6)—inconsistent correlative deductions and credits for certain related corporations; and

(f) section 1312(7)—basis of property corrected after erroneous treatment of a prior transaction.

The fact that the mitigation provisions are founded in principles of equity is apparent from the circumstances to which the provisions apply. For example, if a taxpayer is successful in obtaining a refund with respect to an item erroneously included in income for an open year, it would be unfair if the statute of limitations barred collection of tax on the item in the earlier, correct year. The mitigation provisions open the otherwise barred year and permit the IRS to send the taxpayer a Notice of Deficiency with respect to the omitted item.[39] As is the case with normal deficiency notices, the taxpayer is free to contest the deficiency by either petitioning the Tax Court or paying the tax and filing a claim for refund.

In 1953, Congress expanded the mitigation provisions to include two additional circumstances deemed to warrant adjustment in an otherwise barred year. In one of these circumstances, the taxpayer had a choice of year in which to take a deduction.[40] In the other, the IRS had a choice of year in which to assert that an item not included by the taxpayer in income for any taxable year should have been included.[41] In each case the wrong year is chosen, but by the time the mistake is discovered, the correct year is closed. As is discussed below, a prerequisite for adjustment in these "choice of year" cases is that when the wrong year was chosen, the statute of limitations for both the wrong year and the correct year were open.[42]

38. Benenson v. United States, 385 F.2d 26 (2d Cir. 1967); Gooding v. United States, 326 F.2d 988 (Ct. Cl. 1964).

39. IRC § 1314(b).

40. IRC § 1312(4).

41. IRC § 1312(3)(B).

42. IRC § 1311(b)(2).

Whether dealing with the original "inconsistent position" circumstances of adjustment, or the later "choice of year" circumstances of adjustment, the following five elements define the right to use one of the mitigation provisions and make an adjustment in a closed year.[43]

1. Correction in the error year is barred by a law or rule of law. Section 1311(a).
2. There is a determination. Sections 1311(a) and 1313(a).
3. There is a circumstance of adjustment. Section 1312.
4. There is a condition necessary for adjustment. Section 1311.
5. If present, the two "related taxpayer" issues are addressed. Sections 1313(c) and 1311(b)(3).

The following is a brief overview of these five elements with emphasis on several aspects of mitigation that are not apparent from the language of the Code or the Regulations. The mitigation Regulations are particularly helpful in explaining the statutory provisions and demonstrating their application through examples. Consequently, careful study of the assigned statutory provisions and Regulations is required to gain a working knowledge of these complicated provisions.

A. Error Year Barred by Law or Rule of Law

If correction of the error is not barred by the statute of limitations on assessment or on filing a claim for refund, or by some other rule of law, then there is no need for mitigation. Consequently, the first requisite for application of the mitigation provisions is that a law or rule of law bars correction of the error. While the statutes of limitations on assessment and on claims for refund[44] are most often involved, they are not the only laws that may prevent correction of an error. The Regulations provide other examples of laws that can have the effect of preventing correction of an error and that, like the statutes of limitations, can be mitigated.[45] They include (i) section 6212(c), which limits the IRS's ability to determine another deficiency if a Notice of Deficiency has already been sent to the taxpayer and the taxpayer has filed a petition with the Tax Court and (ii) section 6512, which limits the Service's authority to issue refunds if the taxpayer has filed a petition in the Tax Court.

B. Determinations

An error in a barred year can be corrected under the mitigation provisions only if there has been a "determination."[46] For this purpose, a determination is a judicial or administrative decision or an agreement as to the proper treatment of the item in

43. The party asserting applicability of the mitigation regime bears the burden of proving these elements. *E.g.*, O'Brien v. United States, 766 F.2d 1038, 1042 (7th Cir. 1995).

44. IRC §§ 6501, 6511.

45. IRC § 1311(b)(2).

46. IRC §§ 1311(a), 1313(a).

an open year. The presence of a determination is critical to application of the mitigation rules because without a judicial or administrative decision, or an agreement, on the proper treatment of an item in the open year, there is no basis for changing the treatment of the item in the barred year.

Thus, a decision of the Tax Court, federal District Court, Bankruptcy Court, or Court of Federal Claims that an item is deductible or includible in an open year becomes a "determination" if no notice of appeal is filed and the time for filing such an appeal expires.[47] If the trial court decision is appealed, the decision becomes final once the Court of Appeal's or Supreme Court's decision becomes final.[48] In the case of a judicial decision that has become final, the proper treatment of the item in the open year is conclusively determined. If the same item was erroneously treated in a barred year and if the other requirements of the mitigation provisions are present, the statute of limitations for the barred year is opened for the limited purpose of correcting the error.

Administrative determinations include (i) a closing agreement made under section 7121, (ii) a final disposition of a claim for refund, and (iii) a formal agreement with the Secretary memorialized on Form 2259.[49] These administrative determinations provide a degree of finality as to the proper treatment of the item in the open year because, in effect, the parties have agreed to the proper treatment of the item. This is clear in the case of closing agreements which, in the absence of "fraud or malfeasance, or misrepresentation of a material fact," may not be reopened or modified by the taxpayer or the IRS. Closing agreements become final for this purpose upon approval by the Commissioner.[50]

Claims for refund also can provide the requisite determination about the proper treatment of an item in the open year. Thus, if a taxpayer files a claim for refund based on his failure to take a deduction for the year and the IRS allows the claim, there is agreement as to the proper treatment of the item in that year. If the other requisites are present, the mitigation provisions then open the barred year in which the taxpayer erroneously deducted the same item, thus permitting the IRS to assert a deficiency with respect to that item.

If a claim for refund is filed, the IRS may audit the return and discover one or more omitted items of income or improper deductions. Section 1313(a)(3) and the related Regulations[51] explain that the refund claim filed by the taxpayer may be the

---

47. IRC § 7481(a) (as to Tax Court); Fed. R. App. P. 4(a) (as to District Court); Ct. Fed. Cl. R. 58.1 (as to the Court of Federal Claims). Section 7481(a)(2) provides that if the Tax Court decision is appealed, it will become final if the decision is affirmed or the appeal dismissed and no petition for certiorari has been filed within the allowed time. Tax Court cases handled under the small case procedures are not appealable. Decisions in such cases become final 90 days after the decision is entered. IRC § 7481(b).

48. Fruit of the Loom, Inc. v. Commissioner, 68 T.C. Memo. (CCH) 867, T.C. Memo (RIA) ¶ 94,492 (1994), *aff'd*, 72 F.3d 1338 (7th Cir. 1996).

49. IRC § 1313(a)(2)–(4).

50. IRC § 7121(b); Reg. § 1.1313(a)-2.

51. Reg. § 1.1313(a)-(3)(b).

basis not only for a determination as to each item raised in the refund claim, but also as to each new item raised by the IRS as an offset to the claimed items. The Code and Regulations describe the time when a determination arises with respect to the new items.[52]

A determination as to the proper treatment of the item is also present in the case of a section 1313(a)(4) agreement with the IRS. This is a formal agreement between the taxpayer and the IRS. If a related party is involved, that person must also be a party to the agreement. The terms and conditions of the agreement are spelled out in Form 2259 entitled "Agreement as a Determination Pursuant to § 1313(a)(4) of the Code."

The section 1313(a)(4) agreement is a reasonably quick way of obtaining a determination. For instance, it can be used when a claim for refund is disallowed in whole or in part. In such case, the taxpayer has two years from the date of mailing of the notice of disallowance to commence an action to recover the claimed overpayment. Until that two-year period expires, the claim for refund cannot be the source of a "determination." Rather than waiting two years, the IRS and the taxpayer can create a determination by entering into a section 1313(a)(4) agreement. The section 1313(a)(4) agreement would trigger application of the mitigation provisions and permit the taxpayer to immediately file a claim for refund with respect to the item in the otherwise barred year.

Section 1313(a)(4) agreements, however, are less "final" than the other administrative or judicial determinations. Thus, if after an audit, the taxpayer and the IRS enter into a section 1313(a)(4) agreement, the Regulations say that until the tax liability for the open year becomes final, the taxpayer can still file a claim for refund and the IRS can still assert a deficiency with respect to the open year.[53] Any section 1313(a)(4) agreement with respect to the open year that is changed by any such claim for refund or asserted deficiency will result in a further change in the tax liability for the barred year.

Disagreements about tax liabilities are often resolved when the IRS and taxpayers enter into compromises.[54] Because a compromise or settlement is a result of give and take between the parties whose shared goal is to agree on an appropriate dollar amount to settle the open issues and not necessarily to determine the correct treatment of any item in question, compromises in the open year cannot serve as a determination. For the same reason, section 1311(a) expressly prohibits use of the mitigation provisions to open any barred year to alter any item that was a subject of a compromise.

---

52. IRC § 1313(a)(3); Reg. § 1.1313(a)-3(d).

53. Reg. § 1.1313(a)-4(d).

54. IRC § 7122; Reg. § 301.7122-1. However, the IRS is not permitted to enter into an offer in compromise when a case is still controlled by the Department of Justice. For example, if a taxpayer is paying restitution as part of a criminal tax conviction, the IRS may not enter into a compromise with the taxpayer.

Thus, a compromise in either the open or the barred year in question precludes application of the mitigation provisions.

C. Circumstances of Adjustment

The original circumstances of adjustment and the later "choice of year" circumstances of adjustment are dealt with separately here because the two are treated differently as they relate to the section 1311(b) condition necessary for adjustment requirement. As a preliminary matter, however, it is helpful to understand the equitable thread that connects all of the circumstances of adjustment to which mitigation applies.

1. The Equitable Basis for Mitigation

Most of the circumstances that warrant breaching the bar of the statute of limitations involve an inconsistency between the way an item is treated in an open year and the way it was (or should have been) treated in a barred year. For instance, the circumstance described in section 1312(1), entitled "Double inclusion of an item of gross income," is one in which the taxpayer is required to include an item in income for an open year even though the same item was previously included in income for a barred year. The circumstance described in section 1312(2), entitled "Double allowance of a deduction or credit," is one in which a taxpayer correctly deducts an item in an open year even though the taxpayer previously deducted the same item in a barred year. The double inclusion of an item of income is unfair to the taxpayer and the double deduction of an item is unfair to the IRS. These inequities are most accurately corrected by opening the otherwise barred year and treating the item in that year consistently with the correct treatment of the item as determined with respect to the open year.

There is another consideration, beyond fairness, that supports opening barred years under these circumstances. An important reason underlying statutes of limitations—fear that memories may fail and documentation may be lost with the passing years—has little force with respect to circumstances of adjustment involving inconsistent positions. The process of determining the correct treatment of an item in the open year necessarily presents the parties, or the court, with sufficient facts to determine the proper treatment of the same item in the barred year. This suggests that the prevailing party in the open year should not be able to raise the "memories fail" statute of limitations policy when the party that lost in the open year attempts to correct the erroneous treatment of the same item in a barred year. Similarly, the generally sound principle of finality has little to do with these circumstances of adjustment. In each case, the same factual issues are raised to get the determination of the correct treatment of the item in the open year as would be raised to correct the erroneous treatment of the item in the barred year.

2. The Original Circumstances of Adjustment

Each of the original circumstances of adjustment permits either a refund or an assessment of additional tax in the barred year. These circumstances are relatively straightforward and, with the help of the applicable Regulations, their application can be understood. However, a few comments about sections 1312(3) and1312(7) may help clarify their application.

The section 1312(3) circumstance of adjustment, entitled "Double exclusion of an item of gross income," has two parts. The first part, section 1312(3)(A), deals with items either included in income in the open year, or originally excluded from income in the open year but with respect to which the tax was subsequently paid (normally following an audit). In both cases, the determination is that the item was erroneously included in the open year and should have been included in a barred year. Circumstances falling within section 1312(3)(A) are referred to as "payment double exclusions."

The second part, section 1312(3)(B), deals with items neither originally nor subsequently included in income for the open year which are determined not to be includible in the open year. The basis for the determination is that they should have been included in another year. But, at the time of the determination, the other, correct, year is barred. This might occur when the IRS does not prevail in its assertion that an item of income should have been included in a particular year and by the time that determination is made, the correct year of inclusion is barred. This circumstance of adjustment is referred to as a "nonpayment double exclusion."

As will be seen in section D below, for mitigation to apply, there must be not only a determination and a circumstance of adjustment, but also a condition necessary for adjustment as described in section 1311(b). The condition necessary for adjustment for the section 1312(3)(A) payment double exclusion is generally described as "maintenance of an inconsistent position." The condition necessary for adjustment for the section 1312(3)(B) nonpayment double exclusion (and for a section 1312(4) double disallowance of a deduction or credit) is that both the open and the barred year must be open at the time either the IRS or the taxpayer first selects the year in which to assert that an item of income should have been included (or a deduction or credit taken). The different conditions necessary for adjustment for payment double exclusions and nonpayment double exclusions can produce different outcomes for a taxpayer and can present a trap for the unwary. This difference is elaborated on in subsection D.

The section 1312(7) circumstance of adjustment involves an open-year determination of the basis of property in connection with which there was a prior transaction that either determined or affected the basis of the property. Also, in respect of that transaction there occurred with respect to a taxpayer described in section 1312(7)(B) one of the errors described in section 1312(7)(C). For example, assume that John Thatcher acquired a parcel of commercial property ten years ago in a transaction that he thought qualified for tax-free treatment under the exchange rules in section 1031. Assume also that last year he sold the property at a substantial gain which he reported on his return. John now understands that he should have recognized a gain when he acquired the property because the tax-free exchange attempted at that time failed a critical part of section 1031. Therefore, he files a claim for refund with respect to the gain on the recent sale, using the increased basis he would have if he had properly recognized the gain at the time he acquired the property. The IRS agrees with his position, accepts the higher basis, and allows the requested refund. The question is whether the IRS can now go back through the bar of the statute of limitations and collect the tax due on the previously unreported gain on the exchange of property now known to be a taxable?

On these facts, there is a determination (the allowed claim for refund). There is a section 1312(7)(A) circumstance of adjustment. John is the taxpayer with respect to whom the determination was made, and his error is non-recognition of gain on a prior exchange of property. The statute of limitations on assessing any additional tax with respect to the acquisition year expired long ago. And, the section 1311(b) condition necessary for adjustment is present. Finally, under section 1311(b)(1)(B), the determination adopted a position maintained by the taxpayer (the stepped-up basis) that is inconsistent with the taxpayer's erroneous non-recognition of gain at the time he acquired the property. Since all of the elements necessary for invocation of the mitigation provisions are satisfied, the IRS may open John's closed year for the sole purpose of collecting tax due on the gain realized on the acquisition of the property.

3. The Choice of Year Circumstances of Adjustment

In 1953, Congress expanded the mitigation provisions to include two additional circumstances that warrant adjustment notwithstanding the fact that the statute of limitations on assessment barred correction of the error. Under one of these circumstances of adjustment, the taxpayer chose the wrong year in which to take a deduction. By the time the IRS obtained a determination disallowing the deduction for the open year, the statute of limitations for the correct year expired. Under the normal statute of limitations rules, this results in disallowance of the deduction in the open year with no way to correct the error in the closed year—a double disallowance of the deduction. Under the mitigation provisions, so long as both years were open when the taxpayer selected the erroneous year for the deduction, the otherwise barred, correct year of deduction is opened for one year after the determination to allow the taxpayer to claim the deduction.[55]

Under the second 1953 circumstance of adjustment, a nonpayment double exclusion, upon audit of a taxpayer's return, the IRS chose the wrong year in which to include an otherwise omitted item of income. By the time the taxpayer, who did not pay the proposed deficiency, prevailed in excluding the item of income from the open year, the statute of limitations for the correct year of inclusion expired. Under the normal statute of limitations rules, this would result in exclusion of the item in the open year and no way to correct the erroneous exclusion in the barred year—a nonpayment, double exclusion. As in the case of the double disallowance of a deduction, so long as both years were open when the IRS selected the erroneous year of inclusion, the barred, correct year is opened for one year to allow the IRS to assert the tax.

---

55. IRC § 1314(b). This one-year limitations period was at issue in *El Paso CGP Co., L.L.C. v. United States*, 748 F.3d 225 (5th Cir. 2014) (using the statutory mitigation rules to allow the IRS to net a corporation's deficiencies from closed years against its overpayment in a prior year). *See also* Robin Greenhouse & R. Christy Vouri, *Riding the Mitigation Train Through El Paso*, Tax Notes, May 12, 2014, at 693.

As in the case of the circumstances of adjustment based on inconsistent positions, the circumstances of adjustment based on choice of year produce unfair results (double disallowance of a deduction or double exclusion of an item of gross income) in situations that do not necessarily deserve statute of limitations protection. Issues relating to the item in the open year are resolved on the basis of the same facts necessary to determine the proper treatment of the item in the barred year.

D. Conditions Necessary for Adjustment

Section 1311(b) establishes "conditions necessary for adjustment" that are different with respect to each of the two broad categories of circumstance of adjustment—the original circumstances of adjustment based on inconsistent positions and those based on choice of year.

1. Section 1311(b)(1): The Original Circumstances of Adjustment

In the case of the original "inconsistent position" circumstances of adjustment, the condition necessary for adjustment is that the position maintained by the prevailing party in the determination "is inconsistent with the erroneous inclusion, exclusion, omission, allowance, disallowance, recognition, or nonrecognition" in the barred year.[56] The determination-year prevailing position could be one maintained by the IRS (disallowance of a deduction or inclusion of an item of income) or by the taxpayer (allowance of a deduction or exclusion of an item of income). In either case, the barred-year inconsistent position is taken either by the taxpayer who obtained the determination or, as is explained in Section E below, by a related taxpayer.

The courts disagree as to the manner in which an inconsistent position must be maintained. Some courts (following a Senate Finance Committee report) require that the inconsistency must be actively maintained.[57] Other courts have reached different results even on similar facts because they hold that the requisite inconsistency may be maintained either actively or passively.[58] The divergent positions among the courts are illustrated in the following example.

Gus is a partner in XYZ partnership. He contributes a portion of his partnership interest to two trusts, one created for the benefit of his wife and the other for the benefit of his son. Gus and each of the trusts report their respective shares of the partnership's income on their income tax returns for 20x0. In 20x3, the IRS audits Gus' return, refuses to recognize the two trusts as bona fide partners, and treats the trusts' shares of the partnership income as income to Gus. This results in Gus having a deficiency of $10,000. He pays the deficiency in full in 20x3 (in part by a credit of the tax erroneously paid on the income by the two trusts). In 20x4, Gus files a timely

56. IRC § 1311(b)(1).

57. *See, e.g.*, Illinois Lumber & Material Dealer's Ass'n Health Ins. Trust v. United States, 794 F.3d 907, 911–13 (8th Cir. 2015), *rev'g* 113 AFTR2d 1937 (D. Minn. 2014); Commissioner v. Estate of Weinreich, 316 F.2d 97 (9th Cir. 1963); Glatt v. United States, 470 F.2d 596 (Ct. Cl. 1972).

58. *See, e.g.*, Chertkof v. Commissioner, 649 F.2d 264 (4th Cir. 1981); Yagoda v. Commissioner, 331 F.2d 485 (2d Cir. 1964).

claim for refund based on the $10,000 deficiency he paid. The Commissioner disallows the claim. Gus then petitions the District Court seeking a refund of the tax he paid, taking the position that the two trusts should be recognized. The District Court agrees with Gus and in 20x6 enters a decision that becomes final, recognizing the two trusts as partners and allowing the claim for refund (which included the amount of tax originally paid by the trusts and credited to Gus' liability). The IRS sends Gus a check for $10,000 plus interest, and then sends notices of deficiency to the two trusts for tax they should have paid as partners in 20x0. However, by that time, the statute of limitations on assessing additional tax against the trusts has expired.

In the Second Circuit this would be an inconsistent position.[59] The determination by the District Court adopted a position maintained by Gus that the two trusts were partners in XYZ and should therefore have included their respective shares of the partnership's income in their returns. This is inconsistent with the IRS's erroneous exclusion of the respective shares of the partnership's income from the trusts' returns. The statutory requirements for application of the mitigation provisions, particularly the inconsistent position requirement, are satisfied and mitigation would apply to allow the IRS to collect tax on the income for the otherwise barred year.

However, courts requiring that the inconsistent position be actively maintained would *not* find an inconsistent position under these facts because the trusts did not actively seek to avoid tax by asserting the statute of limitations.

Here, the trusts had maintained a correct position on the original return and the IRS made the incorrect determination that the trusts were not partners. The equitable underpinning for application of the mitigation provisions by the IRS is not present here when the trusts filed their original returns correctly. The IRS cannot rely on its error in disregarding the trusts as the basis for establishing the inconsistent position element necessary for application of the mitigation provisions.

2. Section 1311(b)(2): The "Choice of Year" Circumstances of Adjustment

In the case of "choice of year" circumstances of adjustment, section1312(3)(B) nonpayment double exclusion and section 1312(4) double disallowance of a deduction, the condition necessary for adjustment is that at the time the decision is made (by the IRS or the taxpayer) to account for the item in the wrong year the correct year is still open. For example, assume that the IRS identifies an item of income that the taxpayer received but never reported and includes the item in a deficiency notice relating to year two. Also assume that the taxpayer prevails in Tax Court on his theory that the item of income should not be reported in year two because it was actually income in year one, but that by the time the Tax Court opinion becomes final, year one is barred by the statute of limitations. If at the time the IRS asserted that the item was includible in year two, the Service could have asserted that the item was includible in year one, then a condition necessary for adjustment with respect to that

59. *See Yagoda*, 331 F.2d at 490–91.

item exists. Thus, if both year one and year two were open when the IRS selected one of the years as the year of inclusion, then the IRS is not penalized for selecting the wrong year.[60]

The double disallowance of a deduction circumstance of adjustment, section 1312(4), has a similar condition necessary for adjustment requirement.[61] If a taxpayer reports an item as deductible in year two, and the IRS later obtains a determination that the item was properly deductible in year one, a condition necessary for adjustment is present if, at the time the taxpayer first maintained in writing that he was entitled to the deduction in year two, he was not barred from taking the deduction in year one. Again, it is not intended that the taxpayer be penalized for initially selecting the wrong year at a time when both years were open.

There is a compelling reason why the condition necessary for adjustment for the two choice of year circumstances of adjustments is relatively restrictive. If the section 1311(b)(1) "inconsistent position" condition necessary for adjustment were applicable to the two choice of year circumstances of adjustment then, in effect, there would be no statute of limitations with respect to these circumstances of adjustment. Assume that the IRS discovers an item of income that a taxpayer should have included in a now barred year. Without section 1311(b)(2), in order to open the barred year for mitigation purposes, all the IRS would have to do is assert that the item is properly includible in *any* open year. Ultimately, the taxpayer would likely get a final decision of the Tax Court that the item was not includible in the open year. The position maintained by the taxpayer in Tax Court would be inconsistent with the taxpayer's erroneous exclusion of the item in the barred year, thereby providing the IRS with a section 1311(b)(1) condition necessary for adjustment. In such case, all the elements for application of the mitigation provisions to open the barred year are present—the correct year is closed, there is a final decision of the Tax Court (a determination), there is a section 1312(3)(B) nonpayment double exclusion circumstance of adjustment, and an inconsistent position condition necessary for adjustment.

Thus, in connection with a nonpayment double exclusion, if all that is required to have a condition necessary for adjustment is that the taxpayer prevail in the open year, the IRS could use the mitigation provisions to open any barred year in which there was an omitted item of income. Such inappropriate use of the mitigation provisions is precluded by operation of the section 1311(b)(2) condition necessary for adjustment. It requires that the correct year be open at the time the IRS first asserts in a deficiency notice that the item should be included in another (as it turns out, incorrect) open year. A similar analysis with respect to the section 1312(4) double disallowance of a deduction will demonstrate that, in effect, there would be no statute of limitations in the double disallowance of a deduction case if all that is necessary is that the prevailing party in the open year take an inconsistent position.

60. IRC § 1311(b)(2)(A).
61. IRC § 1311(b)(2)(B).

E. Related Parties

It is possible under the mitigation provisions for a determination obtained by a taxpayer to open a barred year with respect to a "related" taxpayer. Assume that the IRS asserts a deficiency against a husband for an item of income omitted from his return. Assume also that the deficiency is sustained by the Tax Court and that the Tax Court's opinion is now final. Finally, assume that the husband's wife erroneously included the same item in income in her separate return for the same year and that by the time of the Tax Court judgment relating to the treatment of the item by her husband is final, the taxable year in which she erroneously included the item is barred. The erroneous inclusion of the item by the wife, who is a "related party," can be corrected through the mitigation provisions even though the necessary determination was obtained in a judicial proceeding between the husband and the IRS.

For purposes of this example, a related taxpayer is a taxpayer who, during the taxable year in which the error occurred, stood in one of the relationships specified in section 1313(c) with the taxpayer who obtained the determination. It is not necessary that the relationship exist throughout the error year—that it exists "at some time" during the year is sufficient.[62] The specified relationships include that of husband and wife.

Two points about related taxpayers deserve mention. First, the concept of related taxpayers applies to most of the circumstances of adjustment set forth in section 1312. However, it does not apply to the section 1312(7) circumstance of adjustment relating to the erroneous determination of basis. It is possible that an error in determining basis in a barred year can be corrected with respect to a taxpayer other than the one who obtained the determination, but the section 1313(c) related-party concept is not applicable. Section 1312(7) contains its own related-taxpayer rule.

Second, if the IRS is using mitigation to assess tax against a related taxpayer in an otherwise barred year, there is an additional timing rule. Under section 1311(b)(3), the relationship must have existed at the time the taxpayer who obtained the determination

> first maintains the inconsistent position in a return, claim for refund, or petition (or amended petition) to the Tax Court for the taxable year with respect to which the determination is made, or if such position is not so maintained, then at the time of the determination.[63]

F. Amount and Method of Adjustment

When mitigation is available, the error in the otherwise barred year is corrected by the taxpayer filing a claim for refund (if correction of the error results in an overpayment), or by the IRS issuing a Notice of Deficiency (if correction of the error results in a deficiency). In either case, the amount of the adjustment is determined

62. Reg. § 1.1313(c)-1.
63. IRC § 1311(b)(3).

by correcting only the "treatment of the item which was the subject of the error."[64] If correction of the error and the resulting change in gross or taxable income affects other items relating to the computation of tax (such as the limitation on charitable deductions), then those other items must be taken into consideration in determining the amount of the adjustment.[65] Also, penalties and interest "wrongfully collected" and traced to the error are included in the amount of the adjustment.[66] The IRS takes the position that any overpayment may be applied to a taxpayer's agreed upon but unassessed liabilities.[67] However, neither the taxpayer nor the IRS can raise any other issue in connection with the computation of the amount of the adjustment or as a set-off against the adjustment.[68]

If the adjustment causes an increase in tax liability, the deficiency is collected under the normal deficiency procedures including the issuance of a Notice of Deficiency. The notice must be issued within one year from the date of the determination. Similarly, if the adjustment results in a decrease in tax liability, the refund is obtained under the normal procedures applicable to obtaining a refund. In this case, the claim for refund must be filed within one year from the date of the determination.

G. Evaluation of the Mitigation Provisions

Few see the statutory mitigation rules as resoundingly successful. For three reasons, one may fairly wonder whether the game is worth the candle. First, as the preceding discussion makes clear, the mitigation regime is horrendously complicated. As one court noted, the regime "was complex and controversial when first enacted, has been frequently amended, and has spawned conflicting judicial interpretations that are hard to reconcile."[69]

Second, at the end of the day, having waded through the numerous elements and exceptions, the lawyer usually concludes that the mitigation rules do not mitigate. In the clear majority of cases, one or another element is not satisfied, so relief is unavailable. The client pays for the research and analysis but rarely receives a happy answer.

Third, good lawyering often renders resort to the statutory rules unnecessary. Chapter 9 described protective refund claims. At the first sign of possible controversy

---

64. IRC § 1314(a).

65. Cory v. Commissioner, 261 F.2d 702 (2d Cir. 1958).

66. *Id.*

67. CCA 200727015 (Mar. 27, 2007). The issue is not settled. Courts have held for the IRS in several cases but have avoided propounding a broad rule. El Paso CGP Co., L.L.C. v. United States, 748 F.3d 225, 230–33 (5th Cir. 2014); Philadelphia & Reading Corp. v. United States, 944 F.2d 1063, 1064 (3d Cir. 1991).

68. *See Lewis*, 284 U.S. at 283; Reg. § 1.1314(c)-1(a).

69. Illinois Lumber & Material Dealers Ass'n Health Ins. Trust v. United States, 794 F.3d 907 5347 (8th Cir. 2015); *see also* Daniel Candee Knickerbocker, Jr., *Mysteries of Mitigation: The Opening of Barred Years in Income Tax Cases,* 30 Fordham L. Rev. 225, 258 (1961) (noting that, because of the complexity, "we are likely to see some hard cases decided in harsh ways and others in total disregard of the statute"); John A. Lynch, Jr., *Income Tax Statute of Limitations: Sixty Years of Mitigation—Enough, Already!!,* 51 S.C.L. Rev. 62, 87 (1999) (noting "[t]he opacity of the mitigation provisions").

as to the proper year in which an item should be reported or as to the proper taxpayer to report it, the tax representative should protect his or her client by filing a protective refund claim. Doing so prevents expiration of the limitations period as to a refund claim, obviating the need to try to reopen closed years. Moreover, even if the statutory rules did not exist, the party—whether the taxpayer or the IRS—sometimes could achieve a satisfactory result under one or another of the judicial rules described in this chapter.

Problems

1. Thurston had purchased some property in Panama City, Florida (known as the Redneck Riviera) in 20x0 for $1,000,000. He intended to build condominium apartments for sale to the public on the property, and started the necessary land use and related work. He soon realized that the project would take longer and require more work than he had originally intended. So in January 20x3 he abandoned the project and exchanged the property with an unrelated third party for a parcel of oceanfront property on Amelia Island, Florida. That property was worth $1,500,000 at the time of the exchange.

During the year 20x3, Thurston was married to Gwen, but they filed separate returns. Thurston reported wages of $150,000 and a tax liability of $27,500 on his return. He believed that his activities with respect to the Parma Beach property had not gone so far as to preclude the application of section 1031 to the exchange. So he did not report the gain realized on the exchange based on the position that section 1031 applied.

Thurston and Gwen were not getting along and were divorced in August 20x4. The divorce was amicable. The property settlement provided that Thurston would transfer title to the Amelia Island property to Gwen. She knew that Thurston had obtained a property in exchange to which section 1031 applied, so she presumed that her basis in the property would be the same as Thurston's under section 1041(b).

Gwen sold the Amelia Island property in December 20x6 for $3,000,000. She reported long-term capital gain on her timely filed federal income tax for the year in the amount of $2,000,000.

The real estate lawyer who represented Gwen in the sale contacted you in mid-20x7. She told you that although she was not a tax lawyer, she did not think that Thurston's 20x3 exchange of the Panama City property the Amelia Island property should have qualified for section 1031 treatment. She would like to refer the matter to you for your opinion.

After review of the facts and conducting some search, you concluded that the 20x3 exchange in fact did not qualify under section 1031. On your advice, Gwen timely filed a claim for refund for the year 20x6, taking the position that her basis in the Amelia Island property was actually $1,500,000 and that her long-term capital gain should have been $1,500,000, not $2,000,000.

The IRS conducted an examination of Gwen's 20x6 return in response to her claim for refund. Several significant errors were discovered with which Gwen agreed. The

IRS agreed that the 20x3 transaction should not have been treated as a section 1031 exchange. Fortunately, however, Gwen's refund was entirely offset by the deficiency and tax attributable to the agreed errors. Gwen's claim for refund was therefore denied, the IRS mailed its Notice of Disallowance to Gwen on December 30, 20x7.

(a) Is the IRS barred from proceeding against Thurston for the tax that he failed to pay for 20x3 because he improperly treated the 20x3 transaction as a section 1031 exchange?

(b) What steps will the IRS take procedurally to assert its claim against Thurston for 20x3?

(c) What will be Thurston's defense? How should he lodge the defense procedurally?

2. Pete was a financial consultant in private practice. Most of his clients were in the healthcare business. During the last few months of 20x2, he had completed a project for Debbie and Sue, who owned and operated a group of outpatient surgical centers. They used the calendar year and the cash method of accounting for tax purposes. The project had been very successful, but Pete's invoice for service rendered has not yet been paid.

Pete saw Mary and Sue at a reception a few days before Christmas in 20x2. Sue wished him happy holidays and handed him a check for $50,000 in payment of his invoice. Pete told Sue to hold onto the check for now. He suggested that she mail it to him a few days before the end of the year. She and Mary would still get a deduction in 20x2, but he wouldn't receive the check until 20x3, which meant that he wouldn't have to report it as income until then. That plan seemed fine for Sue, so she did as Pete suggested.

Pete received the check from Sue in the mail on January 2, 20x3. His timely filed tax return for 20x2 did not report the $50,000. But, as planned, it was reported on his timely filed tax return for 20x3. The tax due was paid in full in the timely manner. He did not receive extensions of time to file his returns for either 20x2 or 20x3.

The IRS conducted an examination of Pete's 20x2 return. After some unsuccessful attempts to settle the issues, the IRS issued a Notice of Deficiency to Pete dated March 30, 20x5, asserting that is 20x2 return failed to include the $50,000.

Pete timely filed a petition in the Tax Court asking the court to redetermine the deficiency determined by the IRS. The case was tried and briefed. The Tax Court ruled for the Commissioner. The decision became final on September 30, 20x7.

(a) Can Pete now obtain a refund of the taxes he paid on the $50,000 consulting fee for the year 20x3?

(b) What should Pete have done as soon as he received the Notice of Deficiency for 20x2?

3. Titanic Corp. used the calendar year and the accrual method of accounting for tax purposes. During 20x2, Titanic incurred expenses in connection with one of its projects in the aggregate amount of $300,000. Although the expenses were clearly deductible, the proper year for the deduction, either 20x2 or 20x3, was not clear. On

the advice of its tax consultants, Titanic deducted the $300,000 for the year 20x3. Titanic's returns for all years were filed timely.

The Internal Revenue Service conducted an examination of Titanic's 20x3 return during the year 20x5. The Agent conducting the examination also reviewed Titanic's returns for the two years 20x2 and 20x4. The Agent decided that the $300,000 of expenses were properly deductible in the year 20x2 and disallowed the deduction for the year 20x3. The Agent also disallowed some of the other deductions in 20x3 in the aggregate amount of $80,000. The Revenue Agent's Report, dated August 15, 20x5, proposed a deficiency in income tax for the year 20x3 in the aggregate amount of $130,000.

Titanic paid the proposed $130,000 deficiency for the year 20x3 in September 20x5, and filed a claim for refund, arguing that all the deductions for the year 20x3 for proper. The claim for refund was denied in full in January 20x6. Titanic immediately filed suit for a refund in the U.S. District Court, arguing that the denial of the deductions for 20x3 was improper.

After pleadings and discovery were complete, counsel for Titanic proposed a settlement, which called for the $300,000 deduction to be disallowed but the $80,000 of other deductions to be allowed.

The Justice Department, representing the United States, accepted the proposal. The settlement was finalized in stipulation signed by the parties in November 20x6. The District Court then dismissed the suit with prejudice. Titanic soon received a portion of the refund it had claimed attributable to the $80,000 in allowable expenses.

It is now February 20x7. Titanic has asked for advice as to whether it can claim a refund for the year 20x2 based on taking the $300,000 deduction that had been disallowed for 20x3.

(a) Can the error (disallowance of the $300,000 deduction for both the years 20x2 and 20x3) be corrected?

(b) Is the denial of the claim for refund for 20x3 a determination? Explain why or why not.

(c) What steps should Titanic have taken with respect preserving the deduction for the year 20x2 when the Agent denied the deduction of $300,000 for 20x3?

(d) What provision should Titanic have included in its settlement of the lawsuit?

4. David has been a good athlete his whole life. He was a star receiver in high school and was recruited by many universities with major football programs. His collegiate athletic career was equally successful. He won many awards and was drafted to play professional football. He signed a lucrative professional contract and was "set for life."

One of the provisions of his contract entitled him to a bonus of $250,000 if his receiving yards surpassed a certain level for the season, including post-season games. He accumulated enough yardage during the 20x1 season to become entitled to the bonus. In fact, he reached the bonus level in December 20x1, before the post-season games even began. His contract made it clear that he was entitled to payment of the bonus for the 20x1 season in December. He didn't ask for the bonus in December, however, and in fact didn't receive it until February 20x2 when it was paid to him together with some post-season earnings. The bonus was not reported on his 20x1 tax return, the intention being to report it on his 20x2 return.

David and his wife engaged an attorney in early 20x3 for estate planning services. She reviewed his professional football contract, tax returns, and other documents in order to gather the information she needed. She advised David (as well as the accounting firm that prepared his returns and his financial consultant) that the bonus should not be reported on his 20x2 return, which was due soon. Instead, he should, but was not legally required to, file an amended return for 20x1 to include the bonus in income for that year. After considering the advice, David and his financial team decided not to include the $250,000 bonus in income for 20x2, but at the same time decided against filing an amended return for 20x1. David's 20x2 return reported gross income of $900,000. Both the 20x1 and 20x2 returns were timely filed, without extensions of time to file.

In mid-20x7, the Internal Revenue Service began an examination of David's tax returns for all open years. The Agent also asked for copies of returns for some of the closed years, including 20x0 through 20x3. The Agent, who was a professional football fan, knew that David was a star receiver and had been entitled to bonuses. He noticed that the bonus for receiving yards for the 20x1 season was not included in income for any of the years. After reviewing David's bank accounts, he realized that the receiving bonus for the 20x1 season had been deposited in David's bank account in February 20x2. The Agent concluded that the $250,000 bonus should have been included in income for that year, and issued a Revenue Agent's Report that included it in income for 20x2. The Report did not propose any other changes.

David filed a protest and was granted an Appeals Conference. His lawyers asserted that the $250,000 bonus should not be treated as income for 20x2. The Appeals Officer rejected the argument and on August 15, 20x8 issued a statutory Notice of Deficiency for the year 20x2. The only issue was whether the $250,000 bonus should have been included in income for that year.

David timely filed a petition in the U.S. Tax Court for a redetermination of the deficiency. David's attorneys suggested that he pay the tax and accrued interest while the case was pending before the Tax Court in order to stop the running of interest. They told David that if he were to be successful in Tax Court, the payment would be refunded. David paid the tax as they suggested.

The Tax Court decided the case in David's favor in a decision that became final on June 15, 20x0. The Court agreed with David's arguments that the bonus should have been income in 20x1, and, pursuant to Code section 6512(b), ordered a refund of the tax paid by David for 20x2, together with interest.

On August 1, 20x0, the Internal Revenue Service issued a statutory Notice of Deficiency to David for the year 20x1, stating that the $250,000 bonus was taxable in that year. Can the error (exclusion of the $250,000 bonus from income for both the years 20x1 and 20x2) be corrected?

5. (a) Yolanda filed her 20x2 tax return timely. The return included an item of income in the amount of $27,500. In July 20x7, she realized that the item was properly includable in income for the year 20x4, not 20x2. So she filed an amendment to her 20x4 return, and paid additional tax and interest. In December 20x7, she filed a claim for refund for the taxes she had paid for 20x2 attributable to the $27,500 item of income. Will the December 20x7 claim for the refund of taxes paid for the year 20x2 to be granted?

(b) Assume instead that Yolanda inadvertently included the $27,500 item in income on both her 20x2 and 20x4 returns, and paid taxes on it for both years. The correct year for the inclusion was 20x4. At a point in time when both years are open, Yolanda asked for your advice. You consider two options. One option would be to file a claim for refund for 20x2. The other option would be to file a claim for refund for 20x4, fully expecting it to be denied on the merits. What strategy would call for waiting for the time to file suit on the denial, two years, to expire, thus resulting in a "determination." Assuming that all other elements for mitigation were present, Yolanda would be entitled to a refund for 20x2. Is there an advantage to filing the claim for 20x4, instead of 20x2? If so, what is the advantage? Does the strategy present any problems?

6. Mervin had been in the real estate business for many years. He had bought and sold so much property that his tax advisors told him he was a "dealer" for tax purposes. One of the properties owned by Mervin was located in Miami-Dade County, Florida. Mervin entered into an agreement in November 20x1 to exchange that property for some real property owned by Gloria, an unrelated third party, located in Broward County, Florida.

The Agreement provided that there would not be a closing until Gloria had the Broward County property rezoned so that Mervin could build a car wash business on the property. Gloria was able to accomplish the rezoning in mid-20x2 and informed Mervin that she was ready to close. Mervin refused to close, however, because he wanted to build a six-bay car wash and the approval Gloria had obtained would permit only a four-bay car wash.

Litigation between Mervin and Gloria ensued. Mervin took the position that Gloria had not met the contractual condition for closing, that is, a proper rezoning. Unfortunately for Mervin, however, the language of the agreement was not specific enough to support his position and the litigation was resolved in Gloria's favor in late 20x3. The closing occurred in May 20x4. Mervin did not treat the transaction as a like-kind exchange and included the gain from the exchange on his 20x4 return. Because of other items, however, Mervin paid no tax on the gain.

The Internal Revenue Service conducted an examination of Mervin's returns for the year at issue. The Revenue Agent's Report (30-day letter) took the position that the entire gain was taxable in 20x2, the year in which Gloria obtained the required rezoning. Mervin did not ask for an Appeals Conference and a statutory Notice of Deficiency (90-day letter) was issued to Mervin for the year 20x2. Mervin did not file a petition in the Tax Court, and the IRS assessed the deficiency soon thereafter. A notice and demand for payment of the tax followed. Mervin paid the tax and filed a claim for refund, arguing that the gain was not taxable until 20x4, the year of the closing. Mervin argued that even if it was income for an earlier year, it wasn't income in 20x2 because the litigation was not resolved until a later year. The IRS denied the claim for refund, and Mervin filed a suit for refund in the U.S. District Court.

In 20x7, the District Court held that the IRS was correct in its assertion that the income should be recognized in an earlier year, but that 20x3 was the proper year because the lawsuit was settled in that year. The District Court ordered that Mervin was entitled to a refund of the tax paid for 20x2.

After the time for filing an appeal had passed, the IRS issued a statutory Notice of Deficiency to Mervin for 20x3, which by then was a barred year, determining that the gain from the exchange should have been reported in that year.

Mervin asserted the affirmative defense that the statute of limitation barred the year 20x3. Will Mervin's defense be successful?

7. Vernon liked cars his whole life. His passion was "tricking out" cars to make them look unusual and go as fast as possible. His venture into the car repair business was not successful because he spent too much time on each job. Car racing was popular in his area, so he built a dirt racetrack with grandstands for Saturday night stock car races. He hoped he could make money by charging fees to the owners for entering cars in the races and charging admission fees to the fans. That business was successful almost immediately, and soon Vernon was running 10 races every Saturday night. Stock car fans were flocking to the track from all around to participate, look at the cars, and watch the races.

Vernon liked to stand in the middle of the track with a "starter's flag" to begin each race and then at the finish line to waive the "checkered flag" for the winter. Even though he had been warned that this was a dangerous practice, he was in his glory and wouldn't listen to the warnings.

On August 20x1, while Vernon was in his usual spot in the middle of the track starting a race, two of the stock cars lost control. Unfortunately, they hit Vernon at the same time. The funeral was held a few days later.

Vernon's wife, Sally Mae, was appointed the personal representative of his estate. Vernon had amassed quite a fortune in the stock car racing business and in his investments. His last few individual income tax returns were very complicated. His estate adopted the calendar year for federal income tax purposes and timely filed all his tax returns without extensions.

In late 20x2, the Internal Revenue Service began an examination of Vernon's final return for the short year that ended on the date of his death in August 20x1. The return had been timely filed and was not a joint return. The Revenue Agent's Report, issued on March 30, 20x3, took the position that some payments received by Vernon from a cattle operation in which he had invested should be treated as ordinary income and not as non-taxable return of capital as had been reported on the return.

Your firm served as Vernon's counsel and was handling the administration of his estate. You were asked to prepare a Protest in response to the Revenue Agent's Report. The Protest was filed timely on April 30, 20x3, and a conference with an Appeals Officer ensued. You took the position at the Appeals Conference that even if the Revenue Agent was correct in her position that the amounts received from the cattle operation should be ordinary income instead of return of capital, Vernon had sustained substantial losses during the short year (that ended in August 20x1) in another of his businesses, a fertilizer business, which had not been reported on the return and which would more than offset the ordinary income. As a result, there should not be any deficiency.

You had agreed to extend the statute of limitations until December 31, 20x5 for the short year that ended in August 20x1.

The Appeals Officer did not view your arguments favorably and issued a statutory Notice of Deficiency on January 31, 20x4. On February 15, 20x4 you timely filed a petition in the U.S. Tax Court seeking redetermination of the deficiency determined in the Notice of Deficiency. Your position asked the Court to take the losses from Vernon's fertilizer business into consideration in determining the deficiency.

The court issued its opinion on November 1, 20x7. The court held that the payments from the cattle operation were ordinary income, not a return of capital as had been reported originally. The court agreed that the losses from the fertilizer business should be deductible as ordinary losses from a transaction entered into for-profit. The court did not agree, however, that Vernon's short year that ended in August 20x1 was the correct year for the loss deduction. The court opinion said that, because the fertilizer business continued into early 20x2 before it went out of business, the losses were properly deducted in that year.

It is now January 15, 20x8. You have been asked to provide advice with respect to the deductibility of the losses from the fertilizer business for the year 20x2. Deducting those losses would result in a refund for the year 20x2, but the statute of limitations for claiming a refund is closed.

What is your advice? You may assume that the estate would be entitled to ordinary loss from fertilizer business for the year 20x2. Restrict your answer to the statute of limitations and mitigation issues. Do not discuss any substantive or estate tax issues.

Chapter 11

Penalties

Part A: Penalties for Failure to File or Pay Timely

IRC: Skim §§6012, 6081; 6151(a); skim 6166(a), (g)(3); 6651, 6654(a)–(d)(1), (e); 7491(c); 7502(a), (b); 7503

Regs.: §§1.6081-3(a)(1)–(3), -4(a)–(c); 1.6161-1(a), (b); 301.6651-1(a)(1)–(3), (c), (e), (g)

Case: Russell v. Commissioner, T.C. Memo. 2011-81 (skip facts)

IRM: IRM 1.2.12.1.5 para. 2, 4 and 5

I. General

The Code imposes upon taxpayers a variety of due dates for filing tax returns and paying tax. To encourage taxpayers to meet the deadlines, the law establishes an array of penalties, some civil and some criminal.[1] The most significant of the civil sanctions that address these failures are penalties (i) for not prepaying the required amount of tax liability (the "estimated tax penalty"), (ii) for not filing returns timely (the "late filing penalty"), and (iii) for not paying taxes timely (the "late payment penalty"). For taxpayers already in difficult financial straits, these penalties, plus interest on the outstanding balance, may be particularly burdensome.[2]

1. Penalty Policy Statement 20-1 (formerly P-1-18) (IRM 1.2.20.1.1) states:
   1. Penalties are used to enhance voluntary compliance.
   2. The Internal Revenue Service has a responsibility to collect the proper amount of tax revenue in the most efficient manner. Penalties provide the Service with an important tool to achieve that goal because they enhance voluntary compliance by taxpayers. In order to make the most efficient use of penalties, the Service will design, administer, and evaluate penalty programs based on how those programs can most efficiently encourage voluntary compliance.
   3. Penalties encourage voluntary compliance by:
      1. demonstrating the fairness of the tax system to compliant taxpayers; and
      2. increasing the cost of noncompliance.

2. In FY 2015, the IRS assessed over 40 million civil tax penalties of all kinds, totaling over $24 billion. By far the largest category involved income taxes of individuals, estates, and trusts, constituting about 31.9 million penalties totaling over $12 billion. Next came employment taxes, with about 6.3 million penalties totaling just over $4 billion. Other categories included business income tax, excise tax, estate and gift tax, and non-return penalties (including penalties as to tax return preparers and

In order to fully appreciate the subject of this chapter, students should review the portions of Chapter 2 that discuss what constitutes a return for filing purposes, what the due dates are for filing returns and making payments, and how one can get extensions when timely filing or payment is not possible.

II. Prepaying Tax Liability

Congress requires taxpayers to pay almost their entire tax liability during the year it is earned rather than wait until the return is filed in March or April of the next year. One of the reasons for this requirement is the government's need for continuous infusions of revenue. However, the obligation to prepay also protects taxpayers from getting to the date payment and finding they did not set aside enough money to meet the obligation.

Section 6654 does two things: it establishes for individual taxpayers[3] the guidelines for how much of their income tax and self-employment tax needs to be paid during the year on a "pay-as-you-go" (PAYGO) basis,[4] and it imposes a penalty for underpaying the required amount. Subject to various exceptions to be discussed later, the rule is that individuals must prepay 90% of their current year's liability. If the taxpayer does not adequately prepay the liability, a penalty is imposed by applying the underpayment rate to the amount of the underpayment of estimated tax for the period of underpayment.

PAYGO is most often accomplished by having the taxpayer's employer withhold income tax from wages. It is also frequently satisfied by the taxpayer making quarterly estimated payments or by the taxpayer requesting that one year's overpayment be applied to the following year's liability.

Taxpayers whose only source of income is wages and who properly complete Form W-4[5] usually satisfy the 90% requirement. This is because Publication 15 (Circular E), the government-created tables used by employers to determine the amount to be withheld from wages, provides a reasonable estimate of the employee's tax liability for the year from that source. However, if the Form W-4 overstates the number of allowances or dependents, the amount withheld may be inadequate, forcing the taxpayer to make quarterly estimated tax payments to avoid the section 6654 penalty.

---

information returns and reports). The most frequently assessed civil penalty was failure to pay, representing over half of assessed return penalties. 2016 IRS *Data Book* at Table 17.

3. Although the focus of this chapter is on individuals and on Form 1040, the late filing and late payment penalties also apply to the filing of most other tax returns and the payment of most other taxes. The rules for corporations are similar but not identical. *See* IRC § 6655.

4. IRC § 6654(d)(1)(B)(i).

5. The Form W-4 informs a person's employer of his or her filing status and number of dependents. This provides the employer with a basis to determine the amount of federal income tax to withhold from the person's earnings. The filing status and the number of dependents claimed on the W-4 do not have to be the same as that claimed on the Form 1040. The Form W-4 is meant to estimate the person's full-year tax liability.

Example (1): Karin is a single person with no children. Her only source of income during 20x1 is from her job at ABC Company. She plans to take the standard deduction rather than itemize deductions when she files her Form 1040. On the Form W-4 she submits to ABC, she reports herself as single with one allowance. From each weekly paycheck of $1,000, ABC Company withholds $160 per Circular E. When she files her Form 1040 in early 20x2, she will have prepaid $8,320 ($160 x 52 weeks) toward her income tax liability. Assuming her tax liability is about $7,800, she will be adequately prepaid and, in fact, entitled to a refund of $520.

Example (2): Same facts as example (1), except that Karin plans to itemize her deductions when she files her Form 1040. She estimates her itemized deductions at $14,150. Using the W-4 worksheet, she reports that she is entitled to four allowances. As a result, ABC withholds $117 for income taxes from each paycheck. When she prepares her Form 1040, she will have had $6,084 prepaid through withholding. Assuming she claims $14,150 as itemized deductions, her tax liability for 20x1 will be about $5,400 and she will be entitled to a refund of $684. On the other hand, if she does not itemize and uses the standard deduction when filing her Form 1040, she would be under-withheld by $1,716 ($7,800 less $6,084). Since $6,084 is less than 90% of $7,800, she would be subject to the section 6654 penalty.

Besides withholding, taxpayers may prepay their taxes by means of quarterly estimates. Taxpayers who have significant sources of income other than wages, such as dividends, interest, gains, rents, and royalties, or who have income from a sole proprietorship or partnership, are the most likely candidates for having to make estimated quarterly tax payments.[6] For calendar year taxpayers, estimated tax payments, while commonly referred to as quarterly estimated payments, are actually due on the 15th of April, June, and September of the current tax year and the 15th of January of the following tax year.[7] Taxpayers are generally required to pay 25% of their annual estimated tax on or before each installment payment due date.

Example: Margo is a self-employed graphic designer. Her net earnings from self-employment for 20x1 are $52,000. She is a single person and has no dependents. Her itemized deductions are $14,150. Her income tax liability for 20x1, based on the first example above, is about $7,800. However, she must also pay Social Security and Medicare taxes at 15.3% of her net earnings from self-employment. This amounts to approximately $7,950. Margo

6. Taxpayers who have significant income that is not subject to withholding must be financially self-disciplined. If they failed to pay estimated taxes on a quarterly basis, they not only will find themselves liable for the penalty under section 6654 but they will also find themselves burdened with a large tax liability. This is especially true for self-employed individuals, as they have to PAYGO not only for income taxes but also for the 15.3% self-employment tax.

7. IRC § 6654(c).

would have to make quarterly estimated tax payments of 90% of $15,750 ($7,800 + $7,950), or $14,175, to satisfy her estimated tax liability.

A. Calculating the Penalty

Section 6654(a)(1) sets the penalty rate at the underpayment rate established under section 6621.[8] For purposes of the penalty, the underpayment rate is a simple interest rate; it is not compounded daily.[9]

The penalty is calculated based on the "underpayment period," which is the number of days from the payment due date to the earlier of (a) the date the payment is received, or (b) the 15th day of the fourth month following the close of the taxable year, which is the due date of the return without regard to extensions, usually April 15th of the following year. Each underpaid installment period must be computed separately. The length of an underpayment period is not reduced by an extension of time to pay the tax.

The amount of the underpayment of estimated tax is defined as the excess of (1) the required installment over (2) the amount, if any, of the installment paid on or before its due date.[10] Payments of estimated tax are credited against the unpaid portion of the required installment that is most overdue at the time of the payment, unless the taxpayer elects otherwise. By contrast, withheld taxes are divided evenly among all four installments,[11] unless the taxpayer completes and attaches Form 2210 to the return indicating a choice to apply the withholding to the period in which it was actually withheld.

Whether a taxpayer has met the 90% requirement is determined based on the amount of tax reported on the original return. Even if the tax is later adjusted because of an audit or the filing of an amended return, the amount of the underpayment remains the same. An exception exists when an amended joint return is filed after separate returns, in which case the penalty is based on the joint return.[12]

B. Defenses to the Estimated Tax Penalty

If the taxpayer has not met the 90% requirement, the IRS automatically assesses the penalty and sends the taxpayer a notice and demand for payment. The section 6654 penalty is not entitled to deficiency procedures. Most available defenses are pre-

---

8. Taxpayers are not subject to estimated tax penalties if their tax liability is less than $1,000, after subtracting amounts withheld from wages and other payments/credits during the year. Further, no estimated tax penalty will be imposed on taxpayers who had no liability for the preceding (12-month) tax year and who were U.S. citizens or residents throughout the preceding tax year. IRC § 6654(e).

9. IRC § 6622(b).

10. IRC § 6654(b).

11. IRC § 6654(g).

12. IRM 20.1.3.2.1.1.2.

sented to the Service by individuals completing a Form 2210.[13] Taxpayers may attach the completed forms to their tax returns, seeking nonassessment in the first place. Alternatively, if the IRS assesses the penalty automatically, one can request its abatement by sending in the form after the balance due notice is received.

As was true for the initial determination of whether the taxpayer failed to prepay 90% of the current year's liability, most of the defenses to the penalty are mathematical. The most frequently employed exception allows the taxpayer to demonstrate that the amount paid during the year equals or exceeds 100% of the tax shown on the preceding year's return.[14] The purpose of this exception is to make it possible for taxpayers to estimate the amount they must prepay based solely on the tax paid in the previous year, thus avoiding having to continuously update estimated tax calculations for changing circumstances.

> **Example**: Robert is a single individual whose tax liability for 20x4 was $15,000. He changes jobs in 20x5 and receives a 100% increase in salary. Even though Robert's income tax liability may more than double in 20x5, he can still pay only $15,000 in estimated taxes and avoid the section 6654 penalty. (If his adjusted gross income in 20x4 was over $150,000, he would be required to prepay $16,500 (110% of $15,000)). He does not need to go to an accountant during 20x5 to estimate his tax liability for the year.

A less frequently used defense to the estimated tax penalty is established in section 6654(d)(2). Under this method, the amount that must be prepaid is determined under a method that annualizes income. This method allows estimated tax payments to be made as income is earned. The annualized installment method works best for taxpayers who receive the greater portion of their income late in the year and, therefore, did not have a duty to prepay earlier in the year.

There exist two subjective defenses to the section 6654 penalty. Under section 6654(e)(3)(A), the IRS may waive the estimated tax penalty if it determines that the imposition of the penalty would "be against equity and good conscience" because of a casualty, disaster, or other unusual circumstances. This is not necessarily equivalent to reasonable cause. Requests for such a waiver must be submitted in writing and signed by the taxpayer.

Finally, a taxpayer may be eligible for a waiver of the penalty under section 6654(e)(3)(B) if in the tax year in which the payments came due, or in the preceding tax year, the taxpayer either retired after having attained the age of 62 or became dis-

---

13. Similar exceptions apply to corporations and are presented on Form 2220.

14. IRC § 6654(d)(1)(B)(ii). In the case of a taxpayer with adjusted gross income over $150,000 ($75,000 for married filing separately) in the preceding year, the required amount is 110% of the prior year's liability.

According to IRM 20.1.3.2.1.1(5), last year's tax, for these purposes, is determined exclusive of tax resulting from a deficiency or an amended return filed after the due date of the current year's return.

abled and the underpayment is due to reasonable cause and not willful neglect. There is no established procedure to raise these defenses, but a letter should suffice.

III. Failure to File Returns Timely

A. Due Dates, Extensions, and Substitutes for Return

As more fully discussed in Chapter 2, the Code establishes due dates for all returns that must be filed with the Service. If a taxpayer does not have the information needed to complete the return by its due date, an extension of time to file can be requested. Regulation § 1.6081-4 allows an automatic six-month extension without a signature, explanation or payment[15] for individuals who must file an individual income tax return if they submit a timely, completed application for extension on Form 4868 "Application for Automatic Extension of Time to File a U.S. Individual Income Tax Return."[16] Extensions are taken into account in determining whether the return filing is timely and whether assessing the late filing penalty is appropriate.[17]

Taxpayers who fail to file returns by the extended due date are at risk of being targeted by the IRS.[18] Once a nonfiling situation is identified, the Internal Revenue Manual directs the assigned agent to review the case for fraud.[19] If there appear to be indications of fraud, the agent is instructed to prepare a referral to the Criminal Investigation Division.[20]

If there are no apparent indications of fraud, the agent is instructed to contact the nonfiler to request that all delinquent returns be filed.[21] If the taxpayer still fails to

---

15. Prior to 2008, a taxpayer who sought an extension to file also had to make a reasonable estimate of the tax liability and pay the difference between what was estimated and what had already been paid in. Crocker v. Commissioner, 92 T.C. 899 (1989). While payment is no longer required to effect an extension to file, interest begins to accrue as of the original due date.

16. Tax returns for other taxpayers have varying extension periods pursuant to Regulations under IRC §6081. For example, partnerships get five months (Reg. § 1.6081-2) and C Corporations generally get six months (IRC § 6081(b)).

17. *See generally* IRM 20.1.2 (section discussing the failure to file penalty). An extension to file only extends the time to file. It does not extend the date for payment. Although an extension to file is automatic, an extension to pay is difficult to obtain. IRM 20.1.2.1.3.1(6). *See* Chapter 2.

18. In addition to whatever penalties may apply and regardless of reasonable cause to avoid the imposition of penalties, a late filed return may result in the taxpayer being denied a discharge of the tax debt for failing § 523(a)(1)(B)(i) of the Bankruptcy Code. *See* In re Mallo, 774 F.3d 1313 (10th Cir. 2014) (an untimely 1040 Form, filed after the IRS has assessed the tax liability, is not a tax "return" for purposes of the section of the Bankruptcy Code excepting from discharge any tax debt for which a return was not filed or given), *cert. denied*, 135 S. Ct. 2889 (2015); *see also* In re McCoy, 666 F.3d 924 (5th Cir. 2012).

19. IRM 4.12.1.4; 5.1.11.6.

20. IRM 5.19.2.5.4.2; 5.1.11.4.7; 5.1.11.6.

21. IRM 5.1.11.2.

do so, the Service will prepare a Substitute for Return (SFR) for the taxpayer from the information in its computer under the authority of section 6020(b).[22]

B. Failure to File Penalty (FTF)

When a return is not timely filed, the government automatically asserts a late filing penalty under section 6651(a)(1). The taxpayer can avoid the penalty if the failure to file timely was due to "reasonable cause and not willful neglect."[23] The amount of the late filing penalty (also referred to as the failure to file penalty and abbreviated by the IRS as FTF) is the product of three variables:

- The Penalty Rate,
- The Penalty Period, and
- The Net Amount of Tax Due.

The rate of the FTF penalty is generally 5% of the amount of tax due for each month or fraction of a month that the return is late, up to a maximum of 25%.[24] The maximum rate is reached after only four months and one day. If the failure to file is fraudulent, the penalty is increased to 15% per month, up to a maximum of 75%.[25] Since one of the variables is the net amount of tax due, if a taxpayer does not owe anything or is due a refund, there can be no penalty.

The FTF penalty accrues from the due date of the tax return to the date the IRS actually *receives* the return. If an extension to file is granted, the extended due date becomes the date on which the penalty begins to accrue.[26] If the return is received after the due date or the extended due date but mailed before it, section 7502 applies. However, if the return is mailed after the due date, the date that the return actually reaches the Service is the receipt date. *See* Chapter 2. The FTF penalty is imposed based on the number of months, including any fraction of a month, during which the failure to file continues.

---

22. IRM 4.12.1.8.4. When the IRS prepares SFRs, it is likely that the tax liability will be greater than what it would have been if the taxpayer filed the return. This is so because the IRS generally prepares SFRs in a manner that tends to artificially increase the tax liability. For example, the IRS includes as income the gross proceeds of a sale rather than the gain after reduction for basis, allows the taxpayer only one exemption and the standard deduction rather than itemizing deductions, and utilizes a filing status of married filing separately if the taxpayer is married rather than married filing jointly. *See, e.g.*, Meyer v. Commissioner, T.C. Memo. 2013-268.

23. IRC § 6651(a)(1); *see also* IRM 20.1.2.1.4.1.

24. Where a tax return showing a balance due is more than sixty days late, taking into account any extensions of time to file, the minimum failure to file penalty is not less than the lesser of $205 or 100% of the net tax required to be shown on the return, unless the failure is due to reasonable cause and not willful neglect. IRC § 6651(a)(1); IRM 20.1.2.2.7.4. The minimum penalty will be indexed for inflation for returns filed after 12/31/14 and increase in $5.00 increments. "Tax Increase and Prevention Act of 2014, Pub. L. no 113-295, section 108, 128 Stat. 4010 (Jan. 4, 2014).

25. IRC § 6651(f).

26. *See* IRM 20.1.2.1.3.1.1 (rules where extensions were not granted or were voided).

Example: Assume Allison got a valid extension to October 15, 20x4, relative to her 20x3 tax return. She mails the return on November 14, 20x4, and the IRS receives it on November 17, 20x4. The return is two months late (October 16–November 15 is one month and November 16–17 is a second month) as the valid extension period is given full weight in determining the number of months the return is late.

The FTF penalty is calculated as a percentage of "net amount due,"[27] which is the amount of tax required to be shown on the return, reduced by any tax payments made, or credits allowed, *on or before* the prescribed due date for payment of the tax.[28] That date will nearly always be the statutorily prescribed due date for the return. In this regard, extensions to file are disregarded. Thus, payments made after the due date, generally April 15th for Form 1040, do not reduce the amount of the penalty. Net operating losses or credit carrybacks similarly do not reduce the base upon which the penalty is computed.

Example: Assume the facts of the previous example involving Allison. Assume further that (i) her tax liability for the 20x3 tax year is $27,000, (ii) her withholding was $10,000, (iii) she paid $5,000 with the extension, and (iv) she paid the $12,000 balance when she filed the return on November 17, 20x4. Her net amount due would be $12,000, which represents the tax shown on the return ($27,000) less payments made on or before April 15 ($15,000). As she is deemed to be two months late, the penalty is $1,200.

The "tax required to be shown on the return" includes not only the tax shown as due on the return as filed but also tax later determined to be due as the result of an examination.

Example: Assume in the previous examples that the IRS examines Allison's return one year later. Allison and the IRS agree that Allison's correct tax should have been $47,000, thus giving rise to a tax deficiency of $20,000. A penalty of $2,000 ($20,000 times 10%,) will be assessed along with the deficiency in tax. Thus, in total, Allison's late filing penalty is $3,200 ($1,200 + $2,000, or, put another way, 10% x $32,000 [the difference between the $47,000 tax required to be shown on the return and the $15,000 tax paid on or before the due date]).

C. Fraudulent Failure to File

Section 6651(f) provides for an increased civil penalty (15% per month, up to 75%) if the failure to file a return is fraudulent.[29] This penalty is usually imposed

---

27. *See* IRC § 6651(b) (heading).

28. IRC § 6651(b)(1).

29. Both the fraudulent failure to file penalty and the 75% accuracy-related fraud penalty under section 6663 can apply if the taxpayer originally failed to file for fraudulent reasons but, when filed, did so fraudulently. Of course, the bases on which the penalties would be calculated are different; the fraudulent failure to file is based on the number of months late whereas the fraud penalty under section 6663 is based strictly on the amount of the underpayment.

when no return is filed. By contrast, when a return is filed but fraudulently so, the civil fraud penalty of section 6663 applies.

Fraudulent failure to file generally involves evidence of intentional wrongdoing on the part of the taxpayer with the specific purpose of evading a tax known, or believed, to be owed. The IRS bears the burden of proving fraud by clear and convincing evidence.[30] If the IRS is unable to sustain its burden of proof on the fraud issue, the basic failure to file penalty, 5% a month, up to a maximum of 25%, may still be imposed.

The IRS considers the following factors, among others, to be indicators of fraud:

- History of non-filing or late filing, and an apparent ability to pay;
- Repeated contacts by the Service;
- Knowledge of the filing requirements (i.e., advanced education, business (especially tax) experience, record of previous filing, etc.);
- Experience of the taxpayer in tax matters such as a law professor, CPA, or tax attorney;
- Failure to reveal or attempts to conceal assets;
- Age, health, and occupation of the taxpayer;
- Substantial tax liability after withholding credits and estimated tax payments;
- Large number of cash transactions, payment of personal and business expenses in cash when cash payment is unusual, and/or the cashing (as opposed to the deposit) of business receipts;
- Indications of significant income per Information Return Processing documents (*i.e.*, substantial interest and dividends earned, investments in IRA accounts, stock and bond transactions, or high mortgage interest paid);
- Refusal or inability to explain the failure to file; and
- Prior history of criminal tax prosecutions for Title 26 violations.[31]

IV. Failure to Pay Tax Timely (FTP)

Section 6151 establishes the due dates for paying tax. Generally, it is the same as the date for filing the associated return. Extensions to pay under section 6161 may be requested for up to six months but, in the case of income taxes, they are difficult to secure. In order to get an extension to pay, Regulation section 1.6161-1(b) requires the taxpayer to establish that paying timely would create an undue hardship. An extension of time to pay the tax, however, does not affect the accruing of interest, which runs from the original due date.[32]

30. IRC § 7454.
31. IRM 25.1.7.2(1). For an expanded list of indicators of fraud, see IRM 25.1.2.3.
32. IRC § 6601(b)(1).

If a taxpayer does not pay taxes by the due date, as extended, a failure to pay (FTP) penalty will be imposed. There are two distinct FTP penalties: (1) the failure to pay the tax shown as due on the return (section 6651(a)(2)) and (2) the failure to pay an assessed deficiency (section 6651(a)(3)).[33]

A. Failure to Pay the Tax Shown as Due on the Return

While the estimated tax payment obligation in section 6654 requires taxpayers to prepay their tax liabilities, section 6651(a)(2) imposes a penalty on those who fail to pay the balance shown as due on the return by the due date, unless the failure is due to reasonable cause and not willful neglect. The late payment penalty is generally 0.5% (1/2%) of the unpaid tax for each month, or fraction thereof, that the payment is late, up to a maximum of 25% (fifty months).

To encourage taxpayers to address their obligation to pay, the penalty is reduced to 0.25% (1/4%) per month during periods in which the taxpayer is making payments pursuant to a section 6159 installment agreement.[34] Conversely, the penalty rate increases from 1/2% to 1% during certain "advanced" collection proceedings, *i.e.*, on the earlier of (i) the eleventh day after a notice of intent to levy is issued under section 6331(d), or (ii) the date notice and demand for immediate payment is given on a jeopardy assessment under section 6331(a).[35]

This penalty applies to all individual, corporate, trust, and estate income tax returns, employment tax returns, estate and gift tax returns, and certain excise tax returns. A substitute for return (SFR) completed by the IRS is treated as a "real" return for purposes of determining the failure to pay penalties.[36]

---

33. When a taxpayer has filed a petition in bankruptcy, section 6658 may provide relief from late payment penalties. Section 6658(a) provides, in part, that "[n]o addition to the tax shall be made under section 6651, 6654, or 6655 for failure to make timely payment of tax with respect to a period during which a case is pending under title 11 of the United States Code...." Section 6658 applies to tax arising before the taxpayer files a bankruptcy petition if (l) the petition was filed before the due date of the return or (2) the date for making the addition to the tax occurs on or after the day on which the petition was filed. The term "pending" is not defined in section 6658.

In Rev. Rul. 2005-9, 2005-1 C.B. 470, the IRS sought to clarify when a bankruptcy case is pending. A bankruptcy case is commenced by filing a petition with the bankruptcy court pursuant to sections 301 through 304 of the Bankruptcy Code. A case is "pending" for purposes of section 6658 after the debtor files a petition with the bankruptcy court. A bankruptcy case is no longer pending for purposes of section 6658 when it is closed or dismissed. *See* Carey v. Saffold, 536 U.S. 214, 219–20 (2002) (consulting Webster's Third International Dictionary for the ordinary meaning of the word "pending," the Court determined that a state court application for collateral review remains pending "until the application has achieved final resolution").

34. IRC § 6651(h); IRM 20.1.2.2.8.1.2; SCA 200135025 (July 24, 2001) (reduction in rate takes place when the installment agreement is accepted by the IRS, not when it is submitted by the taxpayer).

35. IRC § 6651(d). Once the penalty rate is increased, it applies for all subsequent months for that particular assessment, subject to the same maximum of 25%.

36. However, for the penalty to apply, the substitute for return must be properly prepared and executed (by the Secretary). *E.g.* Cabirac v. Commissioner, 120 T.C. 163 (2003). The requisite procedures are described in Reg. § 301.6020-1(b); Chief Counsel Notice CC-2007-005 (Feb. 4, 2007).

The failure to pay penalty is a percentage of the amount shown as tax on the return after subtracting amounts that have been withheld, estimated tax payments, partial payments, and other applicable credits. For purposes of computing the late payment penalty for any month, the tax liability is reduced by any payments of tax made on or before the beginning of each month.

The failure to pay penalty runs for the number of months, or part thereof, from the payment's due date through the date on which the IRS receives payment. The due date of a tax payment is generally the date on which the return is statutorily required to be filed, determined with regard to extensions of time *to pay*, but without regard of extension of time *to file*. A "month" is measured from the date in a calendar month to the date numerically corresponding to it in the succeeding calendar month.[37]

B. Failure to Pay Tax Deficiency

Recall that when the IRS examines a taxpayer's return and determines a deficiency, that amount is not assessed until the deficiency procedures have run their course. Once the deficiency is assessed, the IRS issues a notice and demand for payment. If the additional amount owed is not paid within twenty-one days of notice and demand (ten days in the case of tax liabilities over $100,000), section 6651(a)(3) imposes the failure to pay penalty on the deficiency amount 0.5% (½%) for each month or fraction thereof the amount outstanding until the tax is paid.

With minor variations discussed below, the section 6651(a)(3) failure to pay penalty is calculated in the same manner as the section 6651(a)(2) penalty. And like the other failure to timely act penalties, the section 6651(a)(3) penalty does not apply if the taxpayer shows that the failure was due to reasonable cause and not willful neglect. The total section 6651(a)(3) penalty cannot exceed 25%. The section 6651(a)(3) penalty is not included in a notice of deficiency. The IRS may proceed to collection if the penalty is not paid after notice and demand.[38]

The penalty imposed is computed based on the assessed but unpaid amount stated in the notice, less the amount of any partial payments made on the deficiency. Thus, the monthly penalty is computed on the portion of the assessment that remains unpaid as of the beginning of each month.

C. Combined Late Filing and Late Payment Penalties

Taxpayers who file late also often pay late. If the section 6651(a)(1) failure to file penalty and the section 6651(a)(2) failure to pay penalty apply for the same month,

---

37. Since, in calculating a late payment penalty, the payment is per se late and has passed "the last day ... for performing [an] act," the "timely mailed is timely paid" rule of section 7502 and the weekend/holiday rule of section 7503 do not affect the determination of the number of months a payment is late. Reg. §§ 301.6651-1(b)(3), 301.7502-1(a).

38. Burke v. Commissioner, T.C. Memo. 2009-282.

or fraction of a month, the amount of the failure to file penalty is reduced by the amount of the failure to pay penalty for that month.[39]

For this purpose, it is important to note that the base of the failure to file penalty is different than the base for the failure to pay penalty. The base for the failure to file penalty is the correct amount of the tax liability (*i.e.*, "the amount required to be shown as tax on [the] return") reduced by the portion of the tax "paid on or before the date prescribed for payment ...."[40] Because the failure to file penalty is based on "the amount *required to be shown* as tax on [the] return," the amount of the penalty will be increased in the event that the return understated the actual tax liability. Also, note that the base is not reduced by any amount that is paid late. Thus, late payment, even of the entire amount of the tax "required to be shown," will not stop the accrual of the penalty unless the return is filed at that time.

The base for the failure to pay penalty is determined monthly and is the amount of the tax actually shown on the return, reduced by "the tax which is paid on or before the beginning of [the] month."[41] In this case, late payments made before filing the late return will reduce both the late payment penalty and the offset of the failure to file penalty. Because the base of the failure to pay penalty, the amount shown on the return reduced by the amount paid, cannot exceed the amount shown on the return, subsequently determined deficiencies will not increase the base for the penalty. However, the section 6651(a)(3) penalty applies when an assessment is not paid within 21 days from the date of the IRS's notice of tax due and demand for payment.

V. The Reasonable Cause Defense

The late filing and late payment penalties are avoided if the taxpayer establishes that there was reasonable cause for the lateness and that it was not due to willful neglect. Reasonable cause is defined as an inability to file or to pay, which arises despite one's exercise of ordinary business care and prudence that is due to circumstances beyond the control of the taxpayer.[42] Willful neglect is defined as a conscious, intentional failure to do what is required or a reckless indifference to the requirement. Since the requirement for successfully arguing reasonable cause tends to encompass a concurrent showing of the absence of willful neglect, courts and the IRS generally discuss both exceptions under the heading of "reasonable cause" alone. A taxpayer wishing to assert the reasonable cause defense as to section 6651 penalties must submit to the IRS a written statement, under penalties of perjury, explaining why the taxpayer has reasonable cause for the

39. IRC § 6651(c)(1).

40. IRC § 6651(a)(1), (b)(1).

41. IRC § 6651(a)(2), (b)(2).

42. Reg. § 301.6651-1(c); IRM 20.1.1.3.2; *see also* Estate of Cederloff v. United States, 2010 WL 3548901 (D. Md. 2010) (holding that reasonable cause was lacking for filing an estate tax return a year after the extended filing deadline and rejecting the defense of reliance on a tax advisor).

delinquency.[43] "Failure to submit such a written statement to the IRS precludes a [taxpayer] from making a 'reasonable cause' showing for the first time in federal court."[44]

Reasonable cause determinations are based on the facts and circumstances of each case. The burden of proving reasonable cause is on the taxpayer, but in a court proceeding the IRS has the burden of producing evidence (known as the "burden of production") that it is appropriate to apply the penalty to the taxpayer in the first place.[45] In making a determination of whether there is reasonable cause, the IRS considers the following, among other factors:[46]

- Whether the taxpayer's reasons address the penalty imposed;
- The taxpayer's payment and penalty history;
- The length of time between the event cited as a reason for noncompliance and the subsequent compliance;
- Whether the event that caused the taxpayer's noncompliance could have reasonably been anticipated; and
- Whether the taxpayer exercised ordinary business care and prudence to meet the requirement as soon as possible, even if late.

A. Situations That Might, Depending on the Circumstances, Qualify as Reasonable Cause

1. Reliance on a Tax Advisor or Other Third Person

Normally, a taxpayer cannot shift blame for his or her late filing or payment to another, such as to one's tax advisor, employee, or spouse. Everyone is deemed to know of his or her obligation to file and pay and is expected to learn when these obligations are due. Case law, however, distinguishes between those situations where a tax advisor or third person has the ministerial duty to file or pay on the taxpayer's behalf, and those situations where a tax advisor gave substantive advice regarding the requirements.[47] Reasonable cause may exist in the latter situation.

---

43. Reg. §301.6651-1(c)(1).

44. Brown v. United States, 43 Fed. Cl. 463, 467 (1999) (quoted by Kuretski v. Commissioner, 755 F.3d 929 (D.C. Cir. 2014)).

45. IRC §7491(c).

46. Reg. §301.6651-1(c); IRM 20.1.1.3.2.2.

47. *E.g.*, United States v. Boyle, 469 U.S. 241 (1985). The teaching of *Boyle* continues to be parsed and massaged. *E.g.*, Estate of Thouron v. United States, 752 F.3d 311 (3d Cir. 2014) (describing three categories of late-filing and late-payment cases); Baccei v. United States, 632 F.3d 1140, 1148–49 (9th Cir. 2011) (also rejecting an exigencies argument for reasonable cause because it was not timely raised and holding that *Boyle* applies to late-payment as well as to late-filing cases); Knappe v. United States, 713 F.3d 1164 (9th Cir. 2013) (rejecting the defense); Estate of La Meres v. Commissioner, 98 T.C. 294 (1992) (upholding the defense). For a particularly egregious case in which reasonable cause was denied, see *Specht v. United States*, 2015 WL 74539 (S.D. Ohio 2015) (unbeknownst to executor, attorney, who had previously prepared the decedent's will and had more than 50 years' experience in estate planning, was privately battling brain cancer and either intentionally or unintentionally deceived executor with regard to the status of an extension for the filing of the estate's tax returns and did not file return timely).

2. Death, Serious Illness, or Unavoidable Absence

The death, serious illness, or unavoidable absence of the taxpayer, or the death or serious illness of a member of the taxpayer's family, may constitute reasonable cause.[48] In the case of an entity, the incapacity must relate either to the individual having the sole authority to take the action required of the entity, or to a member of that individual's family.

In making the determination as to whether an illness constitutes reasonable cause, courts focus on the severity and duration of the illness. The incapacity must be so severe that the taxpayer could not function during the period, and so sudden that the taxpayer could not reasonably make plans for handling his or her financial affairs during the illness. Mental illness, drug or alcohol dependency, battered spouse situations, issues of old age, infirmity, and mental incapacity may also provide a basis for reasonable cause.

Though one may have reasonable cause for late action because of death or illness for some period, the waiver does not apply forever. At some point, the IRS will expect the taxpayer to file or pay. Too great a delay might vitiate the earlier reasonable cause. Where the taxpayer continues to work or take care of other normal business matters during his or her alleged incapacity, reasonable cause generally does not exist.[49]

3. Erroneous Advice from the IRS

Pursuant to Regulation section 301.6404-3, the IRS must abate the portion of any penalty attributable to *written* erroneous advice furnished to the taxpayer by an IRS employee if: (1) the advice is reasonably relied on by the taxpayer; (2) the advice is issued in response to a specific written request for advice by the taxpayer; and (3) the taxpayer provided adequate and accurate information in connection with the request. Reasonable reliance does not continue after the taxpayer is put on notice that the prior written advice no longer represents the IRS's position.

The IRS may abate a penalty for reasonable cause where the taxpayer relies on *oral* advice from an IRS employee.[50] To claim the waiver, the taxpayer must show that the IRS was supplied with complete and accurate information and that he or she exercised ordinary business care and prudence in relying on the IRS's advice. Meeting this burden of proof may be extremely difficult relative to oral advice, unless the taxpayer kept a written record of all dealings with the IRS, including meetings, telephone calls, correspondence, and the name of the IRS representative involved.

4. Fire, Casualty, Natural Disaster, or Other Disturbance

A fire, casualty, natural disaster, or other disturbance may constitute reasonable cause if the taxpayer exercised ordinary business care and prudence but was unable

48. IRM 20.1.1.3.2.2.1.

49. Barber v. Commissioner, T.C. Memo. 1997-206.

50. IRM 20.1.1.3.2.2.5, 20.1.1.3.3.4.1, 20.1.1.3.3.4.2.

to comply with tax obligations due to circumstances beyond his or her control.[51] Good recordkeeping and contemporaneously filed claims with the police and insurance company help establish the truth of the defense. In the case of a significant disaster affecting numerous taxpayers, the IRS generally provides special guidance for penalty relief. In addition, unconnected with natural disasters, the IRS sometimes grants administrative relief as to late filing/late payment penalties or accuracy-related penalties.[52]

5. Service in a Combat Zone

An individual serving in the U.S. Armed Forces, or in support thereof, in an area designated by the President as a "combat zone" has until 180 days after the "period of combatant activities" or period of continuous qualified hospitalization attributable to an injury received while serving in such combat zone, to file a return and pay the tax.[53] This extension also applies to the taxpayer's spouse.

6. First Time Abatement

The Internal Revenue Manual provides an option for penalty relief for the failure to file and failure to pay penalties if the following are true for the taxpayer:[54]

- Has not previously been required to file a return or has no prior penalties (except the estimated tax penalty) for the preceding 3 years on the same tax, and
- Has filed, or filed a valid extension for, all currently required returns and paid, or arranged to pay, any tax due.

7. Automatic Reasonable Cause for Late Payment if Payment within 90% of Tax Liability

Under Regulation section 301.6651-1(c)(3), if there is an extension of time to file, and payment of the tax balance due is made with a timely filed extended return, the taxpayer is deemed to have acted reasonably if the amount shown as due on the filed return is less than 10% of the taxpayer's total tax liability. If the balance due is more than 10% of the total tax or if it is not paid with the return, the penalty applies to the total balance due from the original due date.[55]

> Example (1): Meg obtained an automatic extension of time to file her 20x1 tax return from April 15, 20x2, until October 15, 20x2. She files her return on October 9, 20x2, reflecting a tax liability of $30,000 and a credit for with-

---

51. IRM 20.1.1.3.2.2.2.

52. *E.g.*, IR-2014-66 (May 22, 2014) (pilot program to alleviate penalties on certain small businesses for not filing reporting documents as to non-ERISA retirement plans); IR 2012-31 (Mar. 7, 2012) (as part of Fresh Start initiative, providing grace period as to failure-to-pay penalties of certain wage earners and self-employed persons).

53. IRC § 7508. Filing an extension under sections 7508 or 7508A will not change the date on which the return is "last due, including extensions" for purposes of the Bankruptcy Code or the ordering rules for the discharge of the tax in bankruptcy proceedings. Rev. Rul. 2007-59, 2007-2 C.B. 582.

54. IRM 20.1.1.3.6.1.

55. Reg. § 301.6651-1(c)(3).

holding of $20,000. She pays the $10,000 balance due when she files. Meg is liable for a late payment penalty of $200 (0.5% times 4 months times $10,000). Even though Meg had a four-month extension of time to file her return, she did not have an extension of time to pay.

Example (2): Assume in example (1) above, Meg paid $8,000 on April 15, 20x2, when the automatic extension form was filed. When she files her return on October 9, 20x2, she pays the additional balance due of $2,000. Meg qualifies for the reasonable cause safe harbor since 90% of the liability was paid by the due date.

B. Situations That Generally Do Not Qualify as Reasonable Cause

1. Mistake or Forgetfulness

A taxpayer's or a subordinate's mistake as to the proper treatment of a particular item[56] generally does not demonstrate ordinary business care and prudence and therefore is not a basis of reasonable cause. The same is true for one's forgetfulness[57] or carelessness. Absent affirmative reliance on erroneous advice of counsel, a good faith but mistaken belief will not relieve a taxpayer from the penalty.

2. Time and Business Pressures

The taxpayer's heavy workload does not constitute reasonable cause for failure to perform a required act. People exercising ordinary business care and prudence do not take on assignments that prohibit them from fulfilling their legal obligations within prescribed times. Similarly, the time pressure of a taxpayer's agent (e.g., a return preparer) cannot excuse a taxpayer's failure to file a return or pay timely.

3. Records Unavailable

Unavailability of records is generally not considered reasonable cause for a taxpayer's failure to file a return. Rather, the taxpayer must estimate the tax liability based on the best information available and, where necessary, obtain an extension of time to file. However, if a proper return cannot be filed because information remains unavailable despite ordinary business care and prudence by the taxpayer, there is reasonable cause. For example, in *Dejoy v. Commissioner*,[58] the court held there was reasonable cause where the principals in an accounting firm that provided services to the taxpayer ceased practice and disappeared, taking many of the taxpayer's business and financial records with them.

---

56. IRM 20.1.1.3.2.2.4.
57. IRM 20.1.1.3.2.2.7.
58. T.C. Memo. 2000-162. *See also* IRM 20.1.1.3.2.2.3.

4. Ignorance of the Law

Ignorance of the law, in and of itself, does not constitute reasonable cause.[59] This includes, for example, a taxpayer's erroneous belief (not based on professional advice) that no return is required, a lack of knowledge as to the correct due date, or an erroneous belief that the proceeds of a transaction were not taxable. Ordinary business care and prudence requires that all taxpayers be aware of their tax obligations.

On the other hand, ignorance of the law in conjunction with other facts and circumstances, such as one's limited education or lack of experience with taxes and penalties, may support a claim of reasonable cause. For example, where the IRS has not provided any guidance as to difficult and complex issues, reasonable cause may exist for a position taken in good faith. Similarly, a taxpayer may have reasonable cause if there is a recent change in the tax law or forms of which the taxpayer could not reasonably be expected to know.

5. Constitutional Objections and Religious Beliefs

Neither constitutional objections nor religious beliefs are valid reasons for failing to file a return or failing to pay the required tax. The Fifth Amendment privilege against self-incrimination extends only to a taxpayer's refusal to answer specific questions on the return and does not constitute reasonable cause sufficient to justify a taxpayer's complete refusal to act at all. Presenting only these kinds of arguments in a court may result in imposition of a frivolous argument penalty under section 6673.[60]

6. Lack of Funds

A claim of insufficient funds is never reasonable cause for failing *to file* a return. Lack of funds, however, may be an acceptable reason for failure to pay a tax if the taxpayer can demonstrate that, despite the exercise of ordinary business care and prudence, the taxpayer either lacked the funds to pay the tax or would experience an "undue hardship" if paid on time.[61]

In determining whether a taxpayer lacked funds, all of the facts and circumstances of the taxpayer's financial situation are considered, including the amount and nature of one's expenditures in light of assets, the funds one could reasonably expect to receive, and one's investment practices.[62] Insolvency before the tax payment date, leading

---

59. IRM 20.1.1.3.2.2.6.

60. Hawkins v. Commissioner, T.C. Memo. 2008-168.

61. *See* Reg. § 301.6651-1(c); IRM 20.1.1.3.3.3. *Compare* Fran Corp. v. United States, 164 F.3d 814 (2d Cir. 1999) (financial difficulties as a defense is a facts and circumstances determination in all late payment situations), *with* Brewery, Inc. v. United States, 33 F.3d 589 (6th Cir. 1994) (financial difficulties may be a reason for not paying income taxes timely but it is never a "reasonable cause" with respect to depositing employment taxes).

62. *See* In re Arthur 's Indus. Maint., Inc., 1992 WL 132563 (Bankr. W.D. Va. 1992), *aff'd*, 1993 WL 79206 (W.D. Va Jan. 7, 1993).

to a petition in bankruptcy, is significant evidence of an inability to pay. Inability to pay due to the embezzlement by employees, however, indicates a lack of ordinary business care and prudence.[63] A taxpayer who cannot claim "lack of funds" may still qualify for the reasonable cause exception for late payment if he or she would suffer "undue hardship" if the tax is paid when due.[64]

VI. How and When to Dispute "Late" Penalties

A. Some Filing and Payment Penalties May Be Automatically Assessed and Others Are Entitled to Deficiency Procedures

When a taxpayer files a return or makes a payment, sections 6201(a)(1) and 6213(b)(4) authorize the IRS to automatically assess the tax shown on the return or the amount paid, respectively. If the return or payment of tax shown on the return is late, the IRS may automatically (summarily) assess appropriate penalties. Since the penalties are computed based on the information on the self-assessing return, they too are treated as self-assessing.[65] As a result, taxpayers normally learn that the IRS assessed such a penalty when they receive a notice and demand for its payment.[66]

By contrast, if the IRS determines a deficiency in tax, a late filing penalty attributable to, and calculated as a percentage of, the deficiency will be added to the deficiency amount. It cannot be assessed automatically because the amount is not known until a deficiency is finally determined. The penalty, as part of the overall deficiency, is entitled to the same deficiency procedures as the underlying tax.[67]

1. General

A taxpayer believing that a good reason for filing or paying late exists can seek to avoid the automatically assessed portion of the penalty by writing an explanation of the circumstances either when filing the return, or after the IRS sends a notice of the assessment of the penalty. If the Service persists in assessing the penalty despite the explanation, the taxpayer may seek administrative review of the determination by filing a protest with the Appeals Office. This can be done either before or after paying the assessment.[68]

If the taxpayer and the Appeals Office cannot reach a settlement, the taxpayer may seek judicial review. If the penalty was automatically assessed, review is with the Dis-

63. Conklin Bros. of Santa Rosa, Inc. v. United States, 986 F.2d 315 (9th Cir. 1993).

64. See Reg. § 1.6161-1(b) discussing "undue hardship" in the context of getting an extension of time to pay.

65. IRC § 6665(b).

66. *See* IRM 20.1.1.4.2.

67. IRC § 6665(b)(1); IRM 20.1.1.4.2.

68. Except to the extent taxpayers are entitled to the Collection Due Process (CDP) procedures in sections 6320 and 6330, there is no statutory right to an administrative hearing or judicial review before the self-assessing variety of late filing or late payment penalties must be paid.

trict Court or Court of Federal Claims. If the penalty was part of a deficiency, review is available in all courts hearing tax matters.[69]

> **Example (1)**: Rochelle files her 20x1 tax return on June 23, 20x2, after she had failed to request an extension. The return reflects a tax liability of $50,000, the entire amount of which is paid with the return. Since both the return and the payment are treated as being three months late (from April 15, 20x2), the combined penalties will be $7,500.[70] The penalties will be assessed summarily, unless a letter is sent with the return explaining the reason for the lateness and the IRS accepts the explanation. Interest for the period April 15, 20x2 to June 23, 20x2 will also be assessed.[71]
>
> If no letter of explanation accompanies the return or the IRS did not accept the position advanced, the IRS will send Rochelle a notice of the assessment and a demand for payment. As there is no tax due, the notice would be only for the penalties in the amount of $7,500 (5% x $50,000 x three months) and interest. At this point, Rochelle may request waiver (or abatement) of the penalties on the basis of reasonable cause or, if applicable, first time offense. If the IRS denies the request, Rochelle can protest the determination to the Appeals Office. If the appeal is denied, her principal avenue for challenging the assessment in court is to pay the full amount, file a claim for refund (Form 843), and then file a complaint in District Court or the Court of Federal Claims.
>
> **Example (2)**: Some time after Rochelle files her 20x1 return, the IRS examines it. In a notice of deficiency, the IRS makes a variety of adjustments, resulting in a deficiency in tax of $80,000. Due to the fact that the return was filed three months late, the notice of deficiency would include a deficiency associated with the penalties of $12,000 (15% of $80,000—the [additional] amount required to be shown as tax on [the] return). Being deficiencies, both the $80,000 tax and the $12,000 penalty are entitled to pre-assessment/pre-payment administrative review and Tax Court review. If Rochelle convinces the IRS or the Tax Court of the reasonableness of the late filing and the late payment, not only will she not owe the $12,000 penalty attributable to the deficiency, but she is also entitled to a refund of the $7,500 she paid earlier for the penalties assessed on her 20x1 return.

2. What to Include in the Presentation

The late filing and late payment penalties can be avoided only upon a showing that the lateness for the filing or payment was due to reasonable cause and not due

69. In addition to the more traditional methods for presenting a "reasonable cause" defense, discussed in the text, one may (i) file an offer in compromise based on doubt as to liability, (ii) request a Collection Due Process hearing, or (iii) submit an Application for a Taxpayer Assistance Order.

70. Since the period of the late filing and the late payment overlap, the combined penalties are 5% per month ([5% – .5%] + .5%). IRC § 6651(c).

71. Interest runs on the penalty amount from the date the return was due until the date the IRS receives payment. IRC § 6601.

to willful neglect. Therefore, the presentation should contain evidence establishing that the taxpayer exercised ordinary business care and prudence yet was still unable to meet his obligation through no fault of his own. By requiring the penalty to be imposed "unless" the failure is due to reasonable cause, the statute precludes any partial waiver of the penalty. The IRS must either waive or impose the penalty in full. Despite this, the Appeals Office can settle a penalty for any amount if there are hazards to the government that would occur by litigating the issue.

A request for non-assertion or abatement should be accompanied by supporting documentary evidence and legal authority whenever possible. This might include death certificates, doctor's statements, insurance statements, police or fire reports, etc. The IRS may request additional information if it is needed to make a determination.

3. Burden of Proof and Burden of Production in Court Proceedings

If settlement with the IRS is not possible and the matter has to be tried, section 7491(c) applies and creates a labyrinth with respect to which party has the various burdens.[72] Section 7491(c) provides:

> Notwithstanding any other provision of this title, the Secretary shall have the burden of production in any court proceeding with respect to the liability of any individual for any penalty, addition to tax, or additional amount imposed by this title.

If the taxpayer assigns error to the Commissioner's penalty determination in the petition, the challenge generally will succeed unless the Commissioner produces evidence that the penalty is appropriate. If the taxpayer does not challenge a penalty by assigning error to it (and is, therefore, deemed to concede the penalty), the Commissioner need not plead the penalty and has no obligation under section 7491(c) to produce evidence that the penalty is appropriate.[73]

Assuming the penalty determination is put in issue by the taxpayer, section 7491(c) requires the Commissioner to produce evidence that it is appropriate to impose the relevant penalty, addition to tax, or additional amount (collectively, penalty). However, the Commissioner is not required to introduce evidence regarding lack of reasonable cause, substantial authority, or similar provisions. The conference report explains the respective obligations of the Commissioner and a taxpayer under section 7491(c) as follows:

> Further, the provision provides that, in any court proceeding, the Secretary must initially come forward with evidence that it is appropriate to apply a particular penalty to the taxpayer before the court can impose the penalty. This provision is not intended to require the Secretary to introduce evidence of elements such as reasonable cause or substantial authority. Rather, the

---

72. *See* Wheeler v. Commissioner, 127 T.C. 200 (2006), *aff'd*, 521 F.3d 1289 (10th Cir. 2008).

73. Swain v. Commissioner, 118 T.C. 358 (2002) (a taxpayer who fails to assign error to a penalty is deemed under Tax Court Rule 34(b)(4) to have conceded the penalty, notwithstanding that the Commissioner failed to produce evidence that the imposition of the penalty is appropriate).

> Secretary must come forward initially with evidence regarding the appropriateness of applying a particular penalty to the taxpayer; if the taxpayer believes that, because of reasonable cause, substantial authority, or a similar provision, it is inappropriate to impose the penalty, it is the taxpayer's responsibility (and not the Secretary's obligation) to raise those issues.[74]

VII. Conclusion

The penalties discussed in this part of the chapter pertain to when returns or taxes are not filed or paid in a manner prescribed by the Code. The penalties discussed in the next part of the chapter concern situations where the return contains errors in the treatment of items necessary to the calculation of taxable income.

Problem — Part A

1. Tom filed his federal income tax return for 20x4 on November 29, 20x5. He had not applied for an extension of time to file. He was married but filed separately from his spouse. The return showed adjusted gross income of $250,000 and a tax liability of $70,000. His employer had withheld $35,000 in federal income tax from his compensation. His return for 20x3 had reflected a tax liability of $50,000, and an overpayment of $5,000, which he had directed be applied to his 20x4 tax liability. He had also timely paid estimated tax for 20x4 of $10,000, in four equal quarterly installments of $2,500 each. He paid the balance of the tax due for 20x4 with his return.

(a) Will Tom owe additions to tax for 20x4 for either late filing or late payment, or both?

(b) If so, how much will the additions be?

(c) Is Tom liable for an addition to tax for underpayment of estimated tax?

2. Now assume that Tom had filed an application for extension of time to file his 20x4 return until October 15, 20x5.

(a) Will he owe additions to tax for 20x4 for either late filing or late payment, or both?

(b) If so, how much will the additions be?

3. Now assume that the Internal Revenue Service conducted an examination of Tom's 20x4 return. The Revenue Agent proposed disallowing the deductions taken by Tom for business expenses of $20,000 and for charitable contributions of $10,000, resulting in additional tax of $7,500. Tom agreed with the Agent. How would this affect your answers to questions 1(a), (b) and (c)?

4. Now assume the following facts. How would each affect your opinions as to whether the additions apply?

---

74. H. Conf. Rpt. 105-599 at 241, 1998-3 C.B. at 995.

(a) Tom was generally in good health, but caught the flu shortly before the return was due.

(b) A hurricane unexpectedly came through his area shortly before the return was due. The hurricane caused substantial damage to Tom's property.

(c) Tom's tax advisor had failed to advise him of the correct due date for the return and prepayment requirements.

(d) His tax advisor had given him incorrect advice with respect to the deductibility of the business expenses and the charitable contributions.

(e) Tom became very busy with work at about the time the return was due.

(f) This is the first time in 20 years that Tom was filing his income tax return late.

5. If you believe that one or more of the facts set forth in problems 4(a)–(f) above qualify for avoidance of the additions to tax, what procedure should Tom follow?

Part B: Accuracy-Related and Fraud Penalties

IRC: §§ 6404(f), (g); 6662; 6663; 6664(a)–(c); 6665; 6751; 7491(c)

Regs.: §§ 1.6662-1; -2(a)–(c); -4 (all except (c), (g)); 1.6664-1, -2(a)–(c)(1)(3)(i)–(iii), -3(a), (b), -4(a), (b)(1), (c)(1), (2), (h)

Case: Addington v. Commissioner, 205 F.3d 54 (2d Cir. 2000) (opinion by Judge Sotomayor) (only read portion of opinion discussing negligence penalty)

Rulings: Rev. Proc. 2014-15

Forms: 8275, 8275R

I. Introduction

Many taxpayers facing the prospect of proposed adjustments to taxable income must also confront the imposition of a group of penalties codified in sections 6662–6664 that are commonly known as the "accuracy-related penalties." The term "accuracy-related penalties" encompasses several separate and distinct penalties, including those imposed for reporting positions that were (i) negligent, (ii) not adequately disclosed and which lacked substantial authority, (iii) substantially misvalued, or (iv) fraudulent.

A. Procedures Regarding Assessment

The accuracy-related penalties are calculated as a percentage of the deficiency owed by the taxpayer. They are assessed and collected in the same manner as deficiencies in tax, meaning the taxpayer is entitled to certain procedural rights before they are assessed.[75] Specifically, a taxpayer can challenge the proposed penalties first by filing a protest with the Appeals Office and, if necessary, by filing a petition in the Tax Court.[76]

B. IRS's Burden of Production Relative to the Penalty

In the past, when a section 6662 penalty was proposed against a taxpayer in the thirty-day letter or Notice of Deficiency, the Service usually provided an open-ended pro forma catch-all statement that did little to describe which inappropriate conduct was being penalized. Such generic statements left it to the taxpayer to determine what he or she did wrong. Thus, deciding what evidence to produce to refute the assertion of the penalty was difficult and costly.

But now, under section 7491(c), the IRS has the burden of production in any court proceeding[77] with respect to a taxpayer's liability for a penalty. The IRS must come forward with specific evidence supporting the application of a particular penalty to the taxpayer. If the IRS fails to meet its burden, the penalty is denied. If the IRS meets its burden, the taxpayer has the burden to produce evidence to defend against the penalty, such as establishing substantial authority, reasonable reliance on a professional advisor, or the like.

II. Calculating the Penalty

The accuracy-related penalties in section 6662 are imposed at the rate of 20% of that portion of an underpayment of tax attributable to any of the following transgressions listed in section 6662(b):

- Negligence or disregard of rules and regulations;
- Substantial understatement of income tax;
- Substantial income tax valuation misstatement;
- Substantial overstatement of pension liabilities;
- Substantial estate or gift tax valuation understatement;

---

75. IRC § 6665(a). These rights, generally known as "deficiency procedures," are discussed in Chapters 3, 6, and 8.

76. Many times taxpayers and their advisors do not focus on the penalty during the examination phase, and even fail to address the issue at Appeals or in court. This is a mistake. If the IRS prevails on the deficiency, the taxpayer can still significantly reduce the liability by defeating the penalty asserted by the IRS. The taxpayer must be prepared to present evidence and the legal basis as to why the penalty should not apply.

On the other side, there is concern that the IRS sometimes is insufficiently attentive to accuracy-based penalties, particularly during the correspondence examinations which constitute the bulk of tax audits. *See* Treasury Inspector General for Tax Administration, *Accuracy-Related Penalties Are Seldom Considered Properly During Correspondence Audits* (2010-30-059) (June 4, 2010).

77. The statute does not affect the taxpayer's burden during administrative proceedings before the IRS. However, it is safe to assume that once the matter is before the Appeals Office, the Service's burden of production will be considered a possible "hazard of litigation."

- Tax benefits disallowed because of the economic substance doctrine;[78]
- Understatements involving undisclosed foreign financial assets; or
- An "inconsistent estate basis"[79] if the basis of property claimed on a return exceeds the basis as determined under section 1014(f).

The rate for the three penalties involving valuations increases to 40% on any portion of an underpayment attributable to a "gross" valuation misstatement. A gross valuation misstatement is one that is twice as large as the misstatements that give rise to the 20% penalty.[80] The 40% penalty rate also applies to "nondisclosed noneconomic substance transactions"[81] and "undisclosed foreign financial asset transactions."[82]

The fraud penalty of section 6663 is equal to 75% of the portion of the underpayment which is attributable to fraud. If the government proves that any portion of an underpayment is attributable to fraud, section 6663(b) says the *entire* underpayment shall be treated as attributable to fraud, except with respect to any portion of the underpayment that the taxpayer establishes (by a preponderance of the evidence) is not attributable to fraud.

A. Stacking of Penalties

Prior to 1989, penalties were applied to the entire underpayment. Now, the accuracy-related penalties are applied only to that portion of the underpayment attributable to the particular type of behavioral transgression involved. Stacking of several penalties for the same adjustment is no longer permitted.[83] That is, only 20% (or 40% as the case may be) can be imposed against any portion of a tax underpayment, even if more than one of the section 6662 misconduct bases is present. For instance, a taxpayer may be subject to the negligence penalty and the valuation misstatement penalty with respect to overvalued art that was contributed to a charitable organization. However, only a single 20% penalty can be asserted on the portion of the underpayment attributable to this item.[84]

While stacking is prohibited, the Regulations establish a series of "ordering" rules in the event different elements of the section 6662 penalty apply to different portions

---

78. Unlike the other penalties in section 6662, there is no reasonable cause defense to an economic substance doctrine penalty. *See* § 6664(c)(2).

79. There is an "inconsistent estate tax basis" if the basis of property claimed on a return exceeds the basis as determined under section 1014(f). *See* § 6662(k). Added by The Surface Transportation and Veterans Health Care Choice Improvement Act of 2015, Pub. L. 114-41, 129 Stat. 443 (July 31, 2015). Its effective date was July 31, 2015.

80. IRC § 6662(h).

81. IRC § 6662(i).

82. IRC § 6662(j).

83. Reg. § 1.6662-2(c).

84. IRM 20.1.5.2. The prohibition against "stacking" of penalties does not preclude the Service from alleging penalties in the alternative. For example, the IRS can assert that the taxpayer was negligent or met the conditions for imposition of the substantial understatement penalty. This alternative allegation approach is quite common in statutory notices of deficiency where the Service wants to insure that every conceivable basis for the application of the penalty is raised.

of an underpayment.[85] Normally, the order is not significant since the 20% rate of the penalty is the same regardless of which penalty applies. However, where fraud (75%) or a 40% penalty is asserted on some of the adjustments and the 20% accuracy-related penalty is asserted on others, the ordering rules are important.

The Regulations specify that, in determining the amount of tax on which the penalties are calculated, taxable income is increased first by adjustments on which no penalties are asserted, then by adjustments on which the 20% penalty is asserted, followed by the 40% and 75% penalties.[86] The effect of this is to calculate the more significant penalties at the highest marginal rates, thus increasing the cost of the penalties.

> **Example:** Sigmund's taxable income for 20x1 as reflected on the filed return is $100,000 and the tax liability is $21,000. The Service examines the return and makes three adjustments to taxable income in the amounts of $20,000, $30,000, and $40,000, claiming a total underpayment in tax of $27,000. The IRS asserts no penalty with respect to the $20,000 adjustment, a 20% negligence penalty on the $30,000 adjustment, and a 40% gross valuation penalty on the $40,000 adjustment.
>
> The ordering rules dictate that the $20,000 item be given effect first in determining what portion of the $27,000 understatement is free of misconduct. To do this, one would add $20,000 to the $100,000 on the return, calculate the tax on $120,000 and subtract the $21,000 tax previously paid. The result is the deficiency on the $20,000 adjustment. On these facts, no penalty would be charged against this portion of the understatement.
>
> After that, one would add the $30,000 adjustment to the $120,000 amount, calculate the tax on the $150,000, subtract the tax from the previous step, and apply a 20% penalty to the difference.
>
> Finally, one would add the $40,000 adjustment to $150,000 ($100,000 income on return plus the first two levels of adjustment), calculate the tax attributable to it, subtract the tax from the previous steps, and apply a 40% penalty to the difference.

The section 6662 penalty can only be applied to a return filed by the taxpayer.[87] If no return is filed by the taxpayer, other penalties, such as the failure to file penalty, may be applicable, but section 6662 and section 6663 do not impose additional layers of sanction.[88] This is also true for substitute for returns (SFRs) filed by the IRS.

B. What Is an Underpayment?

Since the section 6662 penalty can only be imposed on that portion of the tax underpayment attributable to the proscribed conduct, it is important to understand

85. Reg. § 1.6664-3.
86. Reg. § 1.6664-3(b).
87. IRC § 6664(b); Reg. § 1.6664-2(c).
88. Reg. § 1.6662-2(a).

what an underpayment is. While its definition in section 6664(a) is hard to comprehend, basically an "underpayment" is the amount by which the tax imposed by the Code exceeds the tax shown on the original return.[89] Normally, an underpayment for section 6662 purposes is the same as the deficiency in tax. The definitions part company, however, where a qualified amended return was filed (see discussion next) or, with respect to the substantial understatement penalty, where the taxpayer either had substantial authority for the reporting position or disclosed the relevant facts affecting the item's tax treatment (see discussion in Section III below). If either of these two situations applies, the amount of the underpayment will be less than the amount of the deficiency by the tax attributable thereto.

A number of cases have explored the meaning of "underpayment" for purposes of sections 6662 and 6663.[90] Most recently, Congress amended section 6664 to make the rule the same as that for taxes.[91]

C. Impact of Filing a "Qualified Amended Return"

As stated, an amended return that meets the definition of a "qualified amended return" (QAR) may limit one's exposure to accuracy-related penalties. This is so because the adjustments to taxable income shown on a QAR are treated as if they were reflected correctly on the originally filed return.[92] In order for an amended return to be considered a QAR, it must be "voluntary." This means that the amended return must be filed before the earliest of:

- The date the taxpayer is first contacted by the IRS concerning any examination (including a criminal investigation) with respect to the return;
- The date a promoter of an abusive tax shelter is first contacted by the IRS concerning an examination of that person for an activity with respect to which the taxpayer claimed any tax benefit on the return directly or indirectly through the entity, plan, or arrangement;
- In the case of an investor in a pass-through item (such as a partnership or S corp.), the date the pass-through entity is first contacted by the IRS in connection with an examination of the return to which the pass-through item relates;
- The date on which the IRS serves a "John Doe" summons relating to the tax liability of a person, group, or class that includes the taxpayer with respect to an

89. *Id.* A late filed return that also contains an understatement of tax, however, will be subject to both the late filing penalty and an accuracy-related penalty.

90. *E.g.*, Snow v. Commissioner, 141 T.C. 238 (2013) (holding that "underpayment" includes the difference between the amount stated on the return as withheld from the taxpayer's wages and the amount actually withheld); May v. Commissioner, 137 T.C. 147 (2011) ("underpayment" includes overstated withholding credits), *aff'd*, 2013 WL 1352477 (6th Cir. 2013), *cert. denied*, 134 S. Ct. 682 (2013); Feller v. Commissioner, 135 T.C. 497 (2010) (upholding Reg. §§ 1.6664-2(c)(1) & (g) (Example 3)).

91. Consolidated Appropriations Act of 2016, Pub. L. No. 114-113, Div. Q, § 209, 129 Stat, 2242

92. IRC § 6664(a); Reg. § 1.6664-2(a).

activity for which the taxpayer claimed any tax benefit on the return directly or indirectly; or

- The date on which the Commissioner announces, by revenue ruling, revenue procedure, notice, or announcement, a settlement initiative to compromise or waive penalties, in whole or in part, with respect to a listed transaction.[93]

An amended return satisfies the definition of a QAR even if it is filed *solely* to make a disclosure to avoid the substantial understatement penalty. This might happen, for example, where the amended return does not report additional tax due but includes a Form 8275 disclosing an aggressive reporting position.[94]

III. The Negligence Penalty

The section 6662(b)(1) penalty applies to any portion of an underpayment attributable to negligence or disregard of rules or regulations. It is useful to think of this section as having two separate components—negligence and the disregard of rules or regulations. As compared to the more mechanical bases for the other accuracy-related penalties, the negligence penalty is determined only after all the facts and circumstances are considered. In addition, although the IMPACT-created penalties are of a more recent vintage, the negligence penalty has been part of the tax laws from time immemorial. As a result, there is a significant body of case law one can consult to "put flesh on the bones" of what constitutes negligence.

A. Negligence

"Negligence" is a failure to make a reasonable attempt to comply with the tax laws.[95]

It includes failure to exercise ordinary and reasonable care in the preparation of a tax return, as well as failure to keep adequate books and records or substantiate items properly.[96] Regulation section 1.6662-3(b)(1) gives several examples of what constitutes negligence.

With respect to return reporting positions, one is negligent if the position taken lacks a reasonable basis,[97] a standard of tax reporting significantly higher than "not frivolous" or merely arguable.[98] Regulation section 1.6662-3(b)(3) says that the *process*

---

93. Reg. § 1.6664-2(c)(3)(i). Reg. § 1.6664-2(c)(3)(ii) states that for taxpayers who have claimed tax benefits from undisclosed listed transactions, the QAR filing period is terminated once the IRS requests information about the transaction from anyone who made a tax statement for the benefit of the taxpayer or gave material aid, assistance, or advice to the taxpayer. The date of a settlement initiative announcement for a listed transaction in which penalties are compromised or waived is the date by which a QAR must be filed.

94. Reg. § 1.6664-2(c)(4).

95. IRC § 6662(b)(1); IRM 20.1.5.7.1.

96. Reg. § 1.6662-3(b)(1).

97. Reg. § 1.6662-3(b)(1).

98. Reg. § 1.6662-3(b)(3).

employed in evaluating whether a reporting position is reasonable is the same as that employed in deciding whether a reporting position has substantial authority for the section 6662(b)(2) penalty, even though the *standards* for determining exposure to each are different. The negligence regulations do not place a percentage on the level of confidence one must have in the reporting position for it to be deemed reasonable. However, practitioners generally place it at somewhere between a 15% and 20% chance of success on the merits if the position were litigated.[99]

As in other areas of the law, negligence is defined in the tax content as the failure to do what a reasonable and prudent person would do under the circumstances.[100] Indicators of negligence run the gamut. The Internal Revenue Manual instructs agents to consider the following when deciding whether to assert the negligence penalty:

- Have previous returns been filed timely?
- Have penalties been assessed in other years?
- Did the taxpayer fail to keep adequate and accurate books and records?
- Did the taxpayer fail to maintain adequate internal controls for processing and reporting business transactions?
- Did the taxpayer fail to report all income accurately, and was he or she unable to offer a reasonable explanation for the error?
- Did the taxpayer overstate deductions or credits, including claiming clearly improper or exaggerated amounts, unsubstantiated by facts or documentation?
- Did the taxpayer use descriptions for deductions that were meant to conceal the true nature of the item in question?
- Did the taxpayer fail to explain items questioned by the Service?
- Did the taxpayer take actions to ensure that the return preparer did not have all the necessary and appropriate information to prepare a correct and/or timely return?[101]

A penalty is not appropriate if the law was unsettled or if a taxpayer, acting in good faith, made a mistake of law or fact. Reliance on a professional advisor can absolve the taxpayer of liability for the penalty.[102]

B. Disregard of Rules and Regulations

The disregard element of the section 6662(b) penalty base "includes any careless, reckless or intentional disregard of rules and regulations."[103] The rules and regulations

99. Burgess W. Raby & William L. Raby, *Reasonable Basis vs. Other Tax Opinion Standards*, 73 Tax Notes 1209, (Dec. 9, 1996).

100. *See, e.g.*, Neely v. Commissioner, 85 T.C. 934 (1985).

101. IRM 4.10.6.2.1.

102. *See* Henry v. Commissioner, 170 F.3d 1217 (9th Cir. 1999) (taxpayer had no obligation to independently verify his tax liability after advice given by accountant); Chamberlin v. Commissioner, 66 F.3d 729 (5th Cir. 1995); Sim-Air, USA, Ltd v. Commissioner, 98 T.C. 187 (1992).

103. IRC § 6662(c); Reg. § 1.6662-3(b)(2).

to which one must adhere to avoid the penalty include the Code, temporary and final Regulations, revenue rulings, and notices issued by the IRS and published in the Internal Revenue Bulletin.[104]

"Careless" disregard occurs when a taxpayer fails to exercise reasonable diligence to determine the correctness of a return position that is contrary to a rule or regulation.[105] The disregard becomes "reckless" if the taxpayer makes little or no effort to ascertain whether a rule or regulation exists, under circumstances that are a substantial deviation from the conduct expected from a reasonable person.[106] An "intentional" disregard is one in which the taxpayer is aware of the rule or regulation being disregarded.[107]

Imposing the penalty for disregard of the rules and regulations is inappropriate even if the taxpayer's position is contrary to a revenue ruling or an IRS notice, if the taxpayer's position has a "realistic possibility of being sustained on its merits."[108] The "realistic possibility" standard is also found under section 6694, and is interpreted to require a showing that there is a better than one-in-three chance of prevailing on the merits of the position.[109]

C. Impact of Disclosure on the Section 6662 Negligence or Disregard of the Rules and Regulations Penalty

While Regulation section 1.6662-3(c)(1) states: "[n]o penalty under section 6662 (b)(1) may be imposed on any portion of an underpayment that is attributable to a position contrary to a rule or regulation if the position is disclosed ... and, in case of a position contrary to a regulation, the position represents a good faith challenge to the validity of the regulation," the scope of this exception is narrowed in Regulation section 1.6662-7. Only the penalty for disregarding rules or regulations, but not the penalty for negligence, may be avoided by adequate disclosure of a return position and then only so long as the position has at least a reasonable basis. The exception was designed to make it possible for taxpayers to challenge rules and regulations without incurring a penalty. Disclosure gives the IRS notice of, and an opportunity to respond to, the challenge. As a general rule, disclosure for these purposes should be made on Form 8275 (or Form 8275-R for positions inconsistent with a Regulation), which should be attached to the taxpayer's return or qualified amended return.[110]

---

104. See IRC sections 6034A(c)(5), 6037(c)(5), and 6222(d) for situations where inconsistent reporting of information provided the taxpayer on Forms K-1 would likely be considered "disregard."

105. Reg. § 1.6662-3(b)(2).

106. *Id.*

107. *Id.* The failure of a taxpayer to put in place an adequate information reporting system after acknowledging the inadequacy of its current system also may constitute intentional disregard. Bale Chevrolet Co. v. United States, 620 F.3d 868 (8th Cir. 2010).

108. Reg. § 1.6662-3(b)(2).

109. Reg. § 1.6694-2(b)(1).

110. Reg. § 1.6662-3(c)(2). From a practical perspective, if one is contemplating taking a position contrary to a revenue ruling or notice, one must weigh whether disclosure is the best way to avoid the penalty. One can avoid the penalty either by disclosing the position or meeting the reasonable

IV. The Substantial Understatement Penalty

Congress added the substantial understatement penalty to discourage taxpayers from attempting to take advantage of the low audit rate by taking aggressive tax return positions unsupported by significant authority. The penalty applies when the IRS asserts a "substantial understatement" of income tax in situations where the taxpayer did not have substantial authority for a tax return position and failed to disclose the relevant facts affecting the item's tax treatment.

Compared with the facts and circumstances analysis associated with the negligence and fraud penalties, this penalty is more mechanically determined. The only issues that require analysis are whether the taxpayer consulted the appropriate authority, what weight should have been placed on the supporting and opposing authorities, and whether there was adequate disclosure of positions that lacked substantial authority.

The following is a brief overview of the substantial understatement penalty with emphasis on several aspects that are not apparent from the language of the Code and the Regulations. Regulation section 1.6662-4 is particularly helpful in explaining the law and its application. Consequently, the assigned statutory provisions, Regulations, and revenue procedure should be carefully studied.[111]

An understatement is defined as the excess of the amount of tax required to be shown on the return for a taxable year over the amount of tax shown on the return.[112] An understatement is substantial if it exceeds the greater of 10% of the tax required to be shown, or $5,000.[113] The penalty applies to any tax imposed by Subtitle A, i.e., income, self-employment, and withholding tax on nonresident aliens and foreign corporations.

> **Example**: Johnny Rose files his 20x1 income tax return showing taxable income of $50,000 and a corresponding tax liability of $8,000. A subsequent IRS examination determines that Johnny's taxable income is $70,000 with a corresponding tax liability of $14,000. There is no substantial authority for Johnny's tax reporting positions and no qualifying disclosures, so the entire $6,000 in-

---

basis standard. Accordingly, disclosure makes sense only if the merits of the position do not meet the reasonable basis standard. That said, having to meet one's burden to prove reasonable basis will certainly be more time-consuming, costly, and hazardous than making a disclosure.

The provisions of Regulation section 1.6662-4(f)(2), which permit disclosure in accordance with an annual revenue procedure for purposes of the substantial understatement penalty, do not apply for purposes of this section. See the text accompanying Section III.

111. The IRS annually publishes a revenue procedure updating rules for disclosure to reduce section 6662(d) understatement penalties and section 6694(a) preparer penalties. *See, e.g.*, Rev. Proc. 2016-13, 2016-4 I.R.B. 290; *see also* IRM 20.1.5.8.

112. IRC § 6662(d)(2)(A). This is reduced by any rebates.

113. IRC § 6662(d)(1)(A); Reg. § 1.6662-4(b). In the case of a corporation other than an S corporation or a personal holding company (as defined in section 542), there is a substantial understatement of income tax for any taxable year if the amount of the understatement for the taxable year exceeds the lesser of 10% of the tax required to be shown on the return for the taxable year (or, if greater, $10,000), or $10,000,000. IRC § 6662(d)(1)(B).

crease in tax liability is treated as an understatement. Because the $6,000 understatement exceeds the greater of (i) 10% of the tax required to be shown on the return (i.e., 10% of $14,000, or $1,400) or (ii) $5,000, the understatement is considered substantial. Accordingly, assuming the good faith/reasonable cause exception of section 6664 does not apply, an accuracy-related penalty equal to 20% penalty of the $6,000 understatement ($1,200) will apply.

In order to encourage taxpayers to take responsible reporting positions or to disclose those positions that were more aggressive, Congress provided that an understatement is reduced to the extent (i) there is substantial authority for the taxpayer's treatment of a questionable item[114] or (ii) the relevant facts affecting the item's tax treatment are sufficiently disclosed on the return.[115] In essence, if there is appropriate authority for a position or there is adequate disclosure, the item is treated as if it were initially reported on the income tax return properly.

Example: Assume all the facts in the previous example except that on the 20x1 return, Johnny adequately disclosed the facts giving rise to $11,000 of the adjustment to income and that he has a reasonable basis for the position. The tax on the disclosed item is removed from the understatement for purposes of the penalty. The tax on the $9,000 remaining portion of the understatement would be less than $5,000. Therefore, Johnny's understatement for the year is not "substantial" and the substantial understatement penalty is avoided.

"Substantial authority" for a reporting position is met only after reviewing many types of authority, such as the Code, Regulations, IRS pronouncements, decisions of the courts, and legislative history, and objectively concluding that the weight of authorities in support of the treatment is substantial in relation to those supporting a contrary position. The weight of authority in favor of a position is likely substantial if there is at least a one in three chance of succeeding on the merits if the case were litigated.[116] If the reporting position is attributable to a tax-shelter item,[117] the understatement is reduced for substantial authority only if the taxpayer reasonably believed that the tax treatment of the items was more-likely-than-not the proper tax treatment.

Similar to the disclosure rules with respect to the disregard penalty, for purposes of the substantial understatement penalty, disclosure is accomplished either by attaching a disclosure statement (Form 8275 or Form 8275-R) to the tax return or qualified

---

114. Reg. § 1.6662-4(b)(4). The taxpayer must have substantial authority at the end of the tax year or when the return is filed.

115. For tax returns due after December 31, 1993, disclosure does not reduce the understatement unless the item or position is disclosed on the return and has a reasonable basis and is properly substantiated, or the taxpayer has kept adequate books and records with respect to the item or position. Reg. § 1.6662-4 (e)(2).

116. While the accuracy-related penalty regulations do not quantify what is meant by "substantial," Regulation section 1.6694-2(b)(1) quantifies the perhaps similar term "realistic possibility" (the standard required of a practitioner to sign a tax return as a preparer) as a position that has approximately a one in three, or greater, likelihood of being sustained on its merits.

117. See IRC section 6662(d)(2)(C)(ii) for a definition of a tax shelter item.

amended tax return[118] or by complying with the dictates of annual revenue procedures issued by the Service for this purpose.[119] If the reporting position is attributable to a tax shelter item, disclosure has no effect on the amount of the understatement.[120]

V. Substantial Valuation Misstatements

The substantial valuation misstatement component of the accuracy-related penalty applies if the value of property (or its adjusted basis) is substantially in error.[121] It applies to overvaluations, in the case of income tax (section 6662(e)),[122] or undervaluations, in the case of estate or gift taxes (section 6662(g)).[123]

A. Substantial Income Tax Overvaluations

There is a substantial valuation misstatement for income tax purposes if the value or adjusted basis of property on a return is 150% or more of the correct value or adjusted basis.[124] The penalty amount on substantial valuation misstatements is 20% of the underpayment attributable to the substantial valuation misstatement. Under section 6662(h), a special 40% penalty applies to gross valuation misstatements, i.e., where the value or basis of any property claimed on an income tax return is 200% or more of the correct amount.[125]

---

118. Courts have also held that a disclosure statement is adequate if it reasonably apprises the Service of the nature and amount of the potential controversy. *See* Schirmer v. Commissioner, 89 T.C. 277, 285–86 (1977); Dibsy v. Commissioner, T.C. Memo. 1995-477. If the disclosure statement fails to include all of the above, misrepresents the facts, or is too general to reasonably apprise the Service of the potential controversy, the disclosure exception does not apply. *See also* IRM 20.1.5.7.2.1.

119. Reg. § 1.6662-4(f)(2); As of the date this book goes to press, the most recent revenue procedure is Rev. Proc. 2016-13, 2016-4 I.R.B. 290. By and large, the revenue procedure does not require the taxpayer to do anything more than complete the designated schedules as fully as one would expect to do anyway and attach whatever documentation might be required by the instructions for the schedule.

120. Reg. § 1.6662-4(g)(1)(iii).

121. It may also apply with respect to a section 482 transaction. However, the discussion will only consider value and basis issues outside the section 482 context. See Reg. § 1.6662-6. There is also a penalty for substantial overstatements of pension liabilities in section 6662(f). The latter penalty is not addressed in this chapter.

122. Reg. § 1.6662-5; *see also* IRM 20.1.5.9.

123. If one of the valuation misstatement penalties applies to the taxpayer, the person who prepared the appraisal may be subject to a penalty under section 6695A.

124. IRC § 6662(e)(1). The percentage changed from 200% to 150% in the Pension Protection Act of 2006, Pub. L. No. 109-280, § 1219(a)(1)(A), 120 Stat. 780, effective for returns filed after August 17, 2006. Many of the decided cases are older and will still reflect the 200% threshold.

125. Regardless of the amount of overvaluation, if the property's correct value or basis is determined to be zero, the 40% gross valuation penalty will apply. Reg. § 1.6662-5(g). The percentage changed from 400% to 200% in the Pension Protection Act of 2006, Pub. L. No. 109-280, § 1219(a)(1)(A), 120 Stat. 780, effective for returns filed after August 17, 2006. Many of the decided cases are older and will still reflect the 400% threshold.

With the exception of the possible application of the section 6664 reasonable cause defense, the application of this penalty is purely mechanical. If an underpayment is attributable to a valuation misstatement of 150% or more and if it exceeds the threshold amount of $5,000 for individuals and $10,000 for corporations (other than S corporations or personal service corporations), the penalty applies.

> **Example (1)**: Ms. Philanthropic donated a painting to the local art museum. She took a deduction of $150,000, which she believed was the painting's fair market value based on a qualified appraisal she obtained.[126] The IRS examined her return and valued the painting at $90,000. Ms. Philanthropic's underpayment resulting from the $60,000 valuation adjustment is $15,000. Since the reported valuation is 167% of the final valuation, the 150% threshold is satisfied. In addition, since the underpayment of $15,000 attributable to the overvaluation exceeds $5,000, the dollar limitation is met. Thus, the IRS will assert the 20% penalty and Ms. Philanthropic will have to establish that she qualifies for relief under section 6664(c).
>
> **Example (2)**: If the final adjusted value in example (1) above were $70,000, the amount reported of $150,000 would then exceed the final adjusted amount by more than 200% ($150,000 divided by $70,000 = 214%). The 40% gross valuation misstatement penalty would apply to the applicable underpayment.

The Regulations provide important rules to implement the provision and should be consulted by the student. For example, the determination as to whether there is a valuation misstatement is done on a property-by-property basis.[127] Also, Regulation section 1.6662-5(a) does not allow a taxpayer to avoid this penalty by disclosing that the valuation might be too high.

Similar rules apply if the taxpayer misstates his basis in a transaction. For example, assume Mr. Investor reports a gain of $40,000 on the sale of stock for $90,000 with a reported adjusted basis of $50,000. If it is later determined that the adjusted basis was only $30,000, the percentage that the basis was overvalued would be 167%. Assuming the underpayment exceeded $5,000, a 20% penalty would apply.[128] And if the final adjusted basis was determined to be $20,000, a 40% penalty would apply.

---

126. A taxpayer will not be considered to have reasonably relied in good faith on advice unless the requirements of Regulation section 1.6664-4(b) and (c) are met. This may require more than merely obtaining a qualified appraisal. In addition, when charitable deduction property is involved, the taxpayer must meet the requirements in Regulation section 1.6664-4(h).

127. Reg. § 1.6662-5(f)(1).

128. Resolving a circuit split, the Supreme Court has held that absence of economic substance can constitute a basis misstatement for purposes of the substantial valuation/basis misstatement base of the § 6662 penalty. United States v. Woods, 134 S. Ct. 557 (2013), *see also* NPR Invs., LLC v. United States, 740 F.3d 998 (5th Cir. 2014) (discussing *Woods*).

Regulation § 1.6662-5(g) applies the valuation misstatement penalty to cases in which the taxpayer has a zero basis. The *Woods* taxpayer did not challenge the validity of the regulation, so the Court assumed its validity for the purposes of the case. A commentator and amicus, however, has offered an argument against the validity of the regulation, based on the proposition that the percent by which

B. Substantial Estate and Gift Tax Undervaluations

The accuracy-related penalty also applies to substantial estate or gift tax valuation understatements. If the property's value claimed on the estate or gift tax return is 65% or less of the correct value, there is a substantial understatement.[129] The 20% penalty applies to the underpayment attributable to the substantial understatement, although no penalty applies if the underpayment attributable to the substantial understatement is $5,000 or less.

Under section 6662(h), the penalty increases to 40% if the property's value is grossly understated, i.e., the value claimed on the return is 40% or less of the property's correct value.[130] As with the valuation misstatement penalty, disclosure on the return does not avoid this penalty.

VI. The Fraud Penalty

Section 6663(a) states, "[i]f any part of any underpayment of tax required to be shown on a return is due to fraud, there shall be added to the tax an amount equal to 75 percent of the portion of the underpayment which is attributable to fraud." As compared to the other accuracy-related penalties where the burden is by a preponderance of the evidence and the government merely has the burden of production in court proceedings, the entire burden of proof with respect to fraud is on the government[131] by the "clear and convincing" standard.[132] If the government proves that any portion of an underpayment is attributable to fraud, section 6663(b) says that the *entire* underpayment shall be treated as attributable to fraud, except with respect

---

claimed basis exceeds zero is always—as a mathematical matter—undefined, thus cannot satisfy the statutory threshold. This issue has been raised in one of the seemingly endless rounds of the *Petaluma* tax shelter saga. *See* Andy S. Grewal, Petaluma *and the Limits of Treasury's Authority*, 144 Tax Notes 479 (July 28, 2014).

In some tax shelter cases, courts have dismissed penalties when the taxpayer artfully conceded the deficiency. *See* Jeremiah Coder, *Self-Serving Concessions and Penalty Avoidance*, 134 Tax Notes 1583 (Mar. 26, 2012). Presumably, the combination of *Woods* and the strict liability penalty for violating the economic substance doctrine, *see* IRC § 6662(b)(6), will bring down the curtain on this strategy.

129. The percentage for the basic undervaluation changed from 50% to 65% and for the gross undervaluation from 25% to 40% in the Pension Protection Act of 2006, Pub. L. No. 109-280, § 1219(a)(1)(A), 120 Stat. 780. effective for returns filed after August 17, 2006. Many of the decided cases are older and will still reflect the older thresholds. *See also* IRM 20.1.5.11.

130. *Id.*

131. IRC § 7454.

132. Tax Ct. R. 142(b). The government may be able to meet its burden utilizing res judicata and collateral estoppel. See Chapter 5 for a detailed discussion of this. Section 6663 seems to have its shadow over another penalty section. Section 6701 establishes a penalty against those who assist or advise taxpayers to take return positions they know or have reason to know will result in understatement of tax. The word "fraud" does not appear in section 6701. Nonetheless, some courts see it as fraud-like in substance. The courts are split as to whether section 6701 knowledge must be proved by a preponderance of the evidence or by clear and convincing proof. *See, e.g.,* Carlson v. United States, 754 F.3d 1223 (11th Cir. 2014) (describing the circuit split and adopting the "clear and convincing" view).

to any portion of the underpayment which the taxpayer establishes, by a preponderance of the evidence, is not attributable to fraud.

Tax fraud is often defined as an intentional wrongdoing on the part of a taxpayer with the specific purpose of evading a tax known or believed to be owing.[133] Evasion involves some affirmative act to evade, defeat, or pay a tax. A good list of examples of affirmative acts is found in the Internal Revenue Manual, where agents are instructed to look for "badges of fraud."[134] These badges of fraud include, but are not limited to:

- Understatement of income (e.g., omissions of specific items or entire sources of income, failure to report substantial amounts of income received),
- Fictitious or improper deductions (e.g., overstatement of deductions, personal items deducted as business expenses),
- Accounting irregularities (e.g., two sets of books, false entries on documents),
- Obstructive actions of the taxpayer (e.g., false statements, destruction of records, transfer of assets, failure to cooperate with the examiner, concealment of assets),
- A consistent pattern over several years of underreporting taxable income,
- Implausible or inconsistent explanations of behavior,
- Engaging in illegal activities (e.g., drug dealing), or attempting to conceal illegal activities,
- Inadequate records,
- Dealing in cash,
- Failure to file returns, and
- Education and experience.

The "willful blindness" doctrine holds that knowledge or willfulness can be inferred when the taxpayer or defendant went to lengths to deliberately avoid acquiring knowledge of the facts or law. Although problematic if used without care, this doctrine is generally accepted.[135]

Usually, the taxpayer's state of knowledge is a matter for trial. It may be decided via summary judgment, however, when the situation is quite clear. In a case involving the section 6701 penalty on advisors who knew the position they recommend would lead to understatement of the taxpayer's liability, the court granted summary judgment to the government because "in this case there is but one conclusion ...

133. Tax evasion is to be contrasted with tax avoidance. The former is illegal; the latter is not. Taxpayers have the right to reduce, avoid, or minimize their taxes by legitimate means. One who avoids tax does not conceal or misrepresent, but shapes and preplans events to reduce or eliminate tax liability within the parameters of the law.

134. IRM 25.1.6.3(2); 20.1.5.14.1. For an expanded list of indicators of fraud, see IRM 25.1.2.3.

135. *See* John A. Townsend et al., Tax Crimes Ch. 2B, Section III.C (2d ed. 2015). For use of this doctrine in a civil fraud case, see *Fiore v. Commissioner*, T.C. Memo. 2013-21 (upholding the penalty against a formerly prominent estate planning attorney).

it is implausible that a trained tax preparer would believe that personal expenses such as a home repair project or a personal vacation could be deducted as business expenses."[136]

Where one intentionally understates income or overstates deductions with the intent to evade tax, that person is potentially liable for both criminal and civil tax penalties. The elements constituting fraud are substantially the same for both civil and criminal purposes. Civil fraud penalties are in addition to any criminal fine imposed under section 7201 et seq.[137] It is difficult to state with specificity why the government pursues one case of underreporting or non-filing as a criminal case and another only civilly. One factor is whether the government believes it can meet its burden of proving willfulness beyond a reasonable doubt.[138] Other factors include whether prosecution of the target has sufficient publicity value to justify expending on a criminal investigation and prosecution the limited resources of the IRS and the Department of Justice and whether there are mitigating circumstances that diminish the case's jury appeal, such as the target's extreme ill health.

In order to prove its case that the taxpayer fraudulently attempted to evade taxes, the government utilizes either the direct (or specific items) method of proof or one of several indirect methods. When direct proof does not exist to reconstruct a taxpayer's financial transactions, indirect methods of proof,[139] such as the expenditures method or the bank deposits method, are used. The government tends to use indirect methods when the defendant deals in cash and has not maintained adequate records from which to reconstruct income. The indirect methods rely primarily on circumstantial evidence. It is common for the government to use more than one method in proving its case.

A. Statute of Limitations and Fraud

The statute of limitations for assessing a deficiency in tax and associated penalties is generally three years from the due date of the return or its filing date, whichever is later. Where fraud is established, either civil or criminal, the statute of limitations on assessment is unlimited. In a fraud penalty case, the court may assess a penalty against one of the spouses for understatement of the couple's tax attributable to his or her fraudulent intent while declining to impose an accuracy-related penalty against

---

136. United States v. Lovlie, 102 AFTR2d 5654 (D. Minn. 2008).

137. Schachter v. Commissioner, 113 T.C. 192 (1999), *aff'd*, 255 F.3d 1031 (9th Cir. 2001), cert. denied, 534 U.S. 826 (2001). Applying both civil and criminal penalties is not a violation of the Double Jeopardy Clause of the Constitution. Helvering v. Mitchell, 303 U.S. 391, 299 (1938); Grimes v. Commissioner, 82 F.3d 286 (9th Cir. 1996).

138. This typically requires proof that the person knew and understood the duty to file and report properly, and yet affirmatively chose to underreport or to not file.

139. *See, e.g.*, Holland v. United States, 348 U.S. 121 (1954) (net worth analysis); United States v. Johnson, 319 U.S. 503 (1943) (expenditures method); United States v. Soulard, 730 F.2d 1292 (9th Cir. 1984) (bank deposits method). A discussion of these methods is beyond the scope of this book. Good explanations and examples can be found at IRM 9.5.9.

the innocent spouse.[140] By contrast, under section 6531(a), a criminal indictment or information for fraud must occur within six years of the commission of the offense, usually the due date of the return.

When the government decides to pursue a criminal investigation, it usually suspends all action on the civil case.[141] The principal reason for doing so is a concern that the taxpayer might utilize the rules of discovery in the civil case to discover evidence involved in the criminal investigation. Other reasons include fear that the IRS and the Department of Justice might take inconsistent positions in the parallel cases and the desire to avoid placing excessive demands on the witnesses. However, especially in many recent tax shelter investigations, the government has been proceeding civilly and criminally simultaneously.

Because criminal cases can take years to work their way to resolution, the normal three-year civil statute of limitations on assessment usually will have expired by the time the civil case is resuscitated. If the government cannot prove fraud or a greater than 25% omission of gross income,[142] or if the taxpayer was smart enough not to extend the statute of limitations by executing Form 872 or 872-A, the taxpayer escapes liability. However, if the IRS successfully proves that the return was prepared fraudulently, not only has the government met its burden for purposes of the fraud penalty, but it has also satisfied the conditions necessary to extend the statute of limitations on assessment.

B. Res Judicata and Collateral Estoppel

Rather than being put to the task of proving fraud in the civil phase of the controversy, the government may be able to take advantage of the collateral estoppel doctrine to prove its case. If the government earned a conviction under section 7201 for evasion, the collateral estoppel doctrine spares it the burden of proving fraud a second time for assessment purposes in the civil case. This is because the government must prove guilt beyond a reasonable doubt to gain a criminal conviction, while in a civil tax fraud case, the government is only required to prove fraud by clear and convincing evidence, a lesser standard.

On the other hand, if the government was not successful in the criminal evasion case or if the taxpayer was convicted of some other offense, such as section 7206(1) perjury, collateral estoppel does not apply and the IRS is obligated to prove fraud in

---

140. Black v. Commissioner, T.C. Memo. 2007-364. The extended limitations period of section 6501(c)(1) for assessing taxes based on a fraudulent return may apply even if the evasion is attributable to his tax return preparer and not his own. Allen v. Commissioner, 128 T.C. 37 (2007). *Contra* BASR Partnership v. United States, 795 F.3d 1338 (Fed. Cir. 2015).

141. *See* Taylor v. Commissioner, 113 T.C. 206 (1999) (the decision to suspend the civil examination is not a purely "ministerial act" and a taxpayer is not entitled to suspension of interest under IRC section 6404(e)), *aff'd* 9 Fed. Appx. 700 (9th Cir. 2001); IRM 9.5.13.2; CCA 200250001 (July 23, 2002) (CDP hearing postponed while criminal investigation is pending).

142. IRC § 6501(e).

the civil case to get an extended civil statute of limitations and to carry the section 6663 penalty.[143]

VII. The Reasonable Cause Exception

Section 6664 provides that the accuracy-related penalty does not apply to any portion of an underpayment if it is established that there was reasonable cause for the position and the taxpayer acted in good faith.[144] Regulation section 1.6664-4(b)(1) provides that this determination is made on a case-by-case basis, taking into account all facts and circumstances. The Regulations state that the "most important factor is the extent of the taxpayer's effort to assess the taxpayer's proper tax liability."[145]

Reasonable cause relief is generally granted when the taxpayer exercises ordinary business care and prudence in determining his or her tax obligations. "[E]xperience, knowledge and education of the taxpayer" are factors to be considered in determining if an honest misunderstanding of fact or law constitutes reasonable cause and good faith.[146] An isolated computational or transcriptional error generally is consistent with reasonable cause and good faith.

The reasonable cause defense has met the cyberspace age. In one case, the court rejected the taxpayer's argument that his Google search provided reasonable cause for his failure to report his IRA distributions.[147] Famously (or infamously), Treasury Secretary Tim Geithner, in his confirmation hearing implausibly explained his tax derelictions by blaming his tax preparation software. Unsurprisingly, later taxpayers have asserted the "Geithner defense" against accuracy-related penalties. Thus far, none of these taxpayers have succeeded.[148]

In one recent case, the IRS asserted the section 6662 penalty as to the section 36 "first-time homebuyer" credit erroneously claimed by the taxpayer who happened to be an accountant. The Tax Court rejected the penalty. Stating that the taxpayer "though he is an accountant, is not a lawyer," the court concluded that the taxpayer had "acted with good faith and had reasonable cause [on the particular facts] for believing that he was entitled to the FTHBC."[149]

---

143. *See* Wright v. Commissioner, 84 T.C. 636 (1985); Del Vecchio v. Commissioner, T.C. Memo. 2001-130, *aff'd*, 37 Fed. Appx. 979 (11th Cir. 2002). An extended discussion of the topic is in Chapter 5. *See also* Anderson v. Commissioner, 698 F.3d 160 (3d Cir. 2012), *cert. denied*, 133 S. Ct. 2797 (2013); John A. Townsend, *Collateral Estoppel in Civil Cases Following Criminal Convictions*, 2005 TNT 4-28 (Jan. 3, 2005).

144. Reg. § 1.6664-4(a); *see* IRM 20.1.5.6.1.

145. See Reg. § 1.6664-4(f) for special rules applicable to corporate tax shelter items.

146. Reg. § 1.6664-4(b)(1).

147. Woodard v. Commissioner, T.C. Summary Op. 2009-150 (nonprecedential).

148. *E.g.*, Lam v. Commissioner, T.C. Memo. 2010-82 (2010). *See generally* Rodney P. Mock & Nancy E. Shurtz, *The TurboTax Defense*, 15 Fla. Tax Rev. 443 (2014).

149. Goralski v. Commissioner, T.C. Memo. 2014-87; *see also* Chandler v. Commissioner, 142 T.C. 279 (2014) (rejecting the IRS's argument that, because the taxpayer "had a law degree and worked as a business consultant, he should have known his appraiser had overvalued the easements.... [E]ven well-educated taxpayers like petitioner must rely heavily on the opinions of professionals.").

In another recent case, the taxpayer was a lawyer, and indeed was a leading tax lawyer at a major law firm and former General Tax Counsel for CBS. The IRS asserted that the taxpayer had made improper withdrawals from this IRAs, and it asserted the section 6662 penalty. The taxpayer's substantial knowledge of tax law was an important factor in the court's upholding the penalty.[150]

When a taxpayer asserts the reasonable cause defense, this puts into issue the taxpayer's state of mind. This forfeits any attorney-client privilege the taxpayer may have had as to tax opinion letters the taxpayer received from his, her, or the entity's lawyer.[151]

A. Reliance on Advice of Tax Professionals

A taxpayer's good faith and reasonable reliance on a professional tax advisor will normally insulate the taxpayer from the imposition of the accuracy-related penalties where the advisor was provided with all the information needed to render a well-informed opinion.[152] In addition, the taxpayer must prove that he or she actually relied on professional advice,[153] and that the reliance was both reasonable and in good faith.[154] The sophistication or expertise of the taxpayer is relevant in determining whether a taxpayer's reliance is in good faith or reasonable.[155] Reliance may not be

---

150. Bobrow v. Commissioner, T.C. Memo. 2014-21. *Bobrow* has other points of interest as well. The approach taken by the taxpayer had repeatedly been endorsed by the IRS previously, including in a proposed regulation. Prop. Reg. § 1.408-4(b)(4)(ii). But the IRS changed its view. IRS publications are not binding, and taxpayers rely on them at their own risk. *E.g.*, Miller v. Commissioner, 114 T.C. 184 (2000), *aff'd sub nom.* Lovejoy v. Commissioner, 293 F.3d 1208 (10th Cir. 2002). As stated in Chapter 1, proposed regulations are not controlling.

The IRS inconsistency aspect of the case gave rise to interesting briefs and an unpublished opinion. Bobrow v. Commissioner, T.C. Memo. 2014-21 (2014) (opinion on order). In response, the IRS announced that it would apply its new view (the view accepted by the court in *Bobrow*) only on a deferred prospective basis. Ann. 2014-15, 2014-16 I.R.B. 973 (also withdrawing the proposed regulation). For discussion of the IRS inconsistency issue, see Steve R. Johnson, *An IRS Duty of Consistency: The Failure of Common Law Making and a Proposed Legislative Solution*, 77 Tenn. L. Rev. 563 (2010).

151. AD Investment 2000 Fund LLC v. Commissioner, 142 T.C. 248 (2014); *see also* Schaeffler v. United States, 113 AFTR2d 2246 (S.D.N.Y. 2014).

152. *See* United States v. Boyle, 469 U.S. 241, 246 (1985) ("When an accountant or attorney advises a taxpayer on a matter of tax law, such as whether a liability exists, it is reasonable for the taxpayer to rely on that advice."); Reser v. Commissioner, 112 F.3d 1258 (5th Cir. 1997); Reg. § 1.6664-4(b), (c). In *Henry v. Commissioner*, 34 Fed. Appx. 342 (9th Cir. 2002), the Ninth Circuit not only held that the IRS's assertion of a negligence penalty when the taxpayer relied on the advice of counsel was wrong, but also found it was not substantially justified and awarded attorney's fees and costs. (Note: Since the Ninth Circuit did not select *Henry* for publication, one should check the applicable court rules to determine whether such unpublished cases can be cited.)

153. Regulation section 1.6664-4(c)(2) identifies "advice" as any communication setting forth the analysis or conclusion of a person (including a professional tax advisor), other than the taxpayer, provided to or for the benefit of the taxpayer and on which the taxpayer relies, directly or indirectly, with respect to the imposition of the IRC section 6662 penalty.

154. *See* DeCleene v. Commissioner, 115 T.C. 457 (2000) (taxpayer's reliance on counsel with respect to a complex IRC section 1031 exchange was justified).

155. *See* Cramer v. Commissioner, 64 F.3d 1406 (9th Cir. 1995) (accuracy-related penalties upheld on sophisticated taxpayers), cert. denied, 517 U.S. 1244 (1996); Heasley v. Commissioner, 902 F.2d

reasonable or in good faith if the taxpayer knew, or reasonably should have known, that the advisor lacked knowledge in the relevant aspects of tax law.[156]

There are two strains of reliance defense cases. One is relatively indulgent, drawing its inspiration from *United States v. Boyle*.[157] The other is relatively strict, following the spirit of the regulation. The split is evident in tax shelter cases. Some decisions analyze opinions given to taxpayers remarkably strictly, even hypercritically.[158] Some of these decisions appear to be driven by the belief that the taxpayer plainly knew what was afoot, that he knew he was buying a bogus contrivance purely for tax savings.[159] Other courts, however, are much less hostile to the defense.[160]

Under a formulation gaining increasing popularity, the defense will succeed only if the taxpayer establishes all of three conditions: (1) the advisor was a competent professional with sufficient expertise to justify reliance; (2) the taxpayer gave the advisor reliable and complete information; and (3) the taxpayer actually relied on the advice and did so in good faith.[161]

Appraisals may provide insulation from the accuracy-related penalties as to a valuation error. To test the taxpayer's supposedly good faith and reasonable reliance on the appraisal, the IRS and the courts consider factors such as the appraisal's underlying assumptions, the appraiser's relation to the taxpayer or to the activity in which the property is used, and the circumstances under which the taxpayer obtained the appraisal.

380, 383 (5th Cir. 1990) (unsophisticated moderate-income taxpayers held to a more forgiving standard); Estate of Robinson v. Commissioner, T.C. Memo. 2010-168 (finding reasonable cause in the personal representative's reliance on a disbarred enrolled agent because the personal representative was unsophisticated in tax matters, did not know of the disbarment, and genuinely believed the ex-agent was competent).

156. The Regulations provide fairly detailed minimum requirements, which must be satisfied in order to justify a finding that the taxpayer's reliance on the advice of a professional was in good faith or reasonable. Reg. § 1.6664-3.

157. 469 U.S. 241 (1985).

158. *E.g.*, Canal Corp. v. Commissioner, 135 T.C. 199, 218022 (2010); *see also, e.g.*, Howard M. Weinman, *Canal Corp. and penalty Protection*, J. Tax Prac. & Proc., Dec. 2010–Jan. 2011, at 33.

159. *E.g.*, Gustashaw v. Commissioner, T.C. Memo. 2011-195, *aff'd*, 696 F.3d 1124 (11th Cir. 2012).

160. *E.g.*, Whitehouse Hotel Ltd. Partnership v. Commissioner, 755 F.3d 236 (5th Cir. 2014) (reversing the Tax Court on the penalty issue and criticizing the "excessively high standard of proof for actual reliance" used by the Tax Court); American Boat Co., LLC v. United States, 583 F.3d 471 (7th Cir. 2009); Heasley v. Commissioner, 902 F.2d 380, 386 (5th Cir. 1990) ("The IRS should not exact every penalty possible in every case where taxpayers pay less than the full amount of tax due."); Klamath Strategic Inv. Fund, LLC v. United States, 472 F. Supp. 2d 885 (E.D. Tex. 2007), *aff'd as to this issue*, 568 F.3d 537 (5th Cir. 2009). *See generally* Dwaune Dupree & Ken Jones, *Reasonable Cause: Reliance on Tax Advisors*, J. Tax. Prac. & Proc. Dec. 2013–Jan. 2014, at 19; Michelle M. Kwon, *Dysfunction Junction: Reasonable Tax Advisors with Conflicts of Interest*, 67 Tax Law. 403 (2014).

161. Neonatology Associates, P.A. v. Commissioner, 115 T.C. 43 (2000), *aff'd*, 299 F.3d 221 (2000). In one case of this line, the court found the taxpayer's reliance to be reasonable despite the fact that the advisor had embezzled over $1 million, a fact of which the taxpayer was unaware. Thomas v. Commissioner, T.C. Memo. 2013-60.

B. Special Rules Apply to Charitable Deductions

Special reasonable cause/good faith rules apply to valuation misstatements attributable to charitable deduction property.[162] These rules provide generally that a taxpayer may demonstrate reasonable cause and good faith only if the taxpayer obtains a "qualified appraisal" from a specially defined qualified appraiser, and if the taxpayer made a good faith investigation of the value of the contributed property. A qualified appraisal must be made not earlier than 60 days before the date of contribution and not later than due date of the return (or the filing date of an amended return) on which the donation is first claimed.[163] The appraisal must contain specific information and the appraisal fee cannot be based on a percentage of the appraised value.[164]

VIII. Tax Shelter Penalties

Stiff penalties are an important part of the attack on tax shelters. Earlier, we noted that the defenses to the substantial understatement basis of the section 6662 penalty are weaker as to tax shelters. Yet Congress concluded that even sterner measures were required. As a result, Congress enacted section 6662A in 2004 and amended it in 2010.

A. Penalty as to Reportable Transactions

The American Jobs Creation Act of 2004[165] added to the rules applicable to tax shelters a new accuracy-related penalty that applies to listed transactions and reportable transactions with a significant tax avoidance purpose (hereinafter referred to as a "reportable avoidance transaction"). The penalty rate and defenses available to avoid the penalty vary depending on whether the transaction was adequately disclosed.

1. Disclosed Transactions

In general, a 20% accuracy-related penalty is imposed on any understatement attributable to an adequately disclosed listed transaction or reportable avoidance transaction.[166] The only exception to the penalty is where the taxpayer satisfies a more stringent reasonable cause and good faith exception (hereinafter referred to as the "strengthened reasonable cause exception"), which is described below. The strength-

162. Reg. § 1.6664-4(h)(1).

163. IRC § 6664(c)(3); Reg. § 1.170A-13(c)(5).

164. Reg. § 1.170A-13(c)(3). These strict appraisal rules supplant a broader "reasonable cause" defense that existed before 2006.

165. Pub. L. 108-357, Title VIII, § 812(a), 118 Stat. 1577 (2004).

166. IRC § 6662A.

ened reasonable cause exception is available only if the relevant facts affecting the tax treatment are adequately disclosed, there is or was substantial authority for the claimed tax treatment, and the taxpayer reasonably believed that the claimed tax treatment was more likely than not the proper treatment.[167]

2. Undisclosed Transactions

If the taxpayer does not adequately disclose the transaction, the strengthened reasonable cause exception is not available (i.e., a strict-liability penalty applies), and the taxpayer is subject to an increased penalty equal to 30% of the understatement.[168]

3. Determination of the Understatement Amount

The penalty is applied to the amount of any understatement attributable to the listed or reportable avoidance transaction without regard to other items on the tax return. For purposes of this provision, the amount of the understatement is determined as the sum of (1) the product of the highest corporate or individual tax rate (as appropriate) and the increase in taxable income resulting from the difference between the taxpayer's treatment of the item and the proper treatment of the item (without regard to other items on the tax return), and (2) the amount of any decrease in the aggregate amount of credits which results from a difference between the taxpayer's treatment of an item and the proper tax treatment of such item.[169]

Except as provided in future regulations, a taxpayer's treatment of an item shall not take into account any amendment or supplement to a return if the amendment or supplement is filed after the earlier of when the taxpayer is first contacted regarding an examination of the return or such other date as specified by the IRS.[170]

4. Coordination with Other Penalties

Any understatement upon which a penalty is imposed under section 6662A is not subject to the accuracy-related penalty under section 6662.[171] However, such understatement is included for purposes of determining whether any understatement (as defined in section 6662(d)(2)) is a substantial understatement as defined under section 6662(d)(1).[172] The penalty shall not apply to any portion of an understatement to which a fraud penalty is applied under section 6663.[173]

5. Reasonable Cause Defense

A penalty is not imposed under section 6662A with respect to any portion of an understatement if it is shown that there was reasonable cause for such portion and the taxpayer acted in good faith. Such a showing requires (1) adequate disclosure of

167. IRC § 6664(d).
168. IRC § 6662A(c).
169. IRC § 6662A(b)(1).
170. IRC § 6662A(e)(3).
171. IRC § 6662(b).
172. IRC § 6662A(e)(1).
173. IRC § 6662A(e)(2)(A).

the facts affecting the transaction in accordance with the regulations under section 6011, (2) that there is or was substantial authority for such treatment, and (3) that the taxpayer reasonably believed that such treatment was more likely than not the proper treatment.[174] For this purpose, a taxpayer will be treated as having a reasonable belief with respect to the tax treatment of an item only if such belief (1) is based on the facts and law that exist at the time the tax return (that includes the item) is filed, and (2) relates solely to the taxpayer's chances of success on the merits and does not take into account the possibility that (a) a return will not be audited, (b) the treatment will not be raised on audit, or (c) the treatment will be resolved through settlement if raised.[175]

A taxpayer may (but is not required to) rely on an opinion of a tax advisor in establishing its reasonable belief with respect to the tax treatment of the item. However, a taxpayer may not rely on an opinion of a tax advisor for this purpose if the opinion (1) is provided by a "disqualified tax advisor," or (2) is a "disqualified opinion."[176]

a. Disqualified Tax Advisor

A disqualified tax advisor is any advisor who (1) is a material advisor and who participates in the organization, management, promotion or sale of the transaction or is related (within the meaning of section 267(b) or 707(b)(1)) to any person who so participates, (2) is compensated directly or indirectly by a material advisor with respect to the transaction, (3) has a fee arrangement with respect to the transaction that is contingent on all or part of the intended tax benefits from the transaction being sustained, or (4) as determined under regulations prescribed by the Secretary, has a disqualifying financial interest with respect to the transaction.[177]

A material advisor is considered as participating in the "organization" of a transaction if the advisor performs acts relating to the development of the transaction. This may include, for example, preparing documents (1) establishing a structure used in connection with the transaction (such as a partnership agreement), (2) describing the transaction (such as an offering memorandum or other statement describing the transaction), or (3) relating to the registration of the transaction with any federal, state, or local government body. Participation in the "management" of a transaction means involvement in the decision-making process regarding any business activity with respect to the transaction. Participation in the "promotion or sale" of a transaction means involvement in the marketing or solicitation of the transaction to others. Thus, an advisor who provides information about the transaction to a potential participant is involved

174. IRC §6664(d)(1) and (3). *See* Neonatology Assocs., P.A. v Commissioner, 115 T.C. 43, 99 (2000) (adverting to three elements: (i) was the adviser a competent professional who had sufficient expertise to justify reliance? (ii) did the taxpayer provide necessary and accurate information to the adviser? and (iii) did the taxpayer actually rely in good faith on the adviser's judgment?), *aff'd*, 299 F.3d 221 (3d Cir. 2002).

175. IRC §6664 (d)(4)(A).

176. IRC §6664(d)(4)(B).

177. IRC §6664(d)(4)(B)(ii).

in the promotion or sale of a transaction, as is any advisor who recommends the transaction to a potential participant. In *106, Ltd. v. Commissioner*,[178] the Tax Court formally adopted this definition of a promoter whose opinion one may not rely on as a defense to the penalty: "an adviser who participated in structuring the transaction or is otherwise related to, has an interest in, or profits from the transaction."

b. Disqualified Opinion

An opinion may not be relied upon if the opinion (1) is based on unreasonable factual or legal assumptions (including assumptions as to future events), (2) unreasonably relies upon representations, statements, finding or agreements of the taxpayer or any other person, (3) does not identify and consider all relevant facts, or (4) fails to meet any other requirement prescribed by the IRS.[179]

B. Strict Liability Penalty

To help finance expanded medical care spending, in 2010 Congress codified the economic substance doctrine, under which tax benefits may be denied, even if the transactions comply with the literal provisions of the Code, if they lack sufficient economic effect and non-tax business purpose.[180]

To enforce the newly codified doctrine, Congress enacted new subsection 6662(b)(6), under which claiming tax benefits from transactions lacking economic substance exposes the taxpayer to the 20% penalty. Moreover, under new subsection 6662(i), the penalty rate rises to 40% if the relevant facts as to the transaction were not adequately disclosed on the return.

This is a "strict liability" penalty—the reasonable cause defense under section 6664 is not available in section 6662(b)(6) cases. The penalty can apply to deficiencies and also, under section 6676, to erroneous claims for refunds and credits. As one would expect, both the codified economic substance doctrine and the accompanying strict liability penalty have been sharply criticized by taxpayers and their representatives. They will continue to generate controversy in the years to come.[181]

IX. Conclusion

Taxpayers must treat the imposition of the accuracy-related penalties as a separate issue from the underlying adjustments. From the earliest stage of a tax controversy,

---

178. 136 T.C. 67 (2011), *aff'd*, 684 F.3d 84 (D.C. Cir. 2012)

179. IRC §6664(d)(4)(B)(iii).

180. IRC §7701(o), enacted by the Health Care and Education Affordability Reconciliation Act of 2010, Publ. L. No. 111-152, 124 Stat. 1029.

181. *See generally* Jt. Comm. on Tax'n, *Technical Explanation of the Revenue Provisions of the "Reconciliation Act of 2010," as Amended, in Combination with the "Patient Protection and Affordable Health Care Act," available at* http://www.jct.gov/publications.html; Martin J. McMahon, *Living with the Codified Economic Substance Doctrine*, 128 Tax Notes 31, 38 (Aug. 16, 2010).

they must consider evidence and arguments with respect to the penalties, even if they believe they have a strong position on the underlying tax adjustment. It is a mistake to ignore these penalties, as the amounts at stake can be substantial, and interest runs on the accuracy-related penalties from the due date of the original return. An understanding of how the accuracy-related penalty and the fraud penalty operate, and the available defenses to the penalties, is essential. While the IRS is saddled with the burden of production with respect to penalties, a taxpayer must always be prepared to show why a penalty is inappropriate for the specific behavior attributable to him or her.

Problem

Veronica filed her 20x4 federal income tax return on June 20, 20x5. She had not applied for an extension of time to file. The return reported gross income of $80,000, and a tax liability of $16,000. Her employer had withheld $9,000 in federal income tax. She did not pay any additional amounts in tax either prior to or with the filing of the return.

Veronica also had $16,000 of income from consulting work unrelated to her job. The company that had engaged her as a consultant had sent her a Form 1099 reporting the income, but it had been lost in the mail and never received. She forgot about the income and didn't report it. The additional tax on the income would be $3,200.

The return reported a contribution of antiques (capital gain property) to a local section 501(c)(3) organization. The antiques were to be sold by the donee charity. The antiques were worth $4,000, but Veronica "fudged" on the value, and took a $10,000 deduction. The additional tax based on the correct value would be $1,200.

She also sold some business property for $100,000. She had purchased it years ago for $90,000 and had taken depreciation deductions over the years, leaving her with an adjusted basis of $40,000. But on her return, she used the cost, $90,000, as the adjusted basis and reported a gain of $10,000. If she had used the correct adjusted basis, her additional tax would have been $10,000.

Her return had been prepared by a good friend, Archie, who was a CPA. He had prepared her returns for years. He knew that the correct adjusted basis of the property was $40,000, but went along with using the original cost, $90,000, as the adjusted basis for computing the gain, to save taxes for Veronica. Archie suggested making a disclosure of the basis issue on the return, along with a statement arguing that $90,000 was the correct adjusted basis for this purpose, but Veronica rejected his idea.

Veronica also took a depreciation deduction in the amount of $4,000 on her automobile, based on an alleged business use. In fact, however, her claim of business use was subject to substantial question. In addition, she had failed to keep records of any kind in support of the business use, contrary to the IRS rules for substantiating the business use of a vehicle. The additional tax would be $600.

The IRS conducted an examination of Veronica's 20x4 tax return. The Revenue Agent who conducted the examination proposed deficiencies in tax on account of the foregoing in the amount of slightly more than $15,000.

Veronica engaged Archie to represent her in the examination. Archie advised her that the Agent would likely propose additions to tax as well as the deficiency in tax.

1. What additions to tax is the Agent likely to propose?
2. What is the rate at which each of the additions is calculated?
3. To what base number is each rate applied?
4. What defenses does Veronica have?
5. What is the IRS's burden with respect to the additions?
6. What is Veronica's burden?

Chapter 12

Interest

IRC: §§ 1274(d)(1)(C)(i); 6072(a), (b); 6151(a), (c); 6404(g), (h); 6601(a), (b)(1)–(3), (c), (d)(1), (e)(1)–(3); 6603; 6611(a), (b), (d), (e), (f)(1), (4)(A), (g); 6621(a), (c)(1), (d); 6622; 6631; 7481(c)(1); 7508(a) (skim); 7508A(a) (skim)

Rulings: Rev. Proc. 2005-18; Rev. Rul. 88-97; Rev. Rul. 2014-14

Forms: Skim 843

I. Introduction

Generally, a taxpayer who pays all or part of his tax liability late is required to pay interest on the amount of the underpayment from the last date prescribed for payment to the date it is paid.[1] Conversely, a taxpayer who pays more than his tax liability is entitled to receive interest[2] on the amount of the overpayment (unless the overpayment is designated by the taxpayer as a credit elect overpayment)[3] from the date of the overpayment to a date "preceding the date of the refund check by not more than 30 days. . . ."[4] Determining the amount of the underpayment or overpayment, the beginning and ending dates of the period for which interest is paid, and the applicable interest rate is generally relatively straightforward. A degree of complexity is introduced by provisions designed:

(a) to ease administration of the interest requirements, such as stopping the accrual of interest on refunds for a period up to 30 days prior to the issuance of a refund check;

1. IRC § 6601(a). A notable exception is contained in section 6205 which, under specified circumstances, permits interest-free correction of underpayments of certain employment taxes. Taxpayers other than corporations are not allowed to deduct personal interest paid or accrued during the taxable year. IRC § 163(h). Personal interest includes: interest on the underpayment of individual Federal, State, or local income taxes notwithstanding all or portion of the income in connection with a trade or business.

2. IRC § 6611(a). Any interest received by a taxpayer on an overpayment interest is required to be included in taxable income. IRC § 61(a)(4).

3. A taxpayer may elect to have all or part of the overpayment shown on her return applied to the estimated tax for the succeeding taxable year. This is referred to as "credit elect" by the IRS. In such cases, interest is not normally allowed on the portion of the overpayment so credited. Reg. § 301.6611-1(h)(2)(vii). *See also* IRM 20.2.4.8.5.

4. IRC § 6611(b)(2).

(b) to accommodate items affecting income tax liabilities that have a multi-year impact, such as loss carrybacks;[5]

(c) to encourage or discourage certain conduct by taxpayers, such as prohibiting interest on refunds until the return is in "processible form";[6]

(d) to encourage or discourage certain conduct by the IRS, such as suspending interest on underpayments if the IRS fails to send a notice and demand for payment within thirty days after the taxpayer files, under section 6213(d), a waiver of restrictions on assessment;[7] and

(e) to reduce or increase the otherwise applicable interest rate on certain taxpayers, such as the favorable 2% rate imposed on certain estates which, under the provisions of section 6166, defer paying estate tax with respect to interests in closely held businesses.[8]

The basic rules and the complicating modifications to those rules are discussed below, first with respect to underpayments and then with respect to overpayments. Finally, the scope of the Tax Court's jurisdiction to determine the interest due with respect to underpayments and overpayments is discussed.[9]

II. Interest on Underpayments

A. The Basic Rules

Interest must be paid on the amount of any tax (other than estimated tax payable under sections 6654 and 6655) not paid before the last date prescribed for payment, from the last date to the date payment is received by the IRS.[10] With respect to any tax for which a return is required, the tax is to be paid on or before the due date of the return, determined without regard to extensions.[11] Income tax returns of indi-

---

5. IRC § 6611(f).

6. IRC § 6611(g).

7. IRC § 6601(c).

8. IRC § 6601(j).

9. Software is available for the computation of deficiency and overpayment interest. See, for instance, the website of Decision Modeling, Inc., www.dmitax.com. A taxpayer can request the IRS to provide an explanation of all penalty and interest charges generated by the Penalty and Interest Notice Explanation (PINEX) system. The PINEX notice (Form CP-569) includes a computation and explanation of systemically generated penalty and interest charges. The PINEX also provides screen displays of penalty and interest computations for an immediate response to telephone inquiries. IRM 20.1.2.1.6.2.

10. Reg. § 301.6601-1. The additions to tax set forth in sections 6654 and 6655 for failure to pay estimated tax in a timely manner are, in effect, interest and are therefore excluded from the normal interest rules. IRC § 6601(h). Interest is also not payable with respect to underpayments of federal unemployment tax for a calendar quarter (or other period) required to be paid under section 6157. IRC § 6601(i). Also, in the case of jeopardy assessments, if a notice and demand is made before the last date prescribed for payment, then no interest accrues between the date of the notice and demand and the last date prescribed for payment. IRC § 6601(b)(3); Reg. § 301.6601-1(c)(3).

11. IRC § 6151(a).

viduals and C corporations are due on the fifteenth day of the fourth month (typically April 15th) following the close of the taxable year.[12] Interest accrues from those original return due dates whether or not the taxpayer has obtained an extension of time to file the return[13] or to pay the tax.[14] Interest on tax underpayments paid by noncorporate taxpayers is not deductible; however, interest on tax underpayments paid by corporations is deductible.[15]

The interest rate on underpayments is 3% over the federal short-term rate.[16] This rate applies to all taxpayers—individuals, corporations, estates, etc.—except for certain situations discussed below. The federal short-term rate is determined for the first month in each calendar quarter and applies during the next calendar quarter.[17] The federal short-term rate, in turn, is defined as "the average market yield (during any one-month period selected by the Secretary and ending in the calendar month in which the determination is made) on outstanding marketable obligations of the United States with remaining periods to maturity of three years or less."[18] Interest is compounded daily.[19]

"C" corporations generally pay the rates discussed above. However, a different rule applies to a "C" corporation with a "large corporate underpayment," *i.e.*, any underpayment that exceeds $100,000.[20] The rate on large corporate underpayments increases by 2% to the federal short-term rate plus 5% thirty days after the earlier of: (i) the date of the first letter of proposed deficiency with respect to which the corporation can obtain administrative review; or (ii) the date a notice of deficiency is sent,[21] unless the corporation pays the deficiency in full within 30 days of the issuance of a notice.[22]

A separate, favorable, rate of interest is imposed on qualifying estates under the provisions of section 6166. Qualifying estates may elect to pay the estate tax attributable to interests in closely held businesses up to a maximum of ten equal installments. The first installment can be deferred up to five years from the original payment due date of the tax. In the case of any such election, interest is 2% for the "2% portion" of the deferred estate tax and 45% of the normal section 6601(a) rate (currently the

---

12. IRC § 6072(a). These and related rules are discussed in Chapter 2.
13. IRC §§ 6081, 6601(b)(1).
14. IRC §§ 6161, 6601(b)(1).
15. Reg. § 1.163-9T(a) & (b)(2). The Tax Reform Act of 1986 eliminated the deductibility of most types of interest for individuals. This has resulted in unequal treatment for individuals who must include interest received from the Federal government in gross income but may not deduct interest when paid.
16. IRC § 6621(a). The IRS publishes the rates quarterly in revenue rulings. See, e.g., Rev. Rul. 2016-06, 2016-14 I.R.B 519, which establishes the rates for the second quarter of 2016.
17. IRC § 6621(b)(1).
18. IRC §§ 1274(d)(1)(C)(i), 6621(b)(3).
19. IRC § 6622. However, interest is not compounded daily with respect to the estimated tax penalties under sections 6654 and 6655. IRC § 6622(b).
20. IRC § 6621(c)(3)(A).
21. IRC § 6621(c).
22. IRC §§ 6621(b)(2)(B)(ii).

federal short-term rate plus 3%) for the excess over the "2% portion."[23] The 2% portion is the lesser of (i) the tentative tax on the sum of $1,000,000 (annually adjusted for inflation) reduced by the applicable credit amount in effect under section 2010(c), or (ii) the amount of estate tax that is deferred under section 6166.

Interest normally accrues until the underpayment is paid. However, if the taxpayer pays the amount due within 21 calendar days (10 business days if the amount equals or exceeds $100,000) after the date of notice and demand for payment, then no interest is due for the short period after the date of the notice. Both the "timely mailing (or postmarking) is timely filing" rule in section 7502 and the "Saturday, Sunday, legal holiday" rule in section 7503[24] apply to the 21-/10-day time periods. For those taxpayers that pay within the 21-/10-day period, this rule avoids the necessity for successive interest computations and notices to collect the amount of interest due up to the actual date the tax is paid.

Within 60 days after the IRS assesses a tax, it is required to provide the taxpayer a notice of tax, penalties and interest due and demand for payment.[25] Section 6631 requires the IRS to include in its notice "information with respect to the section of [the Code] under which the interest is imposed and a computation of the interest."

B. Modifications to the Basic Rules

1. Carrybacks to a Year with an Underpayment

If there is a net operating loss, net capital loss, or certain tax credits in a taxable year, it is possible to carry those items back to a previous year. Doing so will normally have the effect of reducing the amount of an income tax liability for the year to which the item was carried.[26] If there was an underpayment of tax in the carryback year, the loss or credit carryback would, in effect, reduce or eliminate the amount of the underpayment. However, the carryback loss or credit does not reduce the underpayment for purposes of determining the interest due with respect to the carryback year's tax until the period beginning after the due date of the return for the year in which the net operating loss, net capital loss, or credit carryback occurs.[27]

2. Suspension of Interest on Underpayments

a. Suspension in Case of Delayed Issuance of Notice of Tax Due

If within 30 days after a taxpayer waives the restrictions under section 6213(a) on assessment and collection of a deficiency in income, gift, estate, or generation-skipping taxes (or certain excise taxes) by executing a Form 870 (or one of its brethren), the

23. IRC § 6601(j).

24. Reg. § 301.6601-1(f)(5)(ii).

25. IRC § 6303.

26. According to section 6601(d)(3)(B), tax credit carryback is defined in section 6511(d)(4)(C), which, in turn, defines credit carryback as "any business carryback under section 39."

27. IRC § 6601(d)(1), (3).

IRS has not sent the taxpayer a notice of tax due and demand for payment, then interest is suspended beginning on the 31st day.[28] The suspension lasts until the date of the notice and demand. Additionally, during the suspension period, no interest is imposed on interest accrued prior to the suspension period.

This thirty-day rule also applies to suspend the accrual of interest if a partner enters into a settlement agreement (under section 6224(c)) that results in the conversion of partnership items into non-partnership items. In such case, the settlement serves as a waiver and interest is suspended with respect to the resulting computational adjustment if the IRS does not send the partner a notice of tax due and demand for payment within thirty days of the settlement.[29]

b. Suspension in Case of Failure to Contact the Taxpayer in a Timely Manner

Section 6404(g) suspends interest if the IRS does not notify an individual taxpayer who filed his return on time of both the amount of his liability and the basis therefore within thirty-six months after the later of the date on which the return is filed or the due date of the return without regard to extensions.[30] While this chapter's focus is interest, it should be noted that the suspension also applies to certain penalties, additions to tax, and additional amounts. Any such suspension ends on the 21st day after "the date on which notice … is provided by the Secretary."[31] This section will apply most often when the IRS is asserting a deficiency.[32]

"For purposes of section 6404(g), the Service provides notice … to the taxpayer if it sends a writing to the taxpayer at his or her last known address and that writing includes the amount of the liability, the basis for that liability, and sufficient information or explanation regarding the adjustment to enable the taxpayer to challenge the adjustment."[33] Examples of valid notices include: notices with an accompanying explanation of items of math errors, "Underreporter Program" notices, revenue agent reports, and notices of deficiency.[34] In addition, the service of a pleading alleging an increased deficiency in a Tax Court proceeding will be sufficient notice.[35] Presumably,

---

28. IRC § 6601(c).

29. *Id.* This provision is repealed for partnership taxable years beginning after Dec. 31, 2017. Bipartisan Budget Act of 2015, Pub. L. No. 114-74, § 1101(f)(9)(g), 129 Stat. 584 (2015). See Part B of Chapter 6.

30. Reg. § 301.6404-4.

31. IRC § 6404(g)(3)(B).

32. Reg. § 301.6404-4(a) provides guidance on applying section 6404(g) to amended returns and other signed documents that show increased tax liability, as well as to amended returns that show decreased tax liability.

33. Chief Counsel Notice N(35)000-172 (2000 ARD 959-3), 2000 IRS Chief Counsel Notice Lexis 11 *3; *see also* Reg. § 301.6404-4.

34. *Id.*

35. *Id.* at *4. However, if the parties agree to an increased deficiency in a stipulated decision, "the stipulated decision and a letter transmitting such decision to the petitioner for signature will constitute notice of the liability." *Id.*

the date of mailing of the notice establishes the time that the notice is "provided" to the taxpayer.[36]

The Senate Committee Report to the 1998 Reform Act explained the reasoning behind this provision as follows.

> The Committee believes that the IRS should promptly inform taxpayers of their obligations with respect to tax deficiencies and amounts due. In addition, the Committee is concerned that accrual of interest and penalties absent prompt resolution of tax deficiencies may lead to the perception that the IRS is more concerned about collecting revenue than in resolving taxpayer's problems.[37]

While promptly providing taxpayers notice of the nature and extent of their liability is an admirable goal, providing noncompliant taxpayers an interest and penalty holiday if they are not quickly notified of their noncompliant behavior is difficult to justify. As a result, section 6404(g)(2) denies the suspension for:

(a) late filing and late payment penalties under section 6651;[38]

(b) interest, penalties, additions to tax, or additional amounts in a case involving fraud;

(c) interest, penalties, additions to tax, or additional amounts with respect to tax liabilities reported on the return;

(d) any criminal penalty;

(e) interest, penalties, additions to tax, or additional amounts gross misstatements; or

(f) interest, penalties, additions to tax, or additional amounts reportable transaction with respect to which the facts are not adequately disclosed (under section 6664(d)(1)) or to any listed transaction as defined in section 6707A(c).

Gross misstatements for this purpose include any substantial omission of gross income that triggers the six-year statute of limitations under section 6501(e) as well as any gross valuation misstatements as defined in section 6662(h).[39] Reportable and listed transactions are both generally defined in section 6707A(c) as transactions that the Secretary determines to involve tax avoidance or tax evasion.[40]

---

36. *See id.* at *5 (examples suggest, although do not state directly, that the time of mailing will be the time that notice is "provided").

37. S. Rep. No. 105-174, note 20, supra, at § 3305.

38. It is not clear why this exception is necessary. Interest suspension only applies to timely filed returns. If the return is timely, there can be no section 6651(a)(1) penalty. Also, interest suspension is expressly not applicable to "any tax liability shown on the return." IRC § 6404(g)(2)(C). This covers the section 6651(a)(2) penalty.

39. Reg. § 301.6404-4(b)(4).

40. Reg. § 301.6404-4(b)(5). In Rev. Proc. 2007-21, 2007-1 C.B. 613 (guidance for challenging penalties under sections 6707 and 6707(A); CCA 201021021 (Apr. 20, 2010) (guidance as to sections 6111 and 6707).

As discussed in Section II.B.3.below, section 6404(h) grants the Tax Court jurisdiction to review IRS decisions as to interest abatement.[41]

c. Suspension in the Case of a Presidentially Declared Disaster or Terroristic or Military Action

The IRS also has the authority, under section 7508(A), to suspend the accrual of interest (as well as any penalty, additional amount, or addition to tax) for a period of up to one year if the taxpayer is "affected by a Presidentially declared disaster ... or a terroristic or military action...."

d. Sec. 6603. Deposits Made to Suspend Running of Interest on Potential Underpayments[42]

Section 6603(a) provides that a taxpayer may make a cash deposit with the Service that can be used to pay certain taxes. Section 6603(b) states that, to the extent that a deposit is used by the Service to pay tax, the tax shall be treated as paid on the date the deposit is made for purposes of computing interest on underpayments under section 6601.

Section 6603(c) provides that the Service will return to the taxpayer any amount of a deposit that the taxpayer so requests in writing unless the amount has previously been used to pay tax or the Service determines that collection of tax is in jeopardy. Section 6603(d) authorizes the payment of interest on a deposit that is returned to the taxpayer to the extent (and only to the extent) that the deposit is attributable to a disputable tax, defined in section 6603(d)(2) and (3). Section 6603(d)(4) provides that the rate of interest is the Federal short-term rate determined under section 6621(b), compounded daily. Deposits shall be returned to the taxpayer on a last-in, first-out basis.[43]

To receive interest under section 6603, a taxpayer must comply with the provisions of Revenue Procedure 2005-18.[44] To the extent that a deposit exceeds the proposed liability for which it was deposited, that amount may be returned to the taxpayer, with interest under section 6603, without the need for the taxpayer to file a claim for refund. Any excess deposit generally will be returned only if tax collection is not otherwise in jeopardy.[45]

An undesignated remittance will normally be treated as a payment and applied first to any outstanding liability for taxes, then penalties, and finally interest.[46] Two exceptions to the general treatment are:

---

41. In *Corbalis v. Commissioner*, the Tax Court held that it has jurisdiction over section 6404(g)-type cases (in addition to those under section 6404(e)).

42. This topic is also discussed in Chapter 9, Section II.A.

43. H.R. Conf. Rpt. 108-755 to American Jobs Creation Act of 2004, Pub. L. No. 108-357, § 903(a), 118 Stat. 1418 (2004).

44. 2005-1 C.B. 798.

45. *See* W. Scott Rogers, *Section 6603 Cash Deposits to Stop the Running of Interest on a Deficiency: Factors to Consider Before Remitting a Deposit*, Tax Management Weekly Rep., Sept. 13, 2010, at 1221.

46. Rev. Proc. 2005-18, 2005-1 CB 798, § 4.01(2).

(a) any undesignated remittance made by the taxpayer when the taxpayer is under examination but before the Service proposes a liability in writing, will be treated as a deposit if the taxpayer has no outstanding liabilities. The taxpayer will be notified about the status of the remittance and may elect to have the deposit returned before the issuance of an examination report;[47] and

(b) any undesignated remittance in an amount greater than the amount of the deficiency determined by the Tax Court, plus any related interest accrued at the remittance date, will be treated as a deposit to the extent of the excess. The Service will then return the excess amount to the taxpayer after sufficient information indicates that the taxpayer has no other outstanding liabilities.[48]

3. Abatement of Interest Attributable to Unreasonable Errors and Delays by or Advice from the IRS

Section 6404(e)(1) authorizes the IRS, in its discretion, to abate all or any part of any assessed interest "for any period" in two circumstances.[49] First, abatement is appropriate if the interest is on a deficiency "attributable in whole or in part to an unreasonable error or delay by an officer or employee of the Internal Revenue Service ... in performing a ministerial or managerial act." Second, abatement is appropriate if the interest is on a payment of any income, estate, gift, or generation-skipping tax or certain excise taxes "to the extent that any unreasonable error or delay in such payment is attributable to such officer or employee being erroneous or dilatory in performing a ministerial or managerial act...."[50] Generally, requests for abatement of interest are made by filing Form 843 (Claim for Refund and Request for Abatement).

Section 6404(e)(1) points out that an error or delay, any "significant aspect" of which is attributable to the taxpayer (or to a person related to the taxpayer under sections 267(b) or 707(b)(1)),[51] will not be taken into account for abatement purposes.

Another constraint is that abatement is available only for interest accruing after the IRS "has contacted the taxpayer in writing with respect to [the] deficiency or payment."[52] Thus interest cannot be abated during the period from the filing of the return to either the beginning of an audit or, in case the return was filed but all of the tax shown as due was not paid, the demand for payment.

---

47. *Id.* at §4.04.

48. *Id.* at §4.05.

49. The Tax Court has only limited jurisdiction to address issues related to statutory interest. Jurisdiction under section 6404(h) for the court to review the Commissioner's determination under section 6404(e) is lacking unless and until an assessment of interest has occurred and the Secretary has mailed the "final determination not to abate such interest." Williams v. Commissioner, 131 T.C. 54 (2008).

50. *See* Richard A. Levine & Carlton M. Smith, *Interest Abatement Actions—An Important New Avenue for Taxpayer Relief*, 86 J. Tax'n 5 (1997).

51. Reg. §301.6404-2(a)(2).

52. IRC §6404(e)(1); Matthews v. Commissioner, T.C. Memo. 2008-126.

When the interest is on a deficiency or payment resulting from the IRS's conduct, two additional criteria severely limit the IRS's authority to abate: The conduct in question must relate to the performance of a "ministerial or managerial act" and the error or delay in performing that act must be "unreasonable."

Regulation section 301.6404-2(b) and (c) contains brief definitions of both ministerial and managerial acts and provides thirteen examples that give substance to the definitions. The Regulations define ministerial acts as acts which do not involve the exercise of discretion or judgment and that occur "after all prerequisites to the act, such as conferences and review by supervisors, have taken place."[53] Managerial acts take place during the processing of a case and involve "the temporary or permanent loss of records or the exercise of judgment or discretion relating to management of personnel." The determination of the proper application of state or federal law is neither a ministerial nor managerial act. The Regulations do not attempt to define acts that are "unreasonable" although some understanding of the IRS's view of the term can be gleaned from the examples.[54]

A taxpayer's right to abatement of interest under this section is conditioned on conduct by IRS personnel that is deemed to be undesirable. For that reason, persons representing clients during audits should be careful to document throughout the audit the apparent errors or delays caused by IRS personnel with a view to being able to justify application of the abatement rules.

Section 6404(f) authorizes the IRS to abate any penalty or addition to tax attributable to erroneous written advice by the IRS. Abatement under this provision is conditioned on the taxpayer having: (i) requested the advice in writing, (ii) reasonably relied on the advice, and (iii) provided the IRS adequate and accurate information about the matter.[55] The Regulations make clear that when a penalty or addition to tax is abated, any related interest will also be abated.[56]

Taxpayers whose request for abatement of interest has been denied by the IRS may first seek review by the Appeals Office of the IRS and, if that is not successful, may petition the Tax Court to determine whether the denial was an abuse of discretion.[57] Only a taxpayer whose net worth does not exceed the amounts specified in section 7430(c)(4)(ii) is entitled to such judicial review. Under this rule, the maximum net

53. *See* Taylor v. Commissioner, 113 T.C. 206, *aff'd*, 9 Fed. Appx 700 (9th Cir. 2001) (holding that suspension of civil action against the taxpayer pending the outcome of the criminal trial was not a ministerial act).

54. *See* Nelson v. Commissioner, T.C. Memo. 2004-34 (holding that incorrect advice given by the IRS did not constitute ministerial acts for purposes of abating interest).

55. Reg. § 301.6404-3(b)(1).

56. Reg. § 301.6404-3(c)(2).

57. Pub. L. No. 104-168, § 302(a), 110 Stat. 1452, 1457 (1966). On May 21, 2007, the Supreme Court resolved a conflict between the Federal Circuit and the Fifth Circuit on the question of whether the Tax Court has exclusive jurisdiction under section 6404(h) to consider IRS denials of interest abatement claims made under section 6404(e). Hinck v. United States, 550 U.S. 501, 127 S. Ct. 2011 (2007). The Court agreed with the Federal Circuit's opinion in *Hinck v. United States*, 446 F.3d 1307 (Fed. Cir. 2006), that Congress had granted exclusive jurisdiction to the Tax Court and rejected the Fifth Circuit's opinion in *Beall v. United States*, 336 F.3d 419 (5th Cir. 2003), that the district courts can also hear such cases.

worth an individual can have and be eligible for judicial review of an IRS denial of interest abatement is $2 million. For corporations, the limit is $7 million.

The Tax Court has adopted Rules 280-84 relating to actions for review of the IRS's failure to abate interest. The action is commenced by filing a petition and paying the $60 filing fee.[58] Taxpayers must petition the Tax Court "within 180 days after the date of the mailing of the Secretary's final determination not to abate [the] interest."[59] In addition to normal matters pled in a petition, the taxpayer must plead and prove that he qualifies for judicial review under the applicable net worth cap.[60] Decisions of the Tax Court relating to abatement of interest may be appealed in the same manner as other decisions of the court.[61]

4. Interest on Penalties, Additional Amounts, and Additions to Tax

For purposes of determining the period over which interest accrues on penalties, additional amounts, and additions to tax, section 6601(e)(2) divides them into two categories. The first group of penalties—those under sections 6651(a)(1) for failure to file a return on time, 6653 for failure to pay stamp tax, 6662 for accuracy-related penalties, and 6663 for fraud[62]—bears interest from the date that the return is required to be filed, including extensions.[63]

Although these additions to tax are not limited to noncompliance with the income tax provisions, their impact is felt most often in the income tax context. Interest accrues on these additions to tax until they are paid except that if an individual taxpayer pays the amount on the notice and demand for payment within 21 calendar days of the notice, no interest will be charged during that period.[64]

The second category consists of all other penalties, additional amounts, and additions to tax. Interest on these accrues from the date of the notice and demand for payment to the date of payment[65] unless the amount billed is paid within 21 days. If paid within 21 days, no interest is charged.[66]

---

58. The Court of Federal Claims lacks jurisdiction to review interest abatement claims. See the discussion in the previous footnote.

59. Nothing in the Code or Regulations requires the IRS to issue a final determination denying a claim for abatement of interest.

60. Estate of Edward J. Kunze v. Commissioner, T.C. Memo. (CCH) 1999-344 (1999), *aff'd*, 233 F.3d 948 (7th Cir. 2000).

61. IRC § 6404(h)(2)(c).

62. This category also includes the 50% penalty imposed on any person who willfully fails to pay any stamp tax or who willfully attempts to evade or defeat such tax. IRC § 6653.

63. The beginning date of interest for these additions to tax (the date the return was required to be filed including extensions (section 6601(e)(2)(B)) is different from the beginning date of interest on underpayments of tax (the last date prescribed for payment excluding extensions). IRC § 6601(a) & (b)(1).

64. IRC § 6601(e)(3).

65. IRC § 6601(e)(2)(A).

66. IRC § 6601(e)(3). The 21-day period is shortened to 10 business days if the amount for which the notice and demand is made equals or exceeds $100,000. IRC § 6601(e)(3).

III. Interest on Overpayments

A. The Basic Rules

Under section 6511(a), if a taxpayer overpaid his taxes and wishes to get the overpayment refunded, he should file a claim within three years from the time the return was filed or two years from the time the tax was paid, whichever of such periods expires the later.[67] After crediting the overpayment (including corresponding interest) against any other existing tax liability of the taxpayer, such as an unpaid federal or state income tax obligation, and a variety of other debts for which the taxpayer is obligated, the IRS will refund the balance to the taxpayer.[68]

If the claim is filed timely, the taxpayer is generally also entitled to interest on the amount of the overpayment from the date of the overpayment to a date preceding the date of the refund check by not more than 30 days.[69] For purposes of determining the date when the overpayment first occurred, advance payments of tax through withholding, estimated tax payments, and application of prior years' overpayment to the current year's estimated tax payments are deemed paid on the due date (determined without extensions) of the return for the year for which the amounts were withheld or paid. For individuals, that normally means April 15th of the year following the taxable year.[70]

For taxpayers other than corporations, the interest rate on overpayments is the same as the interest rate on underpayments—three percentage points above the federal short-term rate,[71] compounded daily.[72] For corporations, the interest rate on overpayments is just two percentage points over the federal short-term rate for the portion of the overpayment up to and including $10,000, and one-half percentage point over the federal short-term rate for the portion, if any, of the overpayment that exceeds $10,000.[73] It is also compounded daily.[74]

In the case of overpayment of tax on a built-in gain by an S corporation, the Tax Court has held that the higher rate of interest paid to noncorporate taxpayers, rather than the lower rate paid to corporations, is applicable.[75] Interest is recoverable against

---

67. Refund claims of overpayments are discussed in detail in Chapter 9.

68. IRC §6402.

69. IRC §6611(b)(2). Any refund check "tendered" will stop the running of interest. Therefore, taxpayers who receive a refund check in an amount less than they think is correct should deposit the check rather than rejecting it and requesting a check in the amount they think is correct. Accepting the check will not preclude the taxpayer from claiming the additional tax and interest believed to be due.

70. IRC §6611(d).

71. IRC §6621(a)(1).

72. IRC §6622.

73. The Ninth Circuit held that section 6621(a)(1) also applies to interest payable to a corporate taxpayer involved in a wrongful levy. Steven N.S. Cheung, Inc. v. United States, 545 F.3d 695 (9th Cir. 2008).

74. IRC §6622.

75. Garwood Irrigation Co. v. Commissioner, 126 T.C. 223 (2006).

the government only when specifically provided for by statute because only by statute can the government waive its sovereign immunity.[76]

B. Modifications to the Basic Rules

1. Rules Affecting the Period Over Which Interest Is Paid

There are four important exceptions to the general rule that the government must pay interest with respect to overpayments from the date of the overpayment.

- First, no interest is due on an overpayment if the amount claimed on a timely filed return is refunded within 45 days after the last day prescribed for filing the return (determined without regard to extensions of time to file). In the case of a return filed after the last day prescribed for filing the return (determined without regard to extensions of time to file), no interest is due if the overpayment amount is refunded within 45 days of the return being filed.[77]
- Second, if the taxpayer files a claim for refund, no interest is paid for the period after the claim is filed if the refund is paid within 45 days of the claim being filed.[78]
- Third, no interest is paid with respect to an overpayment reported on a return filed after its due date (determined with regard to extensions) for the period ending on the day before the day the return is filed.[79]
- Fourth, no interest is paid with respect to any return that is not in processible form when filed.[80]

2. Netting of Interest for Overlapping Tax Periods

In the 1998 Reform Act, Congress adopted "global interest netting." Under section 6621(d), to the extent that any interest is payable on an underpayment for one year or one type of tax and interest is allowable on an overpayment for another year or another type of tax and there are overlapping periods, the interest rate is zero for the period of the overlap to the extent of the overlapping amount.[81] This rule applies

76. *See* Gandy Nursery Inc. v. United States, 412 F.3d 602 (5th Cir. 2005) (taxpayer not entitled to post-judgment interest on damages awarded under section 7432).

77. IRC § 6611(e)(1). In C.C.A. 200441002, the IRS examined when the 45-day period starts when an income tax return reflecting an overpayment is postmarked on the extended due date for filing the return. The Service adopted a taxpayer-friendly interpretation, finding that the 45-day period starts on the date of the United States postmark.

78. IRC § 6611(e)(2). *See also* Prog. Mgr. Tech. Assist. (July 1, 2008), 2008 TNT 240-9.

79. IRC § 6611(b)(3).

80. IRC § 6611(g).

81. The IRS has dealt with several variations on this theme to which the statute does not necessarily apply. For instance, if the taxpayer reports an overpayment for a given year and receives a refund without interest and it is subsequently determined that there was an underpayment for the year, then interest will be assessed on the portion of the underpayment covered by the amount refunded from the date of the refund. If the underpayment exceeds the amount refunded, interest on the excess will accrue from the due date of the return on which the overpayment was reported. Rev. Rul. 99-40, 1999-2 C.B. 441.

even if different kinds of taxes are involved and even if the rates on the underpayment and overpayment are different.[82] However, interest netting does not apply if one of the periods in question is barred by the statute of limitations.[83]

3. Carrybacks Creating an Overpayment

Net operating loss, net capital loss, and certain tax credit carrybacks may have the effect of reducing the amount of income tax liability for a carryback year. This, in turn, may create an overpayment and entitle the taxpayer to a refund for the year to which the item was carried back. For purposes of determining the amount of interest to which the taxpayer is entitled on the refund, however, the resulting overpayment is deemed not to have occurred before the filing date (determined without regard to extensions) for the year in which the loss or credit giving rise to the carryback occurred.[84] The 45-day period within which the IRS can refund any overpayment without paying interest thereon applies to any refund generated by a carryback.[85] Thus, if the refund is paid within the later of 45 days after the due date of the return for the loss year (determined without regard to extensions) or 45 days after the date the return is filed, then no interest must be paid with respect to any refund generated by the carryback.[86]

A bank acquired other banks by merger. Multiple entities were involved which had multiple tax overpayments and underpayments from pre- and post-merger years. This created considerable confusion as to what netting of interest was allowable. The taxpayer and the IRS litigated test claims based on three merger-related scenarios. The court ruled for the taxpayer as to all three test claims. Holding that the surviving corporation and the acquired corporations were the same taxpayer for section 6621(d) purposes, the court allowed full interest netting. Wells Fargo & Co. v. United States, 117 Fed. Cl. 30 (2014).

82. The rates might be different because of the increased rates on large corporate underpayments and the reduced rates on corporate overpayments in excess of $10,000.

83. Although section 6621(d) refers to interest "payable" and "allowable," which seems to be limited to outstanding underpayments and overpayments, the Conference Committee Report made it clear that netting was to occur "without regard to whether the underpayment or overpayments are currently outstanding." H.R. Conf. Rep. No. 105-599, §3301, at 256 (1998), reprinted at 1998-3 C.B. 747, 1010–11. This is consistent with the fact that in the same Act, Congress amended §6601(f), which deals with a similar issue involving the satisfaction of any tax by a credit, to make §6621(d) apply where the two sections would otherwise overlap. *See also* Federal National Mortgage Association v. United States, 69 Fed. Cl. 89 (2005), *aff'd.*, 469 F.3d 968 (Fed. Cir. 2006) (discussing an uncodified provision which allows taxpayers to request the Service to apply section 6621(d) to periods predating its enactment).

84. IRC §6611(f).

85. IRC §6611(f)(4)(B).

86. *But see* Coca-Cola Co. v. United States, 87 Fed. Cl. 253 (2009) (notwithstanding the 45-day rule, requiring the IRS to pay interest on an overpayment after the IRS examined and adjusted a carryback claim). This case is discussed by Michael J. Grace, Joseph M. Persinger & Gilbert M. Polt, Coca-Cola Company v. U.S.: *6411 Versus 6611 and Other Adventures of Deficiency and Statutory Interest*, 2010 Tax Mgmt. Memorandum 243.

IV. Tax Court Jurisdiction over Interest Determinations

The principal role of the Tax Court in the federal tax system is to provide taxpayers an opportunity for judicial review of determinations by the IRS that income, estate, gift, or generation-skipping taxes have been underpaid. Upon the filing of a petition in Tax Court, the court acquires "jurisdiction to redetermine the correct amount of the deficiency. . . ."[87] If the court finds that the taxpayer actually made an overpayment, it also has jurisdiction to determine the amount of the overpayment.[88]

If the Tax Court determines that there was an underpayment of tax, the IRS will assess[89] the tax determined to be due and send the taxpayer a notice of the amount and demand for payment.[90] At the same time, the IRS will calculate the interest due on the underpayment and will include the interest in the notice and demand for payment.

Although interest is assessed and collected in the same manner as taxes, the deficiency procedures expressly do not apply to interest.[91] This is because once the amount of tax due has been determined, the amount of interest due is purely a mathematical computation.

If the Tax Court determines that the taxpayer actually overpaid the tax, the IRS will normally refund the amount of the overpayment and pay any accrued interest

---

87. IRC § 6214(a). The Tax Court's jurisdiction includes the right to increase the deficiency beyond that set forth in the notice of deficiency. If a petition is filed in the Tax Court in response to a deficiency notice then no assessment and no collection efforts may be made until the decision of the Tax Court becomes final. IRC § 6213(a). Notwithstanding this seemingly broad taxpayer protection, section 7485 makes it clear that assessment or collection of the amount determined by the Tax Court to be due is not stayed by the filing of an appeal unless the taxpayer also files a bond with the Tax Court. The amount of the bond is to be determined by the Tax Court and is to secure payment of the deficiency, interest, additional amounts, and additions to tax. IRC § 7485(a).

88. IRC § 6512(b). If there is any dispute between a taxpayer and the Service (e.g., the Service fails to refund the overpayment determined by the Court or the taxpayer disagrees with the overpayment amount) after 120 days after a Tax Court decision becomes final, the Tax Court, upon motion by the taxpayer, has jurisdiction to enforce refund of overpayment and interest. Tax Ct. R. 260 & IRC § 6512(b)(2). The taxpayer may request that the Tax Court treat his case under the "Small Tax Case" procedures under section 7463. Procedures in such cases are different from those in regular cases. Among other things, the scope of the court's jurisdiction in Small Tax Cases is limited and the court's decisions are not subject to any appellate review. *See* Chapter 8.

89. IRC § 6215.

90. IRC § 6303(a).

91. IRC § 6601(e)(1). The word "taxes" includes the accrued interest related to one's income tax. As such, the Tax Court found it has jurisdiction under section 6015(e)(1) to review the government's denial of equitable relief under section 6015(f) from the taxpayer's liability for the accrued interest. Kollar v. Commissioner, 131 T.C. 191 (2008). Likewise, when a taxpayer executes an agreement to extend the statute of limitations on assessment, such as on a Form 872-A, the agreement applies not only to taxes but also to interest. Estate of Greenfield v. Commissioner, 297 Fed. Appx. 858 (11th Cir. 2008). The statutes of limitations on assessment and collection of interest are the same as for the corresponding taxes. However, interest continues to accrue while collection action on an account is suspended due to various factors (e.g., uncollectibility, an installment agreement, and Tax Court proceedings).

to the taxpayer. If the IRS does not refund the overpayment and pay interest within 120 days after the Court's decision becomes final, upon the taxpayer's motion, the Court may order the IRS to make the refund and pay interest. Tax Court Rule 260 establishes procedures to be followed in connection with such motions.

Whether interest is accrued with respect to an underpayment or an overpayment of tax, as finally determined by the Tax Court, computation of its amount is initially done by the IRS. In 1988, the Tax Court first acquired jurisdiction to redetermine the correct amount of interest arising out of its determinations. Under section 7481(c), the taxpayer has a period of one year after a Tax Court decision becomes final within which to file a motion with the Tax Court for a redetermination of the amount of either the interest to be paid in the case of a deficiency or the interest due to the taxpayer in the case of an overpayment. In the case of interest on a deficiency, the right to a redetermination is conditioned on the taxpayer first paying the full amount of tax, penalties, and interest computed by the IRS.[92] The Tax Court also may hear interest abatement questions as part of the Collection Due Process procedures.[93]

Problem

Paul and Carol, cash basis taxpayers, timely filed their joint federal income tax return for the year 20x2 on August 1, 20x3, after having been granted an extension of time to file until October 15, 20x3. The tax liability shown on the return was $150,000. A total of $35,000 had been paid by withholding from their salaries and $40,000 had been paid in four equal installments of estimated tax in the amount of $10,000 each. The balance of $75,000 was paid at the time the return was filed.

Their 20x2 tax return was selected by the IRS for examination in June 20x4. At the end of the examination, the IRS proposed a deficiency in tax in the amount of $80,000. Paul and Carol asked their lawyer to file a protest with the IRS on their behalf and to request a conference with an Appeals Officer. Unfortunately, however, the Appeals Officer agreed with the proposed deficiency. Paul and Carol were not willing to agree, and the Appeals Officer issued a statutory notice of deficiency in the amount of $80,000 for the year.

Paul and Carol felt strongly about their case, and asked their lawyer to file a petition in the Tax Court for the year. After trial, the Court agreed with Paul and Carol as to $30,000 of the deficiency, but sustained the IRS' determination as to the remaining $50,000. No appeals were filed, and the decision of the Tax Court became final on November 1, 20x5.

Soon thereafter, Paul and Carol received a notice from the IRS, dated November 15, 20x5, demanding payment of $50,000, plus interest, for the year 20x2.

1. What payments are subject to interest? How is the interest calculated?

---

92. IRC §7481(c)(2)(A)(ii); Tax Ct. R. 261. Section 6404(h)(2)(A) contains a curious cross-reference to section 6213 "for purposes of determining the date of the mailing" of the claim for abatement. But, nothing in section 6213 deals with the date of mailing.

93. *E.g.*, Wright v. Commissioner, 571 F.3d 215 (2d Cir. 2009), *rev'g* T.C. Memo. 2006-273.

2. How long do Paul and Carol have to pay the $50,000 deficiency? What would be the result if it is not paid within that time?

3. Assume for this problem 3 that interest rates applicable to the deficiency had risen dramatically. Assume further that Paul and Carol's attorney was aware of the interest, and had told Paul and Carol, prior to the trial in the Tax Court, that the amount of interest was disproportionately large in comparison to the deficiency. The IRS had not proposed penalties, but the interest was so great that it had assumed the appearance of a penalty. Paul and Carol asked whether the disproportionately large amount of interest could be used to their advantage in pre-trial settlement discussions. Could the IRS have agreed to reduce the interest before the trial to encourage Paul and Carol to settle the case? If not, what could the IRS have done to encourage settlement?

4. Assume for this problem 4 that settlement discussions with the IRS Appeals Office before the statutory notice of deficiency was issued were successful. Paul and Carol executed the appropriate Form 870 on July 1, 20x4. The IRS sent them a notice and demand dated December 15, 20x4, for payment of the agreed amount of tax. What are the relevant dates for calculating the interest on the amounts due?

5. Assume for this problem 5 that $10,000 of the $50,000 deficiency determined by the Tax Court is a penalty imposed under IRC section 6673. Would that affect your answer to problem 1 above?

6. Assume for this problem 6 that within a few weeks of receiving the statutory notice of deficiency, Paul and Carol paid the full $80,000 in order to reduce any obligation they might have to pay interest. Will the payment be effective for that purpose? Are Paul and Carol entitled to interest on their $30,000 refund after the Tax Court decided they owed only $50,000?

7. Assume for this problem 7 that in September 20x4, shortly before completion of the examination, Paul and Carol filed their 20x3 return. It included a very large net operating loss that was eligible for carryback both to 20x1 and 20x2 under IRC section 172. The carryback to 20x2 was large enough to reduce their tax liability for that year, as proposed by the IRS during the examination, to zero. How would Paul and Carol's liability for interest on the 20x2 deficiency be affected by the carryback and resulting reduction of the proposed deficiency to zero?

8. Assume for this problem 8 that Paul and Carol filed their 20x2 return on August 1, 20x3, without first obtaining an extension of time to file. Assume further that the total tax liability shown on the return was $50,000, as a result of which they were entitled to a $25,000 refund. The IRS sent Paul and Carol a refund check on September 15, 20x3. Are Paul and Carol entitled to interest on the refund?

Chapter 13

Collection of Tax

IRC: §§ 6159(a)–(b), 6201(a)(1), (d), 6303, 6304, 6320, 6321, 6322, 6323 (skip subsection (e), skim the remaining subsections), 6325, 6330, 6331(a), 6334(a), (e), 6502, 6503(b)–(h) (skim all), 6532 (b), (c), 7122, 7403, 7421, 7426, 7432(a), (b), 7433

I. Introduction

"[T]axes are the life-blood of government, and their prompt and certain availability an imperious need."[1] The overwhelming majority of taxes collected by the IRS are self-reported and paid "voluntarily" by taxpayers. Nonetheless, the enforced collection mechanisms in the Code are of crucial significance. The money they collect, though small relatively, is substantial in absolute terms.[2] More importantly, the possibility of enforced collection encourages taxpayers to pay "voluntarily."

The Code rules governing collection are extensive and complex. The Code equips the IRS with a formidable arsenal of collection devices, stronger than those available to private creditors.[3] Yet, the very power of these devices inspires concern about the possibility of their abuse. Thus, the Code also contains substantial protections for taxpayers and third parties adversely affected by IRS collection activities. This chapter describes the administrative structure through which collection is effected. It then examines key collection devices available to the IRS, administrative and judicial protections available to taxpayers and third parties, and statute of limitations considerations.

---

1. Bull v. United States, 295 U.S. 247 (1935). As Edmund Burke, widely regarded as the founder of modern conservatism, said: "The revenue of the state is the state." *Quoted in* State Tax Notes, Jan. 15, 2007, at 149.

2. In fiscal years 2014 and 2015, enforced collections by the IRS brought in, respectively, about $49 billion and $50 billion. IRS Data Book, 2015, at 43. A series of eight short videos "Owe Taxes? Understanding IRS Collection Efforts" is available on the IRS's website: www.irs.gov.

3. *See, e.g.*, United States v. Whiting Pools, Inc., 462 U.S. 198, 209–10 (1983). Various federal and state laws, such as the Fair Debt Collection Practices Act, limit aggressive debt collection practices. These measures do not apply to the IRS. *E.g.*, Al-Sharif v. United States, 296 Fed. Appx. 740 (11th Cir. 2008) (per curiam).

II. Collection Structure

The collection process typically begins at an IRS service center. Usually, the initial steps are assessment, followed by the issuance by the service center of the first of a series of letters to the taxpayer. The first letter notifies the taxpayer of the nature, amount, and date of the assessment and demands payment. If payment is not made, as many as three more letters may be issued, each spaced several weeks apart. The last of the letters is sent by certified mail and states the IRS's intent to locate assets, levy on them, and perhaps to file notice of the tax lien.

The letters have the effect of satisfying statutory requirements, including the section 6303(a) requirement of notice and demand for payment and the section 6331(d) requirement of notice before levy. Although the letters have this effect, the Code does not require a series of letters.[4] Thus, the series is a matter of policy with the IRS. The IRS can truncate the accustomed series if it chooses.

The letters are designed to induce payment or, at least, to prompt the taxpayer to contact the IRS. If neither payment nor contact ensues, the service center will transfer the case to the Automated Collection System ("ACS") or, less commonly and usually only in large-dollar cases, to a collection specialist known as a revenue officer.

ACS relies on computer searches and telephone contacts. If ACS succeeds in contacting the taxpayer, it will seek financial information in order to facilitate levy. If the taxpayer is represented pursuant to a proper power-of-attorney (Form 2848) filed with the IRS, ACS ordinarily must deal with the representative, not the taxpayer.[5] ACS will attempt to obtain immediate full payment, but it is empowered to accept payments over time.

If ACS fails to collect or to establish an agreement for collection, the case may be transferred to a revenue officer in the field, under the rubric of a Taxpayer Delinquent Account ("TDA").[6] The revenue officer is supposed to contact the taxpayer promptly,[7] but the reality of heavy caseloads sometimes thwarts this command. Once again, the attempt will be to secure full payment or its best feasible alternative. If the revenue officer concludes that there is no worthwhile collection potential, the case will be assigned to Currently Not Collectible ("CNC") status.[8] CNC cases are periodically reviewed and will be returned to active status if new information suggesting collection

---

4. Indeed, the section 6303(a) notice and demand need not even be in writing; oral communication can suffice. *See, e.g.*, Hahn v. United States, 77-1 U.S. Tax Cas. (CCH) ¶ 9334 (C.D. Cal. 1977). The section 6331(d) notice preceding levy, however, must be in writing. If the taxpayer's contact with the IRS is extensive, the taxpayer may be held to have waived receipt of notice and demand. *See, e.g.*, In re Baltimore Pearl Hominy Co., 5 F.2d 553 (4th Cir. 1925).

5. *See* IRC § 7521(b)(2), (c).

6. TDA should not be confused with Taxpayer Delinquency Investigation ("TDI"). In a TDI, a revenue officer is assigned to investigate a taxpayer's failure to file a required return and to procure the missing return.

7. *See* IRM 5.1.10.3.

8. In the jargon of tax practice, putting a case into CNC status is often called "53-ing" the case (after IRS Form 53 used for this purpose).

potential develops. The IRS eventually collects only about 2% of the amounts due on accounts that are designated with CNC status.[9]

Other IRS functions provide support to revenue officers in certain categories of cases. These functions are subject to fairly frequent reorganization.

III. Assessment

Assessment pursuant to section 6201 is the first stage of the collection process. It is key because the IRS cannot legally collect any tax until it has been properly assessed. Assessment must be made within the statute of limitations period, as described in Chapter 5. The assessment itself is a purely mechanical act: the recordation of the liability on the books of the IRS.[10] If the IRS determines that the initial assessment was imperfect or incomplete, it may make supplemental assessments as long as the limitations period remains open.[11]

To protect taxpayers, the Code imposes prerequisites to assessment in some situations. These include the deficiency procedures of sections 6211 through 6215 detailed in Chapter 8.

Certain kinds of taxes—employment taxes and most excise taxes, for instance—are wholly outside the deficiency procedure. Moreover, even taxes generally subject to the deficiency procedures sometimes can be assessed without going through those procedures. For instance, all of the following can be directly assessed: amounts shown on a return but not paid with it, erroneous income tax prepayment credits, mathematical errors, clerical errors, amounts arising out of tentative carryback or refund adjustments, and amounts paid by the taxpayer.[12] In addition, as described in Chapter 7, the deficiency procedures do not apply when jeopardy to collection makes expedited assessment appropriate.

Penalties are assessed and collected in the same manner as the taxes to which they relate.[13] Thus, the accuracy-related penalties and the section 6651 "timeliness" penalties usually can be assessed only after the issuance of a notice of deficiency. However, section 6651 penalties not attributable to a deficiency can be assessed without the issuance of a notice of deficiency. Interest on assessed taxes may be assessed at any time within the limitations period for collection of the underlying taxes.[14] Section 73 provides that amounts received in respect of the services of a child are included in the child's gross income, not his or her parents' income, even if the amounts are not received by the child. Any such amounts assessed against the child "shall, if not paid by the

9. IRS News Release IR-2007-04 (Jan. 9, 2007).
10. The recordation procedures are described in Reg. section 301.6203-1.
11. IRC §6204(a).
12. IRC §§6201(a), 6213(b).
13. IRC §§6665(a)(1), 6671(a).
14. IRC §6601(g).

child, for all purposes be considered as having also been properly assessed against the parent."[15]

In general, the IRS is given substantial latitude in estimating the amount to be assessed when taxpayer records and other evidence do not admit of precision,[16] leaving it up to the taxpayer to establish in litigation what the true liability is. However, if the IRS's determination is based on an information return filed by a third party and if the taxpayer has cooperated with the IRS, section 6201(d) imposes on the IRS "the burden of producing reasonable and probative information" beyond the information return in order to support its determination.

Under section 6404, the IRS has authority to abate unpaid assessments of taxes, other than income, estate, and gift taxes, and in some cases unpaid assessments of interest. Abatement is authorized under various circumstances, including: assessments excessive in amount, made after expiration of the limitations period, or otherwise erroneously or illegally made; small balances that would be uneconomic to collect; amounts attributable to mathematical errors by the IRS; interest attributable to unreasonable errors, delays, or incorrect written advice by the IRS; interest and penalties when the IRS fails to contact the taxpayer; and interest in presidentially declared disaster areas.

IV. Liens

A. Creation and Extent

The assessment begins the collection process. The next step is the IRS notifying the taxpayer of the assessment and demanding payment. Notice and demand are to be made "as soon as practicable, and within 60 days," after the assessment.[17] The notice is to be left at the taxpayer's dwelling or usual place of business or mailed to the taxpayer's last known address.[18]

If the taxpayer neglects or refuses to pay after notice and demand, the general federal tax lien automatically arises under section 6321. The amount of the lien equals the unpaid tax plus any interest, penalties, and costs with respect to it. Section 6322 provides that the general tax lien, once it arises, relates back to the date of assessment and continues until it is satisfied by payment or becomes unenforceable because of expiration of the statute of limitations on collection. In general, under section 6502(a), the collection statute of limitations expires ten years after the date of the assessment. However, under certain circumstances, that period may be extended either generally or as to specific assets. The collection statute of limitations is discussed further in Section IX of this chapter.

---

15. IRC § 6201(c). "Parent" includes any person "entitled to the services of a child by reason of having parental rights and duties in respect of the child." IRC § 73(c).

16. *See, e.g.*, United States v. Fior D'Italia, Inc., 536 U.S. 238, 243–44 (2002).

17. "The failure to give such notice within 60 days does not invalidate the notice." Reg. § 301.6303-1(a).

18. IRC § 6303(a).

Tax practitioners sometimes use the acronyms ASED, CSED, and RSED to refer to the last date on which a statute of limitations is or was open. They are, respectively, the Assessment Statute Expiration Date (see section 6501 discussed in Chapter 5), Collection Statute Expiration Date (see section 6502 discussed in this chapter), and Refund Statute Expiration Date (see section 6511 discussed in Chapter 9).

Taxpayers sometimes argue that the IRS failed to make notice and demand, thus that no tax lien came into existence. These arguments rarely succeed. The courts have been liberal in the kinds of proof of notice and demand they have deemed acceptable.[19]

The section 6321 lien attaches to "all property and rights to property, whether real or personal" of the taxpayer's. The Supreme Court has repeatedly emphasized that this statutory language, and thus the reach of the general lien, is extremely broad.[20] Case law applying the tax lien to particular types of assets and interests underlines this broad reach.[21] Obviously, the lien attaches to property solely owned by the taxpayer in fee simple absolute, but it attaches as well to lesser or weaker interests. For example, it attaches to the taxpayer's interest in jointly owned property,[22] executory contracts,[23] spendthrift trusts,[24] future or contingent property interests,[25] and to property acquired by the taxpayer after the date on which the tax lien came into existence.[26]

For decades, a vexing question was the relationship of state law and federal law in tax lien controversies. However, the following rule is now settled law. In the first stage, one identifies the powers, strings, or controls that the taxpayer has over the asset in question. In the second stage, one decides whether those powers, strings, or controls rise to the level of being "property or rights to property" within the intendment of section 6321, in which case the lien attaches to the taxpayer's interest in the asset. The first stage is a matter of state law (or of whatever other law created the interest or asset). The second stage is a matter purely of federal law. In addition, all post-lien-attachment consequences depend on federal law (except when federal law incorporates state law).[27]

The fact that the second stage is a matter exclusively of federal law means that state law characterizations as "property" or "not property" are irrelevant. For example,

---

19. *See, e.g.*, United States v. Dixon, 672 F. Supp. 503 (M.D. Fla. 1987) (IRS certificate of assessments and payments constitutes proof of assessment). Third parties may not assert that the lien is invalid because of absence of notice and demand. *See, e.g.*, United States v. Lorson Elec., 72-2 U.S. Tax Cas. (CCH) ¶ 9614 (S.D.N.Y. 1972), *aff'd per curiam*, 480 F.2d 554 (2d Cir. 1973).

20. *See, e.g.*, Glass City Bank v. United States, 326 U.S. 265 (1945) ("Stronger language could hardly have been selected to reveal a purpose to assure the collection of taxes").

21. For discussion of case law applying the tax lien in context of numerous types of property interests, see William D. Elliott, Federal Tax Collection, Liens, and Levies ¶ 9.09 (2015).

22. *See, e.g.*, United States v. Trilling, 328 F.2d 699 (7th Cir. 1964).

23. *See, e.g.*, Randall v. H. Nakashima & Co., Ltd., 542 F.2d 270 (5th Cir. 1976).

24. *See, e.g.*, Magavern v. United States, 550 F.2d 797 (2d Cir. 1977).

25. *See, e.g.*, United States v. Solheim, 91-1 U.S. Tax Cas. (CCH) ¶ 50,108 (D. Neb. 1990), *aff'd on other grounds*, 953 F.2d 379 (8th Cir. 1992); Bigheart Pipeline Corp. v. United States, 600 F. Supp. 50, 53 (N.D. Okla. 1984), *aff'd*, 835 F.2d 766 (10th Cir. 1987).

26. *See, e.g.*, Glass City Bank v. United States, 326 U.S. 265 (1945).

27. *See, e.g.*, United States v. Craft, 535 U.S. 274 (2002); Drye v. United States, 528 U.S. 49 (1999); United States v. Rodgers, 461 U.S. 677 (1983).

state law often declares that liquor licenses are privileges, not property. Since state law characterizations are irrelevant, the federal tax lien attaches to a liquor license held by a delinquent taxpayer. State debtor-creditor restrictions also are irrelevant. For example, state law often shields homestead interests or tenancy-by-the-entireties interests from claims of separate creditors of one of the spouses. Yet the federal tax lien attaches to any homestead or entireties interests of the delinquent taxpayer even if his or her spouse owes no tax.[28]

Thus, determining whether the powers the taxpayer has as to the underlying asset are section 6321 property rights, is an exercise in federal law. There is no bright line or single criterion for making this decision. Given the numerous forms that property interests take, there couldn't be. Among the relevant factors are whether the interest is protected by law, has value, is beneficial (as opposed to mere legal title), and is transferable—although not all factors must be present in order to permit an affirmative characterization. The most important consideration may be the extent of control the taxpayer can exercise over the assets.[29]

The general lien under section 6321 is by far the most important federal tax lien. To supplement it, a number of special tax liens exist. For instance, the Code creates special liens as to estate taxes,[30] gift taxes,[31] estate taxes deferred under section 6166,[32] and additional estate tax attributable to property qualifying for special valuation under section 2032A.[33]

The special estate tax lien is imposed, on property in the gross estate, for 10 years from the decedent's death. The special gift tax lien is imposed, on gifted property, for ten years from the date of the gift. These periods contrast with the normal lifespan of the section 6321 lien: ten years from the date of the assessment.

When a special lien applies, typically the general lien does as well. In such cases, the two liens are independent. If one of the liens terminates, the other does not automatically terminate. The continued applicability of the second lien will depend on its own terms.

The IRS also uses nominee liens and alter ego liens. These are broader applications of the normal lien, not special liens. When an individual or entity is holding the taxpayer's property as a subterfuge, the IRS may proceed against the property.[34] It need

28. *E.g.*, United States v. Tyler, 528 Fed. Appx. 193 (3d Cir. 2013) (the tax lien remained on property despite its subsequent transfer into, then transfer out of, tenancy by the entirety). For description of the voluminous case law as to these and other examples, see Steve R. Johnson, *Why* Craft *Isn't Scary*, 37 Real Prop., Probate & Trust J. 439 (2002).

29. *See* Steve R. Johnson, *The Good, the Bad, and the Ugly in Post-*Drye *Tax Lien Analysis*, 5 Fla. Tax Rev. 415 (2002).

30. IRC § 6324(a).

31. IRC § 6324(b).

32. IRC § 6324A.

33. IRC § 6324B. For other special tax liens, see sections 4081, 4901, 5004, and 6311.

34. For factors indicative of nominee status, see *Oxford Capital Corp. v. United States*, 211 F.3d 280, 284 n. 1 (5th Cir. 2000). These factors are much like the factors described in Chapter 15 indicative of fraudulent transfers.

not make a new assessment against the holder or possessor; its lien against the taxpayer is the basis on which the IRS act against the property.[35]

B. Notice of Lien

The IRS is not required to make known the existence of the lien. Often, the IRS does not publicly file or record its lien.[36] When it doesn't, the lien is called a "secret" lien. The lien nonetheless is in force and effect and can serve as the basis of enforced collection against the taxpayer's property and property rights.

When the IRS does decide to file its lien, section 6323(f) directs that it do so in the proper place pursuant to state law. IRS liens which are not filed in accordance with section 6323(f) are ineffective against third parties. There has been an increase in controversies in recent years as to whether the IRS properly filed its liens in particular cases.[37] As to real property, the notice must be duly filed and recorded in the public index of the local office designated by the law of the state in which the property is situated.[38]

As to personalty (whether tangible or intangible), section 6323(f) again provides that the place of filing is the office designated by the law of the state in which the property is situated.[39] Taxpayers not residing in the United States are deemed to reside in the District of Columbia. Business entities are deemed to "reside" where their main executive offices are. This means where major decisions are made, not simply where the bricks and mortar are located.[40]

The personalty/realty distinction is unproblematic in most cases, but special situations occasion special rules. When it is arguable into which category a particular asset falls, the classification is made using state law.[41] Sometimes, assets may change

---

35. For additional discussion of nominee liens, alter ego liens, and related devices, see Chapter 15. Even in the case of real transfers, transfer of the property after the federal tax lien has attached does not remove the lien. "[N]o matter into whose hands the property goes, it passes *cum onere*." United States v. Avila, 88 F.3d 229, 233 (3d Cir. 1996) (*quoting* United States v. Bess, 357 U.S. 51, 57 (1958)).

36. Whether to file notice of the tax lien is a business decision for the IRS: will filing promote collection of the liability? A filed notice of tax lien can negatively affect the taxpayer's ability to borrow or the willingness of others to do business with the taxpayer, reducing the prospect that the taxpayer's future business activities will generate funds to pay the tax liability. On the other hand, the filing of the notice could apply the pressure needed to motivate the taxpayer to find a way to pay. Filing also protects the IRS's interest against certain persons who might otherwise acquire a higher priority interest in the property.

37. *E.g.*, Tracey v. United States, 394 B.R. 635 (1st Cir. B.A.P. 2008); In re Crystal Cascades Civil LLC, 398 B.R. 23 (Bankr. D. Nev. 2008).

38. If that state's law fails to designate any local office or if it designates more than one office, the notice is to be filed with the clerk of the federal District Court for the district where the property is located.

39. If that state's law fails to designate, the personalty is deemed situated where the taxpayer resides when the notice of tax lien is filed.

40. Rev. Rul. 74-571, 1974-2 C.B. 398.

41. *See, e.g.*, Brooks v. United States, 833 F.2d 1136 (4th Cir. 1987).

in character. For instance, natural resources may be realty before extraction but personalty after. Although there is not a great deal of law on the point, it is likely that the character of the property at the time of lien filing would control. If the notice had been filed with the right office based on the property's character, then refiling in another office probably would not be necessary simply on account of subsequent change in the property's character. Still, an abundance of caution might prompt the IRS to make such a secondary filing should it become aware of the transmutation.

Section 6323(f) also governs the form and contents of the notice. A filing satisfying that section's requirements is valid even if it fails to satisfy some requisite under state law. This follows from the fact that federal, not state, law controls all post-lien-attachment consequences. The IRS has developed forms to meet the section 6323(f) requirements.[42]

Inevitably, given the volume of notices filed, some filings contain errors: misspellings, misnumerations, incorrect or incomplete addresses, etc. Many cases have considered whether such errors invalidate the notices. The decisions are not always reconcilable, but the courts usually take a functional approach. Typically, the notice will be invalidated only if the error is such that it would defeat discovery of the lien by a reasonably diligent search.[43] If the taxpayer changes his or her name after the notice filed, the policy of the IRS is to file another notice reflecting the taxpayer's new name as well as his or her "formerly known as" name. When a taxpayer against whom a tax lien is in place moves, the IRS is compelled to use the new address in the filing or refiling of a notice only if the taxpayer timely informs the IRS of the new address.[44]

The normal life of a general tax lien is the ten-year collection limitations period, and initial notices cease to be effective at the end of this time. If the limitations period is extended, the IRS must refile the notice under section 6323(g). The notice will remain continuous if refiled within the "required refiling period," which is "the one-year period ending thirty days after the expiration of 10 years after the date of the assessment of the tax, and ... the one-year period ending with the expiration of 10 years after the close of the preceding required refiling period for [the] notice."

C. Priorities

A federal tax lien does not directly compel payment. Sometimes, the existence or, especially, the filing of the lien does induce payment—in order to remove cloud on title, perhaps, to render the property more readily saleable. Yet there is no assurance that this will happen.

---

42. *See also* Reg. §§ 301.6323(f)-1 (place for filing notice and form of notice), 301.6323(g)-1 (refiling of notice).

43. In re Spearing Tool & Mfg. Co., 412 F.3d 653 (6th Cir. 2005); In re Sills, 82 F.3d 111, 113 (5th Cir. 1996); In re Cennamo, 147 B.R. 540, 543 (Bankr. C.D. Cal. 1992) ("The purpose of the [Notice of Federal Tax Lien] is to give constructive notice, and where there is such notice, a minor defect in filing will be overlooked.").

44. Reg. § 301.6323(g)-1(b)(2).

Thus, the real significance of a tax lien is that it serves as a security device. Those who owe money to the IRS usually owe others as well. Often there aren't enough assets to satisfy all of the creditors' claims. The tax lien is a means by which the IRS protects its position relative to the positions of competing creditors. How successful the lien is in that regard depends on the priorities rules described below.

The current priorities scheme has its roots in the common law rule "first in time, first in right." That rule still governs when no statute applies. Under the common law rule, the claim of the competing creditor would have priority over the tax lien only if that creditor's claim was choate before the assessment date. A claim is not choate until three items have been established: the identity of the creditor, the amount of the debt, and the identity of the property to which the claim attaches.[45] In the tax area, the main purpose of the choateness requirement is to prevent the tax lien from being subordinated to mere contingencies.

In important instances, the common law rule has been modified or displaced by statutes. The most frequently applicable priority statute is section 6323.[46] The section was given its modern form by the Federal Tax Lien Act of 1966 and subsequent amendments.[47] Subsections (a) (b), and (c) of section 6323 protect different sets of third-party creditors. Specifically,

- Section 6323(a) pertains to four categories of third-party creditors: (1) purchasers of property from the taxpayer, (2) holders of security interests in the taxpayer's property, (3) mechanic's lienors, and (4) judgment lien creditors. Under the subsection, the IRS lien yields to the claims of these four groups until notice of the tax lien is filed. Thus, interests of the four groups arising after the tax lien comes into existence but before notice of the tax lien is filed have priority over the tax lien.[48]
- Section 6323(b) creates ten so-called superpriorities, that is, types of interests which "prime" or trump the IRS lien even if the interest arises after notice of the tax lien was filed. Several of the categories are further defined by section 6323(h). There is no single theme that explains the ten superpriorities, but some strands wind through several of the superpriorities. For instance, several reflect the infeasibility or unlikelihood of the third party's checking for federal tax liens in light of the nature of the transaction. Several others are explained by the fact that the transaction increases the value of the taxpayer's property. The IRS is not hurt when the third party is protected to the extent of new money or value

45. *See, e.g.*, United States v. McDermott, 507 U.S. 447 (1993); United States v. City of New Britain, 347 U.S. 81 (1954).

46. Two other specialized sets of rules sometimes come into play. First, 31 U.S.C. sections 191 and 192 involve tax claims against an insolvent estate of a decedent or against a fiduciary in possession of property of an insolvent taxpayer (though one not in bankruptcy). Second, 11 U.S.C. section 507 involves priorities of tax and other claims in bankruptcy cases.

47. For discussion of the 1996 Act, see Steve R. Johnson, *Reforming Federal Tax Litigation: An Agenda*, 41 Fla. St. U.L. Rev. 205, 226–29 (2013).

48. *See, e.g.*, Rev. Rul. 2003-108, 2003-2 C.B. 963 (ruling that section 6323(a) priorities are not affected by actual knowledge of the existence of unfilled tax liens).

made available to the taxpayers. Indeed, the IRS's chance collecting may be enhanced in the long run. Many of the super-priorities are defeated if the third party had actual notice of the tax lien, and one is defeated if the transaction was intended to hinder tax collection. The specific provisions of section 6323 and its Regulations must be reviewed in each case, to identify the peculiarities of the applicable measure(s).[49]

- Finally, section 6323(c) creates another superpriority, this one to protect some security interests arising as a result of commercial financing transactions. A number of pre-1966 cases had held that liens arising from loan agreements providing for future advances did not become choate until the advances actually were made. As a consequence, tax liens filed after the agreement was entered into but before the advance later was made, were held to have priority. Section 6323(c) addresses this and other situations by according priority to security interests in some common commercial financing situations. Section 6323(d) provides implementing rules for one of those situations.

V. Enforced Collection

Unless it engenders "voluntary" payment, the tax lien itself puts no money in federal coffers.[50] The IRS thus will be compelled to engage in enforced collection. Two techniques frequently used by the IRS are (1) administrative levy and sale[51] and (2) judicial sale with distribution of proceeds.

A. Administrative Levy

The IRS's normal approach to enforced collection involves levying on the taxpayer's property, then, in the case of non-cash property, selling it. First, the IRS gains possession of the property through the related measures of levy, seizure, and distraint. These terms are not always given consistent meaning. Sometimes, "levy" is used broadly to encompass seizure and distraint as well.[52] Other times, the terms are used more narrowly, levy referring to taking the taxpayer's property which is in the custody

---

49. For an illustration, see Rev. Rul. 2006-42, 2006-2 C.B. 337 (discussing the procedures a bank should use in asserting the superpriority under section 6323(b)(10)).

50. The IRS distinguishes between voluntary payments and involuntary payments. The latter are amounts received as a result of judicial action or administrative levy. *See, e.g.*, Muntwyler v. United States, 703 F.2d 1030, 1033 (7th Cir. 1983). Taxpayers may designate in writing to which of their outstanding liabilities a voluntary payment will be applied, but the IRS asserts the right to allocate involuntary payments as it wishes. *See, e.g.*, O'Dell v. United States, 326 U.S. 451 (10th Cir. 1964); Rev. Rul. 73-305, 1973-2 C.B. 43.

51. These devices are called "administrative" because the IRS uses them purely on its own. With only a few exceptions, court approval is not required before the IRS levies on or sells property. Nonetheless, the constitutionality of such levy and sale "has long been settled." Phillips v. Commissioner, 283 U.S. 589, 595 (1931).

52. IRC §7701(a)(21) ("The term 'levy' includes the power of distraint and seizure by any means").

or possession of a third party, seizure or distraint referring to taking property directly from the taxpayer. We will follow the first locution, using "levy" encompassingly.

Levy is a provisional remedy only.[53] The levy does not change ownership of the property, only its possession. The IRS becomes the custodian of the property. Thus, the IRS has a duty to protect the property, and the taxpayer generally is entitled to a credit against her liability for the extent to which the property deteriorates in value after levy but before sale.[54] A taxpayer who attempts to forcibly regain possession of the property levied upon, or who corruptly or forcibly attempts to interfere with collection by other means, is guilty of a crime.[55]

The language of section 6331 as to the reach of levy is similar to the language of section 6321 as to the reach of the tax lien. Under section 6331(a), the IRS may "levy upon all property and rights to property [of the taxpayer] or on which there is a lien ... for the payment of such tax."[56] In general, under section 6331(b), a levy extends "only to property possessed and obligations existing at the time [the levy is made]." However, continuing levies—which are effective as well for rights coming into existence after the levy is served—may be made on salaries, wages, and certain other rights to payments.[57] Some types of property are exempt from levy under section 6334. However, the exemptions are generally of limited value. They are designed to avert penury but may be too limited to achieve even that modest objective.[58]

In general, the IRS must notify the taxpayer in writing of its intent to levy at least thirty days before it actually levies, but this requirement does not operate in cases of jeopardy to collection. Section 6331(d) describes the contents of the required notice and the manner in which it must be given.

Levy is prohibited during certain periods. Subject to exceptions, levy may not be made (i) during the pendency of proceedings for the refund of divisible taxes (such as employment taxes), (ii) before the IRS has investigated the status of the property in question, (iii) during the pendency of an offer-in-compromise, or (iv) during the term of an installment agreement provided that the taxpayer is living up to the terms of the agreement.[59] Uneconomic levies—those as to which the expenses of levy and sale would exceed the value of the property—are prohibited.[60] Special approvals are required for levies on principal residences (*ex parte* district court approval) or on

53. *See, e.g.*, United States v. National Bank of Commerce, 472 U.S. 713, 721 (1985).

54. *See, e.g.*, United States v. Pittman, 449 F.2d 623 (7th Cir. 1971).

55. IRC § 7212.

56. For instance, in internal advice, the IRS concluded that it could not seize and sell a taxpayer's season ticket renewals because they are not property or property rights, but it could seize and sell personal seat licenses because they are property rights. FAA 20092102F, Tax Mgmt. Weekly Rep., June 1, 2009, at 723.

57. IRC § 6331(e), (h). *See* Scott A. Schumacher, *Unnecessary Harm: IRS Levies on Social Security Benefits*, Tax Notes, Oct. 16, 2006, at 265.

58. The items listed in section 6334 are exempt from levy but not from the tax lien. *E.g.*, In re Voelker, 42 F.3d 1050, 1051 (7th Cir. 1994).

59. IRC § 6331(i)–(k).

60. IRC § 6331(f). Whether this is a direction purely to the IRS or a judicially operable defense for taxpayers is not yet clear.

certain business assets (higher-level IRS approval). The IRS does not always follow all safeguards applicable to levies.[61]

When the property is in the taxpayer's possession, the IRS levies on it simply by taking it or (if the property is immovable) by providing notice that the property is now in the custody of the IRS. If the taxpayer's property is in the possession of a third party (such as a bank or brokerage house at which the taxpayer has an account), the IRS issues a written notice of levy to the third party. Such notice creates a custodial relationship between the third party and the IRS. The IRS constructively possesses the property until the third party turns it over to the IRS.[62]

There are only two defenses on the basis of which the third party can resist the levy: (1) that the third party neither possesses nor is obligated with respect to any property of the taxpayer or (2) that the property is subject to prior judicial execution or attachment.[63] A third party who improperly fails to honor a levy becomes personally liable in the amount of the property's value (or the amount of the tax liability, if lower) and becomes liable as well for a 50% penalty.[64] A third party who honors the levy is "discharged from any obligation or liability to the delinquent taxpayer and to any other person with respect to such property or rights to property arising from such surrender or payment."[65]

Banks are directed to surrender property "only after 21 days after service of levy."[66] During this period, the taxpayer's account is frozen. The idea is to give the taxpayer and the IRS time to resolve the matter and correct any mistakes before potentially harmful action is taken.

B. Administrative Sale

If what was levied on was money, the IRS will remit it to the Treasury and will credit the taxpayer's account for the payment. If what was levied on was other property, the IRS will need to reduce it to cash by selling it.[67] Alternatively, the IRS may choose to lease levied-on real property, realizing rents therefrom, but this route is not commonly followed.

---

61. Treasury Inspector General for Tax Administration, Fiscal Year 2006 Review of Compliance with Legal Guidelines when Conducting Seizures of Taxpayers' Property (2006-30-113) (Aug. 9, 2006); Treasury Inspector General for Tax Administration, Fiscal Year 2006 Statutory Review of Compliance with Legal Guidelines when Issuing Levies (2006-30-101) (Aug. 4, 2006).

62. *See, e.g.*, Phelps v. United States, 421 U.S. 330, 334 (1975).

63. *National Bank of Commerce*, *supra*, 472 U.S. at 721–22.

64. IRC § 6332(d); *see* Danielle M. Smith, *Bank Levies: Proper Compliance Prevents Hefty Penalties*, Tax Notes, Apr. 17, 2006, at 311.

65. IRC § 6332(e).

66. IRC § 6332(c). For implementing rules, see Reg. § 301.6332-3.

67. If the IRS levies on property but for some reason does not sell it, the taxpayer's account must be credited for the value of the property. *See, e.g.*, United States v. Pittman, 449 F.2d 623, 627–28 (7th Cir. 1971). *But see* McCorkle v. Commissioner, 124 T.C. 56 (2005) (taxpayer made $2 million income tax remittance, but the IRS paid it over to the U.S. Marshals Service pursuant to a court forfeiture order entered in a non-tax case; held: the $2 million payment is not applied to the tax liability).

The principal section governing administrative sale is section 6335. Subsections (a) and (b) require the IRS to give the taxpayer notice of the fact that seizure has been made and of the IRS's intent to sell. Both required notices are to be made "as soon as practicable," and the subsections prescribe the manner in which the notices must be given.[68] The IRS typically issues the notice of sale within 30 days after the notice of seizure, but the two notices may be given simultaneously. The mere fact that a taxpayer does not actually receive the notices "does not negate the constitutional adequacy of the attempt to accomplish actual notice."[69] However, procedural due process requires that the IRS use means of notification that are reasonable under the circumstances.[70]

Section 6335 prescribes when ("not ... less than 10 days nor more than 40 days from the time of giving of [notice of sale]") and where sale may occur. Subsection (e) sets out the manner and conditions of sale, including the minimum sale price (usually at least 80% of the property's forced sale value after subtracting liens on the property superior to the IRS's lien).

If more than one bid meets or exceeds the minimum sale price set by the IRS, the IRS will sell the taxpayer's interest in the property to the highest bidder. Payment must be made via certified or cashier's check. The sale proceeds will be applied first to pay the expenses of sale, then to any specific tax liability on the property, then to the liability on account of which the property was levied on and sold. Should there be any surplus proceeds, they will be credited or refunded to the taxpayer (or other person if legally entitled thereto).[71] If the taxpayer intends to contest the validity of the sale, the taxpayer should not accept any check tendered by the IRS since such acceptance may be viewed as ratification of the sale.[72]

It is important to appreciate that the buyer from the IRS does not necessarily acquire full, free-and-clear ownership of the property. All the IRS can sell is whatever right, title, and interest the taxpayer had in the property.[73] Moreover, the IRS does not warrant the validity of the title or the quality of the property. As a result, a disappointed purchaser has no recourse against the IRS.[74]

Sale extinguishes junior liens (liens with lower priority than the tax lien) on the property as long as the IRS had notified the lienholder of the sale (giving the lienholder the chance to bid at the sale), but the junior lienor has the right to redeem real

---

68. If the IRS fails to give proper notice, the sale may be invalidated. *See, e.g.*, Reece v. Scoggins, 506 F.2d 967, 971 (5th Cir. 1975). However, courts sometimes excuse minor notice defects. *See, e.g.*, Westaire Properties, Inc. v. Tucker, 89-2 U.S. Tax Cas. (CCH) ¶ 9473 (S.D. Cal. 1989).

69. Trimble v. U.S. Dep't of Agriculture, 87 Fed. Appx. 456, 458 (6th Cir. 2003).

70. *Compare* Little Italy Oceanside Invs., LLC v. United States, 115 AFTR2d 5639 (E.D. Mich. 2015) (rejecting due process challenge to IRS tax lien notices), *with* Jones v. Flowers, 547 U.S. 220 (2006) (upholding due process challenge to state notices of tax sale).

71. IRC § 6342.

72. *See, e.g.*, Johnson v. Gartlan, 470 F.2d 1104, 1106 (4th Cir. 1973) (IRS did not comply with rules governing sale but the sale was held valid since the taxpayer cashed the proceeds check).

73. *See, e.g.*, National Bank & Trust Co. v. United States, 589 F.2d 1298, 1302 (7th Cir. 1978).

74. Reg. § 301.6335-1(c)(4)(iii).

property within 180 days after the IRS sells it.[75] As a matter of law, senior liens on the property are not affected by an IRS sale,[76] but elimination of the taxpayer's interest may create practical difficulties for senior lienholders.

The taxpayer has several rights and protections in the sale context, some of them significant. For example, (1) the taxpayer may request the IRS to sell the property within 60 days after the request.[77] (2) Sale of seized property may be stayed during pendency of a Tax Court case as to the merits of the liability.[78] (3) Special rules apply if the IRS determines that seized property is likely to perish or decline greatly in value, or cannot be kept without great expense. If the IRS wishes to sell such property, it must (if practicable) give the taxpayer an appraisal of the property. The taxpayer can get the property back by tendering the appraised price or can stop the sale by posting bond for the amount.[79] (4) Both before sale and, as to real property, for up to 180 days after sale, the taxpayer can redeem levied-on property.[80]

C. Judicial Sale

Administrative levy and sale will not always be practicable. The taxpayer's title may be cloudy, or the property may have multiple owners. As a result, there may be few, if any, potential buyers for administrative sale. In such cases, the IRS may resort to judicial sale under section 7403.

Here are the steps. The IRS, through IRS Counsel's office, authorizes the Department of Justice to bring an action in federal District Court.[81] The action usually is called a lien foreclosure suit although the section is styled "Action To Enforce Lien or To Subject Property to Payment of Tax." Under section 7403(b), all persons having liens upon or claiming interests in the property are joined as parties. Under section 7403(c), the District Court determines the merits of all claims.[82] If the tax lien is found meritorious, the court may effect sale of the whole of the property. The net proceeds of sale are divided among the interestholders in proportion to their interests,

---

75. IRC § 6337(b)(1).

76. *See, e.g.*, Pargament v. Fitzgerald, 272 F. Supp. 553 (S.D.N.Y. 1967), *aff'd per curiam*, 391 F.2d 934 (2d Cir. 1968).

77. IRC § 6335(f).

78. IRC § 6863(b)(3). This situation can arise when the IRS makes jeopardy assessment and levy, and wishes to sell the levied property, before conclusion of Tax Court review of the notice of deficiency. *See* Chapter 7.

79. IRC § 6336.

80. IRC § 6337.

81. *See* IRC § 7401. As described in Chapter 1, the Department of Justice represents the IRS in all courts except the Tax Court. Since nearly all collection cases—both offensive (the Government brings suit) and defensive (the Government is sued by the taxpayer or a third party)—are tried in District Court, the Department of Justice will represent the IRS. Under section 7401, Justice can bring suit in a tax case only if authorized by the IRS.

82. There is no right to a jury in a section 7403 proceeding. *See, e.g.*, Hyde Properties v. McCoy, 507 F.2d 301 (6th Cir. 1974).

with the IRS standing in the shoes of the taxpayer to the extent of the taxpayer's interest in the property or, if less, to the extent of the unpaid tax liabilities.[83]

The District Court is not compelled to grant the Government's request to sell the property. Section 7403(c) is phrased permissively: the court "may" decree sale, not "shall" decree it. Thus, District Courts have some equitable discretion to deny sale. However, that discretion is limited.[84]

Once a District Court has granted the IRS's request for judicial sale, taxpayers sometimes request that the sale be stayed pending appeal. In one fairly typical case, the court denied a stay because (1) the taxpayer was unlikely to prevail on the merits on appeal; (2) the taxpayer would not suffer irreparable injury; (3) other parties would be injured by granting the motion; and (4) a significant public interest existed in prompt enforcement of the revenue laws.[85]

VI. Ancillary Procedures

Numerous additional mechanisms are available to the IRS to assist in tax collection, either to back-stop the devices described above or as alternatives to them. Some of the additional mechanisms are addressed in other chapters, such as jeopardy and termination assessments and levies (Chapter 7), the trust fund recovery tax of section 6672 (Chapter 14), and transferee and fiduciary liability (Chapter 15). Other mechanisms are described below.

Section 7402(a) grants the District Courts, at the behest of the government, the power to issue "writs ... and such other orders and processes, and to render such judgments and decrees as may be necessary or appropriate to the enforcement of the internal revenue laws." The subsection mentions injunctions, writs of *ne exeat republica*,[86] and orders appointing receivers. In addition to section 7402, the All Writs Act, 28 U.S.C. section 1651, provides additional authority for issuance of writs by the District Courts.

An important type of suit under section 7402 is an action to reduce the tax liability to judgment. The principal significance of this approach is that it extends the life of the lien. Under section 6322, the general federal tax lien continues until the liability is paid "or becomes unenforceable by reason of lapse of time." When a suit to reduce the liability to judgment is begun during the limitations period and such judgment

83. If the proceeds allocated to the taxpayer's interest exceed the tax liability, the excess is paid to the taxpayer.

84. *See* United States v. Rodgers, 461 U.S. 677, 703–11 (1983) (setting forth factors to guide the exercise of such discretion).

85. Grass Lake All Seasons Resort, Inc. v. United States, 2005 U.S. Dist. LEXIS 36708 (E.D. Mich. Dec. 15, 2005).

86. *E.g.*, United States v. Barrett, 113 AFTR2d 1842 (D. Colo. 2014); Anthony E. Rebollo, *The Civil Arrest and Imprisonment of Taxpayers: An Analysis of the Writ of Ne Exeat Republica*, 7 Pitt. Tax Rev. 103 (2010).

ultimately is obtained, the tax liability remains enforceable during the life of the judgment.[87] As a practical matter, this eliminates any statute of limitations barrier to tax collection. The government typically uses this device only when the outstanding tax liability is large or the IRS believes that assets to pay the liability will be available after the normal ten-year collection window closes. The government often combines in one action demands to reduce the liability to judgment and to foreclose on the tax lien.

Other types of suits in aid of collection, whether under section 7402 or other sections, include suits to recover refunds made erroneously by the IRS,[88] suits to impose receiverships,[89] suits to open safe deposit boxes, and actions to quiet title.[90] The government also has the ability to intervene in a suit between others that might have the effect of impairing the IRS's interest in the taxpayer's property.[91]

Sometimes, another creditor of the taxpayer may foreclose on or cause sale of property to which the tax lien attaches. If the tax lien is senior, it will remain on the property despite the foreclosure or sale. If the other creditor's claim is senior, the tax lien is terminated if the senior lienor either joins the IRS in a judicial sale or notifies the IRS of its nonjudicial sale.[92] However, if real property of the taxpayer's is subjected to nonjudicial sale, the IRS has the right to redeem the property within 120 days after the sale.[93]

In some instances, the IRS may need or want more information in order to pursue collection. Administratively, the IRS may use summonses in aid of collection under rules largely similar to those governing examination summonses described in Chapter 4.[94] In addition, section 6333 provides that, if levy has been made or is about to be made, the IRS may demand that any person having custody or control of books or records relating to the property, show them to the IRS.

Other procedures also may be invoked. For instance, the government may petition a District Court for a writ of entry, allowing the IRS to enter premises to obtain either information or property. Seizure of property on private property raises constitutional, principally Fourth Amendment, issues. Tax law enforcement is not an exception to constitutional requirements.[95] Accordingly, IRS collection procedures are structured

87. *See, e.g.*, United States v. Hodes, 355 F.2d 746 (2d Cir. 1966).

88. IRC § 7405. *See* Chapter 9, Section III.A.

89. IRC § 7403(d).

90. IRC § 7402(e).

91. IRC § 7424. If the suit is in state court, the government can and usually does remove it to federal District Court under 28 U.S.C. section 1444.

92. IRC § 7425(a), (b). Section 7425(c) contains special rules as to sales and notices. The courts tend to read the section 7425 rules strictly. *See, e.g.*, Alt & RS Coal Corp. v. United States, 461 F. Supp. 752 (W.D. Pa. 1978).

93. IRC § 7425(d). The amount the IRS must pay the purchaser of the property is determined under 28 U.S.C. section 2410(d). *See generally* Note, *Upsetting the Government's Right to Redemption Under Section 7425*, 60 Tax Law. 233 (2006).

94. There are some differences. For instance, the section 7609 special procedures as to third-party summonses apply to examination summonses but not to summonses in aid of collection. IRC § 7609(c)(2)(D).

95. G.M. Leasing Corp. v. United States, 429 U.S. 338, 358–59 (1977).

to conform to Fourth Amendment dictates. The IRS typically first seeks consent of the property owner to entry onto the property. If consent is not forthcoming, the government will seek to obtain a writ of entry.

VII. Administrative and Hybrid Protections for Taxpayers and Third Parties

The collection arsenal available to the IRS is formidable. To mitigate the possible misuse of weapons in that arsenal (and to cushion the blows of even proper use of such weapons), Congress and the IRS have crafted an array of relief devices for taxpayers and third parties harmed by tax collection. These include administrative mechanisms and hybrid (combination of administrative and judicial) mechanisms described in this Section VII and judicial mechanisms described in Section VIII.

A. Relief from Tax Liens

Section 6325 is an important source of relief options. It allows the IRS, typically upon request by the taxpayer or another affected person, to release the tax lien, discharge property from the lien, subordinate the lien to other interests in or claims upon the property,[96] or issue a certificate stating that the lien does not attach to particular property. A release ends the entire lien. The other actions affect the relationship of the lien to particular assets but have no effect on the lien's relationship to other assets.[97]

Substitution agreements often make sense for taxpayers. Measured by the prices actually realized, administrative sales by the IRS do not have an impressive history. The taxpayer often will be able to obtain a higher price by selling the property herself. Thus, a common type of substitution agreement removes the tax lien from property (so that the taxpayer can convey clear title) and imposes the lien instead on the proceeds obtained from the sale. Other types of substitutions are possible but less common.

Each of the types of actions described under section 6325 is largely independent of the other types. Each type differs as to conditions that trigger relief. In addition, some actions require the IRS to grant the relief if the stated conditions exist while other types give the IRS some discretion as to whether to grant the relief.[98] Accordingly, in each case, the taxpayer's representative must focus on the specific relief desired and the particular rules governing that type of relief.

---

96. *E.g.*, Azarri v. Commissioner, 136 T.C. 178 (2011) (holding that the IRS abused its discretion by not considering the taxpayer's request to subordinate the tax lien and by denying its request for an installment agreement).

97. These administrative remedies are exclusive. Rev. Rul. 2005-50, 2005-2 C.B. 124 (ruling that no judicial remedy is available to a third party who seeks a certificate of discharge under section 6325(b)(2)).

98. This difference comes from Congress' use of "shall" in some of the provisions but "may" in others.

Other remedies aim not at the lien and its scope but at the filing of the notice of tax lien. The taxpayer and the IRS may enter into a collateral agreement in which the IRS gains security as to payment of the tax liability in return for which the IRS agrees not to file notice of the lien. Acceptable forms of security include, among others, mortgages, letters of credit, and bonds.[99]

Section 6323(j) authorizes the IRS to withdraw a filed notice of tax lien if (1) the IRS determines that the notice was filed prematurely; (2) the IRS and the taxpayer enter into an installment agreement; (3) withdrawal will facilitate collection; or (4) the IRS and the National Taxpayer Advocate agree that withdrawal is in the best interests of the taxpayer and the IRS. A withdrawn lien is treated as if it never had been filed.

B. Relief From Levies

Section 6343 creates authority for the release of a levy and notice of levy and for the return of property that has been levied on. As is true of section 6325 as well, a variety of relief triggers exist under section 6343. Some types of relief are mandatory under stated conditions while other types are subject to the discretion of the IRS.[100]

C. Taxpayer Assistance Orders

Considering the size of the IRS and the volume and complexity of its work, it is inevitable that some cases will be handled badly. Sometimes clear procedures for handling a type of situation do not exist; sometimes good procedures exist but they are not followed because of staff shortage, human error, or other causes. In 1988, Congress established what has evolved into the current Taxpayer Advocate function to cut across bureaucratic obstacles in IRS operations, including collection.

The Taxpayer Advocate's Office is described in Chapter 1. As relevant here, the office is empowered, under section 7811, to issue a Taxpayer Assistance Order ("TAO") if it determines that the taxpayer is suffering or is about to suffer significant hardship because of the way the IRS is administering the law. The TAO operates, in effect, as an administrative injunction, halting the IRS action in question. Taxpayers request TAOs by submitting Form 911.

D. Installment Agreements

Section 6159 authorizes the IRS to enter into written agreements with taxpayers allowing them to pay their liabilities over time. Formerly, the agreement had to

---

99. For rules governing the use of bonds in this and other collection contexts, see sections 7101 to 7103.

100. In general, the IRS's exercise of its discretion is judicially reviewable. *E.g.*, Vinatieri v. Commissioner, 133 T.C. 392 (2009); CC-2011-005 (Nov. 22, 2010) (following *Vinatieri*).

provide for eventual full payment of the liability. However, the IRS now may enter into partial payment installment agreements.

Installment agreements often are useful options, but there are features that need to be considered. Interest continues to accrue as to the deferred amounts albeit at a reduced rate.[101] Thus, if the taxpayer can raise money from other sources at no interest (for example, by borrowing from a friend or relative), full immediate payment may be less expensive than an installment agreement.

The IRS usually will not entertain an installment agreement offer unless the taxpayer has filed her return and paid her tax for the current year. Section 6159(c) requires the IRS to accept installment agreements under some circumstances. In other circumstances, when acceptance is discretionary with the IRS, the IRS will require the taxpayer to demonstrate his inability to fully pay immediately. The vehicle for this demonstration is a financial statement setting forth in detail the taxpayer's non-tax debts, his assets, and his future income prospects.[102] The IRS may also demand follow-up information if the term of the agreement exceeds a year, and it may modify or terminate the agreement if the taxpayer's financial status improves enough that full payment becomes feasible. The IRS may insist on further conditions memorialized in collateral agreements.

Individuals wishing to enter into an installment payment agreement must pay the IRS a user fee.[103] Individuals owing under $25,000 may apply online for a payment agreement.

E. Offer-in-Compromise

Section 7122 gives the government the authority to compromise tax liabilities.[104] The liberality of the IRS in entering into compromises has varied over time and by geographical area, prompting frequent criticisms in Congress and by practitioners.[105]

If the unpaid amount exceeds $50,000, the IRS cannot accept an offer without first obtaining a written opinion from its Chief Counsel's Office.[106] If the IRS has referred the case to the Department of Justice for prosecution or defense, Justice has exclusive compromise authority until Justice releases the case back to the IRS.[107] Re-

101. *See* IRC § 6601(b)(1), (2).

102. IRS Forms 433-A (Collection Information Statement for Individuals), 433-B (Collection Information Statement for Businesses).

103. Reg. §§ 300.1, 300.2.

104. The ability to compromise tax liabilities has existed since at least the Civil War. Act of March 3, 1863, Ch. 76, § 10.

105. In 2015, approximately 67,000 offers were submitted, and 27,000 were accepted, yielding $205 million. IRS Data Book, 2015, at 43.

106. IRC § 7122(b). An opinion from Counsel must be in the file, but it need not be an affirmative opinion.

107. IRC § 7122(a).

sponding to complaints about inconsistent decisions, the IRS has centralized the processing of offers in compromise.

The taxpayer may submit an offer-in-compromise at virtually any stage of the tax process, including during audit, administrative appeal, and litigation. However, by far the majority of offers are submitted during the collection phase. The offer is submitted on IRS Form 656.[108] The IRS usually suspends collection while it is processing the offer.[109] The IRS may accept the offer as made, may reject it outright, or may negotiate with the taxpayer for better terms.

The IRS returns offers to taxpayers as "not processible" when preconditions are not satisfied. Preconditions typically involve being current on filing returns, paying tax, making required deposits, and providing information.[110] Typically, over 40% of submitted offers are returned to taxpayers because they are "not processible."

Sometimes, as a condition for accepting the offer, the IRS will require the taxpayer to enter into collateral agreements. The most common of them deal with future income, reduction of the taxpayer's basis in assets, and waiver of loss carryovers and other deductions.

The pre-printed language on the Form sets out numerous conditions the taxpayer will be expected to honor. Breach of those conditions can lead to revocation of the compromise. Apart from such breach, the compromise is binding on both parties from the point at which the IRS notifies the taxpayer in writing of the offer's acceptance. However, the agreement may be voided under the conditions described in Regulation section 301.7122-1(d)(5). Contract law principles govern interpretation of an accepted compromise.[111]

There are three bases on which an offer can be accepted: doubt as to liability, doubt as to collectability, and effective tax administration. Doubt as to liability has been a basis for many years, but it is not frequently asserted. Presumably, this is because of the availability of both pre-assessment and post-assessment channels (such as audit reconsideration requests, the Appeals Office, Tax Court review, and refund suits) for challenging the merits of IRS determinations. Nonetheless, an offer based on doubt as to liability may be useful if the taxpayer failed to take advantage of such alternative channels.

Doubt as to collectability is overwhelmingly the most frequent basis for offers. The notion is that, although the taxpayer owes the tax, not even the IRS can "get blood from a stone." The taxpayer will assert that he is now, and foreseeably will remain, unable to pay the entire liability. The taxpayer will offer an amount that rep-

---

108. See Rev. Proc. 2003-71, 2003-2 C.B. 517, for procedures for submitting and processing offers.

109. IRM 5.8.3.7. Revenue Procedure 2003-71, 2003-2 C.B. 517, explains procedures for submitting an offer-in-compromise and the procedures used by the IRS in processing an offer.

110. *E.g.*, IRM 5.8.3.2. *Cf.* Reed v. Commissioner, 141 T.C. 248, 256 (2013) (upholding the discretion of the IRS to refuse to consider "not processible" offers).

111. Reg. § 301.7122-1(c).

resents the present value of the taxpayer's ability to pay. If the IRS accepts the offer, it will take the amount and cancel the remainder of the liabilities.

The IRS will accept an offer based on doubt as to collectability when it is unlikely that the tax liability can be collected in full and the amount offered reasonably reflects collection potential. The IRS's objective is to collect what is collectible as early as possible and at the least cost.[112] Offers are viewed as an alternative to putting a case in CNC (currently not collectible) status. A further objective is to give taxpayers a "fresh start" to help them voluntarily comply with their obligations under the tax system.

The key in doubt-as-to-collectability offers is determining what amount constitutes an adequate offer. Offers may not be rejected solely because the amount of the offer is low.[113] Rather, what matters is whether the offer reasonably reflects collection potential.[114]

Reasonable collection potential reflects at least[115] (i) the quick sale value of the taxpayer's assets plus (ii) the present value of the taxpayer's future income minus necessary living expenses.[116] The taxpayer must provide detailed information in support of these amounts, typically on the 433 series of forms. Under section 7122(c)(2), necessary living expenses are determined by reference to "schedules of national and local allowances" developed by the IRS.[117]

The third basis for accepting an offer—effective tax administration—was added as a result of pressures surrounding the 1998 Reform Act. It is meant to be a flexible category, and it is not widely used.[118] The key authority is Regulation section 301.7122-1(b)(3) and (c)(3).

There is a user fee with respect to most offers-in-compromise. The fee does not apply to offers based on doubt as to liability or offers submitted by low-income taxpayers. The fee may be applied against the offered amount in some situations.[119]

112. IRS Policy Statement P-5-100.

113. IRC §7122(c)(3)(A).

114. Rev. Proc. 2003-71, §4.02(2), 2003-2 C.B. 517.

115. The IRS sometimes also considers amounts that could be collected from third parties (such as transferees) and the amount the taxpayer should be able to raise from assets which may be beyond the effective reach of the IRS (such as property located outside the United States).

116. IRM 5.8.4.3; *see, e.g.*, Porro v. Commissioner, T.C. Memo. 2014-81, at *8.

117. Interesting disputes can occur as to whether particular expenses are necessary. *See, e.g.*, Pixley v. Commissioner, 123 T.C. 269 (2004) (considering whether tithes should be taken into account in determining the taxpayer's ability to pay for offer-in-compromise purposes); Fowler v. Commissioner, T.C. Memo. 2004-163 (2004) (IRS's use of national statistical amount as estimate of taxpayers' expenses, rather than expense figures provided by taxpayers, held to be arbitrary and capricious). *Cf.* Sarasota, Inc. v. Weaver, 2004 U.S. Dist. LEXIS 22515 (E.D. Pa. 2004) (upholding $200 per month cigarette expenses as reasonably necessary for debtor's support and maintenance in Chapter 13 bankruptcy case).

118. *See* Speltz v. Commissioner, 124 T.C. 165 (2005) (holding that the IRS did not abuse its discretion by rejecting an "effective tax administration" offer based on unfair consequences of the alternative minimum tax), *aff'd*, 454 F.3d 782 (8th Cir. 2006); David M. Fogel, *The "Effective Tax Administration" Offer in Compromise*, Tax Notes, Aug. 29, 2005, at 1015.

119. Treas. Reg. §300.3(b). *See* T.D. 9086, 2003-2 C.B. 817. In 2014, the user fee was $186.

IRS policy has been not to consider offers-in-compromise while the taxpayer/debtor is in bankruptcy. After prodding from bankruptcy courts,[120] the IRS announced that it will consider payment proposals made by debtors as part of review of proposed bankruptcy plans.[121]

The Tax Increase Prevention and Reconciliation Act of 2005 ("TIPRA") made important changes to the offer-in-compromise program. A taxpayer making a lump-sum offer (defined as payable in five or fewer installments) must submit, along with the offer, a payment of 20% of the offered amount, in addition to the user fee. Offers not accompanied by the payment will be returned as nonprocessible. If the taxpayer submits a periodic payment offer (consisting of more than five installments), the first proposed installment must be included with the offer.[122]

The IRS has revised Form 656 and issued guidance on the TIPRA changes.[123] There are concerns that participation in the offer-in-compromise program has declined since imposition of user fees and that TIPRA changes will further reduce such participation.[124] More favorably, TIPRA also provides that if the IRS fails to act on an offer within twenty-four months, the offer will be deemed accepted.[125]

F. Collection Due Process

A controversial set of remedies, known as the Collection Due Process ("CDP") rights, is contained in sections 6320 and 6330, added by the 1998 Reform Act. These rights are triggered when the IRS files a notice of tax lien against the taxpayer or before the IRS levies on the taxpayer's property. The taxpayer has a right to hearings on these occasions. The two hearings may be consolidated for efficiency. If two hearings are held, the taxpayer may not raise at the second hearing issues raised at the prior hearing.[126]

The IRS is required to inform the taxpayer of her CDP rights.[127] The taxpayer requests a CDP hearing by filing IRS Form 12153 within 30 days after the notice was

---

120. *E.g.*, In re Peterson, 317 B.R. 532 (Bankr. D. Neb. 2004).

121. Chief Counsel Notice CC-2004-025 (July 12, 2004).

122. IRC § 7122(c)(1)(A), (B).

123. IRS Notice 2006-68, 2006-31 I.R.B. 1; IR-2006-106 (July 11, 2006); FS-2006-22 (July 2006).

124. *See, e.g.*, Richard L. Alltizer & Jeffrey L. Bryant, *TIPRA Further Compromises a Taxpayer's Ability to Compromise*, Taxes, Nov. 2006, at 23; Joseph DiSciullo, *ABA Tax Section Analyzes Offer in Compromise Amendments*, Tax Notes, Oct. 30, 2006, at 451; National Taxpayer Advocate's 2007 Objectives Report to Congress 3–4 (June 30, 2006). The Obama Administration proposed ending this TIPRA requirement.

125. IRC § 7122(f).

126. Reg. §§ 301.6320-1(e), 301.6330-1(e).

127. IRC § 6330(a)(1). The manner of notice and contents of the notice are set out in IRC § 6330(a)(2) and (3). On a "harmless error" theory, defects in the timing or contents of CDP notices often are excused as long as the taxpayer had sufficient opportunity to timely request the hearing. *E.g.*, Golub v. Commissioner, T.C. Memo. 2008-122.

given.[128] If the taxpayer timely files the Form, collection activity and the collection statute of limitations usually are suspended during the CDP process. However, on motion and for good cause shown, the IRS may be allowed to pursue collection even after a CDP appeal has been filed.[129] Taxpayers subject to jeopardy collection proceedings are entitled only to post-levy CDP hearing.[130]

A taxpayer who timely invokes his CDP rights is entitled to both administrative and judicial consideration. First, an IRS Appeals Officer, usually one called a Settlement Officer ("SO"), who has not previously been involved with the case will meet with the taxpayer.[131] The SO must confirm that the IRS has taken the required steps in the collection process. In addition, the taxpayer may raise at the hearing any proper defenses to the lien or levy, spousal defenses, and alternatives (such as an offer-in-compromise or an installment agreement) which the taxpayer may propose to the collection action contemplated by the IRS. The taxpayer can contest her substantive liability for the tax only if she did not receive a notice of deficiency or otherwise have opportunity to challenge the asserted liability.[132]

The SO's decision after the hearing is set forth in a Notice of Determination sent to the taxpayer. If the determination is adverse to the taxpayer, she may obtain judicial review by filing a Tax Court petition[133] within 30 days after the Appeals Office's determination.[134] However, if the IRS determines that the taxpayer is asserting a frivolous position, judicial review and further administrative review are precluded.[135]

The general standard of review is abuse of discretion.[136] However, (1) the Tax Court's sense of abuse of discretion is notably less deferential than that of generalist courts,[137] (2) contrary to the "record rule" used in administrative law cases generally,

---

128. IRC §6330(a)(3)(B).

129. *E.g.*, Burke v. Commissioner, 124 T.C. 189 (2005); CC-2005-007, CC-2005-009 (May 20, 2005).

130. IRC §6330(f).

131. IRC §6330(b)(3); *e.g.*, Moosally v. Commissioner, 142 T.C. 183 (2014). Similarly, to promote impartiality, the SO is supposed to avoid *ex parte* contact with IRS personnel. *E.g.*, Industrial Investors v. Commissioner, T.C. Memo. 2007-93.

132. IRC §6330(c)(2). Liabilities that the taxpayer self-reported on his or her returns may be so contested. Montgomery v. Commissioner, 122 T.C. 1 (2004), *acq.* AOD 2005-03 (Dec. 19, 2005).

133. Before 2006, CDP review was divided between the Tax Court and District Courts based on the issues involved. The Tax Court now has exclusive jurisdiction regardless of the issues. IRC §6330(d)(1).

134. *Id.* As usual (see Chapter 2), this period is extended if the 30th day is a Saturday, Sunday, or legal holiday in the District of Columbia. IRC §7503. Snow days closing federal offices in Washington (including the Tax Court) are considered legal holidays. Guralnik v. Commissioner, 146 T.C. No. 15 (2016).

135. IRC §§6330(g), 6702(b), (c). The IRS's decision in this regard is subject to limited judicial review. *E.g.*, Ryskamp v. Commissioner, 797 F.3d 1142 (D.C. Cir. 2015) (holding that judicial review of the IRS's section 6330(g) determination is limited to verifying that the IRS offered a facially plausible reason for its conclusion).

136. *E.g.*, Goza v. Commissioner, 114 T.C. 176 (2000).

137. *See, e.g.*, Dalton v. Commissioner, 682 F.3d 149 (1st Cir. 2012), *rev'g* T.C. Memo. 2008-165; Steve R. Johnson, *Reasoned Explanation and IRS Adjudication*, 63 Duke L.J. 1771, 1808–11 (2014).

the Tax Court claims the ability to look to evidence outside the record made at the Appeals Office,[138] and (3) liability issues are reviewed on a de novo basis.[139]

A taxpayer who fails to timely request CDP review may request an "equivalent hearing." An equivalent hearing takes place in the Appeals Office under largely the same ground rules as govern CDP hearings. However, collection activity will not be suspended, and judicial review of Appeals' decision is not available.[140]

There have been many studies of IRS collection performance and the effect of the CDP regime on it.[141] The benefits and costs of CDP have been widely debated. What cannot be doubted is that CDP has consumed substantial administrative and judicial resources. CDP is perennially among the most frequently litigated tax issues.[142]

G. Collection Appeals Program

Section 7123(a) directs the IRS to prescribe procedures for early Appeals Office consideration of both examination and collection issues. In response, Appeals operates its Collection Appeals Program ("CAP"). CAP is independent of CDP, and the two sets of procedures differ in material ways.

An attractive feature of CAP is that it is available under more circumstances than is CDP. The taxpayer can invoke CAP (1) before or after the IRS files notice of tax lien, (2) to challenge IRS decisions not to withdraw a notice of lien or not to issue certificates of discharge, subordination, or non-attachment of the lien, (3) before or after the IRS levies on or seizes property, and (4) to contest an IRS decision to deny or to terminate an installment agreement. An unattractive feature is that the Appeals Officer's decision is not subject to judicial review.[143]

H. Collection During Recession

Sharp economic downturns create hardships for many taxpayers. This often leads the IRS to relax the rigors of its collection practice. For example, in some contexts, the IRS has facilitated lien discharges and subordinations for "underwater" taxpayers, raised the dollar thresholds for filing Notices of Federal Tax Lien, facilitated lien with-

138. *See, e.g.*, Robinette v. Commissioner, 123 T.C. 85 (2004), *rev'd*, 439 F.3d 455 (8th Cir. 2006).

139. *See, e.g.*, Chief Counsel Notice 2014-002 (May 5, 2014) (setting out the IRS Chief Counsel's amended CDP Handbook, providing helpful guidance as to many CDP issues).

140. *See, e.g.*, Herrick v. Commissioner, 85 T.C. Memo. (CCH) 1467 (2003).

141. *E.g.*, Government Accountability Office, Little Evidence of Procedural Errors in Collection Due Process Appeal Cases, but Opportunities Exist to Improve the Program (GAO-07-112) (Oct. 2006); Treasury Inspector General for Tax Administration, Fiscal Year 2006 Statutory Review of Compliance with Lien Due Process Procedures (2006-30-094) (June 2006), *available at* www.tigta.gov.

142. *See, e.g.*, National Taxpayer Advocate 2006 Annual Report to Congress, Executive Summary III-1 (Jan. 2007).

143. *See* Rev. Proc. 99-28, 1999-2 C.B. 109.

drawals after payment, and increased the availability of installment agreements, offers in compromise, and penalty relief.[144]

VIII. Judicial Protections for Taxpayers and Third Parties

There also are purely judicial remedies available to taxpayers and third parties aggrieved by overly zealous tax collection. Because of the doctrine of sovereign immunity, the government can be sued only when it has consented to the type of action being brought against it. Some waivers of sovereign immunity are contained in the Code; others are in different statutes.

A. Judicial Remedies in the Code

Subchapter B of Chapter 76 of the Code (sections 7421–7437) provides for suits by taxpayers and third parties against the IRS. We already have discussed some suits, such as refund suits under section 7422 (Chapter 9),[145] actions to review jeopardy and termination assessments under section 7429 (Chapter 7), and recovery of administrative and litigation costs and fees under section 7430 (Chapter 8).

Another significant provision is section 7426. Section 7426(a) authorizes four types of suit against the United States.[146] These are suits for (1) determination that the levy was wrongful,[147] (2) return of surplus proceeds (amounts raised by sale of the property to the extent they exceed the tax liability), (3) funds held as substituted sale proceeds under an agreement to discharge property from the lien to allow its sale, and (4) determination that the interest of the IRS is less than the IRS asserts when, under section 6325(b), other property has been substituted for the taxpayer's property subject to the tax lien.

---

144. *See, e.g.*, SBSE-05-0314-0016 (Mar. 18, 2014); SBSE-05-0313-014 (Mar. 2013); IR-2012-31 (Mar. 7, 2012).

145. Amounts recovered by the IRS as a result of enforced collection can constitute payments, giving rise to the refund remedy as long as the requirements described in Chapter 9 have been satisfied. A third party who paid the taxpayer's liability also may pursue the refund remedy. United States v. Williams, 514 U.S. 527 (1995). Subsequently, the Supreme Court held that suit under section 7426(a) provides the exclusive remedy for wrongful levies. Effectively, this limits the *Williams* refund suit to wrongful liens as to the property of third parties. EC Term of Years Trust v. United States, 550 U.S. 429 (2007); *see* Steve R. Johnson, *Recent Supreme Court Cases Read Remedies Restrictively*, 2614 ABA Sec. of Tax'n News Q. 17 (Summer 2007).

146. Suit cannot be brought against IRS officers or employees individually. IRC § 7426(d). If it is, the United States is substituted as the defendant for the officer or employee. IRC § 7426(e).

147. Wrongful levy suit must be filed within nine months of the service of the levy on the possessor of the property. IRC § 6532(c); Williams v. United States, 947 F.2d 37, 39 (2d Cir. 1991); *see also* Mottaheden v. United States, 794 F.3d 347 (2d Cir. 2015) (rejecting taxpayer's request for equitable tolling of the nine-month period).

As to some of these categories, only a third party, not the taxpayer, may bring the suit. Additionally, as to wrongful levy suits, the third party must have an ownership, possessory, or security interest. An unsecured creditor lacks standing to sue.[148]

A number of sections authorize damages suits by taxpayers or third parties aggrieved by improper IRS collection actions. Recovery of damages is authorized under section 7426(h) for IRS violation of any Code provision, under section 7431 for unauthorized inspection or disclosure of tax returns and return information, under section 7432 for improper failure to release a tax lien, under section 7433 for unauthorized collection actions,[149] and under section 7435 for unauthorized enticement of information disclosure.

The sections typically require that the IRS's improper action or failure was intentional, knowing, or reckless. The amount of damages recoverable typically is capped at stated levels. Frequently, a precondition of recovery is that the taxpayer or other party have exhausted her administrative remedies as to the failure before bringing suit.[150] Damages suits are brought in federal District Court.[151]

B. Judicial Remedies under Other Statutes

Many types of suits as to property allegedly subject to the tax lien are allowed by 28 U.S.C. section 2410(a). The United States can be made a party to actions as to the property commenced in federal District Court or state court (although the government typically will remove state cases to federal court). The suits may be to (1) quiet title as to the property,[152] (2) foreclose on the property (action brought by third-party creditor), (3) partition the property (action brought by non-debtor co-owner), (4) condemn the property (eminent domain action brought by governmental unit), and (5) interplead funds (action brought by third party holding property when faced with conflicting claims by IRS and others). Those seeking relief under 28 U.S.C. section 2410 should scrupulously comply with its requirements.[153]

Filing a bankruptcy petition is a major defensive option for taxpayers confronting serious tax collection.[154] Chapter 1 briefly described the role of the bankruptcy

---

148. *See, e.g.*, Aspinall v. United States, 984 F.2d 355 (10th Cir. 1993).

149. Each attempt by the IRS to improperly collect is an independent violation of section 7433. Kovacs v. United States, 614 F.3d 666 (7th Cir. 2010).

150. Rushing into court without first trying to work the problem out with the IRS constitutes failure to exhaust administrative remedies. Such failure is not jurisdictional but is a frequent cause of dismissal. *E.g.*, Hoogerheide v. IRS, 637 F.3d 634 (6th Cir. 2011) (applying *Arbaugh v. Y&H Corp.*, 546 U.S. 500 (2006)).

151. *See* Steve R. Johnson, *Code Sec. 7433: Damages Against the IRS for Wrongful Collection Actions*, J. Tax Prac. & Proc., Dec.–Jan. 2007, at 27.

152. Only a party claiming an interest in the property has standing to bring a quiet title action. *E.g.*, In re Coppola, 810 F. Supp. 429, 432 (E.D.N.Y. 1992).

153. *See, e.g.*, United States v. Aultman, 2006 Dist. LEXIS 11984 (W.D. Pa. Mar. 6, 2006) (holding that federal tax liens remained on the property because of failure to comply with formal notice requirements under 28 U.S.C. § 2410(b) and IRC § 7425(a)(1)).

154. *See generally* IRS Pub. 908 *Bankruptcy Tax Guide* (Rev. Oct. 2012).

court in tax controversies. For a variety of reasons—including client reluctance or failure to meet eligibility criteria under particular chapters of the Bankruptcy Code—bankruptcy sometimes will not be an option. However, when it is available, bankruptcy always should be compared to more traditional remedies and defensive measures.

Detailed discussion of bankruptcy is beyond the scope of this book, but we will note some salient features. When a taxpayer files a bankruptcy petition, a bankruptcy estate comes into being. All of the taxpayer's assets, except those which are exempt from bankruptcy administration,[155] become the property of the bankruptcy estate, which is directed by a bankruptcy trustee. Depending on when the IRS acquired the assets, the IRS may be required to turn over to the trustee assets of the taxpayer's which the IRS had acquired by levy or otherwise.[156]

Some aspects of the bankruptcy process relate to determination of the extent of liability,[157] but there are at least four significant aspects of bankruptcy bearing on collection.

(1) Under 11 U.S.C. section 362(a), an automatic stay comes into existence when the bankruptcy petition is filed. The stay halts or delays creditor action against property of the debtor or the estate. Because of faulty internal controls, the IRS sometimes violates the automatic stay. When it does, the debtor may be able to recover damages under IRC section 7433(e) or 11 U.S.C. section 362(h).

(2) Along with the bankruptcy petition, the debtor must file extensive schedules of assets and liabilities, and further discovery opportunities exist later. These features may provide the IRS with valuable information to assist future collection. Under 18 U.S.C. section 152, lying as to the information constitutes a crime: bankruptcy fraud.

(3) The various claims against the estate, including tax claims, are paid in a prescribed order. In general, the order is: administrative expenses (such as taxes arising after the petition is filed), secured claims, priority unsecured claims, and general unsecured claims.[158]

(4) Some taxes and other debts are dischargeable. The IRS is prohibited from trying to collect discharged taxes not paid in the bankruptcy process. However, if the tax lien exists, it survives bankruptcy.

---

155. For exemption rules, see 11 U.S.C. section 522. Bankruptcy exemptions and tax exemptions (such as assets exempt from levy under IRC section 6344) are wholly independent. Thus, the IRS may eventually proceed against bankruptcy-exempt property.

156. In return, the IRS is entitled to "adequate protection." *See, e.g.*, United States v. Whiting Pools, Inc., 462 U.S. 198 (1983).

157. For example, the IRS will be compelled to submit claims for the taxes it believes to be owed, and the taxpayer and other creditors can challenge those claims. In addition, the trustee can request prompt determination of new tax liabilities. 11 U.S.C. § 505(b).

158. The filing of notice of the tax lien gives the IRS a secured claim to the extent of its interest in the value of the taxpayer's property. 11 U.S.C. § 506. Some unassessed tax liabilities are entitled to eighth priority status under 11 U.S.C. section 507.

Also relevant to insolvencies is 31 U.S.C. section 3713(a), a superpriority statute. It provides that, in certain nonbankruptcy situations, claims of the United States, including tax claims, are to be paid before the claims of other creditors. This priority attaches upon insolvency and is indefeasible.[159]

C. The Anti-Injunction Act

Section 7421(a) provides that "no suit for the purpose of restraining the assessment or collection of any tax shall be maintained in any court by any person." "The manifest purpose ... is to permit the [IRS] to assess and collect taxes alleged to be due without judicial interference, and to require that the legal right to the disputed sums be determined in a suit for refund."[160]

However, the prohibition is not absolute. The statute itself contains a number of express exceptions. In addition, a very limited judicially created exception exists. It is available only when the taxpayer establishes both that (1) under the most liberal view of the law and the facts, it is clear that the Government cannot prevail on the merits and (2) the taxpayer will suffer irreparable harm for which no adequate remedy at law exists.[161]

Section 7421 is widely thought to be jurisdictional,[162] but some question that.[163] It "does not apply to every lawsuit 'tangentially related to taxes,' "[164] but precisely where the boundaries of the prohibition lie is often controversial.[165]

D. Non-Starters

Eschewing, or ineligible for, the available judicial remedies, some taxpayers have attempted to avail themselves of other remedies—without success. The Federal Tort Claims Act ("FTCA") is a major waiver of sovereign immunity. However, the FTCA does not apply to claims "arising in respect of the assessment or collection of any

---

159. *See, e.g.*, Greene v. United States, 440 F.2d 1304 (Fed. Cir. 2006).

160. Enochs v. Williams Packing & Nav. Co., 370 U.S. 1, 7 (1962). Section 7421 (the Anti-Injunction Act) and 28 U.S.C. sections 2201-2202 (the Declaratory Judgment Act) are coextensive in practical effect. *E.g.*, Ambort v. United States, 392 F.3d 1138, 1140 (10th Cir. 2004). For the history of section 7421, see Steve R. Johnson, *Reforming Federal Tax Litigation: An Agenda*, 41 Fla. St. U.L. Rev. 205, 215–17 (2013).

161. *Williams Packing*, *supra*, at 6–7.

162. *E.g.*, Seven-Sky v. Holder, 661 F.3d 1, 5 (D.C. Cir. 2011), *abrogated on other grounds*, Nat'l Fed'n of Indep. Bus. v. Sebelius, 132 S. Ct. 2566 (2012).

163. *E.g.*, Florida Bankers Ass'n v. U.S. Dep't of Treasury, 799 F.3d 1065, 1074 n.3 (D.C. Cir. 2015) (Henderson, J., dissenting), *cert. denied*, 2016 WL 3129030 (June 6, 2016).

164. Hobby Lobby Stores, Inc. v. Sebelius, 723 F.3d 1114, 1127 (10th Cir. 2013) (en banc) (citation omitted), *aff'd*, 134 S. Ct. 2751 (2014).

165. For example, in the above cited *Florida Bankers* case, two judges of the circuit panel concluded that the Anti-Injunction Act prevented pre-enforcement challenge to a tax reporting regulation while the third judge, agreeing with the district court below, 19 F. Supp. 2d 111 (D.C. 2014), thought that it did not.

tax."[166] Damages suits based on state law also are barred by sovereign immunity and, in some cases, qualified immunity.[167]

In *Bivens*, the Supreme Court created a damages remedy with respect to constitutional violations by government officials and employees.[168] However, a *Bivens* action will not lie if Congress intended to provide an exclusive remedy or if Congress created a statutory scheme that it sees as an adequate substitute for *Bivens*. Accordingly, because of the existence of section 7433 and other Code damages sections, the majority view is that a *Bivens* suit is unavailable with respect to IRS actions.[169]

IX. Statute of Limitations

The IRS can collect only within the statute of limitations ("SOL") period. Under section 6502(a)(1), the normal collection SOL period ends 10 years after the date on which the liability was assessed. In a Supreme Court case, the IRS had properly assessed unpaid employment taxes against a partnership. The Court held that such assessment suffices to extend the SOL to collect tax in judicial proceedings from general partners liable for payment of the partnership's debts.[170]

Many events can extend or suspend the running of the ten-year period. Some of the more important are: the filing of a bankruptcy petition,[171] submission of an offer-in-compromise ("OIC"),[172] filing a request for a CDP hearing or seeking judicial review of the results of a CDP hearing,[173] requesting spousal relief from a joint income tax liability,[174] requesting an installment agreement or appealing the IRS's rejection of an installment agreement,[175] judicial control over or custody of the taxpayer's assets,[176] continuous absence of the taxpayer from the United States for at least six months,[177] and extension of time to pay estate tax under sections 6161(a) or 6166.[178] Many other conditions suspending the SOL are described in section 6501, section 6503, and other sections.

---

166. 28 U.S.C. § 2680(c). *See, e.g.*, Miklautsch v. Gibbs, 90-2 USTC ¶ 50,587 (D. Alas. 1990) (taxpayer unable to recover under FTCA, RICO, or *Bivens*).

167. *E.g.*, Kyler v. Everson, 442 F.3d 1251 (10th Cir. 2006) (also requiring the taxpayer to pay $8,000 in costs as a sanction for filing a frivolous appeal).

168. Bivens v. Six Unknown Named Agents, 403 U.S. 388 (1971).

169. *See, e.g.*, Adams v. Johnson, 355 F.3d 1179 (9th Cir. 2004); Christopher M. Pietruszkiewicz, *A Constitutional Cause of Action and the Internal Revenue Code: Can You Shoot (Sue) the Messenger?*, 54 Syracuse L. Rev. 1 (2004).

170. United States v. Galletti, 541 U.S. 114 (2004).

171. IRC § 6503(h).

172. IRC §§ 6331(i)(5), 6331(k)(1).

173. IRC §§ 6320(e)(1), 6330(e)(1).

174. IRC § 6015(e)(2).

175. IRC § 6331(k)(2).

176. IRC § 6503(b).

177. IRC § 6503(c).

178. IRC § 6503(d).

The collection limitations period may be extended via a consent duly executed by the taxpayer and the IRS.[179] The IRS uses Form 900 for this purpose.[180] To be valid, the Form 900 must be executed on or before the CSED. The 1998 Reform Act amended section 6502(a) to prohibit the IRS from seeking taxpayer consents to extend the collection SOL except in conjunction with an installment agreement or a release of levy.[181]

The IRS sometimes erroneously calculates the CSED. This can adversely affect the IRS because the Service may halt collection in the mistaken belief that the SOL has expired or it may defer collection in the mistaken belief that time remains on the SOL. The taxpayer also can be hurt by being subjected to collection efforts beyond the time for which the taxpayer legally was at hazard.

Sometimes the IRS calculates the CSED automatically by computer; other times, IRS personnel calculate it manually. Unfortunately, the IRS uses multiple computers, not all of which are correctly updated when some of the many events occur which suspend or extend the SOL. In addition, IRS personnel are not always promptly trained as to statutory changes to the suspension or extension conditions or may misinterpret the effect of the statutes applied to complex facts.

The IRS is attempting to address the problems of inaccurately calculated CSEDs. Nonetheless, the wise practitioner will not simply rely on whatever the IRS asserts the CSED to be in a particular case. Instead, the practitioner should independently calculate the CSED whenever relevant in a collection case.

The common law doctrine of laches denies relief to parties who "sleep on their rights." However, "[i]t is well settled that the United States is not ... subject to the defense of laches in enforcing its rights."[182] Thus, IRS collection action which is timely under section 6502 cannot be challenged as untimely under the doctrine of laches.

Problems

Roger was employed by an investment banking and consulting firm. His job was to provide investment advice to customers of the firm who were assigned to him. He also arranged purchases and sales of securities for his customers through the firm. His compensation consisted of a base salary plus commissions. The firm paid Roger on a monthly basis, and withheld income tax from his compensation as required by law.

---

179. For principles governing consents, see Chapter 5.

180. The IRS prefers to obtain the taxpayer's original signature on the Form 900. In some cases, however, it will accept a Form 900 received by facsimile transmission thus bearing only a fax signature. *See* SCA 200504033, 2005 WL 190327 (Jan. 28, 2005).

181. The 1998 Reform Act, section 3461(c)(2), also contained a provision dealing with waivers secured by the IRS in connection with an OIC before December 31, 1999. It provided that any such waiver would expire on the later of December 31, 2003, or on the expiration of the ten-year SOL period.

182. United States v. Summerlin, 310 U.S. 414, 416 (1940); *see, e.g.*, Lucia v. United States, 474 F.2d 565, 570, n.13 (5th Cir. 1973).

Roger was married. His spouse, Sherry, was not employed and had no income. She continued to use her maiden name, Smith, during their marriage. They had filed joint returns for the all years prior to 20x2.

Roger also engaged in frequent purchases and sales of securities for his own account. He often made substantial profits from those transactions. He paid the estimated taxes on a quarterly basis as required. He was having a good year in 20x2, but incurred significant unanticipated losses during the fourth quarter. These losses have the effect of reducing his taxable income for the year, as a result of which he had an overpayment for the year in the amount of $100,000.

For the years prior to 20x2, Roger and Sherry had prepared their own returns using commercial tax preparation software and had filed the returns timely. In February 20x3, the area in which Roger and Sherry lived experienced some very bad storms that resulted in severe flooding. Their home was completely flooded, and they lost all their furniture and most of their possessions. Their computers were damaged beyond repair. All the data, including their income tax data, was lost. As a result, it was not possible for them to file their tax return for 20x2 on a timely basis. So Roger filed for an extension of time to file the return. Roger knew that they would not owe any tax, so he felt confident that obtaining an extension of time to file would be safe.

He and Sherry were in the process of rebuilding their home and reconstructing their records, including their tax records, when in June 20x3 Roger's firm received notice that it was being investigated for numerous violations of securities laws. Roger was interviewed extensively by law enforcement personnel. The preparation and meetings consumed much of his time. Soon the firm went out of business. Fortunately, Roger avoided any personal problems, but he had to find a new job. He was hired by another firm in December 20x3. He immediately went to work rebuilding his client base. Roger's hard work paid off and, by June 20x4, he and Sherry had their home and their cash flow back on track. They filed their 20x3 return timely, but still had not filed their 20x2 return. Roger knew that they would not be subject to penalties because the tax had been overpaid.

Roger experienced good success in his new job. In addition to salary and commissions, his investments were quite profitable. Their tax returns for 20x4 and later years became substantially more complicated than for prior years. So they decided to have their 20x4 and future returns prepared by an accountant. In early 20x5, when the accountant was working on the 20x4 return, Roger told the accountant that they had a big overpayment from the year 20x2 that could be used towards a future tax liability. Roger's new accountant told them that the overpayment would not be needed for 20x4, but that he would keep it in mind for future years.

Sherry's mother, Sally, was experiencing problems taking care of her personal financial matters, so Sherry's name was added to Sally's account at Big Bank. Although all the deposits were made by Sally, either Sherry or Sally could draw on the account at any time.

Roger and Sherry had their accounts at Big Bank as well. Big Bank also had a mortgage on Roger and Sherry's home.

Sherry's sister, Susan, owned a car, which she was not using. Sherry did not have a car, so with Susan's permission, Sherry gladly took over that car. It was titled in the name of "S. Smith," the same name that Sherry used. So she left it titled in the name.

Sherry's father, Steve, had passed away a few years ago. He had owned some property in his name (S. Smith) on a lake a few hundred miles from the city. He left the property to Sherry and Susan on his death. There had not been any probate proceedings, so the property was still in the name of S. Smith.

Roger had a very good year 20x7, but he underpaid his tax for that year. So, after consulting with the accountant, he decided to apply the 20x2 overpayment to the 20x7 tax liability. The joint return was filed timely on October 15, 20x8, after an extension of time to file had been obtained.

Roger received a letter from the IRS in early 20x8 informing them that they could not use the $100,000 overpayment from 20x2 for their 20x7 tax liability because of IRC section 6511(b)(2). Soon thereafter, they received a notice and demand for payment in the amount of $100,000 plus interest and penalties for the year 20x7.

The IRS conducted a search of the public records to determine whether Roger or Sherry owned any property. The IRS discovered an automobile titled in the name of "S. Smith." The IRS knew from tax returns that Sally use that name. A Revenue Officer came to Roger and Sherry's home (the address had been on their last few returns) and saw the car in the driveway. So the IRS issued a notice of levy on the car and seized it right away.

The IRS also discovered the property in the name of "S. Smith" that had been left to Sherry and Susan a few years earlier.

Roger hired a lawyer to commence a malpractice action against the accountant for failing to advise them to take action on a timely basis with respect to the 20x2 overpayment.

1. What actions do you expect the IRS to take to collect the amount due for the year 20x7? What action should Roger and Sherry take?

2. What action should be taken by Sally, Sherry's mother?

3. What action should be taken by Susan, Sherry sister?

4. Big Bank has learned that the IRS has taken collection actions against Roger and Sherry, although the IRS has not yet issued a notice of levy to Big Bank. The bank is concerned that the collection actions might weaken Roger and Sherry's financial position and jeopardize the bank's ability to get paid on its mortgage. What action should the bank take?

Chapter 14

The Section 6672 "Trust Fund Recovery Penalty"

IRC:	§§ 3505; 3509; 6601(e)(2)(B); 6671; 6672; 7202; 7436; 7501
Cases and Rulings:	Rev. Proc. 2005-34; Rev. Proc. 2002-26; Slodov v. U.S., 436 U.S. 238 (1978); Wetzel v. United States, 802 F. Supp. 1451 (S.D. Miss. 1992)
Forms:	Skim 843; 940; 941; 2750; 2751; 2751-AD; 4180

I. Introduction

Owners of failing businesses, confronted with creditors who have already terminated the extension of further credit and who demand cash on delivery (C.O.D.) payment are usually desperate to find funds to keep operating. A ready source within their control is the checking account holding the taxes withheld from employees that are due to be paid over to the IRS.[1] On the belief the business will turn around and they will be able to remedy the situation later, far too many owners do not make the required payment to the government and instead preserve the money for suppliers and other creditors. This frequently goes on for quite a few months, with the amount borrowed from the IRS "pyramiding" one quarter on top of the other to a sizeable amount. Sadly, many of these businesses fail, leaving the withheld taxes unpaid.[2]

---

1. While the discussion in this chapter focuses on the most common situation that causes section 6672 to arise, i.e., employment-related "trust fund" taxes, it is broader than this. Other taxes, such as certain excise taxes, are also collected from third parties and held in "trust" for the government. Their nonpayment likewise brings section 6672 into play. Also, though this chapter focuses on federal tax withheld and owing to the IRS, most, if not all, states have similar procedures they can employ. *See, e.g.*, C.R.S. § 39-21-116.5; Rock v. Dep't of Taxes, 742 A.2d 1211 (Vt. 1999); Nakano v. Commissioner, 742 F.3d 1208 (9th Cir.), *cert. denied*, 134 S. Ct. 2680 (2014); Conway v. Commissioner, 137 T.C. 209 (2011), *aff'd*, 552 Fed. Appx. 724 (9th Cir.), *cert. denied*, 134 S. Ct. 2680 (2014) (both involving section 6672 as to unpaid transportation excise taxes).

2. The failure of the business is the most common scenario causing a trust fund violation. However, there are others, such as when the employer's accounting system or bookkeeping personnel are unsophisticated and fail to assure that the filing and deposit requirements are met or when someone embezzles the funds that were to have been used to pay the employment taxes. For possible ways to minimize employment tax penalty liabilities, see Carol M. Luttati, *How to Secure Penalty Abatement in Cases of Delinquent Employment Taxes Caused by Severe Financial Difficulties*, J. Tax Prac. & Proc., Feb.–Mar. 2011, p. 7.

The large number of taxpayers who repeatedly accumulate employment tax delinquencies continues to be a major compliance problem for the IRS. As of June 30, 2012, the latest date such information is

For businesses that operate as sole proprietorships or general partnerships,[3] any unpaid debts of the business, including the unpaid withheld taxes, are the personal liability of the sole proprietor or general partners.[4] The owners of corporations and multi-member limited liability companies, on the other hand, while normally protected from personal liability for the debts of the business,[5] find this protection does not apply with respect to withheld employment taxes that were not paid over to the government. Instead, section 6672 allows the Service to pierce the limited liability veil and demand payment from any and all individuals who were responsible for the default.[6]

Section 6672, often referred to as either the "trust fund recovery penalty (TFRP)," the "civil penalty," or the "100% penalty,"[7] is a powerful tool in the hands of the gov-

available, employers owed the IRS approximately $14.1 billion in delinquent employment taxes. This total does not include the substantial amount of employment tax delinquencies that the IRS determined were currently not collectible. As of the end of March 2013, the IRS's total dollar inventory of currently not collectible employment tax accounts was $24.9 billion. Treasury Inspector General for Tax Administration, *Trust Fund Recovery Penalty Actions Were Not Always Timely or Adequate 1* (TIGTA No. 2014-30-0345) (May 23, 2014). The IRS intends to take corrective measures in light of the TIGTA report.

3. United States v. Galletti, 541 U.S. 114 (2004) (proper tax assessment against partnership sufficed to extend the statute of limitations to collect tax in judicial proceeding from general partners who were liable for payment of partnership's debts).

4. Reg. section 301.7701-2(c)(2)(iv) was added to treat disregarded entities, such as single-member LLCs, as separate corporations for the purposes of employment tax liability (though not for income tax purposes). T.D. 9356, *Disregarded Entities; Employment and Excise Taxes*, 72 Fed. Reg. 45,891 (Aug. 16, 2007). This rule only applies to wages paid on or after January 1st, 2009. For wages paid prior to January 1, 2009, the sole owner of an LLC that did not elect to be taxed as a corporation is individually liable for all unpaid employment taxes. McNamee v. Department of the Treasury, 488 F.3d 100 (2d Cir. 2007); Littriello v. United States, 484 F.3d 372 (6th Cir. 2007). If state law provides that the owner of a single-member LLC is not liable for the debts of the business, the IRS may not pursue the member individually except to the extent the owner might be liable under section 6672. *See* United States v. Galletti, 541 U.S. 114 (2004) (general partners liable for partnership's employment tax liability because general partners jointly and severally liable for partnership's obligations under state law).

5. In Rev. Rul. 2004-41, 2004-18 I.R.B. 845, the IRS held, citing *United States v. Galletti*, 541 U.S. 114 (2004), that state law determines whether owners of a business can be held liable for unpaid employment taxes of the entity. Since state law generally provides that general partners of a general or limited partnership are jointly and severally liable derivatively for the partnership's obligations, the Service may seek to collect federal tax liabilities incurred by a partnership, such as federal employment taxes, directly (i.e. without resorting to section 6672) from the general partners. *See also* Chief Counsel Notice 2005-003 (Jan. 19, 2005). However, a limited liability company (LLC) taxed as a partnership is different. Since state law affords members protection from the debts of the LLC, the IRS may not pursue the members individually except to the extent they might be liable under section 6672.

6. If a corporation is unable to pay its trust fund taxes, the United States Treasury suffers the loss because the employees from whose wages the taxes are withheld are still credited with the withheld amounts as if they had been paid to the government. IRC § 31.

7. The provision is presently referred to as the "trust fund recovery penalty" because the taxes referred to those the employer is required to hold in trust for the Service. Policy Statement P-5-14, IRM 1.2.14.1.3. Prior to February 1993, section 6672 was commonly referred to as the "100% Penalty." The name was changed since taxpayers (and some practitioners) seemed perpetually confused by the title, often believing that those found liable owed a certain amount of tax and an equal amount, i.e., 100%, as a penalty. In fact, the penalty aspects of the provision are that (i) one is not shielded by the limited liability doctrine, (ii) the penalty is not deductible, and (iii) the penalty is not dischargeable in bankruptcy.

ernment. It creates a unique vehicle for the collection of "trust fund" taxes, i.e., those taxes collected from employees and "held to be a special fund in trust for the United States."[8] Section 6672(a) imposes the penalty on "[a]ny person required to collect, truthfully account for, and pay over any tax ... who willfully fails to collect such tax, or truthfully account for, and pay over any tax, or willfully attempts in any manner to evade or defeat any such tax or the payment thereof...."

The Service usually asserts the penalty against everyone who *might* be liable.[9] The government's motto seems to be: "When in doubt, assert the penalty and let those pursued fight it out among themselves." This policy inevitably leads to a frantic call from someone who says, "I was vice-president of XYZ Corporation until about six months ago. I just got a notice from the IRS saying I owe $125,000 for unpaid employment taxes for 20x4 and 20x5. That isn't possible, is it?"

This chapter attempts to familiarize the student with the law, procedures, and strategies associated with representing someone against whom the IRS is asserting the section 6672 penalty.[10]

II. The Employer's Compliance Duties: Withholding Taxes, Making Payments, and Filing Returns

To understand what the IRS can assess and collect using section 6672, an understanding of the three types of federal employment taxes is necessary. The first type is income tax. This is collected by the employer through withholding pursuant to section 3402. The amount withheld is determined by schedules created by the IRS based on an employee's Form W-4, which lists marital status and number of personal exemptions.

The second type of employment tax is Federal Insurance Contribution Act (FICA), which funds Social Security and Medicare. For wages paid up to a certain amount

8. IRC § 7501.

9. Regardless of the number of persons against whom the liability is assessed, the IRS cannot collect more trust fund taxes than are owed by the business. Thus, even though the IRS might assess the penalty against three persons and so appears to be seeking 300% of the tax, the government can only eventually collect 100% of that which is owed.

10. Section 3505 may also create personal liability for trust fund taxes for persons or businesses that are not employers of the workers. Specifically, section 3505(a) imposes liability on lenders, sureties, and other persons who directly pay the wages of another and fail to withhold the appropriate taxes. Section 3505(b) establishes a penalty of 25% where funds have been supplied to pay wages. In contrast to the penalty under section 6672, which can be assessed and collected administratively, the government must institute legal proceedings in order to collect under section 3505. The government may also seek to have criminal charges filed against a person for failing to pay assessed trust fund recovery penalties. IRC §§ 7201 and 7202. Based on the number of recently reported cases, it is apparent the government is pursuing this avenue with added zeal. *See, e.g.*, United States v. Quinn, 566 Fed. Appx. 659 (10th Cir. 2014); United States v. Easterday, 539 F.3d 1176 (9th Cir. 2008), amended by 564 F.3d 1004 (9th Cir. 2008).

($118,500 in 2016), the total FICA contribution is 15.3% of wages. For wages paid above the annual limit, the contribution drops to 2.9% and is for Medicare only.[11] The burden for FICA taxes, whether at 15.3% or 2.9%, is divided equally between the employee and the employer. The half that represents the employee's portion is collected from the employee by the employer through withholding pursuant to section 3121(a).[12] The other half—the employer's portion—is solely the employer's responsibility and is not withheld from the employee.

The third type of employment tax is referred to as Federal Unemployment Tax Act (FUTA). This tax is exclusively the responsibility of the employer; no portion of it is withheld from the employee.

Employers are regularly required to pay over to, or deposit with, certain designated depository institutions both the employee's and employer's portions of federal income tax and FICA tax.[13] In addition, a business' FUTA tax liability must normally be deposited by the end of the month following each calendar quarter.

Non-agricultural employers are required to file a Form 941 ("Employer's Quarterly Federal Tax Return") on a quarterly basis. The Form 941 return is due on or before the last day of the month following the close of each calendar quarter; in other words, on April 30, July 31, October 31, and January 31.[14] The Form 941 reports the quarterly wages paid, the federal income tax withheld, the sum of the employer's and employees' FICA tax liability and the deposits paid. Any taxes still owed after the deposits are accounted for must be paid with the return. In addition to the quarterly Form 941, the employer is required to annually file a Form 940 ("Employer's Annual Federal Unemployment [FUTA] Tax Return") and to pay the balance due after taking deposits into account.

In the context of employment taxes, the term "trust fund" taxes, i.e., those to which section 6672 applies, refers *only* to taxes that are withheld from employees—federal income tax and the employee's portion of the FICA tax. It does not refer to

---

11. As of January 2013, individuals with earned income of more than $200,000 ($250,000 for married couples filing jointly) pay an additional 0.9 percent in Medicare taxes. IRC § 3101(b). The tax rates shown above do not include the 0.9%.

12. The employer is responsible for withholding the additional 0.9% in Medicare taxes from the wages of the employee if his wages exceed $200,000, regardless of filing status. IRC § 3102 (f).

13. The frequency of the required deposits is dictated by the amount of employment taxes incurred during certain periods. Periods may be as short as one business day or as long as quarterly. Section 6656(a) establishes a penalty to be imposed upon "failure ... to deposit (as required by this title or by regulations ...) on the date prescribed therefor any amount [required to be deposited]." Reg. § 31.6302-1(h)(2)(ii) requires that deposits over $200,000 be made by electronic funds transfer. In several cases, taxpayers have deposited required amounts (over $200,000) timely and in correct amount, but did so manually, not by electronic funds transfer. The courts have upheld imposing the section 6656(a) penalty in such cases. *E.g.*, Commonwealth Bank & Trust Co. v. United States, 114 AFTR2d 5091 (W.D. Ky. 2014).

14. For employers whose annual liability for social security, Medicare, and withheld federal income taxes is $1,000 or less, they can file Form 944 (Employer's Annual Federal Tax Return) instead of the Form 941 and pay these taxes only once a year.

employment taxes, penalties, and interest that the employer itself owes, such as its one-half share of the FICA tax and all the FUTA tax.[15]

III. Liability for Trust Fund Taxes Pursuant to Section 6672

For an individual to be liable under section 6672, it must be determined that he or she (1) was a *responsible person* (2) who *willfully* failed to collect, truthfully account for, and pay over "trust fund" taxes. One can escape liability by proving that either of these elements does not apply. As determinations of the Service are entitled to a presumption of correctness, the taxpayer has the burden of proof and must satisfy it by a preponderance of the evidence.[16]

Though not a separate element, the Internal Revenue Manual (IRM) states that collectibility should be a factor in determining whether the penalty is asserted against an individual. Since the penalty is a derivative liability and its assessment is discretionary, the IRM directs IRS employees not to assess the section 6672 penalty at all if "the financial analysis [of a responsible person] shows ... there is little prospect that, over the collection statute period, the taxpayer will receive any increase in income or acquire assets that will enable the Service to collect any of the penalty [over the collection statute period]."[17]

A. The "Responsible Person" Element

Interestingly, the Code never defines the term "responsible person."[18] That task has been left to administrative rulings and case law. The touchstones for determining whether one is a "responsible person" are the person's "status, duty and authority" within the

---

15. In most situations that are the focus of this chapter, the business has failed to file the returns and pay and deposit the taxes timely. Thus, many penalties will have accrued against the business. The section 6672 penalty cannot be used to impose liability for the late filing or late payment penalties or interest assessed against the *employer* that relate to employment taxes. *See, e.g.*, Williams v. United States, 939 F.2d 915 (11th Cir. 1991). However, once the section 6672 penalty is assessed against a responsible person, that person will have interest accruing on his or her own penalty balance. IRC § 6601(e)(2)(A).

16. *See, e.g.*, Calderone v. United States, 799 F.2d 254 (6th Cir. 1986). For cases applying the two elements, see William Bailey & Ryan Pace, *Trust Fund Recovery Penalty Still Vexing "Responsible Persons,"* Tax Notes, Feb. 10, 2014, at 653 (describing many 2013 cases).

17. IRM 5.7.5.3.

18. The Code defines the term "person" in both sections 6671(b) and 7701(a)(1). Section 6671(b) states that "[t]he term 'person'... includes an officer or employee of a corporation, or a member or employee of a partnership, who as such officer, employee, or member is under a duty to perform the act in respect of which the violation occurs" and section 7701(a)(1) states, more broadly, that "[t]he term 'person' shall be construed to mean and include an individual, a trust, estate, partnership, association, company or corporation."

organization.[19] Knowledge that the taxes are unpaid, while relevant for the *willfulness* factor, is not germane to a determination of the person's status, duty, and authority.

Most commonly, responsibility attaches when a person has the authority to decide which creditors to pay and when to pay them. In short, one is considered responsible if one has the ability to control the purse strings of the business.[20] It is not necessary that the individual have the final word, however.[21] For example, one can be liable if he or she has the authority to pay the IRS but fails to assert that authority when directed by more senior officers to make no payments or pay other creditors instead.[22]

The determination whether an individual has the status, duty, and authority is a factual one. A person's title is not controlling. Nevertheless, acts performed, and positions held, by an individual within the organizational structure tend to indicate "responsibility."[23] Responsibility may be indicated if one has:

- The authority to sign checks.
- Control of the financial affairs of the business.
- Served as an officer, director, or shareholder of the corporation.
- Such duties and responsibilities in the corporate by-laws.
- The ability to hire and fire employees.
- The authority to borrow money for the company.
- The authority to sign and file federal tax returns, particularly the Form 941s, and exercises the authority possessed.
- Dealt with customers and creditors.
- Control over payroll disbursements.
- The ability to direct payments to creditors.
- The final word as to which bills are paid and when.[24]
- Control of the corporation's voting stock.
- Responsibility for making the federal tax deposits.

1. Defense Strategies With Respect to the Responsible Person Element

a. Establish That Individual Did Not Have Status, Duty, or Authority

The most obvious strategy associated with proving one is not a responsible person is proving that the person in question lacked the actual status, duty, or authority to

19. Mazo v. United States, 591 F.2d 1151, 1153 (5th Cir. 1979); *see also* IRM 5.7.3.3.1.

20. Purcell v. United States, 1 F.3d 932 (9th Cir. 1993); *see also* IRM 5.7.3.3.1.

21. *See, e.g.*, Hochstein v. United States, 900 F.2d 543 (2d Cir. 1990); Neckles v. United States, 579 F.2d 938, 940 (5th Cir. 1978).

22. *See* Caterino v. United States, 794 F.2d 1, 5 (1st Cir. 1986).

23. *See* IRM 5.7.3.3.1.1.

24. A person with the final word as to which bills should be paid and when can indicate such person is responsible; however, it is not true the other way around. A responsible person need not have the final word regarding the preference of payments. In many court cases, accountants who merely acted on orders from superiors and would have been fired if they had not done so were considered responsible persons. *See, e.g.*, Brounstein v. United States, 979 F.2d 952, 956 (3d Cir. 1992).

direct the collecting of, accounting for, and paying over of trust fund taxes. This burden is not met merely by proving that someone else had greater power, as several persons within an organization may have the requisite status, duty, and authority.[25]

Persons who are officers or stockholders in a corporation often are responsible. However, officer or stockholder status cannot be the sole basis for a responsibility determination.[26] In rare cases, taxpayers have been able to establish that an officer, such as a secretary or treasurer, or someone with the ability to sign checks, did not have the authority to decide which bills got paid.[27] On the other hand, a person who has the ultimate authority to make the financial decisions cannot avoid responsible person status by either being "willfully ignorant" or delegating the authority to someone else.[28] Nevertheless, if the delegation was so complete as to have rendered the delegator powerless to make financial decisions, such person may avoid responsibility.[29]

b. The "I Was Just Following Orders" Defense

"I was just following orders" is one of the most common defenses raised with respect to the responsible person element. Inequities are particularly likely to occur if the IRS pursues lower-level employees, such as staff bookkeepers or accounts payable clerks, who prepare tax returns or sign checks purely at the direction of someone with decision-making authority.[30] The IRS no longer asserts the penalty against non-owner employees if it can be established that they were "just following orders," and did not exercise independent decisionmaking authority regarding which creditors got paid.[31]

---

25. IRM 5.7.3.3; Heimark v. United States, 18 Cl. Ct. 15 (1989); *see* United States v. Stanton, 37 A.F.T.R.2d (RIA) ¶ 76-1427 (S.D. Fla. 1976) (corporation's vice president was foreman and had no control over or participation in business or financial decisions); In re Clifford, 255 B.R. 258 (D. Mass. 2000) (majority owner kept check-signing vice president and shareholder "in the dark" about finances and retained control over payroll payments).

26. IRM 5.7.3.3.1.1.

27. Vinick v. Commissioner, 205 F.3d 1 (1st Cir. 2000). In *Savona v. United States*, 2007 U.S. Dist. LEXIS 76795 (S.D. Cal. Oct. 15, 2007), the government was denied summary judgment on whether a CEO was a responsible person as a matter of law even though he had check signing authority and had ability to hire and fire employees. The court noted he did not have *significant* control over the businesses' financial affairs because the founder of the business (and former CEO) was the only person able to direct which creditors would get paid.

28. Kinnie v. United States, 994 F.2d 279 (6th Cir. 1993).

29. IRM 5.7.3.3.1.1; Stewart v. United States, 90-1 U.S.T.C. (CCH) ¶ 50,002 (Cl. Ct. 1989).

30. *Compare* Howard v. United States, 711 F.2d 729 (5th Cir. 1983), *and* Roth v. United States, 779 F.2d 1567 (11th Cir. 1986), *with* Jay v. United States, 865 F.2d 1175 (10th Cir. 1989). The defense is much harder to assert when the target is a high-level person. For example, a president and chief operating officer of an airline argued that the company's board of directors had ordered him to pay only those debts needed to keep planes in the air and had divested him of authority to pay taxes. This contention was rejected on both the facts and the law. Ferguson v. United States, 484 F.3d 1068 (8th Cir. 2007) (distinguishing *United States v. Bisbee*, 245 F.3d 1001 (8th Cir. 2001), on the ground that the *Bisbee* involved an individual who had never had the requisite authority in the first place).

31. "[I]ndividuals performing ministerial acts without exercising independent judgment will not be deemed responsible. In general, non-owner employees who act solely under the dominion and control of others, and who are not in a position to make independent decisions on behalf of the business entity, will not be assessed the TFRP. Non-owner employees are those who do not own any stock, interest, or other entrepreneurial stake in the company that employs them.... Officers and

c. Not a Responsible Person at the Time Taxes Withheld

To be subject to liability, a person must be responsible at the time the wages were paid and the taxes withheld; the date the employment tax return was filed is not the critical date.[32] Resignation after the taxes were withheld but before they were paid to the government and before the returns were due does not avoid responsible person status.[33] On the other hand, resignation before or during the accruing of liability not only mitigates the exposure but also goes a long way to establishing lack of willfulness, especially if the person quit because of the defalcation.

Conversely, one who assumes control of a business (or attains the status, duty, and authority) after taxes have accrued and gone unpaid can unwittingly become a responsible person to the extent of the unencumbered funds of the business at the time control of the business is acquired.[34] Exposure is particularly likely if the person merely moved from one position in the company to another position in the company, rather than being newly hired.[35]

B. The "Willfulness" Element

The trust fund penalty applies only if the person who failed to collect, truthfully account for, and pay over the tax did so "willfully." Willfulness, for these purposes, is not defined in the Code[36] and its scope can only be determined by reference to case law. For example, the Tenth Circuit defined willfulness as follows:

> Willfulness in the context of Section 6672, means a voluntary, conscious, and intentional decision to prefer other creditors over the government....

---

higher level employees of a company who are non-owners may still be required to sacrifice their jobs (i.e., quit) to avoid being responsible for the TFRP, rather than obey the orders of an owner to pay other creditors but not to pay current federal trust fund taxes as they become due." *See* IRS Policy Statement P-5-14 (IRM 1.2.14.1.3); IRM 5.7.3.3.1.2.

One important caveat is that the government's position appears to be limited to non-owners and those who would not otherwise be responsible persons. If one is a responsible person, such as a treasurer, one cannot avoid liability simply because of a superior's orders not to pay the tax. Roth v. United States, 779 F.2d 1567 (11th Cir. 1986); *see also* United States v. Rem, 38 F.3d 634 (2d Cir. 1994) (the controlling questions are (1) whether the individual firmly believed that his actual authority was limited to following another's orders; and if so (2) whether such belief was reasonable under the circumstances).

32. Davis v. United States, 961 F.2d 867 (9th Cir. 1992); Vinick v. United States, 205 F.3d 1 (1st Cir. 2000).

33. Long v. Bacon, 239 F. Supp. 911 (S.D. Iowa 1965).

34. Slodov v. United States, 436 U.S. 238 (1978) (dictum).

35. Davis v. United States, 961 F.2d 867 (9th Cir. 1992).

36. It is important to understand that there are different willfulness standards applied in criminal tax cases and in section 6672 cases. The standard in criminal cases is "a voluntary, intentional violation of a known legal duty." Cheek v. United States, 498 U.S. 192 (1991). By contrast, willful conduct for section 6672 purposes merely requires a "voluntary, conscious, and intentional—as opposed to accidental—decision not to remit funds properly withheld to the government." Kalb v. United States, 505 F.2d 506, 511 (2d Cir. 1974) (*quoting* Monday v. United States, 421 F.2d 1210, 1216 (7th Cir. 1970)). Neither requires bad faith or evil intent, though clearly their presence suggests more purposeful conduct. Caterino v. United States, 794 F.2d 1 (1st Cir. 1986); IRM 5.7.3.3.2, 8.25.1.4.2.

> Willfulness is present whenever a responsible person acts or fails to act consciously and voluntarily and with knowledge or intent that as a result of his actions or inaction trust funds belonging to the government will not be paid over but will be used for other purposes ... Proof of willfulness does not require proof of bad motive.... It is the burden of the responsible person to show that he did not willfully fail to remit taxes.[37]

Willfulness is present if (1) the responsible person was aware that the taxes were unpaid and, possessing the power to pay them with funds of the taxpayer entity, decided not to pay the government or to pay other creditors, or (2) the responsible person was "grossly negligent" or acted in "reckless disregard" of the fact that the taxes were due and would not be paid.[38] The latter scenario would arise, for example, if the responsible person was on notice that taxes were past due and, while knowing the business was in financial distress, made no effort to deal with the situation.[39] Even if the responsible person did not have notice that taxes were past due, knowledge of prior failures to pay payroll taxes (even if corrected) will support a finding of reckless disregard or gross negligence if the director fails to take additional steps to guard against such failures in the future.[40]

1. Defense Strategies with Respect to the Willfulness Element

a. Establish That the Responsible Person Did Not Act "Willfully"

While acting either "willfully," in a "grossly negligent" manner, or in "reckless disregard of the facts" may cause liability, being merely careless does not.[41] If a person's conduct was merely negligent and not willful, the person should not be held liable for the penalty. Numerous courts have found that a taxpayer who lacked actual knowledge that the liability existed or lacked actual knowledge that the trust fund taxes had not been paid did not act willfully.[42] For example, an attorney acting on behalf of the corporation, signed checks for employment taxes and entrusted them to the corporate

37. Muck v. United States, 3 F.3d 1378, 1381 (10th Cir. 1993); *see also* Denbo v. United States, 988 F.2d 1029 (10th Cir. 1993).

38. IRS v. Blais, 612 F. Supp. 700 (D. Mass. 1985); *see also* Caterino v. United States, 794 F.2d 1 (1st Cir. 1986); Kalb v. United States, 505 F.2d 506, 511 (2d Cir. 1974); Kinnie v. United States, 771 F. Supp. 842, 851 (E.D. Mich. 1991) ("'willfully' does not mean that the responsible person acted by virtue of a bad motive or the specific intent to defraud the government or to deprive it of revenue.... 'Willfully' means merely that the responsible person had knowledge of the tax delinquency and knowingly failed to rectify it when there were available funds to pay the government"), *aff'd*, 994 F.2d 279 (6th Cir. 1993); United States v. Macagnone, 86 AFTR2d ¶5307 (M.D. Fla. 2000) (holding that the president's failure to inquire about the status of taxes, absent a history of delinquency that would put him on notice to establish a known or obvious risk, did not equal reckless disregard).

39. Denbo v. United States, 988 F.2d 1029 (10th Cir. 1993); Mazo v. United States, 591 F.2d 1151 (5th Cir. 1979); Kalb v. United States, 505 F.2d 506, 511 (2d Cir. 1974).

40. Verret v. United States, 542 F. Supp. 2d 526 (E.D. Tex. 2008), *aff'd*, 312 Fed. Appx. 615 (5th Cir. 2009).

41. Godfrey v. United States, 748 F.2d 1568 (Fed. Cir. 1984); Kalb v. United States, 505 F.2d 506, 511 (2d Cir. 1974).

42. *See, e.g.*, Gustin v. United States, 876 F.2d 485 (5th Cir. 1989); Dudley v. United States, 428 F.2d 1196 (9th Cir. 1970).

president for delivery. The president failed to deliver the checks. The court held that even though the attorney may have been a responsible person and his failure to ascertain whether the checks were deposited may have constituted negligence, his action or inaction was not willful.[43]

b. Establish Reasonable Cause

Responsible persons may also be able to avoid liability if they had reasonable cause for not acting. "Reasonable cause" is a term of art in certain areas of the Code providing a defense to the assertion of a penalty.[44] In the context of the section 6672 penalty, reasonable cause is not explicitly stated as a defense. As a result, the government has argued that reasonable cause has no bearing on the section 6672 penalty. However, the Second, Third, Fifth, and Tenth Circuits, and the Court of Federal Claims, have held that willfulness is mitigated if the taxpayer can show reasonable cause for the failure to pay.[45] For example, one would have reasonable cause if he or she had been advised by counsel that no tax was due,[46] that the tax did not need to be paid,[47] or if others assured the individual that the tax had already been paid.[48] Reasonable cause may also be shown if the business was suffering financial hardships and was unable to pay tax if the business exercised ordinary care and prudence in attempting to pay the tax liability. While a court considers all the facts and circumstances, favoring other creditors over the government weighs against a finding of reasonable cause but a willingness to decrease expenses and personnel in an attempt to pay obligations weighs in favor of finding reasonable cause.[49]

The Tenth Circuit held that the question of liability was for a jury to determine in view of all relevant evidence.[50] The court held that recognizing reasonable cause as a defense avoids a "strict liability" interpretation of the penalty. It noted that certain factual situations are paradigms that "create an expansive web of liability 'as a matter of law' and significantly ease the government's burden." The court indicated that since willfulness in the section 6672 context requires "scienter" on the taxpayer's part, all the facts and circumstances should be considered. However, the court limited the reasonable cause defense to those situations where the jury concludes (1) the individual

---

43. Markewich v. United States, 61-1 U.S.T.C. ¶ 9241 (S.D.N.Y. 1961).

44. *See, e.g.*, IRC §§ 6651(a), 6656.

45. *See, e.g.*, Winter v. United States, 196 F.3d 339 (2d Cir. 1999); Finley v. United States, 123 F.3d 1342 (10th Cir. 1997); McCarty v. United States, 437 F.2d 961 (Ct. Cl. 1971); United States v. Slattery, 333 F.2d 844 (3d Cir 1964); Frazier v. United States, 304 F.2d 528 (5th Cir. 1962).

46. Cross v. United States, 204 F. Supp. 644 (E.D. Va. 1962).

47. Cash v. Campbell, 346 F.2d 670 (5th Cir. 1965), rev'd, 311 F.2d 90 (4th Cir. 1962).

48. Richard v. United States, 72-1 U.S.T.C. ¶ 9267 (C.D. Cal. 1972).

49. Staff IT, Inc. v. United States, 482 F.3d 792 (5th Cir. 2007) (no reasonable cause when business paid all creditors except the government and expanded operations despite failure to pay trust fund taxes); East Wind Industries Inc. v. U.S., 196 F.3d 499 (3d Cir. 1999) (reasonable cause to abate trust fund recovery penalty found when business scaled back operations, and only paid debts/employees necessary to stay in business long enough to pay unpaid employment taxes).

50. Finley v. United States, 123 F.3d 1342 (10th Cir. 1997).

made reasonable efforts to protect the trust funds but (2) those efforts were frustrated by circumstances beyond the person's control.

The First, Seventh, Eighth, and Ninth Circuits,[51] have explicitly rejected the notion that reasonable cause or a justifiable excuse negates willfulness under section 6672. Accordingly, these circuits hold that a taxpayer's intentional actions are willful regardless of whether he or she can provide justification for the action. The reasonable cause defense has been rejected by these courts in situations similar to those in which it has been accepted by the other circuits.

c. Establish There Were No Funds Available at the Time the Person Became a Responsible Person

A particularly troubling situation arises when someone is newly employed by an employer that already owes significant trust fund taxes. In *Slodov v. United States*,[52] the Supreme Court held that a person who took control of a business became a responsible person with respect to existing tax obligations to the extent the business had unencumbered funds at that time available to pay the government. If the business did not possess such funds, or possessed only a limited amount of such funds, the use of subsequently generated money to pay other creditors would not violate the willfulness standard, except to the extent of the then-existing unencumbered funds.[53] This doctrine holds whether the after-acquired money is raised by a contribution to capital or through earnings.

Subsequent decisions have limited *Slodov* to a narrow window. These cases have established that the *Slodov* doctrine does not provide relief if either the person was already a responsible person when the liability arose[54] or the business possessed funds which were not encumbered at that time.[55] Thus, to fully utilize *Slodov*, the person must be a newly responsible person and the business must not have any unencumbered funds at that time.[56]

---

51. Olsen v. United States, 952 F.2d 236 (8th Cir. 1991); Harrington v. United States, 504 F.2d 1306 (1st Cir. 1974); Monday v. United States, 421 F.2d 1210 (7th Cir. 1970); Pacific Nat'l Ins. Co. v. United States, 422 F.2d 26 (9th Cir. 1970). *But see* Gray Line Co. v. Granquist, 237 F. 2d 390 (9th Cir. 1956).

52. 436 U.S. 238 (1978).

53. Davis v. United States, 961 F.2d 867 (9th Cir. 1992); Kenagy v. United States, 942 F.2d 459 (8th Cir. 1991).

54. *Id.*

55. Kenagy v. United States, 942 F.2d 459 (8th Cir. 1991); Honey v. United States, 963 F.2d 1083 (8th Cir. 1992); Huizinga v. United States, 68 F.3d 139 (6th Cir. 1995). A related argument is that there cannot be willfulness if the funds of the business are encumbered. The prevailing view is that "funds are encumbered only where the taxpayer is legally obligated to use the funds for a purpose other than satisfying the preexisting employment tax liability and if that legal obligation is superior to the interest of the IRS in the funds." Honey v. United States, 963 F.2d 1083, 1090 (8th Cir. 1992); *see also* Nakano v. U.S., 742 F.3d 1208, 1211–12 (9th Cir. 2014) (holding that the business's assets were not encumbered as a result of bankruptcy).

56. In re Bewley, 191 B.R. 459 (Bankr. Okla. 1996), *aff'd*, 212 B.R. 668 (N.D. Okla. 1997); *see* Michaud v. United States, 40 Fed. Cl. 1 (1997).

IV. Procedures for Determining Liability for the Penalty

Section 6672 cases are investigated and proposed by Revenue Officers in the IRS Compliance Collection function. Standard IRS procedures, discussed below, include some combination of the following: (1) proposal of the penalty by the Compliance Collection function, (2) assessment of the tax by the IRS, (3) paying a portion of the tax, (4) filing appropriate documents to seek review of the matter by the local office and, if necessary, the Appeals Division, and (5) filing a refund action in federal court.

The IRS identifies late paying employers by means of an IRS program called "FTD (Federal Tax Deposit) Alert." Once a late paying employer is identified, the IRS local office will forward an "FTD Alert Notice" to the employer. FTD Alerts provide an early opportunity to assist and educate delinquent employers before their tax liabilities become too difficult to resolve. If the employer is unable to make required deposits or become compliant, a Revenue Officer will close the Alert, issue Letter 903 (Deposit Requirements for Employment Taxes), and pursue the next collection action, namely, initial contact.[57]

The Manual directs personnel to consider taking all appropriate administrative collection procedures before initiating the Trust Fund Compliance procedure. The most common collection procedures are to consider liens and levies as well as initiating a TFRP investigation.[58]

As part of the TFRP investigation, the Revenue Officer will examine the business's records, such as tax returns, bank records and signature cards, Articles of Incorporation and Bylaws, canceled checks, and corporate minutes and resolutions. If necessary, the Revenue Officer may utilize the IRS's administrative summons power under section 7602 to obtain this information.[59]

The Revenue Officer will also attempt to interview all individuals who might have knowledge of (1) how decisions were made within the organization, (2) who had decisionmaking authority to control which creditors were paid, and (3) who was familiar with the company's financial condition and the status of outstanding tax debts.[60]

At the conclusion of the investigation, the Revenue Officer will decide against whom to propose the penalty. It is almost a certainty that officers, directors and others whose names appear on business documents will be targets if the documentation indicates some level of responsibility for financial matters. For each individual

57. IRM 5.7.1; 5.1.10.3.2.

58. IRM 5.7.2.3.

59. IRM 5.7.4.2.4.

60. In conducting interviews, the Revenue Officer will question potential targets by completing a Form 4180 (Report of Interview with Individual Relative to Trust Fund Recovery Penalty or Personal Liability for Excise Taxes). For non-targets, the Revenue Officer will either interview the person and take notes or send the witness a Form 4181 (Questionnaire Relating to Federal Trust Fund Tax Matters of Employer), asking the person to complete and return it. If a non-target is subsequently implicated as potentially responsible and willful, the Revenue Officer will conduct a personal interview and record it on a Form 4180. IRM 5.7.4.2.2.

identified, the Revenue Officer will prepare a Form 4183 (Recommendation re: Trust Fund Recovery Penalty Assessment) for review by the Revenue Officer's group manager.

The penalty is assessable and does not require a deficiency notice.[61] Nevertheless, the Code requires the Service to hand-deliver or mail to the taxpayer at his or her last known address by certified mail a "60-day letter" (Letter 1153 (DO)), specifying the amount of the penalty and the periods at issue, and stating that the IRS proposes to assess the penalty against the taxpayer personally.[62] In addition to the 60-day letter, the IRS encloses a Form 2751 (Proposed Assessment of Trust Fund Recovery Penalty) that provides the specifics of the proposed assessments and allows the taxpayer to consent to the penalty assessment.[63] Neither the accuracy-related nor civil fraud penalty can be imposed for any noncompliance covered by section 6672.[64] It is enough that the IRS properly mails the notice. If it does so, it is immaterial whether the responsible person actually receives the notice.[65]

A. Protesting the Proposed Penalty to the Appeals Division

After receiving a 60-day letter,[66] a taxpayer can seek Appeals Office review. This can be done before the penalty is assessed. Upon receiving the letter proposing the penalty, the taxpayer has 60 days to file a protest with the Revenue Officer who, after reviewing and commenting on the protest, will forward it to the Appeals Office.[67]

If the 60-day period expires without a response by the taxpayer, the Revenue Officer will assess the penalty. The government will then send the taxpayer a notice of assessment and a demand for payment. The taxpayer may obtain post-assessment review in Appeals by paying a portion of the penalty, filing a claim for refund, and protesting the likely disallowance.[68] Procedurally, this is normally accomplished in the following manner.[69]

---

61. *See* IRC § 6671(a).

62. IRC § 6672(b)(1); IRM 5.7.4.7.

63. The execution of a Form 2751 does not necessarily act as a waiver of the 60-day preliminary notice requirement for a valid tax assessment even though the form states that the taxpayer waives the privilege of filing a claim for abatement after assessment. United States v. Seidel, 2008 U.S. Dist. LEXIS 61799 (N.D. Cal. Aug. 13, 2008).

64. Mason v. Commissioner, 132 T.C. 301 (2009). In a number of cases, including *Nakano* and *Conway*, *supra*, section 6672 targets have argued that the 60-day letter and accompanying material inadequately explained the bases of the proposed assessments. These arguments typically have failed, often on a "harmless error" basis. Steve R. Johnson, *Reasoned Explanation and IRS Adjudication*, 63 Duke L. J. 1771, 1811–13 (2014).

65. IRC § 6672(a) (last sentence).

66. The taxpayer has 75 days from the date of the mailing of the notice of the date of personal delivery to respond timely if the letter was addressed outside of the United States. IRM 5.7.6.1.1. An important advantage to protesting the penalty before it is assessed is that by doing so, assessment of the penalty and, correspondingly, accrual of interest on the penalty, is stayed. IRC § 6601(e)(2); CCA 200235028.

67. *See generally* Rev. Proc. 2005-34, 2005-24 I.R.B. 1233; IRM 5.7.6.1.3.

68. If the taxpayer wishes to suspend collection of the balance of the assessment, he or she must take this action within thirty days and also post a bond in an amount equal to 150% of the amount by which the penalty assessed exceeds the amount of the payment made. IRC § 6672(c).

69. IRM 5.7.7.4.

1. The taxpayer pays the amount of withholding attributable to at least one employee for each quarter in issue.[70]
2. Either concurrently with payment or subsequent thereto, the taxpayer files a Form 843 ("Claim for Refund and Request for Abatement") for each such quarter[71] and attaches an explanation of all factual and legal bases upon which the claim is predicated.[72]
3. An IRS unit, currently called the Advisory office, normally works the claim.
4. If the IRS disallows the claim or does nothing,[73] the taxpayer can pursue the matter within the IRS by filing a protest with the Appeals Office.

In order to properly protest a TFRP assessment when the amount at issue is $25,000 or less, the taxpayer must complete a small case request. If the amount proposed for any tax period exceeds $25,000, the taxpayer may appeal the proposed assessment by submitting a formal written protest.[74] In preparation for filing the protest and meeting with an Appeals Officer, one should conduct a thorough review of all records, documents, and files relating to the taxpayer and the business. Likely sources of information include the taxpayer, third parties and, via disclosure requests, the IRS. One should attach to the protest any supporting documents, evidence, and affidavits tending to prove that the taxpayer was not a "responsible person" or that he or she did not act "willfully," or both.

Thoughtful legal analysis is also critical. There are literally thousands of cases in this area. Each is very fact-specific, and many of the outcomes are contradictory or, at least, in tension with one another. Consequently, one may be able to find cases to cite with facts and law favorable to the taxpayer's position. In addition, the portions of the IRM that support the proposed theory should be examined.

One should use the protest to challenge the Revenue Officer with respect to any inaccurate findings of fact and any incorrect legal assumptions or precedent. The protest should include the taxpayer's version of the facts, his legal argument and the authorities supporting his position.

Even though filed with Appeals, the protest is first reviewed by the Revenue Officer. In instances where the Service has made an obvious mistake, the Revenue Officer

70. Payment of the withholding tax with respect to one employee is sufficient to begin review of the proposed penalty because employment taxes are considered divisible taxes.

71. The relief sought is a refund of the taxes paid within the two years prior to the filing of the claim plus abatement of the balance of the assessment. *See* Chapter 9.

72. Because the arguments made in the claim for refund and the protest are the only ones that the court will review, it is critical that an attorney be involved at this stage to avoid jeopardizing the lawsuit. *See* Chapter 9.

73. Once the Form 843 is filed, the IRS has six months within which to respond. During this six month period, the IRS will do one of several things: (1) agree with the taxpayer that a refund is warranted; (2) send a certified letter, referred to as the Notice of Disallowance, rejecting the claim in whole or in part; (3) send a letter requesting more information; or (4) do nothing. Unless the taxpayer can provide something new that was not considered by the IRS when the Revenue Officer did the examination, it is likely the government will disallow the claim summarily.

74. IRM 5.7.6.1.

may concede the case and not send it on to Appeals. However, if the Revenue Officer does not agree with the taxpayer's position, the Revenue Officer will prepare his or her responses in a memorandum and forward the case to Appeals.[75]

Once the taxpayer and the Appeals Officer have exchanged their views on the evidence and applicable law, they normally attempt to reach a settlement. Any reasonable approach can be the basis of a settlement. This may include liability for certain periods and not for others or liability for a specified percentage or dollar amount of that which was proposed. If the IRS has asserted the same penalty against several persons, it might benefit all or some of the targets to meet and work out a settlement among themselves, propose it to the IRS, and sign Forms 2751-AD to memorialize it. Alternatively, one might negotiate a pro rata settlement with the IRS.

If the Appeals Officer and the taxpayer do not reach an agreement, Appeals will send the case forward. If the case was in 60-day status, it will be sent to the Service Center, where the tax will be assessed. If the case was already in collection and the taxpayer previously filed a refund claim or offer in compromise, the file will be returned to the Collection function for further collection activity.

B. Judicially Appealing an Adverse Determination

Trust fund penalty cases may be litigated in the U.S. District Court, the Court of Federal Claims, or the Bankruptcy Court.[76] Unless it is in connection with a collection due process (CDP) hearing,[77] the Tax Court is not available because the section 6672 penalty is an assessable penalty—a penalty not subject to deficiency procedures.[78] The District Court is the only court in which one can obtain a jury trial. The taxpayer's burden of proof is the same in all courts.[79]

75. IRM 5.7.6.1.8.

76. Since the trust fund penalty is not a dischargeable debt, a bankruptcy action is of little value if discharge is the sole purpose of the petition. 11 U.S.C. §523.

77. IRC §6330(d) confers jurisdiction on the Tax Court to hear all collection due process cases regardless of the type of tax owed. Ginsberg v. Commissioner, 130 T.C. 88 (2008). However, the merits of the assessment are rarely in issue in CDP cases because the taxpayer normally would have had an opportunity for a hearing on the underlying liability, a fact which precludes its being raised in a CDP hearing. IRC §6330; *see, e.g.*, Pough v. Commissioner, 135 T.C. 344 (2010).

78. CDP hearings in Tax Court are increasingly emerging as important vehicles for challenging section 6672 assessments on procedural grounds, as opposed to the underlying liability. *E.g.*, Moosally v. Commissioner, 142 T.C. No. 10 (2014) (Appeals Officer was not impartial as required by section 6320(b)(3)); *Conway, supra* (notices were not validly issued).

The merits of section 6672 assessments can be challenged in CDP hearings only if the taxpayer had not previously had the opportunity to contest the merits. This happened, for example, in *Lepore v. Commissioner*, T.C. Memo. 2013-135, where the notice was properly delivered to the taxpayer's residence but misplaced by the taxpayer's teenage son, who did not tell the taxpayer about arrival of the notice, but not in *Giaquinto v. Commissioner*, T.C. Memo. 2013-150, where the taxpayer knew of and deliberately failed to claim delivery of the appropriately mailed notice.

79. Raleigh v. Illinois Dept. of Revenue, 530 U.S. 15 (2000).

For the District Courts and the Court of Federal Claims, full payment of the tax liability is a jurisdictional prerequisite.[80] However, because the "divisible tax" doctrine applies to employment taxes, a taxpayer need only pay the tax associated with one employee for each of the quarters in dispute in order to place the issues associated with the trust fund liability before the court.[81] Thus, as compared to income or estate tax refund cases in which full payment of the tax may be onerous, the tax cost to litigate the trust fund penalty is not prohibitive. In Bankruptcy Court, of course, prepayment of the tax is not a jurisdictional prerequisite.

A complaint cannot be filed in District Court or the Court of Federal Claims earlier than six months after the claim for refund is filed, unless within that six-month period, the IRS mailed a Notice of Disallowance. A complaint cannot be filed later than two years from the date the IRS mailed the Notice of Disallowance by certified mail. If no Notice of Disallowance is mailed, the time for filing suit is unlimited. These time limitations do not apply to a bankruptcy petition.[82]

Normally, if an action is brought in District Court or the Court of Federal Claims by one of the responsible persons, the IRS will join the others by means of a third-party complaint, so all persons are before the court. Joinder is not possible in a bankruptcy action, though a proof of claim can be equivalent to a counterclaim.

Unless appealed, the decision of the trial court is final regarding the issues of responsible person status and willfulness with respect to each quarter before the court. At that point, the IRS will move to collect or abate the section 6672 penalty.

V. Procedures for Collecting the Penalty

Collection procedures associated with the section 6672 penalty are both similar to and different from those respecting other taxes. With respect to the responsible person individually, the similarities lie primarily in the series of collection notices the responsible person will receive, the opportunity to seek an installment agreement or an offer in compromise or be placed in "currently not collectible" status and the right

80. *See* Chapter 9.

81. *See, e.g.*, Steele v. United States, 280 F.2d 89 (8th Cir. 1960); IRM 5.7.7.4. As a shorthand approach to this, some practitioners say that the taxpayer should pay $100 and designate the payment as being for the particular taxes and quarters. In order to suspend collection activity on the unpaid balance while the claim is considered administratively, the taxpayer must first have complied with section 6672(c)(1) by paying the required minimal amount, filing the refund claim, and posting 150% bond within thirty days of having received the notice of assessment and demand for payment. In order to continue the stay during the judicial phase of the case, the taxpayer must begin a proceeding in the appropriate District Court (or in the Court of Federal Claims) within 30 days after the day on which his claim for refund is denied. Determining the jurisdictionally sufficient amount sometimes is difficult. In one case, the court took a taxpayer-indulgent view in what it perceived to be "an evidentiary catch-22" situation: the section 6672 target could not obtain records to calculate the amount and the government itself was unable to say what payment would suffice. Kaplan v. United States, 115 Fed. Cl. 491 (2014), *vacating* 113 Fed. Cl. 84 (2013).

82. IRC § 6532.

to a collection due process hearing before the IRS. These steps in the collection process are discussed in detail in Chapter 13.

The Code creates one significant difference, though. As discussed above, the only payment required before a judicial decision becomes final is the tax on one employee for each quarter involved. However, to take advantage of this benefit, the taxpayer must act promptly. Section 6672(c) suspends collection activity against those responsible persons who have, within thirty days of having received the notice of assessment and demand for payment, timely paid the minimum amount to file a refund suit, posted bond for 150% of the unpaid balance, filed a claim for refund, and, if the claim is disallowed, filed a lawsuit within thirty days thereafter. Absent jeopardy circumstances, collection is suspended until the matter is finally resolved. The 1998 Reform Act added a new section (i) to section 6331 to state that no levy may be made on the responsible person's assets during the pendency of refund litigation regardless of whether collection activity is suspended under section 6672(c), unless the taxpayer waives this restriction or there is a jeopardy. In addition, section 6330(f) and (h) allow a pre-hearing levy when the IRS has served a "disqualified employment tax levy." A disqualified employment tax levy is a levy connected to the collection of employment taxes "for any taxable period if the person subject to the levy ... requested a hearing ... with respect to unpaid employment taxes arising in the most recent 2-year period before the beginning of the taxable period with respect to which the levy is served."

Other differences result primarily from the fact that since the trust fund liability is derivative of the business's tax liability, there are two levels of taxpayers involved—the business and the individuals. So long as the business remains operating and is a viable collection source, it may be possible to shift the focus of the government's collection efforts from the responsible person to the business.

If the client or another responsible person can influence the actions of the business, assuming the business is still operating, it behooves all the responsible persons for the business to enter into an installment payment plan to pay the trust fund taxes.[83] Within the discretion of the Revenue Officer, assessment of the section 6672 penalty against the responsible persons may be deferred if the business has entered into an installment agreement to pay past due payroll taxes.[84] This normally will be done

83. Alternatively, the business can seek an offer in compromise. However, an offer in compromise at the business level for an ongoing business does not do the individual client much good, as the IRS will require the compromise amount to be the sum of what can be collected from the business and all responsible persons. IRM 5.7.4.9; 5.8.4.20.

84. IRM 5.7.4.8, 5.7.8.4.3, 5.14.7. (The business will have to complete a Form 433-B to prove it cannot afford to pay immediately.) Persuading the IRS to accept an offer in compromise in this area is made more difficult by the fact that the trust fund penalty is not dischargeable in bankruptcy. Nevertheless, if the IRS becomes too aggressive toward either the business or an individual, filing a petition in bankruptcy invokes the automatic stay provisions to stop the government and, under Chapters 11 or 13 bankruptcies, the taxpayer may be able to force the IRS to accept the taxpayer's payment plan. As stated, the decision to withhold collection from the responsible person while the corporation is current on its installment agreement is within the discretion of the IRS. In *Kirkpatrick v. Commissioner*, T.C. Memo. 2014-234, the Tax Court upheld the settlement officer's determination to proceed against the responsible person.

only if the business is paying its payroll taxes on a current basis and is not pyramiding its delinquencies. Even if collection is withheld, the government will likely file a Notice of Federal Tax Lien against the responsible persons who have been assessed the penalty.

VI. Monitoring the Statute of Limitations

A defense based on the expiration of the statutes of limitations (SOL) on assessment or collection can be a wholesale victory for the taxpayer. For this reason, one should consider the SOL in all cases.[85] The SOL for assessing[86] the section 6672 penalty is three years from the later of April 15th following the year in issue, or from the date the return was actually filed.[87] April 15th following the year in issue is the starting point for all quarters of the year, as the quarterly returns are deemed "early filed."[88] The SOL on collection is ten years from the date of assessment.[89]

There are many exceptions to the rules that are likely to apply in section 6672 cases. It is important to recognize that the exceptions that might apply to extend the SOL on assessment or collection with respect to the employment taxes of the business do not normally affect the SOL on assessment or collection of the TFRP against responsible persons.[90] The business and the responsible person are two separate taxpayers.

The most likely exception with respect to the three-year TFRP assessment statute is section 6672(b)(3). It provides that once the 60-day letter is mailed, the SOL does not expire less than 90 days after the letter was mailed or, if a protest is filed with the Appeals Office, not less than 30 days after an administrative determination is rendered. The SOL on assessment may also be extended by timely agreement on Form 2750.[91]

In addition to extensions described in section 6502, extension of the 10-year SOL on collection occurs when the individual (i) submits an offer in compromise or a re-

---

85. *See* IRM 5.7.3.5 et seq.

86. The TFRP is assessed as the "civil penalty" on the IRS's computer. Normally, there is one assessment posted for the entire period for which liability is asserted, rather than separate assessments for each quarter. Taylor v. IRS, 69 F.3d 411, 418–19 (10th Cir. 1995); Stallard v. United States, 12 F.3d 489, 495–96 (5th Cir. 1994). The quarterly details of these "lump sum assessments" are available upon request. Obtaining the detail may be particularly important for SOL purposes, since the assessment may be late for some earlier quarters.

87. Lauckner v. United States, 68 F.3d 69 (3d Cir. 1995); AOD 1996-006, 1996-2 C.B. 1; *see also* IRC § 6672(b)(3); United States v. Jones, 60 F.3d 584 (9th Cir. 1995); Stallard v. United States, 12 F.3d 489 (5th Cir. 1994).

88. IRC § 6501(b)(2).

89. IRC § 6502.

90. In Chief Counsel Advice 200532046, the IRS took the position that the unlimited SOL on assessment with respect to the employment tax return of the business attributable to its fraud also resulted in an unlimited SOL for assessing the TFRP against the responsible person. The IRS cited to *Lauckner*, *supra* note 87, for the proposition that the SOL for the two are linked since the court had held that the SOL begins to run with respect to the responsible person when the employment tax return of the business is filed.

91. IRC § 6501(c)(4).

quest for an installment agreement,[92] (ii) requests a collection due process hearing,[93] or (iii) institutes a refund suit.[94]

Just as the failure of the IRS to comply with the SOL can be a victory for the taxpayer, a missed deadline by the taxpayer can be a "win" for the IRS. Generally, for purposes of section 6672, the SOL for filing an administrative claim for refund is two years from the date of the last payment.[95] However, the statute limits the maximum refund to the amount paid in the two years prior to filing the claim for refund. Once the administrative claim for refund has been filed, the filing of a lawsuit has its own time periods.

VII. General Strategies in Section 6672 Cases

Whether or not the matter is going to be pursued on the merits, there are many strategies to defend against or minimize the impact of section 6672. The following are the most useful.

A. Try to Shift Blame to Others

With respect to liability under section 6672, the taxpayer's best defense often involves trying to shift blame, i.e., helping the government establish the facts and evidence that another individual had the status, duty, and authority to control the purse strings of the company and acted willfully. Even when doing so does not result in an abrogation of liability, shifting blame to others may enlarge the pool of persons and assets available to pay the tax.

In a practical sense, shifting blame means assisting the IRS in developing its case against others by providing evidence pertaining to who the corporate officers were, who had check signing authority, who prepared payroll tax returns, who hired and fired employees, who controlled the corporate finances, and who, in any measure, controlled or otherwise directed or managed corporate affairs.

B. Act to Gain More Time

Another effective tactic is to try to gain more time for the taxpayer in the hope that, in the meantime, another target or the business will pay the employment taxes first. This approach is particularly effective if the other targets have "deep pockets." Extra time is gained when the taxpayer exhausts the administrative and judicial procedures to challenge the government's determination that he or she is liable for the

---

92. IRC § 6331(k)(3).

93. IRC § 6330(e)(1).

94. IRC §§ 6331(i)(5), 6672(c)(4).

95. Though a three-year SOL (from the date the return was filed) normally exists for filing refund claims, it does not apply in IRC section 6672 cases because the taxpayer (the "responsible person") never filed a tax return, the Form 941 is filed by the corporate taxpayer. *See* Kuznitsky v. United States, 17 F.3d 1029 (7th Cir. 1994).

penalty under section 6672. The taxpayer also achieves extra time when he or she enters into an installment agreement, files an offer in compromise, or requests a collection due process hearing.

C. Evaluate Bringing a Suit for Contribution against Other Potentially Liable Persons

While the government will not collect more than the amount of the penalty due, the amount paid by any particular responsible person may be disproportionate to his or her culpability. This is due to the fact that liability for the section 6672 penalty is joint and several and the IRS seeks payment from whomever it can. Because this is a penalty, most states don't enforce or recognize a right of contribution, even if in writing.[96]

Section 6672(d) was added to remedy this. It provides that if more than one person is liable for the 100% penalty, each person who paid the penalty shall be entitled to recover from the other persons who are liable for such penalty an amount equal to the excess of the amount paid by such persons over their proportionate shares of the penalty.[97] An action under section 6672(d) is separate from, and may not be joined or consolidated with, litigation on the merits of the section 6672 liability.[98]

D. Designate Payments to Trust Fund Portion of Assessments

If a taxpayer submits a payment to the government involuntarily, such as by levy or when the taxpayer is in bankruptcy[99] or when payment is made pursuant to an installment agreement or offer in compromise, the IRS applies it in a manner that is in the Service's best interests.[100] For example, if it is a business that is submitting payment, the IRS will apply the payment to accounts with respect to which the SOL is about to expire, to non-trust fund tax liabilities and to penalties and interest incurred at the corporate level before applying it elsewhere.[101] Applying payments in

---

96. United States v. Guerin, 2014-1 U.S.T.C. ¶ 50,272 (N.D. Cal. 2014) (holding that section 6672 liability is joint and several and that the IRS is not required to pursue collection against every responsible person or against the corporation itself before collecting from a particular responsible person).

97. Even though the right exists, one should consider (i) the likelihood of being able to prove the other persons were responsible persons and (ii) whether it would be financially worthwhile to pursue the other persons recognizing that the IRS may have been, or determined that it would be, unsuccessful in collecting from them.

98. *See* Larry A. Campagna & William O. Grimsinger, *Riddles Raised by Those Who Don't Read: Solving Purported Problems with the Right of Contribution Under Code Sec. 6672(d)*, J. Tax Prac. & Proc., Feb.–Mar. 2003, at 15.

99. In *United States v. Energy Resources Co., Inc.*, 495 U.S. 545 (1990), the Supreme Court held that even if a payment is not voluntary because the business is in a Chapter 11 bankruptcy reorganization, the IRS is obligated to follow the direction of the debtor-in-possession corporation if the debtor can establish that payment in that manner is necessary to the success of the reorganization. For example, this burden can be met if designation to the trust fund portion of the business' liability would encourage the responsible persons to stay with the business while it reorganizes.

100. IRM 5.1.2.5.4.1; Rev. Proc. 2002-26, 2002-1 C.B. 746.

101. *Id.*

this manner leaves the "trust fund" taxes still owing and collectible from either the business or the personal assets of the responsible persons while minimizing the risk to the IRS that outstanding balances will be lost to the SOL, discharged in bankruptcy, or become effectively non-collectible due to the collapse of the business. The IRS handles payments made voluntarily by the taxpayer in a manner similarly advantageous to the government when payment is submitted without clear instruction as to which liabilities should be credited.

By contrast, if one makes a payment voluntarily and, in writing, instructs the Service against which tax debts to apply the payment, the Service is obligated to follow these instructions.[102] Specifically, one may direct (1) how much should be applied, (2) to what periods, and (3) for which outstanding taxes.

Designation is very important in the case of trust fund taxes. If the business is still in existence and if one can influence its decisions, it behooves all involved for the business (or the other targets, for that matter) to pay the business's trust fund taxes first. This reduces the outstanding employment tax balance for both the business and all responsible persons alike. Designation is accomplished by transmitting a cover letter instructing that the payment be applied only to trust fund taxes, for all quarters, until they have been fully satisfied.[103]

If the business is considering bankruptcy, a 1990 Supreme Court case can be of great help. In *Begier v. IRS*,[104] the court held that trust fund taxes are not the property of the business but are always the property of the government. Consequently, designated payments of trust fund taxes are not preferential transfers even if made within the ninety-day window prior to filing the petition in bankruptcy.[105] This means that pre-bankruptcy payments of trust fund taxes, even if done solely for the purpose of reducing the liability of responsible persons, cannot be avoided by the trustee and drawn back into the estate as a preference.

E. Try to Settle the Case among the Targets

If there are multiple responsible persons, it may be in everyone's best interest to work together to settle with the IRS, based on some division of the liability, rather than risk the possibility that the IRS may come after one person for the full amount. Clearly, this is of greatest concern for those persons with "deep pockets." But even for shallower-pocketed persons, this method avoids the filing of a Notice of Federal Tax Lien and damage to one's creditworthiness. In exchange for working with the parties, the IRS demands full payment and that each signatory agree not to file a claim for refund.

---

102. IRM 5.1.2.5.4.1, 5.1.28; Rev. Proc. 2002-26, 2002-1 C.B. 746.

103. The IRS has confirmed that it will allow businesses to designate that their payments be applied to the trust fund liability and that the IRS will credit the payments to the trust fund liability even though money is still owed on the non-trust fund liability. IRS Off. Mem. 200838027 (Sept. 9, 2008), *available at* http://www.irs.gov/pub/irs-wd/0838027.pdf.

104. 496 U.S. 53 (1990).

105. 11 U.S.C. § 547.

Problem

Green Tree, Inc. is a local business with 20 employees to whom it pays wages. It regularly withholds federal income tax and FICA contributions from their wages as required by law. Green Tree has both an operating account and a payroll account at the First Bank of Blue. All the wages are paid from the payroll account.

The president and majority shareholder of Green Tree is Alice Green. Alice is also a full-time employee of Green Tree, with check-signing authority on both accounts. She regularly signs payroll checks and frequently signs checks drawn on the operating account as well.

The bookkeeper of Green Tree is Alice's cousin, Tom. Tom is not an officer, director or shareholder of Green Tree, but is a full-time employee. He has check-signing authority on both bank accounts. He rarely signs payroll checks, but frequently signs checks drawn on the operating account. Tom has the responsibility for paying the taxes withheld from the employees' wages to the IRS after each payroll. He is also responsible for the preparation and filing of the quarterly 941 forms and the annual Form 940, and paying the taxes due with those returns, if any.

Green Tree has only one class of stock. Alice owns 55%. Alice's brother, George, who lives in a different state and knows little about the business of Green Tree, contributed some capital in exchange for 30% of the stock. Alice needed the money for the business. She had told George that when Green Tree is sold, in about ten years, he would make a good return on his investment. George takes no role in the management of Green Tree. George has said that he is only an investor and sits on the board of directors only to "watch over" his investment. He receives monthly financial reports that are prepared by Tom, but he barely reads them.

The remainder of the stock is held by some friends and by the Vice President of Green Tree, Terry. Terry is a full-time employee of Green Tree who was promoted to Vice President and given stock a few years ago in recognition of his hard work and loyalty. He works very closely with Alice in the management of the business and views her as his mentor. He is grateful to her for his advancement in the business.

The board of directors of Green Tree consists of three members, Alice, George and Terry. The Board meets once a year at the insistence of Green Tree's lawyer. Alice and Terry attend in person, and George attends by telephone. Tom sends financial reports to the three directors each month.

A few years ago Green Tree encountered some financial difficulty. The revenue was good, but expenses were too high and Alice had made some mistakes in management. So Green Tree borrowed some working capital from First Bank of Blue to "tide it over." Unfortunately, things did not get better and Green Tree was forced to increase the loan. The Bank required Green Tree to allow one of its officers, Leslie, to go over the books and records with Tom regularly and to have a "veto power" over major decisions, including wage increases, bonuses, and expenditures of over a certain amount of money. Leslie monitored the payroll very closely because it was Green Tree's largest expense.

During the last two quarters of 20x4 and the first two quarters of 20x5, Green Tree's financial situation was particularly bad. It used the funds borrowed from the Bank to pay wages to its employees, a practice of which the Bank was fully aware. To preserve its cash, Green Tree did not pay the amounts withheld from the employees' wages for income tax and FICA to the IRS during any of those quarters, nor did it file the required Forms 941 or 940. Tom objected to Green Tree's not making the payments and not filing returns, but Alice told him to "do what he was told" or else he'd be fired. Tom had a big family and needed to keep his job, so he agreed.

In October of 20x4, Alice was involved in a serious automobile accident, and was not able to work. The Bank became very concerned because a lot of Green Tree's revenues were earned during the fourth quarter and Green Tree might have a bad holiday season if Alice couldn't work. The Bank knew that Green Tree had missed some of the tax payments to the IRS, but it was more concerned about getting its loans paid than about the tax payments.

With Alice's consent, the Bank took a more active role until she could return to work full time. Leslie started coming to the Green Tree offices every day, and together with Terry, made the management decisions. Leslie and Terry spoke to Alice every day by telephone so that she would be fully aware of the developments. Terry continued to serve as Vice President and director of Green Tree while Alice was out.

Green Tree held a regular meeting of its board of directors in late December 20x4. George and Alice both attended by telephone. Alice was home recovering from the injuries she had suffered in the accident, and George was at his office in a different state. Leslie attended as well, as a representative of the Bank, although she was not a director. Shortly before the meeting, Tom had circulated a financial report for late December 20x4, which reflected the following as accounts payable:

Federal income tax withheld from employees	$70,000
Social Security and Medicare (FICA) withheld from employees	30,000
Social Security and Medicare (FICA)—employer's portion	30,000
State income tax withheld from employees	10,000
Unemployment compensation tax	7,000

George had only skimmed the report, and hadn't noticed the delinquent taxes. George had heard about the trust fund recovery penalty a few years ago from one of his friends. So he asked, as he usually did, whether the payroll taxes were being paid. Terry said that they were. George accepted Terry's answer, and didn't ask any other questions.

In June 20x5, the Internal Revenue Service contacted Green Tree about the delinquent tax payments. Unfortunately, most of the cash from the holiday season had been used to pay down the Bank loans, leaving Green Tree without much money.

George was furious when he learned about the IRS inquiry and the delinquent taxes. Alice said that she was doing her best to have Green Tree pay the IRS, but George insisted that she step down as president. He brought in Kim, a well-known turnaround specialist, to take over Green Tree on a temporary basis to see if it could be saved. Kim assumed full responsibility and replaced Alice as president of Green Tree as of July 1, 20x5. At that time Green Tree had unencumbered assets of $75,000. The trust fund portion of the delinquent taxes was $125,000; the non-trust fund portion was $50,000.

Kim and Tom met with the Revenue Officer in early July 20x5. After the meeting, Kim directed Tom to pay $75,000 to the IRS, which Tom did. The IRS applied $25,000 to the trust fund portion of the delinquency, and the remaining $50,000 to the non-trust fund portion.

Shortly thereafter, Kim reported back to George that Green Tree could not be saved. Green Tree then proceeded to close its business. Before it went out of business, however, it had another $50,000 in sales. Green Tree, at Kim's direction, used that amount to pay other creditors (and not the IRS).

Alice was very unhappy with Green Tree's going out of business, and felt she could still "make a go of it." So she formed a new corporation almost immediately called Green Life, Inc., which started conducting the same business as had been conducted by Green Tree at the same location as had been occupied by Green Tree. Most of the Green Tree employees, including Tom and Terry, joined Green Life with the same responsibilities as they had had at Green Tree. And most of the old Green Tree customers soon became customers of Green Life.

The board of directors of Green Life consisted of Alice, Terry and Tom. Alice raised $150,000 in capital for Green Life from friends. Under the direction of Alice, Terry, and Tom, Green Life used the full amount to buy equipment and inventory for its new business. It did not use any of the funds to pay the delinquent taxes owed by Green Tree.

1. Before Green Life could actually open its doors to start business, the IRS Revenue Officer contacted Alice, Terry, Tom, George, Leslie, the Bank, and Kim to request information and to schedule interviews in regard to Green Tree's delinquent taxes. Alice, Terry, Tom, the Bank, and Leslie contacted you for advice as to what exposure they might have, if any, for the delinquent taxes. Later that day, George and Kim contacted you with the same question. What would you discuss with each of them?

2. What exposure does each of them have?

3. What are the merits of the IRS's case against each of them?

4. What opportunities for administrative and judicial review would each of them have if the IRS were to propose a trust fund recovery penalty against each.

5. Why did the IRS apply the $75,000 payment the way it did? What should Kim and Tom have done when Green Tree made the $75,000 payment to the IRS?

6. What action would you advise that does not involve the IRS?

Chapter 15

Transferee and Fiduciary Liability

IRC: §§6901(a)–(c), (f)–(i); 6902; 6905; 7421(b); 7701(a)(6)

I. Introduction

Transferee and fiduciary liability are not penalty devices. Instead, they are techniques by which the IRS can collect from secondary persons the taxes that it cannot collect from the primarily liable taxpayer. The core idea behind the mechanisms is easily grasped, but many sharp reefs lurk near the apparently placid surface.

The difficulties in the area come from three tensions. First, many cases require the application of state law as well as federal law. Second, both procedural and substantive principles must be consulted, and they arise from different sources or bodies of law. Third, while it is essential to the fisc that techniques of secondary liability exist, their exercise must be balanced with fairness to the parties. The core ideas behind the devices of transferee and fiduciary liability are discussed below, after which the applicable rules and their sources are described.

II. Core Idea of Nexus

In the first instance, of course, payment of tax is the responsibility of the taxpayer who incurred the liability. When payment from that taxpayer is not forthcoming, however, and enforced collection against the taxpayer is unlikely to prove availing, the IRS may pursue secondary persons.

The concept of nexus is central to secondary collection. It would be fundamentally unfair, indeed it likely would violate due process,[1] to seek collection from a person unconnected to the liability or to its non-payment. Secondary liability is appropriate only when the person to be held secondarily liable either participated in the non-payment or benefitted from it in a meaningful way.

Other chapters already have illustrated this and related ideas. For instance, Chapter 3 discussed spousal relief. The Code permits collection from a spouse who knew of the tax understatement or to whom assets were transferred in order to defeat payment

1. *See* Hoeper v. Tax Comm'n, 284 U.S. 206, 215 (1931). The Supreme Court has upheld the constitutionality of the transferee liability mechanism. Phillips v. Commissioner, 283 U.S. 589 (1931).

of the tax.[2] Chapter 14 discussed the Trust Fund Recovery Penalty. Persons responsible for the payment of trust fund taxes who willfully fail to provide for their payment become secondarily liable for them.[3] The conditions of knowledge, responsibility, or participation in improper transfers in these situations constitute sufficient nexus to visit liability on others. Transferee liability and fiduciary liability also involve the idea of nexus. Consider these scenarios.

Scenario (1): Jesse owes federal income taxes. He has assets sufficient to pay some or all of the taxes, but it's not hard for him to think of friends or relatives whom he would rather endow than the IRS. Specifically, Jesse transfers all his assets to his brother Frank.

If the law allowed this transfer to stand, a valid tax debt would be uncollectible and Frank would have received a windfall. Assuming conditions described later are satisfied, Frank is liable as a transferee for some or all of the unpaid taxes. The nexus that makes this result fair is that Frank's receipt of the assets deprived the IRS of the ability to collect the taxes from Jesse, the primary taxpayer. A legitimate creditor should prevail over a windfall recipient.

Scenario (2): Martha dies. Her children—Carol, Carl, and Clark—are the beneficiaries under Martha's will. Carol also is the executrix of Martha's estate. The estate owes federal estate taxes. However, Carol empties the estate without having paid or made provision for the payment of the estate taxes. She does so either by distributing the assets to the beneficiaries or by paying creditors of lower priority than the IRS.

For the same reason as in Scenario 1, Carol, Carl, and Clark may be liable as transferees. Carol may also be separately liable in her capacity as executrix. The nexus here is that her prematurely distributing the estate's assets or expending them on lower priority claims prevented the IRS from collecting from the estate, the primary taxpayer. Fiduciary liability and transferee liability are independent: Carol is liable as a transferee whether or not she is the executrix and liable as a fiduciary whether or not she is a beneficiary. However, the IRS will not collect the unpaid taxes twice, once from transferees and again from fiduciaries. Transferee and fiduciary liability are collection devices, not penalties.

III. Section 6901 and Related Sections

The starting point in understanding transferee and fiduciary liability is section 6901. Evidencing early awareness of the importance of a secondary liability remedy for the government, section 6901 or its predecessors have been in the law since 1926.[4]

2. IRC §6015(b)(1)(C), (c)(3)(A)(ii), (c)(3)(C), (c)(4).

3. IRC §6672(a).

4. *See* Revenue Act of 1926, §280(a)(1). For discussion of the 1926 enactment and its aftermath, see Note, *What Law Governs Transferee Liability for Federal Income Tax?*, 8 Stan. L. Rev. 261 (1960).

Section 6901(a) provides that certain secondary liabilities generally shall "be assessed, paid, and collected in the same manner ... as in the case of the taxes with respect to which the liabilities were incurred." Thus, the procedures for transferees and fiduciaries are similar to those for primary taxpayers.

The liabilities covered are (i) the liabilities of transferees for federal income, estate, or gift tax, (ii) the liabilities of transferees for other federal taxes "but only if such liability arises on the liquidation of a partnership or corporation, or on a reorganization within the meaning of section 368(a)," and (iii) the liabilities of fiduciaries for federal income, gift, and estate taxes. Pursuant to section 6901(b), such liabilities may be either tax shown on a return or deficiencies.

Subsections (c) through (f) of section 6901 address limitations periods. They incorporate many concepts familiar from Chapter 5 as to tax statutes of limitations generally, with adaptations appropriate to the secondary liability context.

In some situations (mainly involving income, gift, and estate taxes), the IRS is required to assert transferee liability through procedures similar to the deficiency procedures described in Chapter 8. A Notice of Transferee or Fiduciary Liability replaces the Notice of Deficiency. It contains many of the same elements, adapted to the secondary liability context. Section 6901(g) prescribes rules governing such notices. In general, a Notice of Transferee or Fiduciary Liability must be sent to the secondary taxpayer's last known address, a concept having the same meaning for section 6901 purposes as for section 6212(b) purposes.[5] A properly addressed notice is valid under section 6901(g) "even if such person is deceased, or is under a legal disability, or, in the case of a corporation, has terminated its existence."

Section 6901(h) defines "transferee."[6] It provides that the term "includes donee, heir, legatee, devisee, and distributee, and with respect to estate tax, also includes any person who, under section 6324(a)(2), is personally liable for any part of such tax." Regulation section 301.6901-1(b) adds a number of other categories, including a shareholder of a dissolved corporation, an assignee of an insolvent person, a successor to a corporation,[7] and a party to a reorganization described in section 368.

Case law has developed as to transferee status in a variety of contexts, including life insurance beneficiaries, partners, and surviving joint tenants and tenants by the entireties.[8] However, the law is not settled in some areas. For instance, as to surviving

5. For discussion of section 6212(b), see Chapter 8.

6. *See* Jerome Borison, Comment, *Section 6901; Transferee Liability*, 30 Tax Law. 433 (1977).

7. For a case upholding the transferee liability of a successor corporation, see *Self Heating and Cooling, Inc. v. Commissioner*, T.C. Memo. 2004-85.

8. *See also* Rubenstein v. Commissioner, 134 T.C. 266 (2010) (upholding transferee liability with respect to transfer of allegedly exempt homestead property); Griffin v. Commissioner, T.C. Memo. 2011-61 (rejecting transferee liability because sale of business assets and later sale of business were found to be separate transactions); Diebold v. Commissioner, T.C. Memo. 2010-238 (rejecting transferee liability as to beneficiary of martial trust because the beneficiary lacked unilateral power to exercise dominion and control over trust assets); Upchurch v. Commissioner, T.C. Memo. 2010-169 (upholding transferee liability as to persons who received payments from decedent's estate in settlement of litigation as to the will).

tenants by the entireties, the traditional view was that they are not transferees for section 6901 purposes from their deceased cotenants.[9] It is unclear whether this traditional view will survive the Supreme Court's 2002 *Craft* decision.[10]

"Fiduciary" is defined in section 7701(a)(6). The term means "a guardian, trustee, executor, administrator, receiver, conservator, or any person acting in any fiduciary capacity for any person." This concluding "catch all" language contemplates a person acting in a representative capacity for another, not one acting on one's own behalf.[11]

Section 6901 is supported by the remaining sections in chapter 71 of the Code. Specifically, section 6902(a) allocates the burden of proof in transferee liability cases. Section 6902(b) creates special discovery options for transferees in Tax Court cases. Section 6903 provides for the filing with the IRS of notice that a person is acting in a fiduciary capacity. Section 6904 prohibits suits to restrain enforcement of transferee or fiduciary liability, via cross-reference to section 7421. Sections 6904 and 7421(b) make the Anti-Injunction Act[12] applicable to transferee and fiduciary liabilities.

Finally, provisions exist for the relief of liability of executors and other fiduciaries under some circumstances and upon written application. This is provided for estate taxes under section 2204(a) for executors and section 2204(b) for other fiduciaries, and for income and gift taxes under section 6905 for executors. "Executor" is defined slightly differently for the two contexts. For section 6905 purposes, "executor" is defined as "the executor or administrator of the decedent appointed, qualified, and acting within the United States."[13] The term for section 2204 purposes includes such persons plus, if there is no executor or administrator, "any person in actual or constructive possession of any property of the decedent."[14] The executor or other fiduciary can be discharged from liabilities determined by the IRS more than nine months after the written application (or the return, if filed later) was submitted to the IRS, so the practical effect of submitting the application is to accelerate an examination.

The above rules are procedural in nature. Section 6901(a) describes how transferee and fiduciary liabilities are asserted and collected, but it does not itself create or impose liability on any secondary party. The Supreme Court confirmed that in 1958 in the *Stern* case,[15] involving the immediate predecessor of section 6901. The Court held that no federal common law of substantive liability existed, thus that the substantive source for transferee liability could be found, if at all, only in state law.

This statement was somewhat imprecise even in 1958. By now, it is clearly outdated, especially given the creation of a federal fraudulent conveyance statute in

---

9. *See, e.g.*, Tooley v. Commissioner, 121 F.2d 350 (9th Cir. 1941); Rev. Rul. 78-299, 1978-2 C.B. 304.

10. United States v. Craft, 535 U.S. 274 (2002) (holding that the federal tax lien attaches to the tax debtor-spouse's interest in entireties property even when the other spouse doesn't owe tax).

11. Grieb v. Commissioner, 36 T.C. 156 (1961), *acq.* 1961-2 C.B. 3.

12. See Chapter 13 for discussion of the Anti-Injunction Act.

13. IRC § 6905(b); *see* Reg. § 301.6905-1.

14. IRC § 2203; *see* Reg. § 20.2203-1.

15. Commissioner v. Stern, 357 U.S. 39 (1958).

1990, as described in Section IV.C. below. Thus, the real teaching of *Stern* is that section 6901 is a purely procedural section. The substantive source of liability—the rule that *does* create or impose liability on the transferee or fiduciary—lies outside section 6901. To successfully assert transferee or fiduciary liability, the IRS must both identify a substantive basis or source of liability outside section 6901 and assert that liability via the procedures mandated by section 6901 and related sections.[16]

IV. Substantive Bases of Liability

A. Fiduciary Liability

As will be seen, there are many possible substantive bases of transferee liability. In contrast, there is only one substantive basis of fiduciary liability: 31 U.S.C. section 3713(b). This section provides: "A representative of a person or an estate (except a [bankruptcy] trustee ...) paying any part of a debt of the person or estate before paying a claim of the Government is liable to the extent of the payment for unpaid claims of the Government."[17] This language appears to create strict liability. However, as described below, the courts have not interpreted the statute in that fashion.

When such liability attaches, the fiduciary may be liable for the entire amount that he or she paid out (up to the amount of the tax debts)—even if the fiduciary received no personal benefit from the payments. Because of this potential rigor, it has been said that fiduciary liability should attach only when required under "the clearest and most unmistakable reading of [the statute's] precise terms."[18]

In this spirit, a number of defenses have been recognized in various cases. For instance, liability may not be imposed when the fiduciary was relying on advice of counsel or when the fiduciary lacked actual or constructive knowledge of the claims of the government.[19] Also, liability may not be imposed if the debts paid by the fiduciary had higher priority than the government's tax claims.[20] However, the law is

16. The purely procedural nature of section 6901 is explained by history. Before 1926, the government had only a cumbersome response to transfers to defeat tax collection. The government first had to bring suit against the primary taxpayer, then—when that judgment was returned unsatisfied because the transfer had left the primary taxpayer unable to pay—file a bill in equity to set aside the transfer as a fraudulent conveyance. Because of the separation of law and equity, the two actions could not be combined. Moreover, without obtaining the judgment against the primary taxpayer and taking out an execution that was returned unsatisfied, the fraudulent conveyance suit would not lie, because it had not been shown that no adequate remedy existed at law.

17. For this purpose, both assessed and not-yet-assessed amounts are taken into account as tax claims. *E.g.*, United States v. Tyler, 528 Fed. Appx. 193 (3d Cir. 2013) (assessed amounts); Viles v. Commissioner, 233 F.2d 376 (6th Cir. 1956) (not-yet-assessed amounts).

18. Fitzgerald v. Commissioner, 4 T.C. 494 (1944).

19. *Compare* McCourt v. Commissioner, 15 T.C. 734 (1950) (no liability), *with* United States v. Renda, 709 F,3d 472, 484 (5th Cir. 2013) (liability).

20. *See* United States v. Weisburn, 48 F. Supp. 393 (E.D. Pa. 1943).

not settled in those respects. Some decisions have refused to recognize one or another of these extra-statutory exceptions.[21]

Fiduciary liability is not avoided by the executor obtaining a discharge from the local probate court.[22] The executor may request prompt assessment of taxes under section 6501(d), thereby obtaining a discharge of personal liability under section 6905. Alternatively, as a condition of making distributions to them, the executor might obtain a bond from the distributees.

B. Transferee Liability at Law

Section 6901 refers to the liability of a transferee "at law or in equity." Those words relate to the substantive bases of liability. The substantive basis of transferee liability "at law" is either (i) a contract under which the person to be held secondarily liable assumes the obligation of the primary taxpayer or (ii) a federal or state statute other than a fraudulent conveyance statute.

1. Contract

"At law" liability exists if the person to be held liable assumed the primary taxpayer's tax liabilities *and* received assets of the primary taxpayer. Absent a transfer of assets, assumption of the liabilities alone will not suffice to impose transferee liability.[23]

The transfer requirement usually doesn't matter much in this context, however. First, while some assets must be transferred, the IRS is not required to prove their value.[24] Second, it is rare for one to assume liabilities without getting anything in return. The typical context of assumption occurs when a purchaser buys the assets of a going concern and assumes its liabilities—a situation which features a transfer of assets. Third, the IRS often would have an alternative remedy in assumption-without-transfer situations since the IRS might be viewed as a third-party beneficiary under state contract law.

Thus, the other requirement—that there was an assumption of the tax liability—is the more important element. Courts typically hold that an assumption of "all the liabilities" of a transferor includes assumption of tax debts,[25] but only those that are valid and enforceable at the time of the assumption.[26] Courts have disagreed as to whether assumption of liabilities includes tax liabilities arising from the sale itself.[27]

---

21. *E.g.*, United States v. Stiles, 114 AFTR2d 6809 (W.D. Pa. 2014) (finding no room in section 3713 for a "reliance on attorney" defense). Also as to the possible "reliance on attorney" defense, see *United States v. Renda*, 709 F.3d 472, 484 (5th Cir. 2013); United States v. Shriner, 113 AFTR2d 1360 (D. Md. 2014); United States v. MacIntyre, 110 AFTR2d 5151 (S.D. Tex. 2012).

22. *See, e.g.*, Viles v. Commissioner, 233 F.2d 376 (6th Cir. 1956).

23. Denton v. Commissioner, 21 T.C. 295 (1953).

24. *See, e.g.*, Bos Lines, Inc. v. Commissioner, 354 F.2d 830 (8th Cir. 1965).

25. *See, e.g.*, California Iron Yards Corp. v. Commissioner, 82 F.2d 776 (9th Cir. 1936).

26. *See, e.g.*, Diamond Gardner Corp. v. Commissioner, 38 T.C. 875 (1962), *acq.*, 1963-2 C.B. 4.

27. *Compare* Reid Ice Cream Corp. v. Commissioner, 59 F.2d 189 (2d Cir. 1932) (no), *with* Shepard v. Commissioner, 101 F.2d 595 (7th Cir. 1939) (yes).

Not strictly a contract, but akin to one, is an agreement between the transferee and the IRS consenting to transferee liability. Under section 6213(d), a primary taxpayer may consent to assessment in lieu of receiving a Notice of Deficiency. A similar option exists for secondary taxpayers. A transferee may execute IRS Form 2045 "Transferee Agreement" admitting to transferee liability in return for the IRS not making an assessment against the transferor. Although Form 2045 is an agreement, it differs in several respects from a contractual basis of "at law" liability. First, the form is rendered legally operable through the doctrine of estoppel, not contract. A party who executes a Form 2045 will be estopped from subsequently contesting liability as a transferee.[28] Second, a Form 2045 provides more than just a substantive basis of liability; it resolves all potential issues—procedural as well as substantive—in the IRS's favor.

2. Federal Non-Fraudulent-Conveyance Statute

The most frequently asserted federal "at law" basis of substantive liability is section 6324. Under section 6324(a)(2), transferees from the decedent's estate are personally liable for unpaid estate tax. Under section 6324(b), donees are personally liable for their donor's unpaid gift taxes. These sections constitute a substantive basis of liability, and the persons identified in sections 6324(a)(2) and 6324(b) are within the definition of "transferee" in section 6901(h). Transferee liability also can arise in certain situations involving the transfer of assets between private foundations.[29]

3. State Non-Fraudulent-Conveyance Statute

The principal state non-fraudulent conveyance statutes are (i) laws as to distribution of assets of an estate, (ii) laws prescribing treatment of corporate liabilities in the event of organic changes such as mergers, consolidations, and liquidations, (iii) Bulk Sales Acts, and (iv) the successor liability doctrine, under which a legal entity which, in substance, is a continuation of a prior entity may be held liable for that entity's debts, including unpaid tax liabilities.[30]

States typically have statutes that address distribution of probate assets of an estate before claims against the estate have been fully satisfied. Although such statutes theoretically are available to the IRS as a substantive basis of liability, they rarely are used in transferee liability cases. Code section 6324 is a familiar and comprehensive basis of liability, covering non-probate as well as probate assets. Thus, the IRS prefers section 6324 as the basis of liability in estate situations.

Commonly, state corporate laws make the survivor of a merger or a consolidation liable for the debts of the merged or consolidated entities. Such liability sometimes is conceived of as primary, but the laws can serve as the substantive basis of transferee

28. *See, e.g.*, Bellin v. Commissioner, 65 T.C. 676 (1975).

29. IRC § 507(b)(2) & (c). However, distribution of assets from one private foundation to another, which transfers were part of a court-approved settlement did not give rise to transferee liability. PLR 200808043 (Feb. 22, 2008).

30. *See, e.g.*, ILM 200847001, 2008 TNT 227-13 (applying Puerto Rico law).

liability. In addition, state laws prescribe who shall be responsible for any unpaid debts of a dissolved or liquidated corporation. Frequently, distributee shareholders of the corporation are rendered responsible. Again, the state laws are available as the foundation for transferee liability.

A "bulk sale" entails the transfer as an aggregate, and other than in the ordinary course of the business, of a major portion of the inventory or other assets of the business. A bulk sale can imperil the position of creditors of the transferor business. To guard against this, many states have enacted creditor protections in their bulk sale statutes. Article 6 of the Uniform Commercial Code is a model for such laws. Such statutes provide that a bulk sale is ineffective against creditors of the transferor unless the transferor is required to give the transferee schedules of property and creditors and the transferee notifies creditors of the transfer. If a transferee fails in this duty, there is a substantive "at law" basis of transferee liability against it as to unpaid tax debts of the transferor.[31] Similar issues may arise from the sale of assets in the context of receiverships.[32]

C. Transferee Liability in Equity

A substantive basis of transferee liability exists if the transfer from the primary taxpayer to the person sought to be held liable constitutes a fraudulent conveyance. Fraudulent conveyance is an equitable remedy with deep roots in Anglo-American law. A fraudulent conveyance statute was enacted in England in 1571.[33] All states in the United States have had fraudulent conveyance regimes, whether based on the statute of 1571, another statute, or the common law.

There was (and, to a lesser extent, remains today) great confusion and variation among state fraudulent conveyance laws. As a result, work was begun in 1915 which led to promulgation of the Uniform Fraudulent Conveyance Act (the "UFCA"). Some version of it was adopted by 25 American jurisdictions. A major review in the 1980s led to the Uniform Fraudulent Transfer Act (the "UFTA"). Many states that had adopted the UFCA switched to the UFTA. Currently, about a half dozen U.S. jurisdictions continue to use the UFCA in part or whole, and over 40 use the UFTA in part or whole.

Before 1990, the federal government had no comprehensive fraudulent conveyance statute of its own, so it generally had to rely on state laws when seeking collection from transferees. This changed with the adoption of the Federal Debt Collection Procedures Act of 1990.[34] Subpart D of the Act (entitled "Fraudulent Transfers Involving Debts") is a federal fraudulent conveyance statute.

---

31. The schemes that prompted states originally to enact bulk sales acts are less dangerous today because of changes in business practices, commercial law, and civil procedure. Accordingly, the National Conference of Commissioners of Uniform State Laws and the American Law Institute recommend that states repeal their bulk sales statutes as unnecessary. A revised Article 6 is still published, however, for states choosing not to repeal.

32. *E.g.*, Whelco Industrial, Ltd. v. United States, 526 F. Supp. 2d 819 (N.D. Ohio 2007).

33. Statute of 13 Elizabeth, ch. 5 (1571).

34. This Act became effective on May 20, 1991. It constitutes Title XXXVI of the Crime Control Act of 1990, Pub. L. 101-647, 104 Stat. 4789, 4933.

Accordingly, today, the government has available to it, as a substantive source of transferee liability in equity, either the 1990 federal fraudulent conveyance statute or the applicable state fraudulent conveyance statute.[35] The government can choose which source to proceed under. In cases in which the IRS is represented by the Chief Counsel's Office, the IRS rarely has asserted the 1990 federal statute as the basis of substantive liability. It has been more frequently asserted in cases in which the IRS is represented by the Department of Justice.

Some of the salient features common to fraudulent conveyance statutes are described below. However, generalization will not do for the attorney in practice. In each transferee liability case, the attorney must advert to the precise fraudulent conveyance statute on which the government is relying or may rely. The attorney must consider the particular—sometimes peculiar—terms of that statute. Typically, a transfer will be deemed within the statute if it is either actually or constructively fraudulent.[36]

The importance of the particulars of the statute under which liability is asserted is underlined by the cases involving so called Midco tax shelters used to avoid payment of corporate income tax on sales of business assets within a year of stock sales. The results of litigation have been mixed.[37] The Administration has proposed legislation to more clearly impose liability.[38]

In one prominent Midco case, the Tax Court rejected the IRS's attempt to first recharacterize the transactions under federal anti-abuse law, then to use Virginia law as the substantive basis of transferee liability with respect to the recharacterized transactions. The court held that Virginia law was the sole applicable law and that Virginia fraudulent conveyance law has no substance-over-form doctrine allowing recharacterization.[39]

1. Actual Fraud

A transfer is actually fraudulent if, in making it, the transferor had a definite purpose of defeating creditors. This adverts to the mental state of the transferor. In many states, it is irrelevant whether the transferee knew of or colluded in the transferor's intent. However, there are differences among the states on this point, as on many

---

35. The "applicable" statute is the one of the state in which the transfers occurred. *See, e.g.*, Fibel v. Commissioner, 44 T.C. 647 (1965). In theory, this could present choice-of-law issues in cases with complicated facts as to multistate activities. In practice, though, such controversies have been rare.

36. *E.g.*, United States v. Weisman, 102 AFTR2d 6874 (M.D. Fla. 2008) (rejecting the government's constructive fraud theory on summary judgment because the transferor was not insolvent but allowing the government's actual fraud theory to proceed to trial).

37. *E.g.*, Diebold Foundation, Inc. v. Commissioner, 736 F.3d 172 (2d Cir. 2013), *vacating & remanding* Salus Mundi Foundation v. Commissioner, T.C. Memo. 2012-61; *see also* Salus Mundi Foundation v. Commissioner, 776 F.3d 1010 (9th Cir. 2014) *rev'g & remanding* Salus Mundi Foundation v. Commissioner, T.C. Memo. 2012-61; Sloane v. Commissioner, T.C. Memo. 2016-115; Shockley v. Commissioner, T.C. Memo. 2015-113.

38. *See* Staff of Joint Comm. on Taxation, *Description of Certain Revenue Provisions Contained in the President's Fiscal Year 2014 Budget Proposal* 163–71 (Dec. 2013) (JCS-4-13).

39. Julia R. Swords Trust v. Commissioner, 142 T.C. 317 (2014).

other points as to fraudulent conveyance. Direct proof of actual fraudulent intent seldom is available. Thus, the common approach is that such intent may be inferred from the surrounding circumstances, from so-called "badges of fraud." Such badges include that:

- the transfer was to a relative, close friend, corporate insider, or entity under common control;[40]
- the transferor retained some possession, control, or use of the property even after its transfer;
- the transfer was concealed;
- before the transfer was made, the creditor had initiated or threatened to initiate legal action against the transferor to collect the debt;
- all or most of the transferor's assets were conveyed;
- the transferor absconded;
- the transferor removed or concealed assets;
- the consideration given by the transferee was less than reasonably equivalent to the value of the assets conveyed;
- the transferor was insolvent at the time of the conveyance or was rendered insolvent by the transfer or the series of transfers of which it is a part;[41] and
- the transfer occurred shortly before or shortly after a substantial debt was incurred.

There is no formula for the application of the badges of fraud. Obviously, the more badges that are present, the better the IRS's chance of prevailing. Still, the IRS may prevail even if only a few of the badges are present, as long as they are clear. The question always is the general impression that emerges as to the character of the transaction from the totality of the circumstances.[42]

2. Constructive Fraud

Constructive fraud can be established without any showing of intent or purpose. A conveyance is constructively fraudulent as long as it had the *effect* of hindering or impeding the creditor in collecting the debt. Typically, this effect will exist when both (i) the transferee rendered inadequate consideration (usually, in money or money's worth) and (ii) the transferor was insolvent at the time of the conveyance or was rendered insolvent by it.[43]

---

40. In one case, a taxpayer was facing multi-million dollar assessments as a result of his participation in bogus tax shelters. To defeat collection, he and his wife divorced and he transferred his assets to his "ex-spouse." Applying the eleven factors set out in state (Massachusetts) law, the court held that the divorce was a sham and the transfers were actually fraudulent. United States v. Baker, 116 AFTR2d 5674 (D. Mass. 2015).

41. As to the "series of transfers" idea, see, e.g., *Drew v. United States*, 367 F.2d 828 (Ct. C1. 1966).

42. *E.g.*, McGraw v. Commissioner, 384 F.3d 965 (8th Cir. 2004) (upholding transferee liability based on actual fraud).

43. *E.g.*, Suchar v. Commissioner, T.C. Memo. (CCH) 2005-23 (2005) ; *see also* Rubenstein v. Commissioner, 134 T.C. 266 (2010) (holding that care rendered for many years by a transferee son for his aged transferor father did not constitute adequate consideration; also rejecting the transferee's

A requirement common to both the actual and constructive fraud theories is that the IRS has exhausted its remedies against the primary taxpayer before proceeding against the putative transferee. This is inherent in the theory that transferee liability is *secondary* liability. However, the requirement is applied pragmatically. Equity does not require performing a futile act.[44] The IRS need not, as a condition of pursuing the putative transferee, first issue a Notice of Deficiency or take other action against the transferor if the transferor is insolvent[45] or, if an entity, has been dissolved.[46]

V. Procedural Aspects

Once a substantive theory of liability exists, that theory is applied through the procedures established by section 6901 and related sections. State rules matter insofar as they affect the substantive source of liability but are irrelevant as to procedure. Procedure is controlled by the federal rules. For example, assume the IRS is relying on a state fraudulent conveyance statute which contains a shorter statute of limitations than section 6901 establishes for transferee liability. The state limitations period will not limit the IRS's remedy. That period is procedural, and transferee liability procedures are provided by federal, not state, law.[47]

A. Incorporated Procedures

Section 6901 provides that transferee liabilities are "assessed, paid, and collected in the same manner and subject to the same provisions and limitations as" the underlying taxes. Non-exclusively, the Regulations provide that the rules so made applicable include those related to:

(i) Delinquency in payment after notice and demand and the amount of interest attaching because of such delinquency;

(ii) The authorization of distraint and proceedings in court for collection;

(iii) The prohibition of claims and suits for refund; and

(iv) In [income, gift, or estate tax cases], the filing of a petition with the Tax Court of the United States and the filing of a petition for review of the Tax Court's decision.[48]

A number of unfortunate decisions have identified what they call "the procedural elements" of transferee liability that the IRS must establish in addition to the basis

equitable estoppel argument based on the IRS's previous decision not to attempt to effect collection as to the property).

44. *See, e.g.*, Benoit v. Commissioner, 238 F.2d 485 (1st Cir. 1956).

45. *See, e.g.*, Coca-Cola Bottling Co. of Tucson, Inc. v. Commissioner, 37 T.C. 1006 (1962), *aff'd*, 334 F.2d 875 (9th Cir. 1964).

46. *See, e.g.*, Dillman v. Commissioner, 64 T.C. 797 (1975).

47. *See, e.g.*, Bresson v. Commissioner, 111 T.C. 172 (1998), *aff'd*, 213 F.3d 1173 (9th Cir. 2000).

48. Reg. § 301.6901-1(a)(3).

of substantive liability. These elements are said to be (1) that the transferee received property of the transferor; (2) that the transfer was for inadequate consideration; (3) that the transfer was made during or after the period for which the transferor's liabilities accrued; (4) that the transferor was insolvent before or because of the transfer, or the transfer was one of a series of property distributions that rendered the transferor insolvent; (5) that the IRS made all reasonable efforts to collect from the transferor and further efforts would be futile; and (6) the value of the transferred property.[49]

These decisions misconstrue the nature of transferee liability. First, most of the identified elements are substantive in nature and cannot be rendered procedural merely by the wave of the judicial wand. Second, the enumeration mixes discrete bases of substantive liability. The enumeration most closely reflects constructive fraud in equity, and is overly restrictive or simply wrong if the asserted substantive theory is either actual fraud in equity or fraud at law.

These decisions seem to be an attempt to create what the Supreme Court said in *Stern* did not exist: a federal common law of transferee liability. Recourse, in different cases, to fifty state fraudulent conveyance statutes, a federal statute, contracts, and the array of state and federal non-fraudulent-conveyance laws is messy, so the temptation to create a federal common law of transferee liability is understandable.[50] Yielding to the temptation, though, is wrong. The cases asserting the above six so-called "procedural elements" of transferee liability ignore both the Supreme Court's teaching in *Stern* and the multiplicity of the sources of substantive liability.[51]

B. Statute of Limitations

Section 6901 contains detailed limitations rules, which control over any conflicting limitations rules governing the substantive basis of liability. In fiduciary liability cases, the limitations period extends until the later of (i) one year after the liability arises or (ii) the expiration of the period for collection of the tax.[52]

In transferee liability cases, section 6901(c) directs that the starting point is the limitations period against the transferor, as measured under the 6501 rules described in Chapter 5. That period is unaffected by the subsequent death or dissolution of the transferor.[53] To the limitations period against the transferor is added an additional period. That period is one year as to an initial transferee plus an additional year as to each later-stage transferee (i.e., a transferee receiving from a prior transferee, rather

---

49. *See, e.g.*, Gumm v. Commissioner, 93 T.C. 475 (1989), *aff'd without opinion*, 933 F.2d 1014 (9th Cir. 1991).

50. Presumably, the temptation would lose some allure were the IRS to routinely rely on the federal fraudulent conveyance statute in preference to state fraudulent conveyance statutes in "in equity" cases.

51. For example, in one case, the court rejected the transferee's argument that the IRS was required first to pursue collection from the transferor. The law of the state (Wisconsin) imposed no such exhaustion-of-remedies obligation. Shockley v. Commissioner, T.C. Memo. 2015-113.

52. IRC §6901(c)(3).

53. IRC §6901(e).

than from the primary taxpayer/transferor), with the additional period capped at three years.[54]

Assessment or non-assessment against the transferor is irrelevant for this purpose. Assessing against the transferor before the limitations period has run does not contract the limitations period with respect to the transferee, nor does omitting assessment against the transferor have this effect. However, if the limitations period to assess against the transferor expires before the conveyance of assets to the transferee occurs, the transferor's tax liability is extinguished and there can be no transferee liability.[55]

Under section 6901(c), the limitations period with respect to an initial transferee is four years from the due date or filing date of the transferor's return,[56] whichever is later. However, the period may be longer. The limitations period as to the transferor may be expanded by conditions stated in sections 6501 and 6503.[57] Moreover, the additional period with respect to the transferee(s) may be expanded by a number of events, including transfers by one transferee to another,[58] consents to extend,[59] issuance of a notice of transferee liability,[60] and armed service by the transferee in a combat zone.[61]

C. Burden of Proof

Most transferee liability cases are tried in the Tax Court. Section 6902(a) creates a split burden of proof in Tax Court cases. The petitioner bears the burden as to whether the transferor owes tax while the IRS bears the burden as to whether the petitioner is liable as a transferee for the transferor's unpaid tax. Section 7491 does not affect this allocation since, under section 7491(a)(3), the general provision of section 7491(a)(1) yields to other, more specific burden-of-proof rules—like section 6902(a). The applicable standard of proof typically is preponderance of the evidence.[62]

"Burden of proof" for this purpose means the risk of nonpersuasion.[63] Within the overall allocation of that risk, the burden on specific issues may vary. The notion that specific rules control over general ones will sometimes put the burden of proof

---

54. IRC § 6901(c)(1), (2).

55. *See, e.g.*, Illinois Masonic Home v. Commissioner, 93 T.C. 145 (1989).

56. The normal three-year period against the transferor under section 6501(a) plus an additional year under section 6901(c)(1).

57. One case involved interpreting section 6503(a)(1) (suspending the limitations period during the pendency of a proceeding challenging a Notice of Delivery). Shockley v. Commissioner, 686 F.3d 1228 (11th Cir. 2012) (holding that the section applied, thus that the section 6901(c) period remained open), *rev'g* T.C. Memo. 2011-96.

58. IRC § 6901(c)(2).

59. IRC § 6901(d).

60. IRC § 6901(f) (suspending the running of the limitations period).

61. IRC §§ 6901(i), 7508.

62. *But see* Shockley v. Commissioner, T.C. Memo. 2015-113 (appearing to suggest, but not holding, that the IRS had "to prove the elements of transferee liability by clear and convincing evidence" because the law of the state (Wisconsin) used that standard).

63. See Chapter 8 for more detailed discussion of the burden of proof.

on the IRS on particular issues. For instance, if the IRS were to raise a new issue, not contained in the notice of transferee liability, increasing the transferor's alleged liabilities, the IRS typically would bear the burden on that issue.[64] Also, if the IRS were to assert fraud penalties against the transferor, the IRS likely would bear the burden as to them.[65]

Although the risk of nonpersuasion does not shift, the burden of going forward on particular issues can shift between the parties. In general, once the IRS has established a *prima facie* case on the "petitioner liable as transferee" issue, the burden of going forward on it shifts to the petitioner.[66] For instance, once the IRS shows that there was a transfer of valuable assets, the burden shifts to the petitioner to establish the value of any consideration he or she alleges to have given to the transferor in return.[67]

The allocation of burdens between the IRS and the putative secondary taxpayer is somewhat surprising. Commonly, the law puts the burden of proof on the party closest to the transactions, thus best able to adduce in court the relevant facts. But a transferee may not know much about the transactions that gave rise to the transferor's tax liabilities (as to which issue the transferee does have the burden under section 6902), while the transferee was involved in the transactions (the transfers) on which liability as a transferee will hinge (as to which issue the transferee does not have the burden under section 6902).

Yet, there are some counters to these anomalies. As to the "transferor's liability" issue, transferors and transferees often are closely related, perhaps giving the transferee some opportunity to know or find out about the transferor's transactions. Moreover, as described below, section 6902(b) gives the petitioner special discovery options to facilitate shouldering the burden. As to the "transferee's liability" issue, allocation of the burden to the IRS likely reflects concern about trying to collect one person's liability from another person. Before the system will permit that, the IRS will have to convince a court that it's really necessary.

The foregoing section 6902 rules apply only in the Tax Court. When transferee liability cases are tried in a refund forum, the normal refund action burden of proof rules discussed in Chapter 9 apply. The plaintiff must establish his or her entitlement to a return of funds, and thus bears the burden on the "transferee's liability" issue as well as the "transferor's liability" issue.[68]

D. Discovery

Both the IRS and the party to be held secondarily liable are entitled to whatever discovery is available under the rules of the court in which the case is tried. But a putative transferee may need discovery not only from the IRS but also, on the issue

64. *See* Tax Ct. R. 142(a).

65. *Cf.* IRC § 7454(a).

66. *See, e.g.*, Noell v. Commissioner, 22 T.C. 1035 (1954).

67. *See, e.g.*, Alonso v. Commissioner, 78 T.C. 577 (1982).

68. *See, e.g.*, Wehby v. Patterson, 60-2 U.S. Tax Cas. (CCH) ¶ 9611 (N.D. Ala. 1960).

on which he or she bears the burden of proof, from the transferor as well. Responding to this need, section 6902(b) creates special discovery opportunities, but only in the Tax Court—a fact which may influence the forum in which the putative transferee chooses to bring the case.

Under section 6902(b), the putative transferee/petitioner shall, upon application to the Tax Court, be entitled "to a preliminary examination of books, papers, documents, correspondence, and other evidence of the taxpayer or a preceding transferee of the taxpayer's property." That court

> may require by subpoena ... the production of all such books, papers, documents, correspondence, and other evidence within the United States the production of which ... is necessary to enable the transferee to ascertain the liability of the taxpayer or preceding transferee and will not result in undue hardship to the taxpayer or preceding transferee.

What if a putative transferee is denied such discovery because the transferor's books and records were lost or destroyed? This denial does not require that the case be resolved in the putative transferee's favor, particularly when there exists secondary evidence or sources of information.[69]

E. Privity

Transferors and their transferees are deemed to be in privity.[70] This has various consequences. For example, an admission by the transferor may be viewed as a vicarious admission by the transferee. Also, if the IRS and the transferor litigated, the result thereof may have res judicata or collateral estoppel effect.[71]

F. Right to Contribution

Transferees are severally liable. When there are multiple transferees, the IRS may proceed disproportionately, or even exclusively, against one or some of them.[72] For example, assume the transferor owes $50,000 in taxes and gave $50,000 on the same day to each of his three children: Agnes, Bill, and Clara. The IRS could choose to go against only Agnes, leaving Bill and Clara alone.

As described in Chapter 14, when there are multiple responsible persons as to the unpaid trust fund taxes of a business, section 6672(d) creates a cause of action whereby a responsible person disproportionately burdened by IRS collection can obtain con-

---

69. Kreps v. Commissioner, 42 T.C. 660 (1964), *aff'd*, 351 F.2d 1 (2d Cir. 1965).

70. *See, e.g.*, Estate of Egan v. Commissioner, 28 T.C. 998 (1957), *aff'd*, 260 F.2d 779 (8th Cir. 1958).

71. *E.g.*, United States v. Davenport, 484 F.3d 321 (5th Cir.), *cert. denied*, 552 U.S. 1076 (2007) (holding that a transferee contesting transferee liability for gift tax was bound by a Tax Court decision as to gift tax liability of the transferor). *But see* United States v. Botefuhr, 309 F.3d 1263 (10th Cir. 2002) (holding that a transferee was not bound by stipulations made by the transferor in a prior proceeding).

72. *See, e.g.*, Phillips-Jones Corp. v. Parmley, 302 U.S. 233 (1937).

tribution from the less burdened or unburdened responsible persons. There is no comparable rule in section 6901 or allied sections. Arguably, rights to contribution may exist under state law, but the law in this regard is not well developed.[73]

VI. Extent of Liability

A fiduciary is liable for the lesser of the primary taxpayer's liabilities (including interest and penalties) or the amount that the fiduciary wrongly paid out. A transferee is liable for the transferor's unpaid taxes (including interest and penalties) for the year in which the transfer occurred and prior years.[74] A transferee is not liable for the transferor's liabilities for years after the transfer took place.

In "in equity" transferee cases, the transferee's liability is capped at the value of the assets transferred, plus interest if allowed under the rule providing the basis of substantive liability in the case.[75] For this reason, proof of the value of the transferred assets is part of the IRS's *prima facie* case. "Value" for this purpose means the date-of-transfer fair market value of the transferred assets minus any consideration given by the transferee. Consideration includes any debt assumed by the transferee which burdens the transferred assets. If, incident to the transfer, the transferee pays other debts of the transferor, the payment counts as consideration only if those other debts had priority over the tax debts. Any assets that the transferee reconveys to the transferor before receiving the Notice of Transferee Liability are disregarded; they cannot form a basis of liability.

In "at law" transferee cases, the transferee's liability usually is not capped. That is, the extent of that liability may exceed the value of the assets received by the transferee. However, this depends upon the contents of the rule of law which provides the basis of substantive liability. That rule may impose a cap reflecting the value of the transferred assets or some alternative measure.

Interest can be tricky in transferee liability cases.[76] There are three stages at which interest may come into play. First, the transferor's liability will include interest computed pursuant to the normal rules of sections 6601 and 6621.[77] Second, interest on what liability the transferee is determined to bear accrues (again at the IRC rates) from the date of issuance of the Notice of Transferee Liability until the date the transferee pays those liabilities.[78] Third, interest also may run for the period between the

73. *See* Steve R. Johnson, *Unfinished Business on the Taxpayer Rights Agenda: Achieving Fairness in Transferee Liability Cases*, 19 Va. Tax Rev. 403 (2000).

74. *See, e.g.*, Stuart v. Commissioner, 144 T.C. No. 235 (2015); Papineau v. Commissioner, 28 T.C. 54 (1957).

75. *See, e.g.*, Yagoda v. Commissioner, 39 T.C. 170 (1962), *aff'd*, 331 F.2d 485 (2d Cir. 1964).

76. *Compare* Baptiste v. Commissioner, 29 F.3d 1533 (11th Cir. 1994), *with* Baptiste v. Commissioner, 29 F.3d 433 (8th Cir. 1994) (two brothers were transferees of their deceased father's estate and were substantively liable under section 6324(a). The circuits disagreed as to whether the transferees' liability for interest was capped by the value of the assets transferred to them).

77. See Chapter 12.

78. *See, e.g.*, Mysse v. Commissioner, 57 T.C. 680 (1972).

transfer and the issuance of the notice. However, the IRC is not the source of this third-stage interest. Third-stage interest is available only if authorized by the body of law that provides the basis of substantive liability, and only at the rate prescribed by that body of law.[79] The cases and rulings make fine factual distinctions in this area and often are in conflict.[80]

As stated in Chapter 13, tax liabilities sometimes are dischargeable in bankruptcy. A relatively rarely litigated issue is whether transferee liabilities can be discharged incident to the transferee's bankruptcy. Construing conflicting statutes, the Tenth Circuit has held that the dischargeability of transferee liabilities should turn on the dischargeability of the underlying tax.[81]

Similar confusion exists with respect to liability for interest in donee liability situations. In a Fifth Circuit case, the donee was liable under section 6324(b) for the donor's unpaid gift taxes. The IRS contended that interest could be charged even beyond the value of the transferred property. Reversing the district court on this point, withdrawing its own original opinion, and over a dissent, a panel of the Fifth Circuit rejected the IRS's contention.[82]

VII. Alternatives to Transferee and Fiduciary Liability

The mechanisms of transferee and fiduciary liability are non-exclusive or cumulative remedies. That is, they are among the remedies available to the IRS but are far from the only ones. The IRS may choose to pursue transferee or fiduciary liability or, in preference to them, any other remedy which may be better in the given situation.[83]

For example, the government sometimes prefers to bring a fraudulent conveyance action in federal District Court instead of issuing a Notice of Transferee Liability as-

---

79. *See, e.g.*, Stansbury v. Commissioner, 104 T.C. 486 (1995), *aff'd*, 102 F.3d 1088 (10th Cir. 1996).

80. In internal advice, the IRS took the following position. When there is a transfer giving rise to transferee liability and the value of the transferred assets is less than the transferor's liability, interest may be charged against the transferee, with the accrual of interest beginning when the IRS makes notice and demand for payment. ECC 2008480685 (Aug. 19, 2008), 2008 TNT 232–46.

A circuit court has held, however, that a transferee is liable for interest before the Notice of Transferee Liability is issued only if state law creates such liability. On this point, the Circuit Court reversed the Tax Court, which had imposed prejudgment interest under federal law. The courts agreed that the transferee may not reduce his liability by amounts he returned to the transferor. Schussel v. Werfel, 758 F.3d 82 (1st Cir. 2014), *aff'g in part & rev'g in part*, T.C. Memo. 2013-32.

81. McKowen v. IRS, 370 F.3d 1023 (10th Cir. 2004) (holding the transferee liability to be nondischargeable because the underlying income tax was nondischargeable).

82. United States v. Marshall, 116 AFTR2d 5694 (5th Cir. 2015) *aff'g in part, rev'g in part & remanding* 109 AFTR2d 2469 (S.D. Tex. 2012).

83. *See, e.g.*, United States v. Chrein, 368 F. Supp. 2d 278, 283 (S.D.N.Y. 2005) (holding that the IRS may pursue its remedies against the transferor and need not assert transferee liability against a transferee).

serting a fraudulent conveyance statute as the source of substantive "in equity" liability.[84] A principal difference is what the government gets if it wins. If the government prevails in a fraudulent conveyance action, the result is the reconveyance to the transferor of legal title to the assets.[85] Then, the IRS will levy against those assets in the transferor's hands pursuant to the assessments made and liens existing against him or her. In contrast, if the IRS prevails in a transferee liability case, the result is a money judgment against the transferee, which the IRS will assess and collect from the transferee.

The Uniform Fraudulent Transfer Act—which has been substantially adopted by a number of states—allows a creditor to, among other remedies, recover a money judgment against a transferee.[86] Accordingly, in appropriate cases, the IRS might obtain a money judgment against a transferee via the transferee liability procedures (including possible Tax Court proceedings) or the Department of Justice might obtain a money judgment on the IRS's behalf against the transferee via a fraudulent transfer suit in District Court.

When the government proceeds under state fraudulent transfer law, difficult questions can arise as to the relationship of federal and state law in the case. In one case, the government brought suit under Colorado's version of the Uniform Fraudulent Conveyance Act, seeking to collect taxes owed by a defunct corporation from the corporation's sole shareholder. The action was brought after expiration of Colorado's statute of limitations but within the ten-year federal collection period as to the corporation. Over a dissent, the circuit panel upheld the timeliness of the suit despite the fact that the IRS had assessments only against the corporation, not the shareholder.[87]

Transferee liability and fraudulent conveyance theories also should be distinguished from nominee and alter ego liens and levies. Nominee and alter ego mechanisms are availed of when the IRS already has assessments against the primary taxpayer and the taxpayer's property is being held by another, without a formal conveyance of legal title to the property to that other.[88] They also may be used when the transferee really has no identity and existence separate from the transferor, such as when a sole shareholder routinely ignores corporate formalities, hopelessly blurring any line between the two. In such cases, the property remains the taxpayer's, and the IRS can levy on

---

84. Fraudulent conveyance actions are equitable in nature. Thus, there is no right to jury trial. *E.g.*, United States v. Harrison, 273 Fed. Appx. 315 (5th Cir. 2008).

85. *See, e.g.*, United States v. Patras, 544 Fed. Appx. 137 (3d Cir. 2013) (setting aside the transfer and imposing personal judgment against the transferee).

86. *See* United States v. Verduchi, 434 F.3d 17 (1st Cir. 2006); Steve R. Johnson, *Using State Fraudulent Transfer Law To Collect Federal Taxes*, Nevada Lawyer, June 2006, at 14.

87. United States v. Holmes, 727 F.3d 1230 (10th Cir. 2013), *cert. denied*, 134 S. Ct. 1938 (2014); *see* Lori McMillan, *Transferee Shareholders and the Long Arm of the IRS,* Tax Notes, Oct. 14, 2013, p. 223.

88. *E.g.*, United States v. Lena, 2008-1 U.S.T.C. ¶ 50,403 (S.D. Fla. 2008). For defensive measures, see William D. Elliott, *Coping with a Nominee Lien*, Taxes, May 2011, at 13.

it directly, without the necessity of either bringing a fraudulent conveyance suit or issuing a Notice of Transferee Liability.[89]

Other possibilities exist as well. For instance, as noted earlier, section 6901 was enacted to give the IRS a more expeditious procedure than the original trust fund doctrine. But that doctrine survived enactment of section 6901. Thus, although it doesn't happen often, the IRS may still rely on that doctrine in appropriate cases.[90] Fraudulent conveyances may also be attacked under the Bankruptcy Code in a bankruptcy case.[91]

Problems

1. Predator Corp. and Target Corp. were unrelated. Both used the calendar year for federal income tax purposes. Predator had thousands of shareholders and was traded on the New York Stock Exchange. Target was closely held by four individuals who owned the shares equally. Target owned some technology that had proven very successful in its manufacturing business. All four of Target's shareholders had been involved with Target since it was organized and had been instrumental in the development of the technology. Target had timely filed all of its federal income tax returns, without extensions of time to file, and had timely paid all taxes shown to be due on the returns.

Predator was anxious to acquire Target's technology. After negotiations, an agreement was reached between Predator and Target pursuant to which Target would be merged into a wholly owned subsidiary of Predator, Predator-Sub, under state law. The Target shares would be converted into Predator common stock valued at $3,000,000 and cash in the amount of $500,000 ($750,000 in stock and $125,000 in cash per shareholder).

The merger agreement was very short and did not address assumption of liabilities. The merger was closed, and the merger papers filed with the appropriate state authorities on June 30, 20x6. Target's corporate existence ended on that day for state law purposes. On July 20, 20x6, Target's final federal corporate income tax return for its short year ended June 30, 20x6 was filed, and all taxes shown to be due on the return were paid.

Neither Predator, Predator-Sub, nor Target was insolvent at the time of the merger, nor was either rendered insolvent as a result of the merger. The amount of stock issued and cash paid by Predator was determined by the board of directors of Predator

---

89. *E.g.*, Grass Lake All Seasons Resort, Inc. v. United States, 96 AFTR2d ¶ 2005-6072 (E.D. Mich. 2005), *judgment entered*, 96 AFTR2d ¶ 2005-6548 (E.D. Mich. 2005). In Dalton v. Commissioner, 135 T.C. 393 (2010), *rev'd*, 682 F.3d 149 (1st Cir. 2012), a CDP case, the Tax Court rejected an IRS levy action with respect to unpaid trust fund recovery penalties. The Tax Court held, contrary to the IRS's contention, that the taxpayers had no nominee interest in the property. The Circuit instructed the Tax Court that the standard of review the Tax Court had applied was insufficiently deferential, and the circuit court held that the IRS's determination of nominee status was a reasonable interpretation of the applicable state law.

90. *See, e.g.*, Leighton v. United States, 289 U.S. 506 (1933).

91. *E.g.*, BFP v. Resolution Trust Corp., 511 U.S. 531 (1994).

after having an appraisal of the value of Target, including its technology, prepared by an independent valuation company. The Target Board of Directors had conducted a similar appraisal.

In January 20x7, the IRS began an examination of Target's returns for the years 20x4 and 20x5, and the short year ended June 30, 20x6. The examinations did not take long. There was no review by the IRS Appeals Office, and on August 10, 20x7, the IRS issued a Notice of Transferee Liability to Predator-Sub proposing deficiencies in corporate income tax of Target in the aggregate amount of $400,000, plus penalties and interest. Fraud was not proposed nor did the IRS propose that any amount had been omitted from gross income.

In addition, the IRS argued that certain individuals who had received compensation from Target for services rendered during the year 20x5 and the short year ended June 30, 20x6, had been incorrectly classified by Target as independent contractors. The IRS argued that they should have been treated as employees, and that Target should have paid employment taxes for them. So in addition to the proposed transferee liability for the deficiency in income taxes, the Notice of Transferee Liability also proposed transferee liability for employment taxes in the amount of $200,000.

a. Is Predator-Sub potentially liable for any taxes of Target?

b. If so, which ones?

c. Is the liability of Predator-Sub for the taxes of Target subject to any limit?

d. If so, what is the limit?

e. What is the burden of proof of Predator-Sub with respect to possible transferee liability for the taxes of Target? Of the IRS?

f. What is the period of limitations applicable to the transferee liability of Predator-Sub for the taxes of Target?

g. What procedure should Predator-Sub follow to dispute the possible transferee liability for income tax? For employment tax?

h. What court or courts have jurisdiction to hear the dispute?

2. Looking Glass, Inc. was engaged in the manufacture and sale of eyeglass frames. Its sole shareholders were Fred and Sally. Looking Glass had initially been very successful but had suffered financial setbacks in recent years, primarily attributable to mismanagement by Fred. Looking Glass had used all its available cash to pay expenses and didn't pay income taxes as shown on its returns for the years 20x3 and 20x4 in the approximate aggregate amount of $175,000. The 20x3 and 20x4 corporate income tax returns were filed timely, without extensions, but the taxes were not paid.

Bill and Carol had some experience in the eyeglass frame business and thought they could conduct a successful business with the assets of Looking Glass, which included primarily machinery and real property. So they organized a new corporation called Close Look, Inc. Close Look purchased the Looking Glass stock owned by Fred and Sally for a total purchase price of $125,000, evidenced by the promissory note of Close Look. The note was secured by a pledge of the Looking Glass stock.

The closing was held on September 30, 20x5. Fred and Sally agreed to indemnify Close Look against claims by the IRS for the unpaid income tax of Looking Glass through the closing date. Looking Glass was dissolved as of February 10, 20x6, and its assets transferred to Close Look as part of the dissolution process. Looking Glass was rendered insolvent by the transfer of its assets to Close Look. The value of the assets transferred was $135,000. Looking Glass received no consideration in the transfer.

Shortly after the dissolution of Looking Glass and the transfer of its assets to Close Look, the IRS issued a Notice of Transferee Liability to Close Look for the unpaid corporate income tax of Looking Glass for 20x3 and 20x4.

a. Is Close Look liable for the unpaid corporate income tax of Looking Glass?

b. What arguments will the IRS make in support of its position?

c. What defenses will Close Look assert?

d. Is the liability of Close Look for the taxes of Looking Glass subject to any limit?

e. If so, what is the limit?

f. What are the burdens of proof that must be borne the IRS?

Table of Cases

See page number for complete citation.

A

Abatti v. Commissioner, 644 F.2d 1385 (9th Cir. 1981), 251 n.112

Abeles v. Commissioner, 91 T.C. 1019 (1988), 225, 230 n.16, 231 n.18

Abraitis v. United States, 709 F.3d 641 (6th Cir. 2013), 211 n.36

AD Global Fund, LLC v. United States, 67 Fed. Cl. 657 (2005), *aff'd,* 481 F.3d 1351 (Fed. Cir. 2007), 186 n.117

AD Investment 2000 Fund LLC v. Commissioner, 142 T.C. 248 (2014), 355 n.151

Adamowicz v. United States, 531 F.3d 151 (2d Cir. 2008), 116 n.49

Adams v. Commissioner, T.C. Memo. 1978-152, *aff'd,* 609 F.2d 505 (4th Cir. 1979), 8 n.18

Adams v. Johnson, 355 F.3d 1179 (9th Cir. 2004), 407 n.169

Addington v. Commissioner, 205 F.3d 54 (2d Cir. 2000), 338

AICPA v. IRS, 114 AFTR2d 6451 (D.D.C. 2014), 28 n.82

Al-Sharif v. United States, 296 Fed. Appx. 740 (11th Cir. 2008), 379 n.3

Alamo Nat'l Bank of San Antonio v. Commissioner, 95 F.2d 622 (5th Cir. 1938), 294

Alaska Dep't of Envtl. Conservation v. EPA, 540 U.S. 461 (2004), 33 n.115

Albury v. United States, 88-2 U.S. Tax Cas. (CCH) ¶ 9511 (S.D. Fla. 1988), 206 n.7

Alioto v. Commissioner, T.C. Memo. 2008-185, 94 n.68

Allen v. Commissioner, 128 T.C. 37 (2007), 157 n.85, 353 n.140

Allen v. McCurry, 449 U.S. 90 (1980), 164 n.118

Alonso v. Commissioner, 78 T.C. 577 (1982), 448 n.67

Alpha I, L.P. *ex rel.* Sands v. United States, 86 Fed. Cl. 126 (2009), 173 n.25

Alt & RS Coal Corp. v. United States, 461 F. Supp. 752 (W.D. Pa. 1978), 394 n.92

Altera Corp. v. Commissioner, 145 T.C. No. 3 (2015), 29 n.89, 42

Am. Milling, LP v. Commissioner, T.C. Memo. 2015-192, 173 n.32, 180 n.75

Am. Mining Cong. v. Mine Safety & Health Admin., 995 F.2d 1106 (D.C. Cir. 1993), 29 n.86

Am. Standard Inc. v. Commissioner, 602 F.2d 256 (Ct. Cl. 1979), 28 n.80

Ambort v. United States, 392 F.3d 1138 (10th Cir. 2004), 406 n.160

American Boat Co., LLC v. United States, 583 F.3d 471 (7th Cir. 2009), 356 n.160

American Radiator & Standard Sanitary Corp. v. United States, 318 F.2d 915 (Cl. Ct. 1963), 269 n.37

Andantech L.L.C. v. Commissioner, 331 F.3d 972 (D.C. Cir. 2003), 186 n.118

Anderson v. Commissioner, 698 F.3d 160 (3d Cir. 2012), *cert. denied,* 133 S. Ct. 2797 (2013), 354 n.143

Andrews v. Commissioner, T.C. Memo. 2010-230, 177 n.56

Anonymous v. Commissioner, 127 T.C. 89 (2006), 238 n.57

Apache Bend Apts., Ltd. v. United States, 964 F.2d 1556 (5th Cir. 1992), *rev'd,* 987 F.2d 1174 (5th Cir. 1993), 6 n.6

Arbaugh v. Y&H Corp., 46 U.S. 500 (2006), 404 n.150

Arbitrage Trading, LLC v. United States, 108 Fed. Cl. 588 (2013), 172 n.21

Arthur Young & Co., United States v., 465 U.S. 805 (1984), 117 n.53

Arthur's Indus. Maint., Inc., In re, 1992 WL 132563 (Bankr. W.D. Va. 1992), *aff'd,* 1993 WL 79206 (W.D. Va 1993), 333 n.62

Aspinall v. United States, 984 F.2d 355 (10th Cir. 1993), 404 n.148

Atchison, Topeka & Santa Fe Ry. Co. v. Pena, 44 F.3d 437 (7th Cir. 1994), 31 n.97

Auer v. Robbins, 519 U.S. 452 (1997), 31 n.102, 32 n.110

Aufleger v. Commissioner, 99 T.C. 109 (1992), 159 n.90

Aultman, United States v., 2006 Dist. LEXIS 11984 (W.D. Pa. 2006), 404 n.153

Auth v. United States, 79-2 U.S. Tax Cas. (CCH) ¶ 9726 (D. Utah 1979), 207 n.15

Automobile Club of Michigan v. Commissioner, 353 U.S. 180 (1957), 37 n.139

Avila, United States v., 88 F.3d 229 (3d Cir. 1996), 384 n.35

Azarri v. Commissioner, 136 T.C. 178 (2011), 395 n.960

B

Baccei v. United States, 632 F.3d 1140 (9th Cir. 2011), 66 n.131, 329 n.47

Bachner v. Commissioner, 109 T.C. 125 (1997), *aff'd,* 172 F.3d 859 (3d Cir. 1998), 264 n.21

Badaracco v. Commissioner, 464 U.S. 386 (1984), 148 n.35, 149 n.43, 152

Baker, United States v., 116 AFTR2d 5674 (D. Mass. 2015), 444 n.40

Bale Chevrolet Co. v. United States, 620 F.3d 868 (8th Cir. 2010), 345 n.107

Ball, United States v., 326 F.2d 898 (4th Cir. 1964), 209 n.28

Ballard v. Commissioner, 544 U.S. 40 (2005), 242 n.70

Baltimore Pearl Hominy Co., In re, 5 F.2d 553 (4th Cir. 1925), 380 n.4

Balunas v. Commissioner, 546 F.2d 415 (3d Cir. 1976), 162 n.110

Bank of Nova Scotia, United States v., 691 F.2d 1384 (11th Cir. 1982), *cert. denied,* 462 U.S. 1119 (1983), *further proceedings,* 722 F.2d 657 (11th Cir. 1983), *appeal after remand,* 740 F.2d 817 (11th Cir. 1984), *cert. denied,* 469 U.S. 1106 (1985), 120 n.61

Baptiste v. Commissioner, 29 F.3d 433 (8th Cir. 1994), 450 n.76

Baptiste v. Commissioner, 29 F.3d 1533 (11th Cir. 1994), 450 n.76

Baral v. United States, 528 U.S. 431 (2000), 277 n.74

Baranowicz v. Commissioner, 432 F.3d 972 (9th Cir. 2005), 97 n.79

Barbados #7 v. Commissioner, 92 T.C. 804 (1984), 177 n.54

Barber v. Commissioner, T.C. Memo. 1997-206, 330 n.49

Barkett v. Commissioner, 143 T.C. 149 (2014), 141, 156 n.79

Barney v. IRS, 618 F.2d 1268 (8th Cir. 1980), 126 n.87
Barrett, United States v., 113 AFTR2d 1842 (D. Colo. 2014), 393 n.86
Barrow v. Commissioner, T.C. Memo. 2008-264, 164 n.119
Bartman v. Commissioner, 446 F.3d 785 (8th Cir. 2006), 94 n.67
Baskin v. United States, 135 F.3d 338 (5th Cir. 1998), 71 n.165
BASR Partnership v. United States, 795 F.3d 1338 (Fed. Cir. 2015), 157 n.85, 353 n.140
BASR Partnership v. United States, 113 Fed. Cl. 181 (2013), 157 n.85
Bassing v. United States, 563 F.3d 1280 (Fed. Cir. 2009), 172 n.24
Beall v. United States, 336 F.3d 419 (5th Cir. 2003), 371 n.57
Beard v. Commissioner, 72 T.C. 766 (1984), *aff'd*, 793 F.2d 139 (6th Cir. 1986), 146 n.24
Beatty v. Commissioner, T.C. Memo. 2007-167, 87 n.47
Bedrosian v. Commissioner, 358 Fed. Appx. 868 (9th Cir. 2009), 188 n.134
Bedrosian v. Commissioner, 143 T.C. 83 (2014), 188 n.133
Beery v. Commissioner, 122 T.C. 184 (2004), 98 n.86
Begier v. IRS, 496 U.S. 53 (1990), 431
Bellin v. Commissioner, 65 T.C. 676 (1975), 441 n.28
Benderoff v. United States, 398 F.2d 132 (8th Cir. 1968), 155 n.74
Benenson v. United States, 385 F.2d 26 (2d Cir. 1967), 297 n.38
Benjamin v. Commissioner, 66 T.C. 1084 (1976), *aff'd*, 592 F.2d 1259 (5th Cir. 1979), 122 n.66, 165 n.121
Bennett v. Commissioner, 30 T.C. 114 (1958), 158 n.88
Benoit v. Commissioner, 238 F.2d 485 (1st Cir. 1956), 445 n.44
Berg v. Commissioner, T.C. Memo. 1993-77, 231 n.25
Berry v. Westover, 70 F. Supp. 537 (S.D. Cal. 1947), 210 n.29
Bess, United States v., 357 U.S. 51 (1958), 385 n.35
Bewley, In re, 191 B.R. 459 (Bankr. Okla. 1996), *aff'd*, 212 B.R. 668 (N.D. Okla. 1997), 421 n.56
BFP v. Resolution Trust Corp., 511 U.S. 531 (1994), 454 n.91
Bigheart Pipeline Corp. v. United States, 600 F. Supp. 50 (N.D. Okla. 1984), *aff'd*, 835 F.2d 766 (10th Cir. 1987), 383 n.25
Billings v. Commissioner, 127 T.C. 7 (2006), 94 n.67
Bisbee, United States v., 245 F.3d 1001 (8th Cir. 2001), 417 n.30
Bivens v. Six Unknown Named Agents, 403 U.S. 388 (1971), 407 n.168
Black v. Commissioner, T.C. Memo. 2007-364, 353 n.140
Blonien v. Commissioner, 118 T.C. 541 (2002), 173 n.28
BMC Softwear, Inc. v. Commissioner, 780 F.3d 669 (5th Cir. 2015), 23 n.65
Bob Jones Univ. v. Commissioner, U.S. 461 U.S. 574 (1983), 34 n.122
Bobrow v. Commissioner, T.C. Memo. 2014-21 (2014), 355 n.150
Bokum v. Commissioner, 94 T.C. 126 (1990), *aff'd*, 992 F.2D 1132 (11th Cir. 1993), 83 n.35, 85
Bos Lines, Inc. v. Commissioner, 354 F.2d 830 (8th Cir. 1965), 440 n.24
Bosarge v. United States Dept. of Educ., 5 F.3d 1414 (11th Cir. 1993), 279 n.83
Botefuhr, United States v., 309 F.3d 1263 (10th Cir. 2002), 449 n.71
Boultbee v. Commissioner, T.C. Memo. 2011-11, 234 n.38
Bova v. United States, 80 Fed. Cl. 449 (Fed. Cl. 2008), 275 n.62

Bowen v. Georgetown Univ. Hosp., 488 U.S. 204 (1988), 36 n.135
Bowles v. Seminole Rock & Sand Co., 325 U.S. 410 (1945), 31 n.102
Boyle, United States v., 469 U.S. 241 (1985), 329 n.47, 355 n.152, 356
Boyter v. Commissioner, 668 F.2d 1382 (4th Cir. 1981), 90 n.57
Brach v. United States, 107 AFTR2d 1242 (Fed. Cl. 2011), 282 n.99
Bradford v. Commissioner, 796 F.2d 303 (9th Cir. 1986), 115 n.41
Bragg v. Commissioner, 102 T.C. 715 (1994), 257 n.132
Branerton v. Commissioner, 61 T.C. 691 (1974), 238 n.61
Braswell v. United States, 487 U.S. 99 (1988), 123 n.71
Bresson v. Commissioner, 111 T.C. 172 (1998), *aff'd,* 213 F.3d 1173 (9th Cir. 2000), 445 n.47
Brewery, Inc. v. United States, 33 F.3d 589 (6th Cir. 1994), 333 n.61
Broadhead v. Comm'r, 14 T.C.M. 1284 (1955), 63 n.113
Brockamp, United States v., 519 U.S. 347 (1997), 275 n.61, 276 n.67
Brooks v. United States, 833 F.2d 1136 (4th Cir. 1987), 385 n.41
Brounstein v. United States, 979 F.2d 952 (3d Cir. 1992), 416 n.24
Brown v. United States, 391 F.2d 653 (Ct. Cl. 1968), 150 n.48
Brown v. United States, 43 Fed. Cl. 463 (1999), 329 n.44
Buder, Estate of, v. Commissioner, 372 F. Supp. 2d 1145 (E.D. Mo. 2005), *aff'd,* 436 F.3d 936 (8th Cir. 2006), 293
Bull v. United States, 295 U.S. 247 (1935), 291–92, 379 n.1
Burke v. Commissioner, 124 T.C. 189 (2005), 401 n.129
Burke v. Commissioner, T.C. Memo. 2009-282, 327 n.38
Burnet v. Willingham Loan & Trust Co., 282 U.S. 437 (1931), 150 n.46
Bush v. United States, 599 F.3d 1352 (Fed. Cir. 2010), *vacated,* 400 Fed. Appx. 556 (Fed. Cir. 2010), 188 n.133
Busse v. United States, 542 F.2d 421 (7th Cir. 1976), 270 n.43
Bussell v. Commissioner, 130 T.C. 222 (2008), 217 n.63

C

Cabirac v. Commissioner, 120 T.C. 163 (2003), 326 n.36
Calderone v. United States, 799 F.2d 254 (6th Cir. 1986), 415 n.16
California Iron Yards Corp. v. Commissioner, 82 F.2d 776 (9th Cir. 1936), 440 n.25
Campbell v. Commissioner, 59 T.C. Memo. (CCH) 236 (1990), *aff'd & rev'd* , 943 F.2d 815 (8th Cir. 1991), 13 n.31
Canal Corp. v. Commissioner, 135 T.C. 199 (2010), 356 n.158
Candyce Martin 1999 Irrevocable Trust v. United States, 739 F.3d 1204 (9th Cir. 2014), 187 n.126
Capehart, Estate of, v. Commissioner, 125 T.C. 211 (2005), 90 n.58
Carey v. Saffold, 536 U.S. 214 (2002), 326 n.33
Carlson v. United States, 754 F.3d 1223 (11th Cir. 2014), 350 n.132
Carlton, United States v., 512 U.S. 26 (1994), 3 n.2, 36 n.13
Carpenter Family Invs., LLC v. Commissioner, 136 T.C. 373 (2011), 31 n.103
Casa de La Jolla Park, Inc. v. Commissioner, 94 T.C. 386 (1990), 23 n.67, 26 n.73
Cash v. Campbell, 346 F.2d 670 (5th Cir. 1965), *rev'd,* 311 F.2d 90 (4th Cir. 1962), 420 n.47

Caterino v. United States, 794 F.2d 1 (1st Cir. 1986), 416 n.22, 418 n.36, 419 n.38
CC&F W. Operations, Ltd. Partnership v. Commissioner, T.C. Memo. 2000-286, *aff'd,* 273 F.3d 402 (1st Cir. 2001), 154 n.70
Cemco investors, LLC v. United States, 515 F.3d 749 (7th Cir. 2008), 37 n.138
Cemco Investors LLC v. United States, 515 F.3d 749 (7th Cir.), *cert. denied,* 555 U.S. 823 (2008), 182 n.90
Cennamo, In re, 147 B.R. 540 (Bankr. C.D. Cal. 1992), 386 n.43
Centex Corp. v. United States, 486 F.3d 1369 (Fed. Cir. 2007), 256 n.127
Cerrito, Estate of, v. Commissioner, 73 T.C. 896 (1980), 23 n.31, 233 n.31
Chamberlain v. Kurtz, 589 F.2d 827 (5th Cir.), *cert. denied,* 444 U.S. 842 (1979), 126 n.85
Chamberlin v. Commissioner, 66 F.3d 729 (5th Cir. 1995), 344 n.102
Chandler v. Commissioner, 142 T.C. 279 (2014), 354 n.149
Charlton v. Commissioner, 114 T.C. 333 (2000), 88
Cheek v. United States, 498 U.S. 192 (1991), 418 n.36
Cheesecake Factory, Inc. v. United States, 111 Fed. Cl. 686 (2013), 235 n.43
Chenoweth v. Clinton, 181 F.3d 112 (D.C. Cir. 1999), 4 n.3
Chertkof v. Commissioner, 649 F.2d 264 (4th Cir. 1981), 304 n.58
Cheshire v. Commissioner, 115 T.C. 183 (2000), *aff'd,* 282 F.3d 326 (5th Cir. 2002), 85, 86, 88
Chevron, U.S.A., Inc. v. Natural Res. Def. Council, Inc., 467 U.S. 837 (1984), 31–32, 31 n.98, 41–42
Chimblo v. Commissioner, 177 F.3d 119 (2d. Cir. 1999), 180 n.74
Chrein, United States v., 368 F. Supp. 2d 278 (S.D.N.Y. 2005), 126 n.88, 451 n.83
Christians v. Commissioner, T.C. Memo. 2003-130, 158 n.88
Chrysler Corp. v. Brown, 441 U.S. 281 (1979), 29 n.86
Cinema '84 v. Commissioner, 412 F.3d 366 (2d Cir.) *cert. denied sub nom,* 176 n.46
City of New Britain, United States v., 347 U.S. 81 (1954), 387 n.45
City Wide Transit, Inc. v. Commissioner, T.C. Memo. 2011-279, *rev'd,* 709 F.3d 102 (2d Cir. 2013), 157 n.85
Clarke, United States v., 134 S. Ct. 2361 (2014), 116 n.49
Clarke v. United States, 553 F. Supp. 382 (E.D. Va. 1983), 213 n.45
Cleveland Indians Baseball Co., United States v., 532 U.S. 200 (2001), 34 n.121
Clifford, In re, 255 B.R. 258 (D. Mass. 2000), 417 n.25
Clintwood Elkhorn Mining Co., United States v., 128 S. Ct. 1511 (2008), 263 n.11
Clodfelter v. Commissioner, 527 F.2d 754 (9th Cir. 1975), 232 n.29
Clovis I v. Commissioner, 88 T.C. 980 (1987), 180 n.76
Coca-Cola Co. v. United States, 87 Fed. Cl. 253 (2009), 375 n.86
Coca-Cola Bottling Co. of Tucson, Inc. v. Commissioner, 37 T.C. 1006 (1962), *aff'd,* 334 F.2d 875 (9th Cir. 1964), 445 n.45
Cohan v. Commissioner, 39 F.2d 540 (2d Cir. 1930), 48 n.25
Cohen v. Commissioner, T.C. Memo. 1987-537, 84 n.38

Cohen v. United States, 853 F. Supp. 2d 138, 143 (D.D.C. 2012), *aff'd*, 751 F.3d 629 (D.C. Cir. 2014), 29 n.88
Cohen v. United States, 297 F.2d 760 (9th Cir. 1962), 209 n.28
Colony, Inc. v. Commissioner, 357 U.S. 28 (1958), 141, 154–55
Columbia Gas Sys., Inc. v. United States, 70 F.3d 1244 (Fed. Cir. 1995), 148 n.35
Commissioner v. [Party Name]. *See* [Party Name], Commissioner v.
Commonwealth Bank & Trust Co. v. United States, 114 AFTR2d 5091 (W.D. Ky. 2014), 414 n.13
Commonwealth Energy, United States v., 235 F.3d 11 (1st Cir. 2000), 272 n.47
Comparini v. Commissioner, 143 T.C. 274 (2014), 124 n.77
Computer Programs Lambda, Ltd. v. Commissioner, 89 T.C. 198 (1987), 177 n.54
Computer Science Corp. v. United States, 50 Fed. Cl. 388 (2001), *appeal dismissed,* 79 Fed. Appx. 430 (Fed. Cir. 2003), 38 n.146
Computervision Corp. v. United States, 445 F.3d 1355 (Fed. Cir. 2006), 268 n.34
Conklin Bros. of Santa Rosa, Inc. v. United States, 986 F.2d 315 (9th Cir. 1993), 334 n.63
Connelly v. Commissioner, T.C. Memo. 1982-644, 155 n.77
Conway v. Commissioner, 137 T.C. 209 (2011), *aff'd,* 552 Fed. Appx. 724 (9th Cir.), *cert. denied,* 134 S. Ct. 2680 (2014), 411 n.1
Cook v. Tait, 265 U.S. 47 (1924), 120 n.59
Coppola, In re, 810 F. Supp. 429 (E.D.N.Y. 1992), 404 n.152
Corson v. Commissioner, 114 T.C. 354 (2000), 96 n.76, 96 n.79
Cory v. Commissioner, 261 F.2d 702 (2d Cir. 1958), 308 n.65
Costantino v. TRW, Inc., 13 F.3d 969 (6th Cir. 1994), 23 n.65
Coulton v. Commissioner, T.C. Memo. 2005-199, 149 n.40
Council of British Societies in Southern California v. United States, 42 AFTR2d 6014 (C.D. Cal. 1978), 122 n.67
Countryside Limited Partnership v. Commissioner, 132 T.C. 347 (2009), 123 n.74
Craft, United States v., 535 U.S. 274 (2002), 383 n.27, 438 n.10
Cramer v. Commissioner, 64 F.3d 1406 (9th Cir. 1995), 355 n.155
Cramer v. Commissioner, 517 U.S. 1244 (1996), 355 n.155
Crocker v. Commissioner, 92 T.C. 899 (1989), 65 n.122
Crosley Corp. v. United States, 229 F.2d 376 (6th Cir. 1956), 295 n.32
Cross v. United States, 204 F. Supp. 644 (E.D. Va. 1962), 420 n.46
Crystal Cascades Civil LC, In re, 398 B.R. 23 (Bankr. D. Nev. 2008), 385 n.37
Curr-Spec. Partners, L.P. v. Commissioner, T.C. Memo. 2007-289, *aff'd,* 579 F.3d 391 (5th Cir. 2009), *cert. denied,* 560 U.S. 924 (2010), 186 n.118
Cyclone Drilling Inc. v. Kelley, 769 F.2d 662 (10th Cir. 1985), 231 n.23

D

Dalton v. Commissioner, 682 F.3d 149 (1st Cir. 2012), 401 n.137
Dalton v. Commissioner, 135 T.C. 393 (2010), *rev'd,* 682 F.3d 149 (1st Cir. 2012), 453 n.89
Daniels v. United States, 88-1 U.S. Tax Cas. (CCH) (N.D. Ga. 1987), 212 n.41

Daniels v. United States, 88-1 U.S. Tax Cas. (CCH) (N.D. Ga. 1988), 213 n.49

Davenport, United States v., 484 F.3d 321 (5th Cir.), *cert. denied,* 552 U.S. 1076 (2007), 449 n.71

Davey, United States v., 543 F.2d 996 (2d Cir. 1976), 114 n.38

David Dung Le M.D. Inc. v. Commissioner, 114 T.C. 268 (2000), *aff'd,* 22 Fed. Appx. 837 (9th Cir. 2001), 234 n.39

Davis v. United States, 961 F.2d 867 (9th Cir. 1992), 418 n.32, 418 n.35, 421 n.53

DeCleene v. Commissioner, 115 T.C. 457 (2000), 355 n.154

Dejoy v. Commissioner, T.C. Memo. 2000-162, 332

Del Vecchio v. Commissioner, T.C. Memo. 2001-130, *aff'd,* 37 Fed. Appx. 979 (11th Cir. 2002), 354 n.143

Deloitte & Touche USA LLP, United States v., 610 F.3d 129 (D.C. Cir. 2010), 117 n.54

Denbo v. United States, 988 F.2d 1029 (10th Cir. 1993), 419 n.37, 419 n.39

Denton v. Commissioner, 21 T.C. 295 (1953), 440 n.23

Detroit Trust Co. v. United States, 130 F. Supp. 815 (Ct. Cl. 1955), 282 n.96

Dewberry, In re, 158 B.R. 979 (Bankr. W.D. Mich. 1993), 38 n.143

Diamond Gardner Corp. v. Commissioner, 38 T.C. 875 (1962), 440 n.26

Dibsy v. Commissioner, T.C. Memo. 1995-477, 348 n.118

Diebold Foundation, Inc. v. Commissioner, 736 F.3d 172 (2d Cir. 2013), *vacating & remanding* Salus Mundi Foundation v. Commissioner, T.C. Memo. 2012-61, 443 n.37

Diebold v. Commissioner, T.C. Memo. 2010-238, 437 n.8

Dillman v. Commissioner, 64 T.C. 797 (1975), 445 n.46

DiNatale v. United States, 12 Ct Cl. 72 (1987), 282 n.101

Dingman v. Commissioner, T.C. Memo. 2011-116, 148 n.37

Dirks v. Commissioner, T.C. Memo. 2004-138, 22 n.63

Dixon, United States v., 672 F. Supp. 503 (M.D. Fla. 1987), 383 n.19

Dixon v. Commissioner, 132 T.C. 55 (2009), 256 n.127

Dobson v. Commissioner, 320 U.S. 489 (1943), 17 n.47

Dominion Resources, Inc. v. United States, 681 F.3d 1313 (Fed. Cir. 2012), 30 n.96, 42

Dominion Resources, Inc. v. United States, 97 Fed. Cl. 239 (2011), *rev'd,* 681 F.3d 1313 (Fed. Cir. 2012), 270 n.39

Donahue v. United States, 33 Fed. Cl. 600 (1995), 269 n.38

Doyle, United States v., 482 F. Supp. 1227 (E.D. Wis. 1980), 213 n.45

Doyle, United States v., 482 F. Supp. 1227 (E.D. Wis. 1980), *app. dismissed,* 660 F.2d 277 (7th Cir. 1981), 213 n.45

Doyle, United States v., 660 F.2d 277 (7th Cir. 1981), 213 n.45

Drake Oil Tech. Partners v. Commissioner, 211 F.3d 1277 (10th Cir. 2000), 183 n.93

Drew v. United States, 367 F.2d 828 (Ct. C1. 1966), 444 n.41

Drye v. United States, 528 U.S. 49 (1999), 383 n.27

Dudley v. United States, 428 F.2d 1196 (9th Cir. 1970), 419 n.42

Dudley's Commercial & Indus. Coating, Inc. v. United States, 292 F. Supp. 2d 976 (M.D. Tenn. 2003), 27 n.77

Dupont v. Commissioner, 118 F.2d 544 (3d Cir. 1941), 252 n.114

Durden v. Commissioner, T.C. Memo. 2012-140, 49 n.28

Dutton v. Commissioner, 122 T.C. 133 (2004), 83 n.31

Dynamo Holdings Limited Partnership v. Commissioner, 143 T.C. 183 (2014), 116 n.50

E

East Wind Industries Inc. v. U.S., 196 F.3d 499 (3d Cir. 1999), 420 n.49

Easterday, United States v., 539 F.3d 1176 (9th Cir. 2008), *amended by* 564 F.3d 1004 (9th Cir. 2008), 413 n.10

EC Term of Years Trust v. United States, 550 U.S. 429 (2007), 403 n.145

Edward J. Kunze, Estate of, v. Commissioner, T.C. Memo. (CCH) 1999-344 (1999), *aff'd,* 233 F.3d 948 (7th Cir. 2000), 372 n.60

Egan, Estate of, v. Commissioner, 28 T.C. 998 (1957), *aff'd,* 260 F.2d 779 (8th Cir. 1958), 449 n.70

Ehrmann v. Commissioner, T.C. Summary Op. 2014-96, 93 n.64

E.I. DuPont de Nemours & Co. v. Davis, 264 U.S. 456 (1924), 149 n.43

El Paso CGP Co., L.L.C. v. United States, 748 F.3d 225 (5th Cir. 2014), 294 n.23, 303 n.55, 308 n.67

Ellen Ann Hinckley, In re, 256 B.R. 814 (Bankr. M.D. Fla. 2000), 56 n.73

Elliott v. Commissioner, 113 T.C. 125 (1999), 57 n.79

Elman, United States v., 110 AFTR2d (RIA) 6993 (N.D. Ill. 2012), 94 n.68

Energy Resources Co., Inc., United States v., 495 U.S. 545 (1990), 430 n.99

Enochs v. Williams Packing Co., 370 U.S. 1 (1962), 210 n.32, 406 n.160, 406 n.161

Erdahl v. Commissioner, 930 F.2d 585 (8th Cir. 1991), 86 n.44

Erhmann v. Commissioner, T.C. Summary Op. 2014-96, 92 n.62

Estate of [Party Name]. *See* [Party Name], Estate of

Eurodif S.A., United States v., 555 U.S. 305 (2009), 33 n.116

Evans v. United States, 672 F. Supp. 1118 (S.D. Ind. 1987), 212 n.44

Ewing v. Commissioner *(Ewing I),* 118 T.C. 494 (2002), *rev'd,* 439 F.3d 1009 (9th Cir. 2006), 94 n.68

Ewing v. Commissioner *(Ewing II),* 122 T.C. 32 (2004), 94 n.68

Ewing v. United States, 914 F.2d 499 (4th Cir. 1990), 266 n.28

Exxon Mobil Corp. v. Commissioner, 484 F.3d 731 (5th Cir. 2007), 174 n.35

F

Fain v. Commissioner, 129 T.C. 89, 92 (2007), 96 n.79

FDA v. Brown & Williamson Tobacco Corp., 529 U. S. 120 (2000), 41

Fears v. Commissioner, 129 T.C. 8 (2007), 174 n.37

Fed. Nat'l Mortgage Ass'n v. United States, 379 F.3d 1303 (Fed. Cir. 2014), *cert. denied,* 552 U.S. 1139 (2008), 32 n.109

Fed. Nat'l Mortgage Ass'n v. United States, 69 Fed. Cl. 89 (2005), *aff'd,* 469 F.3d 968 (Fed. Cir. 2006), 375 n.83

Feller v. Commissioner, 135 T.C. 497 (2010), 342 n.90

Ferguson v. United States, 484 F.3d 1068 (8th Cir. 2007), 417 n.30

Fern, United States v., 696 F.2d 1269 (11th Cir. 1983), 103, 115 n.43

Fibel v. Commissioner, 44 T.C. 647 (1965), 443 n.35
Fidelity Equipment Leasing Corp. v. United States, 462 F. Supp. 845 (N.D. Ga. 1978), *vacating in part*, 47 AFTR2d (P-H) ¶81-1117 (N.D. Ga. 1981), 214 n.53
Finkelstein v. United States, 943 F. Supp. 425 (D. N.J. 1996), 282 n.96
Finley v. United States, 123 F.3d 1342 (10th Cir. 1997), 420 n.45, 420 n.50
Fior D'Italia, Inc., United States v., 536 U.S. 238 (2002), 382 n.16
Fiore v. Commissioner, T.C. Memo. 2013-21, 352 n.135
First Charter Financial Corp. v. United States, 669 F.2d 1342 (9th Cir. 1982), 150 n.49
Fitzgerald v. Commissioner, 4 T.C. 494 (1944), 439 n.18
Flora v. United States, 362 U.S. 145 (1960), 249 n.109, 261, 274 n.56
Flora v. United States, 362 U.S. 145 (1960), *aff'd on reh'g*, 357 U.S. 63 (1958), 282 n.100
Florida Bankers Ass'n v. U.S. Dep't of Treasury, 19 F. Supp. 2d 111 (D.C. 2014), 406 n.165
Florida Bankers Ass'n v. U.S. Dep't of Treasury, 19 F. Supp. 3d 111 (D.D.C. 2014), *vacated & rem'd*, 799 F.3d 1065 (D.C.Cir. 2015), 35 n.129, 73 n.175, 121 n.64
Florida Bankers Ass'n v. U.S. Dep't of Treasury, 799 F.3d 1065 (D.C. Cir. 2015), 28 n.82, 406 n.163, 406 n.164
Florida Bankers Ass'n v. U.S. Dep't of Treasury, *cert. denied*, 2016 WL 3129030 (2016), 406 n.163
Florida Power & Light Co. v. United States, 375 F.3d 119 (D.C. Cir. 2004), 38 n.143
Fowler v. Commissioner, T.C. Memo. 2004-163 (2004), 399 n.117
Fran Corp. v. United States, 164 F.3d 814 (2d Cir. 1999), 333 n.61
Frazier v. United States, 304 F.2d 528 (5th Cir. 1962), 420 n.45
French v. United States, 79-2 U.S. Tax Cas. (CCH) ¶9538 (E.D. Okla. 1979), 206 n.8
Freytag v. Commissioner, 501 U.S. 868 (1991), 16 n.45
Friedland v. Commissioner, T.C. Memo. 2011-90, 124 n.77
Friedman v. Commissioner, 53 F.3d 523 (2d Cir. 1995), 85 n.40
Frieling v. Commissioner, 81 T.C. 42 (1983), 232 n.28
Friko Corp. v. United States, 91-1 U.S. Tax Cas. (CCH) ¶50,195 (D.D.C. 1991), 212 n.40
Fruit of the Loom, Inc. v. Commissioner, 68 T.C. Memo. (CCH) 867, T.C. Memo (RIA) ¶94,492 (1994), *aff'd*, 72 F.3d 1338 (7th Cir. 1996), 299 n.48
Fund for Animals, Inc. v. Rice, 85 F.3d 535 (11th Cir. 1996), 30 n.95
Funk v. Commissioner, 687 F.2d 264 (8th Cir. 1982), 16 n.43
Furst v. United States, 678 F.2d 147 (1982), 268 n.33

G

GAF Corp. v. Commissioner, 114 T.C. 519 (2000), 182 n.87
Galin v. IRS, 563 F. Supp. 2d 332 (D. Conn. 2008), 296 n.36
Galletti, United States v., 541 U.S. 114 (2004), 143 n.8, 407 n.170, 412 n.3, 412 n.4, 412 n.5
Gandy Nursery Inc. v. United States, 412 F.3d 602 (5th Cir. 2005), 374 n.76
Garavaglia v. Commissioner, T.C. Memo. 2011-228, *aff'd*, 521 Fed. Appx. 476 (6th Cir. 2013), 165 n.120

Gardner v. United States, 213 F.3d 735 (D.C. Cir. 2000), 127 n.89
Garner v. Commissioner, 42 T.C. Memo. (CCH) 1181, T.C. Memo (P- H) ¶ 81,542 (1981), 295 n.31
Garwood Irrigation Co. v. Commissioner, 126 T.C. 223 (2006), 373 n.75
General Mills, Inc. v. United States, 123 Fed. Cl. 576 (Ct. Fed. Cl. 2015), 185 n.110
Germantown Trust Co. v. Commissioner, 309 U.S. 304 (1940), 148 n.38
Ghidoni, United States v., 732 F.2d 814 (11th Cir. 1984), *cert. denied,* 469 U.S. 932 (1984), 122 n.65
Giaquinto v. Commissioner, T.C. Memo. 2013-150, 425 n.78
Gibson v. Commissioner, 264 Fed. Appx. 760 (10th Cir. 2008), 233 n.34
Gingerich v. United States, 77 Fed. Cl. 231 & 78 Fed. Cl. 164 (2007), 187 n.127
Ginsberg v. Commissioner, 130 T.C. 88 (2008), 425 n.77
Ginsburg v. Commissioner, 127 T.C. 75 (2006), 186–87
Glass City Bank v. United States, 326 U.S. 265 (1945), 383 n.20, 383 n.26
Glatt v. United States, 470 F.2d 596 (Ct. Cl. 1972), 304 n.57
Glenn v. Oertel Co., 97 F.2d 495 (6th Cir. 1938), 152 n.55
G.M. Leasing Corp. v. United States, 429 U.S. 338 (1977), 394 n.95
Godfrey v. United States, 748 F.2d 1568 (Fed. Cir. 1984), 419 n.41
Golden v. Commissioner, T.C. Memo, 2007-299, *aff'd,* 548 F.3d 487 (6th Cir. 2008), *cert. denied,* 556 U.S. 1130 (2009), 84 n.37
Golsen v. Commissioner, 54 T.C. 742 (1970), *aff'd,* 445 F.2d 985 (10th Cir. 1971), 242 n.73, 250 n.110
Gonzales v. Oregon, 546 U. S. 243 (2006), 41
Gooding v. United States, 326 F.2d 988 (Ct. Cl. 1964), 297 n.38
Goralski v. Commissioner, T.C. Memo. 2014-87, 354 n.149
Goza v. Commissioner, 114 T.C. 176 (2000), 401 n.136
Graham County Soil and Water Conservation Dist. v. United States *ex rel.* Wilson, 559 U. S. 280 (2010), 41–42
Grand Jury Investigation M.H., In re, 648 F.3d 1067 (9th Cir. 2011), 74 n.175
Grapevine Imports, Ltd. v. United States, 71 Fed. Cl. 324 (2006), 160 n.99
Grass Lake All Seasons Resort, Inc. v. United States, 96 AFTR2d ¶ 2005 (E.D. Mich. 2005), 453 n.89
Grass Lake All Seasons Resort, Inc. v. United States, 2005 U.S. Dist. LEXIS 36708 (E.D. Mich. 2005), 393 n.85
Gray Line Co. v. Granquist, 237 F. 2d 390 (9th Cir. 1956), 421 n.51
Green Gas Delaware Statutory Trust v. Commissioner, T.C. Memo. 2015-168, 179 n.73
Greenberg's Express Inc. v. Commissioner, 62 T.C. 324 (1974), 236 n.44
Greene v. United States, 440 F.2d 1304 (Fed. Cir. 2006), 406 n.159
Greener Thapedi, United States v., 398 F.3d 635 (7th Cir. 2005), 272 n.47
Greenfield, Estate of, v. Commissioner, 297 Fed. Appx. 858 (11th Cir. 2008), 376 n.91
Greenwald v. Commissioner, 142 T.C. 308 (2014), 173 n.27, 173 n.31
Grieb v. Commissioner, 36 T.C. 156 (1961), 438 n.11
Griffen v. Commissioner, T.C. Memo. 2004-64, 246 n.97

Griffin v. Commissioner, T.C. Memo. 2011-61, 437 n.8
Grimes v. Commissioner, 82 F.3d 286 (9th Cir. 1996), 352 n.137
Guerin, United States v., 2014-1 USTC ¶ 50,272 (N.D. Cal. 2014), 430 n.96
Gumm v. Commissioner, 93 T.C. 475 (1989), *aff'd,* 933 F.2d 1014 (9th Cir. 1991), 446 n.49
Guralnik v. Commissioner, 146 T.C. No. 15 (2016), 401 n.134
Gustashaw v. Commissioner, T.C. Memo. 2011-195, *aff'd,* 696 F.3d 1124 (11th Cir. 2012), 356 n.159
Gustin v. United States, 876 F.2d 485 (5th Cir. 1989), 419 n.42

H

Hahn v. United States, 77-1 U.S. Tax Cas. (CCH) ¶ 9334 (C.D. Cal. 1977), 380 n.4
Hall v. United States, 132 S. Ct. 1882 (2012), 34 n.123
Hamilton v. Commissioner, 13 T.C. 747 (1949), 234 n.37
Hammernik v. Commissioner, T.C. Memo. 2014-170, 93 n.63
Hanesworth, In re, 1991 U.S. App. LEXIS 13886 (10th Cir. 1991), 58
Hardt v. Reliance Standard Life Ins. Co., 560 U. S. 242 (2010), 41
Harlan v. Commissioner, 116 T.C. 31 (2001), 157 n.84
Harrington v. United States, 504 F.2d 1306 (1st Cir. 1974), 421 n.51
Harrison, United States v., 273 Fed. Appx. 315 (5th Cir. 2008), 452 n.84
Harvey v. United States, 730 F. Supp. 1097 (S.D. Fla. 1990), 213 n.47
Haskin v. United States, 444 F. Supp. 299 (C.D. Cal. 1977), 212 n.42
Hatch v. Commissioner, 364 Fed. Appx. 401 (10th Cir. 2010), 151 n.51
Hawkes v. IRS, 467 F.2d 787 (6th Cir. 1972) *appeal after remand,* 507 F.2d 481 (6th Cir. 1974), 125 n.81
Hawkins v. Commissioner, T.C. Memo. 2008-168, 333 n.60
Hayes v. Commissioner, T.C. Memo. 1989-327, 84 n.39
Hayman v. Commissioner, 992 F.2d 1256 (2d Cir. 1993), 86 n.44
Healer v. Commissioner, 115 T.C. 316 (2000), 147 n.30
Heasley v. Commissioner, 902 F.2d 380 (5th Cir. 1990), 355–56 n.155, 356 n.160
Heating and Cooling, Inc. v. Commissioner, T.C. Memo. 2004-85, 437 n.7
Heckman v. Commissioner, T.C. Memo. 2014-131, *aff'd* 788 F.3d 845 (8th Cir. 2015), 155 n.75
Heckman v. Commissioner, 788 F.3d 845 (8th Cir. 2015), 153 n.67
Heimark v. United States, 18 Cl. Ct. 15 (1989), 417 n.25
Helvering v. Mitchell, 303 U.S. 391 (1938), 352 n.137
Henry v. Commissioner, 170 F.3d 1217 (9th Cir. 1999), 344 n.102
Henry v. Commissioner, 34 Fed. Appx. 342 (9th Cir. 2002), 355 n.152
Herrick v. Commissioner, 85 T.C. Memo. (CCH) 1467 (2003), 402 n.140
Higgins v. Commissioner, 312 U.S. 212 (1941), 34 n.121
Hinck v. United States, 446 F.3d 1307 (Fed. Cir. 2006), 371 n.57
Hinck v. United States, 550 U.S. 501 (2007), 226 n.3, 371 n.57
Hinckley, In re, 256 B.R. 814 (Bankr. M.D. Fla. 2000), 79 n.12
Hobby Lobby Stores, Inc. v. Sebelius, 723 F.3d 1114 (10th Cir. 2013), *aff'd,* 134 S. Ct. 2751 (2014), 406 n.164

Hochstein v. United States, 900 F.2d 543 (2d Cir. 1990), 416 n.21
Hodes, United States v., 355 F.2d 746 (2d Cir. 1966), 394 n.87
Hoeper v. Tax Comm'n, 284 U.S. 206 (1931), 435 n.1
Holland v. United States, 348 U.S. 121 (1954), 352 n.139
Holmes, United States v., 727 F.3d 1230 (10th Cir. 2013), *cert. denied,* 134 S. Ct. 1938 (2014), 452 n.87
Home Concrete Supply, LLC, United States v., 132 S. Ct. 1836 (2012), 33 n.118, 34 n.123, 154–55, 156–57
Honey v. United States, 963 F.2d 1083 (8th Cir. 1992), 421 n.55
Hoogerheide v. IRS, 637 F.3d 634 (6th Cir. 2011), 404 n.150
Hotel Equities Corp. v. Commissioner, 546 F.2d 725 (7th Cir. 1976), 151 n.54
Howard v. United States, 711 F.2d 729 (5th Cir. 1983), 417 n.30
Howell v. United States, 1992 U.S. App. LEXIS 32709, 231 n.25
Huffman v. Commissioner, 978 F.2d 1139 (9th Cir. 1992), 255 n.126
Huizinga v. United States, 68 F.3d 139 (6th Cir. 1995), 421 n.55
Hunter v. Commissioner, T.C. Memo. 2004-81, 231 n.22
Hyde Properties v. McCoy, 507 F.2d 301 (6th Cir. 1974), 393 n.82

I

Ibrahim v. Commissioner, 788 F.3d 834 (8th Cir. 2015), 79 n.10
Illinois Lumber & Material Dealers Ass'n Health Ins. Trust v. United States, 794 F.3d 907 (8th Cir. 2015), 308 n.69
Illinois Lumber & Material Dealer's Ass'n Health Ins. Trust v. United States, 794 F.3d 907 (8th Cir. 2015), *rev'g* 113 AFTR2d 1937 (D. Minn. 2014), 304 n.57
Illinois Masonic Home v. Commissioner, 93 T.C. 145 (1989), 447 n.55
In re [Party Name]. *See* [Party Name], In re
Industries Inc. v. United States, 349 F.3d 574 (2003), 293 n.16
Insulglass Corp. v. Commissioner, 84 T.C. 203 (1985), 156 n.79
IRS v. Blais, 612 F. Supp. 700 (D. Mass. 1985), 419 n.38
Isley v. United States, 272 Fed. Appx. 640 (9th Cir. 2008), 263 n.16
Israel v. Everson, 2007-1 USTC ¶ 50,319 (S.D. Iowa 2005), *aff'd,* 210 Fed. Appx. 549 (8th Cir. 2007), 210 n. 35
Israel v. United States, 356 F.3d 221 (2d Cir. 2004), 277 n.72
Izaak Walton League v. Marsh, 655 F.2d 346 (D.C. Cir. 1981), 29 n.90

J

Jackson v. Commissioner, T.C. Memo. 2002-44, 269 n.38
Jade Trading, LLC v. United States, 598 F.3d 1372 (Fed. Cir. 2010), 175 n.38
James v. United States, 366 U.S. 213 (1961), 107 n.15
Janis, United States v., 428 U.S. 433 (1976), 236 n.45
Janis v. Commissioner, T.C. Memo. 2004-117, 294 n.28
Jay v. United States, 865 F.2d 1175 (10th Cir. 1989), 417 n.30
Jewell v. United States, 548 F.3d 1168 (8th Cir. 2008), 171 n.5
Jewell v. United States, 749 F.3d 1295 (10th Cir. 2014), 119 n.57
John C. Hom & Assocs. Inc. v. Commissioner, 140 T.C. 210 (2013), 225, 230 n.14, 234 n.39

Johnson, United States v., 319 U.S. 503 (1943), 352 n.139
Johnson v. Gartlan, 470 F.2d 1104 (4th Cir. 1973), 391 n.72
Jones, United States v., 60 F.3d 584 (9th Cir. 1995), 428 n.87
Jones v. Flowers, 547 U.S. 220 (2006), 391 n.70
Jones v. Liberty City Glass Co., 332 U.S. 524 (1947), 264 n.22
Jordan v. Commissioner, 134 T.C. 1 (2010), 165 n.121
Josephberg, United States v., 562 F.3d 478 (2d Cir. 2009), 149 n.39
Juell v. Commissioner, T.C. Memo. 2007-219, 84 n.37
Julia R. Swords Trust v. Commissioner, 142 T.C. 317 (2014), 443 n.39
Justice, In re, 817 F.3d 738 (11th Cir. 2016), 147 n.24

K

Kaffenberger v. United States, 314 F.3d 944 (8th Cir. 2003), 269 n.37
Kalb v. United States, 505 F.2d 506 (2d Cir. 1974), 418 n.36, 419 n.38, 419 n.39, 419 n.41
Kallich v. Commissioner, 89 T.C. 676 (1987), 245 n.87
Kandi v. United States, 2006 U.S. Dist. LEXIS 2687 (W.D. Wash. 2006), 37 n.140
Kanter, Estate of, v. Commissioner, T.C. Memo. 2006-46, 245 n.85
Kanter v. IRS, 478 F. Supp. 552 (N.D. Ill. 1979), 126 n.87
Kaplan v. United States, 133 F.3d 469 (7th Cir. 1998), 176 n.47
Kaplan v. United States, 115 Fed. Cl. 491 (2014), *vacating* 113 Fed. Cl. 84 (2013), 426 n.81
Karagozian v. Commissioner, T.C. Memo. 2013-164, *aff'd,* 595 Fed. Appx. 87 (2d Cir. 2015), *cert. denied,* 136 S. Ct. 370 (2015), 292 n.15
Keil v. Commissioner, T.C. Memo. 2005-76, 239
Kellam v. Commissioner, T.C. Memo. 2013-186, 77
Kenagy v. United States, 942 F.2d 459 (8th Cir. 1991), 421 n.53, 421 n.55
King v. Burwell, 135 S. Ct. 2480 (2015), 31 n.106, 41, 42
King v. Commissioner, 115 T.C. 118 (2000), 77, 96 n.76, 96 n.79
King v. Commissioner, 116 T.C. 198 (2001), 89–90
King v. Commissioner, T.C. Memo. 2006-112, 273 n.55
Kinnie v. United States, 771 F. Supp. 842, 851 (E.D. Mich. 1991), *aff'd,* 994 F.2d 279 (6th Cir. 1993), 417 n.28, 419 n.38
Kirkpatrick v. Commissioner, T.C. Memo. 2014-234, 427 n.84
Klamath Strategic Inv. Fund, LLC v. United States, 472 F. Supp. 2d 885 (E.D. Tex. 2007), 356 n.160
Klamath Strategic Inv. Fund, LLC v. United States, 568 F.3d 537 (5th Cir. 2009), 37 n.139, 356 n.160
Knappe v. United States, 713 F.3d 1164 (9th Cir. 2013), 329 n.47
Knollwood Mem'l Gardens v. Commissioner, 46 T.C. 764 (1966), 148 n.34
Kollar v. Commissioner, 131 T.C. 191 (2008), 376 n.91
Kovacs v. United States, 614 F.3d 666 (7th Cir. 2010), 404 n.149
Kovacs v. United States, 739 F.3d 1020 (7th Cir. 2014), 256–57 n.131
Kovel, United States v., 296 F.2d 918 (2d Cir. 1961), 112 n.32
Kovens v. Commissioner, 91 T.C. 74 (1988), 244 n.83

Kovitch v. Commissioner, 128 T.C. 108 (2007), 95 n.70
Kreps v. Commissioner, 42 T.C. 660 (1964), *aff'd,* 351 F.2d 1 (2d Cir. 1965), 449 n.69
Kretchmar v. United States, 9 Cl. Ct. 191 (1985), 136 n.109
Krock, Estate of, v. Commissioner, T.C. Memo. 1983-551, 77, 79 n.11
Kuretski v. Commissioner, 755 F.3d 929 (D.C. Cir. 2014), 329 n.44
Kuretski v. Commissioner, 755 F.3d 929 (D.C. Cir. 2014), *cert. denied,* 135 S. Ct. 2309 (2015), 16 n.45
Kuznitsky v. United States, 17 F.3d 1029 (7th Cir. 1994), 429 n.95
Kyler v. Everson, 442 F.3d 1251 (10th Cir. 2006), 407 n.167

L

La Meres, Estate of, v. Commissioner, 98 T.C. 294 (1992), 329 n.47
Laing v. United States, 423 U.S. 161 (1976), 210 n.33
Lam v. Commissioner, T.C. Memo. 2010-82 (2010), 354 n.148
Landgraf v. USI Film Prods., 511 U.S. 244 (1994), 36 n.132
Lantz v. Commissioner, 607 F.3d 479 (7th Cir. 2010), 82 n.27
Lauckner v. United States, 68 F.3d 69 (3d Cir. 1995), 428 n.87
Leatherstocking 1983 Partnership v. Commissioner, 296 Fed. Appx. 171 (2d Cir. 2008), 177 n.55
Leighton v. United States, 289 U.S. 506 (1933), 454 n.90
Lena, United States v., 2008-1 USTC ¶ 50,403 (S.D. Fla. 2008), 452 n.88
Leonard v. United States, 85 Fed. Cl. 435 (2009), 282 n.98
Lepore v. Commissioner, T.C. Memo. 2013-135, 425 n.78
Lesavoy Foundation v. Commissioner, 238 F.2d 589 (3d Cir. 1956), 37 n.139
Levi v. Commissioner, T.C. Memo 2015-118, 57 n.79
Levy v. Commissioner, 76 T.C. 228 (1981), 234 n.36
Lewis v. Commissioner, 523 F.3d 1272 (10th Cir. 2008), 44 n.4
Lewis v. Reynolds, 284 U.S. 281 (1932), 252 n.116, 267–68, 281 n.94, 293 n.20
Lewis v. Reynolds, 284 U.S. 281 (1932), *modified by,* 284 U.S. 599 (1932), 264 n.21, 291 n.11
Liebovich v. United States, 104 AFTR2d 5976 (Fed. Cl. 2009), 187 n.127
Liti v. Commissioner, 289 F.3d 1103 (9th Cir. 2002), 257 n.134
Little Italy Oceanside Invs., LLC v. United States, 115 AFTR2d 5639 (E.D. Mich. 2015), 391 n.70
Littriello v. United States, 484 F.3d 372 (6th Cir. 2007), 412 n.4
Llorente v. Commissioner, 649 F.2d 152 (2d Cir. 1981), 247 n.102
Logan Trust v. Tigers Eye Trading, LLC, 616 Fed. Appx. 426 (D.C. Cir. 2015), 173 n.33
Long, United States v., 618 F.2d 74 (9th Cir. 1980), 149 n.41
Long v. Bacon, 239 F. Supp. 911 (S.D. Iowa 1965), 418 n.33
Looper v. Commissioner, 73 T.C. 690 (1980), 232 n.29
Loretto v. United States, 440 F. Supp. 1168 (E.D. Pa. 1977), 211 n.38
Lorson Elec., United States v., 72-2 U.S. Tax Cas. (CCH) ¶ 9614 (S.D.N.Y. 1972), *aff'd per curiam,* 480 F.2d 554 (2d Cir. 1973), 383 n.19
Lovejoy v. Commissioner, 293 F.3d 1208 (10th Cir. 2002), 355 n.150
Loving v. IRS, 742 F.3d 1013 (D.C. Cir. 2014), 31 n.107, 40–41

Loving v. IRS, 742 F.3d 1013 (D.C. Cir. 2014), *aff'g* 917 F. Supp. 2d 67 (D.D.C. 2013), 69 n.151

Lovlie, United States v., 102 AFTR2d 5654 (D. Minn. 2008), 352 n.136

Lovlie, United States v., 2008 U.S. Dist. LEXIS 85458 (D. Minn. 2008), 155 n.75

Ltd. v. Commissioner, 136 T.C. 67 (2011), 172 n.22

Lucia v. United States, 474 F.2d 565 (5th Cir. 1973), 408 n.182

Luhring v. Glotzbach, 304 F.2d 560 (4th Cir. 1962), 129 n.95

Lundy, Commissioner v., 516 U.S. 235 (1996), 276 n.66

M

Maarten Investerings Partnership v. United States, 2000-1 U.S. Tax Cas. ¶ 50,241, 85 AFTR2d P-H 2000-1086 (S.D.N.Y. 2000), 184 n.100

Macagnone, United States v., 86 AFTR2d 5307 (M.D. Fla. 2000), 419 n.38

MacIntyre, United States v., 110 AFTR2d 5151 (S.D. Tex. 2012), 440 n.21

Magavern v. United States, 550 F.2d 797 (2d Cir. 1977), 383 n.24

Maguire Partners v. United States, 104 AFTR2d 7839 (C.D. Cal. 2009), *aff'd,* 444 Fed. Appx. 190 (9th Cir. 2011), 37 n.138

Maier v. Commissioner, 119 T.C. 267 (2002), *aff'd* 360 F.3d 361 (2d Cir 2004), 96 n.76

Maine Med. Center v. U.S., 675 F.3d 110 (1st Cir. 2012), 151 n.51

Mallo, In re, 774 F.3d 1313 (10th Cir. 2014), *cert. denied,* 135 S. Ct. 2889 (2015), 322 n.18

Maloney v. Commissioner, 51 T.C. Memo. (CCH) 572 (1986), 136 n.107

Manhattan Gen. Equipment Co. v. Commissioner, 297 U.S. 129, 135 (1936), 35 n.130

Manko v. Commissioner, 126 T.C. 195 (2006), 137 n.111

Mannella v. Commissioner, 631 F.3d 115 (3d Cir. 2011), 82 n.27

Mannella v. Commissioner, 132 T.C. 196 (2009), *rev'd,* 631 F.3d 115 (3d Cir. 2011), 81 n.24

Manos v. Commissioner, T.C. Memo. 1989-442, 232 n.29

Marco v. Commissioner, 25 T.C. 544 (1955), 295 n.32

Markewich v. United States, 61-1 USTC ¶ 9241 (S.D.N.Y. 1961), 420 n.43

Marriott Int'l Resorts, L.P. v. United States, 437 F.3d 1302 (Fed. Cir. 2006), 126 n.86

Marshall, United States v., 116 AFTR2d 5694 (5th Cir. 2015) *aff'g, rev'g & rem'g* 109 AFTR2d 2469 (S.D. Tex. 2012), 451 n.82

Martin v. Commissioner, T.C. Memo. 2000-346, 88–89

Martin v. United States, 895 F.2d 992 (4th Cir. 1990), 270 n.43

Martinez, United States v., 564 F.3d 719 (5th Cir. 2009), 177 n.55

Martinez v. United States, 333 F.3d 1295 (Fed. Cir. 2003), 255 n.119

Martinez v. United States, 101 Fed. Cl. 688 (2012), 151 n.51

Mason v. Commissioner, 132 T.C. 301 (2009), 423 n.64

Matthews v. Commissioner, T.C. Memo. 2008-126, 370 n.52

May v. Commissioner, 137 T.C. 147 (2011), *aff'd,* 2013 WL 1352477 (6th Cir. 2013), *cert. denied,* 134 S. Ct. 682 (2013), 342 n.90

May v. United States, 2015 U.S. Dist. LEXIS 76962 (D. Ariz. 2015), 161 n.101

Mayo Found. for Med. Educ. & Research v. United States, 562 U.S. 44 (2011), 28 n.81, 31 n.99, 34 n.120
Mazo v. United States, 591 F.2d 1151 (5th Cir. 1979), 416 n.19, 419 n.39
McCarty v. United States, 437 F.2d 961 (Ct. Cl. 1971), 420 n.45
McCorkle v. Commissioner, 124 T.C. 56 (2005), 390 n.67
McCourt v. Commissioner, 15 T.C. 734 (1950), 439 n.19
McCoy, In re, 666 F.3d 924 (5th Cir. 2012), 147 n.24, 322 n.18
McCoy v. Commissioner, 57 T.C. 732 (1972), 85 n.41
McDermott, United States v., 507 U.S. 447 (1993), 387 n.45
McDonald, Estate of, v. United States, 79-1 U.S. Tax Cas. (CCH) ¶9182 (N.D. Cal. 1979), 208 n.21
McElrath v. United States, 102 U.S. 426 (1880), 183 n.98
McGee v. Commissioner, 123 T.C. 314 (2004), 82 n.26
McGraw v. Commissioner, 384 F.3d 965 (8th Cir. 2004), 444 n.42
McKay, In re, 430 B.R. 246 (Bankr. M.D. Fla. 2010), 149 n.40
McKowen v. IRS, 370 F.3d 1023 (10th Cir. 2004), 451 n.81
McMillan v. United States, 64-2 USTC (CCH) ¶9720, 14 AFTR 2d (P-H) 5704 (S.D. W.Va. 1964), 295
McNamee v. Dep't of Treasury, 488 F.3d 100 (2d Cir. 2007), 412 n.4
McNeely, Estate of, v. United States, 2014-1 USTC ¶60,679 (D. Minn. 2014), 280 n.85
Mead Corp., United States v., 533 U.S. 218 (2001), 31 n.100, 32 n.109
Meier v. Commissioner, 91 T.C. 273 (1988), 164 n.118
Menard, Inc. v. Commissioner, 130 T.C. 54 (2008), 293 n.19
Mesher v. United States, 736 F. Supp. 233 (D. Or. 1990), 222 n.88
Mettenbrink v. United States, 71 AFTR2d (RIA) ¶93-3642 (D. Neb. 1991), 208 n.18
Meyer v. Commissioner, T.C. Memo. 2013-268, 323 n.22
Michaud v. United States, 40 Fed. Cl. 1 (1997), 421 n.56
Middleton, United States v., 246 F.3d 825 (6th Cir. 2001), 103 n.1
Miklautsch v. Gibbs, 90-2 USTC ¶50,587 (D. Alas. 1990), 407 n.166
Miller v. Alamo, 992 F.2d 766 (8th Cir. 1993), 256 n.127
Miller v. Commissioner, 114 T.C. 184 (2000), 355 n.150
Mills v. United States, 890 F.2d 1133 (11th Cir. 1989), 271 n.45
Ming, Estate of, v. Commissioner, 62 T.C. 519 (1974), 225, 235 n.42
Mitchell, Estate of, v. Commissioner, 250 F.3d 696 (9th Cir. 2001), 150 n.50
Mitchell, United States v., 463 U.S. 206 (1983), 263 n.16
Mobil Corp. v. United States, 52 Fed. Cl. 327 (2002), 270 n.39
Mobil Corp. v. United States, 67 Fed. Cl. 708 (2005), 269 n.37
Monday v. United States, 421 F.2d 1210 (7th Cir. 1970), 418 n.36, 421 n.51
Monge v. Commissioner, 93 T.C. 22 (1989), 231 n.22
Montgomery v. Commissioner, 122 T.C. 1 (2004), 401 n.132
Monumental Life Insurance Co., United States v., 440 F.3d 729 (6th Cir. 2006), 118 n.56
Moore, In re, 359 B.R. 665 (Bankr. E.D. Tenn. 2006), 150 n.46
Moore, United States v., 627 F.2d 830 (7th Cir. 1980), 149 n.41
Moore v. Commissioner, T.C. Memo. 2007-156, 83 n.30

Moore v. U.S. House of Representatives, 733 F.2d 946 (D.C. Cir. 1984), 4 n.3
Moosally v. Commissioner, 142 T.C. 10 (2014), 425 n.78
Moosally v. Commissioner, 142 T.C. 183 (2014), 401 n.131
Morgan v. United States, 958 F.2d 950 (9th Cir. 1992), 214 n.54
Morse v. Commissioner, T.C. Memo. 2003-332, *aff'd*, 419 F.3d 829 (8th Cir. 2005), 164 n.116
Mosel, United States v., 738 F.2d 157 (6th Cir.1984), 149 n.41
Motor Vehicle Mfrs. Ass'n v. State Farm Mut. Auto Ins. Co., 463 U.S. 29 (1983), 30 n.94, 42
Mottaheden v. United States, 794 F.3d 347 (2d Cir. 2015), 403 n.147
Muck v. United States, 3 F.3d 1378 (10th Cir. 1993), 418–19
Muntwyler v. United States, 703 F.2d 1030 (7th Cir. 1983), 388 n.50
Murphy v. Commissioner, 129 T.C. 82 (2007), 179 n.68
Mysse v. Commissioner, 57 T.C. 680 (1972), 450 n.78

N

Nakano v. Commissioner, 742 F.3d 1208 (9th Cir.), *cert. denied,* 134 S. Ct. 2680 (2014), 411 n.1
Nakano v. U.S., 742 F.3d 1208 (9th Cir. 2014), 421 n.55
Napoliello v. Commissioner, 655 F.3d 1060 (9th Cir. 2011), 182 n.88
National Bank & Trust Co. v. United States, 589 F.2d 1298 (7th Cir. 1978), 391 n.73
National Bank of Commerce, United States v., 472 U.S. 713 (1985), 389 n.53, 390 n.63
Nat'l Cable & Telecomms. Ass'n v. Brand X Internet Servs., 545 U.S. 967 (2005), 33 n.117
Nat'l Fed'n of Indep. Bus. v. Sebelius, 132 S. Ct. 2566 (2012), 406 n.162
Neal, Commissioner v., 557 F.3d 1262 (11th Cir. 2009), 86 n.44
Neckles v. United States, 579 F.2d 938 (5th Cir. 1978), 416 n.21
Neely v. Commissioner, 85 T.C. 934 (1985), 344 n.100
Nehrlich v. Commissioner, 327 Fed. Appx. 712 (9th Cir. 2009), 178 n.57
Nehrlich v. Commissioner, T.C. Memo. 2007-88, 178 n.57
Nelson v. Commissioner, T.C. Memo. 2004-34, 371 n.54
Neonatology Associates, P.A. v. Commissioner, 115 T.C. 43 (2000), *aff'd,* 299 F.3d 221 (2000), 356 n.161
Neonatology Assocs., P.A. v. Commissioner, 115 T.C. 43 (2000), 359 n.174
Neonatology Assocs., P.A. v. Commissioner, *aff'd,* 299 F.3d 221 (3d Cir. 2002), 359 n.174
New Millennium Trading, L.L.C. v. Commissioner, 131 T.C. 275 (2008), 174 n.37
New York Football Giants, Inc. v. Commissioner, 117 T.C. 152 (2001), 189 n.139
Nichols v. Birdsell, 491 F.3d 987 (9th Cir. 2007), 280 n.85
Nihiser v. Commissioner, T.C. Memo. 2008-135, 94 n.65
Nis Family Trust v. Commissioner, 115 T.C. 523 (2000), 247 n.98
Noell v. Commissioner, 22 T.C. 1035 (1954), 448 n.66
Norwood, United States v., 420 F.3d 888 (8th Cir. 2005), 116 n.48
NPR Inv. LLC v. United States, 732 F. Supp. 2d 676 (E.D. Tex. 2010), 180 n.75

NPR Inv. LLC v. United States, 740 F.3d 988 (5th Cir. 2014), 33 n.115
NPR Invs., LLC v. United States, 740 F.3d 998 (5th Cir. 2014), 349 n.128
Nussdorf v. Commissioner, 129 T.C. 30 (2007), 172 n.23

O

Obergefell v. Hodges, 135 S. Ct. 2584 (2015), 50 n.33, 79 n.9
O'Brien v. United States, 766 F.2d 1038 (7th Cir. 1995), 298 n.43
O'Dell v. United States, 326 U.S. 451 (10th Cir. 1964), 388 n.50
O'Dwyer v. Commissioner, 266 F.2d 575 (4th Cir. 1959), 236 n.44
O'Gilvie v. United States, 519 U.S 79 (1996), 271–72 n.47
Olive v. Commissioner, 139 T.C. 19 (2012), *aff'd* 792 F.3d 1146 (9th Cir. 2015), 247 n.99
Olpin v. Commissioner, 270 F.3d 1297 (10th Cir. 2001), *aff'g* T.C. Memo. 1999-426, 58
Olsen v. Helvering, 88 F.2d 650 (2d Cir. 1937), 229 n.13
Olsen v. United States, 952 F.2d 236 (8th Cir. 1991), 421 n.51
106 Ltd. v. Commissioner, 136 T.C. 67 (2011), 360
106 Ltd. v. Commissioner, *aff'd,* 684 F.3d 84 (D.C. Cir. 2012), 360
Ordlock v. Commissioner, 533 F.3d 1136 (9th Cir. 2008), 99 n.89
Ottawa Silica Co. v. United States, 699 F.2d 1124 (5th Cir. 1983), 270 n.40
Oxford Capital Corp. v. United States, 211 F.3d 280 (5th Cir. 2000), 384 n.34

P

Pacific Gas and Electric Co. v. United States, 417 F.3d 1375 (Fed. Cir. 2005), 272 n.47
Pacific Nat'l Ins. Co. v. United States, 422 F.2d 26 (9th Cir. 1970), 421 n.51
Page v. Commissioner, 86 T.C. 1 (1986), 246 n.91
Palomares v. Commissioner, T.C. Memo. 2014-243, 80 n.18, 269 n.38
Pansier v. United States, 2011 U.S. Dist. LEXIS 45539, 151 n.54
Papineau v. Commissioner, 28 T.C. 54 (1957), 450 n.74
Pargament v. Fitzgerald, 272 F. Supp. 553 (S.D.N.Y. 1967), *aff'd per curiam,* 391 F.2d 934 (2d Cir. 1968), 392 n.76
Parker, In re, 515 B.R. 337 (Bankr. M.D. Ala. 2014), *aff'd,* 634 Fed. Appx. 770 (11th Cir. 2015), 257 n.131
Parker Hannifin Corp. v. United States, 71 Fed. Cl. 231 (2006), 270 n.41
Pate v. United States, 949 F.2d 1059 (10th Cir. 1991), 97 n.81
Patras, United States v., 544 Fed. Appx. 137 (3d Cir. 2013), 452 n.85
Paulson v. United States, 78 F.2d 97 (10th Cir. 1935), 272 n.47
Peery v. Commissioner, 610 Fed. Appx. 566 (6th Cir. 2015), 243 n.74
Pennoni v. United States, 86 Fed. Cl. 351 (2009), 281 n.93
Perry v. Commissioner, T.C. Memo. 2010-219, 279 n.78
Petaluma FX Partners, LLC v. Commissioner, 591 F.3d 649 (D.C.C. 2010), 173 n.31, 175 n.38, 249 n.106
Petaluma FX Partners LLC v. Commissioner, 131 T.C. 84 (2008), 249 n.106
Petaluma FX Partners LLC v. Commissioner, 135 T.C. 581 (2010), 249 n.106
Peterson, In re, 317 B.R. 532 (Bankr. D. Neb. 2004), 400 n.120

Phelps v. United States, 421 U.S. 330 (1975), 390 n.62
Philadelphia & Reading Corp. v. United States, 944 F.2d 1063 (3d Cir. 1991), 308 n.67
Phillips-Jones Corp. v. Parmley, 302 U.S. 233 (1937), 449 n.72
Phillips v. Commissioner, 272 F.3d 280 (2d Cir. 2002), 177 n.55
Phillips v. Commissioner, 283 U.S. 589 (1931), 388 n.51, 435 n.1
Pircher v. United States, 2009-1 USTC ¶ 50,138 (W.D. Tex. 2008), 211 n.37
Pittman, United States v., 449 F.2d 623 (7th Cir. 1971), 389 n.54, 390 n.67
Pixley v. Commissioner, 123 T.C. 269 (2004), 399 n.117
Pollock v. Commissioner, 132 T.C. 21 (2009), 95 n.69
Pollock v. Farmers' Loan & Trust Co., 158 U.S. 601 (1895), 3 n.1
Popowski, United States v., 110 AFTR2d (RIA) 6997 (D.S.C. 2012), 94 n.68
Poppe v. Commissioner, T.C. Memo. 2015-205, 22 n.61
Porro v. Commissioner, T.C. Memo. 2014-81, 399 n.116
Porter v. Commissioner, 132 T.C. 203 (2009), 95 n.71
Portillo v. Commissioner, 932 F.2d 1128 (5th Cir. 1991), *rev'd on other grounds*, 988 F.2d 27 (5th Cir. 1993), 247 n.102
Posner, Estate of, v. Commissioner, T.C. Memo. 2004-112, 294 n.28
Potter v. Commissioner, T.C. Memo. 2014-18, 152 n.57
Pough v. Commissioner, 135 T.C. 344 (2010), 425 n.77
Powell, United States v., 379 U.S. 48 (1964), 116 n.47
Powell v. Commissioner, 891 F.2d 1167 (5th Cir. 1990), 255 n.126
Prati v. United States, 81 Fed. Cl. 422 (2008), 188 n.131
Prestop Holdings, LLC v. United States, 96 Fed. Cl. 244 (2010), 188 n.132
Price v. Commissioner, 887 F.2d 959 (9th Cir. 1989), 84 n.37, 86 n.44
Prince v. Commissioner, 138 T.C. 270 (2009), 217 n.64
Prince v. Commissioner, 133 T.C. 270 (2009), 210 n.31
Principal Life Ins. Co. v. United States, 95 Fed. Cl. 786 (2010), 143 n.9, 265 n.24, 266 n.28, 294 n.21
Principal Life Ins. Co. v. United States, 116 Fed. Cl. 82 (2014), 236 n.44
Proske, Estate of, v. United States, 2010 WL 2178968 (D.N.J.2010), 65 n.127
Purcell v. United States, 1 F.3d 932 (9th Cir. 1993), 416 n.20
Pyo v. Commissioner, 83 T.C. 626 (1984), 231 n.25

Q

Quick, Estate of, v. Commissioner, 110 T.C. 440 (1998), 243 n.75
Quinn, United States v., 566 Fed. Appx. 659 (10th Cir. 2014), 413 n.10

R

R. H. Stearns Co. v. United States, 291 U.S. 54 (1934), 294
RadioShack Corp. v. United States, 566 F.3d 1358 (Fed. Cir. 2009), 271 n.46
Raleigh v. Illinois Dept. of Revenue, 530 U.S. 15 (2000), 425 n.79
Ramirez v. Commissioner, 87 T.C. 643 (1986), 208 n. 23
Randall v. H. Nakashima & Co., Ltd., 542 F.2d 270 (5th Cir. 1976), 383 n.23
Raskob v. Commissioner, 37 B.T.A. 1283 (1938), *aff'd sub nom*, 252
Rauenhorst v. Commissioner, 119 T.C. 157 (2002), 38

Raymond v. Commissioner, 119 T.C. 191 (2002), 80 n.14
Reece v. Scoggins, 506 F.2d 967 (5th Cir. 1975), 391 n.68
Reed v. Commissioner, 141 T.C. 248 (2013), 398 n.110
Reid Ice Cream Corp. v. Commissioner, 59 F.2d 189 (2d Cir. 1932), 440 n.27
Reigler v. United States, 546 U.S. 1004 (2005), 176 n.46
Reisman v. Caplin, 375 U.S. 440 (1964), 115 n.45
Rem, United States v., 38 F.3d 634 (2d Cir. 1994), 418 n.31
Renda, United States v., 709 F.3d 472 (5th Cir. 2013), 439 n.19, 440 n.21
Reser v. Commissioner, 112 F.3d 1258 (5th Cir. 1997), 86 n.44, 355 n.152
Reuter v. Commissioner, T.C. Memo. 1985-607, 155 n.75
Revis v. United States, 558 F. Supp. 1071 (D.R.I. 1983), 204 n.2
Rexworthy, United States v., 457 F.3d 590 (6th Cir. 2006), 123 n.72
R.H. Donnelley Corp. v. United States, 684 F. Supp. 2d 672 (E.D.N.Y), *aff'd,* 641 F.3d 70 (4th Cir. 2011), 267 n.32
Rhone-Poulenc Surfactants & Specialties, L.P. v. Commissioner, 114 T.C. 533 (2000), *appeal dismissed,* 249 F.3d 175 (3d Cir. 2001), 186 n.116
Rhone-Poulene Surfactants & Specialties, L.P. v. Commissioner, 114 T.C. 533 (2000), 160 n.99
Richard v. United States, 72-1 USTC ¶ 9267 (C.D. Cal. 1972), 420 n.48
Rickman, Estate of, v. Commissioner, T.C. Memo. 1995-545, 229 n.13
Rickman, United States v., 638 F.2d 182 (10th Cir. 1980), 149 n.41
Ridgely v. Lew, 55 F. Supp. 3d 89 (D.D.C. 2014), 31 n.107, 69 n.152
Rigas v. United States, 2011-1 USTC ¶ 50,372 (S.D. Tex. 2011), 284 n.118
Rigas v. United States, 2011 U.S. Dist. LEXIS 46730 (S.D. Tex. 2011), 247 n.101
Riley v. United States, 118 F.3d 1220 (8th Cir. 1997), 38 n.143
River City Ranches #1 Ltd. v. Commissioner, 401 F.3d 1136 (9th Cir. 2005), 177 n.55
Robinette v. Commissioner, 123 T.C. 85 (2004), *rev'd,* 439 F.3d 455 (8th Cir. 2006), 402 n.138
Robinson, Estate of, v. Commissioner, T.C. Memo. 2010-168, 356 n.155
Robinson v. Boyle, 46 AFTR2d (P-H) ¶ 80-5078 (E.D. Va. 1980), 213 n.51
Robinson v. United States, 95 Fed. Cl. 480 (2011), 271 n.44
Rock v. Dep't of Taxes, 742 A.2d 1211 (Vt. 1999), 411 n.1
Rodgers, United States v., 461 U.S. 677 (1983), 383 n.27, 393 n.84
Roschuni v. Commissioner, 44 T.C. 80 (1965), 157 n.84
Rosenman v. United States, 323 U.S. 658 (1945), 265 n.24
Roski, Estate of, v. Commissioner, 128 T.C. 113 (2007), 66 n.134
Roth v. United States, 779 F.2d 1567 (11th Cir. 1986), 417 n.30, 418 n.31
Rowe v. Commissioner, T.C. Memo. 2001-325, 90 n.56
Royal Denim for Import & Export, Inc. v. United States, 371 F. Supp. 2d 569 (S.D.N.Y. 2005), 209 n.27
Rubenstein v. Commissioner, 134 T.C. 266 (2010), 437 n.8, 444 n.43
Rule, Estate of, v. Commissioner, T.C. Memo. 2009-309, 232 n.26
Russell v. Commissioner, T.C. Memo. 2011-81, 317

Russian Recovery Fund Ltd. v. United States, 101 Fed. Cl. 498 (2011), 185 n.113, 186 n.118, 187 n.126

Ryskamp v. Commissioner, 797 F.3d 1142 (D.C. Cir. 2015), 401 n.135

S

Sala v. United States, 552 F. Supp. 2d 1167 (D. Colo. 2008), *rev'd,* 613 F.3d 1249 (10th Cir. 2010), 37 n.138

Salus Mundi Foundation v. Commissioner, 776 F.3d 1010 (9th Cir. 2014) *rev'g & rem'g* Salus Mundi Foundation v. Commissioner, T.C. Memo. 2012-61, 443 n.37

Samueli v. Commissioner, 132 T.C. 336 (2009), 171 n.5

Sarasota, Inc. v. Weaver, 2004 U.S. Dist. LEXIS 22515 (E.D. Pa. 2004), 399 n.117

Savona v. United States, 2007 U.S. Dist. LEXIS 76795 (S.D. Cal. 2007), 417 n.27

Scar v. Commissioner, 814 F.2d 1363 (9th Cir. 1987), 236 n.45

Schachter v. Commissioner, 113 T.C. 192 (1999), *aff'd,* 255 F.3d 1031 (9th Cir. 2001), *cert. denied,* 534 U.S. 826 (2001), 352 n.137

Schaeffler v. United States, 113 AFTR2d 2246 (S.D.N.Y. 2014), 355 n.151

Schell v. United States, 84 Fed. Cl. 159 (2008), *aff'd,* 589 F.3d 1378 (Fed. Cir. 2008), *cert. denied,* 562 U.S. 897 (2010), 181 n.82

Schering-Plough Corp. v. United States, 2007-2 USTC ¶50,831 (D.N.J. 2007), 38 n.143

Schirmer v. Commissioner, 89 T.C. 277 (1977), 348 n.118

Schulz v. IRS, 413 F.3d 297 (2d Cir. 2005), 115 n.45

Schussel v. Werfel, 758 F.3d 82 (1st Cir. 2014), *aff'g & rev'g,* T.C. Memo. 2013-32, 451 n.80

Schuster v. United States, 765 F.2d 1047 (11th Cir. 1985), 214 n.54

Schwartz v. Commissioner, 128 T.C. 6 (2007), 245 n.86

Schweiker v. Hansen, 450 U.S. 785 (1981), 27 n.77

SECC Corp. v. Commissioner, 142 T.C. 225 (2014), 227 n.5

Seidel, United States v., 2008 U.S. Dist. LEXIS 61799 (N.D. Cal. 2008), 423 n.63

Seneca, Ltd. v. Commissioner, 92 T.C. 363 (1989), *aff'd,* 899 F.2d 1255 (9th Cir. 1990), 176 n.46

Servants of Paraclete v. Does, 204 F.3d 1005 (10th Cir. 2000), 243 n.76

Seven- Sky v. Holder, 661 F.3d 1 (D.C. Cir. 2011), 406 n.162

Shapiro, Commissioner v., 424 U.S. 614 (1976), 210 n.32

Shapiro v. Commissioner, 73 T.C. 313 (1979), 222 n.87

Shasta Strategic Inv. Fund, LLC v. United States, 2014 WL 3852416 (N.D. Cal. 2004), 153 n.65

Shell Oil v. EPA, 950 F.2d 741 (D.C. Cir. 1991), 30 n.92

Shepard v. Commissioner, 101 F.2d 595 (7th Cir. 1939), 440 n.27

Shockley v. Commissioner, 686 F.3d 1228 (11th Cir. 2012), 447 n.57

Shockley v. Commissioner, *rev'g* T.C. Memo. 2011-96, 447 n.57

Shockley v. Commissioner, T.C. Memo. 2015-113, 443 n.37, 446 n.51, 447 n.62

Shook v. United States, 713 F.2d 662 (11th Cir. 1983), 295 n.31

Shriner, United States v., 113 AFTR2d 1360 (D. Md. 2014), 440 n.21

Sills, In re, 82 F.3d 111 (5th Cir. 1996), 386 n.43
Silverman v. Commissioner, 116 F.3d 172 (6th Cir. 1997), 87 n.48
Silverman v. Commissioner, T.C. Memo. 1996-69, *rec'd* 116 F.3d 172 (6th Cir. 1997), 84 n.36
Silverman v. Commissioner, T.C. Memo. 1996-69, *rec'd* 116 F.3d 172 (6th Cir. 1997), 83 n.35
Sim-Air, USA, Ltd v. Commissioner, 98 T.C. 187 (1992), 344 n.102
Skidmore v. Swift & Co., 323 U.S. 134 (1944), 31 n.100, 32 n.108
Sklar v. Commissioner, 549 F.3d 1252 (9th Cir. 2008), 38 n.143
Slattery, United States v., 333 F.2d 844 (3d Cir 1964), 420 n.45
Sloane v. Commissioner, T.C. Memo. 2016-115, 443 n.37
Slodav v. United States, 436 U.S. 238 (1978), 411, 418 n.34, 421
Smiley v. Citibank (South Dakota) N.A., 517 U.S. 735 (1996), 33 n.113
Smith v. Brady, 972 F.2d 1095 (9th Cir. 1992), 255 n.122
Smith v. Commissioner, 133 T.C. 424 (2009), 227 n.7
Smith v. Commissioner, 140 T.C. 48 (2013), 234 n.37
Smith v. United States, 107 AFTR2d 1228 (D. Conn. 2011), 256 n.128
Snap-Drape, Inc. v. Commissioner, 98 F.2d 194 (5th Cir. 1996), 37 n.139
Snodgrass v. United States, 834 F.2d 537 (5th Cir. 1987), 270 n.43
Snow v. Commissioner, 141 T.C. 238 (2013), 342 n.90
Snow v. Commissioner, 142 T.C. 413 (2014), 243 n.78
Snow W. Enterprises, Inc. v. Commissioner, 723 F.3d 857 (7th Cir. 2013), 243 n.78
Solheim, United States v., 91-1 U.S. Tax Cas. (CCH) ¶ 50,108 (D. Neb. 1990), *aff'd,* 953 F.2d 379 (8th Cir. 1992), 383 n.25
Sotiropoulos v. Commissioner, 142 T.C. 269 (2014), 227 n.6
Soulard, United States v., 730 F.2d 1292 (9th Cir. 1984), 352 n.139
South Carolina State Ports Auth. v. Fed. Maritime Comm'n, 243 F.3d 165 (4th Cir. 2001), *cert. denied,* 535 U.S. 743 (2002), 16 n.45
Spearing Tool & Mfg. Co., In re, 412 F.3d 653 (6th Cir. 2005), 386 n.43
Specht v. United States, 2015 WL 74539 (S.D. Ohio 2015), 329 n.47
Speltz v. Commissioner, 124 T.C. 165 (2005), *aff'd,* 454 F.3d 782 (8th Cir. 2006), 399 n.118
Spurlock v. Commissioner, 118 T.C. 155 (2002), 147 n.32
Staff IT, Inc. v. United States, 482 F.3d 792 (5th Cir. 2007), 420 n.49
Stallard v. United States, 12 F.3d 489 (5th Cir. 1994), 428 n.86, 428 n.87
Stanley v. Commissioner, 81 T.C. 634 (1983), 79 n.13
Stansbury v. Commissioner, 104 T.C. 486 (1995), *aff'd,* 102 F.3d 1088 (10th Cir. 1996), 451 n.79
Stanton, United States v., 37 AFTR2d (RIA) ¶ 76-1427 (S.D. Fla. 1976), 417 n.25
Steele v. United States, 280 F.2d 89 (8th Cir. 1960), 426 n.81
Stern, Commissioner v., 357 U.S. 39 (1958), 438 n.15
Steven N.S. Cheung, Inc. v. United States, 545 F.3d 695 (9th Cir. 2008), 373 n.73
Stevens v. Commissioner, 872 F.2d 1499 (11th Cir. 1989), 86 n.44

Stevens v. United States, 2007 WL 2556592 *amended*, 2007 WL 2688466 (N.D. Cal. 2007), 269 n.37
Stewart v. United States, 90-1 USTC (CCH) ¶ 50,002 (Cl. Ct. 1989), 417 n.29
Stiles, United States v., 114 AFTR2d 6809 (W.D. Pa. 2014), 440 n.21
Stobie Creek Inv. LLC v. United States, 82 Fed. Cl. 636 (2008), *aff'd*, 608 F.3d 1366 (Fed. Cir. 2010), 37 n.138
Stocker v. United States, 705 F.3d 225 (6th Cir. 2013), 62 n.109
Stone Canyon Partners v. Commissioner, T.C. Memo. 2007-377, 188 n.134
Stone v. White, 301 U.S. 532 (1937), 291 n.11, 292–93 n.16
Strategic Housing Finance Corp. v. United States, 608 F.3d 1317 (Fed. Cir. 2010)., 255 n.119
Strategic Housing Finance Corp. v. United States, 608 F.3d 1317 (Fed. Cir. 2010), *cert. denied*, 131 S. Ct. 1513 (2011), 271 n.46
Strategic Housing Finance Corp. v. United States, 86 Fed. Cl. 518 (2009), 255 n.119
Stuart v. Commissioner, 144 T.C. No. 235 (2015), 450 n.74
Suchar v. Commissioner, T.C. Memo. (CCH) 2005-23 (2005), 444 n.43
Sugarloaf Fund LLC v. Commissioner, 141 T.C. 214 (2013), 185 n.111
Sullivan, United States v., 274 U.S. 259 (1927), 107 n.14
Sullivan v. U.S., 618 F.2d 1001 (3d Cir. 1980), 143 n.7
Summerlin, United States v., 310 U.S. 414 (1940), 408 n.182
Summit Vineyard Holdings LLC v. Commissioner, T.C. Memo. 2015-140, 176 n.49
Superior Trading, LLC v. Commissioner, T.C. Memo. 2012-110, *aff'd*, 728 F.3d 676 (7th Cir. 2013), 243 n.75
Surowka v. United States, 909 F.2d 148 (6th Cir. 1990), 62 n.107
Swain v. Commissioner, 118 T.C. 358 (2002), 336 n.73
Sylvestre v. United States, 978 F.2d 25 (1st Cir. 1992), 119 n.57
Syring v. United States, 112 AFTR2d 4197143 (W.D. Wis. 2013), 26 n.28, 266 n.28

T

Taproot Admin. Servs., Inc. v. Commissioner, 133 T.C. 202 (2009), *aff'd*, 679 F.3d 1109 (9th Cir. 2012), 31 n.101
Tax Analysts v. IRS, 416 F. Supp. 2d 119 (D.D.C. 2006), 126 n.86
Tax Liabilities of John Does, In re, 96 AFTR 2d 6656 (N.D.N.Y. 2005), 119 n.58
Taxation with Representation Fund v. IRS, 485 F. Supp. 263 (D.D.C. 1980), *aff'd & rem'd*, 646 F.2d 666 (D.C. Cir. 1981), 125 n.81
Taylor v. Commissioner, 113 T.C. 206 (1999), *aff'd*, 9 Fed. Appx 700 (9th Cir. 2001), 353 n.141, 371 n.53
Taylor v. IRS, 69 F.3d 411 (10th Cir. 1995), 428 n.86
Terrell v. Commissioner, 625 F.3d 254 (5th Cir. 2010), 95 n.69
Testan, United States v., 424 U.S. 392 (1976), 263 n.16
Texas Heart Inst., United States v., 755 F.2d 469 (5th Cir. 1985), 117 n.51
Thomas v. Commissioner, T.C. Memo. 2013-60, 356 n.161
Thompson v. Commissioner, 137 T.C. 220 (2011), *rev'd*, 729 F.3d 869 (8th Cir. 2013), 227 n.6
Thouron, Estate of, v. United States, 752 F.3d 311 (3d Cir. 2014), 329 n.47

303 West 42nd St. Enterprises, Inc. v. IRS, 181 F.3d 272 (2d Cir. 1999), 109 n.18
Tigers Eye Trading, LLC. v. Commissioner, 138 T.C. 67 (2012), 188 n.130, 250 n.110
Tigers Eye Trading LLC v. Commissioner, T.C. Memo. 2009-121, 175 n.40
Tipton v. Commissioner, 127 T.C. 214 (2006), 96 n.79
Tooley v. Commissioner, 121 F.2d 350 (9th Cir. 1941), 438 n.9
Torrisi v. Commissioner, T.C. Memo. 2011-235, 92 n.62
Tracey v. United States, 394 B.R. 635 (1st Cir. B.A.P. 2008), 385 n.37
Trans Mississippi Corp. v. United States, 494 F.2d 770 (5th Cir. 1974), 134 n.104
Transco Exploration Co. v. Commissioner, 949 F.2d 837 (5th Cir. 1992), 25 n.72
Transpac Drilling Venture 1982- 12 v. Commissioner, 147 F.3d 221 (2d Cir. 1998), 177 n.55
Tri-State Hosp. Supply Corp. v. United States, 341 F.3d 571 (D.C. Cir. 2003), 263 n.16
Trilling, United States v., 328 F.2d 699 (7th Cir. 1964), 383 n.22
Trimble v. U.S. Dep't of Agriculture, 87 Fed. Appx. 456 (6th Cir. 2003), 391 n.69
Tucek v. Commissioner, 198 F.3d 259 (10th Cir. 1999), 183 n.93
Tyler, United States v., 528 Fed. Appx. 193 (3d Cir. 2013), 384 n.28, 439 n.17

U

Uinta Livestock Corp. v. United States, 355 F.2d 761 (10th Cir. 1966), 136 n.109
Union Pac. R. Co., Commissioner v., 86 F.2d 637 (2d Cir. 1936), 295 n.32
United States Shoe Corp., United States v., 523 U.S. 360 (1998), 3 n.2
United States v. [Party Name]. *See* [Party Name], United States v.
Upchurch v. Commissioner, T.C. Memo. 2010-169, 437 n.8
USA, LP v. Commissioner, 771 F.3d 654 (9th Cir. 2014), 174 n.35

V

Valero Energy Corp. v. United States, 569 F.3d 626 (7th Cir. 2009), 123 n.74
Validus Reins., Ltd. v. United States, 786 F.3d 1039 (D.C. Cir. 2015), 31 n.99, 32 n.109, 33 n.119
Van Arsdalen v. Commissioner, 123 T.C. 135 (2004), 96 n.79
Van Brunt v. Commissioner, T.C. Memo. 2010-220, 233 n.33
Varjabedian v. United States, 339 F. Supp. 2d 140 (D. Mass. 2004), 213 n.50, 214 n.52
Vaughn v. Rosen, 523 F.2d 1136 (D.C. Cir. 1975), 126 n.84
Verduchi, United States v., 434 F.3d 17 (1st Cir. 2006), 452 n.86
Verret v. United States, 542 F. Supp. 2d 526 (E.D. Tex. 2008), *aff'd*, 312 Fed. Appx. 615 (5th Cir. 2009), 419 n.40
Vesco v. Commissioner, 39 T.C.M. 101 (1979), 295 n.33
Viles v. Commissioner, 233 F.2d 376 (6th Cir. 1956), 439 n.17, 440 n.22
Vinatieri v. Commissioner, 133 T.C. 392 (2009), 396 n.100
Vinick v. Commissioner, 205 F.3d 1 (1st Cir. 2000), 417 n.27
Vinick v. United States, 205 F.3d 1 (1st Cir. 2000), 418 n.32
Voelker, In re, 42 F.3d 1050 (7th Cir. 1994), 389 n.58

Vons Cos., Inc. v. United States, 51 Fed. Cl. 1 (2001), 236 n.44
Voss v. Commissioner, 796 F.3d 1051 (9th Cir. 2015), 32 n.109, 42
Vulcan Oil Tech. Partners v. Commissioner, 110 T.C. 153 (1998), 183 n.93

W

Wagenet v. United States, 104 AFTR2d 7804 (C.D. Cal. 2009), 282 n.96
Walker v. United States, 650 F. Supp. 877 (E.D. Tenn. 1987), 212 n.44
Wall Indus. v. United States, 10 Cl. Ct. 82 (1986), 269 n.37
Waltner v. Commissioner, T.C. Memo. 2014-133, 163 n.113
Waterman v. United States, 113 AFTR2d 1169 (S.D. Ohio 2014), 18 n.49, 188 n.131
Webb v. United States, 850 F. Supp. 489 (E.D. Va. 1994), 275 n.61
Wehby v. Patterson, 60-2 U.S. Tax Cas. (CCH) ¶9611 (N.D. Ala. 1960), 448 n.68
Weimerskirch v. Commissioner, 596 F.2d 358 (9th Cir. 1979), 247 n.102
Weimerskirch v. Commissioner, 67 T.C. 672 (1977), 247 n.102
Weiner v. United States, 389 F.3d 152 (5th Cir. 2004), 172 n.20
Weiner v. United States, 389 F.3d 152 (5th Cir. 2004), *cert. denied,* 544 U.S. 1050 (2005), 180 n.74, 185 n.114
Weinreich, Estate of, Commissioner v., 316 F.2d 97 (9th Cir. 1963), 304 n.57
Weisbart v. U.S. Dept. of Treasury, 222 F.3d 93 (2d Cir. 2000), 272 n.5, 272 n.48, 272 n.51
Weisburn, United States v., 48 F. Supp. 393 (E.D. Pa. 1943), 439 n.20
Weisman, 102 AFTR2d 6874 (M.D. Fla. 2008), 443 n.36
Welch v. Helvering, 290 U.S. 111 (1933), 113 n.36, 246 n.93
Wellek v. United States, 324 F. Supp. 2d 905 (N.D. Ill. 2004), 206 n.6, 213 n.48
Wells Fargo & Co. v. United States, 112 AFTR2d 5380 (D. Minn. 2013), 117 n.54
Wells Fargo & Co. v. United States, 117 Fed. Cl. 30 (2014), 375 n.81
Wendland v. Commissioner, 728 F.2d 1249 (9th Cir. 1984), *cert. denied,* 469 U.S. 1034 (1984), 28 n.80
Wendland v. Commissioner, 79 T.C. 355 (1982), *aff'd,* 739 F.2d 580 (11th Cir. 1984), 28 n.80
Westaire Properties, Inc. v. Tucker, 89-2 U.S. Tax Cas. (CCH) ¶9473 (S.D. Cal. 1989), 391 n.68
Wetzel v. United States, 802 F. Supp. 1451 (S.D. Miss. 1992), 411
Wheeler v. Commissioner, 127 T.C. 200 (2006), *aff'd,* 521 F.3d 1289 (10th Cir. 2008), 336 n.72
Whelco Industrial, Ltd. v. United States, 526 F. Supp. 2d 819 (N.D. Ohio 2007), 442 n.32
White & Case v. United States, 22 Cl. Ct. 734 (1991), 179 n.69
Whitehouse Hotel Ltd. Partnership v. Commissioner, 755 F.3d 236 (5th Cir. 2014), 356 n.160
Whiting Pools, Inc., United States v., 462 U.S. 198 (1983), 405 n.156
Whitney v. United States, 826 F.2d 896 (9th Cir. 1987), 137 n.110
Wichita Terminal Electric Co. v. Commissioner, 162 F.2d 513 (10th Cir. 1947), 241 n.67
Wichita Terminal Electric Co. v. Commissioner, 6 T.C. 1158 (1946), 241 n.67
Williams, United States v., 489 Fed. Appx. 655 (4th Cir. 2012), 73 n.175

Williams, United States v., 514 U.S. 527 (1995), 270–71, 403 n.145
Williams-Russell & Johnson v. United States, 371 F.3d 1350 (11th Cir. 2004), 264 n.21
Williams v. Commissioner, 92 T.C. 920 (1989), 217 n.62
Williams v. Commissioner, 131 T.C. 54 (2008), 370 n.49
Williams v. Commissioner, 1993 U.S. App. LEXIS 34203 (9th Cir. 1993), 240 n.64
Williams v. United States, 947 F.2d 37 (2d Cir. 1991), 403 n.147
Williams v. United States, 939 F.2d 915 (11th Cir. 1991), 415 n.15
Wilshire, Estate of, v. United States, 2008 U.S. Dist. LEXIS 91920 (S.D. Ohio 2008), 269 n.37
Wilson v. Commissioner, 705 F.3d 980 (9th Cir. 2013), 95 n.71
Wilson v. Commissioner, T.C. Memo. 2007-127, 88 n.49
Wind Energy Tech. Assocs. III v. Commissioner, 94 T.C. 787 (1990), 179 n.71
Windsor, United States v., 133 S. Ct. 2675 (2013), 50 n.33, 79 n.9
Winnett v. Commissioner, 96 T.C. 802 (1991), 148 n.36, 148 n.37
Winter v. Commissioner, 135 T.C. 238 (2010), 144 n.14
Winter v. Commissioner, 135 T.C. 238 (2012), 189 n.139
Winter v. United States, 196 F.3d 339 (2d Cir. 1999), 420 n.45
Wise Guys Holdings, LLC v. Commissioner, 140 T.C. 193 (2013), 180 n.75
Wolpaw v. Commissioner, 47 F.3d 787 (6th Cir. 1995), 25 n.72
Wood, Estate of, v. Commissioner, 909 F.2d 1155 (8th Cir. 1990), 62 n.107
Woodard v. Commissioner, T.C. Summary Op. 2009-150, 354 n.147
Woods, United States v., 134 S. Ct. 557 (2013), 6 n.9, 173 n.33, 175 n.39, 193 n.3, 349 n.128
Wright v. Commissioner, 571 F.3d 215 (2d Cir. 2009), 377 n.93
Wright v. Commissioner, 84 T.C. 636 (1985), 164 n.117, 354 n.143
Wrightsman Petroleum Co. v. United States, 35 F. Supp. 86 (Ct. Cl. 1940), *cert. denied,* 313 U.S. 578 (1941), 271 n.45

Y

Yagoda v. Commissioner, 39 T.C. 170 (1962), *aff'd,* 331 F.2d 485 (2d Cir. 1964), 304–5, 304 n.58, 305 n.59, 450 n.75

Z

Zackim v. Commissioner, 887 F.2d 455 (3d Cir. 1989), *rev'g* 91 T.C. 1001 (1988), 235 n.41
Zedner v. United States, 547 U.S. 489 (2006), 296 n.35
Zolla, United States v., 724 F.2d 808 (9th Cir. 1984), 231 n.25

Table of Statutes

One asterisk (*) indicates sections of I.R.C. and Regulations before BBA. Two asterisks (**) indicate sections of I.R.C. and Regulations revised by BBA as amended. See page number for complete citation.

ACT OF MARCH 3, 1863 . . . 397 n.104

ADMINISTRATIVE PROCEDURE ACT (ADA) . . . 28, 201, 227 n.5, 236, 254–55

ALL WRITS ACT . . . 393

AMERICAN JOBS CREATION ACT OF 2004
generally . . . 66–67
Section
812(a) . . . 357
814 . . . 160–61
903(a) . . . 369 n.43

ANTI-INJUNCTION ACT (IRC § 7421) . . . 28 n.82, 121 n.64, 145 n.20, 197, 210, 406, 406 n.165, 438

BANKRUPTCY ABUSE PREVENTION AND CONSUMER PROTECTON ACT OF 2005 . . . 19 n.56

BIPARTISAN BUDGET ACT OF 2015 (BBA)
generally . . . 14, 170, 193–94, 195–96, 198–201, 367 n.29
Section
1101(d) . . . 200 n.56
1101(g)(1) (not codified) . . . 194 n.5
1101(g)(4) (not codified) . . . 194 n.6
6231 to 6235 . . . 197–98

BULK SALES ACT . . . 441, 442 n.31

CODE OF FEDERAL REGULATIONS (C.F.R.)
Title 26 . . . 21
Title 31
§ 10.22 . . . 115 n.44
§ 1010.350 . . . 73 n.175
pt. 10 . . . 11 n.28
subtitle A, pt. 10 . . . 68 n.148
Title 31 (former)
§§ 10.4(c), 10.5(b), 10.6(d)(6) & (e)(3) . . . 69 n.150

COLORADO REVISED STATUTES . . . 411 n.1

CONSOLIDATED APPROPRIATIONS ACT OF 2016 . . . 342 n.91

CRIME CONTROL ACT OF 1990 . . . 442 n.34

CURRENCY AND FOREIGN TRANSACTIONS REPORTING ACT . . . 43 n.1, 73 n.175

DECLARATORY JUDGMENT ACT... 406 n.160

DEFENSE OF MARRIAGE ACT (DOMA)...50 n.33

DEFICIT REDUCTION ACT OF 1984... 279 n.80

E-GOVERNMENT ACT OF 2002...237 n.55

EMERGENCY ECONOMIC STABILIZATION ACT OF 2008...70 n.159

ENERGY IMPROVEMENT AND EXTENSION ACT OF 2008...56 n.72

EQUAL ACCESS TO JUSTICE ACT (EAJA)...255

FEDERAL COURTS IMPROVEMENT ACT OF 1982...18

FEDERAL DEBT COLLECTION PROCEDURES ACT OF 1990...279 n.83, 442–43

FEDERAL INSURANCE CONTRIBUTION ACT (FICA)...413–14

FEDERAL TAX LIEN ACT OF 1966... 387–88

FEDERAL TORT CLAIMS ACT (FTCA)... 406–7, 407 n.166

FEDERAL UNEMPLOYMENT TAX ACT (FUTA)...414

FOREIGN ACCOUNT TAX COMPLIANCE ACT (FATCA) OF 2010... 73–74

HEALTH CARE AND EDUCATION AFFORDABILITY RECONCILIATION ACT OF 2010...360 n.180

HIRING INCENTIVES TO RESTORE EMPLOYMENT (HIRE) ACT OF 2010...74 n.176

HOUSING ASSISTANCE TAX ACT OF 2008...56 n.71

INTERNAL REVENUE CODE (I.R.C.)
generally...4, 5
Section
11**...195 n.8
31...412 n.6
61(a)(4)...363 n.2, 363 n.4
63(c)...50 n.31
63(c)(4)...50 n.31
66...98–99
73(c)....382 n.15
151(d)(4)...50 n.31
170(a)(1)...49 n.28
170(b)...50 n.32
170(f)(8)...49 n.28
172...275 n.58
183(e)...161
213(b)(4)....143 n.13
267(b)...359, 370
274(d)...48, 246 n.97
446(b)...7
482...348 n.121
501(c)(3)...219
507(b)(2) & (c)...441 n.29
513(a)...63 n.111
513(b)...63 n.111
552(a), (b), (c)...126
552(b)(3), (5), (7)...126
701(a)(36)(A)...70 n.156
701(a)(36)(B)...70 n.156
702(c)...155 n.74, 157 n.84
707(b)(1)...359, 370
754*...173
761(a)*...178

771* to 776* . . . 169
775(a)(1)(A)* . . . 169 n.2
775(a)* . . . 171 n.7
775(b)(2)* . . . 171 n.7
871 . . . 120 n.60
881 . . . 120 n.60
905(c)(1) . . . 227 n.6
982 . . . 121
1014(f) . . . 294 n.27, 340, 340 n.79
1101(f)(9)(g)** . . . 367 n.29
1212 . . . 275 n.59
1274(d)(1)(C)(i) . . . 365 n.18
1291 to 1298 . . . 220
1294(c)(3) . . . 220 n.76
1311 . . . 298
1311 to 1314 . . . 263 n.15, 276 n.64, 296–98
1311(a) . . . 298, 298 n.46
1311(b) . . . 301, 302, 303
1311(b)(1) . . . 304–5, 306
1311(b)(1)(B) . . . 303
1311(b)(2) . . . 297 n.42, 298 n.45, 305–7
1311(b)(2)(A) . . . 306 n.60
1311(b)(2)(B) . . . 306 n.61
1311(b)(3) . . . 298, 307 n.63
1312 . . . 298
1312(1) . . . 301
1312(3)(A) . . . 302
1312(3)(B) . . . 297 n.41, 302, 306
1312(7) . . . 307
1312(7)(A) . . . 303
1312(7)(B), (C) . . . 302–3
1313(a) . . . 298, 298 n.46
1313(a)(2) to (4) . . . 299 n.49
1313(a)(3) . . . 300 n.52
1313(a)(4) . . . 300
1313(b)(3) . . . 307
1313(c) . . . 298, 307
1314(a) . . . 308 n.64
1314(b) . . . 297 n.39, 303 n.55
1366(c) . . . 157 n.84
2001(a) . . . 51 n.38, 51 n.40
2001(c) . . . 52 n.47
2002(b) . . . 52 n.47
2007 . . . 51 n.41
2010(c) . . . 51 n.43
2101– 2108 . . . 52 n.46
2103 . . . 51 n.44
2106 . . . 51 n.40, 51 n.44
2201– 2202 . . . 406 n.160
2203 . . . 438 n.14
2204(a), (b) . . . 438
2503(b)(1), (2) . . . 52 n.50
2503(e) . . . 52 n.51
2523(a) . . . 53 n.52
2523(b) . . . 53 n.52
26511(a) . . . 271
26511(b)(2) . . . 271
3102(f) . . . 414 n.12
3401to 3406 . . . 261 n.1
3505(a), (b) . . . 413 n.10
4955 . . . 219
6001 . . . 48, 118 n.55
6011 . . . 68, 161
6011(e) . . . 46 n.12
6011(e)(3) . . . 46 n.12
6011(e)(3)(B) . . . 46 n.14
6011(a) . . . 118 n.55
6012 . . . 161
6012(a) . . . 49
6012(a)(1) . . . 49–50
6013 . . . 50
6013(a) . . . 79 n.10
6013(a)(1) . . . 51 n.36
6013(b) . . . 79 n.10
6013(c) . . . 51 n.35
6013(d)(1) . . . 50 n.34
6013(d)(3) . . . 50, 56 n.73, 57 n.81, 79
6013(g) . . . 51
6013(h) . . . 51 n.37
6015 . . . 50, 77–78, 80–82, 96, 98–99, 99, 226
6015(b) . . . 83 n.32
6015(b)(1)(B) . . . 83–84
6015(b)(1)(C) . . . 436 n.2
6015(b) . . . 78, 81
6015(c) . . . 78, 87, 90, 91
6015(c)(2) . . . 90 n.58

6015(c)(3)(A)(ii)...436 n.2
6015(c)(3)(C), (c)(4)...436 n.2
6015(e)...94 n.67
6015(e)(1)...80 n.19, 98 n.86, 98 n.87
6015(e)(2)...98 n.88, 407 n.174
6015(e)(2)....81 n.19
6015(f)...78, 78 n.5, 82, 83, 92–94
6018(a)(1)...51 n.42
6018(a)(2)...52 n.48
6018(a)(3)...52 n.49
6019...52–53
6019(3)...53 n.53
6020(a)...146 n.24
6020(a)...59
6020(b)...59, 147
6031...60 n.93
6031– 6039J...44, 53–54
6034A(c)(5)...345 n.104
6035...294 n.27
6037(c)(5)...345 n.104
6038(c)...54 n.56
6038D...74
6039E...53 n.55
6039G...53 n.55
6041– 6050W...44, 47, 54–55
6042...54 n.58
6045(e)...54 n.62
6045(e)(2)...54 n.61
6045(f)...54 n.62
6045A...56 n.72
6050A...54 n.59
6050I...54
6050I(f)...55
6050N...54 n.60
6050W...56, 56 n.71
6051– 6053...47
6055– 6056...44
6061...147 n.26
6061(a)...56
6061(b)...57 n.76
6062...57 n.77
6063...57 n.78
6064...147 n.26
6065...56 n.74, 146 n.24, 146 n.25, 147 n.26
6072...149 n.45
6072(a)...59 n.88, 365 n.12
6072(b)...59 n.89
6075(a)...61 n.99, 149 n.45
6075(b)(1)...61 n.101
6075(b)(2)...61 n.102
6081...365 n.13
6081(b)...65 n.124
6091(b)...148 n.36, 208 n.20
6103...71–72
6103(a)...71
6103(e)(8)...97–98
6103(h)(3)(B)...123 n.70
6103(p)(3)...71 n.166
6110(k)(3)...25
6111...368 n.40
6111(b)(1)...66 n.139
6111(b)(1)(A)...66 n.136
6111(b)(1)(B)...66 n.137
6112...66 n.139
6151...325
6151(a)...364 n.11
6151(c)...63 n.111
6159...66 n.136, 396–97
6159(c)...397
6161...65, 365 n.14
6161(a)...65 n.129, 407
6161(b)(1)...65 n.130
6163(a)...66 n.132
6163(b)...66 n.133
6164...275 n.58
6164(a)...220
6164(h)...220 n.75
6166...407
6166(a)...66 n.134
6201(a)...115, 381 n.12
6201(a)(1)...143 n.12, 334
6201(c)...382 n.15
6201(d)...117–18
6201(e)...144 n.16
6204(a)...381 n.11
621(a)(1)...373 n.73

6211 . . . 147, 228
6211– 6213 . . . 158 n.89
6211(a) . . . 229
6211(b)(1) . . . 208
6211– 6213 . . . 136, 137
6212 . . . 228, 228 n.9, 232
6212(b) . . . 230 n.17, 437
6212(b)(2) . . . 230 n.16
6212(c) . . . 235 n.41
6212(d) . . . 228 n.8
6213 . . . 377 n.92
6213(a) . . . 145, 216, 228 n.10, 232 n.27, 233, 366–67, 376 n.87
6213(a), (b) . . . 205
6213(a), (c) . . . 145 n.21
6213(b) . . . 381 n.12
6213(b)(1), (2) . . . 282–84
6213(b)(1), (g)(2) . . . 144 n.14
6213(b)(3) . . . 265 n.26
6213(b)(4) . . . 334
6213(d) . . . 145 n.19, 441
6213(d). . . . 144 n.15
6213(f)(1) . . . 234 n.35, 235
6213(h)(2) . . . 227 n.6
6214(a) . . . 235 n. 40, 376 n.87
6214(b) (amended) . . . 251 n.111
6215 . . . 376 n.89
6215(d) . . . 230 n.16
6221* . . . 171–72, 175 n.41, 182 n.89
6221(a)** . . . 195 n.7
6221(b)(1)(A)**, (B)**, (C)** . . . 196 n.17
6221(b)(1)(D)(i)** . . . 196 n.18
6221(b)(1)(D)(ii)** . . . 196 n.19
6221(b)(1)(E)** . . . 196 n.20
6221(b)(2)(A)** . . . 196 n.21
6221(b)(2)(B)**, (C)** . . . 196 n.22
6222* . . . 171 n.10, 175
6222(a)* . . . 175 n.41
6222(a)** . . . 199 n.46
6222(b)* . . . 175 n.42
6222(b)** . . . 199 n.47
6222(c)(1)**, (2)** . . . 199 n.49
6222(c)* . . . 175 n.43
6222(d) . . . 345 n.104
6222(e)** . . . 199 n.48
6223*– 6225* . . . 171 n.11
6223(a)(1)* . . . 178 n.60
6223(a)** . . . 197 n. 24, 197 n.25, 197 n.27
6223(b)(1)**, (2)** . . . 197 n.25
6223(b)* . . . 178 n.64, 197 n.24
6223(c)(3)* . . . 179 n.68
6223(d)(1)* . . . 179 n.69
6223(e)(2)* . . . 179 n.73
6223(e)(3)* . . . 179 n.72
6223(f)* . . . 180 n.75
6223(g)* . . . 176 n.47
6223(h)* . . . 179 n.67
6223** . . . 195 n.7
6224(a)* . . . 180 n.77
6224(c) . . . 367
6224(c)(2)* . . . 182 n.91
6224(c)(3)* . . . 176 n.48
6225(a)(1)** . . . 195 n.9
6225(a)(2)** . . . 195 n.9
6225(a)* . . . 179 n.70, 184 n.106
6225(b)(1)(a)** . . . 195 n.10
6225(c)** . . . 196 n.13
6225(d)(1)** . . . 195 n.11
6225(d)(2)** . . . 195 n.12
6226* . . . 171 n.12, 180, 184 n.106
6226(a)* . . . 176 n.50, 182 n.92, 183 n.95
6226(a)** . . . 196 n.15
6226(a)(1) . . . 283 n.107
6226(a)(2)* . . . 183 n.95
6226(b)* . . . 184 n.103
6226(b)(1)* . . . 182 n.92, 183 n.96
6226(b)(2)*, (4)* . . . 184 n.104
6226(b)(3)* . . . 184 n.105
6226(b)**, (c)** . . . 196 n.14
6226(c)* . . . 185 n.111
6226(d)* . . . 185 n.111
6226(e)(1)* . . . 184 n.100
6226(e)(3)* . . . 184 n.101
6226(e)* . . . 183 n.99, 185 n.112
6226(f)* . . . 183 n.97
6227* . . . 171 n.5

6227(a) . . . 283 n.106
6227(a)(2)* . . . 185 n.109
6227(a)** . . . 198 n.41
6227(b)** . . . 198 n.42
6227(c) . . . 283 n.109
6227(c)** . . . 199 n.43
6227(c)(1) . . . 283 n.110, 284 n.111
6227(c)(2)(A)(ii) . . . 284 n.113
6227(c)(2)(A)(iii). . . . 284 n.115
6227(c)(2)(A). . . . 283 n.108
6227(d)(2) . . . 284 n.112
6227(d)(4) . . . 284 n.113
6228* . . . 171 n.5
6228(a)(1) . . . 284 n.116
6228(a)(1)(B) . . . 284 n.114
6228(a)(1)* . . . 176 n.51
6228(a)(2) . . . 284 n.117
6228(a)(4) . . . 284 n.118
6228(b)* . . . 185 n.110
6229(a)* . . . 179 n.70, 185–86, 185 n.114, 187
6229(b)* . . . 176 n.49, 186 n.119
6229(b)(3)* . . . 187
6229(c)(1)* . . . 186 n.120
6229(c)(2)* . . . 186 n.121
6229(c)(3)* . . . 186 n.122
6229(c)(4)* . . . 186 n.123
6229(d)* . . . 187 n.127
6229(e)* . . . 188 n.128
6229* . . . 160, 171 n.13, 186–87
6230* . . . 171 n.11
6230(a)(1)* . . . 181 n.85
6230(a)(2)(A)(i)* . . . 182 n.87
6230(b)(1) . . . 284 n.111
6230(b)(1)* . . . 174 n.35
6230(c)(1)(A)(ii)*, (2)(A)* . . . 185 n.110
6230(c)* . . . 185 n.110
6230(e)* . . . 177 n.52
6231* . . . 175 n.41
6231(a)** . . . 197 n.28
6231(a)(1)(B) . . . 60 n.93
6231(a)(1)(B)(i)* . . . 177 n.56, 196 n.23
6231(a)(2)(B)* . . . 178 n.65
6231(a)(3) . . . 290 n.10
6231(a)(3)* . . . 172 n.14
6231(a)(4)* . . . 172 n.16
6231(a)(5)* . . . 172 n.17, 181 n.84
6231(a)(6)* . . . 181 n.83
6231(a)(7)(B)* . . . 177 n.54
6231(a)(9)*, (10)* . . . 178 n.66
6231(b)** . . . 197 n.29
6231(b)(1)(C)* . . . 181 n.82
6231(c)* . . . 177 n.55
6231(c)** . . . 197 n.30
6231(g)* . . . 178 n.59
6232(a)** . . . 197 n.31, 199 n.44
6232(b)** . . . 197 n.32
6232(c)** . . . 197 n.34
6232(d)** . . . 197 n.33
6233* . . . 170 n.4, 178 n.59
6234* . . . 174 n.34
6234(a)* . . . 174 n.34
6234(a)** . . . 198 n.35
6234(b)** . . . 198 n.36
6234(c)**, (d)** . . . 198 n.37
6234(e)** . . . 198 n.37
6234(g)(1)* . . . 174 n.34
6235(a)(1)** . . . 198 n.38
6235(a)(2)**, (3)** . . . 198 n.40
6235(b)**, (c)**, (d)** . . . 198 n.39
6240(b)(2)* . . . 171 n.9
6240*– 6255* . . . 169, 171
6241(3)** . . . 199 n.53
6241(4)** . . . 199 n.50
6241(6)(A)** & (B)** . . . 200 n.55
6241(7)** . . . 199 n.51
6241(8)** . . . 199 n.52
6255(a)* . . . 171 n.7
6303 . . . 366 n.25
6303(a) . . . 230 n.17, 376 n.90, 380, 382 n.18
6305 . . . 279 n.82
6315 . . . 261 n.2, 265 n.23
6320 . . . 226, 334 n.68
6320—6330 . . . 217
6320(a)(2)(C) . . . 230 n.17
6320(e)(1) . . . 407 n.173
6321 . . . 383–85

6322 . . . 382
6323(a) . . . 387
6323(b) . . . 387–88
6323(c) . . . 388
6323(f) . . . 385–86
6324 . . . 441–42
6324(a) . . . 384 n.30, 450 n.76
6324(a)(2) . . . 437, 441
6324(b) . . . 384 n.31, 441
6324A . . . 384 n.32
6324B . . . 384 n.33
6325 . . . 395–96
6325(b) . . . 403
6325(j) . . . 396
6330 . . . 226, 334 n.68
6330(a)(1) . . . 400 n.127
6330(a)(2)(C) . . . 230 n.17
6330(a)(3)(B) . . . 401 n.128
6330(c)(2) . . . 401 n.132
6330(c)(2)(B) . . . 262 n.8, 262 n.9
6330(d) . . . 425 n.77
6330(d)(1) . . . 401 n.133
6330(e) . . . 80–81 n.19
6330(e)(1) . . . 407 n.173, 429 n.93
6330(f) . . . 208 n.19, 401 n.130
6330(g) . . . 401 n.135
6331(a) . . . 208, 389
6331(b) . . . 389
6331(d) . . . 380
6331(d)(2)(C) . . . 230 n.17
6331(e), (h) . . . 389 n.57
6331(f) . . . 389 n.60
6331(i)(5) . . . 407 n.172, 429 n.94
6331(i)– (k) . . . 389 n.59
6331(k)(1) . . . 407 n.172
6331(k)(2) . . . 407 n.175
6331(k)(3) . . . 429 n.92
6332(c) . . . 390 n.66
6332(d) . . . 390 n.64
6332(e) . . . 390 n.65
6333 . . . 394
6334 . . . 389 n.58
6335 . . . 391
6335(a), (b) . . . 230 n.17
6335(f) . . . 392 n.77
6336 . . . 392 n.79
6337 . . . 392 n.80
6342 . . . 391 n.71
6343 . . . 396
6401 . . . 264 n.21
6401(a) . . . 264 n.21, 294 n.22, 294 n.23
6401(b) . . . 63 n.117, 261 n.1
6402 . . . 63 n.118, 81 n.26, 263 n.18, 373 n.68
6402(a) . . . 270–71, 278–79
6402(b) . . . 261 n.4
6402(c) . . . 279 n.79
6402(d) . . . 279 n.80
6402(d)(3)(D) . . . 279 n.84
6402(e) . . . 279 n.81
6402(f) (amended) . . . 279 n.84
6402(g) . . . 280 n.86
6404 . . . 226
6404(b) . . . 215
6404(e) . . . 369 n.41
6404(e)(1) . . . 370, 370 n.52
6404(f) . . . 371
6404(g) . . . 367–68
6404(g)(2) . . . 368
6404(g)(2)(C) . . . 368 n.38
6404(g)(3)(B) . . . 367 n.31
6404(h)(2)(A) . . . 377 n.92
6404(h)(2)(c) . . . 372 n.61
6405(a) . . . 4
6411(b) . . . 285 n.119
6416 . . . 264 n.20
6501 . . . 208, 298 n.44, 383, 407, 447
6501(a) . . . 48 n.23, 113, 273 n.53, 289 n.5
6501(a)* . . . 185 n.114, 186
6501(b) . . . 150 n.47
6501(b)(1) . . . 48 n.22, 63 n.111, 289 n.5
6501(b)(2) . . . 428 n.88
6501(b)(3) . . . 147 n.28
6501(c) . . . 153, 164 n.117
6501(c)(1) . . . 157 n.85, 157 n.86, 162, 164, 290 n.9
6501(c)(10) . . . 160–61

6501(c)(4) . . . 152 n.61, 153 n.62, 289 n.6, 428 n.91
6501(c)(4)(B) . . . 113 n.35
6501(c)(4)* . . . 186 n.119, 187
6501(c)(8) . . . 161 n.106
6501(c)(9) . . . 162 n.107
6501(d) . . . 110 n.28
6501(e) . . . 153, 289 n.7, 353 n.142, 368
6501(e)(1)(B) . . . 154
6501(e)(1)(B)(i) . . . 154, 155–56
6501(e)(1)(B)(ii) . . . 154, 154 n.69
6501(e)(1)(B)(ii)(I) . . . 154 n.69
6501(e)(2) . . . 153 n.66, 154 n.66
6501(e)(3) . . . 153 n.66, 154 n.66
6502 . . . 82, 383, 428 n.89
6502(a)(1) . . . 407
6503 . . . 158–59, 252 n.113, 253 n.117, 407, 447
6503(a) . . . 232 n.30, 289 n.8
6503(a)(1) . . . 447 n.57
6503(b) . . . 407 n.176
6503(c) . . . 407 n.177
6503(d) . . . 407 n.178
6503(h) . . . 159 n.92, 159 n.93, 407 n.171
6503(j) . . . 116 n.46, 160
6503(j)(2) . . . 160 n.96
6511 . . . 82, 273, 298 n.44, 383
6511(a) . . . 262 n.10, 271 n.46, 273 n.54, 276–77, 289 n.1, 373–74
6511(a)* . . . 184 n.107
6511(b) . . . 276 n.65
6511(b)(2) . . . 276–78
6511(b)(2)(B) . . . 277–78 n.74
6511(c) . . . 263 n.13, 289 n.2
6511(c)(1) . . . 273–74 n.55, 275 n.60
6511(d) . . . 263 n.12
6511(d)(1) . . . 274 n.57, 289 n.3
6511(d)(2) . . . 289 n.4
6511(d)(2)(A) . . . 275 n.60
6511(d)(4)(C) . . . 366 n.26
6511(h) . . . 263 n.14, 275 n.61, 276 n.63
6512 . . . 280 n.88, 298
6512(b) . . . 263 n.17, 376 n.88
6512(b)(2) . . . 281 n.89, 376 n.88
6513(a) . . . 272 n.49, 276 n.69
6513(b) . . . 272 n.50, 277 n.71
6514(a) . . . 271 n.47
6515 . . . 82
6515(b) . . . 82–83
6515(c) . . . 83
6521 . . . 296 n.37
6532 . . . 426 n.82
6532(a)* . . . 184 n.108
6532(a)(1) . . . 281 n.95, 282 n.96
6532(a)(2) . . . 282 n.99
6532(b) . . . 271 n.47
6532(c) . . . 403 n.147
6601 . . . 335 n.71, 450
6601(a) . . . 363 n.1
6601(a), (b)(1) . . . 372 n.63
6601(b)(1) . . . 325 n.32, 365 n.14
6601(b)(1), (2) . . . 397 n.101
6601(c) . . . 136, 364 n.7, 367 n.28
6601(d)(1), (3) . . . 366 n.27
6601(d)(3)(B) . . . 366 n.26
6601(e) . . . 144 n.17
6601(e)(1) . . . 152 n.59, 229, 376 n.91
6601(e)(2)(A) . . . 372 n.65, 415 n.15
6601(e)(2)(B) . . . 372 n.63
6601(e)(3) . . . 372 n.64, 372 n.66
6601(g) . . . 152 n.59, 381 n.14
6601(j) . . . 364 n.8
6601(j) 366 n.23
6603 . . . 265–66, 369–70
6603(a) . . . 369
6603(b) . . . 369
6603(c) . . . 369
6603(d) . . . 369
6603(d)(2), (3), (4) . . . 369
6604 . . . 382
6611(a) . . . 363 n.2
6611(b)(2) . . . 373 n.69
6611(b)(3) . . . 374 n.79
6611(d) . . . 373 n.70
6611(e)(1) . . . 374 n.77
6611(e)(2) . . . 374 n.78
6611(f) . . . 364 n.5, 375 n.84
6611(f)(4)(B) . . . 375 n.85

6611(g) . . . 374 n.80
6612(a) . . . 229–30
6621 . . . 450
6621(a) . . . 365 n.16
6621(a)(1) . . . 373 n.71
6621(b) . . . 369
6621(b)(1) . . . 365 n.17
6621(b)(2)(B)(ii) . . . 365 n.22
6621(b)(3) . . . 365 n.18
6621(c) . . . 365 n.21
6621(c)(3)(A) . . . 365 n.20
6621(d) . . . 375 n.83
6622 . . . 365 n.19, 373 n.72, 373 n.74
6622(b) . . . 320 n.9
6651 . . . 368, 381–82
6651(a) . . . 420 n.44
6651(a)(1) . . . 323 n.23, 323 n.24, 372
6651(a)(1), (2) . . . 65, 327–28
6651(a)(1), (b)(1) . . . 328 n.40
6651(a)(2) . . . 64–65, 147, 326, 368 n.38
6651(a)(2), (3) . . . 327
6651(a)(2), (b)(2) . . . 328 n.41
6651(a)(3) . . . 326
6651(b) . . . 324 n.27
6651(b)(1) . . . 324 n.28
6651(c)(1) . . . 328 n.39
6651(d). . . . 326 n.35
6651(f) . . . 323 n.25, 324–25
6651(h) . . . 326 n.34
6652 . . . 54
6653 . . . 372
6654(a)(1) . . . 320
6654(b) . . . 320 n.10
6654(c) . . . 319 n.7
6654(d)(1)(B)(i) . . . 318 n.4
6654(d)(1)(B)(ii) . . . 321 n.14
6654(d)(2) . . . 321
6654(e) . . . 320 n.8
6654(e)(3)(A) . . . 321
6654(e)(3)(B) . . . 321–22
6654(g) . . . 320 n.11
6656 . . . 420 n.44
6656(a) . . . 414 n.13
6658(a) . . . 326 n.33
6662 . . . 154 n.69, 339, 340–41, 372
6662(b) . . . 339–40, 358 n.171
6662(b)(1) . . . 343, 343 n.95
6662(b)(1)* . . . 175
6662(b)(6) . . . 360
6662(b)(8) . . . 294 n.27
6662(c) . . . 344 n.103
6662(d)(1) . . . 358
6662(d)(1)(A) . . . 346 n.113
6662(d)(1)(B) . . . 346 n.113
6662(d)(2) . . . 358
6662(d)(2)(A) . . . 83 n.33, 346 n.112
6662(d)(2)(C) . . . 285 n.125
6662(d)(2)(C)(ii) . . . 347 n.117
6662(e) . . . 348–49
6662(e)(1) . . . 348 n.124
6662(f) . . . 348 n.121
6662(g) . . . 350
6662(h) . . . 340 n.80, 350, 368
6662(i) . . . 340 n.81
6662(j) . . . 340 n.82
6662(k) . . . 294 n.27, 340 n.79
6662A . . . 67, 357 n.166
6662A(b)(1) . . . 358 n.169
6662A(b)(2) . . . 67 n.142
6662A(c) . . . 67 n.143, 358 n.168
6662A(e)(1) . . . 358 n.172
6662A(e)(2)(A) . . . 358 n.173
6662A(e)(3) . . . 358 n.170
6663 . . . 157 n.86, 324 n.29, 350 n.132, 372
6663(a) . . . 350–51
6664 . . . 349, 354
6664(a) . . . 341–42, 342 n.92
6664(b) . . . 341 n.87
6664(c)(2) . . . 340 n.78
6664(c)(3) . . . 357 n.163
6664(d) . . . 358 n.167
6664(d)(1) . . . 359 n.174, 368
6664(d)(3)(A) . . . 67 n.143
6664(d)(4)(A) . . . 359 n.175
6664(d)(4)(B) . . . 359 n.176
6664(d)(4)(B)(ii) . . . 359 n.177
6664(d)(4)(B)(iii) . . . 360 n.179

6665(a) . . . 152 n.59, 339 n.75
6665(a)(1) . . . 381 n.13
6665(a), (b) . . . 229 n.12
6665(b) . . . 144 n.16, 334 n.65
6671 . . . 152 n.59
6671(a) . . . 144 n.16, 381 n.13, 423 n.61
6671(b) . . . 415 n.18
6672 . . . 64 n.119, 226, 282, 393, 411–13, 418–19
6672(a) . . . 423 n.65, 436 n.3
6672(b) . . . 230 n.17
6672(b)(1) . . . 423 n.62
6672(b)(3) . . . 428–29, 428 n.87
6672(c) . . . 282 n.103, 423 n.69, 427–28
6672(c)(1) . . . 426 n.81
6672(c)(4) . . . 429 n.94
6672(d) . . . 430
6673 . . . 256 n.127, 333
6673(a)(2) . . . 257
6674 . . . 118
6676 . . . 285
6676(a), (b) . . . 285 n.124
6676(c) . . . 285 n.126
6694 . . . 70
6694(a) . . . 69, 152 n.60
6694(a)(2)(C) . . . 285 n.125
6694(b) . . . 69, 152 n.60
6695 . . . 69 n.155, 152 n.60
6698 . . . 54 n.57, 60 n.93
6698(a) . . . 60 n.93
6699 . . . 54 n.57
6700 . . . 152 n.60
6701 . . . 152 n.60, 351–52
6701(b) . . . 47 n.15
6702 . . . 149 n.42
6702(a) . . . 149 n.45
6702(b), (c) . . . 401 n.135
6707 . . . 368 n.40
6707(A) . . . 368 n.40
6707(a) . . . 227 n.7
6707A . . . 67
6707A(c) . . . 368
6721(a) . . . 55 n.64
6721(d) . . . 55 n.65
6721– 6724 . . . 55
6724(a) . . . 55 n.66
6851 . . . 204, 205, 209–10
6851(a)(1) . . . 205, 207 n.13, 207 n.16
6851(a)(3) . . . 208 n.24
6851(b) . . . 208
6851(d)(1) . . . 218 n.65
6851(d)(2) . . . 218 n.67
6851(e) . . . 209
6852(a) . . . 219
6852(a)(4) . . . 219 n.72
6852(b)(1) . . . 219 n.71
6852(b)(2) . . . 219 n.74
6861 . . . 206
6861(a) . . . 205, 209 n.26
6861(c)–(g) . . . 209 n.25
6861(g) . . . 210 n.30
6862 . . . 206
6862(a) . . . 205, 209 n.26
6863 . . . 215
6863(a) . . . 215 n.56, 219 n.74
6863(a), (b)(2) . . . 215 n.58
6863(b) . . . 215 n.57
6863(b)(3) . . . 217 n.61, 392 n.78
6863(c) . . . 216 n.59, 217 n.61
6863(c)(3)(A) . . . 216 n.60
6864 . . . 220 n.75
6867 . . . 221
6867(a) . . . 221 n.81
6867(b) . . . 221 n.82
6867(b)(3) . . . 221 n.84
6867(c) . . . 221 n.85
6867(d) . . . 221 n.83
6871(a) . . . 220 n.77
6871(b) . . . 220 n.78
6901 . . . 445, 450
6901(a) . . . 438–39
6901(a)—(c) . . . 437
6901(c) . . . 447
6901(c)(1) . . . 447 n.56
6901(c)(1), (2) . . . 447 n.54
6901(c)(2) . . . 447 n.58
6901(c)(3) . . . 446 n.52
6901(d) . . . 447 n.59

7431–7435 . . . 15 n.38
7432 . . . 404
7433 . . . 404
7433(e) . . . 405
7434(a) . . . 118
7435 . . . 71, 404
7436 . . . 15 n.39, 226 n.4
7436(a) . . . 227 n.5
7441 . . . 16 n.45
7441-7487 . . . 16
7443A . . . 17 n.46
7453 (amended) . . . 241 n.69
7454 . . . 163 n.115, 246 n.96, 325 n.30, 350 n.131
7454(a) . . . 158 n.88, 448 n.65
7459 . . . 241 n.70, 242 n.72
7460 . . . 242, 242 n.72
7460(b) . . . 242 n.71
7461(a) . . . 237 n.54
7463 . . . 376 n.88
7463(a)(1) . . . 245 n.86
7463(a), (b) . . . 19 n.54
7463(b) . . . 245 n.88
7476 . . . 15 n.39
7477(a) . . . 227 n.5
7477– 7479 . . . 15 n.39
7478(a) . . . 227 n.5
7479(a) . . . 227 n.5
7481 . . . 145 n.21, 243 n.77, 244 n.84
7481(a) . . . 299 n.47
7481(a)(2) . . . 299 n.47
7481(c)(2)(A)(ii) . . . 377 n.92
7482 . . . 244 n.79
7482(a)(1) . . . 18 n.48, 244 n.82
7482(a)(2) . . . 244
7482(a)(3) . . . 145 n.21
7482(b)(1) . . . 200 n.54
7482(b)(1), (2) . . . 19 n.55
7485 . . . 145 n.21, 245 n.85
7485(a) . . . 376 n.87
7491 . . . 246–47 n.97, 247
7491(a)(1), (3) . . . 447–48
7491(a)(2) . . . 114 n.40
7491(b) . . . 120
7491(c) . . . 247 n.100, 329 n.45, 336–37, 339
7501 . . . 413 n.8
7502 . . . 63–64, 150–51, 150 n.50, 151 n.54, 233, 233 n.32, 327 n.37, 366
7502(a) . . . 61–62
7502(f) . . . 61 n.103, 151 n.52
7502(f)(2) . . . 62 n.104
7503 . . . 62, 63–64, 150, 366, 401 n.134
7508 . . . 331 n.53, 447 n.61
7508(A) . . . 369
7517 . . . 127
7521 . . . 130
7521(a), (b) . . . 122
7521(b)(2), (c) . . . 380 n.5
7525 . . . 123
7525(a)(3)(A) . . . 122 n.69, 123 n.69
7601(a) . . . 115
7602(c) . . . 118
7602(c)(3) . . . 118
7602(d) . . . 123
7603(a) . . . 115 n.42
7605 . . . 122
7605(a), (b) . . . 122
7608(c) . . . 111 n.29
7609 . . . 159
7609(a) . . . 119
7609(a)(2) . . . 230 n.17
7609(b) . . . 119
7609(c)(2)(D) . . . 394 n.94
7609(c)(2), (f), (g) . . . 118
7609(d) . . . 119
7609(e) . . . 119, 159 n.95
7609(f) . . . 119
7609(i)(3) . . . 118
7611 . . . 123
7623 . . . 111, 123–24
7623(b) . . . 111 n.30, 123 n.76
7623(b)(4) . . . 124 n.77
7701(a) . . . 79 n.10
7701(a)(1) . . . 49 n.30, 415 n.18
7701(a)(21) . . . 388 n.52
7701(a)(36) . . . 69–70
7701(a)(36)(B) . . . 70 n.156

7701(a)(6)...438
7701(o)...360 n.180
7703...50 n.34
7704(a)*...178
7704*...169
7803(a)...8 n. 13
7803(a)(1)...8 n. 14
7803(c)(2)(B)(ii)...40
7803(d)...7
7805...20, 36–37
7805(b)...36
7805(b)(1)...36
7805(b)(3)...36 n.137
7805(b)(8)...37
7805(e)(2)...20 n.58
7805(f)...35
7806 (b)...5
7811...11 n.27, 396
7811(d)...159 n.91
8021(e)...6 n.10
8023...4
9100...70–71

INTERNAL REVENUE CODE OF 1939...5

INTERNAL REVENUE CODE OF 1954...5

INTERNAL REVENUE CODE OF 1986...5

IRS RESTRUCTURING AND REFORM ACT OF 1998
generally...262
§1001(a)(4)...131 n.96
§3202(a)...275 n.61

OFFSHORE VOLUNTARY DISCLOSURE PROGRAM...74 n.175

OMNIBUS BUDGET RECONCILIATION ACT OF 1981...279 n.79

PENSION PROTECTION ACT OF 2006
Section
§1219(a)(1)(A)...348 n.124, 348 n.125, 350 n.129
§85(a)...251 n.111
§858(a)...293 n.19

PERSONAL RESPONSIBILITY AND WORK OPPORTUNITY RECONCILIATION ACT OF 1996...279 n.81

PRIVACY ACT OF 1974...127

PROCEDURAL REGULATIONS
Proc. Reg.
§601.105(j)...135 n.105
§601.108...4 n.5
§601.201...26 n.75
§601.202...136 n.106
§§601.101—801.6...20 n.57
§601.601(d)(2)(v)(e)...37 n.141

PROTECTING AMERICANS FROM TAX HIKES ACT OF 2015...193 n.1, 241 n.69

PUB. L. NO. 104-168 (1966)
§302(a)...371 n.57

PUBLIC LAW NO. 114-74 (2015)
Title XI, §1101...155 n.74, 156 n.83

REGULATORY FLEXIBILITY ACT (REGFLEX)...35

REVENUE ACT OF 1926...436 n.4

REVENUE ACT OF 1978...5 n.7

SMALL BUSINESS AND WORK OPPORTUNITY TAX ACT OF 2007...285 n.123

SMALL BUSINESS JOBS ACT OF 2010... 67

SSI EXTENSION FOR ELDERLY AND DISABLED REFUGEES ACT OF 2008... 279 n.84

STATUTE OF 13 ELIZABETH, CH.5 (1571)... 442

SURFACE TRANSPORTATION AND VETERANS HEALTH CARE CHOICE IMPROVEMENT ACT OF 2015
generally... 59 n.89, 60 n.94, 154–55, 156, 340 n.79
Section
2004... 294 n.27
2006... 59 n.90

TAX EQUITY AND FISCAL RESPONSIBILITY ACT OF 1982 (TEFRA)
generally... 5, 14, 150
Section
6229... 160
6662... 154 n.70

TAX INCREASE PREVENTION AND RECONCILIATION ACT OF 2007 (TIPRA)... 400, 400 n.124

TAX REFORM ACT OF 1969... 5

TAX REFORM ACT OF 1976... 52 n.48

TAX REFORM ACT OF 1998... 77 n.3
generally... 7, 9, 11, 12, 83, 86, 87, 118, 132, 251–52 n.112, 256, 268, 274, 399, 400, 427
Section
§ 1001... 9 n.20, 204 n.3
§ 1001(a)(4)... 131 n.96
§ 1203(b)(6) (not codified)... 112 n.34
§ 2001(a)... 45 n.7
§ 3461(c)(2)... 408 n.181
§ 4021... 7
§ 6061(b)... 47
§ 6621(d)... 374–75

TAX RELIEF AND HEALTH CARE ACT OF 2006... 94 n.67, 94 n.68

TREASURY REGULATIONS
Treas. Reg.
generally... 21, 22
§ 1.1294-1T(e)(5)... 220 n.76
§ 1.1313(a)-(3)(b)... 299 n.51
§ 1.1313(a)-2... 299 n.50
§ 1.1313(a)-3(d)... 300 n.52
§ 1.1313(a)-4(d)... 300 n.53
§ 1.1313(c)-1... 307 n.62
§ 1.1314(c)-1(a)... 308 n.68
§ 1.162-17(d)(2)... 49 n.26
§§ 1.163-9T(a), (b)(2)... 365 n.15
§ 1.170A-13(b)(2)(ii)... 49 n.27
§ 1.170A-13(c)... 49 n.27
§ 1.170A-13(c)(3)... 357 n.164
§ 1.170A-13(c)(5)... 357 n.163
§ 1.274-5... 48 n.25
§ 1.274-5T... 48 n.25
§ 1.408- 4(b)(4)(ii) (proposed)... 355 n.150
§ 1.6001-1(a)... 48 n.20
§ 1.6001-1(e)... 48 n.20, 48 n.21
§ 1.6011-4... 66–67, 67–68
§ 1.6011-4(b)(4)... 68 n.147
§ 1.6011-4(c)(3)(i)(E)... 68 n.145
§ 1.6011-4(d)... 161 n.103, 161 n.104
§ 1.6011-4(e)... 161 n.102, 161 n.103
§ 1.6012-1(a)(4)... 57 n.80
§ 1.6012-1(a)(5)... 57 n.79, 58 n.82
§ 1.6012-1(b)(3)... 57 n.79
§ 1.6015-1(a)(2)... 81 n.20
§ 1.6015-1(b)... 79 n.12
§ 1.6015-1(c)... 83 n.31
§ 1.6015-1(d)... 80 n.17
§ 1.6015-1(e)... 82 n.29
§ 1.6015-1(j)... 78 n.3

§ 1.6015-2(b)...80 n.15, 80 n.16, 83 n.33
§ 1.6015-2(c)...85 n.40
§ 1.6015-2(d)...87 n.47, 87 n.49
§ 1.6015-3(b)(1), (2)...90 n.57
§ 1.6015-3(c)(2)...88
§ 1.6015-3(c)(2)(v)...88 n.50
§ 1.6015-3(d)...84, 90 n.58
§ 1.6015-5...82 n.28
§ 1.6015-5(b)(1)...82 n.27
§ 1.6015-5(b)(2)...81
§ 1.6015-5(b)(3)...81 n.23, 81 n.24
§ 1.6015-6(a)(1)...95 n.72, 96 n.74
§ 1.6015-6(b)...95 n.73
§ 1.6015-7(b)...95 n.70
§ 1.6015-7(c)...80 n.19, 98 n.87
§ 1.6015-7(c)(2)(i)...98 n.86
§ 1.6031(a)-(b)(1)...60 n.96
§ 1.6031(a)-1(b)(2), (3)...60 n.97
§ 1.6045-4(g)...54 n.63
§ 1.6050I-1(e)(2)...54 n.63
§ 1.6050W-1...56 n.71
§ 1.6072-2(a)...59 n.89
§ 1.6072-2(b)...59 n.91
§ 1.6081-1(a)...65 n.128
§ 1.6081-1(b)(1)...65 n.125
§ 1.6081-2...322 n.16
§ 1.6081-2(a)(1)...64 n.120
§ 1.6081-4...322
§ 1.6091- 2...208 n.20
§ 1.6109- 2...69 n.149
§ 1.6161-1(b)...325, 334 n.64
§ 1.6411- 2T...285 n.121
§ 1.6411-3T...285 n.121
§ 1.66-4(j)(2)(ii)...82 n.28
§ 1.6662-2(a)...341 n.88
§ 1.6662-2(c)...340 n.83
§ 1.6662-3(b)(1)...343 n.96, 343 n.97
§ 1.6662-3(b)(2)...344 n.103, 345 n.105, 345 n.108
§ 1.6662-3(b)(3)...343 n.98
§ 1.6662-3(c)(1)...345
§ 1.6662-3(c)(2)...345–46 n.110
§ 1.6662-4...346
§ 1.6662-4(b)...346 n.113
§ 1.6662-4(b)(4)...347 n.114
§ 1.6662-4(d)(3)(iii)...23 n.68, 26 n.74
§ 1.6662-4(e)(2)...347 n.115
§ 1.6662-4(f)(2)...348 n.119
§ 1.6662-4(g)(1)(iii)...348 n.120
§ 1.6662-5...348 n.122
§ 1.6662-5(a)...349
§ 1.6662-5(f)(1)...349 n.127
§ 1.6662-5(g)...348 n.125, 349 n.128
§ 1.6662-6...348 n.121
§ 1.6664-2(a)...342 n.92
§ 1.6664-2(c)...152 n.56
§ 1.6664-2(c)(3)(i)...343 n.93
§ 1.6664-2(c)(3)(ii)...343 n.93
§ 1.6664-2(c)(4)...343 n.94
§ 1.6664-3...341 n.85, 356 n.156
§ 1.6664-3(b)...341 n.86
§ 1.6664-4...354 n.144
§ 1.6664-4(b)...349 n.126, 355 n.152
§ 1.6664-4(b)(1)...354 n.146
§ 1.6664-4(c)...349 n.126, 355 n.152
§ 1.6664-4(c)(2)...355 n.153
§ 1.6664-4(f)...354 n.145
§ 1.6664-4(h)...349 n.126
§ 1.6664-4(h)(1)...357 n.162
§ 1.6694- 2(b)(1)...347 n.116
§ 1.6694-2(b)(1)...345 n.109
§ 1.6851-1(a)(1)...205 n.4
§ 1.6851-1(a)(3)...207 n.13
§ 1.6851-2(a)(1)...218 n.66, 218 n.67
§ 1.6851-2(a)(2)...218 n.68
§ 1.6851-2(b)(1)...219 n.70
§ 1.6851-2(b)(1)(i)...218 n.69
§ 1.761-2(a)(1), (2)...53 n.54
§ 20.2203-1...438 n.14
§ 20.6001-1(a)...48 n.20
§ 20.6018-1(a)...51 n.42
§ 20.6018-1(b)...52 n.48
§ 20.6075-1...61 n.100
§ 20.6081-1(d)...65 n.127
§ 31(a)...63 n.116
§ 31.6302-1(h)(2)(ii)...414 n.13

§§31.6413(a)-1 to 31.6413(c)(1) . . . 264 n.20
§300.1 . . . 397 n.103
§300.2 . . . 397 n.103
§300.3(b) . . . 399 n.119
§301.6011-2 . . . 46 n.10, 46 n.12
§301.6011-3(a) . . . 60 n.95
§301.6011-7 . . . 46 n.12
§301.6011-7(a)(3) . . . 46 n.14
§301.6020-1 . . . 59 n.87
§301.6020-1(b) . . . 326 n.36
§301.6203-1 . . . 143 n.8, 143 n.10, 381 n.10
§301.6211-1(a), (b) . . . 228 n.11
§301.6212-2(a) . . . 230 n.19
§301.6221-1(d)* . . . 174 n.37
§301.6223(g)-1(a)(1)* to (3)* . . . 176 n.47
§301.6223(g)-1(b)(1)(ii)* . . . 180 n.81
§301.6223(h)-1(a)* . . . 179 n.67
§301.6223-1(b)* . . . 178 n.59
§301.6224(a)-1* . . . 180 n.78
§301.6224(c)-3(c)(3)* . . . 183 n.93
§301.6226(e)- (a)(1)* . . . 183 n.99
§301.623(c)- 5(a)* . . . 177 n.55
§301.6231(a)(1)-1(b)(2)* . . . 178 n.57
§301.6231(a)(3)-1(a)(3)* . . . 173 n.30
§301.6231(a)(3)-1* . . . 172 n.15
§301.6231(a)(5)-1(b)* . . . 173 n.29
§301.6231(a)(6)-1(a)(1), (3)* . . . 182 n.88
§301.6231(a)(6)-1(a)(2)* . . . 181 n.86
§301.6231(a)(6)-1(a)(3)* . . . 182 n.88
§301.6231(a)(7)-1(b)* . . . 176 n.45
§301.6231(a)(7)-1(l)(1)(iv)* . . . 177 n.55
§301.6231(a)(7)-1(l)* . . . 177 n.53
§301.6231(a)(7)-1* . . . 176 n.46
§301.6231(a)(7)-2* . . . 176 n.46
§301.6303-1(a) . . . 382 n.17
§301.6323(f)-1 . . . 386 n.42
§301.6323(g)-1 . . . 386 n.42
§301.6323(g)-1(b)(2) . . . 386 n.44
§301.6335-1(c)(4)(iii) . . . 391 n.74
§301.6402-2(b)(1) . . . 268
§301.6402-3(a) . . . 266 n.30, 268 n.36
§301.6402-5(a)(1) . . . 279 n.82
§301.6404-2(a)(2) . . . 370 n.51
§301.6404-2(b), (c) . . . 371
§301.6404-3 . . . 330
§301.6404-3(b)(1) . . . 370 n.55
§301.6404-3(c)(2) . . . 370 n.56
§301.6404-4 . . . 367 n.30
§301.6404-4(a) . . . 367 n.32
§301.6404-4(b)(4) . . . 368 n.39
§301.6404-4(b)(5) . . . 368 n.40
§301.650(c)-1(f) . . . 162 n.107
§301.6501(b)-1(a)* . . . 186 n.115
§301.6501(e)-1(a)(1)(iii) . . . 154–55
§301.6511(b)-1(b)(1)(i) . . . 278 n.75
§301.6601-1 . . . 364 n.10
§301.6601-1(c)(3) . . . 364 n.10
§301.6601-1(f)(5)(ii) . . . 366 n.24
§301.6651-1(b)(3) . . . 327 n.37
§301.6651-1(c) . . . 328 n.42, 329 n.46, 333 n.61
§301.6651-1(c)(1) . . . 329 n.43
§301.6651-1(c)(3) . . . 331–32, 331 n.55
§301.6651-1(c)(3)(i) . . . 64 n.123
§301.6852-1(b) . . . 219 n.73
§301.6852-1(c) . . . 219 n.74
§301.6861-1(a) . . . 206 n.5
§301.6861-1(f)(1) . . . 215 n.55
§301.6862-1(a) . . . 204 n.3, 206 n.5
§301.6863-1(a) . . . 215 n.56
§301.6863-2(a) . . . 216 n.60
§301.6867-1(a) . . . 221 n.81
§301.6867-1(d) . . . 221 n.84
§301.6867-1(e) . . . 222 n.86
§301.6867-1(f) . . . 221 n.83
§301.6871(a)-2(a) . . . 220 n.79
§301.6871(b)-1(c) . . . 220 n.80
§301.6901-1(a)(3) . . . 445 n.48
§301.6905-1 . . . 438 n.13
§301.7122-1 . . . 300 n.54
§301.7122-1(c) . . . 398 n.111
§301.7122-1(d)(5) . . . 398
§301.7429-2(b) . . . 212 n.42
§301.7430-2(c)(5) . . . 256 n.129

§ 3727 . . . 271 n.44
§ 5317 . . . 43 n.1
§ 5321 . . . 43 n.1
§ 5322 . . . 43 n.1
§§ 5311– 5332 . . . 43 n.1
Title 38 . . . 6 n.8
Title 44 . . . 237 n.55

UNITED STATES CONSTITUTION
Amendments
Fourth . . . 4, 394–95
Fifth . . . 4, 74 n.175
Article I
section 7, clause 1 . . . 4 n.3
section 8 . . . 16
section 8, clause 1 . . . 3, 13 n.32
section 9, clause 4 . . . 3
Article II . . . 16
Article III . . . 13, 16

UNITED STATES MODEL ESTATE AND GIFT TAX TREATY OF 1980 . . . 52 n.45

UNITED STATES TROOPS READINESS, VETERANS CARE, KATRINA RECOVERY, AND IRAQ ACCOUNTABILITY APPROPRIATIONS ACT OF 2007 . . . 70 n.157

WORKER, HOMEOWNERSHIP, AND BUSINESS ASSISTANCE ACT OF 2009 . . . 46 n.13

Table of Secondary Authorities

See page number for complete citation.

ACTIONS ON DECISIONS

AOD

generally . . . 23 n.66

1996-006 . . . 428 n.87

2000-09 . . . 276 n.70

2004-04 . . . 269 n.37

2005-03 . . . 401 n.132

2006-02 . . . 272 n.47

2012-07 . . . 95 n.71

BOOKS

Federal Tax Collection, Liens, and Levies (2015) (Elliott) . . . 383 n.21

Federal Tax Research (2014) (Richmond) . . . 27 n.78

The FOIA Information Manual (2013) (Gidiere III) . . . 126 n.83

IRS Data Book (2013) . . . 225 n.1

IRS Data Book (2014) . . . 8 n.15, 10 n.23, 11 n.25, 11 n.27, 55 n.67, 109 n.19

IRS Data Book (2015) . . . 105 n.8, 106 n.13, 109 n.19, 125 n.82, 127 n.90, 379 n.2, 397 n.105

IRS Data Book (2016) . . . 44 n.3, 144 n.14, 317–318 n.2

IRS Practice and Procedure (rev. 2016) (Saltzman & Book) . . . 57 n.75, 280 n.87

A Practitioner's Guide to Innocent Spouse Relief: Proven Strategies for Winning Section 6015 Tax Cases (2014) (Nadler) . . . 77–78 n.3, 78 n.4

A Practitioner's Guide to Tax Evidence: A Primer on the Federal Rules of Evidence as Applied by the Tax Court (2013) (Larson) . . . 241 n.68

Tax Crimes (2015) (Townsend et al.) . . . 11 n.24, 15 n.41, 70 n.160, 351 n.135

The United States Tax Court: An Historical Analysis (2014) (Dubroff & Hellwig) . . . 16 n.44

CHIEF COUNSEL ADVISORY

CCA

200107035 (Jun. 16, 2001) . . . 148 n.35

200149032 (Oct. 22, 2001) . . . 147 n.27

200235028 . . . 423 n.66

200250001 (July 23, 2002) . . . 353 n.141

200441002 . . . 374 n.77

200518001 (Mar. 29, 2005) . . . 147 n.31

200532046 . . . 428 n.90

200606001 (Oct. 27, 2005) . . . 78 n.7

200651015 (Dec. 22, 2006) . . . 146 n.24

200727015 (Mar. 27, 2007) . . . 308 n.67

200738010 . . . 137 n.110

200802030 (Oct. 12, 2007) . . . 78 n.8

CCA (Jan 9, 2008) . . . 163 n.111

200848045 (July 17, 2008) . . . 274 n.56

200918021 (May 1, 2009) . . . 296 n.37

200952051 (Dec. 7, 2009) . . . 176 n.49

201021021 (Apr. 20, 2010) . . . 368 n.40

201023053 (June 11, 2010) . . . 155 n.78

201024059 (June 18, 2010) . . . 162 n.107

201030030 (July 30, 2010) . . . 185 n.111

201044006 (Nov. 5, 2010) . . . 282 n.96

201052003 (Aug. 2010)...62 n.106
201108036 (Feb. 25, 2011)...57 n.78, 99 n.90
201109019 (Mar. 3, 2011)...177 n.54
201110011 (Mar. 11, 2011)...271 n.47
201116017 (Apr. 22, 2011)...269 n.37
201321022 (May 2, 2013)...273 n.52
201402003 (Oct. 31, 2013)...273–274 n.55
201526007 (June 26, 2015)...274 n.56
201526013 (June 2, 2015)...277 n.73
2101033030 (Aug. 20, 2010)...293 n.19

CHIEF COUNSEL NOTICE
CCN
2003-014 (May 8, 2003)...38 n.145
2003-015...95 n.72
2004-025 (July 12, 2004)...400 n.121
2004-026...94 n.68
2004-036 (Sept. 22, 2004)...131 n.98
2004-036 (Sept. 22, 2004),...131 n.98
2005-003 (Jan. 19, 2005)...412 n.5
2005-011 (May 20, 2005)...88 n.50
2005-011 (May 20, 2005)....96 n.79
2006-017 (Aug. 17, 2006)...137 n.112
2007-003 (Jan. 19, 2007)...26 n.76
2007-005 (Feb. 4, 2007)...326 n.36
2008-22-026 (May 30, 2008)...59 n.87
2009-027 Aug. 26, 2009...171 n.10
2013-011...95 n.71
2014-002...402 n.139
2014-002 (May 5, 2014)...402 n.139
N(35)000-172 (2000 ARD 959-3)... 367 n.33

COURT OF FEDERAL CLAIMS
Rule 58.1...299 n.47

FEDERAL RULES OF APPELLATE PROCEDURE
Rule 4a...299 n.47

FEDERAL RULES OF CIVIL PROCEDURE
Rule 26(b)(4)...238

FEDERAL RULES OF EVIDENCE
generally...241, 245

FIELD SERVICE ADVICE
Field Attorney Advice
FAA 2009102F (June 1, 2009)...389 n.56
FAA 20075001F (Dec. 14, 2007)...285 n.120
FSA
FSA 200126019 (Mar. 30, 2001)....157 n.85

FINANCIAL ACCOUNTING STANDARDS BOARD
FASB Interpretation 48...72–73

GENERAL COUNSEL MEMORANDA
G.C.M.
generally...28
38786 (Aug. 13, 1981)...274 n.56

GOVERNMENT ACCOUNTABILITY OFFICE (GAO)
generally...6
Large Partnerships: Growing Population and Complexity Hinder Effective IRS Audits (GAO- 14-746T) (July 22, 2014)...188 n.135
Little Evidence of Procedural Errors in Collection Due Process Appeal Cases, but Opportunities Exist to Improve the Program (GAO- 07-112) (Oct. 2006)...402 n.141
Tax Gap: A Strategy for Reducing the Gap Should Include Options for Addressing Sole Proprietor Noncompliance (GAO- 07-1014) (July 2007)...56 n.69

4183...422–423
4506-T...143 n.11
4549...79 n.10, 144 n.15, 158 n.89, 269
4768...65
4868...62 n.105, 64–65, 64 n.121, 65 n.129, 269 n.37, 322–323
8082...171 n. 5
8275...343, 345, 347–348
8275-R...345, 347–348
8300...54–55
8379...80 n.18, 97–99, 269 n.38, 280
8453...47
8526...228 n.8
8822...231–233
8857...80–81, 80 n.18, 80 n.19, 81, 96 n.74, 269 n.38
8868...46
8886...67–68, 161
12153...81 n.23, 400–401
W-2...55 n.68, 105, 117
W-4...318–319, 413

I.R.S. INFORMATION/NEWS RELEASES
IR
IR-2003-27...175 n.44
IR-2004-100...110 n.24
IR-2005-33...47 n.19
IR-2006-106...400 n.123
IR-2007-04...381 n.9
IR-2010-45...63 n.114
IR-2011- 8...261 n.3
IR-2011-32...110 n.21
IR-2011-94...74 n.175
IR-2012-4...55 n.68
IR-2012-31...403 n.144
IR-2014-66...331 n.52
IR-2014-67...63 n.114
IR-2014-73...74 n.175
IR-2014-75...69 n.154
IRS Press Release
May 9, 2013 (07:19 EDT)...121 n.63
Prepared Remarks of John Koskinen, Comm. of IR
Apr. 2, 2014...261 n.5
Written Testimony of John Koskinen, Comm. of IR
2014 Filing Season and Improper Payments, May 2014...262 n.5
IRS Actions to Reduce Improper Payments, July 2014...262 n.5

I.R.S. NOTICES
Notice
generally...13–14, 20, 23
2004-83...62 n.105
2006-68...400 n.123
2008-12...69 n.155, 70 n.156
2008-111...68 n.147
2010-60...74 n.177
2010-67...56 n.72
2011-34...74 n.177
2011-70...82 n.28
2013-78...110 n.26
2013-79...110 n.26
2015-38...62 n.104
2015-63...48 n.26
2016-23...194 n.4, 200 n.57, 201 n.59, 201 n.60

I.R.S. POLICY STATEMENTS
Statement 4–7...9 n.19
Statement 8-2...134 n.103
Statement 20-1 (formerly P-1-18)...317 n.1
Statement P-5-14...412 n.7, 417–418 n.31, 418 n.31
Statement P-5-100...399 n.112

I.R.S. PUBLICATIONS
Number/Title (or citation)
1, Your Rights as a Taxpayer (2014)... 24 n.69
901, U.S. Tax Treaties...73 n.175
908, Bankruptcy Tax Guide (2012)... 404 n.154
1345, Handbook for Authorized IRS *e-file* Providers of Individual Income Tax Returns... 46 n.11

1345A, Filing Season Supplement for Authorized IRS *e-file* Providers of Individual Income Tax Returns... 46 n.11
1346, Electronic Return Filing of Individual Income Tax Returns... 46 n.11
3112, The IRS *e-file* Application and Participation... 46 n.11
3598, The Audit Reconsideration Process (2012)... 111 n.31
4163, Modernized e-file (Mef) Information for Authorized IRS *e-file* Providers of Forms 1120/ 1120 S... 46 n.11
4837, Achieving Quality Examinations Through Effective Planning, Execution, and Resolution (3- 2010)... 110 n.23
7225, History of Appeals: Appeals at 60 Years (1987)... 11 n.25
9086, 2003- 2 C.B. 817... 399 n.119
9356, Disregarded Entities; Employment and Excise Taxes (2007)... 412 n.4
9380, Substitute for Return, 2008-1 C.B. 718... 59 n.87
9425, Section 6707A and the Failure To Include on Any Return or Statement Any Information Required To Be Disclosed Under Section 6011 with Respect to a Reportable Transaction, 2008- 2 C.B. 1100... 68 n.146
9455, 2009-2 C.B. 239... 160 n.97
9504, 2010- 2 C.B. 670... 56 n.72
9510, 2011- 6 I.R.B. 453... 72 n.171
9584, 77 Fed. Reg. 23,391- 01 (2012)... 73 n.175
9675, 79 Fed. Reg. 41127- 02 (2014)... 44 n.2
IRS, Tax Gap Estimates for Tax Years 2008–2010 (2016)... 104 n.3
IRS Establishes Five-Year Duration on Continuous Audits of Taxpayers, Tax Mgmt. Weekly Rep., Dec. 4, 2006... 123 n.75
IRS Oversight Board, Electronic Filing 2014 Annual Report to Congress (2014)... 45 n.8
Postings to the EFS Bulletin Board... 46 n.11
U.S. Dep't of Treasury, Understanding IRS Guidance—A Brief Primer (2005)... 27 n.78

LAW REVIEW/LAW JOURNAL ARTICLES

ABA Section of Taxation Proposal as to Audit of Partnerships, 32 Tax Law. 551 (1979) ... 170 n.3
Agostino, Frank & Tara Krieger, Federal Employment Misclassification, J. Tax Prac. & Proc. (2015)... 109 n.17
Alltizer, Richard L. & Jeffrey L. Bryant, TIPRA Further Compromises a Taxpayer's Ability to Compromise, Taxes (2006)... 400 n.124
Alm, James & Jay A. Soled, Improving Tax Basis Reporting for Passthrough Entities, Tax Notes (2014)... 55 n.68
Asimow, Michael, Public Participation in the Adoption of Temporary Tax Regulations, 44 Tax Law. 343 (1991)... 35 n.128
August, Jerald David, Mandatory Disclosure of Uncertain Tax Positions on Income Tax Returns Filed by Corporate Taxpayers: The IRS's New Weapon, Practical Tax Law. (2011)... 73 n.173
Bailey, William & Ryan Pace, Trust Fund Recovery Penalty Still Vexing "Responsible Persons," Tax Notes (2014)... 415 n.16
Banoff, Sheldon I. & Allan G. Donn, Who Can Sign a Partnership's or LLC's Tax

Returns? Simple Questions; Complex Answers, J. Tax'n (2010)...57 n.78

Banoff, Sheldon I. & Richard M. Lipton, Who Can Sign an LLC's 1065 Tax Return? It's Still Not Clear, J. Tax'n (2011)...57 n.78

Barnes, Amy & Robert E. Dallman, Opportunities for Taxpayers to be Reimbursed for Costs Incurred in Tax Audits and Cases, J. Tax'n (2011)... 255 n.125

Beaulieu, Curtis, New Audit Rules for Partnerships: Heartburn for MLPs, Tax Notes (2015)...200 n.58

Bennett, Alison, IRS Concerned by Tax Court Proposal to Allow Redacted Petitions, Official Says, Tax Mgmt. Weekly Rep. (2007)...238 n.56

Blank, Joshua D., Reconsidering Corporate Tax Privacy, 11 N.Y.U.J.L. & Bus. 31 (2014)...71 n.164

Borison, Jerome, Comment, Section 6901; Transferee Liability, 30 Tax Law. 433 (1977) ...437 n.6

Bowen, Nancy T., A Trap for the Unwary: Is the Six- Year General Statute of Limitation an Outside Limit for Refund Suits?, Practical Tax Law. (2009) ...282 n.96

Bowen, Nancy T., Strategies for Defending Against Discovery Requests for Tax Returns, Tax Notes (2009)...72 n.168

Boynton, Charles *et al.*, A First Look at Schedule M- 3 Reporting and Schedule UTP, Tax Notes (2014)...117 n.55

Brauner, Yariv, What the BEPS?, 16 Fla. Tax Rev. 55 (2014)...74 n175

Callahan, Thomas J., *et. al.*, Joint Committee Refund Review: Twelve Questions to Consider, J. Tax Prac. & Proc. (2008)...4 n.5

Camp, Bryan T., The Mysteries of Erroneous Refunds, Tax Notes (2007)... 272 n.47

Camp, Bryan T., Presumptions and Tax Return Preparer Fraud, Tax Notes (2008) ...157 n.85

Camp, Bryan T., Tax Return Preparer Fraud and the Assessment Statute of Limitations, Tax Notes (2007)...157 n.85

Chabot, Christine Kexel, Selling *Chevron*, 67 Admin. L. Rev. 481 (2015)...31 n.104

Chase, Robert S., II, *et al.*, The FBAR Reset: Final Regulations Provide Mixed Guidance, Tax Notes (2011)... 73 n.175

Chief Counsel Notice CC- 2003-014 (May 8, 2003), *in* 2003 Tax Notes Today 93-7 (2003)...38 n.145

Click, David L., LMSB's Industry Issue Focus Initiative: What Does It Achieve?, Tax Notes (2007)...110 n.25

Clukey, Nathan, Benefits of Shifting the Burden of Proof to the IRS Are Limited, 1999 TNT 20-136 (1999)...247 n.97

Coder, Jeremiah, Self-Serving Concessions and Penalty Avoidance, 134 Tax Notes 1583 (2012)...350 n.128

Coder, Jeremiah, Tax Court Proposes Numerous Rule Changes, Tax Notes (2009)...238 n.59

Cohen, Mary Ann, How to Read Tax Court Opinions, 1 Hous. Bus. & Tax. L.J. 1 (2001)...242 n.72

Cohen, N. Jerold & William E. Sheumaker, When It's Broke, Fix It! It's Time for TEFRA Reform, Tax Notes (2013)...189 n.137

Conference Proceedings, The Tax Legislative Process—A Critical Need, 10 Amer. J. Tax Pol'y 99 (1992)...4 n.4

Crimm, Nina J., Tax Controversies: Choice of Forum, 9 B.U. J. Tax L. 1 (1991)...15 n.42, 248 n.105

Cummings, Jasper L., Jr., Relief for Late Regulatory Elections, Tax Notes (2013)... 71 n.162

Davis, William R., LB&I Commissioner Announces Sweeping Changes, 2015 TNT 181-1 (2015)...10 n.22

DiSciullo, Joseph, ABA Tax Section Analyzes Offer in Compromise Amendments, Tax Notes (2006)...400 n.124

Dizdarevic, Melissa A., Comment, The FATCA Provisions of the HIRE Act: Boldly Going Where No Withholding Has Gone Before, 79 Fordham L. Rev. 2967 (2011)... 73 n.173

Dubroff, Harold & Charles M. Greene, Recent Developments in the Business and Procedures of the United States Tax Court, 52 Alb. L. Rev. 33 (1987)... 16 n.44

Dupree, Dwaune & Ken Jones, Reasonable Cause: Reliance on Tax Advisors, J. Tax. Prac. & Proc. (2013–2014)... 356 n.160

Elliott, Amy S., Camp Draft Forgoes Unified Passthrough Regime, Tax Notes (2014) ...189 n.141

Elliott, William D., Coping with a Nominee Lien, Taxes (2011)...452 n.88

Elliott, William D., Tax Practice—Assessment Irregularities, J. Tax Prac. & Proc.(2010) ...142 n.7

Fahey, Diane L., Is the United States Tax Court Exempt from Administrative Law Jurisprudence when Acting as a Reviewing Court?, 58 Clev. St. L. Rev. 603 (2010) ...255 n.120

FBA Conference on Writing Tax Law, 35 Fed. B.J. 76 (1978)...4 n.4

Ferreira, G. Michelle & Claudia A. Hill, Innocent Spouse: Untying the Tax Knot, J. Tax Proc. & Prac. (2008–2009)...78 n.3

Fichtner, Jason & Jacob Feldman, The Hidden Cost of Tax Compliance, Mercatus Center, George Mason Univ. (2013)...44 n.3

Finley, Janene R. & Allan Karnes, An Empirical Study of the Change in the Burden of Proof in the United States Tax Court, 6 Pitt. Tax Rev. 61 (2008) ...247 n.97

Fogel, David M., The "Effective Tax Administration" Offer in Compromise, Tax Notes (2005)...399 n.118

Fogg, T. Keith & Calvin H. Johnson, Amended Returns—Imposing a Duty to Correct Material Mistakes, Tax Notes (2008)...63 n.113

Ganguly, Maya, Tribunals and Taxation: An Investigation of Arbitration in Recent U.S. Tax Conventions, 29 Wis. Int'l L.J. 735 (2012)...74 n.175

Gerzog, Wendy C., *Bruder:* The Extent of Equitable Recoupment, Tax Notes (2006) ...293 n.18

Grace, Michael J., *et al.*, Coca- Cola Company v. U.S.: 6411 Versus 6611 and Other Adventures of Deficiency and Statutory Interest, Tax Mgmt. Memo. 243 (2010)...375 n.86

Green, Eric L., Making the IRS a Qualified Offer It Can't Refuse: Using Qualified Offers to Help Settle Tax Cases and Obtain Reimbursement of Costs, J. Tax Prac. & Proc. (2010)... 256 n.129

Greenaway, Thomas D., Choice of Forum in Federal Civil Tax Litigation, 62 Tax Law 31 (2009)...248 n.105

Greenhouse, Robin & R. Christy Vouri, Riding the Mitigation Train Through El Paso, Tax Notes (2014)...303 n.55

Grewal, Amandeep S., Mixing Management Fee Waivers with *Mayo,* 15 Fla. Tax Rev. 1 (2014)...34 n.125

Grover Hartt, III & Jonathan L. Blacker, Judicial Application of Issue Preclusion in Tax Litigation: Illusion or Il-

lumination?, 59 Tax Law 205 (2005)...164 n.116
Harvey, J. Richard "Dick," Schedule UTP Guidance—Initial Observations, Tax Notes (2010)...73 n.173
Haxton, Britt, Note, The Section 6166 Balancing Game: An Examination of the Policy Behind *Estate of Roski v. Commissioner*, 62 Tax Law. 525 (2009)...66 n.134
Hickman, Kristin E., A Problem of Remedy: Responding to Treasury's (Lack of) Compliance with Administrative Procedure Act Rulemaking Requirements, 76 Geo. Wash. L. Rev. 1153 (2008)...29 n.87
Hickman, Kristin E., Administering the Tax System We Have, 63 Duke L.J. 1717 (2014)...104 n.5
Hickman, Kristin E., Coloring Outside the Lines: Examining Treasury's (Lack of) Compliance with Administrative Procedure Act Rulemaking Requirements, 82 Notre Dame L. Rev. 1727 (2007)...29 n.87
Hickman, Kristin E., IRB Guidance: The No Man's Land of Tax Code Interpretation, 2009 Mich. St. L. Rev. 239 (2009)...31 n.101
Hoffer, Stephanie, Hobgoblin of Little Minds No More: Justice Requires an IRS Duty of Consistency, 2006 Utah L. Rev. 317 (2006)...295 n.33
Hoffman, William, E- Filing Grows, but IRS Budget Hampers Progress, Tax Notes (2014)...45 n.8
Inventory of IRS Guidance Documents—A Draft, Tax Notes (2000)...27 n.78
IRS Establishes Five-Year Duration on Continuous Audits of Taxpayers, Tax Mgmt. Weekly Rep. (2006)...123 n.75
Joe, Michael & Crystal Tandon, IRS Issuing New "Soft Notice" to Underreporting Taxpayers, Tax Notes (2008)...107 n.16
Johnson, Steve R., After the Cheering, Problems, 31 ABA Sec. of Tax'n News Q. 1 (2012)...156 n.80
Johnson, Steve R., An IRS Duty of Consistency: The Failure of Common Law Making and a Proposed Legislative Solution, 77 Tenn. L. Rev. 563 (2010) 37 n.142, 296 n.34, 355 n.150
Johnson, Steve R., *Auer/Seminole Rock* Deference in the Tax Court, 11 Pitt. Tax Rev. 1 (2013)...32 n.111
Johnson, Steve R., Code Sec. 7433: Damages Against the IRS for Wrongful Collection Actions, J. Tax Prac. & Proc. (2007)...404 n.151
Johnson, Steve R., The Dangers of Symbolic Legislation: Perceptions and Realities of the New Burden-of-Proof Rules, 84 Iowa L. Rev. 413 (1999)...114 n.40
Johnson, Steve R., Explanation and IRS Adjudication, 63 Duke L. J. 1771 (2014)...423 n.64
Johnson, Steve R., The Good, the Bad, and the Ugly in Post- *Drye* Tax Lien Analysis, 5 Fla. Tax Rev. 415 (2002)...384 n.28
Johnson, Steve R., How Far Does Circular 230 Exceed Treasury's Statutory Authority?, 146 Tax Notes 221 (2015)...69 n.153
Johnson, Steve R., Loving and Legitimacy: IRS Regulation of Tax Return Preparation, 59 Vill. L. Rev. 515 (2014)...69 n.151
Johnson, Steve R., The 1998 Act and the Resources Link Between Tax Compliance and Tax Simplification, 51 U. Kan. L. Rev. 1013 (2003)...104 n.6
Johnson, Steve R., Preserving Fairness in Tax Administration in the *Mayo Era,*

32 Va. Tax Rev. 269 (2012)...28 n.82, 31 n.103

Johnson, Steve R., Reasoned Explanation and IRS Adjudication, 63 Duke L.J. 1771 (2014)...30 n.96, 236 n.46

Johnson, Steve R., Recent Supreme Court Cases Read Remedies Restrictively, 2614 ABA Sec. of Tax'n News Q. 17 (2007)...403 n.145

Johnson, Steve R., Reforming Federal Tax Litigation: An Agenda, 41 Fla. St. U. L. Rev. 205 (2013)...13 n.33, 170 n.3, 210 n.34, 226 n.2, 242 n.70,

244 n.80, 281 n.94, 282 n.100, 387 n.47, 406 n.160

Johnson, Steve R., The Rise and Fall of *Chevron* in Tax: From the Early Days to *King* and Beyond, 2015 Pepperdine L. Rev. 14 (2015)...31 n.104

Johnson, Steve R., The Taxpayer's Duty of Consistency, 46 Tax L. Rev. 537 (1991)...294 n.26

Johnson, Steve R., Unfinished Business on the Taxpayer Rights Agenda: Achieving Fairness in Transferee Liability Cases, 19 Va. Tax Rev. 403 (2000)...450 n.73

Johnson, Steve R., Using State Fraudulent Transfer Law To Collect Federal Taxes, Nev. Law. (2006)...452 n.86

Johnson, Steve R., Why *Craft* Isn't Scary, 37 Real Prop., Probate & Trust J. 439 (2002)...384 n.28

Johnson, Steve R.,The Danger of Symbolic Legislation: Perceptions and Realities of the New Burden- of-Proof Rules, 84 Iowa L.Rev. 413 (1999)... 247 n.97

Johnson, Steve R.,The Doctrine of Judicial Estoppel, Nev. Law. (2003)...296 n.35

Johnson, Steve R.,The Duress or Deception Defense to Joint and Several Spousal Liability, Tax Prac. & Proc. 15 (2004–2005)...79 n.12, 87 n.49, 96 n.74

Johnson, Steve R., The E.L. Wiegand Lecture: Administrability- Based Tax Simplification, 4 Nev. L.J. 573 (2004) ...189 n.138

Johnson, Steve R., The Future of American Tax Administration: Conceptual Possibilities and Political Realities, 7 Colum J. Tax L. 5 (2016)...104 n.6, 201 n.61

Johnson, Steve R., The Phoenix and the Perils of the Second Best: Why Heightened Appellate Deference to Tax Court Decisions is Undesirable, 77 Or. L. Rev. 235 (1998)...18 n.49, 244 n.82

Jones, Philip N., The Burden of Proof 10 Years After the Shift, Tax Notes (2008)... 247 n.97

Kafka, Gerald A., Choice of Forum in Federal Civil Tax Litigation (Part I), Practical Tax Law. (2011)...248 n.105

Kafka, Gerald A., Choice of Forum in Federal Civil Tax Litigation (Part II), Practical Tax Law. (2011)...248 n.105

Kay, Bradley D., Whether the Statutory Language of Code Sec. 6501(c)(1) Should be Amended, J. Tax Prac. & Proc. (2013– 2014)...157 n.85

Keenan, John, *et al.*, Supplemental Claims: Acceptable Amendment or New Claim?, Tax Adviser (2011)...270 n.39

Keneally, Kathryn & Charles P. Rettig, The End of an Era: The IRS Closes in on Offshore Bank Accounts, J. Tax Prac. & Proc. (2009)...121 n.62

Knickerbocker, Daniel Candee, Jr., Mysteries of Mitigation: The Opening of Barred Years in Income Tax Cases, 30 Fordham L. Rev. 225 (1961)...308 n.69

Kroh, Eric, IRS Signs 1-Year Extension of Free File Alliance Partnership, Tax Notes (2014)...47 n.18

Kroh, Eric, JCT Will Review a Refund if It's Big Enough, Tax Notes (2014)...4 n.5

Kummer, Michael, The De Novo Doctrine: Irrelevant to Irrelevancy in Civil Tax Litigation, 14 Fla. Tax Rev. 115 (2013)...236 n.44

Kurtz, Jerome, Auditing Partnerships, Tax Notes (2012)...170 n.3

Kwon, Michelle M., Dysfunction Junction: Reasonable Tax Advisors with Conflicts of Interest, 67 Tax Law. 403 (2014)...356 n.160

Larry A. Campagna & William O. Grimsinger, Riddles Raised by Those Who Don't Read: Solving Purported Problems with the Right of Contribution Under Code Sec. 6672(d), J. Tax Prac. & Proc. (2003)...430 n.98

Lederman, Leandra, (Un)Appealing Deference to the Tax Court, 63 Duke L.J. 1835 (2014)...18 n.48, 244 n.82

Lederman, Leandra, Arbitrary Stat Notices in Valuation Cases, or Arbitrary Ninth Circuit?, Tax Notes (2001)...246 n.92

Lederman, Leandra, The Fight Over "Fighting Regs" and Judicial Deference in Tax Litigation, 92 B.U.L. Rev. 643 (2012)...33 n.114

Lederman, Leandra, Reducing Information Gaps to Reduce the Tax Gap: When Is Information Reporting Warranted?, 78 Fordham L. Rev. 1733 (2010)...56 n.70

Leeds, Mark, Passive—Aggressive: IRS Releases Initial Guidance on FATCA Rules, Tax Mgmt. Weekly Rep. (2010)...74 n.177

Levine, Richard A., & Carlton M. Smith, Interest Abatement Actions—An Important New Avenue for Taxpayer Relief, 86 J. Tax'n 5 (1997)...370 n.50

Lunder, Erika K., *et al.*, Constitutionality of Retroactive Tax Legislation (Cong. Res. Serv. Report R42791) (2012)... 36 n.131

Luscombe, Mark A., Tax Protestors: Is the IRS Turning the Corner?, Taxes (2007) ...104 n.4

Luscombe, Mark A., The Tax Gap and the Growth of Third-Party Reporting, Taxes (2010)...56 n.70

Luttati, Carol M., How to Secure Penalty Abatement in Cases of Delinquent Employment Taxes Caused by Severe Financial Difficulties, J. Tax Prac. & Proc. (2011)...411 n.2

Lynch, John A., Jr., Burden of Proof in Tax Litigation Under I.R.C. §7491—Chicken Little Was Wrong!!, 5 Pitt. Tax Rev. 1 (2007)...247 n.97, 248 n.103

Lynch, John A., Jr., Income Tax Statute of Limitations: Sixty Years of Mitigation—Enough, Already!!, 51 S.C.L. Rev. 62, 87 (1999)...308 n.69

Maule, James E., Instant Replay, Weak Teams, and Disputed Calls: An Empirical Study of Alleged Tax Court Judge Bias, 66 Tenn. L. Rev. 351 (1999)...18 n.51, 244 n.81

Mazza, W., Taxpayers Privacy and Tax Compliance, 51 U. Kan. L. Rev. 1065 (2003)...71 n.163

McMahon, Martin J., Jr., & Ira B. Shepherd, Privilege and the Work Product Doctrine in Tax Cases, 58 Tax Law. 405 (2005)...123 n.73

McMahon, Martin J., Living with the Codified Economic Substance Doctrine, 128 Tax Notes 31 (2010)...360 n.181

McMahon, Stephanie H., An Empirical Study of Innocent Spouse Relief: Do Courts Implement Congress's Legislative Intent?, 12 Fla. Tax Rev. 629 (2012)...78 n.4

McMahon, Stephanie H., What Innocent Spouse Relief Says About Wives and the Rest of Us, 37 Harv. J. of Law & Gender 141 (2014)...79 n.12

McMillan, Lori, Transferee Shareholders and the Long Arm of the IRS, Tax Notes (2013)...452 n.87

Mock, Rodney P. & Nancy E. Shurtz, The TurboTax Defense, 15 Fla. Tax Rev. 443 (2014)...354 n.148

Moore, Schuyler M., New Regulations Violate Regulatory Flexibility Act and Executive Order 12291, 36 Tax Notes 805 (1987)...35 n.128

Morgan, Ed, International Tax Law as a Ponzi Scheme, 34 Suffolk Transnational L. Rev. (2011)...73 n.174

Nardiello, Chad D., Is It a Partnership Item?, Tax Notes (2013)...172 n.18

New Strategic Plan Emphasizes Better IT, "Big Data" to Improve Taxpayer Services, Tax Mgmt. Weekly Rep. 887 (2014)...45 n.8

Note, Interpreting a Visigothic Spanish Civil Law Tradition to Trump the Internal Revenue Code: Section 6015's Uneven Application in Community Property States, 63 Tax Law. 553 (2010)...99 n.89

Note, Revenue Ruling 2007- 51; Why the IRS is Keeping Your Money, 59 Syracuse L. Rev. 311 (2008)...279 n.78

Note, Upsetting the Government's Right to Redemption Under Section 7425, 60 Tax Law. 233 (2006)...394 n.93

Note, What Law Governs Transferee Liability for Federal Income Tax?, 8 Stan. L. Rev. 261 (1960)...436 n.4

Olson, Nina E., More Than a "Mere" Preparer: Loving and Return Preparation, Tax Notes (2013)...104 n.7

Pettig, Charles P., New IRS Guidelines Limit FBAR Penalties, J. Tax Prac. & Proc. (2015)...74 n.178

Pettig, Charles P., Nonfilers Beware: Who's That Knocking at Your Door?, J. Tax Prac. & Proc. (2006)...56 n.69, 104 n.4

Pierce, Richard J., Jr., What Do the Studies of Judicial Review of Agency Actions Mean?, 63 Admin. L. Rev. 77 (2011)...32 n.112

Pietruszkiewicz, Christopher M., A Constitutional Cause of Action and the Internal Revenue Code: Can You Shoot (Sue) the Messenger?, 54 Syracuse L. Rev. 1 (2004)...407 n.169

Porter, David B., Where Can You Litigate Your Federal Tax Case?, Tax Notes (2003)...15 n.42, 248 n.105

Prescott, Peter A., Jumping the Shark: The Case for Repealing the TEFRA Partnership Audit Rules, 11 Fla. Tax Rev. 503 (2011)...189 n.138

PricewaterhouseCoopers, Emergence of New Examination Approach—Joint Audits, 2011 TNT 129- 40 (2011)...73 n.175

Puckett, James M., Embracing the Queen of Hearts: Deference to Retroactive Tax Rules, 40 Fla. St. U.L. Rev. 349 (2013)...36 n.131

Raby, Burgess J.W. & William L. Raby, Protecting the Protective Refund Claim, Tax Notes (2003)...274 n.56

Raby, Burgess W. & William L. Raby, Reasonable Basis *vs.* Other Tax Opinion Standards, 73 Tax Notes 1209, (1996)...344 n.99

Rebollo, Anthony E., The Civil Arrest and Imprisonment of Taxpayers: An Analysis of the Writ of Ne Exeat Republica, 7 Pitt. Tax Rev. 103 (2010)...393 n.86

Rettig, Charles P., At- a-Glance: The Internal Revenue Service, Its Mission and Function, J. Tax Prac. & Proc. (2006)...9 n.19

Rogers, W. Scott, Section 6603 Cash Deposits to Stop the Running of Interest on a Deficiency: Factors to Consider Before Remitting a Deposit, Tax

Mgmt. Weekly Rep. (2010)...369 n.45
Rogovin, Mitchell & Donald L. Korb, The Four R's Revisited: Regulations, Rulings, Reliance, and Retroactivity in the 21st Century: A View from Within, 46 Duq. L. Rev. 323 (2008)...28–29 n.78
Sadler, Alex E. & Daniel G. Kim, Scope of Pretrial Discovery: A Key Difference in Litigating Tax Cases in the Tax Court and Refund Tribunals, J. Tax Prac. & Proc. (2009)...238 n.61
Schneider, Steven S., FIN 48 for Tax Lawyers—Accounting for Uncertainty in Income Taxes, 2007 Tax Mgmt. Memo. 139...72 n.169
Schumacher, Scott, Innocent Spouse, Administrative Process; Time for Reform, Tax Notes (2011)...78 n.3, 78 n.4
Schumacher, Scott A., Magnifying Deterrence by Prosecuting Professionals, 89 Ind. L.J. 511 (2014)...74 n.175
Schumacher, Scott A., Unnecessary Harm: IRS Levies on Social Security Benefits, Tax Notes (2006)...389 n.57
Scott, Paul D., Tax Whistle-Blowers To Receive Increased Rewards, Tax Notes (2007)... 111 n.30
Sheehy, Frances D., The Right to Intervene in Innocent Spouse Cases Disappears when the Affirmative Defense of Innocent Spouse is Withdrawn, Fla. B.J. (2013)... 97 n.79
Sheppard, Hale E., It's in the Mail, Right? Recent Decision Emphasizes Limitation on the Mailbox Rule, Practical Tax Law. (2008)...233 n. 34
Sheppard, Hale E., Seeking Cost Reimbursement in Cases of First Impression: Zealous Advocacy or Pushing Your Luck?, Practical Tax Law. (2007)...256 n.127
Sheppard, Lee A., Should Corporate Tax Returns Be Disclosed?, Tax Notes (2014)...71 n.164
Skarlatos, Bryan C. & Joseph Septimus, Can an Innocent Taxpayer Be Subject to an Unlimited Statute of Limitations Because of the Return Preparer's Fraud?, J. Tax Prac. & Proc. (2013- 2014)...157 n.85
Slawson, W. David, Constitutional and Legislative Considerations in Retroactive Lawmaking, 48 Cal. L. Rev. 216 (1960)...35 n.130
Smith, Danielle M., Bank Levies: Proper Compliance Prevents Hefty Penalties, Tax Notes (2006)...390 n.64
Susswein, Donald B. & Ryan P. McCormick, Fixing the Partnership Audit Process, 2015 TNT 193- 19 (2015)...189 n.136, 189 n.142
Townsend, John A. & Lawrence R. Jones, Jr., Interpreting Consents to Extend the Statute of Limitations, 98 Tax Notes Today (1998)...153 n.64
Townsend, John A., Burden of Proof in Tax Cases: Valuation and Ranges, Tax Notes (2001)...246 n.92
Townsend, John A., Collateral Estoppel in Civil Cases Following Criminal Convictions, 2005 TNT 4- 28 (2005)... 354 n.143
Trivedi, Shamik & Jeremiah Coder, TEFRA Raises Complex Jurisdictional Issues, Judge Says, Tax Notes (2012) ...188 n.129
Ungerman, Josh O. & Matt L. Roberts, Buckle Your Seatbelts: Employment Taxes Are Back in Vogue and It Will Be a Bumpy Ride, J, Tax Prac. & Proc. (2015)...109 n.17
Usman, Jeffrey Omar, Constitutional Constraints on Retroactive Civil Legislation: The Hollow Promises of the Federal Constitution and Unrealized

Potential of State Constitutions, 14 Nev. L.J. 63 (2013)...36 n.136
Vance, David E., Unconstitutional Vagueness and the Tax Code, Tax Notes (2014)...44 n.3
Velarde, Andrew & Jaime Arora, District Court Authorizes John Doe Summonses to 5 U.S. Banks, Tax Notes (2013)...74 n.175
Watt, Timothy J. & Thomas L. Evans, Requesting 9100 Relief, Tax Adviser (2008)...71 n.162
Weinman, Howard M., Canal Corp. and penalty Protection, J. Tax Prac. & Proc. (2010–2011)...356 n.158
Wilkins, William J., Implications of *Home Concrete,* 31 ABA Sec. of Tax'n News Q. 25 (2012)...156 n.80
Wilson, Margaret C., The Variance Doctrine: No Forks in the Road to Refunds, 55 Tax Law. 605 (2002)...283 n.105
Wood, Robert W. & Dashiell C. Shapiro, Tax Payments and Waivers Voided by Duress, Tax Notes (2014)...153 n.65
Yin, George K., Saving the IRS, 2014 TNT 87- 5 (2014)...71 n.164

NATIONAL TAXPAYER ADVOCATE

generally...11
2006 Annual Report to Congress, Executive Summary 111-1 (Jan. 2007)... 117 n.52, 402 n.142
2007 Objectives Report to Congress (June 30, 2006)...400 n.124

PRIVATE LETTER RULINGS

PLR

generally...25
200808043 (Feb. 22, 2008)...441 n.29
200842012 (July 18, 2008)...66 n.134

REVENUE PROCEDURES

generally...22

Rev. Proc.

64-22...9 n.19
68-16...136 n.106
78-12...206 n.10
84-35...60 n.93
84-58...265 n.25
94-67...136 n.106
98-54...228 n.8
99-21...276 n.63
99-28...129 n.92, 402 n.143
2002-26...430 n.100, 431 n.102
2002-67...129 n.93, 129 n.94
2003-19...96 n.75, 96 n.76
2003-36...110 n.24
2003-40...129 n.93
2003-61...87 n.49
2003-71...398 n.108, 398 n.109, 399 n.114
2003-84...53 n.54
2005-13...253 n.117
2005-18...265–266, 265 n.25, 265 n.27, 369, 369 n.46
2005-24...423 n.67
2005-26...161, 161 n.105
2005-32...122 n.68
2007-20...67 n.144, 68 n.147
2007-21...368 n.40
2007-40...46 n.9
2008-20...68 n.147
2009-14...110 n.20
2010-16...231, 231 n.21, 231 n.24
2011-25...46 n.12
2012-18...131 n.96
2013-23...87 n.49
2013-30...70 n.161
2013-34...80 n.14, 92–93, 98 n.85
2014-18...70 n.161
2014-42...69 n.154
2014-61...51 n.43
2014-63...132 n.101
2015-40...110 n.26
2015-41...110 n.22
2015-44...132 n.100

2015-53...50 n.31, 51 n.43, 52 n.50, 53 n.52
2015-55...44 n.5
2016-1...24 n.70
2016-13...346 n.111, 348 n.119
2016-22...129 n.95

REVENUE RULINGS
Rev. Rul.
generally...21
54-415...157 n.84
72-42...150 n.46
73- 305...388 n.50
74-571...386 n.40
76-511...268 n.35, 278 n.75
78-299...438 n.9
79-178...157 n.87
80-7...97 n.82
87-41...109 n.18
90-91...23 n.64
99-40...374 n.81
2003-80...159 n.93
2003-118...387 n.47
2004-41...412 n.5
2004-88...177 n.56
2005-9...326 n.33
2005-17 to 2005-21...149 n.42
2005-50...395 n.97
2005-59...79 n.10
2006- 42...388 n.49
2006-11...173 n.26
2007-51...279 n.77, 279 n.78, 285 n.122
2007-52...280 n.85, 285 n.121
2007-53...285 n.121
2007-59...331 n.53
2013-17...50 n.33, 79 n.9
2016-06...365 n.16

SENATE REPORTS/HEARINGS
S. Rpt. No. 105- 174, 105th Cong., 2d Sess. 59 (1998)...91 n.60, 368
Testimony, J. Russell George, hearings before Senate Comm. on Appropriations... 8 n.16

SERVICE CENTER ADVICE
SCA
199924056 (Apr. 20, 1990)...97 n.82
200504033 (Jan. 28, 2005)...408 n.180

STAFF OF JOINT COMM. ON TAXATION
Description of Certain Revenue Proposals Contained in the President's Fiscal Year 2014 Budget Proposal (Dec. 2013)...124 n.78, 443 n.38
Description of Certain Revenue Proposals Contained in the President's Fiscal Year 2016 Budget Proposal (Sept. 2015)...9 n.21, 106 n.12, 124 n.79, 171 n.9
General Explanation of Tax Legislation Enacted in 2015, JCS-1-16, (Mar. 14, 2016)...193 n.2
Study of General Disclosure Provisions (Jan. 28, 2000)...71 n. 165
Technical Explanation of the Revenue Provisions of the "Reconciliation Act of 2010," as Amended, in Combination with the "Patient Protection and Affordable HealthCare Act"...360 n.181

TAX COURT RULES (FED. TAX CT. R.)
Rule
26(b)...236 n.49
27...236 n.48, 237–238
37...237 n.53
39...162 n.109, 163 n.112, 246 n.95
41...235 n.40
41(a)...238 n.58
70...238 n.59
70(b)(3)...238 n.60
70(c)...238
91(a)(1)...239–240
91(f)...240 n.63
141(f)(1)...177 n.52
142...246 n.94, 246 n.96
142(a)...163 n.112, 246 n.95, 448 n.64
142(a)(2)...246 n.97
142(b)...350 n.132
143...240 n.66

143(g) . . . 240 n.65
143 (amended) . . . 241 n.69
155 . . . 242
160 . . . 230 n.15
161 . . . 243 n.74
162 . . . 243 n.74
171 . . . 246 n.90
173(b) . . . 237 n.52
174 . . . 245 n.89
182(b) . . . 241 n.70
183 . . . 241–242 n.70
241(g) . . . 177 n.52
248 . . . 177 n.52
260 . . . 376 n.88
261 . . . 377 n.92
280-84 . . . 372
325(b) . . . 96 n.78
Form 2 . . . 237 n.51

TECHNICAL ADVICE MEMORANDUM
T.A.M.
200429009 . . . 58 n.86
Technical Memo.
TAS-13-0614-005 . . . 11 n.27

TREASURY CIRCULAR
Circular 230 . . . 11–12, 31, 68–69, 122 n.69
Circular E . . . 318–319

TREASURY INSPECTOR GENERAL FOR TAX ADMINISTRATION
generally . . . 7–8
Accuracy- Related Penalties Are Seldom Considered Properly During Correspondence Audits (2010-30-059) (June 4, 2010) . . . 339 n.76
Amended Tax Return Filing and Processing Needs to be Modernized to Reduce Erroneous Refunds, Processing Costs, and Taxpayer Burden (TIGTA 2014-40-028) (July 9, 2014) . . . 262 n.6
Amended Tax Return Filing and Processing Needs to be Modernized to Reduce Erroneous Refunds, Processing Costs, and Taxpayer Burden (TIGTA No. 2014- 40-028) (Apr. 25, 2014) . . . 264 n.19
Deficiencies Exist in the Control and Timely Resolution of Whistleblower Claims (2009) . . . 124 n.79
Expansion of the Delinquent Return Refund Hold Program Could Improve Filing Compliance and Help Reduce the Tax Gap (TIGTA No. 2014- 30-023) (June 3, 2014) . . . 262 n.5
Fiscal Year 2006 Review of Compliance with Legal Guidelines when Conducting Seizures of Taxpayers' Property (2006- 30-113) (Aug. 9, 2006) . . . 390 n.61
Fiscal Year 2006 Statutory Review of Compliance with Legal Guidelines when Issuing Levies (2006-30-101) (Aug. 4, 2006) . . . 390 n.61
Fiscal Year 2006 Statutory Review of Compliance with Lien Due Process Procedures (2006-30-094) (June 2006) . . . 402 n.141
Fiscal Year 2015 Statutory Review of Compliance with the Freedom of Information Act 4 (Sept. 18, 2015) . . . 126 n.84
New Legislation Could Affect Filers of the Report of Foreign Bank and Financial Accounts, but Potential Issues Are Being Addressed (2010-30-25) . . . 74 n.178
Trust Fund Recovery Penalty Actions Were Not Always Timely or Adequate 1 (TIGTA No. 2014- 30-0345) (May 23, 2014) . . . 412 n.2
WEB SITES
Decision Modeling, Inc. . . . 364 n.9
Free File products . . . 47 n.18
I.R.S. . . . 379 n.2
IRS Data Book, 2016, Table 2 . . . 44 n.3
IRS e-filing publications . . . 46 n.11

IRS forms and instructions...45 n.6
on-line tools for tax professionals...47 n.19
Tax Court...17
tax relief in disasters...65 n.126

Index

A

AARs (administrative adjustment requests), 198–99, 283–84

abatements, by IRS
- first time abatement, 331
- of interest, 226, 370–72, 382
- in section 7429 cases, 215
- in termination/jeopardy assessments, 215

accountants, 416–21
- "I was following orders" defense strategy, 417
- newly hired, existing taxes owed and, 421
- resignation, withholding taxes responsibility, 418
- "responsible person" element, defense strategy, 416–17
- willfulness, definition, 418–19
- willfulness defense strategies, 419–21

ACS (Automated Collection System), 380–81

"adequate return" filing, SOL and, 146–49
- proper filing, 148
- proper form, 147–48
- signature, 146–47
- sufficient information, for tax calculation, 148–49

administrative adjustment requests (AARs), 198–99, 283–84

administrative levies, 203 n.1, 388–90

Administrative Procedure Act rules. *See* APA (Administrative Procedure Act) rules

administrative sales, 390–92

administrative sources/authorities, 20–28

aliens, termination assessments and departure of, 218–19

announcements, notices and (IRS), 23

Anti-Injunction Act, 406

APA (Administrative Procedure Act) rules, 28–34
- antiquity *vs.* contemporaneity, 34
- "arbitrary and capricious" reviews, 30
- "bootstrapping," 32–33
- deference, case law, 30–32
- notice/comment, 28–30
- phantom regulations, 34
- policy inconsistency, 33
- regulations *vs.* case law, 33–34, 40–42
- Tax Court *vs.* district courts in using, 254–55

appeals, to determinations
- Appeals Office review, for TFRP assessment, 423–25
- late payments, judicial review, 334–36
- late payments, trial proceedings, 336–37

appeals, to examinations, 127–37
- Appeals Office, data on, 127
- choosing, benefits *vs.* drawbacks, 133–35
- closing agreements, 135–37
- conclusion of, no-change cases, 135
- of docketed cases, 129–30
- Fast Track Settlement program, 129
- generally, 19
- Ninety-Day Letters, 137
- precedent considerations, 250–51

procedures, 130-33	transferee/fiduciary liability in, 451
Protest filing, 128	Bankruptcy Court
RARs, 128	deficiency determinations,
section 7429 reviews, 211-12, 214	jurisdiction, 254
Thirty-Day Letters, 128, 137	equitable considerations, 251
unagreed cases, 137	as forum, for tax cases, 18–19, 249
ASED (Assessment Statute Expiration	litigation costs, 253
Date), 383	refund suits in, 263
as SOL issue, 141–42, 162	section 7430 awards, 256–57
summary assessments, 144	BBA (Bipartisan Budget Act of 2015), 14,
assessment procedures, SOL and, 141–67	170–71. See also partnerships, exami-
adequate return filing, 146–49	nation of (BBA)
ASED, 141–42	bonds, in section 7429 cases, 215–16
burden of proof, 163–64	burden of proof
deficiency assessments, 144–45	burden of production and, 336–37, 339
exceptions, to SOL, 152–62	by government, in fraud penalty cases,
extension/suspension, of SOL, 113–14	352
general rule, 149–52	in section 7429 cases, 213–14
joint tax return filers, 165	SOL issues, 163–64
pleading SOL, 162–63	in Tax Court, 246–48
	transferee liability, 447–48
process, generally, 142–43, 381	transferee natinty, 447–46
res judicata, collateral estoppel and, 164–65	C
SOL issues, 162	"C" corporations (domestic)
summary (automatic) assessments,	filing returns, 59, 365
143-44	interest rates, underpayments and, 365
termination/jeopardy assessments,	CAP (Collection Appeals Program), 402
145-46	carrybacks
attorney's fees, 222, 255-57	corporate NOL carrybacks, 220
audits. See examinations, of returns	creating overpayment, interest on, 375
Automated Collection System (ACS),	quick refunds, 284-85
380-81	SOL for, 275
	to underpayment year, 366
В	cash, possessors of large amounts, 221-22
bankruptcy	C.B. (Cumulative Bulletin), 21
collection and, 404-6	CDP (Collection Due Process) rights pro-
designation of voluntary payments,	visions, 217, 400-402, 407
strategy, 430-31	CEP (Coordinated Examination Program)
fraudulent conveyances, 453	109-10
generally, 15	charitable deductions, accuracy-related
of partnerships, SOL and, 200	penalty for, 357
receivership and, deficiency	churches, examinations/investigations of,
assessment, 220	123, 219
SOL suspension and, 159, 407	
그는 그녀가 있었다. 경기 그렇게 가지 않는 것 같아.	

civil actions (miscellaneous), 14–15. *See also* collection, of tax; examinations, of returns; termination/jeopardy assessments
CNC (Currently Not Collectible) status, 380–81
collateral estoppel
privity and, 449
res judicata and, 164–65, 353–54
collection, of tax, 379–410. *See also* spousal relief
actions, generally, 14
administrative levies, 388–90
administrative sales, 390–92
administrative structure, 380–81
Anti-Injunction Act, 406
appeals program, 402
assessment, 381–82
Bivens suits, 407
due process, 226, 400–402
installment agreements, 396–97
judicial remedies, in Code, 403–4
judicial remedies, in other statutes, 404–6
judicial sales, 392–93
levies, relief from, 396
lien priority, 386–88
liens, creation/extent of, 382–85
liens, notice of, 385–86
liens, relief from, 395–96
offer-in-compromise, 397–400
overview, 379
during recession, 402–3
SOL and, 407–8
sovereign immunity waiver, 406–7
TAOs, 396
writs, by District Courts, 393–95
Collection Appeals Program (CAP), 402
Collection Due Process (CDP) rights provisions, 217, 400–402, 407
Collection Statute Expiration Date (CSED), 383, 408
Congress, tax role of, 4–6
"Blue Books," 6, 6 n.9
GAO, 6
Internal Revenue Code, structure of, 5
Joint Committee on Taxation, 4
Revenue Codes, 5
tax statutes, committee process, 4
consistency, duty of, 290
APA rules and, 33
by government, 295–96
in partnerships (BBA), 199
in partnerships (TEFRA), 175, 182–83
by taxpayer, 294–95
Coordinated Examination Program (CEP), 109–10
corporations
accumulated earnings tax adjustment, by IRS, 126–27
CEP and LIFE, 109–10
corporate NOL carrybacks, 220
correspondence examinations, 108
Court of Federal Claims
appeals, generally, 19
forum, for tax cases, 18, 249
litigation costs, 253
precedent considerations, 250–51
refund jurisdiction of, 263, 281–83
section 7430 awards, 256–57
TFRP review, 226, 282
"variance," definition, 269–70, 283
cross-border tax evasion, 74 n.175, 120–21
CSED (Collection Statute Expiration Date), 383, 408
Cumulative Bulletin (C.B.), 21
Currently Not Collectible (CNC) status, 380–81

D

damages, for improper IRS collection actions, 404
deference
antiquity *vs.* contemporaneity, 34
"bootstrapping," 32–33
case law, 30–32
case law *vs.* regulations, 33–34
policy inconsistency, 33

deficiency determination, litigation of, 225–58. *See also* Notice of Deficiency
additional deficiency notices, issuance of, 234–35
APA issues, 254–55
attorney's fees/costs, 255–57
burden of proof in, 246–48
case overview, 236–45
deficiency, definition, 228–29
disposition, speed of, 254
forum, choice of, 248–55
forum, comparison of options, 251
forum, precedent of court and, 250–51
interest determinations, 253, 376–77
jurisdiction, 235, 249, 254
litigation costs, 253–54
new issues, 251–52
Notice of Deficiency, 227–33
overview, 225–27
payment considerations, 249
petition, timely filing of, 233–34
publicity concerns, 254
small tax cases ("S" cases), 245–46
standard of review, 235–36
Tax Court data, 225 n.1
taxes subject to, 229
deficiency procedure, in assessments, 113 n.37, 144–45
deficiency actions, generally, 13–14, 381
direct/immediate assessments and, 205
in partnerships, 183–85
Department of Justice, 12–13
determination letters, 26
DIF (discriminate function) audit selection process, 105
discovery
in section 7429 cases, 213, 214
in Tax Court, 238
transferee/fiduciary liability and, 248–49
District Courts (federal)
appeals, generally, 19
dispositions, speed of, 254
equitable considerations, 251
forum, for tax cases, 16, 249
litigation costs, 253
payment considerations, in deficiency determinations, 249
precedent considerations, 250–51
publicity concerns, 254
refund jurisdiction of, 263, 281–83
section 7430 awards, 256–57
termination/jeopardy assessments, expedited review in, 226
TFRP review, 226, 282
"variance," definition, 269–70, 283
writs, as collection devices, 393–94
duty of consistency. *See* consistency, duty of

E

e-filing initiative, of IRS, 45–47
"economic level" audit selection process, 106
Electronic Tax Administration Advisory Committee (ETAAC), 45–46
ELPs (electing large partnerships), 169–70
employment tax audits, 109
employment tax withholdings, by employers, 413–15
equitable recoupment doctrine, 291–93
estate returns
equitable recoupment doctrine, 291–93
estate tax audits, 109
filing returns, location, 61
filing thresholds, 51–52
interest rates, underpayments and, 365–66
liens, on estate taxes, 384
substantial undervaluations, 350
ETAAC (Electronic Tax Administration Advisory Committee), 45–46
evasion, by tax payers. *See* cross-border tax evasion
examinations, of returns, 103–39
appeal request, 125
appeals process, 127–35
audio recording, of interviews, 122
audit selection process, 104–7

audit strategies/choices, 111–14
conclusion, administrative appeal or, 135–37
income approximation, 119–20
Information Document Request, 114
international information gathering, by IRS, 120–22
IRS disclosure, means to compel, 125–27
IRS summons enforcement, 115–17, 394
noncompliance rate, 103–4
overview, 103
private letter ruling request, 125
protections/defenses, for taxpayers, 122–23
summons, collections and, 394
summons, on multinational banks/financial institutions, 120–21
third party summons, enforceability of, 117–19
transaction planning, by taxpayer, 124–25
types of, 108–11
whistleblower awards, 123–24
executive branch, tax role of, 6–13
Department of Justice, 12–13
IRS, 8–12
Treasury Department, 7–8

F

FATCA (Foreign Account Tax Compliance Act), 73 n.175, 120
FBAR (Foreign Bank and Financial Account) forms, 73 n.175
Federal Tort Claims Act (FTCA), 406–7
FICA (Federal Insurance Contribution Act), 413–14
fiduciary liability. *See* transferee/fiduciary liability
field examinations, 108
final partnership administrative adjustment (FPAA), 178, 283
FOIA (Freedom of Information Act) of 1966, 125–26
Foreign Account Tax Compliance Act (FATCA), 73 n.175, 120
Foreign Bank and Financial Account (FBAR) forms, 73 n.175
foreign corporations
audits of, international information gathering by IRS, 120–22
cross-board tax enforcement, 73–74 n.175
filing returns, time/place, 59
foreign reporting requirements, 73–74
letters rogatory, 121
forum, for tax cases
Bankruptcy Court, 18–19
choice of, 15
Court of Federal Claims, 18
District Court, 16
Tax Court, 16–18
FPAA (final partnership administrative adjustment), 178, 283
fraud penalty, 350–54
burden of proof, by government, 352
fraud, SOL and, 352–53
fraudulent FTF penalty, 324–25
overview, 350–52
res judicata, collateral estoppel and, 164–65, 353–54
tax fraud, definition, 351
transferee liability, fraudulent conveyance theories and, 451–53
"willful blindness" doctrine, 351–52
FTF (failure to file) penalty, 323–24
FTP (failure to pay) penalty, 325–28
as due on return, 326–27
late filing/late payment penalties, combined, 327–28
overview, 325–26
tax deficiency, 327
FUTA (Federal Unemployment Tax Act), 414

G

GAO (Government Accountability Office), 6
"Geithner defense," against accuracy-related penalties, 354
gift returns
  filing returns, location, 61
  filing thresholds, 52–53
  liens, on gift taxes, 384
  SOL exception, gift tax as to transfer, 161–62
  substantial estate/gift tax undervaluations, 350
"global interest netting," 374–75

I

illegal activities, 15, 221–22. *See also* fraud penalty
"imputed underpayment," 193–94
income tax returns. *See also* penalties, for FTF/FTP
  amended returns, 264
  children, income received by, 381–82
  defense, estimated tax penalty, 320–22
  elections, making/failure to make, 70–71
  extensions, file/pay, 64–66
  FICA, employer's duty to withhold, 413–14
  filing due date, 59–61
  filing location, 61–63
  filing thresholds, 49–50
  FUTA, employer's duty to withhold, 414
  "informal claims" for refunds, 268–69
  information, confidentiality of, 71–72
  interest rate, on overpayments, 373
  joint returns, 50–51
  overpayment collection, 261–62
  payments, time/place, 63–64
  prepaying, by quarterly estimates, 319–20
  prepaying, by withholding, 318–19
  reportable transactions, 66–68
  signing/verifying, 56–59
  withhold taxes, employer's duty to, 413
"infection" audit selection process, 107
"informants" audit selection process, 107
"information matching" audit selection process, 105–6
information returns, 53–56
  persons subject to special provisions, 53–54
  reporting expansion, 55–56
  transactions with other persons, 54–55
installment agreements, with IRS, 396–97
interest, 363–78
  in donee liability situations, 451
  interest abatements, 226, 370–72
  interest determinations, jurisdiction for, 253, 376–77
  on overpayments, 372–75
  overview, 363–64
  penalties, SOL and, 152, 372, 381
  in transferee liability cases, 450–51
  on underpayments, 364–72
Internal Revenue Bulletin (I.R.B.), 21
Internal Revenue Manual (IRM), 26–27, 123
"An Introduction to United States Tax Court" (video), 236
IRS (Internal Revenue Service), 8–12
  ACS, 380
  "burden of production," in court proceedings, 329, 336–37, 339
  CAP, 402
  CDP hearings, 262
  CID, 11
  collections/spending by, 8
  determination letters, 26
  disaster, terroristic/military action, interest suspension and, 369
  e-filing initiative, 45–47
  "Electronic Reading Room," website, 23
  enforced collections by, data on, 379 n.2
  failure to timely contact, interest suspension and, 367–69
  fiduciary liability, assertion of, 439–40

FTD Alert, 422
IRM, 26–27
letters, generally, 380
notices and announcements, 23
Office of Chief Counsel, 10–11
OPR, 11–12
organizational chart, 39 *fig.*
other government sources, in tax, 27–28
OVDP, 74 n.175
penalty assessments, data on, 317–18 n.2
PLRs, 24–26
regulations, 20–21
reorganization, divisions of, 9–10
Revenue Procedures (Rev. Proc.), 22
revenue rulings, 21
TAMs, 26
Taxpayer Advocate Service (TAS), 11, 396
TFRP investigation by, 422–23
transferee liability at law, assertion of, 440–42
transferee liability in equity, assertion of, 442–45

J

joint and several liability
anti-avoidance rules, in section 6015(c), 87, 226
in joint tax returns, 58, 79
res judicata/final administrative determination, 82
joint tax returns, 50–51, 79–87
amount due, 80
assessment of, statute of limitations, 80–81 n.19, 98 n.88, 165
duress, relief for, 79–80
election for relief, 80–82
innocent spouse liability, 86–87
innocent spouse rule, 82–86
joint and several liability, 58, 79
res judicata, 82
signing requirement, 57–59
understatement/omitted income, 83–86
judicial branch, tax role of, 13–19
appeals, 19
bankruptcy cases, 15
bankruptcy court, 18–19
civil actions, 14–15
collections actions, 14
Court of Federal Claims, 18
criminal tax cases, 15
deficiency actions, 13–14
district courts, 116
refund actions, 14
Tax Court, 16–18
TEFRA and BBA actions, 14
trial courts, choice of, 15
judicial estoppel, 296
judicial sales, 392–93

L

Legal Business and International Division (LB&I), 10
letters, from IRS
determination letters, 26
generally, 380
letters rogatory, foreign corporations, 121
Ninety-Day Letters, 137
PLR request, 125
PLRs, 24–26
"60-day letters," TFRP penalty, 423
Thirty-Day Letters, 128, 137
levies. *See also* termination/jeopardy assessments
administrative levies, 203 n.1, 388–90
collection activity, electing spouse, 81
jeopardy levies, 210
relief from, 396
liability, for taxes (under TFRP), 415–21
"responsible person" element, defense strategies, 415–18
"willfulness" element, defense strategies, 415–21
liens. *See also* CDP (Collection Due Process) rights provisions
alter ego/nominee liens, 384–85, 452–53

creation and extent of, 382–85
notice of, 385–86
notice of, errors in, 386
personalty/realty distinction, 385–86
place of residence, 385
relief from, 395–96
"secret" liens, 385
special liens, 384
state *vs.* federal law controversies, 383–84

LIFE (Limited Issue Focused Examinations), 109–10

LLCs (limited liability companies), 176–77

M

malpractice, partnerships and (BBA), 201–2

mitigation provision elements, SOL and, 276, 296–98
amount/method of adjustment, 307–8
choice of year circumstances, 303–4, 305–6
circumstances of adjustment, 297, 301–4
determinations, 298–301
equitable basis for mitigation, 301
error year barred, 297–98, 298
evaluation of, 308–9
necessary conditions for adjustment, 304–6
original circumstances, 301–3, 304–5
overview, 289–91
related parties, 307

N

NAP (Notice of Administrative Proceeding), 197

National Taxpayer Advocate, 40

negligence penalty, 343–45
disclosure, impact of, 345
element, disregarding rules, 344–45
negligence, definition, 343–44

NFPA (Notice of Final Partnership Adjustment), 197

Notice of Administrative Proceeding (NAP), 197

Notice of Deficiency
for cash possession, 221–22
content/form of, 229–30
FPAA *vs.*, 184–85
in jeopardy assessments, 209–10
"last known address," mailing to, 230 n.17
mailing of, 230–33
in section 7429 cases, 216, 217
SOL exception, to assessment, 158–59
in Tax Court, jurisdictional conditions, 227–28
in termination assessments, 208–9
timeliness of, 163

Notice of Final Partnership Adjustment (NFPA), 197

Notice of Proposed Partnership Adjustment (NPPA), 197

notices, announcements and (IRS), 23

"notoriety" audit selection process, 107

NPPA (Notice of Proposed Partnership Adjustment), 197

O

offer-in-compromise, 397–400
acceptance, bases for, 398–99
bankruptcy and, 400
collateral agreements, 398
preconditions, 398
process, 397–98
SOL and, 407
user fee, 399

office audits, 108

OPR (Office of Professional Responsibility, IRS), 11–12

OVDP (Offshore Voluntary Disclosure Program), 74 n.175

overpayments, interest on, 373–75
basic rules, 373–74
carrybacks creating overpayment, 375
interest period, rules on, 374
overlapping tax periods, 374–75

software to compute, 364 n.9
overpayments/claims for refund, 261–88
AARs, 283–84
amended returns, 264
"claim," requirement, 268–70
Court of Federal Claims, refund jurisdiction of, 281–83
deposits *vs.* payments, 265–66, 369–70
District Court, refund jurisdiction of, 281–83
due *vs.* properly due taxes, 266–68
extension of SOL, filing claim and, 263, 273–74
lookback provision (section 6511(b)(2) limitation), 276–78
"offset doctrine," 267–68
overpayment, definition, 264
overview, refund claims processes, 261–64
penalty, 285
quick refunds, for tentative carry-backs/refund adjustments, 284–85
refund diversion, 263, 278–80
SOL, special rules for income tax, 274–76
Tax Court, refund jurisdiction of, 263, 265, 280–81
"taxpayer," definition, 270–71
timely filing requirement, SOL and, 271–73

P

partnership representatives (PRs), 196–97
partnerships, examination of (BBA), 193–202
AARs, 198–99, 283–84
adjustment procedures, 197–98
after 2018, application of TEFRA, 194–95
before 2018, application of BBA, 194
consistency rules, 199
effective date, 194
malpractice considerations, 201–2
open issues, 200–201
overview, BBA legislative history, 193–94
partnership-level adjustments, 195–96
potential future challenges to, 201
PRs, 196–97
special rules, bankruptcy, 200
special rules, partnerships outside U.S., 199–200
tiered partnerships, 200 n.58
partnerships, examination of (TEFRA), 169–92
assessment, SOL for, 160, 185–88
consistency, duty of, 175
examination process, 180–83
excluded partnerships, 177–78
filing returns, time/place, 60–61
FPAA, judicial review of, 183–85, 283–84
NBAP, mailing period for, 179–80
NBAP (notice of beginning), 178–79
overview, TEFRA *vs.* ELP *vs.* BBA regimes, 169–71
"partnership items," classification, 171–73
procedural complications, 188–89
procedural inefficiencies, 173–75
settlement, affected items in, 181–82
settlement agreements, consistency with, 182–83
settlement agreements, partnership items, 181
summary reports, 180–81
TMP, role and authority of, 175–77, 283
passive foreign investment companies (PFICs), 220
penalties, for accuracy-related errors, 338–50
assessment procedures, 338–39, 381
burden of production, of IRS, 339
calculation of, 339–43
negligence penalty, 343–45
QAR, impact of filing, 342–43
reasonable cause exception, 354–57
stacking of, 340–41

substantial understatement penalty, 346–48
substantial valuation misstatements, 348–50
tax shelter penalties, 357–60
underpayment, definition, 341–42
penalties, for fraud, 350–54
burden of proof, by government, 352
fraud, SOL and, 352–53
fraudulent FTF penalty, 324–25
overview, 350–52
reasonable cause exception, 354–57
res judicata, collateral estoppel and, 164–65, 353–54
tax fraud, definition, 351
"willful blindness" doctrine, 351–52
penalties, for FTF/FTP, 317–38
calculation of, 320
defense, reasonable cause, 328–34
defenses, estimated tax penalty, 320–22
failure to file timely, due dates/extensions, 322–23
fraudulent FTF, 324–25
FTF penalty, 323–24
FTP penalty, for tax deficiency, 327
FTP penalty, for tax due on return, 325–27
late filing and late payment penalties, combined, 327–28
"late penalties," disputing, 334–37
quarterly estimates, 319–20
withholding, 318–19
penalties, for tax shelters, 357–60
case strategy, for deficiency, 350 n.128
disclosed transactions, 357–58
disqualified opinion, 358–60
other penalties, coordination with, 358
privilege and, 123
reasonable cause defense, 358–60
reasonable cause exception, 354–57
strict liability penalty, 360
understatement amount, determination of, 358
undisclosed transactions, 358
penalties, for unpaid withholding taxes. *See* TFRP
PFICs (passive foreign investment companies), 220
PLRs (private letter rulings), 24–26
private letter rulings (PLRs), 24–26
property
administrative levies against, 388–90
administrative sales, 390–92
judicial sales, 392–93
law suits against IRS, 403–4, 404–5
seizure, by IRS, 394–95
stay of sale, in section 7429 cases, 216–17
tax liens, foreclosures and, 394
tax liens on, 384, 385
tax liens on, priorities, 386–88
PRs (partnership representatives), 196–97
PTPs (publicly traded partnerships), 169–70

Q

QAR (qualified amended return), 342–43
Qualified Settlement Offer rule, 256

R

RAR (Revenue Agent's Report), 128
reasonable cause defense (for FTP tax), 328–34
"burden of production," 329, 336–37, 339
constitutional objections, 333
for death/illness/unavoidable absence, 330
for erroneous advice, from IRS, 330–31
first time abatement, 331
for ignorance of law, 333
for insufficient funds, 333–34
for military service, in combat zone, 331
mistake/forgetfulness, 332
overview, 328–29
payment within 90% of liability, 331–32
pressures, time/business, 332
for records unavailable, 332

for reliance (on tax professionals), 329
for religious beliefs, 333
for tax shelters, 358–60
TFRP liability, 420–21
reasonable cause exception, for accuracy-related penalty, 354–57
charitable deductions, 357
"Geithner defense," 354
overview, 354–55
reliance defense (on tax professionals), 355–56
recession, collection during, 402–3
Refund Statute Expiration Date (RSED), 273, 383
refunds, 14. *See also* overpayments/claims for refund; penalties
regulations
generally, 20–21
inconsistent enforcement of, 37–38
retroactivity of, 35–37
for tax preparers, 40–41
Regulatory Flexibility Act (RegFlex), 35
reporting/record keeping obligations, 43–76
confidentiality, of return information, 71–72
e-filing initiative, 45–47
elections, making/failure to make, 70–71
estate tax returns, 51–52
extensions, of time/payments, 64–66
filing, time/place of, 59–62
foreign reporting requirements, 73–74
gift tax returns, 52–53
income tax returns, joint returns, 50–51
information, persons subject to special provisions, 53–54
information, transactions with other persons, 54–55
information reporting, expansion of, 55–56
overview, 43–45
payments, time/place for, 63–64
record keeping regulations, 48–49
reportable transactions, disclosure of, 66–68
"required records" doctrine, 74 n.175
signing/verifying returns, 56–59
tax return preparers, 66–70
UTP reporting requirements, 72–73
"required records" doctrine, 74 n.175
res judicata
in bankruptcy cases, 220, 263 n.16, 350 n.132
collateral estoppel and, 164–65, 353–54
fraud exception and, 235 n.41
spousal relief and, 82
in Tax Court, 246
"return items" audit selection process, 106–7
Revenue Agent's Report (RAR), 128
Revenue Procedures (Rev. Proc.), 21
Revenue Rulings, 21
RSED (Refund Statute Expiration Date), 273, 383

S

S corporations
filing returns, time/place, 59–60
interest rate, on overpayments, 373–74
section 7429 reviews, 210–14
administrative phase, 212
cash possession, 222
overview, 210–11
post-trial phase, 214
trial phase, 212–14
setoff doctrine, 293–94
Slodov doctrine, 421
Small Business and Self-Employed Division (SB/SE, IRS), 10
SO (Settlement Officer), 401
SOL. *See* statute of limitation (SOL), for assessments; statute of limitation (SOL), for refund claims; statute of limitation (SOL), for tax liens; statute of limitation (SOL), overriding
sovereign immunity, waivers of, 403–7
Anti-Injunction Act, 406

Bivens remedy, 407
Federal Tort Claims Act (FTCA), 406–7
judicial remedies, in Code, 403–4
judicial remedies, in other statutes, 404–6

spousal relief, 77–102
actual knowledge, 435–36
actual knowledge, proving, 87–90
anti-avoidance rules, 91–92
appeal process, 94–95
availability of, 90
collection, SOL and, 98, 407
community property, 98–99
deficiency, allotment of, 90–91
disclosure issues, 97–98
divorce, taxes owed and, 98
joint returns, 50–51, 79–87
nonrequesting spouse, rights of, 95–96
overview, 77–78
remarriage, pre-existing taxes and, 97
threshold requirements, § 6015(f) election, 92–94

statute of limitation (SOL), for assessments
"adequate return" filing and, 146–49
agreement/waiver exception, 152–53
amended returns, 151–52
bankruptcy exception, 159
BBA rules, 198
burden of proof, 163–64
designated summons exception, 160
due date, on weekends/holidays, 150
early returns, 150
exceptions, 152–61
extension/suspension of, 113–14
filing extension, returns filed pursuant to, 151
fraud and, 352–53
fraud exception, 157–58
general rule, 149
gift tax as to transfer exception, 161–62
international transactions exception, 161
joint return filers, 165
late filed returns, 149–50
"listed transactions" exception, 160–61
losses from certain activities exception, 161
mailbox (postmark) rule, 150–51
Notice of Deficiency exception, 158–59, 289
"offset doctrine," 267–68
"offset doctrine" and, in tax overpayments, 267–68
partnership items exception, 160, 290
in partnerships, 185–88
penalties, interest and, 152
pleading, 162–63
res judicata, collateral estoppel and, 164–65, 353–54
spotting issues of, 162
TAO exception, 159, 396
TFRP assessments, 428–29
third-party summons exception, 159
transferee liability exception, 160
25% nonfraudulent income omission exception, 153–57

statute of limitation (SOL), for refund claims, 262–63
for carrybacks of net operating losses, 275
on filing refund claims, 273–74
for "financially disabled" taxpayers, 275–76
on income taxes, 274–76, 289
lookback provision and, 276–78
mitigation provisions, 276

statute of limitation (SOL), for tax liens, 407–8
CDP process and, 400–401
general tax liens, 386
laches doctrine and, 408
suit, to reduce liability to judgment, 393–94

statute of limitation (SOL), overriding, 289–315
amount/method of adjustment, 307–8
circumstances of adjustment, 301–4
conditions for adjustment, 304–6
determinations, 298–301

duty of consistency, by government, 295–96
duty of consistency, by taxpayer, 294–95
equitable recoupment doctrine, 291–93
error year barred, 290, 298
judicial estoppel, 296
mitigation provisions, 276, 296–308
mitigation provisions, evaluation of, 308–9
overview, 289–91
related parties, 307
setoff doctrine, 293–94
strict liability penalty, for tax shelters, 360
substantial understatement penalty, 346–48
disclosure, 347–48
"substantial authority" for reporting position, 347
understatement, definition, 346–47
substantial valuation misstatements penalty, 348–50
substantial estate/gift tax undervaluations, 350
substantial income tax overvaluations, 348–49
summary (automatic) assessments, 143–44

T

TAO (Taxpayer Assistance Order), SOL and, 159, 396
Tax Court. *See also* deficiency determination, litigation of
additional deficiency notices, issuance of, 234–35
appeals, generally, 19, 243–44
arbitration, 239
burden of proof in, 246–48
calendar call, trial, briefs and, 240–41
collection due process in, 226
decision, 241–43
decision, assessment of deficiency after, 244–45
decision, finality of, 243
deficiency, choice of forum for, 248
deficiency, definition, 228–29
deficiency, types of tax subject to, 229
discovery, 238
dispositions, speed of, 254
electronic filing system, 236
equitable considerations, 251
forum, for tax cases, 16–18
interest accrual, 253
"Introduction to United States Tax Court" (video), 236
joint and several liability, relief from, 226
jurisdiction, of interest determinations, 376–77
jurisdiction, of tax deficiency cases, 235, 249, 254
litigation costs, 253–54
notice of calendared case, pretrial orders and, 240
petition, timely filing of, 233–34
pleadings, in deficiency redetermination matters, 238–39
precedent considerations, 250–51
refund jurisdiction of, 263, 265, 280–81
res judicata, 251–52
"S" cases, 245–46
section 7430 awards, 256–57
settlement, 239
stipulations process, 239–40
Tax Court data, 225 n.1
termination/jeopardy assessments, expedited review in, 226
transferee/fiduciary liability challenges, 226
Tax Exempt and Governmental Entities Division (TE/GE), 10
tax-exempt organizations, 219
tax law, sources of, 3–42
administrative law issues, 28–38
administrative sources/authorities, 20–28
Congress, role of, 4–6
executive branch, role of, 6–13
IRS, organizational chart, 39 *fig.*
judicial branch, role of, 13–19

"tax matters partners" (TMPs), 175–77, 196–97, 283
tax preparer software, reasonable cause exception and, 354
tax return advisors/preparers
  disqualified opinion, in reasonable cause defense, 360
  disqualified tax advisor, in reasonable cause defense, 358–59
  "Geithner defense," 354
  regulation of, 40–41, 68–70
  "willful blindness" doctrine, 351–52
tax shelter penalties, 357–60
  case strategy, for deficiency, 350 n.128
  disclosed transactions, 357–58
  disqualified opinion, 358–60
  other penalties, coordination with, 358
  privilege and, 123
  reasonable cause defense, 358–60
  reasonable cause exception, 354–57
  strict liability penalty, 360
  understatement amount, determination of, 358
  undisclosed transactions, 358
tax treaties, 73 n.175
Taxpayer Advocate Service, 11, 396
"Taxpayer Bill of Rights" (TBOR), 23–24
"taxpayer initiation" audit selection process, 107
TDs (Treasury Decisions), 20
Technical Advice Memoranda (TAMs), 26
TEFRA (Tax Equity and Fiscal Responsibility Act of 1982), 169–92
  assessment, SOL for, 160, 185–88
  BBA *vs.*, 14
  consistency, duty of, 175
  examination process, 180–83
  excluded partnerships, 177–78
  filing returns, time/place, 60–61
  FPAA, judicial review of, 183–85, 283–84
  NBAP, mailing period for, 179–80
  NBAP (notice of beginning), 178–79
  overview, TEFRA *vs.* ELP *vs.* BBA regimes, 169–71
  "partnership items," classification, 171–73
  procedural complications, 188–89
  procedural inefficiencies, 173–75
  settlement, affected items in, 181–82
  settlement agreement, consistency with, 182–83
  settlement agreement, partnership items, 181
  summary reports, 180–81
  TMP, role and authority of, 175–77, 283
termination/jeopardy assessments, 203–24
  abatement, 215
  attorney payments, 222
  bond, 215–16
  collection due process rights, 217
  corporate NOL carrybacks, 220
  departing aliens, 218–19
  expedited assessments, justifications for, 205–6
  illegal activities and, 204–5
  interest accrual and, 364 n.10
  jeopardy assessments, consequences of, 209–10, 381
  judicial review, 226
  overview, 203–4
  passive foreign investment companies, 220
  possessors, of large amounts of cash, 221–22
  receiverships, bankruptcies and, 220
  section 7429 reviews, 210–14
  SOL and, 145–46
  stay of sale, 216–17
  tax-exempt organizations, 219
  termination assessments, consequences of, 206–9
  termination *vs.* jeopardy assessments, 204–5
TFRP (trust fund recovery penalty), 411–34
  Appeals Office review, 423–25
  collection procedures, 426–28

defense strategies, 415–21, 429–31
employer's duties, 413–15
installment payment plans, 427–28
judicial relief, 226, 425–26
liability, for taxes, 415–21, 436
liability assessment process, 422–23
overview, 411–13
"responsible person" element, defense strategies, 415–18
SOL and, 428–29
unpaid balance, suspending activity on, 426 n.81, 427
third-party summons, 117–19, 159
Thirty-Day Letters, 128
TMPs ("tax matters partners"), 175–77, 196–97, 283
transferee/fiduciary liability, 435–55
alter ego/nominee mechanisms and, 452–53
"at law" transferee cases, extent of liability, 450
in bankruptcy, 451
burden of proof, 438
contribution, rights to, 449–50
discovery, 448–49
executors, relief for, 438
fiduciary, definition, 437–38
fiduciary liability, 439–40, 450
fraudulent conveyance theories and, 451–53
"in equity" transferee cases, extent of liability, 450
interest, 450–51
IRS procedure, 437
judicial relief, 226
liabilities, in Code, 437
nexus concept, definition, 435–36
overview, 435
privity, 449
procedural elements, 445–46
state law and, 438–39
transferee, definition, 437
transferee liability, burden of proof and, 447–48
transferee liability, SOL and, 446–47
transferee liability at law, 440–42
transferee liability in equity, 442–45
transferee status, case law, 437–38
treasurers, 416–21
"I was following orders" defense strategy, 417
newly hired, existing taxes owed and, 421
resignation, withholding taxes responsibility, 418
"responsible person" element, defense strategy, 416–17
willfulness, definition, 418–19
willfulness defense strategies, 419–21
Treasury Decisions (TDs), 20
Treasury Department, 7–8
trust fund recovery penalty. *See* TFRP

U

underpayments, interest on, 364–72
abatement of interest, for errors/delays by IRS, 370–72
basic rules, 364–66
carrybacks, to underpayment year, 366
penalties, additional amounts/additions to tax, 372
software to compute, 364 n.9
suspension of interest, for deposits, 265–66, 369–70
suspension of interest, for disasters/terroristic or military action, 369
suspension of interest, for failure to timely contact taxpayer, 367–69
UTP (uncertain tax positions) reporting requirements, 72–73

V

venue, in section 7429 cases, 212

W

Wage and Investment Division (W&I), 9–10
whistleblower awards, 123–24